Out of the Kumbla
Caribbean Women
and Literature

edited by
Carole Boyce Davies & Elaine Savory Fido

Africa World Press, Inc.
P.O. Box 1892
Trenton, NJ 08607

© Africa World Press, Inc. 1990

Cover design by Ife Nii Owoo

Library of Congress Catalog Card Number: 88-70199

ISBN: 0-86543-042-X Cloth
        0-86543-043-8 Paper

To the many unsung Caribbean women
who write, sing, tell stories and struggle
to make their voices heard
and
to Tantie Olive who also
"lately danced and joined the ancestors."

Acknowledgments

Marlene Nourbese Philip is acknowledged for granting permission to include "The Absence of Writing or How I Almost Became A Spy" *Fireweed* (Toronto).

Sincere acknowledgments are offered to a number of friends who offered support. We would like to identify Betty Wilson, Marilyn Desmond and Clarisse Zimra who read versons of the introduction and offered useful suggestions. Rafika Merini and Allison Thomas helped proofread galleys. We will be eternally grateful for the patience of our contributors. The Manuscript Center, SUNY, Binghamton and our copy editor, Patricia Lone are also acknowledged.

Finally our children are embraced with love. In particular: Austin Fido and Jonelle and Dalia Davies are recognised for their understanding of their academic mothers' need for time and space to work.

Editors' Note: This collection has been in the press for a substantial time, being completed in 1987. We therefore need to point out that although there is certainly enough validity in the essays and bibliography contained here to more than warrant publication, they understandably cannot refer to anything published after that date, nor do they reflect the development of critical approaches since then in the authors of the essays.

Foreword

Literature is the first of the disciplines. It seems to have grown, in many cultures, from the ritual act of worship and there is therefore a sense in which it may have preceded language since some theorists of the origin of Language speculate that expressive sound probably came before defining sound—cries of ecstasy and anguish before sounds of naming and identification. Because it comes first, it may be regarded as containing all the other disciplines, so that its burden is not only to describe all human experience but also to employ all the possible ways in which that experience may be thought about in order to do so.

This omnibus burden which literature carries has its analogue in any responsible reaction to the work. As Elaine Savory Fido says in this volume,

> criticism . . . becomes the functional action of revealing the bases of judgement and engaging with a work on all levels (after all form is philosophy and as such politics and ideology as well).

The work of women needs to be a part of the literary account of human experience and the critical response to it simply because the account is incomplete without them and up to now they have not had a sufficient place. This is one reason why, for a while at least, we have to have "women writers" and probably also "women critics." It may be, of course, that the women, once admitted, prove to have something significantly different to say and a significantly different manner of saying it. That is not my present point, which is much simpler: women must have a place if the literary account is to be complete; a complete account is, after all, what each discipline strives for.

I am pleased, as doubtless many scholars of the island literatures will be, that the term "Caribbean" here includes francophone and hispanophone as well as anglophone writing. I am encouraged by the perspective that includes and emphasizes the oral tradition, exemplified in Carole Boyce

Davies's study of women in Caribbean oral literature and informing the discourse of several other scholars in this collection. I am particularly delighted that the contributors are not all women.

Above all I am excited by much of what is offered in these essays, by their groaning towards the comprehensive vision of the "wind." There are metaphors—such as that of the "Kumbla" in the title of the collection—which are both resonant and intractable. They serve as symbolic devices in the works and as critical points of convergence. "Kumbla" becomes the calabash in Clarisse Zimra's essay, "l'espace clos" in Elizabeth Wilson's consideration of women's experience in the francophone Caribbean women novelists, and "A-beng" in Lemuel Johnson's commentary on Michelle Cliff's work of that name. The metamorphosis is unintended but evident. A thing turns into something else and at the same time retains its identity and intactness. The association-in-disparity and capacity-for-being-confounded both signify.

The fact of this refracting of perception and experience is represented in the essays in many ways, most explicitly perhaps in Elaine Savory Fido's piece, "Crossroads: Textures of Third World Reality in the Poetry of Four African-Caribbean Women". But the social-status continuum along which Mark McWatt fits Roy Heath's heroines is also a prismatic form. McWatt says, "The irony is that they (the women) are all in fact equal in terms of their status as victims." Perhaps we need a new critical vocabulary, for irony is the beginning of the prism, the impulse to pluralities restrained by a manner of knowing essentially linear: polarity, syllogism, dialectic.

Evelyn O'Callaghan's analysis of the treatment of "mad" women in the work of some female Caribbean novelists, and Lemuel Johnson's study of Michelle Cliff's *A-beng* are especially fine grist for the prismatic mill, as in Clarisse Zimra's essay in which nothing dubs up in all kinds of interesting versions. If we are to find our way into "ontological security," into an affiliation of "all the necessary disconnections and connections," into some statement-of-ourselves-through-time, we need a new way of knowing. If our self-discovering is to take care of the fragments/facets, it cannot neglect one half of the remembering. This book, edited by two women who both practise the business of literature, is a significant contribution to the beginning of the process of finding the necessary vision and including the other half.

Pamela Claire Mordecai

viii

Preface:
Talking It Over: Women, Writing and Feminism

Sometimes it is important to be personal. Despite the calls in the scholarly world to retreat to a safe distance from subjectivity, we know, as women, that it is the submerged life which orchestrates both our strengths and our difficulties. We do not confront the prejudices, ignorance and resentment which seek to silence our voices and prevent our development by pretending to operate within the same intellectual constructs which have long served male control of the world. Disclosure becomes, then, a vital political touchstone for our work, and a means of bringing into the open many hidden aspects of experience which are the secret referents in any conversation, any judgment passed, any alliance made. So, we decided to preface our introduction with a dialogue on some of the major issues which interest us in this field. We posed ourselves several critical questions and what follows are responses. As friends, editors, academics, mothers, women, we have worked together. This is the second time we have tried collaborative writing.[1] In our dialogue, we try to deal with some of the issues which inform this volume of essays, and which seem to us central to the comprehension of women and literature in the Caribbean.

On Caribbean Feminist Dialogue

CBD: I am concerned that there is not sufficient excitement and passion about feminist issues being generated, at least in Caribbean intellectual and activist circles. By this I mean on either side of the question: the critique *or* application of feminist ideologies to the explication and/or analysis of Caribbean reality. Some comparison with other areas is appropriate as it lends some proportion to the comment I am making. In the field of African feminist concerns, there is a strong, ongoing dialogue related to the struggle for liberation in the whole continent as it affects and is affected by the woman in Africa. In Filomina Steady's *The Black Woman Crossculturally*

(1981)[2] there is a significant and comprehensive introduction which outlines some of the important questions that have to be asked. Omolara Ogundipe-Leslie's 'Woman, Culture and Another Development' (*Journal of African Marxists*)[3] is important, as is also the fact that a subsequent special issue of this journal was devoted to "Women and Liberation,"[4] and this took the discussion in more practical and political directions. Work being done on South African women (see for example *South Africa Report*'s[5] special issue) is also raising central questions about women in African societies. My hypothesis is that, in this feminist era, when countries are struggling through questions of liberation in general, the issues of women's emancipation become critical to the understanding of total liberation. Caribbean societies are not engaged in such struggle. But, this does not mean that there is no need for feminist discourse in the Caribbean. Women seem to have great freedom in Caribbean societies, yet we know that women suffer great inequalities within them. In this regard, the Caribbean contributions to Robin Morgan's *Sisterhood is Global* (1984)[6] are perhaps too truncated, too general, with only representative discussion of the large language areas (English, French, Spanish, Dutch). The contrast is stark; the omissions critical. Where, for example, is some discussion of the women's movement in Grenada during the New Jewel government? By contrast, the discussions by Ama Ata Aidoo of Ghana: "To Be A Woman"[7], or Gwendolyn Konie of Zambia: "Feminist Progress—More Difficult than Decolonization"[8] or the piece by Omolara Ogundipe Leslie: "Not Spinning on the Axis of Maleness" have a polemical bite which seems missing in the anglophone Caribbean essay by Peggy Antrobus and Lorna Gordon: "A Journey in the Shaping".[9] Yet, Magaley Pineda's "We Women Aren't Sheep" (on the hispanic Caribbean)[10] is much more incisive. Her argument is that Latin American feminists need to build a movement both rooted in the social changes taking place in the region and yet also centrally concerned with women's issues. She says "We also believe that women must lose our fear of power if we want to become a serious political force" (p. 137).

Yet there have been a few strong essays in the past. I would single out Merle Hodge's 'The Shadow of the Whip' in Orde Coombs (ed.) *Is Massa Day Dead,*[11] and also her "Young Women and the Development of Stable Family Life in the Caribbean".[12] Actually, that whole issue of *Savacou* is a major contribution to this discussion but its promise has not been sustained.

ESF: I know just what you mean. It strikes me that none of us really knew, when we took on this struggle, how political it is, how intertwined with social realities beyond the question of women it is, and how much entrenched power is determined to reduce feminism to a fad, an aberration, a shortlived disturbance to be humoured before we all go back to other things. Yes, the Caribbean can be a relatively conservative place, although Cuban family law is very progressive for women. Feminism also, like any other movement, has its liberals and appeasers, its hangers-on, its fierce radicals and even its demagogues. Like any movement with integrity, it requires that a person live her/his life entirely by its principles, and not many are prepared to go that far at this stage, especially in the Caribbean where small societies exert tremendous pressure for conformity on the individual. But perhaps one should not always expect angry voices, for Peggy Antrobus has actually achieved a great deal in a quiet, persistent way, through her Barbados based Women and Development Unit.[13] One of the differences between the Caribbean, Africa, and African-America is that here creative writers and artists are not yet regarded as central in the fight against sexism—too often feminism is seen as a social science/development issue. Flora Nwapa, for example, in Nigeria, has been a Minister of Government, and is a well known writer (plays, poems, fiction). Her voice is clearly not bound by the conventions of social science or a scholarly inhibition. Similarly, Ogundipe-Leslie is a poet and academician as is Ama Ata Aidoo, and Micere Mugo.

But there are strong and radical women's groups in the region, such as the Caribbean Association for Feminist Research and Action (CAFRA) based in Trinidad, and local groups of an outspoken nature exist in a number of territories (notably Trinidad). CAFRA has creative writers within it and plans a poetry anthology of women's work soon.

The reason I keep linking writing and radical feminism is that in the Caribbean, as you obviously realize, writers like Edward Kamau Brathwaite, Derek Walcott, Aime Cesaire, George Lamming, and Martin Carter have given voice to a political/social movement for change and creative growth through their art. In Africa it has been the same. But literary criticism from the Caribbean has been disappointingly bereft of strong, committed argument, of camps and fierce confrontations such as have characterised the world of Nigerian letters (with writers like Soyinka, Jeyifo, Chinweizu, Ogunbiyi, etc.). There are signs that feminist literary and political activism is able to survive (and flourish even) in women's theatre but not in criticism (Sistren). The point is still that male writers in the Caribbean have a tradition of debate; women need to develop one consciously now.

How Does The Womanist Versus Feminist Discourse Fit Into Our Theoretical Vision Of Caribbean Women?

ESF: Alice Walker's definition of 'womanism'[14] certainly is not the only one we have, but it has become central. She emphasized the cultural aspects of the African community in the United States as a central part of her understanding of womanism. Later Chikwenye Ogunyemi[15] wrote of the separation of black and white feminism along the terms of 'womanist' and 'feminist'. This alerted me to a problem. Whereas I had celebrated Walker's meaning as a positive cultural expression of a particular experience, and whereas I have no difficulty in perceiving some essential differences between feminism in different racial contexts (something which is, however, relative and capable of dissolution in certain circumstances), I found Ogunyemi's thesis too rejecting of feminism to be sensitive to the literature she used as examples. I simply cannot accept that all white feminists are x, y, z, or that all black feminists are either. We are all complexly involved with various intersecting agendas. I therefore set about trying to comprehend the black lesbian viewpoint as represented by two writers (Lorde and Cliff)[16] and in the process I tried new definitions of 'feminist' and 'womanist'. The former, I see as the political agenda of feminism and the latter as the cultural manifestation—women's talk, customs, lore. We are speaking of particularities of feminism and womanism in different places and languages. I think you and I might differ in this—although I know you think Alice Walker's term is short on political involvement and the implications of what McFadden calls 'the conscientisation of men about their need to resolve the gender issue',[17] and that black women from Sojourner Truth to Barbara Smith have been feminist in an important way. I can well sympathize with the desire for separatism (it is sometimes necessary to withdraw, as Walker says, in order to heal, strengthen, define and realize). I would not want to stay there, of course, but eventually return to a positive community of difference.

CBD: Womanism is a strong term for me, but only as an important redefinition of the term feminism for other experiences than those of Western and white women. My other affinity with 'womanism' comes from realising in Alice Walker's documentation of it that it has strong Caribbean roots. Its acceptance by African women writers like Flora Nwapa and by African-American women who do not want to be associated with (white) feminism speaks to this reality. There is a consistent move to find new language to encompass our experience. This comes either in modifying the term by an adjective of some sort: 'Black' feminists (as with Hull, Scott and Smith[18] and other Afro-American feminists); 'African' feminist (as expressed by Filomina Steady and other African and African-American women like historian Rosalyn Teborg-Penn) and which I adopted in the introduction to *Ngambika*; radical or Marxist feminist for some white or black women who find the term feminist too contaminated with bourgeois experience. In an interview with Patricia McFadden, Fatima Babikar Mahmoud[19] of the Sudan, talking on "Women and Liberation," poses an alternative term, "woman consciousness" for the same reason. She considers 'womanism' acceptable but 'woman consciousness' more ideologically sound, as it takes in both men and women. But I also think Patricia McFadden gives a very important redefinition of feminism in a third world context:

> Feminism as perceived by African women is not defined in terms of man-hating . . . those women who are engaged in the anti-colonial, anti-racist struggles in Namibia and South Africa, define their

feminism in the context of national liberation . . . By feminism, African women, (and Third World women generally) mean the [woman's] right to life as a free woman and as a complete social being.[20]

In the end, though I find myself using 'womanist' in a few contexts and 'feminist' in most. A lot of us talk, though, of an "international feminism," a term that gained credence at the Nairobi Women's Conference (1985) and that divorces it from a Western/European or American context and instead addresses women's struggles globally.

How Do We Participate In Caribbean Women's Experience And Womanist/Feminist Responses To It?

CBD: My experience comes as a result of being Caribbean by birth and spending the first eighteen years of my life in the region, and another three years later on as an adult there. The initial experience was obviously strong because now, despite the fact that at least another half of my life has been spent variously in American and Africa, I find my sense of Caribbean life— the food, music, rhythm, sensuality, humour, cadences—still powerful. In a way though, I am both insider and outsider now. I am able to look back critically on the Caribbean woman's experience and draw conclusions, comparing it with the experience of women elsewhere. I also bring to this evaluation a feminist focus that I may not have had without my experience of migration.

For example, I feel a need to go in search of legendary Caribbean women. I need the knowledge of women who are comparable to Sojourner Truth, Harriet Tubman, Fannie Lou Hamer, Angela Davis, Queen Amina, to sustain me. I know they are there, but, it seems there is no history of women's participation in struggle in the Caribbean. What history there is, like Edward Kamau Brathwaite's essay on Caribbean women and slavery, is merely a scratching of the surface. There has to be more substantial work by feminist historians to reveal this kind of information. This is why a feminist consciousness, or at least a woman consciousness, is crucial because it provides the other side of the story.

So far, Grandy Nanny, the Maroon mytho/legendary ancestress is the only one who is somewhat known.[21] According to the myth, Nanny was one of two sisters who were captured in Africa and transported to the Caribbean as slaves. Once in Jamaica, Nanny rebelled and fled to the mountains from where she waged war against the British. Her children 'Nanny yoyo,' became the Maroons. She is described as an *obeah* (conjure) woman *par excellence*, a healer, one who could create food magically and a military leader.

In real life for me, there were a few women who in a minor way approximated the meaning of Nanny. Growing up in a period which spanned the colonial and postcolonial eras, I knew grandmothers who carried dignity, who meant survival and resilience and who came closest to the Nanny ideal. For teachers tried to enforce the colonial educational patterns, cultivating the middle-class, valuing colour and hair as close as possible to the European; female politicians were satellites to Prime Ministers. In my world, the only person who showed shades of resistance to male dominance for me was my aunt Olive, now in her late seventies, who was sometimes disliked for her over confidence and instinctive leadership. Her attempts at feminist assertion were belittled. She was the type of whom it was said in the context of difficult marital situations: 'two man rat can't live in one hole.' Yet she was politically astute, kind, social, spiritual, an excellent public speaker. Now that I look back, I know that her home was one of the undefined, private shelters for battered women and for girls who were ritually thrown out of their homes because they had become pregnant. Officially she held in her home, women's organisation meetings, political campaign meetings, prayer meetings and annual feasts to ancestors, and ran a 'breakfast shed' to provide hot lunches often from her own pocket for school children. Yet, for her, resistance to male domination could not come through confrontation but in the deliberate creation of a female-centered world. The stories of Caribbean womanists like that have still to be told.

At the same time though there were numerous signs of the condition of women which were depressing: street insult and verbal abuse and physical beatings from men; women with scores of children who were forced to beg the 'children's father' for support at his workplace on payday before the money was spent; girls of promise getting pregnant and thereafter losing all the brilliance that they had previously shown, sinking into a round of baby-making for men who saw sex as recreation and women as conquests; all this crowned by an oral culture which endorsed this behavior.

The positive examples were of female-centredness. Women shared child care and gathered to talk. Market women could slice anyone down with a 'cut eye' and a tongue lashing. Some mothers were fiercely independent and determined to raise their children to be successes with or without male support, and many of the latter group migrated in order to make a better life since the Caribbean did not then have the opportunities.

My position on this now is that whilst some features in Caribbean society make for women's strength and can be defined as womanist, there are perhaps more tendencies which make for women's subordination. Often women's attitudes of self-sufficiency perpetuate male peripherality and sometimes irresponsibility. Mothers of sons often encourage frivolous sexuality with lines like "I've let out my cocks so watch your hens."

ESF: I don't have a childhood experience of the Caribbean although I have watched my son's life unfolding here. Sharing some of his perspectives has brought me closer to seeing the experiences which have shaped many of the people I know as adults—play, particular landscapes, schooling, etc.

But I have essentially 'grown up' in the Caribbean—I came here in my twenties and went through divorce and single parenting here—learning everything I needed to know from Caribbean women. I was not a feminist when I first came, and did not become one until I had to deal with the problems that Caribbean women well understand and that made me interested in joining the women's movement here. I have always been impressed by the way in which Caribbean women fight for their families. They are often superlatively resourceful, strong, patient and capable of immense 'grace under pressure.' Since 1980, my personal development has been encouraged and guided by Caribbean women friends, and from them I have learned how to survive, how to support and raise a child alone, how to deal with an innately sexist society, how to maintain self-respect and self-sufficiency in the face of difficulties. Caribbean women can be daunting for men to deal with—although there are some very caring and responsible Caribbean men who defy the stereotypes and who can share parenting with their wives/women. But the strength of the women surely comes from necessity, from being unable to walk away from being left to raise the children.

One facet of Caribbean experience that has involved me has been 'race'—being white and foreign has given me a marginal position in many ways, but one from which I can observe and perceive the remarkable contradictions of the region—full of both racial antagonism and also enormous generosity and cooperation across race. The whole issue of black and white is infinitely complex here, as you know, and whilst simplicities are no doubt reassuring, they can hardly deliver reality in a satisfactory way. For me, the intersection of race and gender and culture tempers all large statements. I could not feel, whatever the particularities of my political position, as a colleague of mine in the women's movement does, that for her a black man always takes precedence over a white woman in her priorities, i.e. race before gender.

This makes me think also that what I often see as feminism (gender before race, etc.) is equally shortsighted. Yes, there will be a necessary political commitment to a cause and race/gender are central and fundamental issues which require deeply rooted support. But the kind of feminism which supports women, good, bad or indifferent, seems to me to create as many problems as it solves. In the Caribbean, we tend to see a gentler version of political action on the part of women, as when Peggy Antrobus popularised the idea that a feminist is anyone, man or woman, who attends to the issue of female oppression and recognises that it is real. Womanism for me is a softer, more flexible option than feminism. Feminism is necessary as protection, as groundbreaking work, as our best route to a new landscape of gender relations. It, like racial politics, is a necessary stage up to a day when everybody can find some just and quiet space in which to live here.

Like you, then, I see the need for drawing men and the condition of men into the discussion of Caribbean women's experience. Men in the Caribbean certainly need to feel that women's issues, and development, need not mean the further erosion of their manhood. I suppose this is why, unlike you, I do not feel particularly impatient with the apparently compromising tone of much Caribbean feminism/womanism—although we have to be vigilant, since some compromise is damaging. As the mother of a son growing up in the Caribbean, I worry about the inadequacy of much fathering here, despite the evidence that there are some staunchly different men amidst the general lack of fathers caring of children. But there is still too much of a division between the level of domestic responsibility accepted by men and that accepted by women. I can learn how to be a good mother, grandmother, sister, here, but I worry that my son has to pick and choose carefully to find male role models who will teach him a balanced way of coping with emotional commitment and public and private responsibility. Feminism/womanism is for me then a way towards better, more honest and complex relations between men and women in the region.

What Kind Of Meaning Does Caribbean Literature Have For Us Now, Especially Looking At It With A Feminist Lens?

ESF: I came to Caribbean writing through African, British, American writing, so to speak, here from a first job and a good experience in Ghana. At that time, in the early seventies, I saw African, Caribbean, Indian, Irish Literatures as primarily anti-colonial. That emphasis has now changed to one of dealing with present post-colonial, or neo-colonial situations in various countries. I am still primarily interested in the way in which Caribbean literature is a confluence of ethnic literatures, primarily African, but an African presence mediated through other influences so that it becomes creole, Caribbean. The feminist lens, then, becomes another way of seeing this complex culture—women's culture and women's place in the world constitute another vital strand of consciousness here.

Of course what this feminist perspective does is to complicate any vision one acquires. Migration has immensely contributed to the shaping of the region, and to its extension in Canada, America, Britain, France, Holland. Most well-know Caribbean writers have an experience of migration, and for some women writers, like Paule Marshall, Audre Lorde, and Jamaica Kincaid, migration is a central inspiration for their creative work.

That is intellectually how I respond, but emotionally, of course, Caribbean writing has now become mine, the new writing, expressing a reality which I understand. Because the region is small, geographically speaking, and can be traversed by telephone or plane reasonably easily, there is a network of connection here (as there has often been in other cultures) between the writers, directors, dancers, etc. Each Caribbean reality has a shape of its own—African, Indian, Amerindian, Chinese, European—and these subdivide and mingle with each other, Yoruba, Ashanti, Igbo, Hindu, Moslem, Portuguese, Spanish, French, British,

Dutch. What I see beginning to happen in the sphere of women's writing now is that Indian women (like Ramabai Espinet from Trinidad) are expressing their reality whereas before it was largely women of African or European descent who were making a contribution as writers. The women's movement has definitely had an important effect in encouraging this. Most of the Indian women writing are feminists.

Lastly, I, too, of course, have an insider/outsider tension in my relation to the Caribbean experience. But since I live and work here, the dynamic of that tension changes from day to day and this has the effect of making a creative response to the environment necessary. This is much in the same way as the migration north has acted as a creative spur to many women of Caribbean descent. It is noticeable how many of these are successful after they move north. There are many, many women who want to write, and who can achieve a little, a few poems, a story or two, or a play, but who lack the confidence to extend themselves further than that. As well, the usual barriers to women's creativity intervene: pressures of work, domestic responsibilities, social life and here even the climate.

CBD: As a girl, I remember borrowing a copy of Sylvia Wynter's *The Hills of Hebron* (1962)[22] from the public library. The book must have been recently published at that time because it was on display and I was attracted to the cover. I read it and it was interesting but, caught as I was in studying all that English colonial literature over and over again, it automatically got relegated to secondary status in my consciousness. In those days the appreciation of literature was linked unfortunately to the taking of the punitive GCE examinations. It was only later, in a university setting, that the meaning of that work came back to me. As an English major in a historically black university in the USA I read American Literature, English Literature (including Victorian, Romantic and other periods), and then, towards my senior year in the midst of the Black Power movement, a white professor began offering us courses in Afro-American literature. Another who had lived for a while in Africa offered courses in African history. A whole new exciting world unfolded. I consciously chose to focus on African literature for my graduate education, and through it doors of new awareness were opened to me. But in studying African literature at Howard University with Leon Damas, one of the founders of Negritude, the Caribbean made its presence felt. Besides, C.L.R. James was teaching Pan Africanism and Wilfred Cartey (*Whispers from a Continent*)[23] was a frequent lecturer and gave a strong Caribbean-centered vision. Elliot Skinner, also originally from Trinidad, taught anthropology courses on Africa and above all, George Lamming visited, lectured and read from his work.

Caribbean literature thus began to intrude on my consciousness, but still as an adjunct to my interest in African literature or Afro-American Literature. Afro-Caribbean scholars were studying Africa and I found that very progressive. My interest in the Caribbean was still to identify African features in it, not to see it on its own terms. My three-year sojourn in Africa and my subsequent readings, though, corrected that and forced me to accept cultural differences and the idea of a unique Caribbean identity; a separate literary tradition. Lamming was still stimulating to me, as was Derek Walcott, C.L.R. James (*Minty Alley* 1971[24]) and the poetry of Edward Brathwaite, especially "Rites of Passage" and "Islands". But Naipaul alienated me, especially when I read of "Miss Blackie," and the black maid in the Biswas household. The self-deprecatory tone of Mr. Biswas colored much of my subsequent taste for Caribbean Literature. So I never could feel the same excitement and involvement that I felt for African and African-American Literature without exorcising the meaning of Naipaul and some other troubling concerns. The connectedness which had begun for me with Lamming and Brathwaite came to fruition with a reading of Merle Hodge's *Crick Crack Monkey* (1970)[25]. It spoke directly to my experience: it was finally a literature that was mine. This sense of participation continued when I read Jean Rhys's *Wide Sargasso Sea* (1966)[26] Antoinette was real to me. So was Tia. So was each subsequent text I read by a Caribbean woman writer, Simone Schwarz-Bart, Paule Marshall, Jamaica Kincaid. Each work added additional frames to the expanding definition of Caribbean woman's identity. A redefinition is taking place and this must inform, for us as critics, how we review this literature, how we write it, how we teach it.

What This Collection Means

CBD: This collection arises out of the need to "bridge the chasms" as our colleague Abena Busia puts it, and fill the voids. It also comes directly out of my own feminist consciousness and Caribbean identity. A text of this sort is long overdue. As with most other literary and accompanying critical traditions, the principal writers and critics of the Caribbean remain male. Feminist criticism is as Gayle Greene and Coppèlia Kahn title their work *Making a Difference* (1985). In their introductory essay they say:

> Feminist scholarship undertakes the dual task of deconstructing predominantly male cultural paradigms and reconstructing a female perspective and experience in an effort to change the tradition that has silenced and marginalised us.[27]

Although there have been some efforts to look at the discourse of women in Caribbean literature, and these are important, there is still comparatively little work done in this field. Hopefully this volume will help to garner some interest as the Caribbean literary tradition can only grow from a multiplicity of critical discourses and progressive awareness of them.

Black and Third World scholars/writers have already challenged feminist scholars/writers for limiting their visions and conclusions about women to studies of American and European authors. The Caribbean text, like the African, or Indian, or Chinese text, remains still peripheral to what the Eurocentric perceive as the central discourses be they feminist, Marxist, traditional or whatever. This collection attempts to make Caribbean literature and feminist criticism interrelate in important ways.

ESF: For me, this collection means collaboration, something which is as Third World as it is feminist to my way of thinking—and something which strikes at the egocentric and hierarchal traditions of critical work which have dominated us so long. It has been hard for colleagues based in the region to find the space and time to complete work, and for me to complete my own. Single-parenting and doing a job which was set up assuming female support at home for a male academic workload is not easy, and here we do not have the time-saving/energy-saving devices of North America that can prolong the working day. But it means a lot to me that you and I have managed across distance and whilst meeting family commitments and demanding workloads, to collaborate on this project. Giving voice to women's concerns means fighting back against the pressures which obstruct women from finishing things, from engaging fully on professional projects over and above those of the working day. So this collection is for me a matter for celebration, as much as the patience of our publisher has to be also.

Carole Boyce Davies
Elaine Savory Fido

NOTES

1. See "African Women Writers" in *History of African Literatures* ed. Oyekan Owomoyela University of Nebraska Press forthcoming.
2. Schenkman Publishing Co., Cambridge Mass., 1981.
3. 5(February 1984) pp. 77-92.
4. 8(January 1986).
5. "Focus on Women" 1:4 (February 1986).
6. Penguin, Harmondsworth, 1984.
7. Morgan, pp. 258-265.
8. *Ibid.*, pp. 742-745.
9. *Ibid.*, pp. 110-126.
10. *Ibid.*, pp. 134-137.
11. *Is Massa Day Dead?: Black Moods in the Caribbean.* New York Anchor/ Doubleday 1974.

12. *Savacou. A Journal of the Caribbean Artists Movement.* Gemini, 1977: pp. 39-44.

13. This unit has successfully run many developmental programmes for women in the islands of the Eastern Caribbean, as well as hosted and sponsored numerous major meetings and seminars on various issues relating to women.It is part of the Extra-Mural Department of the University of the West Indies at Cave Hill.

14. *In Search of Our Mother's Gardens.* Harcourt Brace and Jovanovich, New York, 1983.

15. "The Dynamics of the Contemporary Black Female Novel in English" *Signs* (1985) pp. 64-89.

16. "Feminist and Womanist Discourses in West Indian/American Lesbian Writers". Paper delivered at the Sixth Annual conference on West Indian Literature, St. Augustine Campus, UWI, Trinidad, May 1986.

17. "Women and Liberation: Fatima Babikar Mahmoud talks to Patricia McFadden" *Journal of African Marxists* 8(January 1986), p. 12.

18. Gloria T. Hull, Patricia Bell Scott and Barbara Smith, *All the Women are White, All the Blacks are Men, But Some of us are Brave* New York: The Feminist Press, 1982.

19. *Journal of African Marxists* 8(January, 1986) pp. 10-11.

20. *Ibid.*, p. 3.

21. See Michelle Cliff, *Abeng* The Crossing Press, New York, 1984.

22. Jonathan Cape, London.

23. *Whispers from a Continent: The Literature of Contemporary Black Africa* Random House, New York, 1967.

24. New Beacon Books, London and Port of Spain, 1971. First pub. 1936.

25. Deutsch, London, 1970.

26. Deutsch, London, 1966.

27. London and New York, Methuen, 1985, p. 1.

Table of Contents

Introduction:
Women and Literature
in the Caribbean:
An Overview

Carole Boyce Davies and Elaine Savory Fido

> It used to be enough, but I no longer want my portion meted out . . . [1]
> —Christine Craig

I. Voicelessness and the Critical Context

The concept of voicelessness necessarily informs any discussion of Caribbean women and literature. It is a crucial consideration because it is out of this voicelessness and consequent absence that an understanding of our creativity in written expression emerges. By voicelessness, we mean the historical absence of the woman writer's text: the absence of a specifically female position on major issues such as slavery, colonialism, decolonization, women's rights and more direct social and cultural issues. By voicelessness we also mean silence: the inability to express a position in the language of the "master" as well as the textual construction of woman as silent. Voicelessness also denotes articulation that goes unheard. In practical terms, it is characterized by lack of access to the media as well as exclusion from the critical dialogue. Understanding "voicelessness", immediately puts into perspective the sparseness of the female literary terrain. This further explains the absence of critical discussion of existing works by Caribbean women writers, save perhaps Jean Rhys. The Caribbean woman (writer) then, we are arguing, has been historically silenced in the various "master discourses."

The double marginalization or dual colonization of the Third World woman (writer) has already been demonstrated by a number of scholars in a

1

variety of fields.[2] Gayatri Spivak further identifies a "worlding of the Third
World" by the colonial text which implicates as well the further "worlding"
of the black female text by the feminist text.[3] And this is a site of unresolved
contradiction in that feminist theoretical formulations, though they have
effectively challenged the colonized status of woman and provided the
necessary context for a discussion such as this one, have simultaneously
marginalized the Third World Woman. Chandra Talpade Mohanty in
"Under Western Eyes: Feminist Scholarship and Colonial Discourses"[4]
develops well some of the critical questions involved in Western feminist
assumptions.

Caribbean women's writing then (Caribbean literature in general) has to
be understood first within the context of the various imperialist discourses
and then against them as a rewriting of those discourses. The question of the
Caribbean male writer's struggle for mastery over the language of colonial
discourse (English, French, Spanish) has already been substantially
explored in the various Caliban/Prospero discussions.[5] Kenneth Ramchand
in his landmark *The West Indian Novel and Its Background*[6] provides
some of the historical contexts and the specifics of the colonial educational
arrangements which gave rise to the "West Indian" novel in English. In
Ramchand's study as in Lloyd Brown's *West Indian Poetry,*[7] the primary
voice is the male's: the Caribbean male text assumes primacy. There has
been a long history of women writing in the Caribbean, and it is only through
feminist *re-visioning* that these invisible writers are being seen.[8] Elizabeth
Wilson in her significant introduction to her translation of Myriam Warner-
Vieyra's *Juletáne*[9] states that "prose works by women from the francophone
Caribbean appeared before the end of the nineteenth century, perhaps even
earlier" by women defined as *femmes de couleur* (women of color) (p. v).
Marjorie Engber's[10] bibliography contains many unknown women writers.
In a more balanced reconstruction of Caribbean literary history, we would
find that women writers are critical to our re-defined understanding of
Caribbean literature.

The Caribbean woman's text is now being (re)written and in witnessing a
literature in the process of becoming, the participating critic can only make
tentative statements, mark and observe as she attempts to understand a
literature in the process of unfolding. The critic must struggle as well to find
an appropriate critical voice, wading through the various critical discourses,
to carry her observations.

Out of this voicelessness and absence, contemporary Caribbean women
writers are beginning some bold steps to creative expression. That some of
these writers have responded personally to this enforced silence and also
share the critical voice advances our discussion. For example, Maryse
Condé's deliberate titling of her study *La parole des femmes*[11] is itself a
posing of the "woman's word" into the void. In her essay in this collection

entitled, "The Absence of Writing or How I almost Became a Spy", Marlene I. Philip, a Toronto-based Caribbean woman writer importantly casts the African as woman and goes on to describe how, within the colonial education process, the harnessing of the language and the creation of the image or the word was always accepted as either white or male (even further, Indian male because of Naipaul's pre-eminence in Caribbean fiction). In identifying this absence, Marlene Philip's unquestioning acceptance of the female pronouns "she" and "her" in the identification of the African becomes a critical subversion of masculinist linguistic processes and an inscription of woman in Caribbean (literary) history where the "sexual/textual politics" accepts her absence. This deliberate feminizing of the personal pronoun poses itself as a refinement, or extension, of the Caliban/Prospero, master/slave dialectic. Clarisse Zimra pursues this point in her article entitled "Righting the Calabash: Writing History in the Female Francophone Caribbean Narrative" in this collection. She posits that Afro-Caribbeans can only more honestly "write/right their own origins . . . by discarding the logos of the Father for the silent song of the Mother". Audre Lorde in "The Transformation of Silence into Language and Action" [12] makes it clear that for us, at this point in history, silence is often allied with fear: "fear of contempt, of censure, or some judgement, or recognition, of challenge, of annihilation." It is overall, a fear of self-assertion and of visibility:

> Black women have on one hand always been highly visible, and so, on the other hand [because of distortion of vision] have been rendered invisible through the depersonalization of racism. (p. 42)

Yet, it is an absolute necessity to break through the boundaries of this accepted voicelessness and invisibility which is what women writers, by the very act of creative expression are doing. Mineke Schipper calls women's writing in the "Third World" *Unheard Words*. [13] For it is often not that women do not speak but that they have not been heard or that there has been selective listening.

"A Journey into Speech" is how Michelle Cliff titles her preface to *The Land of Look Behind*. [14] She contends here that enforced fluency, and the logic of expression in English almost rendered her "speechless" when it came to voicing her*self* creatively: "I could speak fluently, but I could not reveal . . . When I began, finally, partly through participation in the feminist movement, to approach myself as a subject, my writing was jagged, nonlinear, almost, shorthand." (p. 12) Cliff continues that it was through reading the work of an African woman writer who shared and expressed a similar troubled relationship with the culture of colonialism that she was able to move to speech from silence. Ama Ata Aidoo of Ghana and her fragmented, eclectic use of form ("part prose, fictional and epistolary, part poetry") and her rage against colonialism provided Cliff with the ability to find *her* form, *her* rage:

> After reading *Our Sister Killjoy*, something was set loose in me, I directed rage outward rather than inward, and I was able to write a piece I called "If I Could Write This in Fire I Would Write This in Fire." In it I let myself go, any thought of approval for my words vanished; I strung together myth, dream, historical detail, observation, as I had done before, but I added native language, tore into the indoctrination of the colonizer, surprised myself with the violence of my words. (p. 16)

For the Caribbean woman writer, the reality of absence, of voicelessness, of marginalization is linked to the necessity to find a form, a mode of expression. This linking simultaneously identifies the politics of woman's writing anywhere with the politics of the subversion of imperialism. Though Caribbean neo-colonial culture accepts physical, bodily expression by women (dance, etc.) and the entertainment of verbal abuse or creative "cussing out" between women, even the popular oral forms like calypso and reggae have been reserved for male expression. Yet, storytelling by older women is sanctioned as a private familial form of creativity and genealogical connection. The liberation of the creative written form for the new Caribbean woman writer has its source in the context of a feminist/womanist consciousness which as Cliff says, transforms the rage into word and simultaneously facilitates the abandonment of the male logos, which results in the dethronement of the phallic master text.

So, Jamaica Kincaid's opening piece in *At the Bottom of the River*[15] titled appropriately "Girl" retraces and simultaneously dismantles this past, this acculturative process for the female with its mandates, warnings, chastisments, repetitions all geared to enforce the sanctioned behavior of the Caribbean womanchild, domestic and limiting; little here supports the expansion of the self. But this is the self that is in the process of being created by being re-created. This is why Kincaid takes the language back to its barest, almost to nursery rhyme as Giovanni Covi insists, totally dismantling given semantic order, multiple-voiced, fragmentary, but constantly stating, questioning, inserting the silenced self in history.

II. Form and Fiction

Creative modes for recent Caribbean women writers, therefore, begin with a search for voice and form. The fragmented narrative that Michelle Cliff talks about above is the expropriation of a number of forms within one communication. Prose, poetry, letters, female history, all become part of this narrative voice. This eclectic, fragmented mode clearly marks all of Michelle Cliff's works to date. It definitely also marks Jamaica Kincaid's *At the Bottom of the River* which the reader perceives as an experience that the critic and reviewer are unable to define. Thus her more conventionally, linearly expressed autobiographical novel *Annie John*[16] uncovers some of the obscure references of *At the Bottom of the River. Annie John* and *At the Bottom of the River* function then double-voicedly as two separate discourses, one encoding, the other decoding, which together become the single text. In that way, Kincaid masters the use of hidden language of slave and private language of woman which, rephrasing Audre Lorde, the critical tools of the master may never reveal.[17] Lorde calls her self-statement, part history, part autobiography, part poetry, a "biomythography".[18]

Michelle Cliff's first work *Claiming an Identity They Taught Me to Despise*[19] is a similar experience for the reader—a cataloguing of experience, a selection of images; a setting down of memories as they flow into the consciousness, all with the female self as center. In the cataloguing, landscape is as prominent as is the self which it surrounds:

> Airplane shadows moved across the mountains, leaving me to clear rivers, dancing birds, sweet fruits. Sitting on a river rock my legs dangle in the water. I am twelve and solitary ("Obsolete Geography," p. 24 *TLLB*).

This is almost the same voice as the one with which Kincaid speaks in *At the Bottom of the River*: "I sit on the porch facing the mountains. The porch is airy and spacious. I am the only person sitting on the porch. I look at myself. I can see myself." (p. 29)

Some similarity in form to Jean Toomer's *Cane*[20] which comes from the allied African-American tradition and was also dubbed as experimental, is perhaps validly identified here. The texture of a character like Fern, who also sits on the porch and in "whose eyes the landscape flows" permeates these texts. Yet, it is a Fern, not mute but speaking, moving from passive to active, expressing her sensations, the meaning of the landscape, the meaning of her life, coming to terms with her self. For the narrative voice has moved from the third person male omniscient to the first person feminine, a doubled female voice of woman-poet-author and woman-speaking-subject.

Betty Wilson's recent discussion of Francophone Caribbean women's writing advances our understanding of the female narrative voice in this tradition. She argues that in many Caribbean women's works, the first person narrative predominates (p. vii). "The autobiographical first person narrative is particularly suited to the woman's introspective journey" (p. viii). Yet this is not to be confused with autobiographical writing. Instead it is an appropriation of a personal narrative form:

It is simply that the structure of the fictional autobiography, journal, diary, letter or other relative 'intimate' genres seem to be the preferred vehicle for expressing feminine/feminist/female consciousness. The autobiographical form allows a sort of re-vision, a radical re-shaping of a life, seen and recounted from the inside, which fits in with a 'problematic' protagonist's attempts to define and order reality. (p. xiii)

The linear, phallocentric form of the male text is often rejected by Caribbean women writers. Just as Afro-American Alice Walker in *The Color Purple*[21], Senegalese Mariama Ba in *So Long a Letter*[22] and Afro-Brazilian Carolina Maria deJesus in *Child of the Dark*[23] have posed formal interventions, Caribbean women's texts are also engaged in the process of radical re-vision and redefinition of what makes a work of art aesthetically female. The quilted narrative, braided or woven as is Sherley Anne Williams' *Dessa Rose*[24] alters the language and mode of fictional narrative discourse.

Besides the "quilted" use of form (quilted here posited as a revision of "fragmented"), the new Caribbean woman's text becomes a locus for the reinscription of the woman's story in history. The sustained, continuing narrative of the storyteller becomes a second alternative, although perhaps more traditional, creative mode. It is a mode beyond first person narration whose formal specifics in Caribbean women's litereature are yet to be clarified. But there are some distinct advances in our understanding of its contours in this collection. Storytelling is central to Simone Schwarz-Bart's *The Bridge of Beyond.*[25] Abena Busia in her article, "That Gift of Metaphor: Symbolic Strategies and the Triumph of Survival in *The Bridge of Beyond*", also in this collection, shows that the text becomes a collective story and Télumée's (the granddaughter's) autobiography becomes Toussine's (the grandmother's) biography. Beyond that, storytelling becomes a central metaphor for the ability to communicate oral history through the generations. The storytelling mode also flourishes in Merle Hodge's *Crick Crack Monkey.*[26] Yet, even when the linear narrative mode is employed, there is yet a thematic quilting of various stories, at times a deliberate appropriation of the structural features of the oral story.

For this reason, perhaps, there is as well a strong presence of the short story as well. Olive Senior won the prestigious Commonwealth literary prize for her volume *Summer Lightning* (1986). Jamaica Kincaid's work appeared first as short stories. Hazel Campbell is also among the growing number of short story writers.

The textual emplottment of history bridges the quilted/fragmented text and the storytelling text. *Abeng*[27] by Michelle Cliff offers this excursion into history, place, self. It explores the twin heritage of the protagonist Clare who meanders between her father's outright identification with empire and the mother's sensitivity to Afro-Caribbean history and her grandmother's ambiguous placement as spiritual but landed mulatto with peasant affinities. But *Abeng*, as Lemuel Johnson indicates in his essay here, is infused with history, with detailed sections in which Clare's story is displaced by accounts of Maroon Nanny and her sister Sekesu, with family history, with colonial history. The father's line of savagery camouflaged by austerity, colonial might and its eventual decay, and the mother's line of Jamaican mulatto/African/peasant identification meet as Clare attempts to wrest control over this self, this identity that is in the process of becoming. But all of this just takes us to the threshold. The activity is there and the many essays on Caribbean women's fiction in this collection expose it.

III. Poetry and Theater

Perhaps it is because poetry can be achieved more easily in conjunction with a busy life, as Ramabai Espinet[28] has said, but certainly poetic output by women in the Caribbean is considerable, and growing. In the Anglophone region, a milestone was the appearance in 1980 of *Jamaica Woman,* [29] an anthology of poetry edited by Pamela Mordecai (herself a poet and encourager of poets) and Mervyn Morris. Several of the poets who appeared in that volume, such as Christine Craig, Lorna Goodison, Gloria Escoffery, Olive Senior, have gone on since to produce volumes of work and to become more established as individual voices. In Trinidad, a number of poets are beginning to establish themselves. Nancy Morejon, the well-known Cuban poet, says in the interview included here that Cuba has a flowering of women's poetry. The Francophone region is better known for women fiction writers (Simone Schwarz-Bart, Maryse Condé, Jacqueline Manicom, Francoise Ega) than for poets. But in the Hispanic Caribbean and in the Dutch-speaking region, there is also considerable poetic activity by women.

Their voices are various. One cannot generalise about tone or subject matter easily, as Mordecai and Morris noted in their introduction to *Jamaica Woman:*

> Because these poets are all women, one may be tempted to raise the issue of whether they are "poets who happen to be women", or something called "woman poet". But that is not the point. The poems are various . . . these poets cannot be said to share a programme or a limited/limiting set of attitudes.
>
> What these poets most noticeably share is a language, flexible in its range . . . We hope that many of these poems give you pleasure in your contact with the things that matter to the poets. That is the purpose. That is the point. (pp. xi-xii)

Outlets for poetry in the region are fairly good, with some new but significant journals in the past few years (*Sargasso* in Puerto Rico, *Pathways* in Jamaica, *The Caribbean Writer* in the US Virgin Islands) adding to the established journals like *Kyk-Over-Al* (Guyana), *Bim* (Barbados), *Focus* (Jamaica) which publish poetry. Self-publication of volumes continues to be important in the region, and as in the case of the Nigerian women writers Buchi Emecheta and Flora Nwapa, Jamaica's Pamela Mordecai and Olive Senior have recently become involved in publishing ventures.

Women poets from the region are also receiving international recognition. Lorna Goodison of Jamaica won the Caribbean Commonwealth Poetry Prize in 1986 and was very successful giving readings in Britain and the United States. Nancy Morejon from Cuba successfully toured the United States in 1985. The forthcoming anthology of Caribbean women's poetry proposed by CAFRA (Caribbean Association for Feminist Research and Action) will make newer women's voices heard. Ramabai Espinet, in her publicity for the anthology, mentions that critical feedback for women poets has been scarce and that they need this kind of response. She hopes that "(t)he publication of this anthology holds out distinct possibilities for the beginning of a real discourse on feminist poets for the Caribbean."[30]

And there are other well established names of Caribbean women writing outside the region: Marlene Philip, Dionne Brand (Canada), Grace Nichols and Jean Binta Breeze (U.K.), Audre Lorde and Michelle Cliff, a number of Haitian and Puerto Rican women poets (U.S.A.), Francophone Caribbean women writers. Despite anxieties about a lowering of literacy standards, indifference to books and reading, and a kind of inertia in relation to language arts in the region, poetry is burgeoning in almost every island and women writers are very prevalent amongst these new voices.

One clear characteristic of this new work is the desire to experiment. Pamela Mordecai's work shows this very much. Her "Mongoose" is disciplined, sharp and very conversational:

> Poems are shorter; the truth
> look-see the mongoose slip into
> the bush. quick, after it.
> won't stay past these few words
>
> Once the sun moving held earth still
> and the stars musical: the swish-
> tailed mongoose etherized on his
> own breathing slept in a red round.[31]

Her "Up Tropic" is terse and sinuous:

More
than I want

to eat
at your feet

or blow you
bright poems

or winnow
your wheat

with the sieve
of my body . . .

God knows

I want
my own greening[32]

But Mordecai also writes in "nation-language," and in every poem tries a form to fit a new perception. This is a major identifying feature of the beginning of a serious poetic voice. It is there in Christine Craig's volume *Quadrille for Tigers* and in Lorna Goodison's first volume *Tamarind Season*.[33] A collective search for new form is clearly taking place.

The oral tradition stands behind much of this work.[34] In all of the Caribbean, poetry functions as part of a broad and complex spectrum from musical forms on the one hand to written, personal lyricism on the other. There is a constant shifting of tone from poem to poem, very often, within the work of single poet, and sometimes, as with Lorna Goodison's work, within a single poem. There is as well interesting cross-fertilization. The successful London-based oral poet, Jean Binta Breeze, has inspired a long poem by the young St. Lucian poet Jane King Hyppolyte. Within the different Caribbean countries there are also interchanges of influence. Mervyn Morris, who has encouraged a number of women poets in Jamaica, wrote the superscription to Beverly E. Brown's *Dream Diary* (1982)[35] a volume of poems published by the Savacou Cooperative associated with Edward Kamau Brathwaite. Dionne Brand[36] is a friend of Ramabai Espinet; both are Trinidadians. Connections like these make the poetry a collective entity, rather than the scattered and individual voices of Caribbean women living thousands of miles apart. The sisterhood aspect of the women's movement has created the space for women to find pleasure in each other's company in other than domestic tasks, church commitments, or frivolous amusements.

Despite increasing activity since the 1950's on the part of women in theater in the region, whether in plays as actresses or backstage support, as directors, sometimes as writers, or in indigenous theatricality such as carnival, there has not been a strong female presence. The major names associated with written theatrical creativity in the region are male (Errol Hill, Derek Walcott, Dennis Scott, Earl Warner, Rawle Gibbons, Michael Gilkes, Kendal Hippolyte, Ken Corsbie, Alwyn Bulley). There have been, however, major contributions from women. For example, Daphne Joseph-Hackett[37] is respected very much in Barbados for her contribution to the development of theater there, as a drama teacher in one of the major secondary schools and as a director/producer of plays. In Trinidad, Beryl McBurnie is a major figure in dance, as is Molly Ahye, and Helen Camps is well known for her direction of an important theatre movement out of which has come some carnival forms of drama. In Jamaica, Hertencer Lindsay, based at the Jamaica School of Drama, was a force behind the PanCaribbean Theatre Company formed 1986 to tour to England with Rawle Gibbons' *I Lawah*[38] and Dennis Scott's *Dog.*[39]

There have been too few parts of substance and originality for women thus far, and the few women dramatists who have been working have not necessarily produced plays which can stand alongside the works of major male dramatists as part of the classic tradition of Caribbean drama. A very important exception to this is the work of Sistren, the theatre group which is based in Jamaica and which focuses on the experience of black working-class women there. Sistren, and its Artistic Director Honor Ford-Smith, have produced a major volume of life histories of Jamaican women, *Lionheart Gal* (1986).[40] Their work is in the form of popular theatre but their scripts are written and may therefore become part of an ongoing theatrical repertoire in the region.

A large part of the problem of getting women extensively involved in theatre in the region has to do with the fact that professional opportunities in drama or dance are very limited and most people must have a full-time job and participate in theatre in their vacations or evenings. This is a strain on energy and frustrating to those who desire to develop their talent fully (many of these leave the region and become professionals elsewhere). But for women there is a greater difficulty: whilst the male absence from the household is a fairly conventional fact of life in the Caribbean, women are still expected to be home, and if they are single-parents, they often have no choice but to restrict their theatrical activities. The result of this is that whereas some young women, single or childless women, and older women whose children are grown may participate, there is little chance that large numbers of women can be fully involved in theatre unless they can create their own support system, as Sistren have tried to do in Jamaica.

Elaine Savory Fido's essay in this volume deals with such recent developments in theater and drama and her previous paper "Radical Woman: Women and Theatre in the Anglophone Caribbean"[41] discussed earlier work in this area. The thesis of the earlier article, i.e., that Sistren's work was a radical breakthrough in form and content, has been supported by the extensive success of the group and their influence on theatrical experimentation elsewhere in the region. Despite the strong conservatism of the Caribbean, there is an equally strong spirit of experimentation and eclecticism which has always characterised Caribbean creativity, and this is certainly a powerful element in women's theater in the region at this time. The earlier work of dramatists like Cicely Waite-Smith (*Uncle Robert*)[42] and others has borne fruit in the sense of there being a small but vital tradition of women writing plays and contributing to theatre despite the problems involved.

The Critical Context for a Caribbean Feminist Poetics

The critical development which this collection marks, has to be viewed against a legacy of Caribbean literary criticism which tended/tends to operate within its colonially-constructed perimeters. In other words, the center of the discussion was/is on the one hand the colonial literary discourse, best typified by the approach of Louis James in his *Islands in Between.*[43] On the other the politics of the resistance to colonialism voiced most eloquently by Aime Cesaire, George Lamming, Ngugi wa Thiong'o, for example. Gordon Lewis in "Some Reflections on the Leading Intellectual Currents that Have Shaped the Caribbean Experience 1950-1984"[44] identifies anti-colonial and post-colonial nationalism. Black power and négritude, and Marxism-Leninism as the three basic ideological formulations which have guided Caribbean thought, each separate and distinct but each clearly interpenetrating the other. These ideological formulations have been clearly expressed in the literature and its criticism.

It is time to argue that a fourth ideological formulation—feminism—now is being seriously articulated. That Gordon Lewis begins his essay "Men, everywhere, behave in response to the conceptions that they carry in their minds of the world around them . . . " (22) identifies his construction of the world from the male standpoint. Nonetheless, the work of Elsa Goveia and Sylvia Wynter, for example, demand to be placed in perspective.

One continuing thread of literary criticism continues to break through the boundaries of colonial/anti-colonial discourse in order to pose an affirmation of an indigenous Caribbean identity and "vernacular" tradition. Work done by Gordon Rohlehr, Edward Brathwaite, J.D. Elder, Maureen Warner-Lewis represents this position. New terms like Brathwaite's "nation language" are created. The culture of the folk, the working-class is privileged.

There is as well a growing body of "regional criticism" coming from the various literary conferences held at the University of the West Indies; so far two texts[45] have been produced from these efforts, as well as the new *Journal of West Indian Literature* (Cave Hill, Barbados). A number of individual endeavors from *critics* based in the United States, Canada, Europe and Africa have made significant contributions to the study of Caribbean literature, including works on individual authors: Sandra Pouchet Paquet's work on George Lamming, Michael Gilkes on Wilson Harris, Gordon Rohlehr on Edward Brathwaite. A number of forthcoming works also add significantly to the corpus of Caribbean literary criticism.

Current work on Caribbean women writers continues this discussion, subverting accepted discourse as it expands it. For we know that radical thought and innovation has not necessarily brought male writers to confront the issue of the role of women in Caribbean societies. George Lamming, who has contributed importantly to the feminist debate through his provocative portrayal of female characters in his fiction, nevertheless made no reference to any woman writer in his piece "The Peasant Roots of the West Indian Novel" (1978)[46] despite the fact of the centrality of women in the peasant culture here in the Caribbean. The point need not be laboured. A consciousness of women in culture and literature has been a recent phenomenon in the Caribbean, as elsewhere. Yet, it should be noted that Lloyd Brown, a Jamaican critic resident in the United States, wrote the first full length study of African women writers and dealt with several women poets in his study *West Indian Poetry* (1978). Bruce King's *West Indian Literature* (1979)[47] includes four essays by women critics (including Rhonda Cobham-Sander and Sandra Pouchet-Paquet whose work is in this collection).

Until recently, the surveys of Caribbean Literature rarely mentioned women. C.L.R. James lamented in the late 1970's that black women in the Caribbean "were not writing." He could recommend only one writer then. Even major female scholars, such as Sylvia Wynter, the writer identified and described by C.L.R. James as an "intellect that is surpassed by nobody in the Caribbean,"[48] did not have the political context and support in which to raise, theoretically, questions about women, although by her work, her presence, her articulations, the issue was raised. For the Caribbean at that time the politics of decolonization was more critical to our existence than was woman's emancipation. Although there have been some areas of serious work in all three major language areas (English, French and Spanish), a sustained critical response to the growing number of women writers and the representation of women in Caribbean literature began to emerge only in the seventies. This we must concede, could only exist within an international feminist climate and the growing body of feminist literary criticism.

However, women's literature is flowering in the '80s and we may identify two major bodies of creative writing by Caribbean women, that done within the region, and that done by women of migration and published in their country of residence, i.e., Canada, Britain, the United States, France, Holland. The latter has received some attention at conferences and in critical studies as extensions of other fields of interest (e.g., African-Caribbean writing as part of the writing of the African diaspora). For example, the conference on the Black Woman Writer in the Diaspora held at the University of Michigan, (October 1985), as well as the U.N. Decade for Women Conference in Nairobi (July–August 1985) encouraged work on African-Caribbean women writers to be linked strongly to that of African-American and African women writers. But there has been less attention paid to writing within the region. As the interview with Nancy Morejon included here makes quite clear, Cuban women writers have been emerging in large numbers in recent times. In Jamaica as well, a significant number of women writers have been publishing volumes of work. Critical response to this contemporary output of Caribbean writers however falls into some major categories, which the collection indicates. Carole Boyce Davies has argued in her essay "Gender and Heritage in the Works of Afro-Caribbean/American Women Writers" in this collection that migration had been as crucial to the generation of Caribbean writers who migrated in the 50s to London as was migration to France for the Négritude writers in the 1930s. The same, therefore, for Caribbean women writers today.

The work on Caribbean women and literature addresses a number of new and developing interests in Caribbean literature. The *Savacou*[49] special issue on Caribbean women in many ways began the discussion in the Anglophone Caribbean. But Filomina Steady's *The Black Woman Cross Culturally*[50] which included an essay by Regine Latortue "The Black Woman in Haitian Society" (pp. 535–536) added to that discussion and has to be credited with posing the study of black women in a cross-cultural fashion, including Africa and the Diaspora. Criticism of Caribbean women's writing is presented here as part of an ongoing examination of Black women's writing and is distinctly a work of cross-examinations.

A second major critical intervention in the Caribbean however, was the publication of the *Bulletin of Eastern Caribbean Affairs*[51] special issue on "The Female Presence in Caribbean Literature" introduced by Elaine Fido. Maryse Condé's *parole des femmes* and Yvette E. Miller's and Charles Tatum's (1977) work on *Latin American Women Writers*[52] additionally contributed significantly towards our understanding of this developing field. The *Kunapipi* special issue edited by Kirsten Holt Petersen and Anna Rutherford published subsequently as *A Double Colonization*[53] and Mineke Schipper's *Unheard Words* include Caribbean and Latin American sections. All of these provide us with a developing body of feminist literary criticism of Caribbean literature.

In the new critical work which is beginning to be established in this field, certain strands can be clearly seen. Critical assessments of women writers is paying attention to their contexts, and as much as possible, responding to the differences between their work/lives and those of male writers. Historical work is important in establishing the early women writers who have been neglected or forgotten. Phyllis Allfrey, Elliot Bliss and others have thus been recently rediscovered as a result of a strong interest in finding out the antecedents of today's women writers. Early women writers of course tend to be white, and despite Edward Brathwaite's apparent dismissal of Jean Rhys and other white creole women writers (1978),[54] they are clearly as important to an understanding of Caribbean literary history as are Herbert deLisser and Thomas Henry Macdermot. National contexts are also being studied, for it is clear that the cultures of certain countries give rise to the developement of women writers more than others. At the present time, Jamaica, Guadeloupe and Cuba seem to have more women writers than other Caribbean countries. Trinidad, home of such intense creativity as the calypso and steelband, and such theatrical developments as Derek Walcott's years with the Trinidad Theatre Workshop, has very few. Many of the writers from countries with turbulent political struggle such as Guyana[55] and Grenada have gone into voluntary exile and are writing from abroad.

Linguistic analysis is often a major part of the critical pieces that reassess established work. Bev Brown's article "Mansong and Matrix: A Radical Experiment"[56] posits that Brathwaite's theory of Caribbean aesthetics, "sun-aesthetics," is "male-centered and inadequate for interpreting writing by Caribbean women". In the process of arguing her thesis, Brown tackles the whole implication of "sun/son" imagery, the male persona presence as central image in Brathwaite's world. Women writers' use of language is a rich area for research. For example, writer Louise Bennett (Mis' Lou) speaks in a Jamaican female voice in both her oral and written poetry, using 'nation language' completely to carry meaning. Jamaican Barbara Gloudon as well uses language in innovative ways. In Barbados, the newspaper column written as the voice of a dialect speaker "Likmout' Lou" is popular, and the definitely female ambiance of the writing is a major part of the success of the pieces. In a similar vein the different language areas of the region (in the sense of the nation-language variants of Spanish, French, English, Dutch) arguably create different cultures for women and these need to be explored.

The ways in which specific aspects of history, political condition and culture impact on the literary creation needs further examination. For example, Elizabeth Wilson, who has an essay on Francophone women writers in this volume, thinks that these writers create heroines who are often haunted by "a deep sense of failure, dislocation and alienation"[57] as compared to Anglophone Caribbean women writers who tend to be more self-affirming. In this respect she sees Jean Rhys' heroines as very similar to those of French Caribbean women writers. Maryse Condé, in her *La Parole des Femmes* (1979) remarks that "A travers le monde, la parole des femmes est rarement triomphante" (113) ["Across the world, women's word is rarely triumphant"] a pessimistic view which is by no means universally held. Astrid Roemer, a Dutch-speaking writer from Surinam, communicates her ambiguity about gender and heritage thus: "I feel closer to the Dutch than to the Africans . . . And yet Africans, black Africans, have something that never fails to move me, that brings me to my knees".[58] In the introduction to *Spanish American Women Writers* (1983)[59] the author of the bibliography, Lynn Ellen Rice Cortina, expresses the hope that in the future, these writers will be examined in a fitting context.

Feminism also needs to be defined as well in relation to the critical context. Feminism has a wide spectrum of meanings, as we have indicated in our dialogue. Located at one, very political, end of this spectrum is the work by lesbian Caribbean writers like Audre Lorde and Michelle Cliff whose frankness and directness is assisted by their residence in the United States. At the other end is the quite serious but tentative attempts of women to write, teach, work within traditional situations, such as the East Indian family, for example, which have built-in inhibitions against open rebellion. In her address to the 1981 Carifesta symposium on women in Caribbean culture, Trinidad feminist activist Marina Maxwell said: " . . . it is a marvel that there have been so many creative women artists in the Caribbean. Too many have fallen silent or been driven underground, smothered by husbands, children or jobs."[60]

Lloyd Brown's charge in the introduction to *Critical Issues in West Indian Literature* that the present interest in women in literature in the Caribbean is another import (pp. 3-4), may well be premature or inadequately phrased. Whereas it is certainly true that the women's movement in the region has been strengthened and developed by contact with outside feminism, it has equally been true that from the beginning Caribbean women have understood that they have a long history of struggle and of valuable experience in dealing with sexism, racism, and class prejudices. They have tried to share this history with other women in the world as much as they have taken ideas from outside. Their traditions (like those of feminists in India, active since c. 1948) have not always been the result of Western feminism, although this has been a tremendous spur to the development of women's confidence worldwide. But it is not a distortion to say that wherever Caribbean women are engaged in women's issues, whether in the region or outside, they bring a special perspective to them. Their particular approach, born of the special character of Caribbean life, its unity-in-diversity, its engagement with human rights issues and with the ensuring of survival in adverse circumstances of all kinds, is the major contribution to world feminism that Caribbean women make.

Despite the relative conservatism of West Indian literary criticism, there is a growing influence of radical critical trends which easily fuses with feminism, as in the work of Indian Marxist/feminist critic Gayatri Spivak[61] with emphasis on the politics of what she calls "master discourse/native informant", and Edward Said who addresses some of the specifics of Third World textualities.[62] Early and pioneering work on Caribbean women writers, done in the 1970's by critics like Marjorie Thorpe and Keane Springer,[63] has now given way to more individually focussed pieces, or to larger and more extensive listings like Brenda Berrian's forthcoming bibliography of Caribbean women writers,[64] Darryl Dance's *Fifty Caribbean Writers* and Anne Adams' forthcoming *Fifty African and Caribbean Women Writers*[65]. But we are still at the very beginning of the establishment of a literary tradition, one which integrates the work of Caribbean women of all races and cultures but which respects their particularities and differences as well. Perhaps the reevaluation of Jean Rhys must come as part of this movement. She has been singled out for extensive critical treatment as a separate writer for a long time,[66] since her reemergence onto the literary scene in the late sixties with *Wide Sargasso Sea* (1966). It may be that now it is time to reintegrate her with the rest of the women writers both in the region and outside who portray Caribbean reality. All language areas, all races, classes, ages, experiences of women comprising the Caribbean need to be studied, but we naturally desire to comprehend each particularly of experience separately before putting it together into the mosaic of the whole.

The resistance movements of Third World societies to colonialism, slavery, racism, and exploitation have always had a great deal to do with harnessing and reconstructing culture, just as Nanny, the Maroon Leader in Jamaica, was a great obeah woman and her magic helped cement her centrality as a warrior and head of her people. The greatest threat to Caribbean life at this time comes from a denial of the spiritual/intuitive/emotional strengths which have developed to sustain the culture in the past. This denial takes the form of adherence to materialism, of attraction to the world of fast foods, video recorders, cars, multi-channel television stations, and attendant attitudes of more concern for the superficial and literal than the deeper meaning of social tradition. Literary studies are deeply involved with the creative values of a society and the art forms a society produces express, above all, those values. The fight before us then is to protect the womanist cultural elements which inform women writers, artists, dancers, dramatists, as well as to connect with the other aspects of the feminist and other political struggles to give women an equal share of socio-economic power. In this struggle, it is important to integrate intellectual pursuits with humane concerns—that intellectual work should never be self-seeking, competitive, or designed to further a career alone—and always with the expressed intention of extending our understanding of Caribbean issues relating to women and society. Thus the poets, novelists, dramatists and academics developing Caribbean literature as a woman's tradition as well might best work towards the same end. This is the tradition of Wilson Harris,[67] of Edward Kamau Brathwaite,[68] or of the theatrical work of Rawle

Gibbons which uses ritual and music to heighten a progressive cultural and political consciousness.

But the most urgent and central concern we must have in the sphere of women's writing is to encourage writing. The first essential is to find all the lost writers-those many, many women all over the region who have poems in drawers and inside books, pieces of fiction unpublished and stored in boxes in the roof. There are daughters who inherit a knowledge of their mother's literary activity as unpublished and confined to obscurity. There is a tremendous potential for major creative traditions amongst women who write here in the Caribbean, and that has to be a large priority for all of us in the future.

The essays in *Out of the Kumbla* collectively address many of the questions raised in this introduction. They share a commitment to reading these often marginalized texts, to doing the spadework for future discussion, to expanding the boundaries of feminist discourse as well as Caribbean literary discourse. As the first major text on Caribbean women and literature, this collection hopes to raise some critical questions and spur the development of a continued, sustained intellectual debate which can only redress the critical lack in Caribbean literary studies. With this collection, then, we present a revitalization of Caribbean literature and criticism and a redefinition of the meaning of Caribbean literature and an expansion of the narrow, Western limits/terms of feminist discourse.

The essays in this collection are less concerned with centrally arguing the relation between male and female text or between Caribbean discourse and Western discourse although these issues are implicitly addressed. Instead, they privilege the many unknown women writers, many unknown even in the Caribbean because of different language areas, the products of distinct colonial spheres. The critics here tend to pursue three methods of critical inquiry: the examination of a number of writers within a given tradition (Puerto-Rican, Francophone, Caribbean-American, for example); the closer reading of a particular author's entire corpus; and the examination of a particular theme in the works of a number of writers. Relatively little time is spent on the male representation of women, but as an ongoing, but not major, discussion it is represented here. An important contribution, for us, is the interview with Nancy Morejon. This because, since Cuba has grappled most explicitly with the problems of race and class which still beset the Caribbean, it is important to see how women writers perceive this reality.

Finally, the critics here do not seem intensely concerned with using or espousing specific theoretical constructs such as post-structuralist, post-modernist, deconstructionist. This should not be read as an avoidance of these contemporary modes of literary inquiry. Where necessary, critics employ the language, theoretical formulations and constructs of a variety of critical positions. The majority of essays, tend, we would argue, to be solidly feminist criticism, yet do not abandon the critique of feminist discourse.

In her essay "The Race for Theory"[69] Barbara Christian states that in contemporary criticism, there is an academic hegemony in which a "reigning academic elite" dominates the mode of criticism which is published and read and which, above all, reifies theory with the result that:

> Among the folk who speak in muted tones are people of color, feminists, radical critics, creative writers, who have struggled for much longer than a decade to make their voices, their various voices heard, and for whom literature is not an occasion for discourse among critics but is necessary nourishment for their people and one way by which they come to understand their lives better. (p. 53)

Henry Louis Gates—often identified in the camp of those applying too easily the theoretical formulations of deconstructionism to black texts—admits in his introduction to *Black Literature and Literary Theory*[70] that black literary criticism is actually a double-voiced or two-toned discourse which is engaged in a simultaneous drawing upon and divergence from the theoretical methodologies employed (13). A plurality of readings is desired for,

> Theory, like words in a poem, does not 'translate' in a one-to-one relationship of reference . . . the critic, by definition, transforms the theory, and, I might add, transforms received readings of the text into something different, a construct neither exactly 'like' its antecedents nor entirely new. (p. 4)

Elaine Showalter in *The New Feminist Criticism*[71] who argues for a "double-voiced discourse" in the feminist reading of the literary text posits that "feminist criticism has flourished in combination with every other critical approach from formalism to semiotics" (p. 3). To end with one final position on tradition (literary and critical), Hortense Spillers in "Cross-Currents, Discontinuities: Black Women's Fiction" states:[72]

> [The] work of black women's writing community not only redefines tradition, but also disarms it by suggesting that the term itself is a critical fable intended to encode and circumscribe an inner and licit circle of empowered texts. (p. 251)

All of these critical references suggest that this collection of Caribbean female criticism is engaged multiple-voicedly with both the female condition and its affirmation as well as the critique of the politics of imperialism and marginalization. Caribbean women's literature and Caribbean feminist literary criticism by their very nature cannot escape this political reality. For us, our writing and critical responses empower as they challenge. "Out of the Kumbla" then signifies for us movement from confinement to visibility, articulation, process. As process, it allows for a multiplicity of moves, exteriorized, no longer contained and protected or dominated. "Out of the Kumbla" is as well a sign for departure from constricting and restricting spaces. It further signifies the taking of control and above all locating ourselves at a different vantage point from which to view the landscape. Makeda Silvera in a creative response to voicelessness titles her collection of personal narratives of Caribbean domestics in Canada, *Silenced*.[73] Yet her very presentation of these women's voices contributes to the "Shattering the Silence". *Out of the Kumbla* is above all an articulation of our presence on the literary landscape.

NOTES

1. "For Artists and Writers" *Quadrille for Tigers* (Sebastopol Ca.: Mina Press, 1984): 61.
2. See essays in Robin Morgan's *Sisterhood is Global* (N.Y.: Doubleday, 1984); Kirsten Holst Petersen and Anna Rutherford, *A Double Colonization* (Denmark, Dangaroo Press, 1986) for example.
3. See e.g., "Three Women's Texts and a Critique of Imperialism" (includes discussion of *Wide Sargasso Sea*) in *Critical Inquiry* (Autumn 1985): 243-261.
4. *Boundary 2. A Journal of Postmodern Literature and Culture* 12 + 13 (Spring & Fall, 1984): 222-358.
5. See Spivak's discussion (fn. 3) and reference to Roberto Fernandez Retamar, "Caliban: Notes Toward a Discussion of Culture in our America." Trans. Lynn Garafola, David Arthur McMurray, and Robert Marquez, *Massachusetts Review*, (Winter-Spring, 1974): 2-72. ALso, Lamming's *The Pleasures of Exile* (London, Michael Joseph, 1960). Sylvia Wynter pursues this discussion here with specific reference to "Caliban's Woman".
6. London: Faber, 1970.
7. London: Heinemann, 1984 (1st. pub. Boston: Twayne, 1978).
8. Ralph Ellison in *Invisible Man* (1952) defines invisibility as a "peculiar disposition" in the eyes of the beholder. Adrienne Rich's concept of feminist *re-visioning* has to be applied in this context as well.
9. London: Heinemann, 1987.
10. *Caribbean Fiction and Poetry*. New York: Center for Inter-American Relations, 1970.
11. Paris, L'Harmattan, 1979.

12. New York: The Crossing Press, 1984: 40-44.
13. *Unheard Words: Women and Literature in Africa, the Arab World, Asia the Caribbean and Latin America.* London: Allison and Busby, 1985.
14. Ithaca, New York: Firebrand Books, 1985: 11-17.
15. Pan Books London 1984/New York: Vintage Books (Aventura), 1985.
16. Pan Books London 1985/New York: Farrar, Straus Groux, 1985.
17. "The Master's Tools Will Never Dismantle the Master's House," *Sister Outsider.* (New York: The Crossing Press, 1984): 110-113.
18. *Zami: A New Spelling of My Name* (Trumansburg, New York: The Crossing Press, 1982.)
19. Watertown, Mass: Persephone Press, 1980.
20. New York, Boni and Liveright, 1923/New York: Harper & Row, 1969.
21. New York: Washington Square Press, 1982.
22. London: Heinemann, 1981. (*Une si longue lettre.* Dakar, Nouvelles Editions Africaines, 1979).
23. *The Diary of Carolina Maria deJesus.* (New American Library, 1962.)
24. New York: William Morrow & Co., Inc., 1986.
25. Heinemann, London, Kingston, Port of Spain 1982. (1st pub. Paris Editions 'du Seuil, 1972).
26. London: Deutsch, 1970.
27. New York: The Crossing Press, 1984.
28. Publicity material for the CAFRA Poetry Anthology, forthcoming, 1988.
29. Kingston: Heinemann, 1980.
30. Publicity for CAFRA anthology, p. 2.
31. *Jamaica Woman*, p. 98.
32. Ibid.
33. Kingston, Institute of Jamaica, 1980.
34. See Louis Bennett, *Jamaica Labrish* Kingston: Sangsters Bookstores Kingston 1966; Erna Brodber *Jane and Louisa Will Soon Come Home*, London: New Beacon Books, 1980 and many other works which clearly grow out of the oral tradition.
35. Kingston: Savacou Cooperative.
36. Canadian-based West Indian poet. See, for example, *Primitive Offensive* Toronto, Williams-Wallace, 1982.
37. See Daphne Joseph-Hackett "Women in Drama" *Journey in the Shaping* ed. Margaret Hope n.d. WAND Barbados, p. 43.
38. Unpublished. Described by the author as "an extended calypso poem."
39. "Dog" is unpublished, and is a grim expose of human relations through the Caribbean metaphor of "dog" as an epithet conveying the lowest possible form of life.
40. London: Women's Press, 1986.
41. In *Critical Issues in West Indian Literature.* Ed. Erica Smilowitz and Roberta Knowles. Parkersburg, Iowa: Caribbean Books, pp. 33-45.
42. UWI Extra-Mural Department, Trinidad 1957. Published under the name Cicely Howland.
43. London: Oxford Univ. Press, 1968.
44. *Cimarron* 1:1 (Spring, 1985), pp. 23-40.

45. See fn. 41 above also Mark McWatt ed., *West Indian Literature and Its Social Context*. Barbados: Dept. of English, 1985.
46. In Edward Baugh, *Critics on Caribbean Literature*. London, Macmillan 1978: 24-26.
47. London: Macmillan.
48. "Wisdom: An Interview with C.L.R. James" by Anthony L. Welch in *Sturdy Black Bridges* eds. Roseann Bell, Bettye Parker, Beverly Guy-Sheftall. Anchor, New York, 1979: 261.
49. *Savacou* 13, Gemini, 1977.
50. Cambridge, Mass.: Schenkman Publishing Co., Inc., 1981.
51. Cave Hill, Barbados: Institute of Social and Economic Research, 11:1 (March-April, 1985).
52. Pittsburgh: Latin American Literary Review, 1977.
53. *Kunapipi* (special double issue on colonial and post-colonial women writers in the Commonwealth). Subsequently published as *A Double Colonization Colonial and Post Colonial Women's Writing*. Denmark: Dangaroo Press, 1986.
54. *Contradictory Omens*. Mona, Jamaica Savacou, 1972: 38.
55. This is not always for reasons of political commitment, but often because the turbulence of political change is unsettling, and greater opportunities lie overseas. Some good work is emerging. Guyanese writer Janice Shinebourne produced *Timepiece* recently (Leeds Peepal Tree Press, 1986).
56. See fn. 53.
57. See fn. 9.
58. *Unheard Words*: 203.
59. New York and London: Garland Press, 1983.
60. In *Journey in the Shaping*. Ed. Margaret Hope n.d. WAND Barbados: 36.
61. See fn. 3 & 5. Her *In Other Worlds* (New York: Routledge, 1988) develops these positions further.
62. Edward Said, *Orientalism* (New York: Random House, 1978) and *The World, the Text, The Critic* (Cambridge: Harvard Univ. Press, 1983). Both Spivak and Said are known for their radical interventions into Western critical hegemony within the space provided by deconstruction.
63. See entries in the bibliography by Jenifier Carnegie attached to this volume. Known since early critical work on the role of women in West Indian Literature, Thorpe has been very centrally concerned with the establishment of literary programmes as part of Women's Studies, and was the first ever female University Dean (of Arts) at U.W.I. Keane Springer's work is referred to in *Journey in the Shaping* see fn. 37.
64. Washington, D.C.: Three Continents Press, forthcoming.
65. Darryl Dance, *Fifty Caribbean Writers* (Greenwood Press, 1986) includes a number of women writers. Anne Adams' companion edition *Fifty African and Caribbean Women Writers*, forthcoming also from Greenwood, will have extensive coverage of Caribbean women.
66. See *Jean Rhys: A Descriptive and Annotated Bibliography of Works and Criticism*. Ed. by Elgin Mellown. (New York, Garland, 1984). There are volumes of critical/biographical writings by numerous critics on Rhys,

including those by Thomas Staley, Peter Wolfe, Carole Angier, Louis James, Helen Nebeker, David Plante.

67. See particularly *Tradition, the Writer and Society* New Beacon Books London 1967. His address to the Caribbean Writers Conference in London November 1986 was concerned with the perception of ancient symbols common to old, traditional world cultures, like the Amerindian, and he linked for example, their use of the tiger symbol to that of Blake, the mystic British poet. He accused intellectuals of largely ignoring real understanding, of operating on a superficial and egotistical level.

68. A number of important writers in the region have worked in a very localised area of spiritual problem—Brathwaite in getting people of African descent to respond once more emotionally, intuitively, to African forms and cultural perspectives, Lamming in trying to make a space for the pride of the black working class, Rhys in dealing with the alienation from the white racist world of the sensitive white West Indian, who also feels shut off from the black world. Harris is a most comprehensive worker towards spiritual health, whose work encompasses everyone—all races, classes, nationalities, and returns us to a plane where good and evil are the fundamental realities, not the categories we were born into. In London, in November 1986, at the Caribbean Writers Conference, Samuel Selvon was physically disciplined by an outraged West Indian woman who found his portrayal of women extremely sexist in a passage he was reading jocularly from his novel *Moses Migrating*. In the ensuing debate about this (in which positions were taken up ranging from strong justification of the assault to strong defence of Selvon's right to write/read what he likes), it became clear that one thing is new and has to be taken into account by male writers-they cannot assume a passive and silent female audience any longer when they present sexism without comment through the characters they invent. But on the other hand, if female consciousness is given to physical responses, then really the issues are not going to be raised long in a healthy and constructive manner.

69. *Culture Critique* 6 (Spring, 1987), pp. 51-63.

70. New York and London: Methuen, 1984.

71. New York: Pantheon Books, 1985.

72. *Conjuring. Black Women, Fiction, and Literary Theory* (Bloomington, Indiana Univ. Press, 1985.)

73. Makeda Silvera, *Silenced*. Toronto: Williams-Wallace Publishers, 1983.

CARIBBEAN WOMEN WRITERS:
SELECTED CREATIVE WORKS TO 1986

Adisa, Opel Palmer. *Bake-Face and Other Guava Stories*. Berkeley: Kelsey St. Press, 1986.

Allfrey, Phyllis. *The Orchid House* (1(53). Washington, D.C.: Three Continents Press, Washington, 1985.

Archer, Beatrice. *Poison of My Hate*. Lusaka: Neczam, 1978.

Bennett, Louise. *Jamaica Labrish*. Jamaica: Sangster Bookstore, 1966.

Brand, Dionne. *Primitive Offensive*. Toronto: Williams-Wallace International, 1982.

Brodber, Erna. *Jane and Louisa Will Soon Come Home*. London: New Beacon Books, 1980.

Brown, Beverly E. *Dream Diary*. Mona Savacou Cooperative, 1982.

Campbell, Hazel. *The Rag Doll and Other Stories*. Mona Savacou, 1978.

Cambridge, Joan. *Clarise Cumberbatch Want to Go Home*. New York: Ticknor & Fields, 1987.

Capécia, Mayotte. *Je suis martiniquaise*. Paris: Corréa, 1948.

_____.*La Négresse blanche*. Paris: Corréa, 1950.

Chauvet, Marie. *Fille d'Haiti*. Paris: Fasquelle, 1954.

_____.*La Danse sur le volcon*. Paris: Plon, 1957.

_____.*Amour, colere et folie*. Paris: Gallimard, 1965.

Cliff, Michelle. *Abeng*. New York: The Crossing Press, 1984.

_____. *Claiming an Identity They Taught Me To Despise*. Watertown, Mass.: Persephone Press, 1980.

_____. *The Land of Look Behind*. New York: Firebrand Books, 1985.

_____. *No Telephone To Heaven*. New York: E.P. Dutton, 1987.

Cobham, Rhonda and Merle Collins. *Watchers and Seekers. Creative Writing By Black Women*. London: Women's Press, 1987.

Conde, Maryse. *Heremakhonon*. Washington, D.C.: Three Continents Press, 1982.

_____. *Une Saison a Rihata*. Paris: Robert Laffont, 1981.

_____. *Segou I. Les Muraille de terre*, Paris, 1984.

_____. *Segou II. La Terre en Miettes*, Paris, Laffront, 1985.

Craig, Christine. *Quadrille for Tigers*. Sebastopol, Ca.: Mina Press, 1984.

Edgell, Zee. *Beka Lamb*. London: Heinemann, 1982.

Ega, Francoise. *Lettres a une Noire*. Paris: L'Harmattan, 1973.

Gilroy, Beryl. *Frangipani House*. London: Heinemann, 1986.

Goodison, Lorna. *Tamarind Season*. Kingston: Institute of Jamaica, 1980.

_____.*I Am Becoming My Mother*. London: New Beacon Books, 1986.

Hodge, Merle. *Crick, Crack Monkey*. London: Deutsch, 1970.

Jones, Marion Partrick. *Pan Beat*. Port of Spain: Columbus Publishers, 1976.

_____. *J'Ouvert Morning*. Port of Spain: Columbus Publishers, 1976.

Kincaid, Jamaica. *Annie John*. N.Y.: Farrar, Straus and Giroux, 1985.

_____.*At the Bottom of the River*. N.Y.: Farrar, Straus & Giroux, 1983.

Lacrosil, Michèle. *Demain Jab-Herma*. Paris: Gallimard, 1967.

_____.*Cajou*. Paris: Gallimard, 1961.

_____.*Sapotille et le serin d'argile*. Paris: Gallimard, 1960.

Lorde, Audre. *Zami: A New Spelling of My Name*. Watertown Mass.: Persephone Press, 1982.

_____.*Our Dead Behind Us*. N.Y.: W.W. Norton, 1986.

_____.*Sister Outsider*, New York: The Crossing Press, 1984.

Marshall, Paule. *Brown Girl Brownstones* (1959). N.Y.: feminist Press, New York, 1981.

_____.*The Chosen Place The Timeless People*. New York, Random, 1969.

_____.*Praisesong for the Widow*. New York: Putnam, 1983.

_____.*Soul Clap Hands and Sing*. Washington, D.C.: Howard Univ. Press, 1986.

_____.*Reena and Other Stories*. New York: Feminist Press, 1984.

Mordecai, Pamela and Morris, Mervyn eds. *Jamaica Woman: An Anthology of Poems*. Kingston: Heinemann, 1980.

Morejon, Nancy. *When the Island Sleeps Like a Wing*. Berkeley, Calif.: Black Scholar Press, 1984.

_____.*Grenada Notebook*. N.Y.: Circulo de Cultura Cubana, New York, 1984.

Nichols, Grace. *i is a long-memoried woman*. London: Karnak House, 1984.

Nunez-Harrell, Elizabeth. *When Rocks Dance*. N.Y.: Putnam, 1986.

Philip, Marlene. *Salmon Courage*. Toronto: Williams Wallace, 1983.

_____.*Thorns*. Toronto: Williams Wallace, 1980.

Rhys, Jean. *Voyage in the Dark* (1934). London: Penguin Harmondsworth, 1969.

_____.*Good Morning, Midnight* (1939). London: Penguin, 1969.

_____.*Wide Sargasso Sea* (1966). London: Penguin, 1968.

_____.*Smile, Please: An Unfinished Autobiography* (1972). London: Deutsch, 1984.

Schwartz-Bart, Simone. *The Bridge of Beyond* (1972). London: Heinemann 1984.

_____.*Ti-Jean L'Horizon*. Paris: Seuil, 1979.

Senior, Olive. *Talking of Trees*. Kingston: Calabash, 1985.

_____.*Summer Lightning*. London: Longman, 1986.

Sistren with Honor Ford-Smith. *Lionheart Gal*. London: Women's Press, 1986.

Warner-Vieyra, Myriam. *As the Sorcerer Said* (1980. London: Longman, 1982.

_____. *Juletane*. Paris: Presence Africaine, 1982. Trans. by Betty Wilson. London: Heinemann, 1987.

Williams, Lorna. *Jamaica Mento*. Port of Spain: Publishing Associates, 1984.

Wynter, Sylvia. *The Hills of Hebron*. (1962) London: Longman, 1984.

PART ONE
Woman Consciousness: Righting History and Redefining Identity in Caribbean Literature

"Woman Consciousness: Righting History and Redefining Identity in Caribbean Literature" is a deliberate attempt to inscribe or reinsert women into Caribbean literary history, or at least to identify their overlooked presence within the various, primary, literary/language traditions (Francophone, Anglophone, Hispanic) which together make up the Caribbean literary corpus. Part One also has an additional preoccupation, the redefinition of issues that include identity and self perception as they relate to women. The womanist consciousness which envelops this section explicitly shapes discussion here, as it does in the rest of this collection, not to express the primacy or singularity of the female, but to fill voids, correct omissions, redress neglects.

We appropriately begin with Elaine Savory Fido's essay "Textures of Third World Reality in The Poetry of Four Afro-Caribbean Women Poets." This essay simultaneously presents the works of some new Caribbean women poets as it addresses the question of woman's position in writing, literary criticism and ideology. The discussion begins with a quotation from Omolara Ogundipe-Leslie on the Third World woman writer's necessary consciousness of "colonialism, imperialism and neo-colonialism as they affect and shape our lives and historical destinies". It goes further to make a number of points on the Caribbean woman writer, therefore, as Third World woman and writer, as well as on the political responsibility of writers and critics as it relates to questions of race, gender, class and nationality. For Elaine Fido then the "Crossroads" becomes metaphor for the current place of these Caribbean women writers "standing within the central space from which all the roads emanate," making choices as far as direction goes. The metaphor takes on additional significance especially since the crossroads is a place of magical significance in many African/Afro-Caribbean societies. The writers she examines, Craig, Goodison, Senior and Phillips do not waver from their commitment to gender, race and class issues; are all poised for movement at the "crossroads" ready to change, develop, grow.

Elizabeth Wilson's essay, " 'Le voyage et l'espace clos'—Island and Journey as Metaphor: Aspects of Woman's Experience in the Works of Francophone Caribbean Women Novelists," locates the woman in questions of Caribbean identity: geography, migration, entrapment. It identifies how journey, exile and alienation are experienced by the Caribbean woman wherever she may be, in the Caribbean, France or Africa. According to Wilson, the Caribbean woman's peculiar "predicament is expressed metaphorically also in terms of clearly defined closed spaces," and she herself often becomes the island, cut-off, marooned. The closed space has the potential of functioning both negatively and positively—but positively only if it is used as cocoon (cf. our titular kumbla *metaphor) from which growth eventually comes. This latter model is expressed by Manicom in* Mon Examen de blanc *which Wilson calls the most militant feminist West Indian work to date and which presents the woman as conscious of the imposed limitations and deliberately rejecting them. For Manicom, the woman's subordination to the male is linked to the colonized position of the French Antilles to France.*

"Writing Home: Gender and Heritage in the Works of Afro-Caribbean/American Women Writers" by Carole Boyce Davies presents another group of Caribbean women writers, North American-based but explicitly Caribbean-identified. By examining such factors as migration, the relationship to the hegemonic United States, the capacity to explore woman to woman relationships along with thematic continuities to the larger body of Caribbean literature, Carole Boyce Davies establishes the importance of defining this group of women writers (Marshall, Kincaid, Lorde, Cliff) within the Caribbean literary tradition.

Sandra Messinger Cypess's "Tradition and Innovation in the Writings of Puerto Rican Women" decries the omission, by literary historians and critics, of significant Puerto Rican women writers in Puerto Rican literary tradition. She points to numerous women who produced works of great literary merit and describes how

Puerto Rican literary tradition actually began with the work of a woman, Maria Bibiana Benitez. Any revised Puerto Rican literary history, therefore, has to accord women their rightful place. Puerto Rican women writers, it becomes clear, reveal a concern for gender and class issues along with their attempts to define their Caribbean identity.

Importantly, a majority of the essays in this section take issue with critical perceptions, at first colonialist and sexist, now neo-colonialist and sexist, which obliterate the existence of the woman, which fail to read the woman's text, which place negative values on women's issues, and which consequently marginalize or even erase Caribbean women writers. Evelyn O'Callaghan in "Interior Schisms Dramatised: The Treatment of the 'Mad' Woman in the Work of Some Female Caribbean Novelists," discusses the work of Jean Rhys, Myriam Warner-Vieyra and Zee Edgell who, along with several other women writers, present women undergoing varying levels of psycho-social dislocation. For O'Callaghan, the 'mad' woman serves as social metaphor for the damaged West Indian psyche, at the same time that it underscores the disfigurement of the female personality under the same colonial stresses but along with the additional victimization that is a fact of life for women in patriarchal societies.

Lemuel Johnson's "A-beng (Re)Calling the Body In(to) Question" uses Michelle Cliff's novel Abeng *as a point of departure for an excursion into the re-writing of the woman's story in Caribbean/ New World societies. Using and critiquing theoretical formulations ranging from the French feminists and psychoanalytic critics to deconstructionists, Johnson follows Cliff in raising Nanny the Maroon to a position of historical prominence. Nanny becomes epigrammatic of the womanist consciousness which informs works like Cliff's. Johnson poses this womanist presence against the symbolic manipulation, and othering, of the female, for example, in the vision of a Derek Walcott.*

"Righting the Calabash: Writing History in the Female Franco-phone Narrative" by Clarisse Zimra similarly takes us back into Francophone Caribbean literary history. It picks up questions of the ideology and genealogy of négritude, the master/slave text and the gender variants of the roman creole. *Zimra, in a fitting rounding off of this section, concludes that "the intolerable absence of the original Father hides the silent presence of a Mother not yet fully understood."*

All of the essays in this section, "Woman Consciousness: Righting History and Redefining Identity in Caribbean Literature," set up some of the contours and perimeters, and deal with many of the theoretical questions with which essays in the rest of the collection grapple. In a way, Part One tends toward broad overviews of thematic concerns across language barriers. Overall, it re-defines Caribbean literary history, conscious of the insertion of female identity in that definition.

Textures of Third World Reality in the Poetry of Four African-Caribbean Women[1]

Elaine Savory Fido

> That the female writer be committed to her *third world reality* and status may lead to disagreements. Being aware of oneself as a third world person implies being politically conscious, offering readers perspectives on and perceptions of colonialism, imperialism and neocolonialism as they affect and shape our lives and historical destinies.
>
> (my italics)
> Omolara Ogundipe-Leslie[2]

Women writers in the third world have a complex series of possibilities to realise in their work, if they choose to effect full consciousness of their situation: race, class, nationality and gender issues intersect in their lives. These different agendas can also become conflicted and cause stress, although women can avoid this by making one or other commitment primary in any given situation, choosing according to the context. I am concerned in this essay with the ways in which four women poets of African-Caribbean descent, three from Jamaica and one from Barbados, determine these priorities in their work, and with how these choices might affect reader response or criticism. It seems to me that the critical act is very much one of deception if the critic pretends to objectivity of judgement. However the attempt is made to avoid prejudice or subjective assessment, this will creep in. It is a good deal worse to claim objectivity or universality when in fact strong personal experience lies underneath the critical theory which interprets the work. It must be remembered that the priorities of the critic also shift.

I have chosen to present the choices which face both writer and critic as an image of the crossroads, that place of mystery and ritual in many third world cultures, which denotes a particular seriousness attached to choices made. Standing within the central space where all roads meet, one can see the choices clearly. At any time, it is possible to decide on one direction and pursue that to the exclusion of all others. Some writers and critics choose only one aspect of their total perception of reality, and by choice pursue that as far as possible to the exclusion of all others. It is of course possible for the consciousness, to return at any time to the collective central space. But for some people the crossroads is only a momentary and tedious pause before embarking on a major direction: for example, women could privilege race agendas over ones of gender. Such fragmented consciousness is encouraged by educational and political agendas which stress the need to make a choice of one commitment as a priority (whether it be subject for study or ideology or belief by which to live one's life).[3] I believe it is a truer perception to realize that we are bound to be less than fully aware of the intersections of various aspects of our complex reality most of the time and to cause ourselves to be as conscious as possible of these limitations by the admission of subjectivity and the analysis of it in both creative and critical work. This position has come to be important in my own critical and creative work as a result of living in the Caribbean (where the known realities of complex intercultural living are enough to make anyone pause who wishes to judge literature on the basis of objective, complete understanding). The perception of literature or of writers from the Caribbean as being able to be confined to large simplicities of race, nationality, color, class or gender is simply a very misguided one. Of course we need some of these categories to sort writers in a fairly crude way for first experience of their work. But very soon, we have to realize that the Caribbean writer is almost inevitably a person of multi-faceted experience.[4] There is really only the choice of dealing with that experience in a integrative manner, of tolerating the differences within the personality, or of ignoring one or other facet of a life. It is not enough to talk of Naipaul, for example, as a Trinidadian, for he is a Trinidadian East Indian male fiction writer with a long and important cultural influence from his adopted country of Britain. All those factors, (and including here are the complex meanings of his particular subculture of East Indian Trinidadian culture) have to be important in judging his work, but it is very important to understand his own choices and priorities as well as ours. Naipaul's work sets up tensions in most readers of African-Caribbean (or African) descent because he reflects in his work, whether consciously or unconsciously the prejudices embedded in Caribbean East Indian culture towards African culture in the Caribbean (a similar prejudice answers this from African to Indian). Similarly, feminists find Naipaul's depiction of women difficult.[5] Sorting out what is justifiable (to reject his prejudices from what is praiseworthy) and the arguable admission of these in the work, and fact (that such attitudes exist in the society Naipaul writes about) is only possible when the fact of writer and reader subjectivity is clearly laid out. Criticism could then proceed beyond the fairly futile ground of deciding between outsider and insider views of a literature (there is a danger here of confining literature to the interpretations of those critics who happen to come from the social milieu of the writer or of privileging outsider views, where these are purportedly more "objective"). It could become a matter of sharing the complexly personal vision of writer and critic as they interact together, which I want to suggest is a major way forward to unlocking the deeper value of writing and reading as communication of a special, profound nature.

I must add here that this kind of acceptance of consciously perceived and analysed subjectivity in the critical stance is very easily brought together with a generally female desire to understand another person outside the strictures of categories (this is by no means an inevitable female trait, but the fact that successful female nurturance of both children and adults has often required a subtle and very complex awareness of the nature of all involved in such transactions) is important.

Criticism then, in this sense, is a self-exploratory act on the part of the critic, understanding that even the apparently objective perception of form in literature is best comprehended with the knowledge that form is philosophy, and as such politics and ideology as well. In this essay, I will examine the poetry of Christine Craig, Lorna Goodison, Esther Phillips and Olive Senior expressions of their present perception of their reality and the reality of their societies. These perceptions are likely to change, for they are all new writers, developing constantly. I, too, as a critic, am on a journey of development, which hopefully will never use the works of writers but rather explore them as a source of knowledge and experience of form and content which can bring me more self-awareness as well as an awareness of the writer's creative power and achievement.

Craig, Senior, Goodison and Phillips are different writers but they share a good deal in a broad sense: three are single mothers, whose emergence as poets has come after the birth of their children. Olive Senior has never married or had children. All four are of African descent: to differing degrees resting identity on their particular sense of racial belonging (in the Caribbean this is not just a matter of race itself but of color and class as well). All four recently produced first volumes of poetry,[6] and Lorna Goodison has just published her third volume and her second won the Commonwealth Poetry Prize for the Caribbean in 1986. These similarities make it the more important that their work is so significantly different, one from the other. Choices of style and craft essentially emanate from the directions each chooses according to her perceptions of her own realities and priorities.

I shall begin with Christine Craig's *Quadrille for Tigers*. Her poem "All Things Bright . . . ", written about a personal moment, is a good example of the effect present in a great deal of her work, namely a presentation of different elements each in an intersecting relation with the other. Craig often writes from that crossroads centre, her poems taking creative energy from a juxtaposition of factors in an experience which she creatively perceives. In this poem, the central persona is a mother, trying to bring up a daughter, concerned with the small details of appearance ("you not going anywhere/ in those dirty shoes") but emotionally hurt by the violence in Kingston through which she must go "Eyes mussed with tears" to take her daughter to school. The daughter, whose sensitivity to the violence in the city is a mark of sharing values with the mother, is also hurt by the world outside the home and her face is "sad,/just at the edges". Good mothering is frustrated by the social chaos, in the sense of not being able to protect the child against all hurts in the environment (and the child's vulnerability is a sign of being able to care). In the poem, we are made to realise how all human relations are enhanced or damaged by the state of society:

> Women's lives shot to stillness
> in small, hot rooms. Men
> bought and sold, holding death bold
> in the gleam of guns,
> a deadly phallic power against the impotence of poverty.[7]

Here Craig does not quite say that economic tensions create sexual tensions, but she shows how one interacts with the other, how the need to be traditionally female and withdrawn (as the daughter in the poem wants to withdraw), and the need to be traditionally male and keep potency through aggression, are both dangerous in the circumstances of extreme economic exploitation. The way in which rhyme and sound patterns (particularly $c, s,$ and p sounds) interact here reinforces the way in which this impression of complex involvement of a number of aspects of social experience is conveyed by verbal meaning.

In another poem in the same volume, "Lost from the Fold", where Craig focuses on a derelict woman who has died in the street, there is a juxta-position of the woman with the rhetoric of religion:

> Can't believe in
> His infinite mercy
> when I see a woman,
> age uncertain, legs
> like gaulins, but crumpled
> across the gutter.[8]

Here again, in this poem, is a strong sense of one perception being cut across by another and changed by it (God is altered by the woman's particular plight. The city is a very present reality, with the image of hunger *skanking* (to *skank*, in slang usage, is to survive on the street, usually used of young men). Male images in the poem are all ones of neglect of the woman. Hunger is Death's "dread" friend (and male by inference as well as Rasta), and Death himself is the only certain kind of entity in the woman's life at this point. The "noble lion/of Judah" is absent. These images of men which have overtones of power and strength contrast with the Sunday School "dove" and "lamb". Even Death, who was good enough to release his victim from her suffering, took his time. The poem is subtle in its anger, but very definite, and again, the interaction of gender issues with economic circumstances which affect everyone in the city (Rastafarianism as the cult of the poor and oppressed is very present here but is redefined in relation to the dead woman) is a strong characteristic of the creative identity of the work.

But the poem which most clearly identifies this interaction of interests is Craig's well known "Crow Poem". The "crow" is a woman whose voice "wants to say things/about blue skies, blond sand", but this Caucasian tourist poster imagery is rejected. Instead, a "rasping carrion croak/jets from my beak/sharp edged". The wordplay ("Illsuited"; "jets") contains the double-layering which informs the poem: again there is a delicate touch to the dilemma and a wry playfulness:

> Perhaps there is out there
> one crow, wheeling over the city dump
> convinced she is a woman.[9]

The cliched imaged of the crow is thus reassembled and revived here by the female consciousness which pervades the poem: at one level it works as a statement about woman's constant sense of physical inadequacy in the face of male desires for "pretty" images and of course, in this case, for "white" tourist cliches of attractiveness, but then the poem shifts and realigns. It is a much more awkward self which becomes the basis of a tentative contact with a loved other:

> I want so much to put
> my arms around you but
> extended they are feathered
> vanes, snapped, tatty things
> no longer curving.[10]

The creative power of "Crow Poem" comes from the delicacy of this brave facing of an alienated self.

Like Craig, Olive Senior writes out of a clear awareness of a conflicted life which is only by effort brought into any kind of control and clarity. She spoke recently[11] of her childhood lived between two homes, a village, "darkskin" one and a "lightskin," middle-class environment, where she was alone and being groomed for status and advancement. In her recent volume, *Talking of Trees*, she uses as a superscription to a section of the book Brecht's statement, "What kind of period is it/when to talk of trees/is almost a crime/because it implies silence/about so many horrors?" and of course this is the source of the book's title as well. Similarly, she quotes Martin Carter "But what the leaves hear/is not what the roots ask". Her vision is often one of aloneness "Alone I will walk through the glass." [12] In "Cockpit Country Dreams" she speaks of father and mother saying different things as "Portents of a split future". [13] There are two cultures here, the father's and the mother's:

> My father said: lines on paper
> cannot deny something that *is*.
> (My mother said: such a wasted life
> is his). [14]

But in the end the poet makes sense of this division:

> Now my disorder of ancestry
> proves as stable as the many rivers
> flowing around me. Undocumented
> I drown in the other's history. [15]

Poetry becomes the balancing point, the crossroads at which all directions have to meet. Like Craig, Senior determines life through an awareness of many directions and contradictions facing the individual, and her poetry becomes the place where at least distances and schisms can be spoken of an accepted:

> One night
> the father
> split
> a house
> in two [16]

Part of the solution to these tensions is the control which poetry gives. In "To the Madwoman In My Yard", the poet speaks with an exasperated understanding and sisterhood but in the end they are divided by the certainty in the poet that "Life Equals Control":

> Yes. Here is what the difference between us
> is about: I wear my madness in. You wear yours out. [17]

Even Senior's use of line order suggests this constant attempt to control and order fragmentation: she experiments a good deal with various formations and these suggest a vigilant awareness of possible rearrangements of reality all the time. Her language, like Craig's, sometimes becomes creole but is mainly international English. Goodison, by comparison, moves in and out of creole increasingly within the same poem, [18] thus suggesting a deep unity within the two forms within her creative centre. But Senior draws a good deal on a sense of African culture, of ancestors who are still present and of rituals, of the African past and its relation to the contemporary experience through family stretching back to slavery, and this provides an emotional base for much of her painful poetry of isolation and displacement:

> Listen child, said my mother
> whose hands plundered photo albums
> of all black ancestors: Herein
> your ancestry, your imagery, your pride . . .
> Listen child, said my father
> from the quicksand of his life:
> Study rivers. Learn everything.
> Rivers may find beginnings
> in the clefts of separate mountains
> Yet all find their true homes
> in the salt of one sea. [19]

It is not only African and European ancestry which Senior can claim but also Arawak:

> . . . Yokahuna as real
> as the Virgin Mary, Coyaba as close as Heaven.
> My spirit ancestors are those
> I choose to worship and that
> includes an I that existed
> long before me. [20]

Both Craig and Senior, then, convey an awareness of life which is complex and which their tightly organised and carefully sensitive poems try to express. Esther Phillips has another kind of mood for most of her poetry so far published. It is much more intensely angry, and often more single-level polemical, than any of the other poets here discussed. This is a necessary part of consciousness in women, a stage of anger which precedes an ability to reintegrate things and balance them. It is part of an awareness of oppression which, as in the Black Arts movement in the 1960's in America, provides a channel for healthy reassessment of the self and for the

demand for greater creative space in which to live. But even though Phillips'
work is frequently moving only in one direction, there is sometimes an
intersection of religious conviction with expression of anger at a woman's
exploitation by a man. I find Phillips' work less interesting now that I would
have done several years ago when I needed to go through this anger myself,
but for a woman who is still trying to express her feelings about a difficult
relation with a man it is going to provide an important and satisfying if
narrow focus. Phillips tends to the large and general in her vision of men. In
"Child Grieving", which presents a small girl sleeping and dreaming of an
absent and irresponsible father, "gone/but loved/with all the adoration/of
your childish dreams." Many of the lines are heavy with a flattening rage:

> I know
> that sigh precedes
> your bitter grief of womanhood,
> when tears, not sighs
> will splash against
> the iron cycle
> that binds your women-folk,
> a repetitious wheel
> where weak men
> come
> and then
> they go.[21]

In "Lonely Women", the rhythm of the language begins to give way under
the weight of anger which is expressed romantically and starkly:

> deep, deep in sleep, he does not dream
> of his dead seed
> on her naked thigh
> not touch
> the crushed rails
> of her heart's
> high Altar.[22]

But in "Tribute (to My Mother)", which I like better, there is a tension set
up between the conflicting images of conventional maternity (loving,
gentle), and the reality of motherhood under stress:

> Now
> I see the hate
> was for your own condition
> your horror
> of entrapment,

that the angry shouts
to the god of fate
were only your Song of Life.[23]

"Half Measures" is a clever poem, where the poet-persona is strong at the end after telling a man to go home to his other woman, "and leave me with nothing./for out of nothing/I can create . . . " Here the situation is a familiar Caribbean one of polygamous male behaviour but the fact that the woman is a creator, a writer, cuts across the bleakness of losing the male lover. The poem does not resolve the tension, the 'yearning belly' remains as a powerful image of a hunger which writing cannot appease.

Phillips' major confrontation, however, comes potentially between her sense of being a woman and her religious conviction. In "Old Woman in Church" she presents a "Tired, old, black woman/bewigged and safety-pinned," who raises her fist in power, "God's power/black power". She hopes for the coming of the Comforter. As in Craig's "Lost from the Fold", this poem reminds that women constitute the bulk of church congregations in the Caribbean (along with their children), and of course also bear the brunt of economic oppression because of the prevalence of poor, single-parent households headed by women. The fist raised is not only an ambiguous Black Power salute but an accusation of God as well. But Phillips' work is less verbally seductive than Craig's, partly because the emotional directness which characterizes it is less suitable for subtlety.

Of all four writers, Lorna Goodison is presently most verbally fascinating, sensuous and musical. Her two volumes of poetry to date, *Tamarind Season* and *I Am Becoming My Mother*, show a progression towards harmony. Less polemical than Phillips, (although some poems, like "Judges" in *Tamarind Season* are very strong) Goodison is a very skilled craftswoman of sounds. In "Judges" the point is partly the rhythm, which beautifully mirrors the Jamaican voice:

I am lining up these words
holding them behind the barrier of my teeth
binding my time as only a woman can.
I have a poem for you judge man.[24]

The placement of "man" here rings with her anger. But often Goodison is a resolver of tensions, as in her poems "For My Mother (May I Inherit Half Her Strength)." The opening lines of this poem declare an awareness of contradictions:

My mother loved my father
I write this as an absolute
in this my thirtieth year
the year to discard absolutes[25]

But the poem becomes very cosy and proceeds to present the portrait of the mother, full of the enchantment of myths, as all of our images of our mothers tend to be. Goodison's image of the emotional texture of her mother's life is honest and emotionally appealing:

> and she cried.
> For her hands grown coarse with raising nine children
>
> for her body for twenty years permanently fat
> for the time she pawned her machine for my sister's
>
> Senior Cambridge fees
> and for the pain she bore with the eyes of a queen
>
> and she cried also because she loved him.[26]

But some of Goodison's poems find the crossroads between gender and race, and are neither strongly polemical nor primarily sensuous and resolving of issues. In "England Seen", for example, there is a very good sense of humour about Icylyn "chief presser hair", who goes "afro" in the summer, and the poem plays with the anxieties of women about looks (particularly here of black women in a white society). Middle-class aspirations are comically treated:

> " . . . and everytime she come here
> she ask me where is the loo
> It don't move from the backyard
> as far as I know . . . "[27]

Goodison occasionally treats class as a theme (as also do Phillips, Senior and Craig). In Goodison, voice of the dialect or creole speaker is much more often interwoven into the texture of the line than it is in the other writers who tend to write either in one linguistic mode or the other in different poems. Goodison's humor is a medium for dealing with potential confrontation. Her portrait of a "rural revolutionary" is very acute:

> my head agrarian
> I know
> Textbook, how it grow.[28]

But for the most part, she is a poet of sensuous language, who is, to judge from her newest work, like "Heartease", is both technically confident and moving towards harmony and healing:

> while the rest of we planting the
> undivided, ever-living
> healing trees . . .
> what a glory
> possibility
> soon come
> HEARTEASE . . . [29]

Whilst her love poems often have a striking imagery ("Guyana Lovesong", "Sea Changes", "On Misplacing Him"), and are sometimes full of feeling, she herself seems humourously aware that sometimes writing about love treads perilously close to romanticism and banality: "I torn from the centre of/some ladies novel".[30] The love poems convey originally what seem to be the nuances of a personal experience "Ah, he was a harsh lover,/left sand and salt in my bed".[31] Her world is one where old archetypes reverberate:

> and sit down cleansed, to tell a rosary of your ancestor's names
>
> a singing chain of ancient names to bind them tight
>
> all those who work evil downward through the night[32]

It may therefore seem churlish to find her rich style, resolving tensions, has any dangers to it, and this is where my own subjectivity as a critic and poet comes in. I acknowledge that Goodison is undoubtedly a poet of the greatest potential in terms of language technique and the ability to weave different aspects of experience together (as for example she uses Catholic and African elements in the passage quoted above). For many readers, this might seem an ideal solution to the tensions which surround us and also to inner conflict. But I find Craig and Senior, remaining clearly aware of different and colliding elements of experience, are the closest to the nature of the life I know. The question really is how we take the different aspects of a life into account: deal with them separately (as often Phillips does), resolve them into a harmonious whole (as Goodison's major recent work seems to want to do), or present them as ever present and shifting elements in the experience, unavoidably separate and troublesome, as in Craig's work.

At the moment, however, it would only be true to say that Goodison is the most achieved of the three writers and that her poetry does give immense satisfaction. Edward Baugh, in his recent paper on Goodison[33] says of her that she has a "redemptive joy of life", which is very true. This presumably partly comes from her confidence in integrating the various aspects of herself. She has said "I am a woman and I'm a writer and I'm going to write

about what I know most about".[34] No writer is likely to stay always with one
direction or style, so we are probably going to see change in the work of all
three poets here discussed. Craig, although desiring that her poems are
easily understood by all readers, finds "so often the ones that seem obscure
are in fact the most realistic".[35] She is simply aware that life is very
complicated, and her poem "Coda" expresses this well, in revealing not
only a powerful and proud consciousness of womanhood but also a desire to
join somehow with men "to make something new together".[36]

There is also the point that many women poets begin from a personal
note, working through personal experiences in different poems, which
become the first volume, and it is only after that we can see a real
development in the direction of a mature voice. Goodison has said that she
started from the personal and now wants to move to the social and
communal. Craig and Phillips are not yet beyond a first volume. So
everything said here is tentative, and I do not want to suggest that I am
ranking these writers as poets in any final qualitative sense. I find it
important that we appreciate that ideological or strongly partisan perspectives have to be able to change and adapt as our vision of literature changes.
There are some strong advantages sometimes to a powerful new understanding of categories which comes from a passionately held and narrow
conviction, and in this context I find Georg Gugelberger's application of
Peter Nazareth's definition of third world writer in his introduction to a
collection of essays on *Marxism and African Literature* important:

> By now it has become clear to me that we have to replace the old
> geographic definition by a class-based progressive definition as Peter
> Nazareth has offered it in his *The Third World Writer:*
> To belong to the Third World is therefore to accept an identity, an
> identity with the wretched of the earth spoken for by Frantz Fanon, to
> determine to end all exploitation and oppression.
> This definition—if adhered to—clearly replaces not only the old
> geographical definition but at the same time the notion of ethnicity
> (race/Africanity) with clear class consciousness.[37]

Gugelberger sees the implications of this as being that Third World writers
will include Blake, Brecht and others who have made the fight against
oppression their major theme. This would only be a logical extension of the
fairly widely accepted idea that a history of oppression makes a country
Third World (Ireland, for example). This seems to be my problem with
some of Goodison's resolutions, that they do not bring to me the
consciousness I perhaps always need to have, of the terrible tensions which
afflict so many societies in the Caribbean and elsewhere. Goodison is
clearly aware of social problems and of poverty, but she is powerfully a
writer of spells, incantations and blessings, which work on a metaphysical

level, almost, to bring us closer together in an atmosphere of harmony and peace. I do not discount this, for perhaps her way of dealing with the pain of her context is to transcend it in a metaphysical way. Certainly she has talked to having to go through pain to write, of not having an easy life and of wishing things were easier.[38] Part of her immensely strong reading presence is that Goodison clearly almost sings her poems as if they were religious verses. But sometimes, it is teasing to receive her hints as to the nature of hidden tensions, details of a life clearly lived across the lines of class or color warfare, as in the line about her father's wooing of her mother "sure in the kingdom of my blue-eyed grandmother".[39] No doubt some readers will object here that I am asking the lyrical territory of poetry to become more socially concerned than perhaps it should, but I am only asking that poetry be able to avoid smoothing out the edges of a rough life wherever possible, and to give a sense of the very real divisions and awkward tensions of being alive in complex modern third world societies, especially as a woman and a poet.

There is a similarity between Phillips' polemic and Goodison's sensuousness, and that is in the resolving qualities of both styles. This is precisely because when a harmony is desired, either for polemical effect or for the establishment of peace and unity of feeling, it is important to sketch in broad strokes. Phillips' images of nature and of the experience of living tend to the general:

> . . . and that there is nothing
> but Oneness
> and nothing worth knowing
> but the Harmony
> of all things[40]

By contrast, Craig seems to me to balance the combative aspects of a live lived in the front line, so to speak, as a woman writer in Jamaica.

Despite finding that Gugelberger and Leslie perceive the third world much as I do, they are both prescriptive, and being an anarchist critic rather than a Marxist one, I cannot not endorse such strong directives entirely. Perception of reality constantly shifts, as the individual adjusts her/his perspective, depending on which of a number of priorities are uppermost at a given time. Perhaps it is enough to suggest that poetry written by the third world woman writer seems likely to have to deal with a great many complexities which are not resolved. Of course there can be no expectation that writers should be alike. Sexism is still rife in the Caribbean, and there seems little possibility of lessening it by appeasing men. This is why Phillips deserves recognition of her courage, as a woman in Barbados where gender conservatisms are intense, in making strongly polemical statements about female anger at male abuse of women.

These four writers, then, articulate directions which are possible in dealing with their lives, with all or some of the following facets: being black, a woman, a writer, from the Caribbean, English-speaking, middle-class, educated, a single mother. For it is all those facets of experience and more which give to the texture of their work its particular character. I find Craig's endearing sense of awkwardness of the crow's wings makes more vivid sense to me as an articulation of the consciousness of a woman who is aware of many things than either Phillips' tendency to polemic or Goodison's wonderful warmth and ability to give a sense of comfort and security through her work. But that is, as I began by saying, because my particular critical and creative responses are turned in a specific direction at the moment. In articulating response to these poets, all of whose work I enjoy and admire, my own present direction is clearer. Perhaps another aspect of feminist and womanist dialogue is that critical response can cease to be a judgemental business and become much more of a musing over the possibilities which literature brings to the life which experiences it. In the process, a few important aspects of the writing ought to be articulated. But in the end, as critic and writer, I want to bless the work of these writers, that they may continue regardless of what criticism may say, praising or not.[41]

NOTES

1. This paper is a revised and extended version of the paper entitled "Crossroads: Third World Criticism and Commitment with Reference to African-Caribbean Women Poets" given at the Fifth Annual Conference on West Indian Literature, College of the Virgin Islands, St. Thomas, May 22-25, 1985 and published in the Proceedings of that Conference, ed. J. Jackson and J. Allis, *West Indian Poetry*, College of the Virgin Islands, USVI, 1986, pp. 41-55. (This was a publication of limited circulation.)

2. "The Female Writer and her Commitment", *The Guardian*, Lagos, December, 1982, II.

3. In "Consciousness and Authenticity: Toward a Feminist Aesthetic", Josephine Donovan, ed., *Feminist Literary Criticism*, Lexington: University Press of Kentucky, 1975, pp. 38-47), Marcia Holly argues that "realism" is the inclusion of important aspects of experience in a given situation. In the case of literary work, this means that single-level polemic is much less realistic than what Holly calls "human orientation", or a wider concern than gender politics. But she sees feminist criticism as a necessary stage in the development of criticism/writing. In the same way, I see Phillips' comparatively narrow focus as a major stage of development of a conscious female voice. Goodison seems to me to reflect a very appealing and attractive possibility for reconciliations of disparate social and personal elements but Craig and Senior seem to me to capture most closely the struggle to live with colliding aspects of experience.

4. Pamela Mordecai, in her paper delivered at the Fifth Annual Conference on West Indian Literature, College of the Virgin Islands, St. Thomas, USVI, May 22-25, 1985, (published in the *Proceedings*, pp. 106-121) and entitled "A Crystal of Ambiguities: metaphors for creativity and the art of writing in Derek Walcott's *Another Life*", rejected dialectical method in favour of a concept of "prismatic reality" as a characteristic of Caribbean thought modes. This is also close to Edward Brathwaite's arguments about the nature of Caribbean reality in his *History of the Voice* (New Beacon Books, London, 1984, p. 6). I was, in the first draft of this paper, attracted to Hegelian dialectic, but have since rethought this position. However, I think all of these approaches are important since they all stress the experiential complexity of Caribbean life.

5. See the essays on Naipaul in Mark McWatt, ed., *West Indian Literature and its Social Context* (Dept. of English, UWI Barbados, 1985); especially Cheryl Griffith, "The Women as Whore in the Novels of V.S. Naipaul", pp. 95-106 and Elaine Fido "Psycho-Sexual Aspects of the Woman in V.S. Naipaul's Fiction", pp. 78-94. It is interesting to note that all the essays collected here on Naipaul and sexuality were conceived and written without the knowledge of any of the others. It was clearly a topic on a good many people's minds in 1984, when the Fourth Conference on West Indian Literature was held at UWI, Barbados at which these papers were presented.

6. Christine Craig, *Quadrille for Tigers*, (Mina Publishing House, Sebastopol, CA, 1984).
    Lorna Goodison, *Tamarind Season*, (Institute of Jamaica, Kingston, 1980); *I am Becoming My Mother*, (New Beacon Books, London, 1986) and *Heartease* (New Beacon Books, London, 1989).
    Esther Phillips, *Poems*, (Poetry Chapbook Series, UWI, Barbados, 1983).
    Olive Senior, *Talking of Trees*, (Calabash, Kingston, 1985).

7. *Quadrille for Tigers*, p. 33.

8. Ibid., p. 13.

9. Ibid., p. 21.

10. Idem.

11. This was during a plenary session on women writers in the Caribbean at the FOCUS 1986 Caribbean Writers Conference, Commonwealth Institute, London, October 23-25, 1986.

12. "Homescape", *Talking of Trees*, p. 1.

13. *Talking of Trees*, p. 3.

14. Ibid., p. 4.

15. Ibid., p. 5.

16. "One Night, The Father", *Talking of Trees*, p. 22.

17. *Talking of Trees*, p. 56.

18. Edward Baugh, in his recent article on Lorna Goodison, "Goodison on the Road to Heartease" in *Journal of West Indian Literature*, Vol. 1, no. 1, (October 1986), pp. 13-22, mentions that Goodison has been "steadily refining her skills at sliding seamlessly between English and Creole", mingling "erudite literary allusion with the earthiness of traditional Jamaican speech, images from modern technology with the idiom of local pop culture". Her voice thus becomes, says Baugh, "at once personal and anonymous, private and

public". I am not sure of the wisdom of becoming linguistically quite so catholic, and my essay makes this clear.

19. *Talking of Trees*, p. 4.
20. "To My Arawak Grandmother", *Talking of Trees*, p. 11.
21. *Poems*, p. 9.
22. Ibid., p. 3.
23. Ibid., pp. 5-6.
24. *Tamarind Season*, p. 54.
25. *I Am Becoming My Mother*, p. 46.
26. Ibid., p. 48.
27. *Tamarind Season*, p. 18.
28. Ibid., p. 74.
29. *Heartease*, p. 8.
30. "Guyana Lovesong", *Tamarind Season*, p. 31.
31. "Seachanges", *Tamarind Season*, p. 65.
32. *Heartease*, p. 1.
33. Baugh, p. 21.
34. Quoted in Baugh, *Journal of West Indian Literature*, p. 17.
35. Back cover, *Quadrille for Tigers*.
36. Ibid., p. 57.
37. *Marxism and African Literature*, (Africa World Press, Trenton, NJ, 1985, p. v).
38. Quoted in Baugh, *Journal of West Indian Literature*, p. 21.
39. "For My Mother (May I Inherit Half Her Strength)", *I Am Becoming My Mother*, p. 46.
40. *Poems*, p. 7.
41. I am trying to consider a kind of criticism which permits bias because it seems to me criticism is only partly about analysing literature (whether on the surface or deeply), and should always be turned also to encouraging the development of new literature and of creative acts of language. Criticism which determines strong reader reaction to a work is healthier than that which purports to be scientific or objective and this disguises bias (rather than omitting it). Writers have strong views about writing, kinds of writing, because they are about something of their own. Their criticism though often very strikingly without balance or moderation, has a passion and involvement often which is very important for the stimulation of feeling about literary work. I am here hoping for a criticism which does not wound the writer but is definitely performed in the context of creative involvement with literature. Here in the West Indies, many critics are also poets, but do not often express their criticism in the same way as their creative work (with the very significant exception of Edward Kamau Brathwaite.)

"Le voyage et l'espace clos" —Island and Journey as Metaphor: Aspects of Woman's Experience in the Works of Francophone Caribbean Women Novelists

Elizabeth Wilson

Francophone Caribbean women's writing shares the preoccupation with the identity crisis or quest common to West Indian writing in general. However, unlike male-authored Caribbean fiction, the quest in women's writing usually ends in withdrawal and isolation and/or flight and evasion, rather than confrontation. Central to the depiction of this quest are the metaphors of the journey and the closed space. The journey is an archetypal symbol, but whereas it is most often a journey-as-initiation—to self-knowledge and/or integration into a community—in Francophone female Caribbean writing, the journey, except in rare instances (for example in Schwarz-Bart's work), takes the form of journey-as-alienation. Self-knowledge often leads to destruction of self.

Mary Jean Green identifies in Quebec women's writing a pattern of "rejection, resistance and liberation" in response to a repressive social system.[1] French Caribbean women's writing, in general, reveals rather a pattern of rejection, resistance, and *attempted* liberation, followed by failure and deeper alienation because of the aborted attempts at revolt. This cycle reproduces itself in the novel form as a circular or closed structure. *"Forme"* and *"fond"* coincide. The narrative form is non-linear. It traces a closed circle and the heroine is in the same hopeless situation (or a worse

one) at the end as at the beginning.[2] The female protagonists are destroyed
both by the strictures of their society and by their futile attempts to escape,
their *tentatives d'évasion* only serving to entrap and alienate them further,
and their only effective liberation being implicit in the act of writing, explicitly
portrayed in several works as the means to achieve relief through a symbolic
reunion with the self, with other women, and with the mother (land) from
which they have been exiled.[3] Several novelists draw upon Césaire's imagery
and make use of two central metaphors to depict woman's condition and her
efforts to escape or change it: the island (a closed space) and the journey or
voyage (*voyage* in French includes both meanings, that is, journey and
voyage). The image of the island is one of isolation, of being marooned. An
island by its very nature is cut off, separate, set apart. Yet, *marronnage* (the
state of being a Maroon), in Caribbean literature, also has positive connotations, the Maroon being primarily a figure of resistance and defiance. The
images therefore are complex, multifaceted, at times even contradictory.
These images have particular resonances in terms of the story of Caribbean
people, a people born of the slave trade.

In the infamous "Middle Passage," that leg of the slavers' journey which
was the voyage from Africa to the West Indies, these two images coalesce
as the slaveship, the *négrier*, becomes the simultaneous embodiment of
incarceration and *déracinement*, confinement and tragic uprootedness,
movement, displacement and rootlessness. In the course of that journey the
African, cruelly chained in the hold of the *négrier*, becomes the *nègre*
imprisoned and trapped in the color of his/her skin. Free men and women
become forcibly transformed in that voyage into an undifferentiated,
dehumanized mass. Africans of all different nations and ethnic groups lose
their identity and become *nègres* and *négresses*, crowded together and
lumped together, to be identified like animals only by their physical
characteristics. The color of their skin for the first time becomes the single
distinguishing factor which gives or rather denies them their identity.

Aimé Césaire's *Return to My Native Land (Cahier d'un retour au pays
natal)*, a seminal work in French Caribbean literature, is an attempt to
reverse and retrace that voyage in order to restore the black man to his
original, pre-slavery state of worth and dignity. The major image of the
Cahier is that of the journey, which functions on several levels. As Ormerod
points out, the title of Césaire's poem

> . . . ostensibly refers to a return to the poet's own island of Martinique
> after years in a state of exile in France. But as the poem unfolds, that
> state of exile is increasingly identified with the inner experience of
> alienation, and the "return" of the title becomes a return to the poet's
> true self through a rediscovery of his African roots.[4]

Francophone Caribbean women writers depict women in their societies as being haunted by this same sense of alienation. Whether she is in the Caribbean, in France, or in Africa, the situation of the black *Antillaise* woman is portrayed as one of confinement and frustration. Her life is depicted as tragically limited and her efforts at resistance doomed to failure. This predicament is expressed metaphorically in terms of clearly delineated and closed spaces: a boat, a cabin, windows, mirrors, rooms, houses, prisons—structures which isolate and alienate the woman from herself and from others. She is an island, cut off, stranded with no life-lines. The journeys she undertakes become a *"voyage d'évasion,"* an attempt to escape, but also, like Césaire's voyage, a journey within, to self-awareness. Both images are dual (double and contradictory) in nature. Thus the Nausicaa, a transatlantic ship in Michèle Lacrosil's first novel, *Sapotille et le serin d'argile*, (*Sapotille and the Clay Canary*) (1960) is both a prison and a refuge. The heroine is confined to her cabin, both the ship and cabin being a metaphor for the woman's condition.[5] The space in the novel is restricted, compartmentalized and stratified. The boat is traveling between the Antilles and France, cut off from both. The decks on board ship mirror the divisions in Caribbean society. The heroine, Sapotille, is on her way to France because she is seeking to flee from her suffocating island society with its prejudices of race and color and false, alienating values. But the reader soon becomes aware that the journey is futile. The boat is not a means of escape but a temporary shelter and a prison—the class structure Sapotille hopes to escape is reproduced, and class divisions are even more strictly enforced in the tiny microcosm of the ship. The heroine's naïve expectations of a classless society in her new, unknown, *"patrie"* [mother/fatherland] point to a voyage which is doomed from the start. She is locked in by her neuroses and prejudices, as she is confined within her cabin, in the world of the ship. As Sapotille recognises at the very outset: "Mon voyage est pourri" (p. 18), ["My trip is ruined"]. Indeed, Sapotille is forced to share her cabin with a childhood companion, the light-skinned daughter of a *député*, a sort of alter-ego, symbolic of all she is trying to flee. Her prison is within.

The initial situation in Mayotte Capécia's work *La négresse blanche [The White Negress]* also metaphorically expresses the ambiguous situation of the woman of color in the French West Indies of the forties. She is a figure of tragic *déchirement*, torn in two. As the novel opens, Isaure, the "white negress," finds herself locked in a room, her own bar, with three white men, two officers and a sailor, whom she says she despises but is forced (or chooses) to serve as customers. Outside the door, in the night, are *nègres* whom Isaure scorns and fears and whom she refuses to admit to her establishment. The situation is symbolic of the colored woman's, (in the original "femme de couleur"), psychological and social incarceration and her dilemma: Assertive, fiercely proud, desirous of being financial independent, Isaure is nevertheless dependent on her white clients and remains a prisoner of her fears and prejudices against blacks, as Clarisse Zimra says, a pawn and a go-between, between two traditionally hostile groups.[6] Capécia's protagonists as well as Lacrosil's, isolated in their own land, choose to abandon their society and for them the journey to France is perceived as the only means of escape from an intolerable, untenable situation.

The journey to France, like the journey to Africa in Maryse Condé's and Miriam Vieyra's novels, thus becomes at once a physical and a psychological voyage, the journey of an alienated, homeless individual in search of the motherland, of a people in exile who have three potential "homelands": the Caribbean, Europe and Africa; of a people deprived of their identity who have a triple heritage: African, European, and Antillean. Caribbean woman, the *assimilée* (a French term for an educated French subject or citizen born into a foreign culture but steeped in the values and traditions of French "culture"), like her male counterpart, is tragically exiled from herself. She is caught in a bind. Isaure locked in her bar and Sapotille in her cabin on the ship are imprisoned, yet paradoxically safe. By isolating themselves, by fleeing, they do not need to, and indeed cannot, rid themselves of their distorted values and point of view.[7]

Maryse Condé's novel, *Une Saison à Rihata*, set in a fictitious African country, opens with a description of the protagonist's house: it is cut off from the rest of the town, a picture of neglect and decay, damp, mildewed, a crumbling reflection of its former colonial glory. The appearance of the house offers a striking parallel to the situation of the family and in particular to that of its *Antillaise* mistress, Marie-Hélène—a stranger in exile and at odds with her surroundings in an alien and hostile society. A brilliant, middleclass woman, married to an African, she had hoped to heal the divisions in herself by a return to her ancestral homeland. Marie-Hélène's life in Africa, however, is characterized by shattered hopes and unfulfilled dreams. She finds herself banished to an isolated and stagnating provincial town and responds to being rejected by Africa by withdrawing from life and from those around her. The journey back has not recovered the lost mother, the mythical Africa, the ancestral homeland. Like Césaire's poet, the Antillean heroine fails to find what she expected. She becomes more cut off, more exiled from herself. The rejection of Africa leads to a corresponding withdrawal from all everyday reality, expressed metaphorically by her physical isolation: Her room becomes her refuge where she rejoins her rejected West Indian homeland through the medium of the dream and the imagination.[8]

Similarly, Suzette and Juletane, the anti-heroines of Miriam Warner-Vieyra's two companion novels (*Le Quimboiseur l'avait dit* and *Juletane*) are figures of dislocation, isolation and alienation, victims of misguided efforts to escape from their initial restricted situations. Both are associated with closed spaces, severely circumscribed worlds. Suzette, a young West Indian girl, confined to her room in an insane asylum in Paris, looks back nostalgically to her island and what had once seemed to be a restricted environment comes to be in retrospect an idyllic paradise. Suzette's selective memory evokes an image of simple, communal life in a tiny village on an island "as big as two coconuts." In terms of the fate of woman's ambitions Vieyra's novels are pessimistic. Suzette affirms that she ought never to have left her village. The journeys to Europe (*Le Quimboiseur...*), and to Africa (*Juletane*), attempts at self-actualization and escape, end in catastrophe. The woman who is not content to limit herself or to "be satisfied with the known domestic world," Suzette seems to suggest, is doomed to failure, to a last state worse than the first, partly because of her society's taboos, but also because of false, misplaced ambition. Juletane in Africa goes mad because she has been betrayed by her husband but also because she is unable to accept and be content with the sort of life typified by her husband's first wife, for whom "the entire universe was limited to a mat under a tree and three children around her" ["Pour elle, tout l'univers s'arrête à une natte sous un arbre et trois enfants autour"].[9]*

Similarly, Suzette in Paris is driven to madness because her dreams too are betrayed. She is exploited and degraded by her ambitious and egotistical *créole* mother (a symbolic representation of Guadeloupe or that part of Guadeloupean society which espouses and pursues white values) and her French lover (her false vision of France). Locked in her hospital room Suzette goes back over the course of her life and remarks: "J'avais choisi une route large et fleurie, elle s'etait transformée en étroit sentier plein d'embûches; mais je devais poursuivre mon chemin, n'ayant pas d'autre choix possible."[10] ["I had chosen a wide, flower-filled road, it had become transformed into a narrow path full of ambushes; but I could not turn back, I had no other choice open to me. . . . "] Having strayed too far from home, now, with no way out, she longs to recover the safe haven of her father's boat, the comfort of the island womb.

The closed space can function generally as both a positive and a negative image. In later West Indian novels it is a trap which forces a confrontation with self, a confrontation often too painful to endure. It is a prison which is accepted and transformed by an effort of the woman's imagination into a refuge from a reality perceived as intolerable.

Marie-Hélène (*Une Saison à Rihata*), stifling in the remote country town of Rihata, completes the process of sequestration by deliberately confining herself to her home and specifically to her room where she escapes into the world of dreams with its occasionally comforting associations and links to her idealized past in Guadeloupe. Similarly, Suzette (*Le Quimboiseur l'avait dit*), locked in her hospital room and slipping fast into an "endless abyss," at first struggles to escape but then, realizing it is too late, resigns herself to her fate and willingly embraces death, which becomes a reunion with her childhood world. Miraculously, when she reaches the bottom of the abyss she seems to find not death but the reassuring, familiar experience of being back in her childhood fishing-village world. The chasm is transformed and in her dreamlike state she is finally reunited with her past self, protected and safe in the bottom of a boat: "Quand j'atteignis le fond, j'eus conscience d'être couchée au fond d'une barque. Tout ce que je pouvais voir du fond de la barque, c'était le large dos d'un homme au torse nu—ses muscles luisants de sueur évoquaient une puissance qui me rassurait—et un tout petit nuage blanc accroché à un ciel bleu."[11] ["When I reached the bottom, I became aware that I was lying in the bottom of a boat. All that I could see from the bottom of the boat was the broad bare back of a man—his muscles shining with sweat evoked a power which reassured me—and a tiny white cloud in a blue sky."] The boat functions as a variation of the island's closed space, a safe comforting haven. Suzette manages in her hallucination to regain the protective maternal womb (here, her father's boat; her mother, having rejected her, is in turn rejected) and the imagined figure of her fisherman father, strong, dependable, completes the image of security. Significantly, her desire to go to Paris following in her mother's footsteps represented a rejection of her black West Indian peasant identity (her mother a light-skinned *petit bourgeois* despised her black fisherman husband). Now the process is reversed. The view from the bottom of the boat, with its clearly delineated and circumscribed perspective, succeeds in blocking out the rest of the world. Suzette out there on the ocean allows herself to see only what she wants to; she is isolated yet safe. However, it is a passive image, she is a child, "la petite Zétou," living out the fairytale destiny which life had denied her and which prefaces the novel: The novel's epigraph is an Antillean proverb: "Là ou confiance te mène, la force ne te fait pas sortir" ("Where confidence leads you, your strength cannot save you"). Suzette's tragic story seems pessimistically to illustrate the wisdom of the dictum and to serve as a cautionary tale.

The journey away from the Caribbean to Europe or Africa and into self ends, in the case of Lacrosil and Vieyra's anti-heroines, with an inability to face the harsh realities they find. They cannot accept either the external or the interior reality and instead choose the escape/alienation of madness or death. The view of woman's destiny presented by these works is negative. Maryse Condé's protagonists suffer a less drastic fate and manage to come to terms in a limited way with their situation. Simone Schwarz-Bart's and Jacqueline Manicom's novels suggest more hopeful yet difficult alternatives.

Manicom's book, *Mon examen de blanc*, is perhaps the most militant "feminist" West Indian work to date.[12] She exploits to the full the possibilities inherent in the central situation of the novel: an operating/

labor room, a hospital in Guadeloupe where a white male gynecologist/ surgeon is assisted by an *Antillaise, femme de couleur* (she is of East Indian origin), an anaesthetist. The relationship between the two colleagues— equally educated, equally skilled, but unequal for other traditional, hierarchical reasons—is cleverly constructed and subtly manipulated by the narrator in order to comment on both the feminine condition and the position of the West Indian *assimilé(e)* and Antillean society in general. Manicom uses the closed space symbolically to represent the heroine's dilemma.

The protagonist of *Mon Examen de blanc* (a créole expression full of ambiguity which literally translated means "my exam in whiteness" or "to be a white person"), the doctor Madévie Ramimoutou, is the victim of many of the same complexes and prejudices as her predecessors. She is, however, acutely aware of the inconsistencies and contradictions in her position. As an educated *femme de couleur* she is cut off from much of her own society. Manicom uses the familiar symbols to express her heroine's isolation and alienation. Madévie is shown mainly in her clinic, the operating room and her tiny living quarters referred to as the "cube." She too has made the journey to France and returned disillusioned. But she is caught between two worlds, as her clinic is, out by the airport in Guadeloupe's Point-à-Pitre, where she watches the planes (links to the *metropole*) and reflects on the distorted image of France she once had, a view common to most of her fellow *Antillais*.

Madévie's journey has embittered and matured her and she consciously separates herself from her former self, "the other Madévie," with whom she no longer wants to identify. But because of her background and French education she cannot easily re-integrate into Caribbean society. She is oriented toward the world of the *békés* (rich, upper-class whites) who look down on their fellow West Indians and who are in turn regarded suspiciously by them. Madévie finds herself confined to the circles of expatriate *"blancs-France."* Symbolic of this isolation are the closed spaces with which she is associated: the clinic, her "cube," the sterile operating room, frequented only by other (white) professionals. Madévie is painfully conscious of the ambiguity of her situation and of the ambivalence of her own attitude to it. Sometimes she welcomes it, because as a member of the privileged class she is safe and protected: "In my restricted space," she says, "I feel protected." ["Dans mon espace limité, je me sens protégée."]

At other times, however, her situation becomes unbearable, and in her vain longing to break out and escape it she is tempted by suicide. She recognizes that her relationship with Cyril, the white doctor, is one of feigned deference and passivity, conditioned by her past experiences and her upbringing. It is Cyril who ironically controls her world or believes he does. Manicom uses the relationship between Cyril and Madévie to portray not only the male/female relationship but also to mirror the relations between the middle-class *Antillais(es)* and the white European, the "*béké-France*." It is explicitly described by the metaphor of the "cube."

> Arrive Cyril. Il s'introduit dans ce cube. Capricieuse géométrie que cette pièce rétrécie qui s'étire quand Cyril est là. Je peux alors si je veux, faire des voyages en hauteur et en profondeur.[13]

> [Cyril arrives. He enters the cube. How capricious the geometry of this cramped, narrow room which expands when Cyril is there. At those times I can, if I want to, experience/explore its heights and its depths.]

The terminology and imagery (deliberately ambiguous) is suggestive not only of a scientific, biological process, consonant with the medical setting, and of the sexual act, but of a psychological reality. Cyril wants to, and does, direct her destiny and she allows him to. He invades and dominates her space. The "cube" is a metaphor not only for Madévie's body, identity, self-image, and existence (the woman *vis-à-vis* the male, here specifically the *femme de couleur* and the dominant "liberating" white male), but for the Antillean middle and upper classes and for Guadeloupe. It signifies the identity and destiny of the French Antilles and their relationship with the *metropole*. Cyril, the "*blanc-France*" (white Frenchman), has locked Madévie into a certain role and path, as she has boxed herself in. He can release her from her prison, expand her "cube," albeit temporarily. When he is with her, she feels differently about her landscape, her space, because by his presence he has conferred value and importance and given it added dimensions. When Cyril is there Madévie feels freed and fulfilled: "And the joyful spring gushed from the clear (pale) rock to flow black and silent in the 'cube'." ["Et la source joyeuse a quitté la roche claire pour couler noire et silencieuse dans le 'cube'."] Again the sexual imagery is explicit and the references to color, "claire," "noire," are hardly fortuitous. But lest the reader still not get the point, the narrator carefully spells it out, again by means of a similar metaphor: Madévie/woman/Guadeloupe, the "tiny red corpuscle" suffocating for lack of oxygen, is dependent on Cyril/man/France for her life and her happiness. In a heavily ironic passage Manicom describes this paradoxical situation. (The narrator's relationship to her story is one of deliberate distancing.) Madévie and her colleague are looking out the window:

> Evidemment je suis malheureuse et j'ai besoin de Cyril. Il faut que je sois malheureuse pour Cyril. Je suis un tout petit globule rouge et il n'y a pas assez d'oxygène dans ce "cube." Cyril Démian m'en apporte. Il me dit rien! Ou si peu de choses...

Généreusement il m'offre le paysage d'en bas. Il me fait cadeau de mon pays: me voilà, les bras chargés de ma savane brûlante, de la mer Caraïbe engloutissant le gigantesque soleil d'or.[14]

[Evidently I am unhappy and I need Cyril. I must be unhappy for Cyril. I am a tiny little red globule (corpuscle) and there is not enough oxygen in this "cube." Cyril Démian brings me some. He says nothing! Or so little . . .

Generously he offers me the landscape beneath us. He gives me my country as a gift. Here I am, my arms loaded with my blazing savannah, with the Caribbean sea swallowing up the huge golden sun.]

Manicom was an avowed feminist and also actively involved in politics and her multi-faceted metaphor functions effectively on several levels in terms of racial, sexual and nationalist politics. The relationship between Madévie, the French West Indian woman of color, and Cyril, the white Frenchman, thus extends beyond a simple preoccupation with any one of these aspects and makes many points at once. In terms of consciousness the protagonist/narrator of *Mon Examen de blanc* has come a long way. But there is still a long way to go. The neuroses and problems have been diagnosed but not removed. Manicom's work recognizes that the situation is indeed complex, but suggests that the solution is to be found in political action and commitment. Manicom sketches the possible lines of a revolt.

Simone Schwarz-Bart's novels, on the other hand, attempt to treat the predicament of the woman and West Indian society at the level of the individual enduring life: self-esteem and self-worth are restored through a process of revalorizing of images and a heritage seen in negative terms by most *Antillais*. Schwarz-Bart reverses the connotations of the closed space and emphasizes only its positive, nurturing aspects. Her heroines' voyages are symbolic interior journeys. Coupled with the defeated, fettered figure is the other face of the islander, that of the hardy intrepid adventurer, braving the elements in order to survive, of the Maroon who lives by wits and is a figure of revolt and resourcefulness. This is the image evoked by the Guadeloupean novelist Simone Schwarz-Bart in the original title of her novel *The Bridge of Beyond* which, in the original French (*Pluie et vent sur Télumée Miracle*) means "Rain and Wind on Télumée, the Miracle woman."[15] Télumée, indeed, is called "*marron sans bois*"—a testimony to her qualities of survival, self-sufficiency, and independence. Here the woman is a figure of strength and resistance and the island, hamlet, boat or room becomes not a negative space but a positive one, not a restrictive enclosure, but a solid base from which to venture out to brave the waters of life, the open sea, that sea which at once protects and threatens, isolates and frees, gives and takes life.

Schwarz-Bart's vision does not deny either history or the realities of island life. Guadeloupe, Télumée's island, is described as "cette île à volcans, à cyclones et moustiques, à mauvaise mentalité": battered by hurricanes, infected with mosquitos and with her share of people who as we say in creole "have bad min" (are bad minded). It is a tiny speck on the map, but for Schwarz-Bart's heroines it is not a land with no past and no history. Schwarz-Bart makes explicit in her work that her concept of the island is at variance with the view of those who consider it unimportant or insignificant. [16] Moreover, it is not necessary to look overseas to Europe or to Africa to find a sense of worth. Schwarz-Bart's heroines struggle resolutely to resist and reject the negative attitudes of the people around them and assert their power to remain afloat and upright, in the waters of life. The Lougandor women journey not to France or to Guinea, but deep within themselves.

Télumée, an old lady, standing in her tiny garden, transcends the limitations of her island and her history and affirms her desire to relive her life, to suffer and to die in exactly the same circumstances. But one must come to terms with the reality in order to transcend it. Whatever hand life deals, one must play it. The Lougandor women, Télumée's clan, accept their destiny, but refuse to be bowed by it. Télumée's life is rooted in positive values and a belief in herself acquired at her grandmother's knee. It is a security conferred by a belief in an alternative vision of reality to which many *Antillais* do not subscribe or have access. Télumée has never "suffered from the exiguity" of her homeland, for, according to Télumée, "the country depends on the size of one's heart." [17] One's reality is conditioned by one's point of view.

Pluie et vent sur Télumée Miracle stresses the importance of individual courage and family solidarity. The novel opens and closes with the image of Télumée, an old woman, resolutely upright in her little garden. The structure of the novel reproduces the cyclical pattern of life, of nature which continually renews itself and the rambling narrative voice recalls events and characters from the family history, patterns which replicate and repeat themselves. Télumée's garden is the privileged, circumscribed space within which she blossoms and flourishes, safe from intruders. It is her plot of land, which she can cultivate and control and which, despite the ravages of the elements, allows her to reap a certain measure of reward and happiness.

Télumée's life is a mirror image and a continuation of the life of her grandmother, the marvelous Toussine, who has triumphed over life's vicissitudes. During a period of great happiness and fulfillment, Toussine's life with Jérémie, her husband, blossoms and prospers within a severely limited and clearly demarcated space; their cottage is clearly separated from the surrounding terrain by paths and bushes, trees and lawn, bounded on all sides by clearly identifiable barriers. Within this tiny space Télumée's grandmother is depicted as being completely fulfilled: "Dans cet espace, elle évoluait avec une sorte d'allégresse permanente, de plénitude, comme si des oeillets d'Inde, des cannes congo, un oranger à colibris suffisaient à combler un coeur de femme." ["In this small space, she moved about with a sort of permanent joy and fulfillment, as if Indian poppies, Congo canes and an orange tree with hummingbirds were all that a woman's heart needed to be full." *Pluie et vent . . .* p. 22, translation mine.] Jérémie and Toussine are cut off from the world of jealous villagers who envy, decry, but finally become accustomed to their happiness. Their prosperity is special and individual, based on their mutual love, industry and separateness.

Similarly, Télumée, sent to live with her grandmother is led across "The Bridge of Beyond" separating her from the ordinary world and bringing her into the mysterious world of the *morne* (hill), with its rich heritage of legend and myth. There, cut off in her grandmother's hut, "la dernière du village, elle terminait le monde des humains" (*Pluie et vent . . .* p. 47) ["the last in the village, it marked the end of the world of human beings" (*The Bridge of Beyond*, p. 28)]. Télumée is initiated into her grandmother's world. Toussine, Queen-without-a-name, symbolically leads the young Télumée safely across the dangerous bridge "ce casse-cou de planches pourries, disjointes, sous lesquelles roulaient bouillonnantes les eaux de la rivière." (*Pluie et vent*, p. 47, translation mine.) ["This neck-breaking structure of rotten, uneven planks, beneath which rushed the frothing, bubbling waters of the river."] In her grandmother's tiny room, isolation from the ordinary world becomes a positive, enriching experience. Télumée feels safe and protected:

> Reine Sans Nom ouvrit la porte et me fit entrer dans la petite pièce qui composait tout son logis. Sitôt que j'eus franchi le seuil, je me sentis comme dans une forteresse, à l'abri de toutes choses, connues et inconnues, sous la protection de la grande jupe à fronces de grand-mère. (*Pluie et vent . . .* p. 47)

> Queen without a Name opened the door and ushered me into the one little room. As soon as I crossed the threshold I felt as if I were in a fortress, safe from everything known and unknown, under the protection of my grandmother's great full skirt. (*The Bridge of Beyond* p. 28)]

Just as Jérémie's love provided for Toussine an ambiance within which to flourish, her grandmother's affection transforms Télumée's world:

> Sous ce regard lointain, calme et heureux qui était le sien, la pièce me parut tout à coup immense et je sentis que d'autres personnes s'y trouvaient, pour lesquelles Reine Sans Nom m'examinait, m'embrassait maintenant, poussant de petits soupirs d'aise. Nous n'étions pas seulement deux vivantes dans une case, au milieu de la nuit, c'était autre chose et bien davantage, me semblait-il, mais je ne savais quoi. (*Pluie et vent . . .* p. 48)

[Under that distant, calm, happy look of hers, the room seemed suddenly immense, and I sensed there were others there for whom Queen Without a Name was examining me, then kissing me with little sighs of contentment. We were not merely two living beings in a cabin in the middle of the night, but, it seemed to me, something different, something much more, though I did not know what. Finally she whispered dreamily, as much to herself as to me: "I thought my luck was dead, but today I see I was born a lucky Negress and shall die one." (*The Bridge of Beyond* pp. 28-29)]

The "case" becomes a protective, nurturing space and Télumée is conscious of an unknown but special place and destiny within a larger framework. Concomitant with the re-valorizing of the closed space, associated with the female and the familiar, is the restoration of the dignity of the term *négresse*. Télumée's grandmother's friend Man Cia counsels her to be a "fine little negress, a real drum with two sides". Télumée is told to keep the underside of the drum intact while the world beats upon the other face. The drum (also a configuration of a closed space) is a symbol of revolt against the white world as Ormerod points out, of "African ancestry, a slave resistance, racial solidarity and rhythmic energy."[18] Télumée has a strong sense of belonging, of her place within the landscape which the *assimilée* lacks.

Women's writing from the French Caribbean, like Caribbean writing in general, continues to be concerned with questions of identity, alienation and the possibility of finding ways to counteract or transcend a situation perceived as painful. The works discussed in this paper draw on Césairean imagery and use a similar pattern of metaphors to express personal and divergent views of Caribbean reality. Hence, the same image or set of images can achieve both positive and negative values according to the moment or the perception of the viewer. The closed space, protective and reassuring for the protagonist who is content to be within, becomes a trap and a prison for the individual who is or should be desperate to get out. The journey within, Schwarz-Bart's narrator suggests, promises more than an escape to France or to Africa. Télumée in her garden is a figure of hope and quiet strength, a tribute to that part of Caribbean womanhood which continues to resist and to endure no matter what restrictions and burdens are placed upon her, while Manicom's Madévie, although still not fully liberated, within the confines of her "cube" transcends her situation by her astute self-scrutiny and her ironic distance. Within recurring patterns there is a progression, a deepening awareness and a cause for hope.

NOTES

*All translations are mine unless otherwise indicated.

1. See Mary Jean Green, "Structures of Liberation: Female Experience and Autobiographical Form in Quebec." *Yale French Studies* 65 (1983), p. 130.

2. Circular objects and spaces are said to symbolize and be associated with the female; see for example Calvin S. Hall, *The Meaning of Dreams* (New York: Harper and Brothers, 1953), p. 93, on the symbolism of circular objects and containers.

3. See for example Miriam Warner-Vieyra's *Le Quimboiseur l'avait dit* and *Juletane* (Paris: Presence Africaine, 1980 & 1982), Michèle Lacrosil's *Cajou* (Paris: Gallimard, 1961) and François Ega's *Lettres à une Noire* (Paris: L'Harmattan, 1973).

4. Beverley Ormerod, *An Introduction to the French Caribbean Novel* (London: Heinemann, 1985), p. 2.

5. Michèle Lacrosil, *Sapotille et le serin d'argile* (Paris: Gallimard, 1960). The ship is a dual image associated with protection and salvation as well as with shipwreck, uncertainty and destruction, see James Hall, *Dictionary of Subjects and Symbols in Art* (London: John Murray, 1974).

6. See Clarisse Zimra, "Patterns of Liberation in Contemporary Women Writers," *L'Esprit Créateur*, XVII:2 (Summer 1977), p. 103.

7. Marie-Denise Shelton describes Lacrosil's heroines as being characterised by "militant neurosis." (Marie-Denise Shelton, "Michèle Lacrosil and Marie Chauvet." Paper read at "Black Women Writers and the Diaspora," Conference at Michigan State University, October 1985.)

8. Maryse Condé, *Une Saison à Rihata* (Paris: Robert Laffont, 1981), p. 23. Translations of relevant portions of this and other works cited are mine unless otherwise indicated.

9. Miriam Warner-Vieyra, *Juletane* (Paris: Présence Africaine, 1982), p. 17.

10. Miriam Warner-Vieyra, *Le Quimboiseur l'avait dit* (Paris: Présence Africaine, 1980), p. 131.

11. Warner-Vieyra, *Le Quimboiseur*, pp. 137, 138.

12. Jacqueline Manicom, *Mon examen de blanc* (Paris: Editions Sarrazin, 1972). Manicom herself was a co-founder of the French feminist group "Choisir" which among other things campaigned vigorously in favor of abortion and women's rights.

13. Manicom, p. 12.

14. Manicom, p. 12. Madévie and Cyril are frequently depicted at the window, often competing for the narrow restricted space. Windows are sometimes associated with passivity, being a spectator (a traditional female role) and with the woman.

15. Quotations in English unless otherwise indicated are taken from Simone Schwarz-Bart, *The Bridge of Beyond (Pluie et vent sur Télumée Miracle)*. Trans. Barbara Bray. Introd. Bridget Jones. (London: Heinemann, 1982). Quotations in French are taken from French text: *Pluie et vent sur Télumée Miracle* (Paris: Editions du Seuil, 1972).

16. See Simone Schwarz-Bart, *Ti-Jean l'Horizon* (Paris: Editions du Seuil, 1979).

17. Schwarz-Bart, *Pluie et vent*, p. 11.

18. Ormerod, p. 120.

Writing Home: Gender and Heritage in the Works of Afro-Caribbean/American Women Writers

Carole Boyce Davies

I.

If we have been traditionally accustomed to thinking of Caribbean literature as male and a critical colonial literature, then it is clearly time for a radical revision. A substantial number of women writers, living both at home and abroad, have emerged, giving different shape and voice to this literature and challenging the preeminence of the largely male writers whom we used to think of as "Caribbean literature." The reality of gender presents, perhaps, the crucial difference between this group of writers and the preceding generation. But because they display all the possible degrees of familial and historical links to the Caribbean world, the identification of a common cultural heritage has been paramount in their self-definition as writers and in their own creative experiences. The result is that a shared exploration of gender and heritage is an inseparable aspect of a singular articulation of cultural identity.

My object here is to reveal the crucial links of creative experience which make Caribbean-American women writers, however diverse their places of birth or context and generation of emigration may be, essential in the redefinition of Caribbean literature. If we accept that the experience of migration was crucially related to the development of Caribbean literary expression, (as witnessed by the proliferation of Caribbean writing with migration to England in the 1950's) then contemporary Caribbean women, writing in the United States, must be accorded a similar place of importance within the growing Caribbean literary tradition.

Several continuities with the larger body of Caribbean literature validate
this position. The reconstruction of Afro-Caribbean cultural experience is
often central to the works of these women. And in this, the thematics of the
search for identity constantly recurs. The evocation of Caribbean landscape is
strong, as are the historical linkages to Africa. And of major importance,
these texts are critically engaged in an anti-hegemonic discourse with the
United States in much the same way that earlier writers waged an anti-
colonial dialogue with Great Britain.

This discussion will focus on the works of four writers: Jamaica Kincaid,
Michelle Cliff, Audre Lorde and Paule Marshall. These are writers who
because they are U.S. based and did not reproduce the anti-colonial text
seem to have forfeited their identity as part of the Caribbean literary
tradition. Although both Jamaica Kincaid and Michelle Cliff were born in
the Caribbean, only Kincaid is listed in Daryl Dance's *Fifty Caribbean
Writers*.[1] Audre Lorde and Paule Marshall were born of Caribbean parents
in the United States, grew up in distinctly Caribbean households in New
York and have defined themselves in various ways as Caribbean-American.
Despite parallel backgrounds, however, only Marshall has gained some
acceptance in Caribbean circles.[2]

Although these are all current writers, it may be useful, while studying
them as a group, to place them each within a historical context. Paule
Marshall and Audre Lorde are of similar chronological age, but Marshall's
first novel, *Brown Girl, Brownstones* (1959)[3] is steeped in the culture of the
first wave of migration. Thus she conveys the conflicting world of a
Caribbean people trying to control their new environment and construct a
Caribbean community in New York. Audre Lorde, in contrast, because of
the time of her presentation of *Zami* (1982)[4] and her explicit lesbian
identification is able, as I will show, to appropriate Caribbean experience in
a distinctly different way. Michelle Cliff connects the more mature view of
Lorde and Marshall to the fresher Jamaica Kincaid. Further, Cliff's world
is that of the bourgeois vacillating between the metaphoric yard and the big
house, while Kincaid deals intimately with peasant/working class experience. But both were born in the Caribbean and know the landscape
intimately. Through their varying contexts, social and ideological positions,
all of these writers are telling crucial parts of the Caribbean story.

II.

The question of identity for Caribbean women writers involves a self-
definition which takes into account both gender and heritage. In all cases it
is difficult to separate heritage/identity questions from gender/identity. So
for the Caribbean-American writer, cultural politics have to be worked out
along with sexual politics.[5] For the Caribbean woman, confronting racial
discrimination, male phallicism and foreign bias, the relationship to

Caribbean identity is problematic. So, the acceptance of heritage cannot come easily as Lorde reveals in *Zami*. For her it is a tortuous passage through adolescence, a rejection of an authoritarian family, a cultivating of female friendships and her independence, and finally a reintegration achieved through a fuller knowledge of her Caribbean female ancestry.

The heritage/ancestry relationship is clearly worked out by Paule Marshall only in her most recent work *Praisesong for the Widow* (1983).[6] In her first work, *Brown Girl, Brownstones*, the conflict for the girl Selina, arises from continual tension between her mother's rigidity and her father's contrasting emotionalism, between the conflicting worlds of Afro-Caribbean society in New York and her separate American experience. The girl's understanding of culture is shaped by the many conversations of the Caribbean working women in the kitchen, the Caribbean diet that is the mainstay of the household, the dialect from which she learns rhythm and poetry and relationships with other Caribbean people, like Suggie, who expose Caribbean sensuality.

Marshall herself spent vacations as a child and as an adult with family in the Caribbean. Her dedications tell the story of this connection with family still Caribbean-based, still strong. *Reena and other Stories*[7] is "In memory of my aunt Branford Catherine Watson ("Bam-Bam"), a West Indian market woman who thought nothing of walking 14 miles to town and back in a day." *Praisesong* is "For my Grandmother", the character she immortalizes in her short story "To Da-Duh in Memoriam (pp. 95-106). It is perhaps necessary to begin this discussion, as Eugenia Collier[8] does, by charting the passage of Marshall's questing character. The child in the story has been taken ostensibly to one of those "vacations" home which we know have more to do with family identification and history than they have to do with holidaying. The story dramatizes the tensions between ancestry and youth, tradition and modernity, African civilization with its tradition of respect for humanity and Western civilization with its often callous disregard for life. The child's identity is a source of the debate which Marshall unfolds. Da-Duh is in a losing battle, pitted against the skyscrapers of New York and the war planes which swoop over Barbados towards the end of her life. For her part, Da-Duh wants to do no more than expose her granddaughter to all the features of her Caribbean, but the child has numerous examples of bigger and better things to counter Da-Duh's canefields. Yet, while the canefields are presented as idyllic, the reality is much more complicated than Collier reads it. For the irony is that canefields are so wedded to Caribbean slavery and oppression of Africans that the child's rejection of them is an important departure from that particular experience and history. Yet her acceptance of America's technological might is another form of slavery. Importantly, Marshall captures that falling away that often occurs between generations. For whereas the grandmother's experience is of slavery and British colonialism, the insidious and also "colonial" relationship to America is also implicit in the child's acceptance of American dominance. Da-Duh's resignation evinces her understanding of this new master/slave dialectic:

> The next morning I found her dressed for our morning walk but stretched out on the Berbice chair in the tiny drawing room where she sometimes napped during the afternoon heat, her face turned to the window beside her. She appeared thinner and suddenly indescribably old.
> "My Da-Duh." I said.
> "Yes, nuh," she said. Her voice listless and the face she turned my way was, now that I think of it, like a Benin mask, the features drawn and almost distorted by an ancient narrow abstract sorrow. (p. 104).

This struggle to maintain heritage in the path of encroaching Western values is pursued relentlessly in all of Marshall's works and is crystallized in *Praisesong*, where the struggle between generations begun in "Da-Duh" takes on greater significance. Here, the protagonist is engaged, with her Great Aunt Cuney, in a dream battle, the outcome of which is that Avey must have a complete immersion into her African heritage in the Caribbean in order to maintain equilibrium. Avey's journey is beset by psychological trauma and physical agony but ends in a soothing resolution during the phase of acceptance and belonging. There is a definite Pan-Africanist focus in the relationship to heritage in *Praisesong* and in several other Marshall works. Connections can be made to writers like Edward Brathwaite, Barbadian by birth, who makes similar identifications. Brathwaite describes an earlier Marshall work as "literature of reconnection"[9] in which the writer purposely attempts to bridge the gap which separates; to create an unbroken path between Africa and the Caribbean, the Caribbean and Afro-America. Importantly, just as *Brown Girl, Brownstones* ends in conflict and departure to the Caribbean, *Praisesong* ends at the point of return to the U.S.A., the journey having been completed. The difference is that a much more controlled protagonist makes the journey in the latter. Avey is now beyond the impetuousness of youth and more fully engaged in the rituals of identification.

Audre Lorde's *Zami*, somewhat like *Brown Girl, Brownstones* but more explicitly, explores the struggle to define a self amid the overwhelming Caribbean culture of the household. The conventions of autobiography allow for a centering of a self caught in the conflicts of a Caribbean/American household which eschews any thought of private individual space: "a closed door is considered an insult" (p. 83). Nevertheless, there is an engagement with Caribbean folk culture through the recalling of folk healing, song-making, the notion of "home" (p. 13). Above all, she is able to make an explicit connection between her lesbianism and the fact that Carriacou women have a tradition of "work[ing] together as friends and lovers." By accepting "Zami," a word still identified negatively in the Caribbean, she is like Michelle Cliff, "claiming an identity" she was taught to despise. The definition of "Zami" is a bold epigraph to the work. And the tension in accepting identity seems to be finally resolved here. Her essay "Grenada Revisited,"[10] for example, is one of the best evaluations of the Grenada invasion and, as I see it, a fitting conclusion to *Zami*. Buttressed by concrete images of Grenada, pre- and post-revolution, she concludes with a tribute to the strength and resilience of the Grenadian people:

> I came to Grenada my second time six weeks after the invasion, wanting to know she was still alive, wanting to examine what my legitimate position as a concerned Grenadian-American was toward the military invasion of this tiny Black nation by the mighty U.S. I looked around me, talked with Grenadians on the street, the shops, the beaches, on porches in the solstice twilight. Grenada is their country. *I am only a relative.* I must listen long and hard and ponder the implications of what I have heard, or be guilty of the same quick arrogance of the U.S. government in believing there are external solutions to Grenada's future.
>
> I also came for reassurance, to see if Grenada has survived the onslaught of the most powerful nation on earth. She has. Grenada is bruised but very much alive. Grenadians are a warm, resilient people (I hear my mother's voice: "Island women make good wives. Whatever happens they've seen worse"), and they have survived colonizations before. *I am proud to be of stock from the country that mounted the first Black english-speaking People's Revolution in this hemisphere* . . . (pp. 188-189)

The heritage/identity question is definitely established in the Grenada essay as is the woman-identification in the acceptance of the term "Zami." But Lorde's expressed connectedness has its impetus from revolutionary Grenada and the sense of possibility which it held. Clearly then, for Lorde, cultural identification has to be addressed along with an overtly, anti-hegemonic discourse. She therefore moves the discussion, beyond a singular Pan-African identification to a fuller acceptance of a gender-identified relationship with history and an ideological consciousness of the meaning of Grenada's thwarted revolution within the context of power, powerlessness, and empowerment.

Michelle Cliff's *Claiming an Identity they Taught me to Despise* (1980)[11] deals head-on with the identity issue even to the expressive titling of her book. It is a lyrical, somewhat autobiographical exploration into identity with gender and heritage comprising this identity. Landscape, history, family, events, places, all become features of her exploration. The movement of the book mirrors the migratory pattern, beginning in the

Caribbean and childhood and moving to adulthood and America. The
sections entitled "Obsolete Geography" and "Filaments" particularly
typify this theme. In the first, we get an extended catalog of Caribbean
fruits, vegetation, details of day-to-day experience like the waxing of parlor
floors, the burying of umbilical cords, the slaughtering of domestic animals.
Much of the identification with "home" comes from the rural grandmother
who maintains continuity with homeland and whose entire being conveys
the multi-faceted composition of Caribbean society. We see her, however,
caught up in the conflict of being privileged, yet poor, white-skinned but
culturally Caribbean. Her mother is a distant, intangible, liminal presence
in her life. The contradictions of surface appearance versus reality, of
camouflage and passing are explored. For this reason she feels affinity with
Antoinette of *Wide Sargasso Sea*.[12] The hybrid creoleness that is
essentially the Caribbean, the necessity of accepting all facets of experience,
history and personhood in the definition of a self become integrated in her
consciousness of her own identity. Personal history, family history and a
people's history and culture all converge.

Cliff, like Lorde, makes even more explicit her connections in her
polemical essays. "If I Could Write This In Fire, I Would Write This in
Fire," in *The Land of Look Behind* (1985),[13] is definite about the politics of
Caribbean identity. Color and privilege are held up and examined. British
colonialism and American colonialism are juxtaposed (pp. 67-68). *Sula*[14]
is recalled, as is *Brown Girl, Brownstones*, and Ama Ata Aidoo's *Our
Sister Killjoy*[15]; so too are W.E.B. DuBois's concept of "Double Consciousness" and Bob Marley and the Rastafarian response. For Cliff as for Lorde
and Marshall, connectedness becomes a reality, "filaments" toughen and
expand:

> The Rastas talk of the "I and I"—a pronoun which they combine
> themselves with Jah. Jah is a contraction of Jahweh and Jehova, but to
> me always sounds like the beginning of Jamaica. I and Jamaica is who
> I am. No matter how far I travel—how deep the ambivalence I feel
> about returning. And Jamaica is a place in which we/they/I connect
> and disconnect—change place. (p. 76)

The works of Jamaica Kincaid, with their forthright acceptance of
Caribbean identity (and of course the fact that she has legally renamed herself "Jamaica") present an explicit identification. Kincaid's works therefore
begin at a different point on the identity/heritage continuum. Having
already accepted Caribbean identity, she can then pursue the meaning of
her woman self as she does in "Girl"; her inner personal self as she does in
"Wingless" and "Blackness," which is a clear redefinition of the concept of
"racial" blackness; her relationship to the landscape and folklore, as she
does in "In the Night" and "Holidays"; and all of these in the title story "At

the Bottom of the River." Both *At the Bottom of the River* and *Annie John*[16] explore the female self in the context of landscape and Caribbean folk culture. Central to both books also is perhaps the best presentation in literature so far of the conflicted mother-daughter relationship.

Heritage and identity are intrinsic to the narrative and have as much significance as the gender issues with which she begins *At the Bottom of the River*. "Girl" begins with a catalogue of rules of conduct for the growing Caribbean girl/woman. These merge into surrealistic images of the Caribbean supernatural world but conclude with her woman-to-woman motif which recurs throughout both texts. In *Annie John*, a similar landscape is created. Here, the maternal grandmother, Ma Jolie, clearly an ancestral presence, is characterized as a mysterious healer who appears on the scene at a time when her granddaughter is experiencing a terrible psychological dislocation which is manifesting itself in physical illness and disorientation. Much of this dislocation is located in Annie's attempts to understand and define herself against her mother. *Annie John* differs from *At the Bottom of the River* in that it is an autobiographical narrative which, as I have argued elsewhere,[17] functions as a decoder of much that is unexplainable in the mysterious world of the first work. But in both, the necessity to identify with, yet separate oneself from, the mother is a central issue. "My Mother" in *River* pursues this maternal identification/separation fully. There is a need for bonding as there is for separate space. The ability of each to separate and thus grow ensures harmony. During the early years, the girl is incapable of delineating a separate self and it is the mother who has to initiate and force the break: "You can't go around the rest of your life looking like a little me" (AJ, p. 26); "Of course, in your own house you might choose another way" (p. 29). The mother's seemingly brutal way of instituting this break produces emotions in the daughter that border on hatred but it is an intense love/hate sequence with much pain and rejection for both women. The child's experience of losing the mother is preshadowed in a seaside experience when the mother disappears from her view for a time.

> A little bit out of the area in which she usually swam was my mother, just sitting and tracing patterns on a large rock. She wasn't paying any attention to me for she didn't know that I had missed her. I was glad to see her and started jumping up and down and waving to her. Still she didn't see me and then I started to cry, for it dawned on me that, with all the water between us and I being unable to swim, my mother could stay there forever and the only way I would be able to wrap my arms around her again was if it pleased her or if I took a boat . . . (pp. 43-44)

This experience follows her descriptions of her mother's earlier attempts to make her swim on her own but the only way she would get in the water was on her mother's back, her arms clasped around her neck—clearly a pleasant but burdensome experience for the mother. Separation becomes a repeated nightmare of loss prefiguring the actual separation between the two at the novel's conclusion.

Annie John is a *bildungsroman* marking the girl's growth from childhood to womanhood and only at the end of the work, close to the point of her departure from the island do we learn that she and her mother share the name Annie John. The exile and departure motif is strong and in a way reminiscent of G's departure in Lamming's *In the Castle of My Skin* (1953)[18] and Tee's exile in Merle Hodge's *Crick Crack Monkey*. [19] Idyllic, but often difficult, childhoods seem a stock feature of Caribbean literature and may be explained by the nostalgia of "writing home." Descriptions of experiences in the colonial schools link this work to other Caribbean novels of childhood. But, more centrally here than in Hodge's works (and in a sense more like Lamming's exploration of the boys' friendships), is the exploration of relationships between girls. Feelings of sameness and the girl/woman-identification that adolescent girls often share, permeate the work. There are several lesbian allusions in the Gwen/Annie and Annie/Red Girl friendships but both Gwen and the Red Girl also appear to be alter egos: Gwen, and the path she chooses, become the rejected persona and the Red Girl with her wildness and freedom the preferred identification for Annie. The same maternal, woman-love image is central to both works: "Now I am a girl, but one day I will marry a woman—a red skin woman with black bramble bush hair and brown eyes, who wears skirts that are so big I can easily bury my head in them." (*River*, p. 11).

In the surreal landscape of *At the Bottom of the River* it is easy to see the maternal image merge with the image of woman love, for the imaginary female love she creates combines her Red Girl friend and her mother. The differentiation that is forced in *Annie John* with its solid autobiographical realism is allowed free poetic exploration into emotions and self in *River*.

> . . . one picture of two women standing on a jetty, one picture of the same two women embracing, one picture of the same two women waving goodbye, one box of matches. Everyday this red-skin woman and I will eat bread and milk for breakfast, hide in bushes and throw hardened cow dung at people we don't like, climb coconut trees . . . Every night I would sing this woman a song; the words I don't know yet, but the tune is in my head. This woman I would like to marry knows many things, but to me she will only tell about things that would never dream of making me cry, and every night over and over, she will tell me something that begins, "Before you were born." I will marry a woman like this, and every night, every night, I will be completely happy (p. 12).

In the haunting world of *At the Bottom of the River* where landscape collides gently with people, there is an Edenic quality to relationships and place and woman-to-woman identification is strong.

In Audre Lorde's *Zami*, this mother-daughter tension similarly propels the daughter to leave home, although in *Zami*, the departure is not shrouded in ritual and infused with exile motifs of ships, water and adieus as it is in *Annie John*. Here, in contrast, the mother's imposition of herself and her values on Audre's life is a crucial motif as is the daughter's distant affection. An early scene in which Audre finds a little playmate but is interrupted by the mother's gargantuan presence becomes emblematic, foreshadowing the mother's constant criticism of her friends and her unwillingness to accept her daughter's individuality. Another poignant scene is the one in which the girl Audre is savoring the sensuality of the pounding of spices. This act coalesces with her new womanhood and good feelings about herself until the mother returns and grabs the pestle out of her hand and teaches her the "correct," but, to the girl, brutal way of pounding spices (pp. 78-79). Much of this scene is wrapped up with her own sexuality, as the harsh "bone jarring" way which she now rejects is another signal of her separation from her mother in whose "kitchen there was only one right way to do anything." It is also a prefiguring or a recreation of her own rejection of phallicism especially as one of the few scenes of maternal tenderness which Audre had envisioned earlier follows. But her departure is inevitable as there are many more examples of coldness than there are of affection.

> When I moved out of my mother's house, shaky and determined, I began to fashion some different relationship to this country of our sojourn. I began to seek some more fruitful return than simple bitterness from this place of my mother's exile, whose streets I came to learn better than my mother ever had learned them. But thanks to what she did know and could teach me, I survived them better than I could have imagined. I made an adolescent's wild and powerful commitment to battling in my own willful eye, closer to my own strength which was after all not so very different from my mother's. And there I found other women who sustained me and from whom I learned other living. How to cook the foods I had never tasted in my mother's house . . . (p. 104).

The symbolization of the house as source of self-definition that is common in Caribbean literature is also prominent in Afro-Caribbean women's literature. The house and its specific rooms become metaphors of self and loci of self-definition, prevalent in Kincaid's two works. In "My Mother", she says, "My mother and I walk through the rooms of *her* house . . . As we walk through the rooms, we merge and separate, merge and separate; soon we shall enter the final stage of our evolution" (p. 60). At the end of her own explorations of self and meaning in "At the Bottom of the River," she constructs another house, which is a trope for her own writer-self emerging: "I looked in, and at the bottom of the river I could see a house, and it was a house of only one room, with an A-shaped roof . . . " (p. 75). Stopping at this house, though, is only one aspect in the movement to heightened self consciousness, but one to which she will return, for the view shifts to landscape, animals, and a microscopic examination of every feature of her being, a shedding away (p. 80) and a concomitant reconstruction and reclamation of her identity as writer. The A-shaped house becomes synonymous with the rudiments of writing: the alphabet[20]. After all of the excursions, the narrator moves into a spare, lit room with the implements of the trade and the necessities for sustenance: a table, a pen, fruit, milk and clothing (p. 82) from which springs her identity.

These same metaphors of house and rooms are present in a variety of modes in all of the works by Caribbean-American women writers. In *Brown Girls, Brownstones* the mother's struggle to acquire a house is one of the central stories. In *Praisesong*, Avey has to move beyond the superficiality of the White Plains home and come to an acceptance of her identity in the sparer circumstances of Rosalie Parvay's (the healer's) house. Michelle Cliff constantly identifies her grandmother's house with its polished floors in *Abeng*[22] and in *Claiming*, and in "If I Could Write This in Fire, I Would Write This in Fire", specifies it as "four rooms, no electricity, no running water. The kitchen was a shed in the back . . . " (p. 58). But there is no sense of the house as her own space. For Audre Lorde in *Zami*, separation from mother and mother's house means temporarily a rejection of ties to the culture in which she had been raised. But in her mature reappropriation of the Caribbean, a wider space is identified. In all cases, the confines of the mother's house have to be extended.

In this spatial expansion of the meaning of home, female elders are crucial links. For Clare in *Abeng*, her friend Zoe, though of similar age, functions effectively as elder in much the same way as had Clary (after whom she is named) to her mother (p. 141). Ma is as central to Tee in *Crick Crack Monkey* as is Great Aunt Cuney to Avey in *Praisesong* and Ma Jolie in *Annie John*. For Lorde, the politics of her lesbianism is seen on a continuum between her female ancestors and the women who sustained her after her departure from her mother's house.

> Their shapes join Linda and Gran' Ma Liz and Gran' Aunt Anni in my dreaming, where they dance with swords in their hands stately forceful steps to mark the time when they were all warriors.
> In libation, I wet the ground to my old heads. (p. 104)

Connections with Paule Marshall's *Praisesong* with its reacceptance of heritage suggest themselves here, especially in the Nation dance with the old women staying the course of history. The connection between gender and heritage is never severed in *Zami* for Audre Lorde consistently identifies with the legendary *women* of her extended family and so makes some explicit personal and political connections. Afro-Caribbean female history is an important pool from which contemporary positive images are constructed.

All of the works in this study locate the definition of female self for Afro-Caribbean female protagonists within the larger exploration of cultural identity. And within this self-definition, as the metaphors of house reveal, the mother-daughter relationship is paramount. In *Brown Girl, Brownstones*, the power struggle played out between Selina and Silla is as central to the novel as is the struggle between the mother and father, or Silla's own struggle for material success. The naming of the two is significant here, for Selina, like Annie John, shares the contradictions of the mother/daughter bond. The creative tension between Silla and Selina similarly prompts the daughter to initiate her own departure. The symbolic tossing away of one of her two Caribbean silver bangles in the wreckage of the brownstones where her early life had been shaped and which closes the novel (p. 310) is a rejection of some aspects of her mother and Caribbean culture but it is also a simultaneous holding on to other features. For she does keep one of those "two heavy silver bangles which had come from 'home' and which every Barbadian-American girl wore from birth." (p. 5)

Michelle Cliff from the start communicates this distancing between mother and daughter, as in *Claiming An Identity* the mother is not as active a presence as the grandmother. In *Abeng*, the same situation occurs for Clare, who while she seems to identify with Kitty is nevertheless alienated from her. Kitty deals emotively with African identification and her femaleness but never struggles with, or fully embraces either. In *Claiming an Identity* the mother/daughter relationship is filtered through a visit to the museum and an exploration of various mother-daughter relationships through time.

My mother and I meet in public places—and move between swathed heads:

We came to this exhibit in part to connect, in part to recollect—but we hold few memories in common: our connections are limited by silences between us. Our common ground is the island where we were born—and we speak in the language spoken here. And we bear a close resemblance, except for eye color. (p. 33)

Through the museum experience, the mother and daughter connect with the meaning of gender and with their European and African legacies. But in the final section, entitled "Separations," a departure similar to those discussed above is effected. Here, it is more emotional than a physical departure for the writer recognizes that the gap between them has become too wide for the nurturing that the mother now needs from the daughter. In response to a story in which a daughter daily suckled her mother from her full breasts while the latter was imprisoned in a Roman prison, Cliff responds:

> I cannot do this for my mother, not merely because I have no milk. I cannot do this for my mother. We have no proximity. My mother has no knowledge of my breasts. . . .
>
> My mother did not nurse me, but my decision not to suckle her is not vengeful. She asks too much of me. She has no knowledge of my breasts, my clitoris, my intelligence. (p. 62)

In her memory and consciousness is another woman who nurtured her.

III.

Students of Caribbean literature have been oriented to think of Caribbean literature only as male; to experience the literature from the point of view of the male writers whose works are the majority and dominate the literary landscape.[22] We are also programmed to live within the narrow confines of language, in most cases, English. Finally, we are used to making certain distinctions based on geography and birth largely derived from colonial conditioning and a European, academic definition of literary place. Thus England was for years recognized as the legitimate literary center of Caribbean writers abroad. The writers based in North America, and there are many—the Haitian women and Puerto Rican women who are writing in New York, Cuban women writing about exile, writers like Marlene Philip in Canada—exist in a strange, hitherto undefined relation to the Caribbean literary tradition.[23] Even when they attain American acclaim as has Jamaica Kincaid, for example, they seem not to belong fully to either tradition. In Lorde's case or Marshall's, there is complete recognition within the Afro-American literary tradition but the Caribbean cultural elements remain submerged.

Migration and fluidity of movement or displacement and rootlessness, intrinsic to the New World experience, fundamental to the meaning of the [African] diaspora are broadening definitions of writers' place. The rigid compartmentalization into geography and national identity which academia forces on writers disintegrates when confronted by writers like Paule Marshall, or Claude McKay or even Olaudah Equiano. One of the benefits of a black feminist critical focus is its attempts to cut across geographic boundaries in search of a sisterhood among Black women beyond the limitations of language and locale. Thus it becomes easier to study women writers beyond the male academic categories. There is an ongoing cross-fertilization, so, allusions to works of other Third World women writers repeatedly appear in the works of a number of these writers: Ama Ata Aidoo appears in the same discussion as does Toni Morrison. For the critic with knowledge of these various allied traditions, all sorts of connections can be made.

An important point of reference in the charting of the ambiguous relationship of the Caribbean-American woman writer and the United States on one hand, the Caribbean on the other, lies in our recognition of that largely female migration, documented by Dolores Mortimer and Bryce-LaPorte.[24] Paule Marshall makes explicit this relationship. For prominent in the picture are determined, hard-working women, grappling with American capitalism while holding on determinedly to their Afro-Caribbean heritage.[25] But there is little idealization of these women at all by these daughter-writers. The mother is presented with all her failings, yet she often remains heroic. Audre Lorde's recent poem "Call" is an example, with its linking of female heroism in the celebrated mytho-legendary figures with the mundane struggles for transcendence of working women:

> We are learning by heart
> what has never been taught...
> you are my given fire tongued
> Oya Seboulisa Mawu Afrekete
> . . . .
> and we are shouting
> Rosa Parks and Fannie Lou Hamer
> Assata Shakur and Yaa Asantewa
> *my mother* and Winnie Mandela are singing
> in my throat...
> Mother loosen my tongue
> or adorn me
> with a lighter burden
> Aido Hwedo is coming... [26]

(emphasis mine)

It is perhaps finally futile to distinguish between writers who, like Cliff or Kincaid, were born in the Caribbean and migrated to the U.S. as young women and those, like Lorde and Marshall, whose parents joined the American working class, educated their children yet gave them a cultural grounding. It is more important that, in their works, some to a larger extent than others, these writers accept their Afro-Caribbean heritage and ancestry and use it creatively. For here are writers who define themselves as products of both experiences; have had direct knowledge of the Caribbean landscape, people, food, and the like; have listened to their parents, relatives and other elders describe the Caribbean homeland; have at times lived in the Caribbean. The surface difference in experience then becomes superficial when one realizes the crucial importance in their art and in their creative impulse, of the shared, common Afro-Caribbean heritage.

There is the definition of a female self at the core of every work. Also present are the distinctly Caribbean themes of identity, of being caught on the border between two culture-areas and of exile and movement. "Writing home," reclaiming and redefining Caribbean female identity, appropriately sums up this particular literary experience.

NOTES

All other page references to these editions appear parenthetically in the text.
1. Daryl Cumber Dance, *Fifty Caribbean Writers. A Bio-Bibliographical Critical Sourcebook* (New York: Greenwood Press, 1986).
2. Paule Marshall was even listed in Marjorie Engber's *Caribbean Fiction and Poetry* (New York: Center for Inter-American Relations, 1970) as Barbadian.
3. (New York: The Feminist Press, 1981).
4. *Zami. A New Spelling of My Name.* (Trumansburg, New York: The Crossing Press, 1982). Audre Lorde defines this work as "bioymythography".
5. Barbara Christian has a useful discussion of this point in "Trajectories of Self-Definition: Placing Contemporary Afro-American Women's Fiction" in *Conjuring* (Bloomington: Indiana University Press, 1985), pp. 233-248. She discusses Lorde and Marshall within Afro-American women's literary tradition.
6. (New York: G.P. Putnam's Sons, 1983). Marshall's other major works include *The Chosen Place, The Timeless People* (New York: Harbourt Brace and World, 1969) and *Soul Clap Hands and Sing* (New York: Atheneum, 1961).
7. (New York: The Feminist Press, 1983).
8. Eugenia Collier, "The Closing of the Circle: Movement from Division to Wholeness in Paule Marshall's Fiction" in *Black Women Writers (1950-1980). A Critical Evaluation* (New York: Anchor Press/Doubleday, 1984), pp. 295-315.
9. Edward Brathwaite, "The African Presence in Caribbean Literature," *Daedalus* 103:2 (Spring, 1974) 73-109.
10. "Grenada Revisited: An Interim Report," in *Sister Outsider. Essays and Speeches* (Trumansburg, New York: The Crossing Press, 1984) 176-190.
11. (Watertown, Mass.: Persephone Press, 1980).
12. (London: Penguin, 1968). First published in 1966. This point, along with the influence of Jean Rhys is pursued fuller in my "Developing a Voice: Creative

Modes in Caribbean Women's Fiction" presented at the 1986 MLA, New York.

13. (Ithaca, New York: Firebrand Books, 1985), pp. 57-76.

14. Toni Morrison, *Sula* (New York: Bantam, 1975).

15. Ama Ata Aidoo, *Our Sister Killjoy or Reflections from a Black-Eyed Squint* (London: Longman, 1977/New York: NOK, 1979).

16. Jamaica Kincaid, *At The Bottom of the River* (New York: Vintage Books, 1985). Stories published between 1978 and 1983 and *Annie John* (New York: Farrar Strauss Giroux, 1985).

17. Carole Boyce Davies, "Developing a Voice. Creative Modes in Caribbean Fiction." Unpublished MLA paper, 1986.

18. (New York: McGraw-Hill, 1953).

19. (London: Andre Deutsch, 1970).

20. A graduate student suggested this to me during discussion of the text.

21. (Trumansburg, New York: The Crossing Press, 1984).

22. Marjorie Engber's bibliography lists quite a few writers including novelists: Phillis Alfrey, Rosa Guy, Lucille Iremonger, Mary F. Lockett, Clara Rosa de Lima, Nancy Marr, Paule Marshall, Jean Rhys, Ada Quayle; one short story writer, Phyllis Cousins, and poets: Iris Tree, Tropica (Mary Adella Wolcott), Una Marson, Stella Mead, Julia Warner Michael, Alma Norman, Harriet Ormsby, Rhoda Mackenzie, Miriam Lyons, Erica B. Lee, Althea Barbara Jones, Vivian Hazell, Edith Daniel, Paula Brown, and Phillis Alfrey. Serious evaluation of these women's works is a matter of urgency, as often the names of women writers mentioned in bibliographies represent the apex of a larger triangle of writers who remain in oblivion. Work being done on Phillis Alfrey, for example, reveals her as a significant talent who somehow remained outside the pale of Caribbean literary criticism. See for example John J. Beston's review "Neglected West Indian Writers. No. 1. Phyllis Alfrey. *The Orchid House*" in *World Literature Written in English* 11 (April-November, 1972), pp. 81-83.

23. Claude McKay, Harlem Renaissance poet and novelist, Jamaican born but resident in New York in the early 1900s and Eric Walrond, Barbadian-born author of *Tropic Death*, and other U.S. based writers had the same uneasy relation in the Caribbean canon. There is more acceptance of them as Caribbean writers now.

24. Delores M. Mortimer and Roy S. Bryce-La Porte, *Female Immigrants to the United States: Caribbean, Latin American and African Experiences* and *Caribbean Immigration to the United States*. (Washington, D.C.: Smithsonian Institution, RIIES Occasional Papers Nos. 1 & 2, 1981 and 1983).

25. Paule Marshall's "From the Poets in the Kitchen" in *Reena*, pp. 3-12 is perhaps the best explanation of this creativity and struggle.

26. Audre Lorde, *Our Dead Behind Us* (New York: W.W. Norton, 1986), pp. 73-75.

Tradition and Innovation in the Writings of Puerto Rican Women

Sandra Messinger Cypess

Any consideration of the tradition of women writers in Puerto Rico should be placed within the context of the social, economic, and political conditions and ideologies which were in effect during the time of its Spanish colonial status and which continue to affect the culture of the Island to the present time. Because of Puerto Rico's initial political status as a marginal colony within the Spanish Empire, it is not until the middle of the 19th century that one can begin to distinguish a native, original body of work that does not imitate the patterns, themes, and characters of the Spanish mother country. It is important to remember that in terms of other Latin American countries, this is considered a late start in the creation of a national literature.[1] The three previous centuries of Spanish rule had permitted relatively little in the way of opportunities for the creation of a literary tradition, for as Antonia Sáez reminds us in her description of the cultural climate of Puerto Rico, life in the colony was regimented with an iron hand, and the inhabitants were deprived of both educational and economic opportunities; from the sixteenth to the nineteenth centuries, no university or other centers of learning were allowed to be established on the Island.[2] The marginal status of Puerto Rico continued to condition cultural circumstances on the island long after 1898, when it was transformed from a colony of Spain to become a possession of the United States.[3]

Olga J. Wagenheim offers a telling analysis of the cultural conditions of Puerto Rican women, who suffered not only "the legacy of colonialism, political intolerance, educational deprivation, economic dependence and exploitation [but] . . . racism, the division of classes, patriarchy, and the mythology of subordination implicit in the religious dogma of Catholicism."[4]

75

Such a context may explain the relative silence, on the part of critics and
historians, regarding the role of women in Puerto Rican society, their
contribution to history as well as their formation as creative writers. For
example, in her study of history textbooks, Isabel Picó documented that
authors of these texts omitted mentioning the role of women and lessened
their importance in practically all the periods studied.[5] Until recently, this
general trend of neglect has been repeated in the presentation of Puerto
Rican literary history, and the figures chosen as the "initiators of the
cultural awakening in Puerto Rico" are generally Miguel Cabrera, Román
Baldorioty de Castro, José Julián Acosta and Alejandro Tapia y Rivera
(Saez, p. 10).

Cabrera's "Coplas del Jíbaro" (1820) is considered among the first
Puerto Rican pieces to reflect a national consciousness. In this poem
Cabrera uses the regional language of the unique Island figure, the *jíbaro*, a
word derived from the Taino word *jiba*, meaning forest. The jíbaro who
lives and works on the land has come to symbolize for many the truly native
Puerto Rican. Cabrera's jíbaro questions the manner in which the Spanish
Constitution relates to its colony and is generally critical of Spain's
relationship to the Island. Though the work was censored and its publication
prohibited, it signalled an expression of a national consciousness in its use
of a unique national language which would be developed further by other
writers throughout the 19th and 20th centuries. It should be understood,
however, that even at this early date in the development of a national
literature, there were women writers who should be recognized as part of the
growing literary tradition of the Island.[6]

In the opinion of Efraín Barradas, "la literatura culta puertorriqueña
nace con la labor, mínima pero eficaz, de una mujer ["the Puerto Rican
cultured literary tradition begins with the minimal but effective work of a
woman]: Maria Bibiana Benítez (1785-1873)."[7] Benítez was a member of a
productive literary family, being the aunt of Alejandrina Benítez (1819-
1879) and the great aunt of José Gautier Benítez, considered the great
Romantic poet of the Island. With the appearance in 1832 of "La ninfa de
Puerto Rico," Maria Bibiana Benítez became the first woman to write a
recognized poem. This ode was followed by further poetic and dramatic
pieces in the Romantic style of the times. Of significance is Benítez's ability
to present abstract Romantic themes of independence and freedom in terms
of Puerto Rican realities, a technique that is continued by contemporary
writers. Her play, *La cruz del Morro (The Cross of Morro Fortress)*
(1862) openly explores a nationalistic theme, the Dutch invasion of the
Island in 1625, and therefore can be included in the tradition of works
dealing with the theme of revolution.

Benítez's play is not the first drama written by a woman in her century;
this distinction belongs to Carmen Hernández de Araújo (1832-1877) who
wrote *Los duedos rivales* in 1846 when she was about 14 years old. In

evaluating the literary production of Hernández de Araújo, Rivera de Álvarez noted that "Fue, en síntesis, esta autora un espíritu dotado de fina sensibilidad que, a no haberse hallado cénido por el empobrecido ambiente cultural de su época, hubiera podido dar obra de mayor relieve literario" ["This author was, in synthesis, a spirit gifted with a fine sensibility which, had she not been curtailed by the impoverished cultural environment of her period, could have been able to offer works of greater literary projection"].[8] Of course, typical for that period, Carmen Hernández de Araújo was able to receive only the most rudimentary education. Yet despite such a handicap, she created literary works comparable with those of well educated male writers of the time.

The one woman writer of the 19th century whose fame has survived to this day is Lola Rodríguez de Tio (1843-1924), one of the most outstanding literary and political figures of her period. A militant *independentista* (Separatist), she wrote "La borinqueña," a poem which calls for the Puerto Rican people to join the armed struggle against Spanish colonialism. Written to the music of a dance already known as "La borinqueña," her poem was inspired by the political events of 1868, referred to as "El gritto de Lares" ["*The Cry of Lares*"]. Although this uprising against Spanish colonial rule, planned by Ramón Emeterio Betances and his followers, failed to achieve its aims, her poem has survived as the anthem for the Separatist movement. Moreover, the poem reveals a Caribbean consciousness that becomes a thematic concern for the women writers of the contemporary period, as noted in this stanza:

Bellísima Borinquen,   Beautiful Borinquen
a Cuba hay que seguir;   You must follow Cuba
tú tienes bravos hijos   You have brave sons
que quieren combatir.   Who wish to do battle.

A revised Puerto Rican literary history must, therefore, include not only Miguel Cabrera and Alejandro Tapia, but also María Bibiana Benítez, Carmen Hernández de Araújo, and Lola Rodríguez de Tio as national writers who foreshadow important themes and figures of the contemporary period. These 19th century women writers, though few in number, and hampered by the sociopolitical obstacles of their culture, nevertheless overcame those barriers to begin a tradition which has continued to the present period.

Despite the works of these women writers, for some contemporary critics, there is no feminine tradition in Puerto Rican letters. The presence of a tradition implies that there is an inherited, established, or customary pattern of thought which is handed down from one generation to another. This continuity is accorded to male writers and their texts, yet when women authors are studied, the typical observation is that of Efraín Barradas:

"Nunca ha habido una tradición femenina en nuestras letras. Nuestras escritoras son excepciones aisladas en una constante o regla masculina. El caso . . . repite el de las letras hispanoamericanas en general" ["There never has been a feminine tradition in our writing. Our women writers are isolated exceptions in a masculine rule or constant. The situation is repeated in Spanish American writing in general"] (p. 405). I would like to comment on various aspects of that observation because I believe there is a discrepancy between the real literary contributions of Puerto Rican women writers and the value assigned them in critical analyses.

It is verifiable that in the majority of studies of Latin American literature, when Puerto Rican authors are included, male writers are mentioned in far greater numbers than women writers. Granted that Alejandro Tapia, Eugenio María de Hostos, Luis Llorens Torres, Luis Palés Matos, have been integrated into the literary canon, whereas Carmen Hernández de Araújo, Lola Rodríguez de Tio, and Soledad Llorens Torres (the sister of the poet, as she is referred to, despite her own innovative poems), are not visible in the popularly recorded literary tradition. Does their omission from the canon negate the presence of a feminine tradition, or their role in the unified literary tradition of their island? I would suggest that the reality presented by most critics regarding the presence of a feminine tradition has more to do with their perspective of that tradition, rather than with the actual literary production of women writers. Granted the number of women writers who were published is small in comparison with the number of men who were able to see their works introduced into the public arena. The lack of quantity, however, is clearly understandable when one remembers that

> "Existen en la sociedad puertorriqueña diversas instituciones y organizaciones que directa o indirectamente fomentan o refuerzan el papel dependiente y subordinada de la mujer" ["There exists in Puerto Rican society diverse institutions and organizations which directly or indirectly stimulate or reinforce the dependent and subordinate role of women."][9]

Let us put aside, then, the quantitative element in regard to tradition, and examine instead the repetition of themes and techniques as verification of the continuity of characteristics among the women writers of the 19th and 20th centuries in Puerto Rico.

It may be that Barradas offered his observation about a lack of a feminine tradition because he based his assessment primarily on individual figures within a given genre. However, when one takes into account the totality of women writers in all genres, then Puerto Rico certainly can boast of a continuous and productive feminine tradition. Using this approach, one can also observe a continuity of themes and preoccupations of the women writers from the 19th to the 20th centuries, an established and customary pattern of thought, which women writers have repeated from one generation to another. What is noteworthy, moreover, is that the same problems treated by women in the 19th century persist into the socio-cultural sphere of the 1970-80's. Nevertheless, the continuity of previous themes does not belie the innovations of the contemporary generation of young women writers. Conversely, the innovations in style and technique need not deny the thematic tradition which has been repeated: an awareness of their Caribbean identity, their fight for freedom, in terms of their gender and class, and their interest in the distinctive features of their homeland.

It should be noted that poetry has been the genre most often associated with women writers in Puerto Rico, as in Latin America in general, because of the greater ease it affords for publication of individual works. In Puerto Rico, there is an acknowledged and rich tradition of women poets, beginning with María Bibiana Benítez (see above), some of whose work has also infiltrated the standard anthologies. A prototypical figure who will serve as another example in the genre of poetry is Julia de Burgos (1914?-1953). Burgos was productive in her lifetime, but remained unacclaimed at her death and only recently has her work received its merited evaluation and esteem. Her books of poems—*Poema en veinte surcos* (1938), *Canción de la verdad sencilla* (1939), *El mar y tú y otros poemas* (1954)—record her personal interests in the classical themes of love, death, and her nostalgia for her homeland and its landscapes, as well as her social concerns regarding political inequities and the need for social justice, themes previously raised by Lola Rodríguez de Tio and Luisa Capetillo. Burgos reveals a contemporary perspective by contributing a feminist note to her concern for workers and social inequality—she criticizes the limited role to which women are relegated in society (see her poem "A Julia de Burgos" as a good example). There are many women poets in contemporary Puerto Rico who have continued in her path: Marina Arzola (1939-1976), María Arrillaga, Carmen Alicia de Cadilla, Angela María Davila, Vanessa Droz, Lolita Lebrón, Violeta López Suria, Carmen Marrero, Magaly Quiñones, Olga Nolla, Etnairis Rivera, Luz María Umpierre, Iris Zavela, to name but a few. (Nuyorican writers like Sandra María Esteves and Nicholasa Mohr argue for a separate tradition.)

While poetic expression by women is accepted and acceptable, their involvement in drama, on the other hand, has received little attention by critics outside the island.[10] It has already been mentioned that women dramatists were active in the 19th century in initiating themes that have continued to this day. It is helpful to recall the presence of Luisa Capetillo (1883-1922) who should be considered one of the key figures in the tradition of women writers in Puerto Rico. She was consciously a feminist, whose actions and literary texts revolved around the major themes of feminine liberation and workers' rights. Her essays and dramatic pieces condemned the double sexual standard, religious hypocrisy and fanaticism, workers' exploitation and female oppression by the dominant patriarchal society. She also proclaimed the rights of women to universal suffrage and free love, and she defended internationalism. The title of her collection of plays indicates her progressive position: *Influencia de las ideas modernas [Influence of Modern Ideas]* (San Juan: Negrón Flores, 1916). The individual pieces are somewhat like essays in dialogue form, clearly stating her denunciation of the economic system and its oppression of women— "Matrimonio sin amor, consecuencia el adulterio;" "La corrupción de los ricos y la de pobres o Cómo se prostituyen una rica y una pobre" ["Matrimony Without Love, Adultery the Consequence," "The Corruption of the Rich and the Poor, or How a Rich Woman and a Poor Woman become Prostitutes." "En el campo, el amor libre" ["Free Love in the Country"] offers her defense of free love, as can be observed from the speech of the heroine Angelina:

> Beautiful girls who have heard this, if you wish to be the mothers of future and conscious generations who are free, do not engage in civil or religious contracts because they are sales and sales are a way of prostitution. Love should be free like the air one breathes, like the flowers that open up to receive the pollen that fertilizes them and carries their scent into the air. You should give love in the same way and prepare to have children out of love.[11]

While Luisa Capetillo may not be an expert dramatist whose technique merits imitation, nevertheless her work is important in the literary tradition for its outspoken treatment of feminist issues, and for its creation of women characters as spokespersons for those progressive ideas. Capetillo's themes have maintained their relevance to the present day because Puerto Rican sociocultural values still reflect a strong patriarchal system. The necessity to repeat her themes is seen in the work of another woman playwright, Carmen Marrero, whose play *¿Por qué no se casa, Señor Senador? [Why don't you Marry, Mr. Senator?*, 1953] deals once again with the double standard which affects women and with their relegation to second class status by the patriarchy.[12]

The concern for the political status of the Island first expressed by María Bibiana Benítez is repeated in *independentista* (Separatist) writing today; it has been noted that one of the early plays of the versatile Myrna Casas (1939), *Eugenia Victoria Herrera* (1964), contributes to this theme.[13] Casas is one of the writers considered as part of the Generation of the Sixties, and has been an active participant in the theatrical life of the Island as dramatist, actress, producer, as well as professor of drama at the University of Puerto Rico. Nevertheless, her many experimental and provocative plays have not received the same attention generated by Luis Rafael Sánchez (1936), who replaced René Marqués as the Puerto Rican playwright most often studied, in large part because of the impressive success of his novel *La Guaracha de Macho Camacho [Macho Camacho's Beat*, 1976]; it should be noted that this text has been considered one of the key works to raise the consciousness of readers to the exciting possibilities of Puerto Rican narrative. While Casas's work has not been as linguistically provocative as Sanchez's, her plays have explored various theatrical techniques and have been innovative in the presentation of feminist themes. Just as *Eugenia Victoria Herrera* explores the role of women in traditional patriarchal families, *Absurdos en soledad [Absurdities in Solitude*, 1963] continues this study of women in society in an absurdist form. Casas's presence in the theatrical life of Puerto Rico should not be considered an anomaly associated with the contemporary period, for she is part of a continuous if ignored tradition of women dramatists on the Island.[14]

In addition to Marrero and Casas, the work of Lydia Milagros González (1942) has also continued the feminine tradition in Puerto Rican dramaturgy. González has been called the most important writer of her period by the critic Jorge Rodríguez;[15] the radical work of her group, "El tajo del alacrán" [The Scorpion's Slash] raises the public's consciousness concerning the problems of the Island. Like Casas, she is involved in every aspect of dramatic production, yet she has broken out of the traditional theatrical space by going out into the street to bring theater to the common people. While this interest in the "pueblo" [the people] is not new in Puerto Rican literature, Lydia Milagros González uses contemporary issues expressed in the language of today to reach both the masses and the upper classes. Plays like "La historia del hombre que dijo que No" ["The Story of the Man who Said No," 1966, revised 1977] and "La nueva vida" ["The New Life," 1969, revised 1977], question traditional values and the identity of the Puerto Rican caught between political problems of statehood versus separatism.[16]

Perhaps the work most representative of the latest tendencies in Puerto Rican theater today, as well as representative of feminist writings, is found in the texts of Zora Moreno (1951). She is a versatile figure, not only a dramatic writer, but a well-known actress and director, who also has her own group, Producciones Flor de Cahillo (Flower of Cahillo Productions). She grew up in the lower class neighborhood called Tokio de Hato Rey, but left to go to New York City, where she worked with Miriam Colon and the Teatro Rodante Puertorriqueno (Puerto Rican Travelling Theater). In 1970 Moreno returned to the Island, and founded a theatrical group called "El gran Quince de la barriada Tokio" [The Great Fifteen of the Tokio Neighborhood]. This group continues to be the most active of the theatrical companies doing popular theater. Whether the critics call it anti-conventional theater, anti-theater, popular theater or even theater of social protest, the work of Zora Moreno is associated with the need to point out the social injustices in her society.

According to Moreno, "The purpose we follow with this group is to raise consciousness, to entertain, educate and promote our Puerto Rican culture" (Playbill). Her dramatic representations use popular music and humor to characterize typical people speaking their own dialects and caught in typical situations of their everyday life in the *barrio* (neighborhood). In some ways one may compare her plays to *La carreta [The Oxcart]* of Rene Marques or the *Máscara puertorriqueña [Puerto Rican Masque]* of Francisco Arriví, in the use of Puerto Rican dialect and the presentation of themes involving racial tensions and acculturation. Despite these apparent similarities, Moreno's special contribution must be recognized in that she adds special attention to the feminine characters and feminist themes in general. For example, in "Dime que yo te diré, o estampas de un arrabal" ("Tell me and I'll tell you, or scenes from a neighborhood," 1975], the particular economic problems of women in contemporary social situations are included. The play is composed of nine fast-paced scenes depicting the lives of the residents in the poor neighborhoods of San Juan and of the inland *jíbaros*. It is the grandmother Juana, however, who can be called the main character and who keeps the people together even after her death. The realization of her loss stimulates the others to declare their mutual need and desire to help each other. Collective group effort instead of passive disinterest in others is shown to be a positive mode of behavior. *Con machete en mano [With Machete in Hand*, 1976] continues her preoccupation with popular traditions and the economic situation by presenting the effect of industrial changes on the lives of the Puerto Rican family. Moreno represents the problems of both women and men as they face the new conflicts brought about by changes in the job market and in technology.

Perhaps her most famous work to date is "Coquí coriundo vira el mundo o Anastasia" ["Coquí coriundo turns the world around, or Anastasia," 1981], which was produced by Flor de Cahillo during the First Spring Theater Festival of the Ateneo Puertorriqueño. The story is based on a true account that appeared in the newspapers in 1979 about a Puerto Rican woman, Adolfina Villanueva who was assassinated by police while attempting to defend her home against eviction. This tragic event also inspired another feminist writer, Maria Arrillaga, to recount poetically her reaction in "This is the World of Terror" from *Frescura 1981* (Río Piedras: Ediciones Mairena, 1981). In Moreno's version, the three acts of the drama depict typical Caribbean customs and music at the same time they focus on the tragedy of the real-life Villanueva family. Antonio and Anastasia, a simple fisherman and his wife with their six children, live happily and independently in a sea-side hut, when the landowner comes to threaten their way of life. The landowner wants to evict them for he plans to build new homes on the valuable land they have inhabited for so many years. This scene calls to mind *La carreta*, in which the jíbaro is also evicted from his land in the name of progress. In Moreno's "Coquí coriundo" the characters are not passive, however, and fight for their land. It is important to note that the person who bravely faces the landowner and shows herself to be valiant in the face of danger is Anastasia, the mother. Overcoming constricting stereotypes of the machista society, she does not back down in the face of his threats, unlike other female figures both on stage and off, but speaks to him directly and fights for her rights. The play follows the tragic ending of the real-life story, and Anastasia, like Adolfina, is killed by the police in her battle to defend her land. Despite the unhappy ending, the play has a positive effect in presenting a female figure as a valiant spokesperson for the rights of the poor. It also shows many happy scenes of family life, with people enjoying good food, good music, and positive family relationships.

Our overview would not be complete without reference to the contemporary short story writers, for more than the novel, the short story is the form most used in narrative today and is undergoing a renovation of great energy and spirit. This energy and spirit is also reflected in the short stories of contemporary women writers, whose production has received serious critical evaluation. Their work is characterized by a preoccupation with popular idiomatic language which dissolves the old barrier between "poetic or literary" language and "popular or vulgar" speech. It is not only that the popular idiom is being used, but that language traditionally called "obscene" has also become part of the literary vocabulary of the women writers. The use of such language has generally been acceptable for males, but its use by women writers ruptures established social tabus concerning acceptable speech and in its sociolinguistic dimension, reflects their anger against the system. The women writers have recognized the relationship between language, power, and sexuality studied by Michel Foucault in his landmark texts *The Archaeology of Knowledge* and *The History of Sexuality*. There is also a renewed exploration of pan-Caribbeanism which had been a theme of the 19th century Puerto Ricans as they questioned their identity vis-a-vis Spain; now it stems from Puerto Rico's relation with the United States and its cultural imperialism on the Island.

Among the younger generation of writers who express the new sensibility in language and form, the work of Rosario Ferre has received increasing critical attention. Her family has been active in Caribbean political life (her father, Luis Ferré, is a former governor of the Island), but rather than enjoy the confined privileges of the wealthy upper class, Ferré has chosen to explore the values of the traditional bourgeoisie from a feminist perspective. Just as Luisa Capetillo had founded the journal *La mujer* in 1910 as a vehicle for her progressive ideas, Ferré and other like-minded writers began *Zona Carga y Descarga [Loading Zone]* in 1972 as a journal committed to literary and sociopolitical change. Her first collection of poems and short stories, *Papeles de Pandora [Pandora's Papers]* (Mexico: Joaquin Mortiz, 1976) reflects her social commitment to feminist ideology. Most of her women protagonists are "ninas buenas" (good girls), the daughters of the bourgeoisie whose experiences cause them to realize their position of subservience in their society. "La muneca menor" ["The Youngest Doll"], "Amalia" "La bella durmiente" ["Sleeping Beauty"], and "Cuando las mujeres quieren a los hombres" ["When Women Love Men"] serve as good examples of her reaction to patriarchal authority, her questioning of the power and status of men in relation to the subjugation of women. As so many other women writers before her (Lorenza Brunet, María Molina, Isabel Cuchi Coll, etc.), Ferré has also written works for children, which can be read as political and social allegories. [17]

"When Women Love Men" has received much critical scrutiny because it epitomizes the exploration of the image of women from a feminist perspective. [18] The story recounts the lives of two very different women whose paths cross because of a man; Isabel Luberza is Ambrosio's legitimate wife, the white woman of the bourgeoisie, symbol of repressed sexuality similar to the wife of Senator Vicente Reinosa in *Macho Camacho's Beat*. If Isabel Luberza functions in the traditional role of women in a patriarchal society, being the "good woman," the other woman, also Isabel, serves as a symbol of the "fallen woman," for she is a prostitute. The particulars of class and race are also explored, for the prostitute is a black woman who depends on white men for her economic sustenance. Despite their different racial and class origins, both women are shown to be objects of the patriarchy. The two women whom society would judge so differently are seen to behave similarly in the economic sphere: they exchange sex for economic support. Their inherent similarity as women is shown stylistically in a number of ways, from their common name, their shared preference for Cherries Jubilee nail polish, (a direct reference to American cultural imperialism), and from the narrative perspective, in the blending of their two narrative points of view. The story shows expert handling of the narrative, and with its verbal facility, thematic sophistication and humor, should maintain a place in the history of the narrative.

The last writer I would like to highlight in this overview is Ana Lydia Vega, co-author with Carmen Lugo Filippi of *Vírgenes y martires [Virgins and Martyrs]* (Rio Piedras: Editorial Antillana, 1981), and the collection *Encancaranublado y otros cuentos de naufragio [Threatening Skies* and Other Stories of Shipwrecks]* (La Habana: Casa de las Ámericas, 1982), which received the "Casa de las Americas Prize" in 1982. Her work also explores the problem of identity within a Caribbean context and the question of cultural unity, and *mestizaje* [admixture of races] that is characteristic of the Caribbean experience. Although her stories are marked by feminist consciousness, the world she depicts also contain a great deal of violence, assassinations, assaults; the reader is hit as well with stylistic world play and humor, that can be noted in the tongue-twister title "encancaranublado," a world typical of the Caribbean, to describe the skies that predict storms (hence my attempt to translate it as "threatening skies"). Like Ferré and co-author Carmen Lugo Filippi, Vega records the rapid and uncertain social and economic changes in Puerto Rico, where both national and personal concepts of identity are under attack. The stories grouped under the first section "Nubosidad variable" ["Variable Clouds"], refer to the different Caribbean nationalities, adrift in the sea of uncertain political status and unsettling social and economic changes. In the title story, "Encancaranublado," Vega brings together protagonists from several Caribbean countries—Haiti, the Dominican Republic, and Cuba—and explores their interactions as they attempt an escape by boat to the United States. Their brush with shipwreck, their subsequent retrieval by the United States Navy, and the ultimate lessons they learn about "Caribbean" solidarity and their place in North American society, can be read as a political allegory in the best tradition of universal political literature.

"Puerto Rican Syndrome" is another exploration of pan-Caribbean identity, using violent actions and images which culminate in the apocalyptic tidal wave that overcomes the Island. Vega parodies the language of the media, of politicians, of those who would convert the Caribbean into a costumbristic island paradise of food, fun, sun and sand. She discounts the paradise in favor of a realistic picture of the problems which confront the people of the Caribbean today, and she offers no easy solutions. Although her themes question traditional social values and the absurdities of colonialism in the tradition of Maria Bibiana Benitez, Lola Rodriguez de Tio, Julia de Burgos, "her language moves with the popular rhythm of the 'salsa,' combining satire, irreverent humor, and biting criticism."[19]

Efraín Barradas has rightly asserted that the so-called Generation of the Seventies has brought about important and exciting technical and linguistic innovations. Among the ten short story writers included in his anthology *Apalabramiento (Word Cont[r]act* (Hanover, N.H.: Ediciones del Norte, 1983), Barradas includes Luis Rafael Sanchez, Manuel Ramos Otero, Juan Antonio Ramos, but also Rosario Ferré, Ana Lydia Vega, Magali García Ramis, and Carmen Lugo Filippi. The inclusion of the women writers in this and other recent anthologies is no longer seen as a special event, because the work of the contemporary women authors is now considered an integral part of the Puerto Rican literary tradition. Although this critical recognition marks the coming of age of women writers and an enlightened perspective on their works, it should be remembered that the tradition of women writers in Puerto Rico is not new—only the critical awareness of that tradition is new. The line of thematic continuity that was limited, suppressed and hidden by the socio-cultural environment now has been re-stated and re-expressed by many voices in a variety of genres.

NOTES

*Unless otherwise indicated, all translations from the Spanish are my own. The asterisk next to a translated title is meant to convey the notion that the translation is an approximation, because the author is engaged in word plays that are difficult to translate into English.

1. Many Puerto Rican critics makes this comment; see for example Jose Emilio Gonzalez, *La poesía contemporánea de Puerto Rico (1930-1960)* (San Juan: Instituto de Cultura Puertorriqueña, 1972), p. 14; Julio Rodríguez Luis, *La literatura hispanoamericana entre compromiso y experimento*, (Madrid: Editorial Fundamentos, 1984).
2. Antonia Sáez, *El teatro en Puerto Rico* (San Juan: Editoria Universitaria, 1950),p. 9. All further references to this text will appear in parentheses.
3. Julio Rodríguez Luis, *La literatura hispanoamericana entre compromiso y experimento*, p. 33; Jose Luis Gonzalez in *El país de cuatro pisos* makes the point that North American colonialism caused an internal upset in the cultural values of Puerto Rico, and has caused the "Northamericanization" of Puerto Rico.
4. Olga Jiménez Wagenheim, "The Puerto Rican Woman in the Nineteenth Century: An Agenda for Research." *Revista/Review Interamericana*. 11 (1981), p. 196.
5. Quoted by Iris G. González, "Some Aspects of Linguistic Sexism in Spanish," *Revista/Review Interamericana*, 11 (1981), p. 208.
6. In my overview of Puerto Rican literature "The Unveiling of a Nation: Puerto Rican Literature in the Twentieth Century" in *The Puerto Ricans: Their History, Culture, and Society*, ed. Adalberto López, (Cambridge: Schenkman Publishing Co., 1980), pp. 283-309, I consciously integrated the works of men and women in Puerto Rico in an attempt to establish a comprehensive perspective. Recent anthologies of Puerto Rican literature also include the texts of both men and women writers; also consult *Personalidad y literatura puertorriqueñas*, eds. Hilda E. Quintana, María Cristina Rodriguez, Gladys Vila Barnes (Santurce: Editorial Playor, 1985).
7. Efraín Barradas, "Reseña a *Vírgenes y martires,*" *Revista/Review Interamericana*, 11 (1981), p. 465.
8. Josefina Rivera de Álvarez, *Diccionario de la literatura puertorriqueña*, Tomo 2, Vol. 1 (San Juan: Instituto de Cultura Puertorriqueña, 1974), p. 737.
9. Celia Fernández Cintrón and Marcia Rivera Quintero, "Bases de la sociedad sexista en Puerto Rico," *Revista/Review Interamericana*, 4, 2 (1974), p. 243.
10. Puerto Rican drama, by both men and women, is the least known of the Island's literary production, as Manuel Galich acknowledges in an issue of *Conjunto* dedicated to Puerto Rican theater. Galich adds, however, that a careful study of dramatic production "es suficiente para descubrir cuan equivocados estamos... cuando creemos que la isla aherrojada carece de una rica tradición y de un vigoroso movimiento contemporaneo en el campo teatral" ["is sufficient to discover how wrong we are when we believe that the captive Island lacks a rich tradition and a vigorous contemporary theatrical movement"] in "Boceto puertorriqueño," *Conjunto*, 25, p. 4.
11. Quoted in Carmen Rivera de Álvarado, "La contribución de la mujer al desarrollo de la nacionalidad puertorriqueña," *La mujer en la lucha hoy*, eds. Nancy Zayas and Juan Angel Silén (Rio Piedras: P.R.: Ediciones KIKIRIKI, 1972), p. 43.

12. See Sandra Messinger Cypess, "Carmen Marrero y su drama feminista," *Explicación de textos literarios*, in press.

13. Although *Eugenia Victoria Herrera* does not refer to the United States's presence in Puerto Rico, its story takes place some time before the War of 1898; it explores the colony's relationship to Spain and the values of the patriarchal system. See Sandra Messinger Cypess, "Women Dramatists of Puerto Rico," *Revista/Review Interamericana*, 9, 1 (1979), pp. 36-37; Cypess, "Myrna Casas y la dramaturgia femenina en Puerto Rico a la luz del estado sociopolítico," *Third Woman Press*, in press; Luz Maria Umpierre, "Inversiones, niveles y participación en *Absurdos en soledad* by Myrna Casas," *Latin American Theatre Review*, 16/1 (Fall 1983), pp. 3-13, places another work of Casas with a feminist perspective (rpt. in *Neuvas aproximaciones . . .*, pp. 59-73).

14. See Cypess, "Women Dramatists," pp. 24-41.

15. Jorge Rodríguez, "Los nuevos dramaturgos: Optimismo y desafío," *El reportero* (11 febrero 1984), p. 19.

16. Lydia Milagros Gonzalez actively participated in the political and cultural events of the '60s and '70s. She published the play texts and a history of the Tajo de Alacrán group in *Libretos para Teatro del Tajo del Alacrán* (San Juan: Instituto de Cultura Puertorriqueña, 1980).

17. Luz María Umpierre, *Nuevas aproximaciones críticas a la literatura puertorriqueña contemporánea* (Rio Piedras: Editorial Cultura, 1983), pp. 91-101.

18. This short story has been translated by Cynthia Ventura in the collection *Contemporary Women Authors of Latin America*, eds. Doris Meyer and Margarite Fernández Olmos (Brooklyn: Brooklyn College Press, 1983), pp. 176-185.

19. Fernández Olmos, "From a Woman's Perspective: The Short Stories of Rosario Ferré and Ana Lydia Vega." *Contemporary Women Authors of Latin America*. Introductory Essays (Brooklyn: Brooklyn College Press, 1983), p. 86.

Interior Schisms Dramatised: The Treatment of the "Mad" Woman in the Work of Some Female Caribbean Novelists

Evelyn O'Callaghan

And then a Plank in Reason, broke,
and I dropped down, and down . . .

Emily Dickinson

Novel's by Caribbean women have increased in number over the last twenty years; in the majority of these, the central character (or characters) is female and in several of these novels she is presented as 'mad.' In Jean Rhys's *Wide Sargasso Sea* (1966)[1] and Myriam Warner-Vieyra's *As the Sorcerer Said* (1982),[2] the protagonist becomes increasingly disturbed and ends up institutionalized as mentally unsound. Zee Edgell's *Beka Lamb* (1982)[3] deals with a 'normal' adolescent whose best friend Toycie becomes severely mentally ill and does not recover. I propose to examine the treatment of the 'mad' girl/woman in these three works.

It must be noted from the outset that many other texts in what is, after all, a small corpus of fiction produced by West Indian women writers, share this characteristic presentation of women. The protagonist in Erna Brodber's *Jane and Louisa Will Soon Come Home* (1980) suffers a physical and mental breakdown, a fragmentation of self out of which she is beginning to emerge whole as the novel ends. A similar process is undergone by the very different central character in Paule Marshall's *Praisesong for the Widow*

(1983). Telumee in *The Bridge of Beyond* (Simone Schwarz-Bart, 1974 &
1982) suffers for a time the loss of her mind. Elizabeth, in Marion Patrick-
Jones's *Jou'vert Morning* (1976) becomes a crazy woman walking in the
streets. Merle Hodge's *Crick Crack Monkey* (1970) portrays young Tee's
personality on the verge of total collapse and withdrawal.

My concern is what we can learn about these literary madwomen and
about the societal contexts of their lives. What is the significance of this
recurring presentation of the female in a state of psychic collapse? To a
certain extent, we learn something of the emotions, thoughts and behaviour
of Caribbean women in various states of mental disintegration. But are
these representations of mental illness medically credible? Since the three
novels portray characters who ultimately suffer some form of psychosis,
withdrawing almost totally from 'reality,' they do not accurately mirror
trends in the distribution of mental disorders among women in the West
Indies.[4] In fact, it would seem only a fairly small minority of women are
afflicted in this way. Nonetheless, the novels describe these severe illnesses
as the end result of earlier disorders (e.g. depression, personality disorder)
not being treated or alleviated,[5] and contain information about some of the
long and short term causes of mental illness[6] as well as credible literary
presentations of several symptoms of psychosocial disorder. My attempt
here is to pursue the idea of the madwoman in the West Indian novel as
social metaphor, and to link authorial treatment of this figure with certain
common assertions about West Indian literature, to be discussed later in the
essay.

There are clear similarities between the three characters in the novels
under study despite differences of historical context, social origin and race.
Suzette (Zetou), Toycie and Antoinette[7] are described in adolescence as
insecure, vulnerable personalities. All three share a history of rejection by
one or both parents, and there is little evidence that physical affection was
shown them in childhood. Growing up, they experience loneliness, lack of
security and helplessness, exacerbated in the cases of Zetou and Antoinette
by physical displacement. Further rejection/betrayal occurs (Zetou's rape
and her mother's betrayal; Toycie's betrayal by Emilio and rejection by the
school authorities; Antoinette's rejection and betrayal by her husband).
The characters are portrayed as reacting with feelings of anger, guilt, fear,
frustration and hopelessness. They exhibit behavioral abnormalities such
as extreme violence, paranoia, and in the case of those whose mental world
we are permitted to enter, hallucinations. They each withdraw from a
hostile world, almost totally cut off from reality. Toycie and Antoinette
have self-destructive tendencies and for Zetou, it is implied, death would be
a welcome release.

Now, it is foolhardy to attempt even a tentative medical diagnosis of a
fictional character. This is clearly pointed out by both Lilliam Feder[8] and
Sandra Gilbert and Susan Gubar[9] in their books on the portrayal and

significance of 'madness' in literary texts. However, although Feder makes it clear that 'attempts at diagnoses of the pathology of fictive characters by literary critics are often anachronistic, not to say absurd . . . ,' she also feels that any study of literary madness requires some knowledge of basic "psychoanalytic theories of mental functioning and psychopathology where they provide essential clues to the symbolic nature and expression of such characters" (*Madness in Literature*, p. 10). Bearing in mind Feder's warning, I nonetheless asked Dr. Belle[10] if the fictional "case studies" of the novels in question bore any resemblance to psychiatric fact, and if so, what type of mental illness the characters might suffer from. After much discussion, she returned the opinion that all three novels appeared to describe a progression from personality disorder through depression to psychosis. In the case of Zetou, she felt that the final pages of the novel "would almost be the classic description of the latter part of a schizophrenic illness," and that the patterns of disintegration of the other two characters could also suggest schizophrenic symptoms.

Attempting to follow Feder's injunction to acquire some knowledge of basic psychoanalytic theory proved somewhat problematic, in that so much of the literature on mental illness seemed to me to be oriented towards a European or North American context. Dr. Belle had pointed out that in different societies/cultures, illness can present in different ways and result from widely varying causes. Hence much of the theory seemed curiously distanced from a West Indian application.

Philip Rack's illuminating study of this problem (1982), cites examples from several ethnic minority groups in Britain to illustrate the point that

> Cultural differences in the manifestations of distress and the way such manifestations are interpreted, represent *diagnostic pitfalls* for the practitioner . . . We have to consider whether a familiar illness (such as endogenous depression) has a different presentation in different cultures; or to put the same question the other way round, whether a familiar symptom has a different meaning in different cultures.[11]

Dr. Roland Littlewood, a psychiatrist with extensive experience of West Indian patients in the United Kingdom, has researched reactive depression in Trinidad[12] and notes that such illnesses have not, until recently, been described outside "the industrialized West." He feels this is probably because "they are seldom identified locally as distinct entities" (p. 275), but are explained in terms of behavior patterns and beliefs embedded in cultural values—for example, depressive symptoms may be explained as part of the state of "Tabanka," which can follow the loss of a sexual partner to another person. Littlewood feels that culture does not only shape illness as an experience, but shapes the very way we *conceive* of illness, so that in explaining patterns of mental illness in a given society, we should "start with the context of indigenous conceptualizations of psychopathology" (p. 276). Lawrence Fisher[13] attempts to do this for the Barbadian situation, and I found his approach very helpful.

However, of the established descriptions and theoretical analyses of schizophrenia, R.D. Laing's famous study, *The Divided Self,*[14] provided a conceptual framework within which I could examine the development of the "madwoman" figure in West Indian fiction as social metaphor. Briefly, Laing's approach is based on an "existentialist/phenomenological" analysis of existence as one's "being-in-the-world," which is of necessity "being-with-others," since one experiences oneself as autonomous only in experiencing the other as "not me." One's experience of self then is as a conscious subject, mind and body integrated, interacting with a world which contains objects, including other persons (who, by analogy, are also presumed to be autonomous, integrated self/body subjects).

But, Laing observes, there are people who do *not* experience themselves or the world in this way—this is the "schizoid" person:

> Such a person is not able to experience himself "together with" others or "at home in" the world but, on the contrary, he experiences himself in despairing aloneness and isolation; moreover, he does not experience himself as a complete person but rather as "split" in various ways, perhaps as a mind more or less tenuously linked to a body, as two or more selves, and so on. (p. 15)

This person suffers from "ontological insecurity"; he/she lacks the sense of unquestioning, self-validating, integral selfhood and personal identity that "normal" people take for granted. Thus he/she seeks isolation, and avoids relationships with other subjects, who may 'absorb' him/her as just another thing in the world of objects; complete isolation is a defense against the threat of complete merging of identity with another.

The ontologically insecure person doesn't even feel an integration of self (mind) and body—the latter is perceived as a detached thing, another object in the world of depersonalized objects. The unembodied "true self" looks on detachedly as the body (the "false self" or "false self system") plays its part/parts. We've all felt such dissociation ("this is like a dream"; "this isn't happening to me"), but for "normal" people the feeling of disembodiment is temporary. This "false self" of the schizoid usually acts according to other people's standards and expectations, having none of its own, thus concealing and protecting the true self. As Laing points out, such compliance with "what other people say I am" is a betrayal of one's true potential, a concept imaginatively conveyed in the 'kumbla'[15] image in Erna Brodber's first novel.

Behind the façade of the false self/selves, the isolated "true self" becomes more and more empty, a vacuum, having no direct connection with the world, omnipotent in fantasy, but *unreal* in actuality.[16] And the more this happens, the more critical the "true self" is of the false self, which it considers to be more and more separate, indeed to *belong* to others, "enemy-occupied territory" as it were. At this point, the schizoid becomes a schizophrenic, becomes psychotic. He/she feels unreal, "dead" and wishes to kill the "self"—*not* the body, but the imprisoning torture-chamber which the "true self" or mind has become. Obviously, denial of being as a means of protecting or preserving being can only lead to insanity.

Laing's often-criticized methods of treating schizophrenics aren't at issue here; his notion, however, of ontological insecurity and its consequences are relevant to the three 'madwomen' discussed here, particularly because, as Elizabeth Abel[17] points out, Laing's attempt to reconstruct the schizophrenic's way of being in *his/her world*, rather than viewing him/her objectively, seems useful to an analysis of characters in *their* literary worlds.

To begin with, Laing's description of the patterns of schizoid/schizophrenic behaviour is similar enough to the novelistic presentations of madness to suggest that the type of mental illness being described is indeed schizophrenia. Consider, for example, the resemblance between the following excerpts: the first describes Zetou's state of mind at the end of *What the Sorcerer Said*, the second is Laing's picture of a deeply distressed (psychotic) young woman.

(i) Now ... no feeling could penetrate my armour of despair. ...
    I was plunged into an alien world, behind a wall of darkness. I could hear people talking and laughing on the other side, but I could not communicate with them ... I was slipping slowly into a bottomless abyss. My first impression was that I was happy to be far from the others, sheltered by my wall.
    But when I realised that at the bottom of the abyss was death, I struggled desperately to get out. The room I entered was empty.
    ... It was too late. There was nobody there. I was still alone. Once more I could feel myself slipping down into the chasm. This time I made no attempt to halt my descent into the valley of darkness. (pp. 72-73)

(ii) ... the more she felt she could not reach other people, that other people could not reach her, and the more she felt herself to be in a world of her own—'They can't get in and I can't get out'—the more this private and closed world of hers became invaded by psychotic dangers from outside ... (p. 166)
    She felt, as she said, that 'she' had recently 'gone right down' and she wanted to get out of 'it' now, before it was too late, and yet she had a feeling that things had gone too far and that she 'could

not hold on to herself' for much longer and that 'it' was 'slipping
away from her' . . . 'I'm losing myself. It's getting deeper and
deeper.' (p. 164)

Similar feelings, responses, even similar images are apparent in both
portrayals.

The picture of Toycie in the mental home (*Beka Lamb*, p. 134),
pretending to study her imaginary schoolwork intently, is reminiscent of
Laing's account of the psychotic trying to "acquire" the reality from which
the "true self" is isolated by copying or imitating forms of behaviour which
are perceived as "real." And in *Wide Sargasso Sea*, there are numerous
passages in which the vivid portrayal of Antoinette's disturbed thoughts and
emotions conform to the schizophrenic symptoms described by Laing—for
example, her perception of the world as meaningless, colourless, unreal (p.
147); the split between her "real" self and the "ghost" self she sees in the
mirror (p. 149); the importance of touching things (her red dress) as a link
with reality (p. 152); her conception of herself as two entities, a "she" and
an "I" (p. 154), and so on.

Abel examines several of Rhys's novels using Laing's paradigm of the
divided self, and concludes that Rhys's "recurrent heroine . . . manifests
several specific symptoms of schizophrenia" (p. 156). In her treatment of
Wide Sargasso Sea, Abel is more interested in the reader's response to the
conflicting portrayals of the "mad" Antoinette's subjective, emotive point
of view and the "sane" Rochester's objective, intellectual perspective. Rhys,
suggests Abel, may be implying that we grant excessive authority to the
latter.

However, I'd like to suggest that several manifestations of the husband's
behavior also bear close resemblance to Laing's key characteristics of the
schizoid, if not the schizophrenic state: his crazed possessiveness regarding
the woman he intends to see completely transformed into "My lunatic. My
mad girl" (p. 136); his deliberate depersonalization of Antoinette into a
doll, a puppet, a marionette; his fear of being engulfed by the tropical
landscape, or the passion of his wife; his insistence on the necessity for
hiding his feelings, protecting the inner vulnerability and lack of security
experienced since childhood (p. 85). Laing's study of the patient "James,"
particularly the details of his relationship with his wife whom, because of his
own ontological insecurity, he depersonalizes into an "it" with a "robot-like
nature," "a machine" (pp. 50-51), helps to illuminate the fictional
Rochester's schizoid personality and suggests that the world view represented by Rochester, apparently sane, sensible and dominant, is actually
flawed and precarious. Indeed, given the husband's own disturbed psychology[18] which inhibits his achieving a sustained one-to-one relationship, many
of Antoinette's responses to him appear very sensible indeed.[19] It is the
mark of Rhys's skill that we enter so fully into Antoinette's mental world (as

Laing would have the therapist enter the schizophrenic's world), that I question whether in fact we *do* "know objectively that Antoinette is mad," as Abel claims.

Laing's paradigm then, provides a helpful analytical framework for the deeper understanding of the type of madness conveyed in the fiction of these three West Indian novelists. I want to suggest also, that the usefulness of this model extends into the realm of *causal* explanation, and leads us toward an exploration of the societies in which these authors wrote/are writing. Abel's study acknowledges the value of *The Divided Self* for her analysis, but feels that the work does not help to "answer a fundamental question: what has reduced these Rhysian heroines to such a helpless and divided state," (p. 186). To do so, she turns to Laing's later work, which develops on the idea that ontological insecurity may be due in part to parental failure to instill a sense of autonomy in the child, valuing instead passive compliance and submission of will as model behaviour. As Abel explains Laing's reasoning,

> This failure leads the child to question (or never to develop) an independent sense of self, to feel susceptible to the control of external forces, and to withdraw from the world in an attempt at self-preservation. (p. 168)

Now almost universally, female children are socialized into "good behaviour"—meaning compliant, obedient, submissive behaviour. Toycie, as we learn in *Beka Lamb*, was a model child, as she's a model young lady; her anxiety to please and to conform is obviously informed by her vulnerable and precarious position in the world as an orphaned, and thus economically dependent woman (see pp. 59-60 in the novel). Thus, Abel suggests, we might postulate that "there is a continuum between the general lack of confidence produced in women by cultural attitudes and the radical lack of sense of self characteristic of schizophrenia." (p. 169) In other words, perhaps the "schizoid" state is a more integral part of women's experience than that of men. Gilbert and Gubar (1979, p. 54) are quite specific about the negative effects of patriarchal socialization on womens' mental (and physical) health: "To be trained in renunciation is almost necessarily to be trained in ill-health, since the human animal's first and strongest urge is to his/her *own* survival, pleasure, assertion . . . " While these authors are mainly concerned with American and European women writers in the 19th century, the link between repression of will leading to self-doubt and illness[20] doesn't seem to me to be limited to any historical period or specific cultural context.

I'd like to use this link between "ontological insecurity," feminine submission and feelings of inadequacy, and "madness," as a departure point for a broader discussion. In this, I want first to outline some specifically West Indian historical/cultural factors which exacerbate the sense of "the divided self"—the emotional and mental state that characterizes the treatment of madness in several novels by Caribbean women; and which has been acknowledged as a recurrent theme in West Indian literature as a whole.

Apart from the general phenomenon of female socialization into submissiveness, what reasons are we given in the novels to explain the lack of a strong sense of self in these young women? Despite different geographical and historical contexts, certain stressful patterns recur. For example, all three grow up in changing societies with increased societal mobility and are subjected to some degree of conflict in their choice of social/sexual roles. Like Toycie, Zetou in *What the Sorcerer Said* conceives of a different future for herself than that of the women in her village since "the idea of having nothing but housework and children to occupy my time later was most depressing" (pp. 28-29). Education is seen as a means towards a job, a career. But Zetou's family thinks education for a girl, particularly the daughter of a fisherman, is useless and even dangerous; while in *Beka Lamb*, the author tells us that "economic necessity forced many creole girls to leave school after elementary education" (p. 34). So that while the goal of education for social mobility is available to them, it is by no means easy to attain.

Rhys's Antoinette, by virtue of her birth and colour, is already a member of the elite; but her family's poverty after Emancipation as well as her mother's creole origins, cause her to be considered socially inferior by the English whites, and a "white cockroach" by the black population: "Old time white people nothing but white nigger now, and black nigger better than white nigger" (p. 21). Like Toycie and Zetou, Antoinette does not fully belong to a stable, cohesive social class, and this factor contributes to her insecurity.

Did such tensions apply to the majority of Caribbean women—black working-class or peasant women? Brodber's study[21] of the images and stereotypes of post-Emancipation women in Barbados, Jamaica and Trinidad, notes that this group was perceived in the earlier period as self-confident, assertive, often financially independent after acquisition of initial capital and rarely dependent on one man. The black women in Antoinette's world, in Zetou's village and Toycie's community *seem* to bear out this generalized view—they earn a living in difficult conditions, raise children, often singlehandedly, and seem unplagued by self-doubts and conflicting social expectations which can lead to ontological insecurity.

But, as Merle Hodge points out in her introduction to Brodber's text (pp. viii-xiii), "ideal" stereotypes of women increasingly imposed by the media and based on upper-class, Euro-cultured values (such as "Excellent Ellen" and "Household Pearl"),[22] can negatively affect the way "real" black working-class women perceive and evaluate themselves. And in fact, closer reading discloses that the novels discussed contain very *few* models of strong, independent, capable women. In *Beka Lamb*, Miss Eila depreciates herself as ugly and unmarriageable and even the strong Granny Ivy cannot legally vote and must live according to her son's rules. The women in Zetou's village merely raise children and serve men; even her self-sufficient grandmother holds the view that a woman's life consists of cooking, mending and housekeeping (p. 22). And in *Wide Sargasso Sea*, the women are virtually all victims: strong-willed Amelie is destined to become the plaything of "rich men in Rio" (p. 116); Aunt Cora, aging and powerless, turns her face to the wall; even the redoubtable Christophine, who knows that a woman must "have spunks" to survive, admits that she too is a fool in dealings with men (p. 91) and is, in the end, frustrated by Antoinette's husband from helping her.

However, the novels are more concerned with the younger women under discussion here, who grow up in changing societies and are expected to adapt and to improve their societal status by behaving according to the standards, the "ideal" stereotypes, of the dominant class or a foreign culture or race. In *Beka Lamb*, for instance, education offers an alternative for girls to 'the washing bowl underneath the house bottom' (p. 2); but to graduate, the black Belizean students must conform to the model imposed by white, foreign educators, must "leap through the hoops of quality purposely held high by the nuns" (p. 112). For many, there is a clash between the norms and expectations of their traditional creole society, which they are expected to deny, and those within the convent gates.

Ramesh Deosaran (1978, p. 15) calls attention to the rapidity of modernization in the Caribbean and notes that while new opportunities and prospects arise as a result, they are often accompanied by an "anti-tradition" attitude which has long-term negative effects on society. In the case of Toycie, whose culture permits sexual indulgence and unmarried motherhood, but whose rise up the social ladder involves emulation of the Virgin Mary, we may see the result of the type of psychological conflict detailed above: the harsh judgment of Toycie is also a judgment of traditional values, seen as backward and immoral by the modern, foreign educators.[23]

Even where internalization of others' standards is successful, there is a price to be paid for the assumption of new social roles. As Zetou comes to realize, her own mother is an outsider in the social world of Paris and must act the part her lover wishes her to play, in order to hide her humble origins: "smoking her Players and talking in a high-pitched voice in what she hoped was a Parisian accent, to give herself airs of a fine lady" (p. 57), but always terrified of revealing a gap in her education or a lapse into the "nigger talk" of her homeland. Again, Antoinette's mother, widowed, impoverished and socially "marooned," plays the part of socialite to catch a wealthy husband and then finds she's expected to collaborate in his efforts to Anglicize the family, despite her awareness of the Jamaican ex-slaves' dangerous hostility to this new regime.

Naturally, confusion and anxiety about social roles overlap with confusion and anxiety about sexual roles. Gilbert and Gubar (1979) image the two polarities of female sexuality as portrayed in Western culture, "the angel in the house"[24] (like "Excellent Ellen") on the one hand and on the other, the witch/whore, a slave to the flesh who entices men to the sins of the flesh.

To choose the former self-image involves firstly, economic dependence on the husband/father and, as Abel (1979, 176) points out, "economic dependence induces psychological dependence and a subsequent loss of confidence that reinforces the fundamental economic dependency." This dependency is clearly portrayed in the character of Antoinette, "sold" for her money and with no legal rights thereafter. Similarly, her mother's lover proposes to marry the powerless Zetou off to a rich man, for his own financial gain.

Secondly, this self-image implies that women have no other aim but to love and serve men, which virtually reduces them to the status of object, having no existence apart from its function. Again, such repression of self leads to psychological stress; as Laing comments, "if an individual needs another in order to be himself, it presumes a failure fully to achieve autonomy, i.e. he engages in life from a basically insecure ontological position" (p. 204).

To identify with the witch/whore stereotype is to incur the wrath of Christian morality, to become, in effect, no better than the prostitute National Vellour, in *Beka Lamb*, a scorned and feared outcast.

The choice between these polarities is dramatized in the case of Toycie. Father Nunez lectures schoolgirls on the choice between the model of the Virgin Mary and that of Eve, who has the power "to unleash chaos upon the world" (p. 90). Like her own mother and many women in her neighborhood, Toycie becomes pregnant out of wedlock. Her nausea, causing her to vomit on the chapel floor, establishes her in the eyes of the nuns as a fallen woman, a source of contamination to be removed from the school before her sins infect others. The message she must learn is that to rise socially, it is necessary not only to break with her creole class but also with its morality— or suffer the consequences.

For Antoinette also, sexuality labels her suspicious. Her repressed English husband cannot understand her passion, although *he* has initiated her into "what's called loving"; indeed, he considers Antoinette's sexual abandon grounds for considering her promiscuous, even unbalanced:

> she thirsts for *anyone*—not for me . . . (a mad girl. She'll not care who she's loving), She'll moan and cry and give herself as no sane woman would—or could. *Or could*. (pp. 135-136)

Loving with body as well as mind, Antoinette finds, is grounds enough for her husband's rejection. Zetou also has been taught to believe in sexual purity, despite the example of her own mother. Despite the fact that she's blameless, her rape by her mother's lover leaves her feeling tainted, guilty, depressed: "I was sharing a man with my mother, I was damning my own soul" (p. 66). For all three characters, confusion and guilt associated with varying models of female sexuality lead toward mental breakdown.

The same process is anatomized in Brodber's *Jane and Louisa Will Soon Come Home*. Sexual maturation for the central character, Nellie, is felt to be a source of shame and men are to be avoided "lest you turn woman before your time" (p. 17). Against this idea of sexual repression is set the antithesis of promiscuity, of woman's womb as a scrap-heap, epitomized by her mysterious cousins who had simply 'dropped' their unwanted children and vanished. Torn between these now-internalized role models, and pressurized by the attitude of sexual freedom at University, Nellie withdraws into yet another female type—the "cracked doll," the dry, cerebral intellectual, emotionally sterile. Clearly this latter role is a defense against her inability to come to terms with the discordant sexual roles attached to the "label called woman."

In the particular West Indian context, anxiety about social and sexual roles[25] is further complicated by the well-documented experience of alienation and negative self-image in the colonized person, who is told to strive towards goals and values imposed from without. Antoinette, barred by her race from solidarity with the African ex-slaves, is rejected as socially inferior by the whites in Jamaica and becomes confused about her very identity: "So between you I often wonder who I am and where is my country and where do I belong and why was I ever born at all" (p. 85). Feelings of self-doubt and alienation are invariably intensified if the colonial migrates to the "motherland." Rack (1982, p. 56) describes at length the phenomenon of "culture shock" affecting migrants to Britain, which occurs "when the psychological cues that help an individual to function in society are withdrawn and replaced by new ones." Such stressful factors combined with climatic change, loss of communal and family support systems, inferior and isolated housing and so on, will naturally affect the migrant's sense of security and stability. Antoinette's reaction to her (forced) migration to England, which she finds cold and unreal—despite her stepfather's attempt to make her into "an English girl" in Jamaica—clearly supports this generalization.

The colonized person who has been educated to identify with the "motherland" is likely to have an even worse problem of adjustment. As Rack (1982, pp. 138-139) observes, "many West Indians came to Britain with high expectations of the welcome they would receive and the standards of tolerance and public morality they would encounter." Instead, they met with intolerance, racism, hostility and suspicion. Certainly, Zetou's reception in Paris is traumatic. Instead of welcome, she finds disillusion-ment, racism (pp. 58, 69) and reminders of her inferiority as a colonial (p. 55)—all of which contribute to her growing experience of ontological insecurity: "I was a solitary piece of flotsam, washed along by life, with nothing to catch on to" (p. 65). Even her own mother, mentally colonized in feeling that "nothing from Cocotier had any value" (p. 45), denies her daughter's worth.

To return, then, to the question of causes for the helpless and divided state of the female characters discussed here, it may be possible to isolate factors that are in some ways specific to post-Emancipation West Indian societies. Anxiety about choice of social (class-based) and sexual role (the latter includes the question of economic dependence); problems posed to psychic security by wholesale adoption of cultural values from the metropolis, and by migration to the "motherland" by the colonized woman—all are important stress factors which must be taken into account in analyzing the mental states of the fictional characters.

Such factors, it is suggested, are partly responsible for the "ontological insecurity," the vulnerability which leads to mental breakdown in the novels. One defense mechanism that may be used to preserve the insecure self against the threatening world is, as Laing explains, the adoption of one or more "false selves," or roles:

> becoming what the other person wants or expects one to become while only being one's "self" in imagination . . . In conformity, therefore, with what one perceives or fancies to be the *thing* one is in the other person's eyes, the false self becomes that thing. (p. 105)

Zetou, for example, responds to the gradual erosion of her sense of self by objectifying her actions in theatrical terminology (p. 62). But in time, she comes to realize the unpleasant role is *not* a temporary one for her "real" self is totally in the power of her "false" self: "I was no longer on stage, playing my part opposite other actors. The curtain would never fall, never, as I was playing my own role." (p. 65)

As Laing explains, to "play one's own role," to become a "thing" for others—whether it's that of "cracked doll," as in Nellie's case, or schoolgirl in a world from which she can't be expelled, in Toycie's—can lead to the situation where the false self becomes virtually autonomous, behaving in ways the inner self loathes but over which it can exert no control.

The inner self, meanwhile, has autonomy only in fantasy or, as Laing puts it, "in games in front of a mirror" (p. 105). Gilbert and Gubar use the metaphor of the mirror's reflection to suggest the dilemma of the 19th century female writer dimly perceiving her true self, trapped behind the glass of patriarchal literary stereotypes.[26] Their comment on this metaphor is particularly apt in the context of Rhys's novel: "To be caught and trapped in a mirror . . . is to be driven inward, obsessively studying self-images as if seeing a viable self" (p. 37). Laing and Gilbert and Gubar could have been describing Antoinette, who is both literally and figuratively obsessed with mirrors as she seeks to choose a "viable self-image" from the models offered her—the picture of the English "Miller's Daughter" (p. 30); her double/opposite, the black Tia (p. 38); the perfect young de Plana ladies at their convent school (p. 46).

As Antoinette becomes more disturbed, the image of the mirror is used to suggest the widening gap between her real and false selves (or role/s):

> The girl I saw in the glass was myself yet not quite myself. Long ago when I was a child and very lonely I tried to kiss her. But the glass was between us . . . (p. 147)

The dissociation becomes more severe ("I saw Antoinette drifting out of the window," she thinks (p. 147); until at the worst stage of her madness, the psychic split is complete and she no longer recognizes herself in the mirror; "*The woman* with streaming hair. *She* was surrounded by a gilt frame but *I* knew her" (p. 154—my emphases).

Laing's paradigm of the true self, isolated from the false self/selves which play out roles to please others, finally "haunted" and driven mad by those selves that become autonomous, seems similar to the process dramatized in the development of the fictional madwomen analyzed here. The choice of roles (self images) is determined by the social context of each novel, but the device of assuming roles is clearly a defensive one. For these characters, reality offers no possibility of integrated self-development—hence Zetou describes herself and her fellow patients as "people for whom madness was the only solution to a desperate situation" (p. 52). However, the defensive strategy is ultimately counter-productive as dissociation occurs, and even the inner self is fragmented in madness.

To an extent, Laing's paradigm can be applied more broadly to concepts of "the West Indian psyche" which have assumed critical orthodoxy over the last 30 years. For example, the existentialist interpretation of the self/other relationship as one of insoluble conflict—as epitomized in the slave/master model described by Hegel[27]—has been applied to the colonized/colonizer contact, and clearly informs the work of several Caribbean writers—George Lamming, for example. Sociologists too, such as Ramesh Deosaran, consider that our Caribbean societies have been forged from and are still based, to some extent, on "pervasive conflict and dominant-submissive relationships" ("Multiculturalism for democratic living," *Caribbean Issues*, IV:I [April 1978] 16).

Again, the Laingian description of the person who defines his/her "self" according to external models at the expense of his/her own autonomy is paralleled by Brodber's findings (1982, p. 55) on female stereotypes. The "ideal" female, as noted above, is one "whose purpose is derived from the existence of another" (father, husband, family), and many women define themselves according to this limiting stereotype, internalizing it as "right."

Female evaluation according to her degree of subservience to the male, clearly invites comparison with the colonized/colonizer relationship, and Anderson (1981, p. 242) has explored this connection in her analysis of *Wide Sargasso Sea*: "In this sense . . . Antoinette emerges as the colonized, the black woman, Rochester as the colonizer, the white man . . . " Thus, the phenomenon of ontological insecurity arising out of an unequal relationship between self and other may be seen to apply beyond the bounds of psychiatric analysis, and to explain some of the negative results of colonial and/or patriarchal oppression.

One such negative result is the well-documented condition of alienation, a condition which is not peculiar to the Caribbean, but has been so often portrayed in the literature—V.S. Naipaul's *The Mimic Men* (1967) is an excellent example—that it has come to be listed as a recurring theme in any definition of that literature. Once more, the "mad" individual as described by Laing, the ultimately isolated outsider, personifies alienation taken to the extreme.

Finally, a common correlate of the colonized, alienated and schizoid condition is the sense of being victimized. Kiev[28] claims that difficulties arise in the treatment of mental patients from underprivileged communities, because they tend to blame society for their problems, and refuse to take responsibility for their own lives. In other words, they tend to feel victimized and powerless. This observation is supported by the findings of Fisher (1978), whose working-class patients in the Barbados Mental Hospital considered their hospitalization as unfair punishment by an adversary with whom they had been in conflict (family member, neighbour, the police), with the complicity of the hospital staff (p. 86). Hence their stay in the asylum reinforced their feelings of powerlessness and frustration.

In addition to the serious dispute which "caused" their admission, patients also reported that they experienced hostility from their home communities in general.[29] People were malicious, wicked and bad-minded to them at home too. Thus, their general feelings were of political powerlessness at the hands of the enemy, the power structure, and their communities. They saw themselves as victimized. As one patient commented to Fisher, "I am not responsible for being here, the people of Barbados are responsible."

Fisher concludes that "Barbadian patients who blame external factors for their current predicament do so with some justification" (p. 104). Their poverty, and the resultant negative self-image of failure, are largely results of the class-structure "which shapes identities and which exercises considerable power over persons" (p. 106). Yet they tend to blame their victimization on individuals and their communities, rather than the larger social system which generates the structure in which they are underprivileged. So although the patients may not see clearly that their dispute is with the social system, there *are* faults in the organization of Barbadian society which cause mentally ill people to feel themselves to be powerless victims.

Of course, this perception of victimization and frustrated powerlessness is not limited to the mentally ill. Helpless impotence in the face of an unjust society and the hopeless, passive state this induces, are common reactions to colonial oppression and the "victim mentality" has been explored in several works of West Indian fiction—in Orlando Patterson's *The Children of Sisyphus* (1964), for example. Mark McWatt's essay, elsewhere in this collection, discusses the work of Roy A.K. Heath in which *all* the characters are in some way victims, regardless of their social status: the men are victims of the now-internalized colonial myth of native inferiority; the women are doubly so, since they are also oppressed by men.

If the woman can be seen as victim in patriarchal culture, the madwoman is victim *par excellence*. As Gilbert and Gubar point out (1979, p. 284), self-imposed victimization such as "self-starvation or anorexia nervosa, masochism, and suicide form a complex of psychoneurotic symptoms that is almost classically associated with female feelings of powerlessness and rage." And Chesler[30] goes so far as to suggest that many women institutionalized in mental hospitals are there in protest against their devalued, powerless female role—they've opted out. As noted in the novels under discussion, the female characters have also "given in"—at least superficially; they assume the pose of passive victim and wish to be left alone, or wish to withdraw into the ultimate isolation—death.

It is possible, then, to note parallels between Laing's theory of the schizoid personality, and portrayals of the damaged "West Indian psyche" in literature—fragmented, alienated and victimized as a result of the colonial or post-colonial conflict. These "symptoms" are to some extent dramatized, in all the novels analyzed here, on a microcosmic scale—in the lives of the individual female characters. It seems possible, then, to note a blurring of distinctions between individuals in a state of breakdown and society in a state of fragmentation: "ontologically insecure" characters stand for a Caribbean society that is itself lacking a strong sense of secure, autonomous self-worth.

Wide Sargasso Sea, I think, illustrates the Laingian paradigm on many levels. Antoinette finds herself divided between cultures, between emotions, between roles/false-selves, between places, even between life and death, until she becomes a "zombie"[31] her "true self" withdrawn and her physical body like a "marionette," enacting empty actions.

The conflict between other/self that precipitates her "madness" is the conflict between man (the domineering exploiter and tamer of nature) and woman (wild, mysterious but ultimately vulnerable and passive nature); but it is also the conflict between the hostile world of society (white *and* black) and the increasingly alienated individual, who fits in with neither group.

And, as previously noted, conflict exists between the colonial Englishman with his "superior" values (which Antoinette both fears and respects), and the colonized native woman with *her* values (which the husband despises, fears and is yet attracted to). So Rhys is not "merely" dealing with Antoinette the "mad" individual, but with Antoinette as metaphor for the madness of her fragmented socio-historical context.

Viewed on these several levels, Antoinette epitomizes the ultimate victim—colonized, alienated, victimized, female, and, finally, mad. The causes, in these novels, lie partly in the characters' personality make-up and personal history, but more with the organization of a social world which allows legal exploitation of women by men, and which trivializes and frustrates female assertion, channeling it into unproductive and self-destructive forms of behaviour.

My point is that the image of the "mad" woman, the ultimate victim, serves as a social metaphor for the damaged West Indian psyche during the period covered in these novels (post-Emancipation to early 1950s). The withdrawn, psychotic state of mind anatomized in the fictional individuals, figures of fragmentation and degeneration, corresponds with the passive "victim mentality" so common in our post-colonial societies, where the ills of the past have not been healed, and the present organization of the power structure seems to be indifferent to the individual or positively hostile to his/her need for self affirmation.

Like their male counterparts, but in a more subtle way and from another perspective, these women writers are dealing with the West Indian "quest for identity"—using the psychic damage and distorted self-image of the individual as metaphors for a kind of pervasive "illness" to which our societies are prone as a result of the colonial encounter. The interior schisms dramatized in fiction may be interpreted as the symptoms of the dangerous lack of ontological security still prevalent in our region—manifested in continuing "outward directedness": continuing regard for foreign culture, denigration of local traditions, the need to seek an elusive "reality" in the metropolis, or to play out roles adopted from imported models/ideals—all revealing a lack of secure pride in our society and its image. If a lesson may be learned from these novels it is that if we continue to avoid such central issues, that way madness lies.

However, rather than end on this pessimistic note, I'd like to touch on an issue in Laing's later work which is raised by both Feder (1980, p. 281) and Abel (1979, p. 173). This concerns Laing's conception of madness as a kind of liberation from false attitudes and values, leading to a rebirth of the "true self." Madness (schizophrenia), seen in this light, may be "breakthrough" as well as "breakdown."

Applying the idea to *Wide Sargasso Sea*, Abel finds in Antoinette's final dream a reaction to the false self or "ghost" she has become, and a movement towards autonomy as she wakes thinking "someone screamed and I thought, *why did I scream*" (p. 155, *Wide Sargasso Sea*). The re-identification of "someone" with "I" suggests a move from the divided state towards a type of wholeness. Abel thinks this progress is further supported by Antoinette's choice of the present tense once she awakes from her dream, a choice which isolates her statement ("Now at last I know why I was brought here and what I have to do" pp. 155-156) from the past tense narration of her madness. Although we know that Antoinette will commit suicide, Abel feels that Rhys wants us to see such an active choice as better than the option of prolonged imprisonment and madness, which was her mother's fate.

Certainly, Rhys herself seemed to intend Antoinette's choice to be a positive one, as her *Letters* (1985, p. 157) make clear: "Lastly: Her end—I want it in a way triumphant!" Suicide may thus be interpreted in this novel as an assertion of will by a hitherto passive victim or, in Gilbert and Gubar's terminology, "an escape into wholeness." John Thieme considers Antoinette's act of self-destruction "double-edged" since "an element of regeneration is involved as she symbolically escapes back to the lost Eden of her childhood."[32]

Regression, however, is hardly progress and I am more inclined to accept Feder's caution about the presently fashionable tendency to associate madness with insight, wisdom. As she points out (1980, p. 281), "Scientific investigations long before Laing recognized in delusions and other forms of mental aberration distorted yet significant communications of deeply suppressed human impulses." Confrontation with suppressed problems, contradictions and frustrations may lead, as with Nellie in Brodber's novel, toward the reconstruction of self—or, in my extended application, to the redefinition of a healthy, secure self-image in a given society. But what is clear from the novels is that in many cases, such as those of Zetou and Toycie, this facing of crucial issues is left too late and the withdrawal into fragmentation is irreversible. For the mental health of the individual and for that of her/his community, the warning is clear.

NOTES

1. Jean Rhys, *Wide Sargasso Sea* (London: Andre Deutsch, 1966 and Harmondsworth: Penguin, 1968). All page references to the latter edition.
2. Myriam Warner-Vierya, *As the Sorcerer Said*, trans. Dorothy Blair (London: Longman, 1982). All page references to this edition.
3. Zee Edgell, *Beka Lamb* (London: Heinemann, 1982). All page references to this edition.

4. Aggrey Burke's data from Trinidad and Tobago ("Socio-cultural determinants of psychiatric disorder among women in Trinidad and Tobago," *West Indian Medical Journal*, 23 (1974) pp. 75-79), lists "affective disorders" (those associated primarily with acute mood changes, such as depression and hypomania) as the most common of the illnesses among the female patients in the psychiatric unit. These are "functional disorders"—that is, there is no demonstrable organic cause, like brain tumour, for the symptoms, so illness is due to environmental stress and/or endogenous factors such as biochemistry and, perhaps, genetic makeup. After the affective disorders, Burke ranks schizophrenia (a psychosis), then neuroses (such as phobias) and finally personality disorders. A small percentage of his sample was categorized "no diagnosis," which consisted of young women with "situation or adjustment reactions" and included attempted suicides. Organic disorders and "other diagnoses" made up the rest of the sample. He notes that most of the patients admitted to the psychiatric unit were in the younger age group (about half were under 25) and that both admission rates and diagnosis categories for the East Indian and African subcultural groups were similar.

   There will be notable differences between admissions to a psychiatric unit in a hospital and to a public mental hospital, which tends to be a "last resort" for the very disturbed or the very poor. But Dr. Ermine Belle, of the Barbados Mental Hospital, also lists depression and hypomania as the most common mental illnesses among admitted patients. After these, come psycho-neuroses, personality disorders and other diagnoses, with psychoses like schizophrenia and manic-depression being much rarer. For further amplification of Dr. Belle's comments, see O'Callaghan (1985).

5. Clearly it is dangerous to make hard and fast assumptions, because the earlier presentations *could* be diagnosed as earlier signs of the psychosis rather than minor disorders.

6. Regional psychiatrist Dr. George Mahy, in "Mental Illness in Barbados and the Eastern Caribbean", *Bulletin of Eastern Caribbean Affairs*, 9:6 (Jan./Feb. 1984) pp. 1-4, comments on the appalling ignorance concerning mental illness in our territories, and the pressing need for mental health education. In addition, Lawrence Fisher (1978) calls attention to the unfortunate fact that West Indian communities tend to withdraw support from people labeled "mad"—this is a derogatory concept—and the consensus of feeling is that the patient is responsible for his/her condition and thus deserves the disgrace. Fictional representations such as those discussed here may go a long way towards correcting such misapprehensions, and educating readers about the very real problems of mental illness as it occurs in the West Indian context.

7. See my previous essay on this subject, "The Bottomless Abyss; 'Mad' Women in Some Caribbean Novels" in *The Bulletin of Eastern Caribbean Affairs*, 11:1 (March/April 1985) pp. 45-58, for my presentation of the three fictional 'case studies'.

8. Lillian Feder, *Madness in Literature* (Princeton: Princeton Univ. Press, 1980).

9. Sandra Gilbert and Susan Gubart, *The Madwoman in the Attic: The Woman Writer and the Nineteenth Century Literary Imagination* (New Haven: Yale Univ. Press, 1970).

10. Dr. Ermine Belle, interviewed by Evelyn O'Callaghan, Barbados Mental Hospital, February 18, 1985.

11. Philip Rack, *Race, Culture and Mental Disorder* (London: Tavistock Publications, 1982) p. 99. An example of this type of confusion surrounds a particular reaction termed "West Indian Psychosis" by some British authors, to which people of Afro-Caribbean descent are more liable. While this *presents* with all the symptoms of mania—an endogenous psychosis—and is often diagnosed as such, further investigation has often proved it to be a stress reaction (see Rack, 1982, pp. 113-116).

12. Roland Littlewood, "An Indigenous Conceptualization of Reactive Depression in Trinidad," *Psychological Medicine*, 15 (1985) pp. 275-281.

13. Lawrence Fisher, "The Barbadian Mental Patient: Conflict and Cultural Form," *Caribbean Issues*, IV:1 (April 1978) pp. 85-108.

14. R.D. Laing, *The Divided Self: A Study of Sanity and Madness* (London: Tavistock Publications, 1960).

15. The "Kumbla" is a kind of protective enclosure, calabash or cocoon, made up of layers of assumed roles and evasions, behind which the fragile self hides its vulnerability. But, as the novel makes clear, "the trouble with the Kumbla is the getting out of the Kumbla. It is a protective device. If you dwell too long in it, it makes you delicate." *Jane and Louisa Will Soon Come Home* (London: New Beacon, 1980) p. 130. Eventually, the self must emerge into the threatening world or risk psychic fragmentation.

16. V.S. Naipaul brilliantly dramatizes this schizoid state in the persona of Ralph Singh, protagonist of *The Mimic Men* (Harmondsworth: Penguin, 1967).

17. Elizabeth Abel, "Women and Schizophrenia: the fiction of Jean Rhys," *Contemporary Literature* XX:2 (Spring 1979) p. 157.

18. See Jean Rhys, *Letters* 1931-66, ed. Francis Wyndham and Diana Melly (Harmondsworth: Penguin, 1985) pp. 263-266 and 269, for further insights into the author's conception of Rochester's emotional dilemma. Additional light is shed on the husband's psychological problems by Paula Anderson, "Jean Rhys' *Wide Sargasso Sea*: The Other Side/Both Sides Now," *Proceedings of First Annual Conference on West Indian Literature*, ed. E. Smilowitz and R. Knowles (St. Thomas: College of the Virgin Islands, 1981) pp. 237-259 and indirectly, by Roland Littlewood, "Jungle Madness: some observations on expatriate psycho-pathology," *International Journal of Social Psychiatry* (in press).

19. On a lighter note, for example, is Rhys' remark on "the *reason* why she [Antoinette] tries to set everything on fire and eventually succeeds. (Personally, I think *that* one is simple. She is cold—and fire is the only warmth she knows in England.)" *Letters*, 1985, pp. 156-157.

20. See Rack (1982, p. 130): "It seems likely that it [oppression] makes people fearful and angry, and causes problems of identification and self-image."

21. Erna Brodber, *Perceptions of Caribbean Women: Towards a Documentation of Stereotypes* (Barbados: Univ. of the West Indies, Institute of Social and Economic Research, 1982).

22. See Brodber (1982, pp. 15-16, 22-24). These stereotypes, promoted by the media after the second world war, portray the ideal woman as the submissive, dutiful daughter/wife/mother who is "delicate, diffident, tender, pleasing,

tactful, suffering and at home" (p. 32); she is the dependent of a man who can afford to keep her and is thus middle-class in aspiration, if not in fact.

Rhonda Cobham's essay in this volume also talks of the chaste, idealized female stereotype perpetuated in post-war Jamaican literature, no longer sexually free and economically independent as in earlier portrayals, but devoted to the home and/or the devout service of God.

23. To an extent, Beka's mother holds views similar to those of the nuns. She wants to move to a "nicer" area, to rid her family of any "low down" habits and associations, even if this means cutting them off from the "old ways"—the traditional culture into which she was born, but which she dismisses as "a bunch of superstition." She learns through her daughter to value Belizean traditions and the beauty of her own land, as much as the imported British flowers she struggles to cultivate in the unsuitable tropical climate.

24. From Coventry Patmore's eponymous novel (London: George Bell and Son, 1885). His view of the male/female relationship is contained in the lines, "Man must be pleased; but him to please/Is woman's pleasure" (p. 73).

25. In a conversation with Dr. George Mahy (November 13, 1985), a respected Barbadian psychiatrist, he expressed the opinion that contemporary educated West Indian women face what they perceive as conflicting obligations to succeed in a career *and* be the perfect housewife and mother, and fear criticism of failure in either sphere as an inadequacy on their part. He felt that this puts tremendous stress on young women, leading at times to depression. So it seems that even the modern "liberated" Caribbean woman experiences role anxieties.

26. Gilbert and Gubar's central thesis is that the madwoman figure, in 19th century literature by women, figures as the writer's double, acting out the authorial anger and anxieties to which women who "attempted the pen" in a male-dominated literary tradition, were subject. Through the device of the madwoman disguise, these conflicting and self-divisive impulses could be safely dramatized, so that the female author was "not submitting while seeming to submit" (p. 322). They suggest that the recurring images of enclosure/escape in female fiction reflect the women writers' anxieties about powerlessness, fear of being trapped in a male world/text.

While not wishing to apply this theory to the female writers under discussion, I suggest that the consistent use of the madwoman in their fiction reflects feelings of female fragmentation, discrepancies between self-image and expected role, the latter becoming limiting to the point of imprisoning. Such concerns, I think, are not limited to women *writers* but apply to women in general—and are imaged in the fictional characters discussed here.

27. "The one is independent, and its essential nature is to be for itself; the other is dependent, and its essence is life or existence for another. The former is the Master, or Lord, the latter the Bondsman." From "Master and Slave," *Critical Sociology: Selected Readings*, ed. Paul Conneston (Harmondsworth: Penguin, 1976) p. 45.

28. A. Kiev, "A gap between psychiatry and underprivileged groups," *Current Perspectives in Cultural Psychiatry*, ed. E. Foulkes, R. Wintrob et al (New York: Halstead Press, 1977).

29. On this, see Rack's comments (1982, pp. 43-45) on the control of deviance in peasant cultures. He notes that the "myth of the close-knit rural community rich in mutual support and good fellowship does not stand up to inspection. Villagers are as full of malice and coercion as any other community . . . " Pressure is towards conformity and the new, the strange and the deviant are distrusted.

Rack's description of highly-structured peasant society norms, given that most West Indians have peasant roots, may shed some light on the noticeable lack of sympathy by Caribbean people for the mentally ill. He explains that in many peasant cultures, severe "mental illness, with its distressing and mystifying qualities, is an obvious subject for magical or supernatural explanations . . . If insanity is inflicted by Gods or ancestral spirits this is attributed to violation of taboos or other misbehaviour, in which case the affliction is in some sense the sufferer's own fault" (p. 121).

30. Phyllis Chesler, *Women and Madness* (New York: Avon, 1972).

31. See Rhys' *Letters*, p. 263.

32. John Thieme, "Apparitions of Disaster: Brontean Parallels in *Wide Sargasso Sea* and *Guerillas*," *Journal of Commonwealth Literature*, XIV:1 (August 1979) p. 123.

A-beng: (Re)Calling the Body In(To) Question

Lemuel A. Johnson

I. Ramgoat-dash-along, or "Parson grinnin' "?

One twentieth-century historian calls [J. Marion] Sims the "Architect of the Vagina". . . . He adapted a spoon handle for the holding open of the vaginal opening, calling it a "speculum." "Introducing the bent handle of a spoon I saw everything as no man had ever seen before. . . . I felt like an explorer in medicine who views a new and important territory." Sims could see himself as Columbus, his New World the vagina. . . . Once Sims sensed his pioneer track . . . he pursued it relentlessly. He gathered up all the vesico-vaginal fistulae he could, embodied in black female slaves (the first three named Anarcha, Lucy, and Betsy), and housed them "in a little building in his yard." For four years he operated and failed, thirty times on Anarcha alone.
—G. Barker-Benfield, *The Horrors of the Half-Known Life*

The men of the Galibi spoke their own language; the women spoke only Arawak.   —Michelle Cliff, *Abeng*

So, in our macho society, the woman, in '85, had once again proclaimed her own sovereignty; she had again become the sexual aggressor. Now, however, she used not only her body language to tease, she was reversing one of the more pervasive and chauvinistic demands, using Crazy's words to taunt, torment, and quite likely, terrify a lot of men. And so in shouting "Suck Me! Suck Me! Suck me soucouyant! Suck Me!" those women were delivering what must easily be the most blatant, and by far the least subtle sexual statement yet to be chorused in a roach march. . . .
—Roy Boyke, "Carnival Is What It Is"

The embedded consciousness with which this essay thus begins is that of history as threat and as condition of possibility. The foundational events involved therefore have a great deal to do with the circumstances and the import, as above, of half-known lives. What such lives might or, in fact, do signify will be developed as much from, and through, *Abeng*'s invocation of Carib and Arawak as from that historical parable in which Michelle Cliff summons up a relevant genealogy of disconnections and connections: "In the beginning there had been two sisters—Nanny and Sekesu. Nanny fled slavery. Sekesu remained a slave. Some said this was the difference between the sisters. It was believed that all island children were descended from one or the other."[1] The *a-beng*, as it will be further sounded here, will therefore resonate and (de)generate within and against a number of Afro-New World foundational issues. These issues converge in a discussion of certain ways of apprehending and re-constituting female (body) space and consciousness, which, borrowing from Louis James's title, I will designate "island-in-between" ways.

The context and the text for such island-in-between re-memberings are necessarily multi-layered, given the dense superimposition of tropes and times: Arawak/Carib and Maroon; Great House/Plantation; Paradise and "the word JAMAICA": "The island rose and sank. Twice." Michelle Cliff thus begins the call to attention in *Abeng*. "During periods in which history was recorded by indentations on rock and shell. This is a book," she continues, "about the time which followed on that time. As the island became a place where people lived. Indians. Africans. Europeans." (p. 3). The nature of the time which followed on the time of rock and shell also allowed—as above—Sims's (gynaecological) backyard specul(ariz)ation with Anarcha.[2] It also allows for the latter-day thrust of Roy Boyke's[3] treatment of a conspicuous and carnival phallocentricity. The phallocentricity may be seen as idiosyncratic, as one "Crazy" and private manifestation; or else it may be taken as generic business or, better, as sexist habit. In which case one may want to extend its business habits into that of Earl Lovelace's Calypsonian in *The Dragon Can't Dance,*[4] Lord Philo: "The Great Fucker"; "The Axe Man."

Further afield, there is, from the African end of things, Ama Ata Aidoo's *Anowa*[5] and its woman-centered situating of black diaspora origins in a nightmare of dismembering parturition. Equally relevant, in that it puts the pre-Middle Passage and New World imprimatur on our Caribbean realities, there is Octavio Paz's[6] reading of La Malinche. Paz represents her, "the very flesh of Indian women," as the prototype of ab-original female bonding and bondage to conquistadorial (in)difference. In the final analysis, then, the implications of such sisters of Anarcha/daughters of La Malinche blood/line in the "elliptical basin of the Caribbean" (Derek Walcott) may be readily anticipated from Walcott's own rather indelicate conception of the ab-original "she" in "the star-apple kingdom": "her sex," so we learn there, "was the slit throat of an Indian"[7].

When, therefore, the *a-beng* (re)calls the body in(to) question through assessments of female *dis*membering and *re*membering, it does so in specific Afro/New World illustrations of what, for example, Elaine Scarry proposes in the theology-defined context of *The Body in Pain, The Making and Unmaking of the World.*[8] She writes, and thus prefaces her project, "the structure of belief and its modulation into material making," that before focusing on scenes centering on made artifacts, she would back up "one step to a very different kind of scene, that in which the human body is perceived to be wounded by the primary Artifact, God."

> The relation between God and human beings is often mediated by the sign of the weapon . . . hovering in space with its most essential feature, its two impossibly different ends, helping both to account for and to demonstrate the power and perfection of the divine and the imperfection and vulnerability of the human. (pp. 182-183)

There are degrees of "creaturely" woundability, of course; they range from the merely *woundable* to the deeply and permanently *wounded.*

With and under her "sign of the weapon" Scarry suggests, but does not, of course, focus in an island-in-between way (with its axe men and other architects of the vagina) on a form of woundability in which the female body is seen as essentially more woundable, or as "simply" and more "naturally" available for (mis)use. Such a focus is especially keen whenever that body and its topography are made the text of preference with(in) which to penetrate and to explore new or half-known worlds. There is, for instance, that "fresh, green breast of a new world" which once "pandered in whispers" north of the Caribbean Sea to Fitzgerald's Dutch sailors and thereafter to Gatsby in *The Great Gatsby.* In the "elliptical basin" of the Caribbean Sea itself there is Edward Brathwaite's[9] "Manchild' in the promised land view of the woman-island body. She blinds, we learn, "but she is locked still in her island/your key will click, responsive to its prick/or heat . . . / . . . an lard how it hot" (p. 28). All in all, the female body comes, or is made to come adorned, or armed, with various but rather predictable "essentials." The fact is that, at bottom, it is always laid out and invested with degrees of suggestiveness that make the woman as much balm as ruined and ruinous fecundity. She is then very much Crazy's carnival Soucouyant. She is also the site of that "sweet pain" into the consciousness of which Clare Savage will descend in *Abeng*: hers is a descent in which lies the promise of sororal and self-affirming womanhood as well as the threat of blood/line.

The last conceiving of the issue is, finally, what we do get in that emblematic flow of blood with which Michelle Cliff brings her *Abeng* to full term. There is, first, Clare Savage's dream of a fight with her friend in which "she picked up a stone and hit Zoe underneath the eye and a trickle of blood ran down her friend's face. . . . And she went over to Zoe and told her she was sorry—making a compress of moss drenched in water to soothe the cut. Then squeezing an aloe leaf to close the wound." There follows, immediately, what Kitty will later explain as the "sweet pain":

> But soon the dream was covered by her consciousness and a sharp pain in her vagina . . . the tops of thighs felt heavy, filled up. She touched herself with her finger and found blood. . . . Perhaps propelled by her dream, perhaps because she could not think of anywhere else to go, she headed for the stream formed by the cascades of water. . . . The numbing of the cold water was wearing off and Clare was slowly becoming accustomed to this new pain in her [now] echoing off the walls of her inside. As the blood lining was breaking away. (p. 165)

It has been an experience, then, in the ritual and bodily facts of which blood, water and (emergent) self-reflection had converged; in which the woman had "folded a linen handkerchief into several layers and pinned it to her underpants. Her face was hot, and she dipped it in the water, catching her own likeness even though it was barely light".

Given such conflations of myth, biology, and state of consciousness, and their varied reproductions in calypso and reggae, or else in self-reflecting fictions, it is hardly surprising that Marina Warner's study of the female body in allegory, *Monuments and Maidens*,[10] should begin in an epigraphic use of Artemidorus: "In dreams, a writing tablet signifies a woman, since it receives the imprint of all kinds of letters." Or that Francis Barker's essays on subjection should suggest, in *The Tremulous Private Body*'s[11] parenthetical reading of Marvell's "To His Coy Mistress," that certain imprintings may be better understood in the context of "the sharp pleasure [which] corresponds to an affect of power in one of its more spectacular forms—the delight to be had from dismembering a woman's body" (pp. 86-87). The subsequent (de)generation of image and narrative, and of relations of power as they affect race, class and gender, can manifest themselves in a variety of ways. There is, for example, that reality which Sims carves out for Anarcha in the (gynaecological) backyard. And then, there is, *intra*-gender, the absence of the form of specul(ariz)ation with Woman which Anarcha experiences from, say, French feminist Luce Irigaray's re-presentation of the speculum. It is an absence that is all the more telling given Irigaray's apparently subversive exploration of the speculum as a male instrument, as a "master discourse" for the invention and further penetration of woman in *Spéculum de l'autre femme*.[12]

The target of the French feminist is, throughout, the sexual and textual politics which engender and nurture the philosophical discourse, that "discourse of discourses." Irigaray's *Speculum* is thus preoccupied with mastering (with God, Artifact, and Female woundability, philosophically-speaking) as that mastering is contained in, and thus as it may be subverted from within, a certain apprehension of (western/white) history. "Irigaray's *Spéculum de l'autre femme*," Toril Moi explains in *Sexual/Textual Politics*, [13] "is shaped like a hollow surface on the model of the speculum/vagina. At the center, the section entitled 'Speculum' is framed by the two massive sections on Freud and Plato respectively." Irigaray presents her own discourse within the middle section, "in the first and last chapters, so framing the seven middle sections dealing mainly with male philosophers from Plato to Hegel" (p. 130). In summary, Irigaray's is a sub/version of discourse and a re-structuring; one in which the master discourse sinks toward and into a new *topos* of containment: "In a phallic, instrumental move the speculum illuminates [. . .] while simultaneously pointing to [the master discourse's] position within the feminine, as if to demonstrate Irigaray's contention that woman constitutes the silent ground on which the patriarchal thinker erects his discursive constructs." (p. 131). There are, as we shall see, problematic issues (ambivalence and ambiguity, aporias, essentialist proportions, gestures of exclusion) in such moves to contain erections that master, or seek to master. Toril Moi underscores the implications for the Irigarayan maneuver in her subsequent discussion of what she calls, succinctly, "the inexorable logic of the Same."

Meanwhile, operating as he is from a number of island-in-between premises in his "Carnival Is What It Is," Roy Boyke works hard to resolve the challenge of "the inexorable logic of the Same" in the language of celebration with which he apprehends the 1985 carnival road march song. He celebrates as effectively womanist a road march re-presenting of the erstwhile mastering discourse contained in *Soucouyant* [14] Given Boyke, what results is, body blow for body blow, a womanist (re)call and response in the course of which the woman proclaims "her own sovereignty." Crazy's macho signature tune is thus sucked into discomfiture by the very terms and obsessions of its own mastering plot. All this happens, moreover, in a public act of revenge which, so to speak, hoists the phallocentric on a petard of its very own erection.

Boyke's reading suggests that what we get is effective containment, as the male sinks under the female. We are offered a road march in the course of which womanspeak does indeed re-invest *Soucouyant*, it so appears, with the power of true subversion. No inexorable logic of the Same rises to suggest that what has taken place is, at bottom, only licensed illusion; a mere *sub/version* and thus an extension of the Other's (male) power. The Boyke understanding of the road march's (re)calling of the body in(to) question therefore suggests ways of re-presenting, to subversive effect, even the most conspicuously phallocentric of texts. As, for example, that calypso, "Women Running Me Down," which, carnival-erect in sexual politics and financial reward, was a very big hit indeed for Lord Philo, the Calypsonian "Great Fucker" and "Axe Man" of *The Dragon Can't Dance:*

All over town, I can't get a rest
Ah never thought I would meet the day when woman is a pest
But I stand up to the test
Because I is the axe man, I is the best. (p. 230)

The question may nonetheless be raised, *pace* Boyke, *pace* Irigaray, as to how recoverable from, and re-useable, are the terms of reference: axe, pest, fucker—and Soucouyant. What if the act of revenge and its presumed empowering are already so contained by the master discourse that all they do is generate even harder forms of penetration and deeper levels of containment? Gayatri Spivak is very persuasive, it is true, when she suggests that there are contexts in which deconstructive and reversal-displacement strategies can be "productively conflictual" when used "to expose the ruling discourse." It is nonetheless possible, as she also suggests, that such strategies may only generate illusory and self-dissolving re-definitions; ones which, as Moi would put it, are "produced exclusively in relation to the logic of the Same." It is obviously such a reading of Irigaray which prompts Monique Plaza to conceive of her as "a patriarchal wolf in sheep's clothing." [15]

The proposition here is that a carnivalesque and *soucouyant* rivalry *by* mimesis cannot *not* entail, so to speak, re-affirmations of a certain world-view; one which, at best, can only allow a licensed and temporary sub/version—never a *subversion*—of itself. Besides which, there are, always, those "prison-house of language" implications which underlie the typically Bakhtinian view that

> In language, there is no word or form that would be neutral or would belong to no one: all of language turns out to be scattered, permeated with intentions, accented. . . . Every word gives off the scent of a profession, a genre, a current, a party, a particular work, a particular man, a generation, an era, a day, and an hour. [16]

Implicit in this "dialogic principle" and in what Jay Caplan calls the "genealogy of the beholder" in *Framed Narratives* is the reasonable enough postulation that "only the mythically and totally alone Adam, approaching a virgin and still unspoken world with its very first discourse, could really avoid altogether this . . . orientation with respect to the discourse of the other." [17]

A womanspeak sub/version can therefore effect no change in relations of power since it cannot lead to a "reorganization of sexual markers within the society as a whole," to continue in the language of *Framed Narratives* (p. 54). For inside the sub/version the authorized version always remains the privileged text. Indeed, the text becomes the only possible context within which the woman will be scented and accented. In short, this implicitly anti-Boyke view now suggests that, given specul(ariz)ation with the body in question, one cannot really road march with *and through* Crazy's Soucouyant and Lord Philo's "Women Running Me Down" to an "other side." This re-assessment also suggests that carnival contexts and texts may not be quite as unreachably self-contained in a carnival *it*-ness; that they may not be as unheadquartered in other relations of power as Boyke might be understood to propose when he writes: "Carnival is what it is. This is the truth that all of us, by now, should count to be self-evident. Yet we persist, Pharisees, Philistines, and scribes, to indulge ourselves in the futile annual ritual of prescribing parameters for the celebration of mas."[18]

If, however, context and text are indeed only seemingly unheadquartered, then bodies may indeed shake, quake, and suck but to no real upheaval. Or else they may move all they want to but can and will only register a reading according to the design(s) of the measuring rod. And, by way of illustration, precisely such a state of affairs would best explain why "Parson grinnin' " in reggae; why the inexorable logic of the Same should "sweet 'im so"— even though "if you was passing/Parson 'prayer' room/you would think it was an earthquake." But his is only a woman-(de)based earthquake from which comes no womanist upheaval as such. The fact of the matter is that the woman has the Word of God under her head; the Son of Man is upon her breast; and the Rod of Correction is in her womb. She has been so laid out because, as Parson put it to her in the master plot, "we have to pray in the nude." And she, why she must "shake thy arse to save thy soul." And the woman does indeed do so: "she shake; she shake. She shake she wais" until, finally, her reaction becomes what it was in any case already plotted out to be—simply master-full: for

> she never had such satisfaction
> so everytime she had problem
> she know just how to solve them
> she shake; she shake; she shake—yeah . . .
> parson grinnin' . . . [19]

And perhaps Parson grinnin' too because when the woman so "over-elocutes" (in Velma Pollard's happy coinage, below) she can only transport him to the way of the world as it ever was at *his* beginning. For given the prior plotting of things, Parson will in any case always assume for himself the right position for "she." The point is that the man was always too well hung (up) to ever *not* hear, for instance, that "Hurt me like that—hurt me—Love me and hurt me! Hurt me hard!" to which Roger Mais's Papacita once, "road marched" Girlie at the climax of one of *Brother Man*'s[20] naked power plays. It is a climax in the making of which Girlie becomes, if you will, the man's master/piece who is, in effect, always being written out into and as a blank page. But then such is the way of the world "wit' dat [and every] falla-line gal, Eva, oh, Eva" (*Abeng*; p. 48).

Michelle Cliff's *Abeng* is quite brisk, and various, in its illustrations of the dangerous seduction of a world-making but female-dismembering Word. Her versions of the inexorable logic of the Same suggest a condition of being taken (out) for which Judith Fetterly[21] has coined the term "immasculation." For in Clare Savage we are shown in one instance, and it is an early one, the unresisting reader as daughter: "Clare's relationship with her father took the form of what she imagined a son would have, had there had been a son." And in another instance her female-ness is seductively contained in the mastering plot of a world-view in which dis/membering of the female is romance—this being the view that we get when patriarch Savage becomes, perhaps involuntarily, high priest and sacrifier in paternal clothing. Clare Savage's father, we learn, was no commonplace dreamer and teller of visions. His were of Atlantis, Stonehenge and Pyramids; of magic and the extraterrestrial; of Armageddon and God's own time. He also dreams of the Aztecs. And through them he reaches back for that affect of power which comes from (dis)membering the female body: "[Mr. Savage] tried to pass these ideals on to his elder daughter—calling her an Aztec princess, golden in the sun. 'Clare, you would have certainly been a choice for sacrifice—you know the Aztecs slaughtered their most beautiful virgins and drank their blood.' It did not occur to Clare to question her father's reading of history— a worldview in which she would have been chosen for divine slaughter" (pp. 9-10).

In a resisting reader response to *Paradise Lost* titled "When Eve Reads Milton: Undoing the Canonical Economy," Christine Froula[22] has relevantly considered the consequence for Eve of such plotting and power: "The master plot of the invention [of Eve and Adam] exists on the condition that Eve 'read' the world only in one way, by making herself the mirror of patriarchal authority." What is thereby erased or contained is the possibility of a consciousness which is not so heavily invested in the name of the Father, in the passions of the Son, and in the "white rush" (Yeats) of *their* need to have the female laid out only in certain ways: gratefully terrified, with loosening thighs ("Leda and the Swan"). In the final analysis, then, and as Monique Plaza makes clear in opposing Irigarayan re-construction so-called, readings which (merely) re-invent sub/versions of master plots can only work out a dangerously "true," because indeed quite circular hermeneutic. The preface explains how and why Irigaray sinks into her own specululm: "Every mode of existence which ideology imputes to women as part of the Eternal Feminine and which for a moment Luce Irigaray seemed to be posing as the result of oppression is from now on woman's essence, woman's being. All that 'is' woman comes to her in the last instances from her anatomical sex, which touches itself all the time. Poor woman"[23]

II. Speculum in a New World?

> Consider an example:
> This woman died young
> And still her laughter echoes in the world
>   . . . .
> All is lost—all is won.
>
> —Jean D'Costa, "In Memoriam"

The complex con/fusion of text and sub/text notwithstanding, it is clear that Irigarayan and carnivalesque sub/versions of Woman cannot take into account the range of foundational events and bloodlines which the *a-beng* relevantly summons out of Africa, the Caribbean, and Latin America. The sexual and racial politics of Irigarayan sub/version offer no really effective way to (re)member the convergence of forces which once b(r)ought and made Anarcha available for (mis)use, be it in calypso and reggae; in Sims's (gynaecological) backyard; or, sadly, in certain feminist considerations of sexual/textual politics. Which, incidentally, is why I find Toril Moi disappointing, even predictable, in the revealing con/fusions with which she reasons and disguises at the end of the first part of her *Sexual/Textual Politics:*

> Some feminists might wonder why I have said nothing about black or lesbian (or black-lesbian) feminist criticism in America in this survey. The answer is simple: this book purports to deal with the theoretical aspects of feminist criticism. So far, lesbian and/or black feminist criticism have presented exactly the same *methodological* and *theoretical* problems as the rest of Anglo-American feminist criticism. . . . It is the *contents* of her work that make the [other] critic's study different, not her method. Instead of focusing on 'women' in literature, the lesbian critic focuses on 'lesbian women', as the black feminist critic will focus on 'black women' in literature." (p. 86)

As, presumably, Moi should have underscored all along that Irigaray and Kolodny, Showalter and even the nay-saying Myra Jehlen focus on *white* women in literature and theory?[24]

The issues involved in a speculum look into the island-in-between world of the sisters of Anarcha and the daughters of La Malinche are complex ones. They are very much magnified in the light of Michelle Cliff's richly problematic quest in *Abeng* for a history and for an ab-original *mythos* with which to speak the New World female presence in "the land of look behind." 'She should have been the daughter of Inez and Mma Ali, and Nanny too—and had she known of the existence of these women, she might have shared her extraordinary passion . . . rather than protecting what she felt was its fragility," so Michelle Cliff writes of a Kitty paralyzed by passionate tenderness and bitter insecurity into believing that, given the way of the world with the body and "the souls of black folk," any "coming brighter day" was irredeemably dis/membered: "lay at the bottom of the sea in lead coffins or scattered through the earth on plantations" (p. 128). Kitty Freeman Savage, in the very richness of the contradictions into which her names sink her, "has forgotten her ancient properties"—to speak now in the language with which Marie Thérèse Foucault recalls the dis/member-ment of Toni Morrison's "tarbaby"[25] (1981: p. 263) from bloodline and ancestry.

Cliff's *Abeng* (re)calls out of and into connections and disconnections. Sometimes, the narrative does so by way of a telling collusion and collision of blood/line and name—as in island-in-between Kitty Freeman Savage and Auschwitz Kitty Hart making a text out of *I Am Alive*. Cliff also works out (of) genealogies in which ancient properties are quickened into dense superimpositions. They converge and impose complex identities upon Arawak Woman and Maroon Nanny; Clare Savage and Anne Frank; and upon "bronze" Inez whom Justice Savage had taken to be his mistress:

> Her mother was a half-blood Miskito Indian, whose people had come from the mountain chain of Central America. Her father was a Maroon, an Ashanti from the Gold Coast. Inez was known as a friend of the slaves on the Savage Plantation. Her mother's ancestors had been among the Indians the Red Coats brought to the island to defeat the armies of the Maroons. But they went over to the Maroon side— lived among them and married with them. Her father and mother settled in the Cockpit country. (p. 33)

They settled, that is, in the deep crevices of the Blue Mountains where, incidentally, the ruins of Nanny's town lie.

Meanwhile, over the mantelpiece of the Savage Great House there "was a picture hung in a gilt frame—a portrait of the judge's wife-in-England: a young woman whose face was framed in curls, her hands folded in her lap, wearing lace and brocade, a bouquet of white roses beside her" (pp. 33-34). Wife-in-England, significantly; and yet not so significantly, after all. For there are degrees of creature-ness, and thus of traffic and trade-ins: "There were few white women on the island during slavery, and so the grandmothers of these people [who need now to (re)member as they sit in a church on a Sunday evening during the mango season] had been violated again and again by the very men who whipped them. The rape of Black women would have existed with or without the presence of white women, of course, but in Jamaica there was no pretence of civility—all was in the open" (p. 19), which is why Justice Savage will have his "nigger wench" (p. 39) on his Paradise Plantation.

Under such circumstances, it is significant that Michelle Cliff's call to (re)member with the *a-beng* (the conch shell used for passing messages *for and against* enslavers) ends both heuristically and in dense ambiguity. It thus matters in *Abeng*'s Afro-New World-ness that, on her way to the Arawak Hotel at Ocho Rios, Clare Savage remembers the Great House, *the* site of her New World (un)becoming, to dismembering affect. She properly conceives of the Great House as the place of bloodline and stone wall, of life and of life arrested: "the salt taste of the walls could indicate to a visitor something, if only a clue, about the time which had passed through them. Maybe there were signs marked on the walls each time they heard a shout—like the slashes on the Rosetta Stone" (p. 32). By the same token, it also matters that the language of Clare's remembrance of the Great House past is appealed to when, at the end, her own body is finally (re)called in(to) question: she slowly became "accustomed to [the] new pain in her. The cramps in the lips of her pussy were now echoing off the walls of her inside. As the blood lining her womb was breaking away" (pp. 165-166).

But the promise of a fully heuristic experience of history, and thus of enlightenment (the deciphering of the Rosetta Stone), is held in check by the obsessive issues from which Clare labors to deliver herself. At the end, so ambivalent are Clare's attempts to bring sign, symbol, and womanhood into plenitude and full presence that the narrative is as much driven to promise full term delivery as it is to threaten miscarriage. We learn of Clare Savage that "She was not ready to understand her dream. She had no idea that everyone we dream about we are" (1985: p. 166). But then, in this her final state of unreadiness Clare's response to the *a-beng* is very much like that of the others, those "they" so ironically overshadowed by the Blue Mountains of Maroon Nanny and her Windward Maroons. "They" did not know their ancestors. "They" did not know of Ashanti or Dahomey. "They" did not know their name for papaya—*pawpaw* was the name of one of the languages of Dahomey. "Some of them were called Nanny, because they cared for the children of other women, but they did not know who Nanny had been" (p. 21). Michelle Cliff has, in any case, appropriately contextualized the problem of consciousness and being in the island-in-between. She invokes for Clare Savage a near-pathological genealogy of racial facts that are very much vexed by fantasies about race:

> The Black or the white. Both perhaps. Her father told her she was white. But she knew that her mother was not. Who would she choose were she given the choice: Miss Havisham or Abel Magwitch? She was both dark and light. Pale and deeply colored. To whom would she turn if she needed assistance? From who would she expect it? Her

mother or her father—it came down to that sometimes. Would her alliances shift at any time? The Black or the white? A choice would be expected of her, she thought (pp. 36-37).

Blood linings thus break away—but not quite through the walls of the Great House and its maddening imperatives, inexorably so, perhaps.

Given the lucidity and the horror of *Abeng*'s way with half-known (widowed) and new (virgin) worlds, it is no easy matter (in a montage now of Cliff titles) to claim identities they taught the losers to despise (1980) in the land of look behind (1985)—when, obviously, the winner names the age (1982). The titles manage to suggest Cliff's way of taking in all "the disconnections and the connections" which issue from the captive and the belaboring body and mind. The titles also suggest her way of working with seemingly extravagant but foundational events in the making of the Americas; ones in which wounding maker and woundable/wounded creature coincide. Such events are conceived of in the fantastic "excesses of the heart;" but then they are Caribbean born and bred, *bruta facta*. They are placed, dated, and named—as happens, typically, when Justice Savage conceives of burning, and does indeed burn, his one hundred slaves alive on the eve of abolition. "To have a nation of Black freedmen, the justice thought, "would be like wearing a garment—he searched his mind [there he will find, "more than once," the Virginian and the Yankee "enlightened thinkers" Thomas Jefferson and Benjamin Franklin] for an analogy—a garment dipped in the germs of the plague." He comes to and becomes his bloodline in a moral descent that was far from original among his own kind: at that moment the slaves were his property; they would burn.

> Lest anyone think the judge's action—which became the pattern of foundation stones and thin dirt gullies Clare saw that afternoon behind the great house, rectangles remembering an event she would never know of—lest anyone think the judge's behavior extreme or insane or frenzied, the act of a mad white man, it should be pointed out that this was not an isolated act on the eve of African freedom in Jamaica (p. 40).

Michelle Cliff thus insists on a vision of history as blood/lines: as "an intricate weave, at the heart of which was enforced labor of one kind or another." The pattern holds from Cape-to-Cairo; from the tea plantations of Ceylon and China to the coffee ones of Sumatra and Colombia. There are, too, "the mills of Lowell. Manchester. Leeds. Marseilles. The mines of Wales. Alsace-Lorraine. The railroads of Union Pacific." Under such circumstances, "Slavery was not an aberration—it was an extreme. . . . To some this may be elementary—but it is important to take it all in, the disconnections and the connections." For to do so would be to better understand the closed economy within which traffic and trade in identities take place; within which, when the carnival turns bitter, the road march becomes the constraining reality of a chain gang and gender shuffle—and why, incidentally, the rod of correction can lay about with a caned sweetness. In short, the pattern of disconnections and reconnections makes very clear indeed the inexorable logic of the Same which binds veiled slavery to slavery-in-fact. And it all therefore explains, predicts, in what is for Cliff the most naked of examples, the subsequent limits of any abolition of slavery in the island-in-between:

> The enslavement of Black people—African peoples—with its processions of naked and chained human beings, whipping of human beings, rape of human beings, lynching of human beings, buying and selling of human beings—made other forms of employment in the upkeep of western civilization seem pale. So slavery-in-fact—which was distasteful to some of the coffee-drinkers and tea-drinkers, who might have read about these things or saw them illustrated in the newspapers the clubs and cafes provided for their patrons, neatly hung on a rack from dowel sticks—slavery-in-fact was abolished, and the freedom which followed on abolition turned into veiled slavery, the model of the rest of the western world. (p. 28)

The fact of the matter is that the Great House never quite burned to the ground: "It was spruced up and made into a flagship for the Paradise Plantation. Fitted with period furniture imported from a factory in Massachusetts which made replicas of antiques. And white plaster dummies from a factory in New York City, which supplied several Fifth Avenue department stores were dressed in nineteenth-century costume, and placed on the verandah and through the rooms" (p. 37).

In Michelle Cliff's arrangement of things woman does not, indeed cannot, exist outside so dynamic a conception of history. *Abeng* does not deliver her packaged and contained in an ahistorical "essentialism." What we have is, instead, *Subject-in-History* participation. And it is one which, incidentally, can be very much conquistadorial. After all, in 1958 Jamaica had two rulers: "a white queen and a white governor." The former was a "rather plain little white woman decked in medals and other regalia—wearing, of course, a crown. Our-lady-of-the-colonies. The whitest woman in the world" (*Abeng:* p. 5). Historical engagement can also be other than conquistadorial. It is in this second context, with its ab-original female types and island-in-between resistance, that Michelle Cliff recreates in Maroon Nanny (at long last!) the complement to and anticipation of Toussaint and of Nat Turner; of Macandal and Christophe. For before all of them, she, Maroon Nanny, was. *Abeng*'s conceptualization of the essential historical gesture is thus determined by the active Subject-in-History which Maroon

Nanny was and becomes. She remains indivisibly present in the intricate weave of *Abeng*'s genealogies and disconnections within which she is always represented as person-in-reality and re-presented as spirit of the deep crevices of the Blue Mountains: of "Cockpits. Places to hide. Difficult to reach. Not barren but deep and magnificent indentations populated by bush and growth and wild orchids—collectors of water—natural goblets" (p. 21). In effect, she was: "there is no doubt at all that she actually existed." But then, because Cliff's conflation of the phenomenal and the numinous is meticulous, (having been) Maroon Nanny remains as historically singular as she is bio-cultural continuity and symbolic expression:

> Now her head is tied. Now braided. Strung with beads and cowrie shells. Now she is disguised as a *chasseur*. Now wrapped in a cloth shot through with gold. Now she stalks the Red Coats as they march toward her cave, where she spins her Akan chants into spells which stun her enemies. Calls on the goddesses of the Ashanti forests. Remembers the battle formations of the Dahomey Amazons. She turns her attention to the hunt. To the cultivation of cassava and yam and plantain—hiding the places for use in case of flight. (p. 19)

Michelle Cliff's mountain stronghold thus continues the hold out for a line of ab-original and female descent through Jamaica's Maroon Nanny, she "who could catch bullets in her buttocks." "A small and old Black woman whose only decoration was a necklace fashioned from the teeth of white men" (p. 21), Maroon Nanny serves to counterpoint that other "rather plain white woman decked in medals. . . . The whitest woman in the world."

Abeng then, through Nanny and her sister Sekesu, makes a point of tracing its genealogy of New World consciousness to a foundational memory-event. The narrative of Clare Savage's developing Carib/ean consciousness thus introduces us, in a narration as ectypal as it is archetypal, to quite elaborate and woman-centered processes of myth-making and *mythos*-recovering: "It was believed that all island children were descended from one or the other. All island people were first cousins" (p. 18). A [saving] myth, Bettina Knapp relevantly proposes in *The Prometheus Syndrome*,[26] is "ectypal (it deals with the existential world) and archetypal (it deals with eternal experiences). Existence on these two levels contains past, present, and future. . . . In that the myth is ectypal, it reveals and relives 'the structure of reality.' It may become the model and prototype of the period or periods that brought it into being; and it reflects in its many transformations and recountings through the centuries, the needs, obsessions, and longings of the individual cultures" (pp. 2-3).

Cliff's narrative settles down to an extended illumination of such a view when, on "an afternoon in March—the month of most rain, the month in which the star apple ripens. Clare sat by herself in the Carib cinema—the first enclosed cinema in Jamaica, named for one of the native peoples of the West Indies" (p. 67). Thereafter what narrative and motion picture generate is enlarged upon, frame by frame, into a sequence of signifiers. They encompass a great deal—even though the island-in-between conclusion to which it all comes does not allow for a "tidy" restoration of ancient properties. *Abeng*'s "first cousins" genealogy is never fully (re)membered because it finds no effective correlation in Kitty's amnesia and bitter paralysis, or in Clare's womanhood but callow and arrested consciousness. The *abeng* persists, notwithstanding. And when the conch shell sounds, it invariably calls up(on) the slave and the maroon, at once invoking and bridging the Middle Passage: "The Galibi practiced scarification—the ritual marking of the skin. Their color was primarily cinnamon and their group later divided into Red Galibi and Black Galibi—the latter having mixed with West African peoples" (p. 67).

Michelle Cliff thus begins her "remembrance of things past" on the right note—with the *Galibi*, who "were all but exterminated by the Spanish conquerors. But they exist not only in the past—there are a few who survive today on a reserve on the island of Dominica" (p. 67). By the same token, her novel's epigraph is a "telling" recognition of resistance and of the self-dissolving threat that history can be. Cliff's dedication is to Jean Toomer and Bessie Head. There then follows an especially apt use of Jamaican Basil McFarlane's poem of (un)becoming:

> To know birth and to know death
> In one emotion,
> To look before and after with one eye. . . .
> To know the World and be without a World:
> In this light that is no light
> This time that is no time, to be
> And to be free. . . .

Abeng's own descent into new world identity is ultimately given focus by Cliff's varied re-presentation of the womanchild in the (com)promised land. Her attempt to work out a womanspeak and New World "seeing-naming-reconstituting," to move in categories generated by Elizabeth Schussler Fiorenza's *In Memory of Her*,[27] make for altogether complex, even precarious, exploration and path-finding.

But then, if one must judge such things from the experience of the manchild in the promised land, any such female ab-original and Carib/ean "surfacing" can perhaps be nothing if not complex and precarious—given the play of, say, Kitty Freeman Savage's unspoken word, as against Boy-Boy's (her husband's) wounded and wounding presence. The manchild seems, after all, to have had much the longer and Great Tradition in such matters. And yet, it presumably matters in Toni Morrison's *Tarbaby*, for instance, that when that manchild, Son, had first looked out upon the (com)promised land, it matters that not even he would look upon it and remain completely whole. It is telling, moreover, that this should be so, given the dominant histories and fictions of his Word: from Caliban and High John de Conqueror to Macandal and Christophe, from Axe Man to Parson. Still, it is from the stacked deck of a myth-making *and* myth-mocking consciousness that Son (be he Crazy or Boy-Boy, Great Fucker or Bigger) "saw the stars and exchanged stares with the moon, but he saw very little of the land, which was just as well because he was gazing at the shore of an island that, three hundred years ago, had struck the slaves blind the moment they saw it". Morrison thus ends the prologue to *Tarbaby*, a prologue which had begun with the easy enough temptation of "He believed he was safe" (pp. 1-5). The truth is, of course, that the threat was always there; that it manifests itself in various narratives of bonding and bondage: Caliban versus Prospero; Man Friday versus Crusoe; King Christophe versus First Consul Bonaparte; *Tarbaby*'s Son losing the "yalla" to "the young man with yellow hair and blue eyes and white skin." And Shine is there, of course—caught between the daughter of the *Titanic*'s Captain and the Shark: "And the Shark said: Shine, Shine, you doing fine, but if you miss one stroke your ass is mine" (trad.).

Still, at the end, there is also a narrative tradition, be it "steady" or carnivalesque and "lickety-split," in which Boy/Son is re-membered into his ancient properties. For *Tarbaby*'s Son, the re-membering is one which, ironically enough, Marie Thesèse Foucault, *abeng*-like, directs: "They are naked and they are blind too . . . their eyes have no color in them," she tells him. "But they gallop; they race those horses like angels all over the hills where the rain forest is, where the champion daisy trees grow." And so

> By and by he walked steadier, now steadier. The mist lifted and the trees stepped back a bit as if to make the way easier for a certain kind of man. Then he ran. Lickety-split. Lickety-split. Looking neither to the left nor to the right. Lickety-split. Lickety-split. Lickety-lickety-lickety-split. (pp. 263-264).

In sum, Shine/High John de Conqueror does have a tradition in which Boy makes it from ship to shore—Mr. Savage's genuine enough terror in *Abeng* notwithstanding: "Mr. Savage had just stepped into the water, when he came running out again—'Shark! Shark!' . . . He claimed a shark had swum up right beside his thigh and touched him" (*Abeng*, p. 10).

Man-making words are plentiful, for sure; and they converge in a Great Tradition with which to signify and to re-member, be it in occult or his/torical circumstances. Not so, it would seem, when and where the womanchild enters; for, to speak now in terms of the topography to which *Abeng* appeals, the hidden crevices of Maroon Nanny's mountain stronghold are little known, difficult to get to, or, quite simply, they have been forgotten. More often than not the womanchild in the compromised land is conceived of as the crying one, from Suriname (Eddy Bruma's "Waran neti-dren;" J.G.A. Koender's' "Mama Afrika e krey fu en pikin")[28] to Mexico (*La Llorona*; Octavio Paz). And in New York, too, "the black girls . . . were crying and their men where looking neither to the right nor to the left. Not because they were heedless, or intent on what was before them, but because they did not wish to see the crying, crying girls split into two . . . nothing could stop their crying and nothing could persuade their men to look to the right or to the left" (Morrison, p. 185).

Such images of the ties that (un)bind in the island-in-between haunt and threaten Michelle Cliff's Kitty and Inez, Octavio Paz's La Malinche, and that ab-original ancestress who, in the pre-Columbian world of the Galibi, could only speak Arawak. Why and how these images (de)generate or (de)mean may be readily deduced from, say, Zora Neale Hurston's *Their Eyes Were Watching God*,[29] in Nanny's perception of the meaning of the acts of conquistadors: "de white man throw de load and tell the nigger man tuh pick it up. He pick it up because he have to, but he don't tote it. He hand it to his womenfolks. De nigger woman is de mule uh de world so far as Ah can see" (p. 29). And, far as one can see, so, too, is *Abeng*'s Kitty, for she is woman continued in Boy-Boy: "Kitty complained that Boy was weak, and that he would never amount to anything; that he was intolerant of too many people; that he lived in another world. She complained that his presence in her life as her husband had essentially been an error—but she seemed to have no desire to change the situation". So "she unpacked . . . fought viciously with Boy, then forgave him. . . . "I wouldn't hit you, Kitty, because I might kill you. Yes, I'd kill you for true," was what Boy sometimes said" (p. 51). In what is tantamount to a palimpsest of such instances of bloodline and conquest, Michelle Cliff's seeing-naming-reconstitution works its way through genealogies of mules and men, aiming, all the while, at Maroon Nanny's act of load-shedding.

Abeng's invocation of the ab-original (Arawak/Carib) and of the conquistadorial cuts very close indeed to those *ur-texts* of the Americas in which, "for true," woman is re-constituted for dismemberment. Cliff's appeal to pre-Columbian relations between Carib male and Arawak female serves as prelude to and template for other post-Columbian *chingon* and *chingada* (Octavio Paz) ties which bind La Malinche to Cortez; Pocahontas to Puritan, and bronze Inez to Justice Savage. For Paz's "Sons of La Malinche," in *The Labyrinth of Solitude*, La Malinche is both victim and complicit, disturbance-generating wound: "It is true she gave herself voluntarily to the conquistador, but he forgot her as soon as her usefulness was over." She is "the very flesh of Indian woman" upon which the conquistador's *chingon* or macho rites and rights have left their mark and word, *la chingada:* "The idea of violence rules darkly over all the meanings of the word, and the dialectic of the 'closed' and the 'open' thus fulfills itself with almost ferocious precision. The *chingon* is the macho, the male, he rips open the *chingada*, the female, who is pure passivity, defenseless against the exterior world." In the final analysis, "she loses her name; she is no one; she disappears into nothingness; she *is* Nothingness"[30]

Elsewhere, in *The Conquest of America*, Tzvetan Todorov traces similar lines of force. He does so in a focused re-presentation of that Mayan woman who dies, devoured by the conquistadors' dogs. "Reduced to a few lines," her/story, for Todorov, "concentrates one of the extreme versions of the relation to the Other. . . . When the Spanish conquistador appears, this woman is no more than the site where the desires and wills of . . . men meet. . . . To kill men, to rape women: these are at once proof that a man wields power and his reward.[31] The ab-original New World Woman "is thrown to the dogs because she is both an unconsenting woman and an Indian woman." And the act, to return to the thesis formulation in *The Tremulous Private Body*, corresponds to an affect of power in one of its more spectacular forms—the delight to be had from dismembering a woman's body.

Abeng (re)calls that body (in)to question within and against such "conquest of America" paradigms. Insisting all the while on her patterns of disconnections and connections, Cliff's narrative aims at affiliation—which is what we get when, for example, *Abeng* looks behind to Galibi-Carib/ean bloodline and (t)race: "Carib was invented by Columbus, and was later changed to *Canibal*—the origin of the English word *cannibal*—because it was said the Galibi ate human flesh." They were, Cliff so celebrates them, a fierce people who opposed the *conquistadores* with skill and power. "The men of the Galibi spoke their own language; the women spoke only Arawak" (p. 67).

Curiously, Cliff stops short of a fuller explanation of the prison-house of language in which the Arawak ancestress is thus contained. For that we need to turn to the longer vision of the way of the world which Cuban Alejo Carpentier gives us in *Explosion in a Cathedral*.[32] The women spoke Arawak because they were victim-breeders for Galibi males who, in their Great Migration search for the Land-in-Waiting, had killed off the Arawak males. (It was, incidentally, this Carib/ean search for the (Mayan) Empire of the North which Isabella and Ferdinand's High Admiral cut to the quick):

> All the males of other races were ruthlessly exterminated, and the women kept for the propagation of the conquering race. Thus there came to be two languages; that of the women, the language of the kitchen and childbirth, and that of the men, the language of warriors, to know which was held to be supreme privilege. (p. 243)

The separation of speech into languages of male privilege and female service and subservience is thus historicized and re-traced to its origins in sexual politics and biological imperatives. The goal is not so much that complementarity implied in *Abeng*'s truncated narration as it is, finally, booty, dismemberment—and breeding, as much with Arawak as, elsewhere, with Trojan or Sabine women.

Although the odyssey of arms and men against which Lawrence Lipking[33] works is a different one from that of the Americas, his "Aristotle's Sister: A Poetics of Abandonment" nonetheless identifies a relevant division of speech and privilege. "In the beginning was an aborted world," is the way in which Lipking begins his re-call of the dismembering of the female Word and thus of its tradition:

> The first example of woman's literary criticism in Western tradition, or more accurately the first miscarriage of a woman's criticism, occurs early in the *Odyssey*. High in her room above the hall suitors, Penelope can hear a famous minstrel sing that most painful of stories, the Greek homecoming from Troy—significantly, the matter of the *Odyssey* itself. That is no song for a woman. She comes down to protest. . . . It seems a reasonable request. But her words meet an immediate brutal rebuff from an unexpected source: her own son Telemachus. . . . Men like to hear the news; women must learn not to take songs so personally! Penelope gives in. Marvelling at the wisdom of her son, she goes back to her room and cries herself to sleep. (pp. 64-65)

And thereupon she sinks into that condition of erasure which Edward Said, in *Orientalism*,[34] so aptly identifies as a state or condition of "existential weightlessness."

When, back on the island-in-between, *Abeng*'s Carib and star apple world becomes Derek Walcott's *The Star-Apple Kingdom*, the miscarriage, so to speak, is a telling one. As we reach conclusion in Walcott's poem of (re)membering we do become increasingly aware of a figure that haunts the phallocentric line of thought and its narration. The particulars of that figure's own history and identity are, however, very much overlaid by the foregrounded egocentricity of the male dreamer—until, that is, "The Star-Apple Kingdom" is, so to speak, held up against the light. When that happens attention is drawn to the way in which the female presence has all along been served up: "The woman's face, had a smile been decipherable/in that map of parchment so rivered with wrinkles,/would have worn the same smile with which he now/cracked the day open and began his egg." The poem's lyrical and near-sollipsistic remembrance and transport now appear to have been powered by a typical Great Tradition traffic and trade in the female body. For example, it is obvious that the body is, for Walcott, the site of the wound which bore, and bears, historical consciousness. And it is just as clear that it does so in the appropriate mastering discourse.

The vision is in reality pan-American, and common enough, being a form of speculation with the female in the course of which she becomes Land-in-Waiting and Virgin Continent which yield milk and honey—but only do so upon being ravished. From the romance and delusion implicit in Walcott/Shabine's knowing in "Flight" of a time "before" (when "these slums were paradise") to *Abeng*'s latter-day and resisting reader use of the Carib cinema, and as recently as "yesterday" in Edward Brathwaite's *Black + Blues*, the Carib/ean picture of discovery and conquest seems rooted in penetration of the female. And so, just "yesterday," in Brathwaite's "Manchild," "the girl raped in the toilet of the Carib cinema by four/fourteen year old yout' . . . /and all her dolours taken." And now it is not surprising that "she will not open her window/for fear of intruders."[35]

Michelle Cliff makes her female protagonist's presence in *Abeng*'s Carib cinema the occasion for a somewhat more complex consciousness of intrusion and dead reckoning. *Abeng*'s "dolours" and "fear" thus occur in or are distributed throughout a history which binds Arawak and Conquistador; Jew(?) and African. The Carib picture show thus ties (down) victim and intruder to the brute facts and deep fictions of "Discovery":

> The Arawak . . . had named Jamaica, Xaymaca, land of springs [but now] existed no longer. (p. 78)
> Christopher Columbus—whose statue stands in the town squares of so many countries of the New World . . . the explorer whose body was buried four times: twice in the Americas, twice, and finally, in Spain—may well have been a Jew himself. . . . He left behind a reputation for dead reckoning—was he in search of a safe place for Jews—a place out of the Diaspora? So many veils to be lifted. (pp. 66-67)
> Columbus discovered—strange verb—discovered Jamaica in 1494, while on his second journey across the curve of the globe for Isabella and Ferdinand, los Reyes Catolicos, the Catholic Monarchs. (p. 66)
> There was a Black man in Columbus' crew—Pedro Alonso Nino. And Black men sailed with Balboa, Ponce de Leon, Cortez, Pizarro, and Menendez. In 1538 Estevanico, a Black explorer, discovered Arizona and New Mexico. For what purposes did these men find themselves on their expeditions. So many intertwinings to be unraveled. (p. 67)

Such, then, are the intertwinings and the veils from within which the Carib/ean woman, had she been fully discernable as *Subject-in-History*, might have been better placed in the star-apple kingdom. Instead, in the world of Walcott's haunted patriarchy, the woman "shrank to a bat that hung day and night/in the back of his brain." The contrast in vision is rather telling, given the resonance (of Caribbean slavery) in Walcott's title—and the deeper echo in Michelle Cliff's *Abeng*. She starts off her female protagonist into the complex connections of the Carib/ean picture show during one "afternoon in March—the month of most rain—the month in which the star apple ripens." In the "elliptical basin" of Walcott's Caribbean, things come to a head somewhat differently; and they reach their climax in a phallocentric consuming of "raped wife, empty mother, and Aztec Virgin."

The Star-Apple Kingdom's "She," we are told, "was as beautiful as a stone in sunrise." She is the stone(-making?) woman whose "voice had the gutturals of machine guns." She seems then to be a latter-day Siren who is, disturbingly enough, in the way of an odyssey to (re)member the oppressed. It is an idyssey embarked upon, and here is the seeming paradox, in her name and on her behalf: because, says Walcott, "her sex was the slit throat of an Indian;" because she was "a black rose of sorrow;" "a black umbrella blown inside out;" etc. And yet she is *the* temptation to disorder, very much the inspiration, it seems, for "khaki deserts where the cactus flower/ detonates like grenades." She is in one instance redeemed in the heuristic image of her "penitential napkins." On the other hand, she cannot *not* transfer her "footbath" allegiance from the (proper) Son of Man to his sub/versions—to Trujillo and Machado; and when not to them then to blood-toxic revolutionaries.

She further cancels the heuristic simply in her failure (inability? refusal?) to "understand." Less ambiguous, of course, is the way in which she fails when, in her final unbecoming, she metamorphoses into that creature of the night, bat. And yet, all the while, to the very deep and serious extent that biology (vagina and womb and blood) is her destiny, she is History as victim. She is the site of a dangerous but seductive aporia which licenses the obviously phallocratic Other in his act of filling in the blank. Transfixed, even transfigured, by conquest in "the name of the Father" she can only generate texts out of which come, and along which lie, a great found(er)ing of phallocentric issues and lines of succession:

> Her sex was the slit throat
> of an Indian, her hair had the blue-black sheen of the crow
> She was a black umbrella blown inside out
> by the wind of revolution, La Madre Dolorosa,
> a black rose of sorrow, a black mine of silence,
> raped wife, empty mother, Aztec virgin
> transfixed by arrows from a thousands guitars,
> a stone full of silence, which, if it gave tongue
> to the tortures done in the name of the Father,
> would curdle the blood of the marauding wolf,

the fountain of generals, poets, and cripples
who danced without moving over their graves
with each revolution; her Caesarean was stitched
by the teeth of machine guns, and every sunset
she carried the Caribbean's elliptical basin
to be the footbath of dictators, Trujillo, Machado,
and those whose faces had yellowed like posters
on municipal walls. Now she stroked his hair
until it turned white, but she would not understand
that he wanted no other power but peace,
that he wanted a revolution without any bloodshed,
he wanted a history without memory,
streets without statures,
and a geography without myth. He wanted no armies
but those regiments of bananas, thick lances of cane,
and he sobbed, "I am powerless, except for love."
She faded from him, because he could not kill;
she shrank to a bat that hung day and night
in the back of his brain. He rose in his dream.[36]

The female body is thus called into service as the vessel in which the body politic is (man)-made and (woman)-unmade. (It is most ironic, of course, that this should be the product of a consciousness which wants, so it tells itself, "a geography without myth.") But then, as Marina Warner notes, "surfaces [can only] define outer limits." Edward Said's term is "exteriority of representation;" for it is clear that the "he" in Walcott, much as he presumes penetration, remains outside the "she"—as "an existential and as a moral fact."[37] The use, then, of maidens as monuments is thus bound by and belied by the nature of skin:

> But skin is porous, sensitive, and yielding: women's skin especially is thought to be soft. It does not evoke images of a surface or outer edge impregnable to externals such as sound vessels must possess in order to be filled and remain full. The body of the woman, when used to represent generalized concepts that strain at absolute definition . . . must have its surfaces reinforced, so that the poor leaky vulnerable bag of skin and bone and flesh . . . can be transformed into a form strong enough to hold within its ambitious contents. . . . The thought that the figure then represents thereby acquires desirable firm outlines and clean definition, cancelling the nebulousness and slipperiness of the concept thus illusorily captured.[38]

Michelle Cliff echoes Warner and Said in her narrative's concern with island-in-between histories of racial and gender misrepresentation. Appropriately, *Abeng*'s New World sensitivity to mis(sing)-representation and "existential weightlessness" is in terms of genocide: "Imagined inhabitants will have few individual characteristics," Cliff writes:

> They will have bizarre features by which they are joined to one another, but none which are specific to themselves. Their primary feature is their difference from white and European Christians. It is *that* heart of darkness which has imagined them less than human. Which has limited their movement. The fantasies of this heart infected the Native tribes of North America with smallpox and with syphillis. Destroyed the language of the Mayans and the Incas. (p. 79)

The truth of the matter is, of course, that because the misrepresented are contained in vulnerable bags of skin and bone and flesh, the "true inhabitants will always be less fearsome than [the] imaginary creatures and therefore easier to conquer." Worse, *Abeng*'s picture shows that they can also be unimaginably, indeed, monstrously easy to erase: "nine million people, including six million Jews, in the death camps of Europe. This is one connection." It is precisely such a found(er)ing of the human in the inhuman which, Cliff insists, had "brought Africans in chains to the New World and worked them to death" (p. 79).

The mis(sing)-representation of the sisters of Anarcha and of the daughters of La Malinche do add, even in the absences, to the chain of traffic and trade in Carib/ean identities. In *Abeng*, the cost is measured by the effect of the absence of Maroon Nanny from, say, Kitty's consciousness; and if not there, then, surely and diaspora-wide, in the finely distilled ironies of the "fact" that "all the blacks are male, all the women are white, but some of us are brave."[39] For some of that "some," however, the consequences of mis(sing)-representation are, as with Maryse Condé's Veronica in *Heremakhonon*,[40] incorrigibly reductive.

Maryse Condé effectively focuses on states of consciousness and of (un)becoming—as they are further compounded by phallocentric privilege and racial insecurity. And she does so, from Caribbean Heroine to African *Heremakhonon*, in her female protagonist's conviction that "Time is a monster with a bloated neck." The *abeng* does (re)call with a sharp-voiced tartness in Condé's *Heremakhonon*. But it does so with so off-key an investment in the "good fuck" (p. 222) that Maroon Nanny's *Subject-in-History* activism ends up being, in Vernonica, self-deprecation and self-dissolving cynicism. The psycho-historical bent is not really surprising, given Condé's approach to "making generations" out of Carib/ean "step" relations; for example, out of step-daughter/step-mother bond(age) as well as out of what one might as well as call ancestral step-lover ties. Condé has relevantly pointed out that "Etre femme et antillaise, c'est un destin difficile à dechiffrer. Pendant un temps, les Antillais on cru que leur quête d'identité passait par l'Afrique. . . . J'aurais aimé que l'Afrique devienne une mère adoptive, mais elle ne peut être une mère naturelle. Les Antilles sont ma mère naturelle et c'est avec elles que j'ai des comptes à regler, comme toute fille avec sa mère, avant de devinir entièrement adulte".[41]

Appropriately, Veronica's desire in *Heremakhonon* is to remember and to be re-membered. It is, for sure, "un destin" made all the more "difficile à dechiffrer" because the attention is so focused on *la chose genitale*. Caribbean Veronica's investment in an ancestral phallocentricity, as *the* means of getting through to the "other side," only results in a myth-making and myth-mocking copulation—in the course of which, once more, she must shake her arse if she is to save her soul:

> This man who is about to take me does not know that I am a virgin of sorts. Of course the wrapper won't be stained with blood and the griotte won't hold it up proudly to reassure the tribe. It will be another blood. Heavier and thicker. . . . [And later she wonders] Don't you ever speak to the women in your bed? He laughs in the dark. . . . But it has always been recognized from time immemorial that pillows are a place for confidences. True, some have nothing to confide. Individuals, sound in body and mind, do exist. So he doesn't want to know who I am, where I come from, what I've come to do so far from home? If he's not interested, he doesn't ask, how can I call up my rab so that they leave me alone? (*Heremakhonon*, pp. 37, 51).

Re-membering thus becomes, to borrow from Jamaican Jean D'Costa, an instance of that "executioner's art" which allows "the doll on a rope's end" to move, but only in response to the rites and rights of "god, man and devil." Which is how and where, appropriately enough, D'Costa fixes the woman upon "reading the life of Mr. Silas Told: slave-trader, sailor, teacher & saint."[42]

Nowhere else, it seems to me, have the foundations for such a vision of diaspora *do-fe-do* connections been as well laid as in Ama Ata Aidoo's *Anowa* with its representation of diaspora origins as dismembering parturition. And, ironically enough, it is sited in Maroon Nanny's other country, in Akan land, when, as the Gold Coast, it had exploded in a holocaustal scattering of the female body. It is of some significance, too, that the key moral issue, enslavement, is linked to a phallocentric traffic in identities: "Did men of the land sell other men of the land, women and children to pale men from beyond horizon who looked like you or me peeled, like lobsters boiled and roasted?" Later, at the other end of the Middle Passage in *Abeng*, Michelle Cliff will recall that it was just such a "Do-fe-do mek guinea come a Jamaica" (p. 19). Aidoo's Anowa remembers that *do-fe-do* (in-fighting) in an adrocentric and nightmare vision of history:

That night, I woke up screaming hot; my body burning and sweating from a horrible dream. I dreamt I was a big, big woman. And from my insides were huge holes out of which poured men, women and children. And the sea was boiling hot and steaming. And as it boiled, it threw out many, many giant lobsters, boiled lobsters, each of whom as it fell turned into a man or woman, but keeping its lobster head and claws. And they rushed to where I sat and seized the men and women as they poured out of me, and they tore them apart, and dashed them to the ground and stamped upon them. And from their huge courtyards, the women ground my men and women and children on mountains of stones. But there was never a cry or a murmur; only a bursting, as of ripe tomato or a swollen pod. (p. 46)

Anowa's vision of the *heremakhonon*'s ruined and ruinous fecundity is effectively linked to the Carib/ean New World of *Abeng* by that corpse-laden container which provides Cliff with a key image. It was dug up, she writes, in 1958 in downtown Kingston. Heavy, still dangerous with a viable plague so many centuries after the Middle Passage, the body-container serves to bridge ravaged motherhood in the Gold Coast and, in Kingston, miscarried motherhood. Thus, when Mad Hannah's son, Clifton, dies his death by water, the drowning summons up images of the "monstrous packing case, made of lead and welded shut," which was uncovered in 1958 close by the Kingston Parish Church, near King's Parade, founded in 1692. The brass plate affixed to the coffin informed the vicar of the church

that the coffin contained the remains of a hundred plague victims, part of a shipload of slaves from the Gold Coast, who had contracted plague from the rats on the vessel which brought them to Jamaica. Others, many others, would have died onboard and their bodies dropped in the sea during the Middle Passage—the route across the Atlantic from Africa—or the Windward Passage—the route from the Atlantic to the islands of the Caribbean Sea. . . . The coffin should be opened on no account, the plaque said, as the plague might still be viable. The vicar commissioned an American navy warship in port to take the coffin twenty miles out and sink it in the sea. (p. 8)

It is this vision of miscarried potential which haunts Kitty into bitter insecurity and paralysis, leaving her, as I have pointed out already, with that belief of hers that the future lay at the bottom of the sea in lead coffins or scattered throughout the earth on plantations. Meanwhile, Mad Hannah's efforts at "following" Maroon Nanny, "she decided she could take no more, and rode up into the hills to find some peace," ends up being a ride to the asylum at Port Maria, where, made undecipherably articulate by grief and insight, she speaks a Word for which there is no audience. "They sent her off to the asylum at Port Maria, where she tried to explain to the people in charge—the light-skinned educated people—about the death of her son and his incomplete and dangerous burial" (p. 66). And so, because *Abeng*'s "land of look behind" had apparently passed through its change-of-life too traumatically,

> [even] men and women who had known Mad Hannah for donkey's years [hounded her]. They didn't stop to consider their actions. To ponder her relationship to magic or to think about her journeys as ceremonies of mourning, as expressions of faith. They thought her foolish and crazy. Now she twitched where she used to stroll. She talked to lizards and spiders and turned away from people on the road. They tried to forget that her actions followed on the death of her son. No . . . no, they said, she had passed through change-of-life too quickly and this made her fool-fool. (p. 65)

What Aidoo and Condé suggest about the trauma associated with Afro-New World motherhood, Michelle Cliff rather graphically develops and complicates. For in *Abeng*'s pluralist conception of things, the Mother is always on the island-in-between. She is Clare Savage's Miss Havisham and the eccentric, impossible kind which she represents, "White English women who had suffered great disappointment" (p. 37)—and Inez, that bronze and Half-Miskito Indian from the mountain chain of Central America, and about whom Justice Savage can say, speaking to Mma Alli, "Bitch, tell me where my nigger wench is" (p. 39).

By the same token, "daughter" can be both nanny's other child and the nanny-wench's own child. The traumatizing ambiguities involved are sometimes "tear-jerker" obvious (*Imitation of Life*); sometimes melo-dramatic with silence ("Her Virginia Mammy," by Chestnutt). Elsewhere they color, so to speak, the vision of Nanny in *Their Eyes Were Watching God*. And in *The Bluest Eye*, Toni Morrison[43] gives us, most poignantly, Pecola Breedlove who, "every night, without fail, . . . prayed for blue eyes. Fervently, for a year she prayed" (p. 40). Meanwhile, her mother, Mrs. Pauline Breedlove suffers the typical mis(sing)-representation which turns her into the "Polly" of the little girl with yellow hair and "infinite quantities of hot, clear water." The result is that "more and more she neglected her house, her children, her man—they were like the afterthoughts one has just before sleep, the early-morning and late-evening of her day" (p. 101). The daughter is, predictably, always the potentially "mixed-up baby". Which is what she is, of course, in *Abeng*'s Clare: "her father told her she was white. But she knew that her mother was not." And, even though pre-empted, the "mixed-up" is no less so in Inez's aborted "thick liquid." "A baby, Inez's people believed, was sacred, but a baby conceived in *bukra* rape would have no soul" (p. 35).

The "mixed-up baby" is not only fashioned in *bukra* rape, of course. There is the "mixing up" which has its origins in the economic imperatives of trade-in and live-in relationships, with their surrogate bonding and bondage. "The familiar violence rose in me," we read in Morrison. "Her [the girl with corn yellow hair] calling Mrs. Breedlove Polly, when even Pecola called her mother Mrs. Breedlove" (p. 86). Meanwhile, on the island-in-between, *Abeng*'s women work within and through conflictual roles:

> The women also served. Cleaned. Mopped. Cooked. Cared for babies lighter than their own. Did other people's laundry. . . . received some cash each week. To their mothers and sister and their aunts they gave some toward the care of their children. They saw these children perhaps once a week, if the children were kept in town. Less often if they were not. Many of these women had never been married, but they kept their children and gave them names and supervised their rearing as best they could. (p. 17)

In the final analysis, so much was "ranged against the upkeep of . . . connections": there was fruit picking in America; factories in the north of England; households and hotels in Kingston: "these men lived-in, as did their wives—over the years these people lost touch" (p. 16). And they lose touch, ironically enough, from being so much contained in and by the Other, from being "like one of the family."

> "Like one of the family" was a reality they lived with—taking Christmas with their employers and saving Boxing Day for their own. "Like one of the family" meant staying in a small room with one light and a table and a bed—listening to a sound system which piped in Radio Jamaica. They waited for tea-time and prepared lap trays dressed with starched and ironed linen cloths. They asked missis for the key to the larder so they could remove caddies of Earl Grey or Lapsang Souchong leaves, tins of sardines, English biscuits, Cross and Blackwell or Tiptree preserves—gooseberry or greengage plum.
> Sometimes this other family became more familiar to them than the people they were closest to. The people they were part of. (p. 17)

And so we have it, finally and ironically: Maroon Nanny miscontained in the existential weightlessness of the nanny and the nigger-wench. Appro-

priately enough, given the bloodline of speechless Arawak, consumed
Mayan, dismembered Aztec Virgin, and emptied mother, female bodies can
only make generations, or fail to do so, only in the pain of deferred, or in the
ecstasy of imagined, connections:

> "Cry-cry baby, suck you mama's titty," children used to taunt one
> another. At twelve Clare wanted to suck her mother's breasts again
> and again—to close her eyes in the sunlight and have Kitty close her
> eyes also and together they would enter some dream Clare imagined
> mothers and children shared. (p. 54)

It can hardly be surprising that strange, mad mutations of maternal desire
occur as they do in the Caribbean Great House, and if not there, then, for
sure, among "the miserable, little huts of Back-O-Wall" in Orlando
Patterson's *The Children of Sysyphus*,[44] where "The man was laughing
and swearing at her, pointing to her large, inflated belly and shoting that it
was only newspaper that was there."

> "Help me, lawd, help me!" she screamed. "Protec' me baby while ah
> kill de bitch!" She sprung forward, but too hastily. A roll of old
> newspaper fell from beneath her ragged skirt. There was a roar of
> laughter as the man grabbed the newspaper and held it in the air,
> holding his nose at the same time. Screaming hysterically that she
> could have a baby too, that she was having a baby, only it was taking a
> little time to come, she started looking frantically about for a brick. (p.
> 23)

The Mother-figure in the literature thus suffers a curious displacement.
She is more a medium than full representation as such, especially so in that
typically claustrophobic and "cruel little house" whose "implacability
panics" Aimé Césaire's[45] return to the native land: "my mother whose feet,
daily and nightly, pedal, pedal for our never tiring hunger, I am even woken
by those never-tiring feet pedalling by night and the Singer whose teeth rasp
into the soft flesh of the night, the Singer which my mother pedals, pedals for
our hunger night and day" (p. 46). The mother-woman moves thus, without
moving. She remains sensitive to the hunger which makes it imperative that
she come to be "like one of the family." So she remains nanny transfixed
rather than Maroon Nanny transfigured. And the inexorable logic of the
Same leaves her with a "daughter" who also seems fated to move without
moving. Clare Savage's condition of being in "the land of the look behind"
is such that, even at the end of *Abeng*, she was not ready to understand her
dream.

Conclusion: We Cannot Live Without Our Lives

> Still, if I could balance
> water on my head I can
> juggle worlds
> on my shoulders
>
> —Olive Senior, "Ancestral Poem"[46]

Whether postponed or otherwise "unauthorized" by the rites and rights of the pen/is, or else by this or that executioner's speculum or art, bending to look into the female self eventually results in recognition, resistance, and re-constitution. The text of a 1979 "3rd World Women" banner, "We Cannot Live Without Or Lives"[47] gets to the point succinctly. The point is similarly made in Michelle Cliff's choice of her activist Subject-in-History, "Nanny, the sorceress, the obeah-woman" (p. 14). And there is, too, Velma Pollard's way with her "Martha." The poem's "desist and live" is, as it were, a future celebration of an autonomous but as yet unliberated consciousness. Here, the *a-beng*'s appeal is to a female Self-in-Waiting, to one who is being called upon to generate issues that are larger than the authorized or the sub/versions of "he," "him," and "his":

> Woman desist
> he cannot hear your flesh
> your tongue and well-springs
> over-elocute
> her spirit speaks.
>
> He tunes you out
> but swings you in
> with habit thrust
> another she infuses all his sense
> whose spirit throbs
> and blows his body
> in your mind
> woman desist
> and live.[48]

Once upon a time, back in the newness of the old days, Elizabeth Barrett Browning's "Runaway Slave at Pilgrim's Point" (1850) had found it necessary, as she felt "the clouds breaking on [her] brain," to announce "I am not mad: I am black." *Abeng* re-presents figure and feature, enlarging the vision and the necessary point: They waged war from 1655-1740,

Michelle Cliff writes of the Windward Maroons. "Nanny was the magician of this revolution—she used her skill to unite her people and to consecrate their battles. There is absolutely no doubt that she actually existed." And even if the ruins of her Nanny Town remain difficult to get to, the *a-beng* does, in fact, (re)call the body in(to) question from those hidden crevices of the Blue Mountains of the island-in-between. The promise in all this is, of course, that when and where Maroon Nanny enters, there and then, in the resonances of the *abeng*, there enters all the necessary disconnections and connections which, nonetheless, make for affiliation. For as Michelle Cliff has most recently written of the nature of things in the land of look behind,[49] "the lone figure on the landscape/ . . . /unaffiliated—unnoticed./This is not how it is."

NOTES

1. Michelle Cliff, *Abeng* (Trumansburg, New York: The Crossing Press, 1984), p. 18.
2. G. Barker-Benfield, *The Horrors of the Half-Known Life. Male Attitudes Toward Women and Sexuality in 19th Century America* (New York: Harper & Row, 1976).
3. Roy Boyke, "Carnival Is What It Is", *Trinidad Carnival* (Port of Spain: Key Publications) No. 13, 1986.
4. Earl Lovelance, *The Dragon Can't Dance* (London: Heinemann, 1979).
5. Ama Ata Aidoo, *Anowa* (London: Longman, 1970).
6. Octavio Paz, *The Labyrinth of Solitude. Life and Thought in Mexico.* Trans. Lysander Kemp (New York: Grove, 1961).
7. Derek Walcott, *The Star-Apple Kingdom* (New York: Farrar, Strauss and Giroux, 1979), p. 51.
8. Elaine Scarry, *The Body in Pain, The Making and Unmaking of the World* (London: Oxford, 1985).
9. Edward Brathwaite Kamau, *Black and Blues* (Benin City, Nigeria: Ethiope, 1977).
10. Marina Warner, *Monuments and Maidens. The Allegory of the Female Form.* (New York: Atheneum, 1985).
11. Francis Barker, *The Tremulous Private Body. Essays on Subjection* (London: Methuen, 1983).
12. Luce Irigary, *Speculum de l'autre femme.* (Ithaca: Cornell University Press, 1985).
14. Editors' note: "Soucouyant" is in Caribbean folk mythology an old hag who sheds her skin and flies around at night, sucking the blood of sleeping victims. (See essay by Carole Boyce Davies elsewhere in this collection.) During the 1985 Carnival season, two calypsoes, one the "road march" tune, resurrected this character but this time with sexual meaning.
15. Moi, p. 146.

16. Tzevtan Todorov, *Mikhail Bakhtin: The Dialogical Principle* (Minnesota, 1984).

17. Jay Caplan, *Framed Narratives. Diderot's Genealogy of the Beholder* (Minnesota, 1985) p. 54.

18. Boyke, p. 10.

19. Max Romeo, "Deacon Wife", Angen Records (Jamaica). Produced by B. Lee, 1976.

20. Roger Mais, *Brother Man* (London: Heinemann, 1961), p. 29.

21. Judith Fetterly, *The Resisting Reader. A Feminist Approach to American Fiction* (Indiana, 1984).

22. Christine Froula, "When Eve Reads Milton: Undoing the Canonical Economy", *Critical Inquiry*, 10:2 (1983), pp. 321-347.

23. Moi, pp. 146-147.

24. See Moi's discussion, pp. 80-86.

25. Toni Morrison, *Tar Baby* (New York: Alfred Knopf, 1981), p. 263.

26. Bettina L. Knapp, *The Prometheus Syndrome* (Troy, New York: Whitson Publishing Company, 1979).

27. Elizabeth Schussler Fiorenza, *In Memory of Her. A Feminist Theological Reconstruction of Christian Origins* (New York: Crossroad, 1985).

28. In *Creole Drum. An Anthology of Creole Literature in Surinam*, eds. Jan Voorhoeve and Ursy M. Lichtveld. Trans. Vernie A. February (New Haven: Yale University Press, 1975).

29. Zora Neale Hurston, *Their Eyes Were Watching God*, (University of Illinois Press, 1978).

30. Paz, pp. 75, 96.

31. *The Conquest of America* (New York: Harper & Row, 1984), pp. 246-247.

32. Alejo Carpentier, *Explosion in a Cathedral* Trans. John Sturrock (New York: Harper, 1979).

33. Lawrence Lipking, "Aristotle's Sister: A Poetics of Abandonment," *Critical Inquiry*, 10:1 (1983) pp. 61-81.

34. Edward Said, *Orientalism* (New York: Vintage, 1979).

35. Brathwaite, p. 28.

36. Walcott, pp. 51-52.

37. Said, p. 21.

38. Warner, p. 258.

39. Editors' note: Full title of Gloria T. Hull, Patricia Bell Scott and Barbara Smith, eds. *But Some of Us Are Brave* (New York: The Feminist Press, 1982).

40. Maryse Condé, *Heremakhonon*, Trans. Richard Philcox (Washington, D.C.: Three Continents Press, 1982).

41. Maryse Condé, "L'Afrique un continent dificil. Entre tien avec Maryse Condé," Marie-Clotilde Jacquey & Monique Hugon, *Notre Libraire* 74 (April-June, 1984), pp. 22-23.

"Being woman and Antillian is a destiny difficult to untangle. At one time, Antillans believed that their quest for identity had to go through Africa . . . I would have liked Africa to become an adoptive mother, but she cannot be a natural mother. The Antilles is my natural mother and it is with her that I have accounts to settle, like any daughter with her mother, before becoming completely an adult."

42. Jean D'Costa, "In Memoriam", "On Reading the Life of Mr. Silas Told," *Jamaica Woman. An Anthology of Poems*, ed. Pamela Mordecai and Mervyn Morris (London: Heinemann, 1980), pp. 13, 15.
43. Toni Morrison, *The Bluest Eye* (New York: Washington Square Press, 1972).
44. Orlando Patterson, *The Children of Sisyphus* (Kingston, Jamaica: Bolivar Press, 1964).
45. Aimé Césaire, *Return to My Native Land.* Trans. John Berger and Anna Bostock (London: Penguin, 1969).
46. In *Jamaica Woman*, p. 77.
47. "Why Did They Die? A Document of Black Feminism," *Radical America* 13:6 (1979), p. 43.
48. In *Jamaica Woman*, p. 62.
49. Michelle Cliff, *The Land of Look Behind* (Ithaca, New York: Firebrand Books, 1985).

Righting the Calabash: Writing History in the Female Francophone Narrative

Clarisse Zimra

> From the earliest of historical time, Africa has remained cut off from all contacts with the rest of the world; it is the land of gold forever pressing in upon itself, and the land of childhood removed from the light of self-conscious history, wrapped in the dark mantle of night.
> —Hegel, *The Philosophy of World History*

The hot trend in current critical persuasion, generally known as "feminist" criticism and the (once) equally fashionable school known as "Marxist" have cut promising swathes in the variegated crop of modern black literature. The latter school's champions claim that an artist is nothing if not the product of HIS material environment, a position congruent with the conviction that the infrastructure mimics the superstructure. The former's exponents retort that a writer is nothing if not the product of HER biological environment, a position just as congruent with the rewriting of his/story. Beyond the relative merits of each approach in isolation, there may yet be a more fertile, joint critical terrain: The intersection of myth and sociohistory. Nowhere is this more obvious than in the case of Caribbean literature through which, Martinican Edouard Glissant claims, course "the deep, hidden whirls of the same historical current."[1] Keeping in mind Mouralis's[2] cautionary words about the specificity of cultural colonization processes, one might expect to find a unified literary corpus birthed from similar historical circumstances.

It has become a (quasi) cliché to assert that Caribbean literature is obsessed with history. Facing the Hegelian void, every writer has claimed the recreation of a collective memory as the imperative of authentic creation. Often, the collective dreamers have turned historians. Two such quests have been exemplary; that of James and Césaire. C.L.R. James started as a novelist but switched to a formidable ideological career with *The Black Jacobins* (1938).[3] In George Lamming's words, this milestone work pressed upon our ignorance, "the fact that there was a history of the area, as distinct from a history imposed upon the area."[4] Providing the black diaspora with counter heroes, it set the French revolution on its ears. As for Aimé Césaire, he was not only the poet of *Cahier* (1937) but the poignant philosopher of *Toussaint Louverture: La Révolution française et le problème colonial* (1960). Of three seminal historical plays, *Une Tempête* (1969),[5] defiantly rewriting the quintessential *agon* of white power, charted the subversion of Eurocentric history on the Caribbean shore. This discovery of an essential Other has made of all writing in the Caribbean a meditation on history.

James and Césaire gave Caribbean literature its two identifying features. First, an ironic reversal of the blessed isle *topos* inherited from the Renaissance. Second, a replay of the primal Caribbean *agon*, Haiti; which, posing the question of legitimacy, continues to define (and defy) the male text. But, reflecting neo-colonialist reality, female narratives remained narrowly intimistic.[6] The protagonist was generally a girl under the tremendous pressure of her social rite of passage into womanhood. Whether accepting it (pre-60s), resenting it (the 70s) or seeing an end to it (post 1980 novels), there was no escaping an identity sex-bound and male-defined. There could be no crossing of the gender bar.

One

> I made up my mind that I would write a book in which Africans or people of African descent, instead of being the object of other people's exploitation and ferocity, would themselves be taking action on a grand scale and shaping others to their needs.
>
> —James, "Preface" to *Black Jacobins*

If Plato first described an Africa deep in the sleep of unself-consciousness, it was Hegel[7] who Eurocentrically posited the black presence outside of history: A blank. Collective memory being either falsified in the white man's records or obliterated by his actions, the only writing—perforce a re/writing or a setting to right—of such an absent past as can be done must be done through imaginary structures "emplotted" (to use Hayden White's terminology) in the text. Yet, White[8] has also shown, somewhat in spite of himself, that there remains irreducible historical residues in all narratives;

what Fredric Jameson[9] (1981) prefers to call, because his ideological grounding is somewhat different, layered sediments, "alluvians." The writing of history in all fiction thus demands the imaginary emplotment of origins that cannot be fully apprehended. Myth is the sign of absence destined to fill in this original blank, erase the presence of the ursurper and reinscribe the true origins into the collective memory. In the Caribbean, Toussaint's struggle thus constitutes the symbolic *agon* of choice in every narrative of the black diaspora, from Césaire to Lamming, Guillèn to Dadié and beyond. Yet, females seem conspicuously absent. It was along Hegelian premises defining Woman as Man's dark continent, his Africa, that Freud posed his famous question. There may, indeed, be a gender variable in Caribbean versions of the original Father.[10] Not necessarily because women write inherently "differently" from men; because they have been socialized other/wise and thus conceive of heroism as Other/defined. If writing His/story is a male prerogative, what happens, then, when the writer is a female?

It is generally thought that the first break with tradition was Guadeloupe's Maryse Condé whose *Hérémakhonon* came out in 1976.[11] There had been precursors. As early as 1957, a full three years before Césaire's *Toussaint*, Haiti's Marie Chauvet had written *La Danse sur le volcan*. For Haitians, the reference was clear; "dancing on a volcano" had been the words Toussaint had thrown in Leclerc's face. Still, with a talented high yellow heroine in the throes of unrequited love, it was more a romance than a historical novel; although it highlighted, with a meticulous attention to historical detail, the comings and goings of a theatrical company in San Domingo on the eve of upheaval. *Volcan* also had a fine psychological study of race relations in the portrait of a free man of color, heir to a white man's plantation, who, consumed by self-hate, treated his slaves with a cruelty which few of his white neighbors could match. True to form, *Volcan* had been preceded by *Fille d'Haiti* (1954), Chauvet's own romp through the negrophobic narrative convention, that self-indulgent side of the mulatto convention usually dealing with a (barely) colored woman too beautiful and too intelligent to be content with her inferior station. One can measure the force of the negrophobic tradition when one realizes that in Haiti, if anything, a high mulatto complexion should have been deemed desirable, rather than the reverse, particularly for a female (Lirius). It seemed that Chauvet was trying her hand at all the conventional plots before trusting to her own instincts. *Fille d'Haiti* had one saving feature; it was the first systematic depiction of a love/hate relationship between a colored mother and her daughter; a plot which Lacrosil would radicalize further by using, instead, a white mother. In 1968 came *Amour, colère et folie,*[12] a surrealistic work which, I have shown,[13] obliquely introduced the question of history in the text; sexual madness being its ruling metaphor, blood its ruling imagery. It consisted of three novellas set in a provincial city under siege, victimized by the forays of the *tontons-macoutes*. Their chief, an ugly black man from the lower classes, wracked by self doubt and usually impotent, took his racial and sexual revenge by torturing and raping the virginal mulatto daughters of the upper classes. Chauvet controlled the tendency toward voyeurism inherent in such a plot by presenting the counter picture of the pristine daughters of the Haitian bourgeoisie as sex starved, sex obsessed and religion mad. The sadistic behavior bordering on madness which bonded master and slaves in *Volcan* now reappeared, more finely tuned. In *Amour, colère et folie*, sexual deviancy, the hidden side of race wars, was presented as the metaphor for unnatural social conditions. Chauvet never had time to confront history directly, her logical next step. Her death turned Condé into a pathbreaker, putting the writer from Guadeloupe in a problematic position on several accounts.

First: Condé did not come into her own as a historical writer until her two volume *Ségou* (1984; 1985).[14] Her first novel very much follows the tradition of rewriting accepted paradigms, albeit in this case, with a vengeance. Second: To throw the fake fathers out of Caribbean history, she stuck to Caribbean pre-history: Africa. The strategy decenters our enquiry so I shall only signal its import. It eviscerated the traditional gender compartmentalization prevailing in the tragic mulatto convention, usually on the Capécia model, revealing the true ideological content of the nobler-than thou (read, whiter-than-thou) undertow running through what the nineteenth century liked to call *roman créole*.[15] It took her two reworkings of the paradigm, *Hérémakhôn* (1976) and *Rihata* (1981), before Condé could break free. Third:—and this is a point which cannot be made too strongly—Condé had a predecessor whose work she knew well in Michèle Lacrosil,[16] a compatriot a good thirty years older. For, as *La Parole des femmes*[17] makes plenty clear, Condé is a writer particularly well aware of her own tradition.

Condé's and Lacrosil's careers overlap in intriguing ways. Born on Guadeloupe, they are both black women from the middle-class. Both were educated in the French system, both started as teachers. Just as it took Condé two somewhat autobiographical novels, it had taken Lacrosil two intensely personal texts (*Sapotile*, 1960; and *Cajou*, 1961) before she turned to history. In her too brief survey, *La Parole des femmes* (1979), Condé pays attention to Lacrosil's first two novels but completely ignores her last; showing the same, uneasy relation to her challenging elder as, say, a Glissant to Césaire or a Brathwaite to James. Harold Bloom, who sees in "the anxiety of influence,"[18] a primarily male pattern of dependency in the western corpus, might do well to look at the Caribbean. Except for *Dieu nous l'a donné* (1972), a searing farce of missed opportunities, Condé has favored Africa. Lacrosil, therefore, remains the first, and perhaps the only one, to have tackled the male competition on its own turf, the recreation of

an insular past. It is time that Lacrosil be given her due among those whom
Claudine Hermann (1976) calls "the tongue-snatchers." [19]

But, from its inception in the seventeenth century, there had been gender
variants in the *roman créole*. The first male version, which I shall call the
avenging paradigm, can be traced to Mrs. Behn's celebrated *Oroonoko, or
The Royal Slave* (1688), [20] which boasted an African prince all the more
admirable for the fortitude which which he greeted bondage and the
constancy with which he remained faithful to his captured princess. That
the male paradigm followed a pattern established by a female writer was an
irony lost on its practitioners. What mattered was the power play between
master and (male) slave in which females became but an erotic pretext: To
titillate in the name of virtue. Adapted for the stage by Southerne in 1695,
the text had a splendid track record all through Europe. Translated into
French by Laplace in 1745, its end was radically altered. Instead of
Oroonoko's futile rebellion and death by (revoltingly graphic) torture in a
Surinam Mrs. Behn knew well—a passage which inspired both the Voltaire
of *Candide* and the Crèvecoeur of *Letters from an American Farmer*—, the
French readers found the African variation of the Noble Savage who,
having won the admiration of the island's governor, was given free passage
back home with his wife and child. The new version sought to have it both
ways, cutting our Mrs. Behn's realistic study of plantation mores to appeal
to Europe's prurience with a story of lovers wronged. Hoffmann[21] has
stressed what the characterization of the royal slave owed to the prevailing
aristocratic tradition, thus accounting for its extraordinary success. There is
no doubt, as Seeber[22] argues, that Mrs. Behn's story was the source for
much of the negrophile literature of the following two centuries, including
Hugo's youthful master text, *Bug-Jargal* (1819)[23] and Mérimée's more
cynical *Tamango* (1829), [24] both of whom have royal origins.

It was the nineteenth century that most clearly demarcated the male
narrative from its female variation. Contaminated by the Noble Savage
semantic charge during the Enlightenment, the black protagonist became,
in the Romantic iconography, the avenger who murders his white master/
father in an explosion of blood. Two of its most celebrated and most
(arche)typal versions are to be found in *Le Mulâtre* (1837), [25] the work of
Louisiana born Victor Séjour, an upper class man of color sent by a wealthy
father to France and who chose to remain; and in *Georges* (1843), [26] the
work of one of the most prolific and popular among the French Romantics,
Alexandre Dumas, who happened to be the grandson of the black common
law wife of a French born officer stationed on the island of Martinique. As
one who never fully claimed his "race", Dumas has been controversial
among the diaspora writers, although C.L.R. James, for one, saluted him as
one of his own (*Kas-Kas*). Secure in his literary fame, he never advertised
his black ancestry but never hid it either (witness the number of jests and

caricatures which hounded him).[27] And, in a quiet way, he vindicated himself with a novel to which few of his contemporaries paid attention, except to confirm their own prejudices. What Dumas's *Georges* and Séjour's *Le Mulâtre* have in common is far more important than the ideological affiliation of their authors. As Hoffman aptly argues, they modulate a favorite Romantic theme, that of the outsider.[28] Social interloper and biological bastard, the Romantic mulatto is forever self-hating. The hero goes by his first name, underlining the matrilineal filiation which, by law, kept him a slave and, as Fanon's example will eventually demonstrate, guaranteed that he become a woman-hater as well. The discovery of the father's identity, which confirms the son's non-identity, triggers a brutal murder. In Séjour's text, for instance, the master's chopped head rolls at the feet of the avenger, murmuring the words, "I am your father." A scene of primal self-birthing to which Césaire, for one, returns time and again throughout his work, the avenging paradigm developed through the Romantic period was well suited to emplotting the Haitian *agon*.

In contrast, the tragic female never achieved autonomous ontological status because, in a fundamentally patriarchal society, she could not lay claim to a name. She could only die, erased ontologically as she had always been semantically. Hoffmann has documented examples of lustful females in the lower tradition of pulp romance geared to the white male's erotic projections. Since such *femmes fatales* tend to die a violent retributive death in the end, as in Paul Féval's *Le Mendiant noir* (1847),[29] their semi-educated audience could have their (racist) cake and eat it too. But the stereotype that stuck came from the higher Romantic tradition whose best example remains Gustave de Beaumont's 1834 *Marie ou l'esclavage aux Etats-Unis*.[30] The story of a noble soul who, because of the invisible drop of black blood, steadfastly refuses to marry the gallant Frenchman who would take her away. She dies, instead, of a broken heart. It goes without saying that a mulatto character, by essence and condition torn between two irreconcilable sets of values, made for perfect tragedy. The Caribbean connection was made by way of New Orleans where Beaumont, who had accompanied Tocqueville through his celebrated American periple, had found his inspiration. I have argued the question of gender variables in the development of *Négritude*[31]; they carry, *mutatis mutandis*, into the evolution of the narrative.

Two

Toutes ces femmes de couleur échevelées, en quête du Blanc, attendent.
                                                              —Fanon, *Peau noire*

[Questing for the white man, all these colored women, dishevelled, wait]

By the twentieth century, the female mulatto character had fused both higher and lower strains; not unexpectedly, since structuralism has taught us that a symbol is always contaminated by its opposite referent. In Capécia's novels,[32] the heroine could be both the self-sacrificing *doudou*, little more than a pet animal whose affections do not run deep (and who can, therefore, be easily discarded since she's expected to recover just as easily); or the conniving Circe who gets what's coming to her and whom it behooves any self-respecting gentleman to discard after use. But dutiful or not, Massa's daughter still was being defined exclusively in terms of the white, male, scale of values.

Precisely because Mayotte Capécia was a second rate writer (and there subsist doubts as to her authorship),[38] she exhibited rather nakedly in her work the racial strictures of her colonial society, what Fanon has decried as the neuroses of the lactification complex. Kept in the comfort she could not afford by a Frenchman who will eventually leave, the empty-headed high yellow woman of *Je suis martiniquaise* (1948) consoles herself with the idea that her son will at least (and at last) look whiter and climb farther than she. The formula was successful and turned up again, barely amended, in a second novel. World War II had just ended in a Gaullist victory. Here was a colonial making points in the *mé*tropole by writing a "true" story deprecating "false" Frenchmen. Her pseudo-autobiographical heroine sailing away to the land of *liberté-égalité-fraternité* vindicated an official policy which was refusing, in a carrot and stick fashion, to grant the islands autonomy.[34] Although she became a tad politicized in *La Négresse blanche* (1950), standing up to her white, Martinique-born mother-in-law, her heroine never really shook off her own prejudices. It was this naked cynicism about bartering sex for material survival that angered Fanon so.

If to recover the past it is necessary to throw out the false fathers, Fanon's career was exemplary. But the writer who, with Sartre, argued that the "cracker" creates the "nigger" much as the anti-semite creates the jew, contradicted his own logic when he put the blame full on the rump of the fundamental Other, the whoring accomplice in Massa's bed. Fanon's outrage jolted a whole generation out of complacency but overlooked, as I have argued,[35] more poignant questions. While *Black Skins, White Masks*[36] devotes plenty of space to the unjust humiliation of the black man, little is spent on the corresponding degradation of the black female. As a good Marxist, Fanon must have known that systemic oppression acts dialectically. Could it be that a double patriarchy left its women no choice but to trade sex for safety? Or is it that women "naturally" enjoy oppression (as they used to enjoy rape). Edouard Glissant's *Le Quatrième siècle* (1964)[37] what he calls a "reconstitution" of three centuries of Caribbean history, perpetrated the same outrage. Black females are given as rewards by the master to his favorite strapping slave. One might dismiss Fanon as a psychiatrist for whom literature was the preserve of neuroses, were it not that the American brothers of the 1960s who devoutly quoted him also believed that liberation by reason of sex should take a back seat to the question of liberation by race. Angela Davis or Kay Lindsey fought, and lost, the same battles that felled Rosa Luxembourg. Female autonomy seldom enters the narrow gate of Marxist paradise.[38]

Such had been the genre when Lacrosil picked up the challenge. Thanks to Fanon's high visibility, Capécia was remembered long after she should have been forgotten and served as pre-text for Michèle Lacrosil's own texts.[39] Suggested by an editor who wanted to capitalize on the successful Capécia's formula (1976 interview), *Sapotille* (1959) and *Cajou* (1960) succeeded, instead, in dismantling the paradigm: The bitter conclusion to the tragic mulatto convention was its own destruction.

It is a black husband who beats her up savagely and causes her to miscarry, not a faithless white man, that Sapotille flees, hoping, like Capécia's heroine, for the freedom of the French shore. This first novel ends, semi-optimistically, with her arrival. The second picks up where the first one ended and finishes it off. Cajou has lived in France a while and is now engaged to a man of integrity. Her tragedy has less to do with French racism than with Caribbean pathology. Fanon had shown that skin gradations lose ontological status in France where everyone is "just a nigger". Obsessed with such gradations, Cajou (like Beaumont's Marie before her) cannot believe that the white man by whom she is with child wants to marry her. Rather than confront the possibility that she is wrong, she commits suicide. Likewise, there is a similar misunderstanding (minus the suicide but with a blighted life) at the center of Carbet's *Au Péril de ta joie*,[40] published in the '70s but started in the late '50s. For the tragic mulatto of the '50s, race is self. Take it away and there's nothing.

Demain, Jab-Herma was written against her editor's wishes (1976 interview); it suffered accordingly. A virtual recluse and shy by temperament, Lacrosil could never deliver the verbal pyrotechnics that imposed the younger Condé on fickle Parisians. Its originality was overlooked. Unlike Chauvet's *Volcan* which used data from the Haitian revolution as backdrop only, *Jab-Herma* was after far more ambitious results: To inscribe an altogether blank text.[41]

Guadeloupe makes an interesting case because its self-birthing is missing from the official record, although its native sons have written its chronicles (Lara 1921;[42] Saint-Ruf 1977;[43] Glissant 1981): Neither standard dictionaries nor ordinary textbooks mention the name of Louis Delgrès, although they do Toussaint. The Haitian remains ideologically safer. He may have been great but he was, ultimately, caged. A good French patriot can, therefore, afford to admire his memory much as Mrs. Behn's readers admired Oroonoko. Furthermore, with the recent example of the Duvalier regime, a good French patriot can still find comfort in the inner conviction that Toussaint's children are not ready for freedom. Delgrès, however, escaped ideological bondage forever. Born free on Martinique, this 30 year old colonel in the republican army led over three thousand of Guadeloupe's armed rebels but a few, brutal weeks. Surrounded by six thousand of Napoleon's troops, Delgrès and three hundred of his men, along with their women and children, blew themselves up in a hilltop fortress on the Matouba. In the ensuing weeks, thousands of people were butchered. But, as Derrida (1974)[44] has shown, memory blanks chart the palimpsest's trace. There always is his/story underneath.

Caliban's island stands at the center of the symbolic web. Its emplotment in a Caribbean text closes Hegel's epistemological circle for the first time in the western discourse. *Jab-Herma* locates itself in the '50s, in the midst of impending African independences, an increasingly problematic platform for *Négritude*; and, on this particular island, sugar riots met with a ferocity that Napoleon's mercenaries would have envied. At the nadir of insular history, collective imagination feeds on what glorious moments from the past can be retrieved. But can such memories be trusted? *Jab-Herma* poses frontally the question that Condé will only gingerly raise ten years later in her first novel: What happens to history when the Father is a fake.

The surface story is simple, its political dimension obvious. Young Philippe arrives on the island to take control of a failing sugar operation owned by a European cartel but run by Constant, former owner of the surrounding plantation, a Prospero fallen from power. New Ferdinand on the blessed isle, Philippe will eventually level Constant's magnificently dilapidated mansion to replace it with a cost efficient factory; throwing out of doors and out of work the army of plantation hands whom Constant kept on the payroll because they had always been at the service of his family.

The subterranean plot is less predictable. First, Lacrosil stands on its sexist head the tragic mulatto paradigm, changing Capécia's configuration to a homoerotic one. The switch underlines the Hegelian structure of interdependence upon which the master-slave relationship is predicated. Not the wish to be LIKE the master, ever imperfect approximation, but the desire to BE the master. (Those who recognize famous Sartrean premises will be glad to know the novel was dedicated to Sartre and Beauvoir.) Mesmerized by Philippe's blue eyed beauty, Cragget, a mulatto who despises his own color, commits a series of murders culminating in his own suicide.

Next, Lacrosil uses intercrossing pairs to bring out the dialectical content of the topos. As white Philippe (the outsider from without) is to the mulatto (outsider from within); so is black Jab-Herma (the voodoo priest) to white Constant (the planters' scion), the young master with whom he was raised. Constant's need for Jab-Herma has the same neurotic intensity as that of Cragget's for Philippe. It leads to the same suicidal temptation, under the sign of the Ancestor: Delgrès, the man "who knew how to choose his own death."

Setting off these two homoerotic pairs in binary opposition, the text poses the question of history as a search for legitimacy. The four are obsessed with Delgrès who, legend says, buried gold on Matouba just before his immolation. Only a voodoo ceremony, conducted with a fetish transported "over water" (i.e. from Africa) by a strange man, will discover it. The mulatto sees Philippe, who arrived bearing a mysterious chest, as this stranger. In a perfect metonymic transference he believes that, to appropriate the gold (the totem of insular origins), is to acquire Delgrès's power (the Law of the legitimate Father). Cragget is triply mistaken. On thematic grounds because Philippe, of course, is not the stranger. On symbolic grounds because, having misinterpreted voodoo, the mulatto kills the wrong victims. And on ethical grounds because, even though he knew who Delgrès was, he has coveted the gold for himself alone. But, from the outset, the legend (and the folk tale which recounts it and therefore represents the collective interpretation thereof) made it quite clear; the treasure must be collectively searched and collectively found: "On se le partagerait" (p. 17). History can only be that which can be shared. That he should seek to steal the hidden powers of the black ancestor (Delgrès) in order to become the white man (Philippe) is the sign of his condition: Claiming the wrong ontology and, therefore, the wrong history. This use of history as the single most important narrative device raises the question of historical discourse: Writing as rewriting. It puts Lacrosil ahead of her times, in line with current feminist theories of decentering, fragmenting the image of the Father in order to question his legitimacy.

Three

> Parce que la mémoire historique fut trop souvent raturée, l'écrivain antillais doit "fouiller" dans cette mémoire, à partir de traces parfois latentes qu'il a repérées dans le réel.
>
> —Glissant, *Le Discours antillais*

> [Because historical facts have been crossed out of collective memory too many times, the Caribbean writer has to "root around", faintly guided by latent traces showing through the real.

The rewriting of Guadeloupe's history occurs in a contrapuntal mode emplotting Guadeloupe's own *agon*, Delgrès' fight whose traces survive in the thick undergrowth of insular memory. The shifting of power from Constant to Philippe brings economic servitude to the former slaves, their new dependence on the French welfare state. It also compels the former master, suddenly bereft of real power, to appropriate the slave's symbolic power, Guadeloupe's past. Once again we find the pairing reversal which, in Lacrosil, signals a flawed vision. Just as the mulatto, pitting himself against (black) Jab-Herma, tried to appropriate Philippe's (white) values;

so now Constant, pitting himself against Philippe's future, claims Jab-Herma's Ancestor.

The mulatto died because he did not have mastery of the signs that constitute the voodoo system. Misreading the symbolic text, he sacrificed the wrong victims, female first born, where he should have used male. Throughout, such references function as signposts of blindness. They are the unidentified trace of the Ancestor, Guadeloupe's self-birthing first born whom the folk always refer to as pure male principle (*"un mâle"*). Likewise Philippe, the outside in charge of law and order, cannot prevent the murders because he cannot penetrate the system for which Delgrès is the cipher. The semiotic level invalidates both quests, leaving us with the other paradigmatic pair, Constant and Jab-Herma.

Their confrontation occurs during a dinner at the mansion when the conversation turns to "explaining" Guadeloupe to the outsider. It would be worth quoting at length were not space so limited, for it is a prime illustration of Lacrosil's technique: Partial versions overlap but never quite mesh, linking the re/w/righting of history with the legitimacy of the verb. Black slave or white master? Who speaks? And on whose behalf? Emplotting whose history?

Each claiming Delgrès as his own, planter and priest trade versions of the past. Philippe, interloper on Caliban's shore who cannot conceive of a race war so primal, disqualifies himself; for innocence is a form of historical blindness. The insular past, hitherto absent from white consciousness, lives neither in the facts, nor within each subjective interpretation thereof, but in the tension, distance and contradictions among the fragments of a contrapuntal narrative:

> —Ils vivaient ici, une région paisible, côte à côte, les anciens maîtres et les anciens esclaves, ah! les mêmes soucis, la même besogne, et malgré les apparences, la même pauvreté. Un jour, un jeune conquérant est venu! [...] Delgrès! ... ah! s'est suicidé: c'était la chose à faire. [...]
>
> Philippe dit, paisiblement:
> —Peut-on savoir qui est Delgrès? [...]
> Jab-Herma intervint [...]
> —Patron, il faut vous imaginer le temps des dernières luttes des esclaves noirs. Nous étions de part et d'autre de la ligne de feu, toi et moi, Monsieur Constant.
> Il insista:
> —Des adversaires, frère blanc. Et aujourd'hui, nous deux.
> Constant s'était repris:
> —Nous n'étions pas des ennemis, Jab. L'esclavage avait été une époque sanglante. Des luttes sanglantes en marquèrent la fin. Et puis les anciens maîtres et les anciens esclaves reprirent la travail côte à

côte. [. . .] *D'ailleurs, à l'époque qui nous intéresse, 1802, il
ne s'agissait pas d'une révolte d'esclaves* C'était autre chose. Une
prise de conscience d'hommes qui, ayant été libres, refusaient de
redevenir des esclaves. *Louis Delgrès était un homme libre. Un
mulâtre.* [. . .]
—Et . . . la révolte a été réprimée?
Constant dit, rudement:
—Je vous crois.
Philippe montra de l'émotion:
—Réprimée, mais pas dans le sang, ce n'est pas pensable?
Sougès et Jab-Herma dirent presque en même temps:
—Ce fut une guerre impitoyable.
—Fraîche et sanglante. [. . .] une tuerie.
Constant les regardait, haletant.
—Delgrès n'avait aucune chance et il le savait. [. . .] Mais quelle vie
aurait-il eue! ou plutôt, quelle mort? Nous l'admirons d'avoir choisi sa
mort (italics mine; pp. 228-235).

[—They used to live here, a peaceful place, side by side, the former
masters and the former slaves shared, ha! common cares, common
chores and, in spite of appearances, a common poverty. One day,
there came a young conquerer! [. . .] Delgrès committed suicide: it
was the one thing left. [. . .]
Peaceably, Philippe enquired:
—And who might this Delgrès be? [. . .]
Jab-Herma cut in [. . .]
—Sir, you'd have to be able to imagine the times of the last slave
struggles. Thou and I stood on either side of the battlefield, Master
Constant.
He insisted:
—Adversaries, then. Yet, today, the two of us.
Constant had regained his composure.
—We never were enemies, Jab. Slavery had been a bloody era.
Bloody struggle signaled its end. Then, former masters and former
slaves resumed work side by side. [. . .] *Besides, for the period under
consideration, 1802, there was no question of slave rebellion.* It was
something else. The self-awakening of men hitherto free, who refused
to return to slavery. *Louis Delgrès was a free man. A free man of
color.* [. . .]
—And, did they put the rebellion down?
Rough, now, Constant replied.
—Better believe it.
Philippe showed some emotion.

—What do you mean, put down. Not in blood. I don't believe it.
(Constant) Sougès and Jab-Herma replied with almost one voice.
—They waged a merciless war.
—A fresh war for blood [. . .] a butchery.
Breathing hard, Constant looked around.
—Delgrès never stood a chance and he knew it. [. . .] But what kind
of a life could he have claimed? Or, rather, what kind of a death? We
admire him for choosing his death.]

Very much the scion of a class which divided the better to conquer,
Constant sees in Delgrès only the "free man of color" of the white history
books and severs the Matouba struggle from the slave revolt altogether.
Simultaneously, he longs for the Renaissance version of his island: Garden
before the Fall. His double self-delusion signals his own ideological
obsolescence. His synchronic notion of history as myth negates temporality.
His love for Constant notwithstanding, Jab-Herma interprets Delgrès's
immolation quite differently, as an integral part of the black fight for
freedom. Situating himself on the other side of the ideological fence, using a
diachronic frame of reference, he removes myth from history, insisting upon
a sequence of time-grounded moments in which to anchor the authentic
Caribbean self.

In these conflictual versions, Lacrosil eliminates all but Jab-Herma as a
legitimate speaker. But this is not to say that she backs up the heroic *agon*
unreservedly. However unflinching his vision of the past, we know nothing
of his future except for the cipher that precedes his name. The Jab-Hermas
of tomorrow may rescue history but only if they read the past correctly.
Constant's failure makes clear that an illusory past invoked to escape the
present can have no relevance to the future. The heroic mode may well be
the ultimate blindness, a misreading of history and of self. This constitutes
an oblique indictment of black ideologies posited on a glorious past, the
Afro-American brothers and *primus inter pares*, the *Négritude* prophets
included.

Two years later, Césaire was to stake his claim on the insular map along
two related axes. First, a political fable of displacement. His *Tempest*
(1969), first performed on African soil, unveiled the original absence:
Caliban had no legitimate Father. Second, a semiotic fable. The heroic
cipher pointed toward quite a different ideology of presence, that of the
primal Mother.[45] More recent writers who know Lacrosil's text well, such
as Simone Schwarz-Bart[46] and Daniel Maximim,[47] have openly followed in
her footsteps.

Female genealogy as ideology of choice is at the heart of *Télumée*
(1972). But in this novel, the biological bond which was left ambiguous in
Plat de porc is discarded in favor of the free choice of an ideologically

autonomous agent. For the chosen Mother (rather than the inherited genitrix) through whom ancestral wisdom is transmitted, is often the childless woman; or, as Schwarz-Bart pointedly calls her, the "nameless one" (Reine sans Nom). If she cares for children, they are not always her biological ones, that she may be the symbolic ideological Mother to a whole people. The female Ancestor with whom story-telling Télumée identifies is, herself, also a story-teller. And so we find the tale within the tale, and the retelling of a retelling, structures of mythopoesis. Not only is the Ancestor's Word the (Lacanian) condition for the narrator's own, it is also an exemplum: what can be set to right/write. Tri-partite versions in Télumée's autobiography reproduce closely similar moments in Reine-sans-Nom's own past. We have seen, with Lacrosil, that history must be that which is shared. For Schwarz-Bart, it is that which must be reproduced, "passed on," passed down and, by the same token, passed "up." A true sign of the mythic dimension.

Closer to Lacrosil in content, Maximin's *L'Isolé soleil* (1981) frontally deals with the writing/righting of a Delgrès legend they know too well: All three, Lacrosil, Schwarz-Bart and Maximin were born on Guadeloupe. Alternating the voice of a male and a female narrator, Maximin sifts through the official archive versions of the rebellion. In their restless obsession with the Matouba, son and daughter end up discarding the Father's versions to invent their own. The daughter's action is more subversive. Half-way into the story, Marie-Gabriel, the daughter, decides to give up the manuscript she has been working on, entitled "L'aire du père," to turn to her dead mother's diary whose rewriting she titles "L'air de la mère;" punning, in so doing, "air" with "area" and "era." But there is obviously more than linguistic wit here. The semantic shift signals a radical re-orienting, relocating of self and origins in the Caribbean corpus; a redefinition of the primal one. The ultimate reading has to do with the superimposition of the mother's "song" over the father's "place-time," his story and territorial preserve, the island. Marie-Gabriel's true pre-text is the closest we come to the oral trace. Not surprisingly, we find in *L'Isolé* the same suspicious male figure we have in *Ti-Jean l'Horizon* (1979), an untrustworthy ancestor. In Maximin's text, the Ancestor is unreliable because he is undecipherable; in Schwarz-Bart's, the Ancestor has misdeciphered. Giving the wrong message, he sent the son on a false African quest from which there was no coming back: " . . . la route est arrêtée."

Maximin's matricial scene "re-opens the way." It occurs on the Matouba, during the self-sacrificial ceremony preceding the explosion; its concluding words: "A bon entendeur, silence." "Let s/he who understands, keep silent." Until Afro-Caribbeans write/right their own origins they will, like Ti-Jean, run the risk of staying in the belly of the beast. This they can only overcome by disregarding the Logos of the Father for the Silent Song of the Mother.

Hence, in the new Caribbean novel, the intolerable absence of the original Father hides the silent presence of a Mother not yet fully understood. Like Michelle Cliff for the Anglophone narrative, Maximin and Schwarz-Bart have charted a new passage and, in so doing, paid brilliant hommage to their own pre-text: Lacrosil's work. It is high time critics do likewise.

NOTES

Unless otherwise indicated, all French publication places are located in Paris. All translations are mine. English references have been provided for less accessible works.

1. Edouard Glissant, *Le discours antillais* (Seuil, 1981), p. 130.
2. Bernard Mouralis, "La littérature négro-africaine: quelle critique pour quelle littérature?", *Interdisciplinary Dimensions of African literature*, ed. Kofi Anyidoho et al (Washington, D.C.: Three Continents Press, 1985), pp. 27-31.
3. C.L.R. James, *The Black Jacobins: Toussaint L'Ouverture and the San Domingo Revolution* (New York: Vintage Books, 1980, first published 1938).
4. In *Kas-Kas: Interviews with Three Caribbean Writers in Texas* (University of Texas at Austin, 1972), p. 13.
5. Aimé Cesaire's major works include *Cahier d'un retour au pays natal* (Présence Africaine, 1939, 1956); *Toussaint L'Ouverture: la révolution francaise et le problème colonial* (Club francais du livre, 1960); *La Tragédie du Roi Christophe* (Présence Africaine, 1963); *Une Saison au Congo* (Seuil, 1966); *Une Tempete* (Seuil, 1969).
6. Cf. *Bulletin of Eastern Caribbean Affairs* (March-April, 1985), special issue on "The Female Presence in Caribbean Literature"; in particular essays by Fido and O'Callaghan. Also Julie Lirius, *Identité antillaise* (Editions Caribeennes, 1979).
7. Frederich Hegel, *Lectures on the Philosophy of World History* (London: Cambridge University Press, 1973).
8. Hayden White, *Metahistory: The Historical Imagination in 19th Century Europe* (Baltimore: Johns Hopkins University, 1973).
9. Frederic Jameson, *The Political Unconscious: Narrative as a Socially Symbolic Act* (Ithaca: Cornell University Press, 1981).
10. I am using categories circulated by what may be called, rather loosely, the Yale school, in the wake of the self-destruction of continental Marxist structuralism. See in particular Henry Louis Gates, *Black Literature and Literary Theory* (London: Methuen, 1984) for the application of linguistic deconstruction to the reading of a black text; Frederic Jameson (1981) on the limits of the socio-critique; and Hayden White (1973) on the structuralist concept of ideological "emplotment". For a thorough trashing of the "Law of the Father" and its attendant questions of legitimacy, Shoshana Felman, *Literature and Psycho-analysis: The Question of Reading: Otherwise* (Baltimore: Johns Hopkins University Press, 1980) which appeared in preliminary form as issue 55/56 of *Yale French Studies* (1977), giving the first English translation of Lacan's (in)famous "Hamlet".

11. Maryse Condé, *Heremakhonon* (Washington, D.C.: Three Continents Press, 1982, first published 1976).

12. Chauvet's works include *Fille d'Haiti* (Fasquelle, 1954); *La danse sur le volcan* (Plon, 1957); *Amour, colère et folie* (Gallimard, 1968).

13. Clarisse Zimra, "Versions of Things Past in Contemporary Caribbean Women Writers," *Explorations: Essays in Honor of Frank J. Jones* (Washington, D.C.: The American Press, 1986), pp. 227-252.

14. Maryse Condé, *Segou I: Les Murailles de Terre.* (Laffont, 1984); *Segou II: La Terre en miettes* (1985). Condé's other creative works beside *Heremakhonon* (1976) include *Dieu nous l'a donne* (Oswald, 1972); *Un Saison a Rihata* (Editions Robert Laffont, 1981).

15. Indeed a choice example was even entitled *Le Negre comme il y a peu de blancs* by Joseph Levallée (1789).

16. Michèle Lacrosil's works include: *Sapotille et le serin d'argile* (Gallimard, 1960); *Cajou* (Gallimard, 1961); *Demain Jab-Herma* (Gallimard, 1967).

17. Maryse Condé, *La Parole des femmes* (L'Harmattan, 1979).

18. Harold Bloom, *The Anxiety of Influence* (London: Oxford University Press, 1973).

19. Claudine Hermann, *Les Voleuses de Langue* (Libraire des Femmes, 1976). Little work of substance has been done on Lacrosil. I have just come across Michael Dash's review of Beverly Ormerod's *An Introduction to the French Caribbean Novel* (London: Heinemann, 1985) in *Caribbean Contact* (October, 1985). Given the quality of Ormerod's previous work on Caribbean fiction, this may be the most useful introduction to Lacrosil yet. On the subject of the inscription of the female in the Caribbean text, see Lemuel Johnson's essay "A-beng: (Re)Calling the Body In(to) Question" in this volume.

20. Aphra Behn, *The History of Oroonoko; or The Royal Slave* (London: Batlesworth and Clay, 1688, 1722).

21. Léon-François Hoffman, *Le Nègre Romantique: Personnage littéraire et obsession collective* (Payot, 1973).

22. Edward D. Seeber, "Oroonoko in France in the XVIIIth Century," *PMLA* (December, 1936).

23. Victor Hugo, *Bug-Jargal* (Club francais du livre, 1967, first published 1819).

24. Prosper Merimee, *Tamango* (Garnier, 1967, first published 1829).

25. Victor Séjour, "Moeurs coloniales: Le Mulâtre, *Revue des colonies* (March 1837).

26. Alexandre Dumas, *Georges* (Folio, 1974, first published 1843).

27. For instance, the 1838 letter to the editor of *La Revue des colonies*, quoted by Hoffman (p. 245) intended to rectify other literary matters but which ended thus "c'est ce que je desire qu'on sache parfaitement, non seulement en France, mais partout ou je compte freres de race et des amis de couleur." [This is what I wish known, not only in France but everywhere I have race brothers and friends of color.] On the matter of *Georges*, Hoffman's introduction to the Folio edition is invaluable.

28. Hoffman, pp. 238-241.

29. Paul Feval, *Le Mendiant Noir*, Roux et Cassanet, 1847.

30. Gustave de Beaumont, *Marie, ou l'esclavage aux Etats-Unis* (Gosselin, 1834; 1836).

31. Clarisse Zimra, "Négritude in the Feminine Mode; The Case of Martinique and Guadeloupe," *Journal of Ethnic Studies*, 12:1 (Spring, 1984), pp. 53-77.

32. Mayotte Capecia, *Je suis martiniquaise* (Paris: Correa, 1948); *La Négresse blanche* (Paris: Correa, 1950).

33. Point made in several conversations with Leonard Sainville (Paris, 1976) and Marie-Magdeleine Carbet (Paris, 1976, 1978). But since we are dealing with the image projected by Capecia's novels and their reception among the French public, whether she was their true author or not is not germane.

34. Having sided against the Petain loyalists who had sailed into their ports, the former colonies of Martinique and Guadeloupe and their dependencies received "departmental" territorial status in 1947, for good services rendered, a situation touted as the beginning of self-sufficiency. Without too much hindsight gloating, we can see that quite the reverse has been true.

35. See my articles: "Patterns of Liberation in Contemporary Women Writers" in *L'Esprit Createur* XVII:2 (1977), pp. 103-114, (Special issue on the Caribbean); "A Woman's Place: Cross-Sexual Perceptions in Race Relations; The Case of Mayotte Capecia and Abdoulaye Sadji," in *Folio*, Special issue on Women Writers (August, 1978), pp. 174-192.

36. Frantz Fanon, *Peau noire, masques blancs* (Paris: Seuil, 1952). Translated as *Black Skins, White Masks* (New York: Grove, 1968).

37. (Seuil, 1964).

38. Re-inventing the wheel, Fritz Gracchus, *Les lieux de la mere dans les societes afro-americaines* (Editions Caribeennes, 1980) has just claimed all over again that the black man was done in with the lustful cooperation of his own "black bitches".

39. Michele Lacrosil's works include *Sapotille et le serin d'argile* (Gallimard, 1960); *Cajou* (Gallimard, 1961); *Demain Jab-Herma* (Gallimard, 1967).

40. Marie-Magdeleine Carbet, *Au péril de ta joie* (Sherbrooke: Lemeac, 1972).

41. The Caribbean text, of course, is always more "blank" for a French reader. The difficult question of intended audience aside, the fact remains that both Chauvet and Lacrosil (and Condé) were first published and read in Paris. They are, therefore, "French-oriented", much in the way their societies are "male-oriented".

42. Oruno Lara, *La Guadeloupe dans l'histoire* (L'Harmattan, 1921, 1979).

43. Germain Saint-Ruf, *L'Epopée Delgrès: La Guadeloupe sous la révolution française* (L'Harmattan, 1977).

44. Jacques Derrida, "White Mythology: Metaphor in the Text of Philosophy", in *New Literary History* 6:1 (1974), pp. 5-74.

45. Rewriting Shakespeare, the only original text which Cesaire kept has to do with Caliban's claim of legitimacy (i.e. history) to Prospero's island through his own witch-mother. Césaire's *Tempest* inscribes back into the collective memory the original matrifocal order. Lamming's 1972 novel, *Water With Berries* (London: Longmans) covers the same epistemological ground.

46. Simone Schwarz-Bart, *Pluie et vent sur Télumée-Miracle* (Seuil, 1972). Trans. as *The Bridge of Beyond* by Barbara Bray (London: Heinemann, 1982); *Ti-Jean l'Horizon*, trans. Barbara Bray, (Seuil, 1979).

47. Daniel Maximin, *L'Isole soleil* (Seuil, 1981).

PART TWO
Constricting and Expanding Spaces: Women in Caribbean Literature

This section, "Constricting and Expanding Spaces: Women in Caribbean Literature," focuses on the representation of women in Caribbean Literature. Included here are several essays which re-evaluate selected male writers from the point of view of the feminist/womanist debate. The list of writers examined here is by no means comprehensive. George Lamming, Wilson Harris, Roy Heath, Garcia Marquez are the primary writers to whom single papers are devoted. In some ways, this may be considered a limited presentation since crucial writers like Edward Brathwaite, Derek Walcott, Vidia Naipaul, and Earl Lovelace (looking only at the Anglophone Caribbean) are not represented in this section. Our own acceptance of this limitation had to do with the scope of this collection and its commitment to be truly representative of the Caribbean, the availability of work given our time constraints and standards, and the general inability in volumes of this sort to include everything.

A further consideration was that since feminist criticism of Caribbean literature has been predominantly "re-vision" with its examination of female images, writers like Walcott and Naipaul have already been subjected to this type of analysis. (See bibliography for essays by Salick, McWatt, Fido, Griffith, Pyne-Timothy for example). The subject has by no means been exhausted in Caribbean criticism. The depiction of women in works by writers like Samuel Selvon or Joseph Zobel, for example, has not yet been undertaken. There is a lot more work to be done and we look forward to seeing these studies soon. Secondly, our approach was to present a range of writers and those whose works have not been the subject of similar inquiry. Thirdly, since this is the first collection of its kind, we are hoping that it will generate some debate and future, wider examinations of Caribbean literature.

One of the major contributions to this discussion of the female in Caribbean literature is a broad, historical examination of Jamaican literature, covering many writers. Included also, is the first major examination of women in one of the most well-known Caribbean writers, George Lamming of Barbados. There is also coverage of oral tradition, a vital aspect of any discussion of [Caribbean] literature in general. This inclusion we believe is a major advance in Caribbean criticism. It is the first critical attempt, that we know, to present analyses of oral and written discourse as integrated aspects of the criticism of Caribbean literature.

The first essay, " 'Woman Is A Nation . . . ' Women in Caribbean Oral Literature" by Carole Boyce Davies, examines three genres: proverbs, folktales and calypso, finding that the depiction of women in these forms is unsurprisingly overwhelmingly negative and, in fact, that women are shown as either consistently evil and despicable, or malleable and unthinking. The category of heroic women, more reflective of social reality remains under-represented in the available oral literature.

The movement of the Jamaican woman from "independent spirit" to "heavy load," from the post-emancipation, turn of the century period to the immediate pre-independence era is the concern of Rhonda Cobham in "Women in Jamaican Literature 1900-1950." The essay relentlessly pursues this shifting depiction from the early works of de Lisser and his contemporaries, through Claude McKay and Basil McFarlane, pausing for a closer look at Una Marson and moving to George Campbell, Vera Bell, Vic Reid and finally Louise Bennett. It becomes clear that African women in the immediate post-slavery period exerted a great deal of independence and freedom which later was constricted by the bourgeois, colonial/Victorian notion of what woman's proper place ought to be.

Women in Guyanese literature are represented in the discussion of Mark McWatt, "Wives and Other Victims: Women in the Novels of Roy A.K. Heath." McWatt takes issue, though, with the persistent portrayal of the "woman as victim" in the entire corpus of Heath: "It is as though Heath were focusing relentlessly on only half of what Wilson Harris calls 'the victor victim statis' ", he says. Moreover, as McWatt further reveals, while man seems to have the possibility of fleeing the oppressiveness of society, woman, in Heath's world, remains trapped, waiting, dependent on man.

Joyce Stewart, in "Woman as Life or 'Spirit of Place': Wilson Harris's Companions of the Day and Night,*" contends that in Harris's complex, symbolic, mythological world, women are portrayed as abstractions or presences. Some substantial, though not enough, work has already been done on Harris, perhaps one of the most challenging of Caribbean writers, but this study of one text, clearly demonstrates that there is much more to be done. Much of the challenge of reading Harris resides in the density of his mythological scaffolding. A feminist approach to this writer will no doubt help to make his work more accessible.*

The work of Gabriel Garcia Marquez is examined in Amparo Marmolejo McWatt's "Victim and Accuser: Contradictory Roles of Women in Gabriel Garcia Marquez's Cronica de Una Muerte Anunciada.*" The essay begins with the bold statement that "only those not familiar with Gabriel Garcia Marquez's works will question his right to be considered a Caribbean writer." The author thus firmly locates Garcia Marquez as Caribbean writer and thus validates our encompassing of the Hispanic and Francophone with the Anglophone traditions in the discussion of Caribbean literature. Her essay reveals how the Latin "machismo," culture, as explored by Garcia Marquez, regulates and constricts women's lives and how his heroine Angela rebels against her society and its traditions.*

"Woman Is A Nation…"
Women in Caribbean
Oral Literature[1]

Carole Boyce Davies

*(This essay is dedicated to the pioneering work
of Prof. J.D. Elder)*

The words "Woman is a Nation…," by themselves, convey a sense of
solidity and empowerment. The reality is different for Caribbean oral
literature, however, for the words that complete the line of this folksong are
"… grumble too much." So while on one hand there is the identification of
a structured, female, political sphere, coupled with the derogatory completing words, the subordination of this "nation" of women becomes clear.
This tendency towards the "putting a woman in her place" seems to
dominate the entire Caribbean oral tradition. The oral literature—which
provides a tremendous amount of material for the study of the development
of traditional and contemporary attitudes to women, and of women towards
themselves—consistently portrays the woman, in the worst extreme, as an
evil, despicable entity or at best, as a malleable, unthinking, submerged
personnage. In at least three categories of the earliest material available—
the proverb, the folktale and the major song form, the calypso—woman's
image is almost uniformly negative.

Caribbean oral literature is still virtually untapped as a cultural/critical
source.[2] Also, almost no close literary examination of the available
Caribbean oral literature has been done, and of course the study of women
in Caribbean oral literature has been of peripheral interest in the critical
discussion so far. J.D. Elder's 1968 study of male/female conflict in
calypso[3], and William Aho's follow-up, 1981 study[4], a tentative attempt by
Esther le Gendre[5], a chapter in Keith Warner's study of the calypso as oral

literature[6], and Maureen Warner-Lewis's study of women in Kumina[7] are the primary works among the few pieces that present women at all. But oral literature, it has been demonstrated, is important for the mere fact that it is the literature of the majority of the people. In addition, the oral tradition not only provides an important bridge to the study of narrative strategies in written form, but it is elemental in the definition of a group's aesthetic and psycho-social dynamics.

This essay explores the image of women in three genres of Caribbean oral literature: the proverb, the folktale, the calypso. It makes a concerted attempt to utilize the early collections, like those of Cundall and Izett, Beckwith and Clews-Parsons and others which lie virtually untouched and unexamined in remote corners of libraries. These collections, while they reveal some clear ethnocentric biases on the part of collectors,[8] can provide us with material for some important conclusions about how women were/are perceived at specific historical periods. The essay further looks substantially at calypso, examining the depiction of women both in politically conscious calypsonians, like the earlier Atilla or the contemporary Black Stalin, as well as in the tradition, generally.

I. Proverbial Wisdom and Womankind

In the introduction to her collection of *Jamaican Proverbs*, Martha Warren Beckwith says in passing, while discussing certain thematic and structural features of the proverbs: "Women are seldom mentioned, and then generally to belittle" (p. 6). Examination of a number of proverb collections supports this early Beckwith statement. There is a preponderance of proverbs that deal with "man" and although man is often used in the generic sense of mankind (e.g. "man sleep in fowl house, but fowl house not him bed" MJH #67),[9] there is a definite masculine character to proverbs and these refer to and define the experiences of the male gender (human and animal) as normative. This is distinct and separate from how women are introduced in proverbial wisdom. It may be fair to say that the proverb is one of the most important sources for documentation of bias against the female. Because they each contain, in capsule, a core of folk wisdom and are used as codes-of-conduct or quick reference points of ancestral wisdom in diverse human situations, this contention has to be taken seriously. Moreover, since there is a whole genre of Caribbean proverbs which are Biblical reinterpre-tations[10] and since it is already well established that the *Bible* contains much which establishes the subordination of women, biblically-derived proverbs therefore lend extra weight to the generally male-focused thrust of many proverbs. So, not only are negative stereotypes of women thus both easily communicated and perpetuated, they are most difficult to demystify. As folk wisdom, they come biblically endorsed, or coded with the ancestral sanction, viz: "As de ole people used to say" or "My grandfather/

grandmother always would say." This legitimacy renders them almost unchallengeable.

The question of the gender of the informant or user, it seems to me, would be appropriately raised here. Although in the Caribbean, women are known to use proverbs with as much facility as men (while in many African societies, for example, proverbs are the preserve of the men, and elders at that), a survey of several collections reveals that informants tend always to be men. In the Beckwith case, although much of the material came from young women students who were asked to write out lists of "old sayings" when they went home on vacation, the principal informant for interpreting these proverbs was one male informant of established reputation in the community and the reader has no way of knowing the gender of original reference source of the proverb. Herskovits, for the Trinidad collection, had one informant, but no gender is identified. And definitely, the Clews-Parsons collections have an overwhelmingly male informant listing. This is not to suggest that women informants would necessarily use proverbs that were generally positive to women, for proverbial wisdom, although male defined and reinforcing patriarchal concepts, tends to become community property. But the gender of the informant may have a lot to do with the context and the kind of material at his/her disposal. Ropo Sekoni, Nigerian scholar of oral literature,[11] argues convincingly that there is usually a more revolutionary "under text" in oral literature which rarely comes to surface; the one that is recorded quite often meets the needs of foreign recorders and of maintaining the status quo of the society at large. These unfortunately become the canonized texts. It may be that this thesis can be applied to Caribbean proverbs about women as to Caribbean oral literature in general. For the proverbs about women in many collections are all questionably negative. Because of our historical distance from the time of collection, it may be difficult to prove this thesis here and no attempt is being made to do so.

My examination of available proverbs reveals that the women who most frequently populate proverbs can be placed in three categories: mothers, old women and women in general. (All numbers refer to list appended). Mothers, human or animal, seem to appear most commonly as self sacrificing, downtrodden but struggling: "Many a mauger cow you see a common a bull mamma" (#44. See also #10, 12, 14, 34, 39, 42, 45, 50, 67). All of these communicate the tedium of motherhood, but also the overwhelming concern and worry for the child's well-being. The proverbs about mothers tend to be the most positive ones of women, communicating a certain heroism. But, there is also a sense of fatalism and self-destructiveness as in "Las' pickney always kill mumma" (#42), and callousness and ingratitude on the part of children as in "Daag say him radder him momma dead dan fe mek mos' night rain ketch him" (#29) or "If you kill pickney gi' momma, momma won't eat, but if you kill momma gi' pickney, pickney wi' eat" (#49). Mothers are portrayed as resourceful but vulnerable. Overall, the images of mothers are mixed in value: positive in the sense of maternal dedication, negative in the sense of the stereotyping and limiting of the female.

Women beyond the childbearing years, though, tend to be seen as more commonly evil. There are a few proverbs which suggest the actual value that the female elder has in the community as in "If you no see mammy, you seek grandy" (#40) and "Ole 'ooman day a fireside, ram goat can't hang himself" (#47). But the majority of proverbs seem to belittle older women and accord them nothing of the honor that African societies do and that sociologists suggest was retained to a large degree in the Caribbean. "Go a cross pass, you see ole 'ooman, no trouble him" (#32) suggests she might be doing obeah and "If you want fe tas'e old 'ooman pepper-pot, (s)cratch ole 'ooman back" (#41) communicates a certain disrespect as does "Trouble make old woman trot" (#54). The Surinamese proverb "You can hide your grandmother but not her cough" (#73) perhaps comes closest to communicating the message of ancestry, resilience and determination that senior women represent in Caribbean society and, as well, the overall conflicting portrayal of senior women.

It must be remembered that a proverb comes to life in its application and one particular proverb may have validity in a number of contexts. Some, for example, which do not contain any textual reference to gender may yet be applied to underline or comment on a certain aspect of female behavior. On the other hand, several of the proverbs which do mention women may not be talking literally about women but, instead, commenting on other human situations. A proverb is, by definition, metaphorical, we know. However, in their rhetorical use of women they set several notions of inequality. I would argue, though, that there are two levels of apprehension: the one which conveys the metaphorical meaning, the other the literal level in which women are objectified.

For the most part, women in proverbs are quite specifically referred to in terms of their relative beauty or ugliness, deceitfulness or faithfulness, service to men or disrespect for them. The proverb "Beautiful woman, beautiful trouble" (#16), for example is consistent with the "deadly to the male" motif. But note the proverb "Ugly woman does give yo' you' dinner on time" (#1) and what that means in terms of wife selection and service to the male. "Obeah man daughter always pretty" (#46) also plays with the concept of beauty and relative connection to the male. Two other proverbs in this category: "Hard push mek mulatto woman keep saddler shop" (#35) and "Brown man wife eat cockroach in a corner" (#20) stress the notion of color, gender and privilege. In the case of the mulatto women, resourcefulness takes the place of relying on favors but what is communicated on the literal level of the proverb is that a beautiful woman is now reduced to having to work. The other (#20) is compatible with proverb No. 1 in high-lighting the notion about what physical features contribute to the making of a good wife. In this case the brown man's wife accepts abuse or distress.

Many proverbs say that women are not to be trusted: "Woman two face like star apple leaf" (#64), "Woman mout and fowl are one" (#60), "Woman no wan fe dance him say him frock short" (#61). Others that she is primarily after material gain: "Basket full, 'ooman laugh" (#16), "Ant follow fat, ooman follow man" (#15) and "Woman an' wood, an' woman an' water, an' woman an' money never quarrell" (#59). Some firmly establish woman as domestic drudge: "Good wife better than estate wagon" (#33) or "Man build the house but woman mek the home" (#43) which has to do with familial roles. But abuse is sanctioned in "Driber fum (flog) his wife fus" (#31). Inequality in male and female children is set in "Marry yo daughter when you can, yo' son when you please" (#65). And in marriage "Two man rat can't live in one hole (#2) enforces the subservience of wives.

It can easily be argued that some proverbs about women which may seem negative in one context, may be seen in a different application as extolling women's ability to endure and survive. For example, "Snake say if him no hol' up him head, female tek him tie wood" (#52) or "When Guinea fowl cry him say, 'woman no fe play' " (#55) or "When man hab trouble 'ooman tek it mek laugh" (#56) or "rum mek man walk an' stagger; rum mek woman si down an' consider" (#51) comment on woman's serious approach to problems.

One can therefore draw a number of conclusions in examining proverbs which deal with women. It is important to reiterate that proverbs utilize any number of references to make moral, philosophical statements on human nature and society in general. The extent to which proverbs deal negatively with males and male experience may warrant analysis for comparative purposes or to further validate or refute my argument here that the proverbial depiction of women and women's lives seems to be fixed, stereotyped and limited. Sonia Lee finds that in African oral literature, "[t]here are no proverbs which admonish man in terms of his particular sex. The moral is directed either to a particular fault such as a lack of judgment and is aimed at a particular [and deviant type of] man."[12] In proverbs criticizing the female, however, she finds that the female species as a whole is attacked and not human weakness in general. The available material reveals that Caribbean proverbs seem to display the same tendency.

II. The Demonic or Foolish Female in the Folktale

The critique of the foibles of human, particularly female, behavior, is starkly revealed in the narrative forms. A survey of the Clews-Parsons collection, *Folklore of the Antilles, French and English*, reveals a wide range of female characters—witch-spouses, gullible wives, dumb wives, unfaithful wives, wicked mothers, murderous mothers, cruel old women (hags, sorceresses, witches, soucouyants), vulnerable daughters, and almost no heroic women. The closest one gets to heroism on the part of women is in the devil's daughter cycle in which one of the devil's daughters, usually the youngest, aids the hero in solving the riddle and defeating her father and consequently allowing her to escape the household. This particular act, much in line with the female function in the heroic mono-myth, has, as its prize, marriage to the hero and does not offer any alterna-tive options to the daughter. The cycle of stories in which the devil is defeated can be read as the struggle against the domineering and patriarchal male, the devil then being the European landed aristocracy (as in Derek Walcott's characterization in *Ti Jean and His Brothers*). In this way the daughter's act is clearly subversive or revolutionary, transferring the devil's power to the poor Jack. Yet the female is never heroic herself but always facilitates the hero's success so that she can escape.

Legendary stories seem the only avenue for the portrayal of heroic women. Darryl Dance in *Folklore from Contemporary Jamaicans*[13] reveals one story, "Nine-Finger Jack," which ascribes some heroism to Captain Morgan's daughters:

> Well the first man that captured Port Royal, his daughter—he had a daughter by a Black woman—and he were a white man. You know being here and alone and all that, he see here now is Black people to move with. He go with a Black woman, and get that girl. *She were a hero.* For imagine (you don't know the distance) but from St. Elizabeth she walk on foot, not on the road, in the bushes, to Morant Bay, where she meet man they call Nine-Finger Jack, you see. And for life-saving sake, she gots to decide that she fall in love with Nine-Finger Jack . . . (p. 97)

The narrative ends with the girl, who remains unnamed in the story, selecting a heroic death with Nine-Finger Jack rather than capitulating to her father.

Few stories of Nanny the Maroon ever surface in collections,[14] which validates the thesis about the more revolutionary stories being submerged. (Michelle Cliff in *Abeng* deliberately includes the Nanny story in her novel). Definitely there are no women of Nanny's stature in the Clews-Parsons collection. Elder's title story "Ma Rose Point" in his 1972 collection of the same name is one of the few of this female heroic genre recorded. In an act of resistance and heroism, Ma Rose, who in this story from Tobago, is described as a Scotch Ibo slave woman, bit into the neck of a white slave driver who was whipping her mercilessly and chewed into his windpipe, not releasing until she had totally destroyed him. Then, rather than accept punishment, she jumped over a cliff and into the sea, giving her name to a local landmark and becoming the type of enduring spirit of place in the local mythology. Even today, Elder reports, fishermen, on rough nights, pour libations into the ocean near Ma Rose Point. This category of strong, heroic women, more reflective of cultural reality remains the exception in folk tales. Instead, the easy narratives of fowl and cockroach and foolish women become the constantly circulated canonical texts.

For this reason, it is necessary to place into context the La Belle Dame Sans Merci cycle which is popularly recycled in places like Guyana and Trinidad, Grenada and the Eastern Caribbean. There is very little reference to this type in the Clews Parsons collection. Instead she is one in a wide range of types. Yet, *La diablesse, Soucouyant* or Old Higue and Mammy Water constantly make the round of collections. In the Elder collection, *Ma Rose Point*, though, there is only one reference to Mammy Water and in it she is not hostile until bothered. In Roy Heath's "The Function of Myth," Alfred Codallo's "The Spirits of Trinidad", and M.P. Alladin's "Folk Stories of Trinidad",[15] *soucouyant* continuously makes her appearance. Esther Le Gendre's question is strongly to the point: "Is it mere chance that some of the most terrifying creatures that haunt our folktales are women?" (p. 37).

The woman in these tales is invariably deadly to the male. The *soucouyant* is an old woman who sucks the blood of unsuspecting victims at night; the *diablesse* is a woman with a cloven hoof who attends dances and lures an unsuspecting suitor to his destruction; Mammy Water promises riches but lures her victims to live with her below the sea and death by drowning is the ultimate result or she is *mamma d'l'eau*, a hag with snakes in her hair. Peter Minshall's creative reinterpretation of this mythology in his carnival presentation "The River,"[16] is therefore commendable. In his portrayal River Mama performs a therapeutic role and is closer to *Yemanja*[17], a beneficient mother at war with Man Crab (technology, the phallic male principle, rape, aggression and the like).

The argument that these evil woman tales are a manifestation of society's fear has some validity. "White lady," a vampirish presence, is clearly symbolic of the society's response to slavery and racism. But the other evil woman tales are problematic. On one hand, they show women having the upper hand. Yet this "fear woman" idea is one aspect of an overall mythology which excludes women from shrines in some cultures, linked in a way to an aboriginal fear of female fertility.[18] The woman therefore becomes the symbolic evil as Eve, Circe, etc. These tales of La Belle Dame Sans Mercie, however, (Stith-Thompson *Motif Index*. Type G264) have an international provenience and may underscore the global perspective on women. One may argue that they are residues of an earlier mythological corpus of political and ritual power. As they exist in the corpus now, however, they serve to reaffirm constantly a 'woman as dangerous' mythology.

Few male characters in the folk literature share this demonic characterization. Lagahou is tame by comparison. The Devil's characterization is one of power.

In a number of tales in which women are ordinary people, the category of mothers poses the most ambiguity. There are several stories in which mothers are sold by children (CP #44) for material gain. These may symbolically refer to slavery and the destruction of families, but along with the tales in which Stupid John scalds his mother to death (CP #217) there may be a kind of Freudian suggestion of the removal of maternal dominance of young men in female-headed households. There are several tales of suffering mothers whose primary role is to tell their sons that there is nothing else to eat and to send them off, on their own, to seek their fortunes—other examples of maternal separation from sons. But the cruel mothers who kill children, give them to the devil, try to drown them for not doing chores or so that they can get more food are the obverse of the cultural norm and may serve to reaffirm the importance of self-sacrificing, positive mothers which the society at large upholds. In this way, they serve as warnings to mothers who have less than maternal intentions.

Zora Neale Hurston reports an interesting story of sororal triumph in which the mother rescues the daughter. The devil had used trickery and stolen the daughter during the mother's absence.

When the girl mother come she didn't meet her daughter and she start crying. And the berries whut she bring for her daughter all grow on her and she went peeping through de bushes growing on her body looking for her daughter. And when she went through, her daughter servant was at the sea taking bath and she hear the mother sing and she went and tell the mistress and she mistress say: "Can you say a word whut you hear the lady sing?"

And she sing: "Angelecky mammy die-er."

De lady daughter run. She say it was her mother. She pull all de vine off her mother and she clean her all up. And she leave her mother there till she went home and pick up all her things and de devil had a witch rooster. And the rooster tell her: "You wash out your bloomers and sprinkle the water all over the grass." If she don't do dat de devil smell all their foot track and know where they went. So she did dat and they left. After they be gone, de devil come home. She had carried de devil rooster wid her.

Usually when de devil come home he crow and de rooster crow back. But when he come dat dat he rooster don't crow, so he couldn't follow, 'cause she done took his witch rooster.

Biddy, biddy bend
My story is end. [19]

Variants of this tale appear in other collections but not with as positive a resolution. In one tale, though, the girl destroys the animal and returns home herself.

The chosen suitor tales, in which a usually gullible girl makes a disastrous choice of mate, usually based on his external appearance or conspicuous display of wealth are interesting cautionary tales. In each case the girl has to be rescued by a very junior brother who knew all along that this man was a devil, a pig or a snake as the case might be. In the case of the snake-husband stories, the phallic symbolism associated with animal conveys other meanings. In one of the stories, the girls is licked all over by the snake in preparation for his swallowing her. She keeps on singing, forcing the snake to stop and respond to her until she is finally rescued. The chosen suitor tales are well known, globally, for instructing girls in the careful selection of mates or at least in the acceptance of parental mate selection.

The trickster cycle of tales, especially the Anancy stories, are notorious for their depiction of the subservience of women at the same time that it makes points about wit, the weak over the strong and so on. Anancy's wife usually goes along with his exploits or shares in the rewards of her husband's trickery. But, perhaps the most blatant example of the trickster turning on his own and showing the extent to which a professional trickster can go is "Nancy Fools His Wife",[20] Anancy tries to eat all his son's food while the mother is out, leaving him to care for the child. The story further shows how Anancy, who has lost part of his arm while trying to steal from a neighbour and is at home recuperating, desires to eat his wife's only two pigs and her entire field of yam. He pretends to be very ill, sends her for the doctor, then takes a back route and pretends he is the doctor, advising that the only way Anancy will recover is if she feeds him the pigs and yams. The storyteller says: "Dese pigs an' de field a yam was all dat dis woman had. But she fool." Believing that this is the only way to save Anancy's life, the wife feeds him one pig the first day and the other the next. The story ends: "Nancy eat every bit a dis an' not gi' his wife an' Little Toukouma any. Dat's de way Anancy fool his wife. Finish."

Is this a cautionary tale? I would argue that while it further extends the trickster cycle of tales, it can be read as a caution to the would-be female dupe to be wary when dealing with a known trickster. And, rather than applauding Anancy's guile, one feels instead a certain sadness for this woman who is so used. In analyzing the trickster tales it may be important to ask: Who is the recipient of this trickery? Is the gain communal or individual satisfaction? There is rare triumph over Anancy's greed, though, in "The Dancing Granny,"[21] who "danced in the morning. She danced at noon and her dancing helped her outwit greedy Ananse."

The collected folktales, as I have described, are short on tales of heroic women, and loaded with those who are trapped, foolish and otherwise not in charge. Yet, there are cruel fathers as there are cruel mothers. The tendency, however is to present the male with much more power and control than the female. Since Caribbean folklore is in many ways a composite of a number of other folk traditions (African, Indian, European, Amerindian, for example), in a sense it has inherited many of the unsavory Old World attitudes to perceiving women.

III. Women in Calypso

I'm sure that you must have read Kipling's tale
The female of the specie is worse than the male (repeat couplet)
That's in tune with the opinion universally
I heard a calypso band was singing lustily
They say—man santapee bad bad
But woman santapee more than bad.
They say—Man santapee bad bad
But woman centipede more than bad.

So goes the opening verse of a calypso by Atilla (c. 1930) in which he sets out to prove that the female of species is much more to be feared than the male. For evidence he cites Biblical stories which describe woman as instrumental in the demise of an otherwise upright man: e.g. Eve in the case of Adam, Delilah in the case of Sampson. Then he turns to nature and points out that in many cases the female carries more hostility or venom (the cobra), or disease (the anopheles mosquito), and of course, the centipede (poison). Significantly, the impetus for this condemnation of women takes its point of departure from the British colonialist writer Rudyard Kipling. Another similar calypso "Man Smart, Woman Smarter" (c. 1937) takes a similar thematic approach as does "Loving Woman is a Waste of Time," sung by the Duke of Iron in which he tells how ungrateful women are to men who give them nothing but love. The parallel between this sentiment and several proverbs about women is striking. Note for example Proverb No. 1 "Ugly woman does give yo' you' food on time" and the Roaring Lion's "Ugly Woman":

An ugly woman gives you your meals on time
And will always try to console your mind
At night when you lie on your cosy bed
She will coax, caress you and scratch your head
And she will never shame her husband at all
By exhibiting herself with Peter and Paul
So from a logical point of view
Always marry a woman uglier than you.
If you want to be happy and live a king's life
Never make a pretty woman your wife
All you've got to do is just what I say

And you'll always be happy and gay
From a logical point of view
Always marry a woman uglier than you.[22]

The uniformity of meaning between this calypso and the proverb raises some interesting questions of transferral of themes across forms: of how certain aphorisms enter the proverbial pool and the reverse. The calypso, it has already been conclusively proven has a very important function in Caribbean society as commentary on social patterns, public and private issues, local political and international affairs. But it also has become obvious that the calypso exhibits a larger proportion of aggression toward women and overt misogyny than do other forms of oral literature. So that while folktales and proverbs are biased against women, endorse female subordination or malign women, the calypso is much more explicit and direct in its hostility to women.

Several researchers have identified this aspect of calypso. Elder (1968) was the first to explore this male/female conflict pointing out the various forms of male aggression and hostility to females in calypso and the possible socio-psychological reasons, rooted in slavery and colonial demoralisation of the male, to explain this ongoing attack. Merle Hodge in her essay "The Shadow of the Whip"[23] furthers this aspect of the Elder thesis. She contends, in part, that hostile male behavior to women, in general, including public verbal abuse and humiliation which the calypso also pursues, is in many ways an emulation and transferral of the hostility the male learned within the plantation system. Keith Warner's very important chapter "Male/Female Interplay in Calypso" in his *Kaiso. The Trinidad Calypso* (pp. 95-111) examines the various thematic and structural movements in what Gordon Rohlehr calls the "phallic calypso."[24] The term Warner uses, "interplay," however, fails to carry the weight of his discussion of this chapter's important material, as there can be little "interplay" with so few women calypsonians to at least represent a woman's point of view. Elma Reyes newspaper articles such as "Woman's Image in Calypso"[25] pursues this issue with conviction.

Themes pertaining to male ego maintenance, sexual prowess and conquest have been present throughout the calypso's history. In part, this may derive from the calypso's generic relationship to African topical songs in which the risque, the obscene and the erotic has a fundamental place. Whether there is the same level of abuse in the African topical song that one finds in the calypso perhaps needs more specific examination. But calypso-singing grew to national and international recognition, as a male-dominated arena with *chantwells* who later became known as calypsonians and stick-fighting men becoming themselves prime examples of male sexuality and prowess. The early stage names spell out this phallic tendency: The Roaring Lion, the Duke of Iron. So calypsonians became local heroes, monarchs, champions in the absence of more substantial heroes. The most renowned of the singers embody these ideas and maintain this *machismo* by singing of actual accounts of seduction of the female, or of having many women seek their company, or their unfailing virility.

As the Mighty Radio sang circa 1937,

> They can't find a lover like me again
> I'm the only lover in Port-of-Spain
> Fifty women now supporting me
> And all of them belonging to high society

The reference to 'high society' is important here. For in many ways the calypso has been one of the few avenues for criticism of class domination, imperialism and colonialism. So some kind of vicarious satisfaction is obtained through the singer's claim to have found a way of besting the middle and upper classes. The difficulty is that the conquest is attained symbolically by subordination of the women.

Early calypsoes and those of the Golden Era of Calypso (1944's-1960's) perhaps set this verbal abuse theme. (Elder in his study found the latter to be the high point and notes that there was a diminution of such abuse in the late 60's with the thrust towards independence.) The calypsoes of "The Golden Era" often accused women of maintaining relationships with men only for material reward, a theme consistent with Proverbs #15, 57, 59. The following calypso (c. 1937) by the Mighty Tiger illustrates that point:

> If you have money and things going nice
> Any woman would call you honey and spice
> If you can't give her a dress and a new pair of shoes
> She'll say she have no uses for you
> When you try to caress her she'll tell you stop
> For she can't take love to a butcher shop
> I'm sure that you will agree that it's true
> If you have no money, dog better than you.[26]

This "No Money No Love" theme as the Mighty Sparrow identifies it in his calypso so titled, appears with fair frequency throughout the tradition. It is a given that the male here is singing of poverty, unemployment, lack of resources to play the role of provider that bourgeois society says he should. A song with this content is clearly a lament about man's inadequacy, but it is also a concomitant enshrining of the notion that women are only after material gain, even though in reality there are enough documented cases of women supporting men and they themselves sing about it. The 1960s' calypso by the Mighty Conqueror, with the same mood and theme, similarly concretizes this stereotyped view of the female:

When a poor man see a woman and he like she bad
He have to lie like if he mad
And tell she he have car, house and property
But if he play honest and tell she the truth
He can't conquer the old brute
Not he, because he brokes and he ain't have no money

Chorus
Money they love
Money they crave
Money will send them to they grave
But not me
They can't spend me money
Chest jumping, behind bumping
They walking in saga thing
Just because they want to spend me dollars etc.

So when you see a pretty woman
With a ugly ugly man
It ain't hard to understand
That he have the things that make she happy
She don't care what she friends and them say about she
Once she gettin the currency
The man could be ugly like sin
But the money is damn good looking.[27]

Is this a calypso about male poverty or female greed? Clearly, to the listener, the "deadly to the male" motif is reinforced. The woman is directly implicated in, at times even made responsible for, the man's unfortunate situation. Her alleged excessive material needs become a direct challenge, embarrassment and finally source of hostility to the man who is unable to fulfill them.

As a direct corollary to the "No Money; No Love" theme, the songs about prostitution, unfaithfulness and mistaken paternity expose further the condemnation. (Keith Warner's chapter examines a number of songs in this genre.) The increased obscenity and lewdness in calypso which accompanied the American occupation of bases in Trinidad is of central importance here. Reports are that prostitution was rampant because of "Yankee" soldiers with money to spend on willing women; this kindled feelings of neglect in the local male. In perhaps the most important response to this corruption of values and the symbolic meaning of "Yankee money," calypsoes ridiculed women in general and jeered at those who were left with babies whose color attested to the white male/black female liaison. The famous "Brown Skin Girl, Stay Home and Mind Baby . . . I going away in a sailing boat and if I don't come back, throw way the damn baby" (or "stay

home and mind baby," alternatively) has to be viewed as a response to this
situation.[28] In fact the verses of the calypso clearly indicate this as did "Rum
and Coca Cola" and the notion of working for the Yankee dollar, which is
another song about prostitution. The following 1948 calypso gives an
account of the situation

> Happy days are here again
> Yankees back in Port-of-Spain
> Trouble in the land with the hustlers
> Trinidad is the headquarters
> Old and young rouge up they face
> Puttin' they bodies in the proper place
> Only waiting for some Yankee
> To join in matrimony
>
> When the first batch of Yankees
> Landed in La Trinity
> You didn't need glasses to see
> Some of the girls had white babies
> Some didn't know the child daddy
> But now they leave them to weep and pine
> With a fatherless child to mind.[29]

And in a similar vein, the calypso "Chinese Children Calling Me Daddy" is
a comment on the growing control of the merchant sector by the Chinese
and their occasional sexual relationships with some black women. Prostitution, however it was regarded morally, led also to obvious independence in
some women who, through it, controlled their own resources. The relative
independence and prosperity of some women became an issue in songs
which lamented the difficulty men faced in making a living:

> I'm such a crooked lad
> I can't get work in Trinidad
> I've tried all technological screws
> I can't eliminate the discrepancy
> Which misfortune brings to my family
> My indescribable unsuccessfulness . . .[30]

Caresser (c. 1937)

Quevedo points out that up through the 1950s, King Radio became the
"choice of the masses" with songs reflecting the people's desires for basic
necessities like electricity and by projecting himself as having upper class
women supporting him in style. (pp. 102-103). The point that has to be
raised with hindsight is the extent to which the achievement of parity is

acquired through political struggle as opposed to men's easy, pimp-like pandering to women for support. [Atilla reports that it was not until ten years after that Radio would sing a calypso directly on a political theme.] Because there is always a surface truth to claims about some women achieving financial success through prostitution, the reality that the majority of women were not engaged in prostitution but were still struggling to feed children is usually masked. Additionally, there is always a tendency on the part of male writers/singers to glamorize prostitution and not show the oppressiveness and dangers inherent in having to sell one's body. It is no wonder, then, that the Mighty Sparrow was able to capture the Calypso King title in 1956 with the famous "Jean and Dinah," a song of Caribbean male dominance over the woman and the reclamation of his "rightful place" from the Yankee usurper. Thus,

> It's the glamour boys again
> We are going to rule Port-of-Spain
> No more Yankees to spoil the fete
> Dorothy have to *take what she get* . . .
>
> Jean and Dinah, Rosita and Clementina
> 'Round the corner posing
> Bet you life is something they selling
> And if you catch them broken
> You can get it *all for nothing*
> Don't make a row
> The Yankees gone and Sparrow take over now.[31]

Elder has already pointed out that home and family life and relationships with women were the most consistent sources of stress for the male. Throughout the history of the calypso this sexual war was waged in an ongoing attempt to put the independent Caribbean female in her place. In his survey of calypso over the period 1850-1960, Elder found that pejorative accounts and derision of women accounted for the highest percentage of songs. Conquest tales, fear of female magic, disgust at women seemed to supplant attack on the real sources of power and authority in the society. In Elder's words,

> Today it is difficult to find songs in which male authoritarian-figures like oppressive governors, policemen, priests, etc. are openly castigated. Has the male figure ceased to cause stress in the Trinidad society? The folksongs in Stages A, B, C above (the periods closest to slavery) are dominated by episodes in which bad-men, tie-pins, unjust judges, wizards etc. are the heroes. But these songs were composed in the pioneer days of Trinidad social history. Nowadays, the characters of

that type have almost lost all of their glamour and their glory. The folksingers have turned their castigation and ridicule upon other human figures—the females in the society. Forty-one females out of the fifty-nine referents occupy the non-endorsement cell [in the Table II]. All through the stages of the calypso evolution, the female moves progressively over the years, as a subject of male preoccupation as much as the victim of his condemnation.[32]

Among the women admonished, young women accounted for the highest percentage of referents. Wives and old women were fairly popular negative referents; mothers were the only positive referents. This is clearly consistent with the findings of our examination of proverbs above.

The reverence afforded mothers represents the only oasis in this desert of verbal aggression and hostility. The Mighty Sparrow, who in many ways is the flagbearer for the various contemporary movements in calypso, has been able to get by unchallenged with the most demeaning characterizations of women: "She was an ole wreck and a nastiness"; "You worse than a dog Theresa." [Keith Warner ably discussed many of the contours of Sparrow's depiction of women: Phallic aggression, the attack on female personal hygiene, covert and overt references to genitalia, endorsement of physical abuse, rejection of paternity are all prominent aspects of the Sparrow corpus of songs (pp. 99-101)] Yet, Sparrow can sing on occasion beautiful ballads of mother's love and the perils a man would face if he does not acknowledge and fulfill his filial obligations to his mother. This tendency to show reverence to the mother in the face of tremendous hostility to all other women is consistent with Latin American *machismo*.[33] The individual man's mother is the virginal saint while all other women are disdained for their weakness in succumbing to male pressure and are therefore no more than bitches.

It is perhaps significant to point out that the collection of calypsoes by Atilla reveals that a calypsonian who has his sights set on social and political inequities concentrates only a small portion of his attention on female denigration.[34] Of the forty-five Atilla calypsoes in his collection, only eight deal with the male/female issue at all. And of that eight only two ("Treat 'Em Rough" and "Man Santapee") can be defined as negative to women. Two others are calypso duets on issues of female sensuality: "Young Girls Touch" with Beginner and "Mamaguy" with Lion. Of the other four, "Guardian Beauty Contest" is decidedly a positive and still relevant critique of the beauty contest syndrome especially when the European/Nordic conception of what a beautiful woman looks like is still the norm.[35] His "Woman Is Not the Weaker Sex" is clearly a feminist calypso. But, "Treat 'Em Rough," though he was careful to make it clear that he was against abuse, still argued for mastery of women: "Teach them, yes, who is the master/Don't be swayed by sentimentality/Or they'll tell their friends that you are a sissy..." Its chorus though clinches the message and leaves enough room for interpretation by the listener:

> Every now and then turn them down
> They'll love you long and they'll love you strong
> You must be robust, you must be tough
> Don't throw no punches but treat 'em rough (p. 154)

Overall, though, the Atilla calypsoes on women all fit into a pattern of making a case that women are not stereotypically fragile. At the same time, though, they communicate that women are often "deadly to the male".

Elder's study was published in 1968 and concluded somewhat optimistically that male verbal aggression was on the wane. William Aho's examination "Sex Conflict in Trinidad Calypsoes 1969-1979" shows, however, that for the period under consideration, among all calypsoes concerned with women, almost for every year examined, they are 100% negative to women. Warner's study, demonstrates that the pattern continues well into the 1980's. He adds additionally, the definition of beautiful and ugly based on Euro-centric concepts, the highlighting of physical defects and in Rohelehr's terms the constant phallic self-projection. A case is made that a fear of female infidelity seems to constantly underlie this projection of female nastiness and there are a few ballads about rejection which are often seen as not being true calypso.

But there are some interesting breakthroughs and the vanguard calypsonians with their undying interest in social and political themes, continue, much like Atilla did earlier, to wage an independent struggle for calypso to be true to its history of social and political commentary. Importantly, their targets are not women. Instead, they identify the true source of oppression as the socio-political system which does not function in the interest of the majority. Valentino is on record as condemning calypsoes of female abuse. Chalkdust sings a calypso parodying the type of sexually-explicit calypso that gets the carnival judges' and the people's attention. Black Stalin's 1985 "Dorothy" performs an impressive feat by using the form and language of the sexual calypso to accomplish the reverse. He says directly that his calypso about "big, fat Dorothy" will have to wait until after all his political themes are exhausted which means also when the world is a more humane place. Barbadian calypsonian Adonijah's recent calypso about women sums up the contemporary thrust:

> I stop and wonder, when I hear Kaiso,
> How dem kaisoman does treat dey woman so.
> Dey singing 'bout woman in a party

Winin' up she bumsie,
While somebody jam she,
Is this all they have to show?

Kaisoman, please lend me your ear,
This is something I think you all should hear
In your search for wealth, in your quest for fame,
Never ever cause your woman shame.

Chorus:
To me she is mother of our children, bearer of life,
My queen, my friend, my woman, my wife.
Come walk with me, hand in hand,
We will guide the youth unto the promised land.

Woman helped to build this nation,
She helped it advance,
So when you sing, please give her a chance.
She cut the cane to make the sugar, make parts for computer,
Is doctor, teacher, lawyer.
She can do more than dance
It takes two, if we must go on,
Without woman, the human race is gone.
Jah Jah know what I sing is true,
Is time to give the woman her due.[36]

This is clearly a 1980s calypso of recognition with an additional influence of Rastafarianism which holds woman as queen, or somewhat patriarchally as daughter. Yet, created with the benefit of the international woman's movement, it is a recognition of the inequity and a need for new modes of perceiving and depicting women in this form of oral literature.

Female Participation and the Question of Performance and Meaning

Calypso underscores the thesis that the gender of singers/performers/oral artists, along with political consciousness, is crucial in transmitting certain attitudes about women. Elder had pointed out as early as 1968, before the growing body of feminist criticism, that "the almost total absence of women as singers of calypsoes in Trinidad is of great significance for the social scientist investigating male/female conflict". Keith Warner in his subsequent study, which unfortunately made no reference to the earlier Elder work on this subject, nevertheless makes several points about this important subject. One is that female calypsonians operate out of a position of numerical and psychological weakness. But although they too draw on the male prowess/female satisfaction theme, they make no attempt to degrade the male, or project themselves as a group. Even more significant, a number of the calypsoes sung by the women have male composers.

In recent years, though, a more pronounced female presence in the calypso singing field was championed by Calypso Rose who became the first female calypso monarch (the title had to be changed from king to monarch to indicate the female presence). Calypso Rose had to survive through rumours of lesbianism and for years had a distinctly androgynous appearance; her stage performance was similar to some male calypsonians like the Mighty Sparrow, including dancing and projecting the microphone as phallus. Singing songs of men, sex and satisfaction: "A man is a man etc.," Rose ably competed with her male peers.

A few younger women singers have now entered the calypso singing field, including the junior calypso competitions in Trinidad. And this becomes crucial, for one sees a definite female response to themes like physical abuse, for example. Singing Francine in a decidedly popular calypso among women, urged women to leave abusive relationships:

> Dog does run away
> Cat does run away
> Child does run away when you treating them bad
> Fowl does run away
> Don't sit down and grieve
> Woman put two wheels on your heels
> Get out![37]

This theme of woman's response to abuse is not new but seems to accompany woman's participation in the tradition. Much like the songs of Afro-American women blues singers, for example, a song quoted by Elma Reyes of Lady Iere in the 1950's laments male aggression:

> You cook dey food
> And you wash dey clothes
> When dey come home vex
> Dey does give you blows[38]

The difference is that whereas in the early calypso there is mainly a recounting of the abuse, in the Singing Francine and Singing Diane calypso "Ah Done Wid Dat" (1980) there is a clear statement about woman's rejection of subservience and abuse. There is even a more progressive statement by one singer—Calypso Stella of Guyana—about men and women sharing family domestic and childrearing responsibility.[39]

The significance of this contemporary female participation, however, attains more importance when one considers the thesis that early in the history of calypso, there was substantial involvement by women. "Mitto

Sampson's Calypso Legends"[40] reveals a female *chantwell*, named Bodicea
in the 19th century. Bodicea is described as a woman who participated in
the same activities as the men in her group: singing, stick-fighting, drinking.
Similarly, Donald Hill has significant documentation, in an unpublished
study of calypso, that there was significant female participation and that
calypso could have been originally a woman's song. To further support the
female calypsonian argument, Atilla's collection includes two calypsoes
from Guadeloupe and Martinique with a decidedly female focus. One of
them, dating from 1906, he explicitly ascribes to a female "kaisonian",
Sophie Mataloney (the same Lady Mataloni to which Donald Hill refers).
Translated from the French patois it is rendered:

> Pauline my child don't worry
> Is the best thing that could happen to you
> Two months' rent you have to pay
> And you can't find your child's father
> Her belly drop drop low, low, low
> Her belly low, low
> And she can't find her child's father (pp. 15-16)

Another one, recorded as pre-1890's by Atilla, is an exploration of the
woman's side of the prostitution charge:

> A year ago I was a girl
> A young little girl in my mother's house
> This year I am a woman
> Fighting to make a living for myself
> Aie Aie
> Shake your body and I will give you
> Naughty girl
> Shake your body and I will give you
> I will give you, I will give you
> A hefty mister (p. 14)

How that early female presence in calypso became reduced to back-up
singing or dancing is worthy of much further examination. It seems,
however, to underscore the phallic developments in calypso and the
circumscribing of woman's space. Even in Lady Iere's case, her participation
in the 1950's seems to have been mitigated by the presence of her husband,
Lord Iere with whom she sometimes sang calypso duets. The available texts
reveal that women's issues such as abandonment and abuse were part of the
thematic configuration of the calypso from the earliest but that this female
presence has remained submerged over the years and up to the present.

One significant development in the creation, performance and reception of calypso, however, is the mass involvement of women in carnival and the singing by them of calypso on the streets. Recent calypsoes like "A Deputy Essential" and "Sorf Man" sung originally by men reflect underlying preoccupation with the male projection. But when re-sung by women, however, they are no longer songs of male privilege but challenges. A calypso like "Sorf Man" which is a rejection of any feminine characteristics in the male—tenderness etc. (read homosexuality) sung by women, forces the man to live up to his phallic projection. But it also carries with it some homophobia and a serious message about the permanence of the phallic in the consciousness of the community. The voicing by women is an interesting piece of dramatic irony for the woman too proclaims her right to have a deputy (lover on the side) which was the male calypsonian's original statement of privilege.[41]

Conclusion

One can observe how, as it relates to the Afro-Caribbean woman, the presentation of women remains constant in the three forms discussed. It is worth reiterating that some of these themes of calypso have remarkable concurrence with the proverb. The ugly woman references, the portrayal of mothers, the condemnation of females, the stereotyping of women as chasers after material wealth or prostitutes at heart and the lack of portrayal of any heroism in women. While the folktale provides a wide selection of female characters, there is a preponderance of the negative and again a lack of female integrity and heroism. In reality, the Caribbean woman's strength and ambition to radically improve her social and economic situation became a direct threat to male superiority. So, in much of the oral literature studied she became "deadly to the male".

I submit therefore that a distinct economic factor and a concomitant need to "put women in their place" are the most important factors determining the treatment of women in the oral literature. As the evidence reveals, the same post-slavery serial polygamy and "friending" relationships which freed man from family obligations, also allowed the woman freedom to develop her finances independently. The result was an increasingly self-sufficient female who could discard those men who contributed nothing. This more than the surface jealousy of unfaithfulness threatened the male ego.

This is most easily validated in the calypso than in the other forms as in this tradition it is easier to date, to identify authorship. The folktale and proverb categories by their very definition have no traceable sources. In calypsoes of the colonial period, therefore, we see the male's struggle to reassert his manhood via the phallic, by attacking the woman who seemed to him to be most directly responsible for his powerlessness. Relative

political and economic progress has removed some of the underlying threats
to the male ego. The struggle for political independence saw the rise of black
male leaders who automatically symbolized black male dominance.
Expulsion of colonial masters and of the "Yankee" presence, further
secured the black male position.

Today and with the influence of the international women's movement,
and of calypsonians more committed to political issues, it is more difficult
for calypso to concentrate on female harassment. Targets are instead
ineffective political leaders, corruption and economic exploitation, the
South African situation.[42] Yet there remains a residue of that earlier
tradition which still makes it entertaining for the male to tell about women
being publicly demeaned or abused. (This is not to condemn the erotic. A
crucial aspect of calypso is its spicy sensuality. What is offensive though is
the abuse or denigration which often accompanies the erotic.) Vanguard
calypsonians have long recognized what and who the real enemies are. But
even there, chatising the female can appear as in Chalkdust's calypso on
identity, "They Ain't See Africa At All"[43] which begins by blaming black
women for ignoring African identification, then moves to black people in
general and certain patterns of avoidance but never identifies black men as
participating in this tendency.

For me, the most positive example is a calypso by Executor, quoted by
Atilla, on the issue of abandonment of a child. It starts off by questioning the
meaning of such a seemingly callous act, graphically describing the child's
sad state. It immediately moves to apportioning equal blame to the father
of the child and then concludes with the agony which the mother must feel
about having committed such an act of cruelty.

> What can a mother mean
> What heartless cruelty is seen
> On the Savannah freezing with cold
> To leave a baby only three days old
> On a rubbish heap
>
> . . .
>
> (3rd Verse)
> But on the mother we must not put all the blame
> Or to her name ascribe all the shame
> For perhaps the man for whom the child she bore
> Was heartless and cruel to the core
> So fearing the wrath of her family
> And the scorn of society
> She placed her own little baby
> To die in misery. (pp. 25-26)

In the folktale tradition, as the Darryl Dance's work reveals, more contemporary collection efforts will open up interesting room for comparing tales at specific historical junctures. For example, a look at the folk literature of post-revolutionary Grenada may provide interesting material. Some earlier individual tales, not in the major collections, as the ones collected earlier by Zora Neale Hurston, need to become part of the canon of Caribbean oral literature. A feminist re-vision of Caribbean oral literature opens a wide range of possibilities for future research.

NOTES

1. This paper is a revised and extended version of a paper titled "Deadly to the Male. Female Images in Caribbean Oral Literature" which was presented at the National Women's Studies Association Conference, Storrs, Connecticut, June, 1981.

2. Since the early collections at the turn of the century and publications like the Elsie-Clews Parsons collections, *Folklore of the Antilles French and English* (New York: American Folklore Society, 3 vols.: 1933, 1936, 1943); *Folklore of Andros Island, Bahamas* (American Folklore Society, 1918); Martha Warren Beckwith, *Jamaica Anansi Stories* (American Folklore Society, 1924), *Jamaica Folklore* (American Folklore Society, 1928); *Jamaica Proverbs* (Negro Universities Press, 1925) and the work of Zora Neale Hurston (1920s-1930s not available in one collection) comparable, ongoing collection projects of the same magnitude have not surfaced. But there have been notable efforts over the years: The work of Daniel Crowley, Roger Abrahams and J.D. Elder (1950s-70s), Edward Brathwaite's research on *Folklore of the Slaves in Jamaica* (1970), Darryl Dance's recent collection (1985) and Louise Bennett's untiring attempts to keep folklore in the popular and literary consciousness. The Szwed-Abrahams bibliography, *Afro-American Folk Culture: An Annotated Bibliography from North, Central and South America and the West Indies*, 2 pts. (New York: Publications of the American Folklore Society, 1978) reveals an interesting assortment of collections and critical discussion which can serve as basis for closer analysis of material available. Work being done in Jamaica by Olive Lewin, Laura Tanna and others is also commendable.

3. Jacob Delworth Elder, "The Male/Female Conflict in Calypso," *Caribbean Quarterly* 14:3 (September, 1968): 23-41.

4. William Aho, "Sex Conflict in Trinidad Calypsoes 1969-1979," *Revista/ Review Interamericana* 11:2 (Spring, 1981): 76-81.

5. Esther Le Gendre, "A Startling New Way to Look at Fairytales," *People* (Trinidad), August, 1975: 37.

6. "Male/Female Interplay in Calypso," Keith Q. Warner, *Kaiso. A Study of the Trinidad Calypso as Oral Tradition* (Washington, D.C.: Three Continents Press, 1982): 95-111.

188 Out of the Kumbla

7. Maureen Warner-Lewis, "The Nkuyu: Spirit Messengers of the Kumina,"
   Savacou (Kingston) 13(Gemini, 1977): 57-78.
8. For example, early collectors like Anderson and Cundall (1910) talk of "showing the class of thought that appeals to the negro mind" (p. 11). For further
   discussion, Roger D. Abrahams, "British West Indies Proverbs and Proverb
   Collections" in *Proverbium* 19(1968): 239-243. It is well known that
   European-American collectors bring to the field their own cultural baggage
   (often racist and sexist) which precludes penetrating to levels of discourse
   which the people save for more appropriate usage.
9. Refers to the Melville J. Herskovits collection, "Trinidad Proverbs," *Journal
   of American Folklore* 59(July-September, 1945): 195-207. For others see
   appended list of proverbs.
10. H.B. Meikle, "Tobago Villagers in the Mirror of Dialect", *Caribbean
    Quarterly* 4:2 (December, 1955): 154+. See also J.J. Thomas, *The Theory
    and Practice of Creole Grammar*, (London: New Beacon Books, Ltd., 1969
    rpt.) for a discussion of the formation of Afro-Caribbean creole folklore and
    language.
11. Discussion at African Literature Association Conference (Michigan, April,
    1986) of thesis developed in book on The Trickster in Nigerian Oral Literature
    (forthcoming).
12. "The Image of the Woman in the African Folktale From the Sub-Saharan
    Francophone Area," *Yale French Studies* 53(1976): 19-29.
13. Darryl C. Dance, *Folklore from Contemporary Jamaicans* (Knoxville: The
    University of Tennessee Press, 1985).
14. See Kenneth Bilby and Filomina Chioma Steady, "Black Women and
    Survival: A Maroon Case" in *The Black Woman Cross-culturally* ed. by
    Filomina Steady (Cambridge, Mass.: Schenckman Publishing Company,
    Inc., 1981): 451-467 for further discussion of some of the Nanny legends.
15. Roy Heath, "The Function of Myth" In *Caribbean Essays* ed. by Andrew
    Salkey, (London: Evans Brothers, 1973): 86-94; Alfred Codallo, "The Spirits
    of Trinidad" *The Guardian* (Trinidad—Independence supplement) August
    26th, 1962, p. 111; M.P. Alladin, *Folk Stories and Legends of Trinidad*, n.p.,
    1968, pp. 22-3; Jacob Delworth Elder, *Ma Rose Point. An Anthology of Rare
    and Strange Legends and Myths from Trinidad and Tobago* (Port-of Spain,
    National Cultural Council, 1972).
16. Text of Peter Minshall, "Callaloo an De Crab" (Trinidad) n.p. 1984.
17. There is a definite distinction to be made between Mammy Water and River
    Mama, *Yemanja*, derived from the Yoruba *Yemoja*, with the same meaning.
    See also H.B. Meikle, "Mermaids and Fairymaids or Water Gods and
    Goddesses of Tobago." *Caribbean Quarterly*, 5:2(February, 1958): 103-107.
18. The beautiful but deadly white woman of mythic proportions recurs in Afro-
    American oral and written literature. See James Weldon Johnson's "The
    White Witch" quoted in Barksdale and Kinnamon, *Black Writers of America*,
    (New York: Macmillan, 1972). See Elaine Savory Fido's discussion in her
    essay "Okigbo's Labyrinths and the Concept of Igbo Attitudes to the Female
    Principle" in *Ngambika, Studies of Women in African Literature*, ed. Davies
    and Graves (Trenton, NJ: Africa World Press, 1986): 223-239 and Merlin
    Stone, *When God Was a Woman* (New York: Dial Press, 1976).

19. Zora Hurston, "Dance Songs and Tales from the Bahamas" *Journal of American Folklore* 43(1930): 309-310. The informant for this tale was a ten year old girl, Edith Knowles.
20. John H. Johnson, "Folk-lore from Antigua, British West Indies", *Journal of American Folklore* 34(1921): 48-50. Informant was George Edwards and his wife.
21. Ashley Bryan, (reteller and illustrator), *The Dancing Granny* (New York: Atheneum, 1977).
22. Quoted in Raymond Quevedo, Atilla's *Kaiso. A Short History of Trinidad Calypso*, ed. by Errol Hill (Trinidad: University of the West Indies, Extra Mural Studies, 1983): 50. This calypso entered American popular culture being recorded subsequently by several singers.
23. Merle Hodge, "The Shadow of the Whip: A Comment on Male/Female Relationships in the Caribbean," in *Is Massay Day Dead*, ed. Orde Coombs (New York: Anchor Books, 1974): 111-118.
24. Gordon Rohlehr, "Sparrow and the Language of Calypso," *Savacou*, 2 (September, 1970): 94.
25. "Women's Image in Calypso" *Trinidad Express*, 19 February 1980 quoted in "Images of Women in Calypso in the Caribbean" *International Women's Tribune Centre Newsletter* 14, 1st quarter, 1981): 8. See also her "What's in a Name? Quite a Lot for the Calypsonians" *Trinidad Express*, February, 1979 and "Women Hold Their Own in Calypso World" *Trinidad Express*, February, 1979.
26. William C. White, "The Calypso Singers" *Esquire*, September, 1937: 46, 106. Entire song quoted in Atilla's *Kaiso*, pp. 102-103.
27. Personal recollection of lyrics.
28. Atilla suggests that this calypso originated in the Grenadines within the context of male travel for employment purposes between the islands but was reinterpreted to convey the usual Yankee abandonment of local women (pp. 18-19).
29. Mitto Sampson, "Old and New Calypsoes Compared" *The Guardian* (Trinidad) January 30, 1945: p. 6 contains some texts.
30. Quoted in "The Calypso Singers", p. 106.
31. Personal recollection of lyrics. But see also Francisco Slinger (The Mighty Sparrow), *120 Calypsoes to Remember* (Port-of-Spain, Trinidad: Caribbean Music Co., 1954). My emphasis.
32. Elder, "The Male/Female Conflict in Calypso", p. 28.
33. Carlos Fuentes, *Tiempo Mexicano* (Mexico, 1978), p. 26.
34. See Appendix I "A Selection of Atilla's Calypsoes" pp. 114-160.
35. While there have been some breakthroughs as in Janelle Commissiong, Miss Trinidad and Tobago 1977, winning the Miss Universe title, the tendency towards European criteria of the beautiful remains. This calypso makes a nice link with the Mighty Sparrow's caricature of Vanessa Williams, the first black woman to win the Miss America title and the scandal of the explicitly sexual photographs which led to the end of her reign. For Sparrow, Miss America's demise becomes symbolic of American decadence as well as the Euro-American fostering of the beauty pageant mentality and the revealing of the female body for public viewing and judging.
36. Mimeographed sheet of lyrics, 1985.

37. Personal recollection. See Keith Warner, *Kaiso* and Elma Reyes, "Women's Image in Calypso" (fn. 25) for fuller quotation of various verses.
38. Quoted in Elma Reyes, "Images of Women in Calypso in the Caribbean", Reyes, p. 8. (See fn. 19 above).
39. Ibid.

> Now me and me man have a policy
> To suit we self and we family
> He does bathe the children
> Comb their hair
> Take them to school without affair
> I doing the cooking, he doing the washing
> And if I baking,
> He helping out with the ironing.

40. Andrew Pearse ed. "Mitto Sampson on Calypso Legends of the Nineteenth Century." *Caribbean Quarterly*, 4:3&4 (March-June, 1956): 260-261.
41. Two "soucouyant" calypsoes were recorded in 1985. Interestingly the negative characteristics of this vampiric, mythological character became sexual metaphor. Lemuel Johnson, elsewhere in this collection quotes a Roy Boyke essay which further discusses this issue.
42. See my "The Politics of African Identification in Trinidad Calypso", *Studies in Popular Culture*, 8:2(1985): 77-94.
43. Lyrics on dust jacket of album "Chalkdust. Kaiso With Dignity" (Trinidad: RH Productions, Inc. 1984).

APPENDIX I
CARIBBEAN PROVERBS ON WOMEN

1. Ugly woman does give yo' you' dinner on time.
2. Two man (smart) rats cyan (can't) live in the same hole.
3. Mo' than one bitch name Liz.
4. No true bride without love.
5. One-one blow kill ol' cow.
6. A good "live-with" better than a bad marriage.
7. Don' put yo' han' in a empty corn jar (don't marry a pauper).
8. If child ain' got mudda, it cyan (can't) cry fo' bub (breast).
9. Pumpkin nevah bear calabash.
10. When hen scratch, she use two feet fe tell the chicken, 'If y'u no fin' i ya, y'u fin' i yonder'.
11. "See me" is one t'ing, but "Come live wid me," dat's another.
12. Hen never mash her pickney hot.
13. Ol' hen make good soup.
14. Mama pickney cry never done.
15. Ant follow fat, 'ooman follow man. ("Ant follow fat" in Bates collection).
16. Basket full, 'ooman laugh.
17. Beautiful 'ooman, beautiful trouble.
18. If you wan' to get at de gal, sweeten de ol' lady mouth.
19. Bad hen don' cackle.
20. Brown man wife eat cockroach in a corner.
21. You axe me fo' court you, you mus axe me mudder too.
22. When cow can' get water fe wash him pickney face, him tek him tongue.
23. Man hab cow, him look fe milk.
24. Two mistress cyan' govern one house.
25. Mudder sen' out pickney; she hands cold, but she heart not cold.
26. If you lub (love) de cow you mus' lub de calf.
27. So cow a grow, so him nose-hole a open.
28. Callalu a swear fe ole 'ooman, ole 'ooman a swear fe callalu".
29. Daag (Dog) say him rader (rather) him momma dead dan fe mek mos' night rain ketch him.
30. Distress mek 'ooman ketch darg-flea two time.
31. Driber fum his wife fus'. (A driver flogs his own wife first).
32. Go a cross pass (crossroad), you see ole 'ooman, no trouble him. (i.e. she might be a sorceress setting obeah and may do you mischief too).
33. Good wife better dan estate wagon.
34. Mumma a ashes better dan mumma a grave.
35. Hard push mek mulatto woman keep saddler shop. (Hard times make even the privileged work for support).
36. If man been know, him neber would a plant nyam in (s)tranger 'ooman grung.
37. If nightingale sing too much, him kill him mumma.
38. Drummer wife neber keep goat kin.
39. [If you] go a pickney mumma yard, you sure fe get something.
40. If you no see mammy, you seek grandy.

41. If you want fe tas'e ole 'ooman pepper-pot, (s)cratch ole 'ooman back.
42. Las' pickney always kill mumma.
43. Man build de house but 'ooman mek de home.
44. Many a mauger (lean) cow you see a common [is] bull mamma.
45. Me know who me mammy/daddy neber know.
46. Obeah man daughter always pretty.
47. Ole 'ooman day a fireside, ram goat can't hang himself.
48. Perfec' 'ooman and white John Crow scarce.
49. If you kill pickney (child) gi' momma, momma won't eat, but if you kill momma gi' pickney, pickey wi' eat.
50. Pig ask him mamma say wha' mek him mout' long so; him say "A no mind, me pickney' dat somet[h]ing mek me long so wi' mek fe you long so too.
51. Rum mek man walk an' 'tagger; rum mek 'ooman si' down an' consider.
52. Snake say if him no hol' up him head, female tek him tie wood.
53. When dainty lady lib well him tek pin fe nyam pea (extreme affectation often comes with good living).
54. Trouble mek ole woman trot.
55. When Guinea fowl cry, him say "woman no fe play" ("don't play with woman").
56. When man hab trouble, 'ooman tek it mek laugh.
57. When money done, love done.
58. When ole 'ooman want fe cry, him say smoke get in him yeye.
59. Woman an' wood, an' woman an' water, an' woman an' money never quarrel.
60. Woman mout' and fowl a one. (i.e. both ungrateful)
61. (W)ooman no wan' fe dance him say him frock short.
62. Market house a 'ooman court-house.
63. (W)ooman rain neber done.
64. (W)ooman two face like a 'tar apple leaf. (The leaf has a white surface and a dark underside).
65. Marry yo daughter when you can, son when you please.
66. Me mamma dead, it no hurt me like juju water wet me a marnin' time.
67. Pickney run wil' when him mumma dead.
68. When you see an old lady run, don't asky why, just run too.
69. Women's breasts are never too heavy for her.
70. You can have several wives but only one mother.
71. A child that doesn't listen to its mother ends up in the snake's mouth.
72. Grandmother's breast is for all children.
73. You can hide your old [grand]mother but not her cough.
75. A woman is like half a cent—you can't make her any smaller.
76. Mother dead, greetings finished.
77. A donkey has children so it can rest its back.

SOURCES

The proverbs above were culled from the following collections: Anderson, Izett and Cundall, Frank. *Jamaica Negro Proverbs*. Ireland: Irish University Press, 1972 (1st pub. 1910); Armbrister, Hilda. "Proverbs from Abaco, Bahamas" *Journal of American Folklore* 30(1917): 274; Bates, William C. "Creole Folk-lore from Jamaica." *Journal of American Folk-Lore* 9(1896): 38-42; Beckwith, Martha Warren. *Jamaican Proverbs*. New York: Negro Universities Press, 1970 (rpt. 1925; Blackman, Margot. "Barbadian Proverbs", *Bim* 11:43 (July, 1966): 158-163; Cleary, Al. *Jamaican Proverbs*. Kingston: Bainbuster, 1971; Courlander, Harold. "Some Haitian Proverbs" in *A Treasury of Afro-American Folklore*. New York: Crown Publishers, Inc., 1976; Crooks, Kenneth B.M. "Forty Jamaican Proverbs." *Journal of Negro History*. 18:1 (January, 1963): 132-143; Herskovits, Melville J. "Trinidad Proverbs ("Old Time Saying So")". *Journal of American Folklore*. 59(July-September, 1945): 195-207; Parsons, Elsie Clews. "Proverbs" in *Folk-Lore of the Antilles, French and English*. 26 (Part III) (1943): 457-487; Schipper, Mineke. "Proverbs" [The Caribbean]. *Unheard Words. Women and Literature in Africa, the Arab World, Asia, the Caribbean and Latin America*. London: Allison & Busby, 1984: 166-167.

Women in Jamaican Literature 1900-1950

Rhonda Cobham

The independent spirit of the black Jamaican woman caught the attention of colonial authorities very early in Jamaican modern history. Christian missionaries, for example, identified the woman's independence, along with the persistence of the practice of obeah, as the two major obstacles in the path of "civilising" the former slaves. Writing in 1899, W.P. Livingstone, then editor of *The Gleaner* states:

> The women earned their livelihood, and lived their own robust, independent life. There was no wooing and winning, and permanent companionship thereafter; they gave themselves to each other as they pleased. To be married was, to a woman, to become a slave, and slavery, with its dark associations, was a yet a stone's throw in the past. She preferred her freedom, and accepted its greater responsibilities with equanimity. It was this unconscious sensuality which proved the greatest obstacle to the development of their character.[1]

Even his strong moral censure of such a lifestyle cannot disguise Livingstone's grudging admiration of the independent spirit of the black women who chose to live in this way. His ambivalence, however, is characteristic of educated opinion in Jamaica at the turn of the century: On the one hand the woman's independence and resourcefulness was admired and often contrasted favourable with the apparent "laziness" of the black man; on the other hand, her sexual freedom was seen as something dangerous and evil, which it was in the interest of the dominant culture to suppress.

It is a historical fact that Jamaican women in the early part of the 20th century were, in comparison to their counterparts in post-Victorian England, both economically and sexually independent. Their lifestyle had its origins in the social patterns evolved during slavery. Rhoda Reddock makes the point that in the West Indies, slave-owners had a vested interest in disregarding the traditional, secondary role of women in the productive sector.[2] Women worked as hard as men and were punished as severely, and in many cases they proved better able to withstand their harsh working conditions. Stable sexual unions were discouraged on the estates, as these made it difficult for individual slaves to be sold or transferred. Female slaves were encouraged not to have children as this reduced the woman's effectiveness at the workplace, and it was considered cheaper to import a full-grown slave than to have to bear the expense of feeding and clothing a slave child until it was old enough to work. These attitudes to family life were sometimes internalised by many slave women. As in the United States, there was a high rate of reported infanticide and abortion among slave mothers, some of whom claimed they would rather kill their children than sentence them to a life of slavery.

After 1838, the pattern persisted with only minor changes. Though Emancipation produced a wave of marriages and a greater desire on the part of black women to have and rear children, both single and married women remained financially independent of men, accepting money for the upkeep of their children when it was available but continuing to work as well. Favoured jobs tended to be forms of self-employment such as higglers, cultivators and seamstresses. When these could not be had, most women sought jobs which were extensions of their domestic roles—as domestic servants, task workers on estates or, toward the end of the 19th century, as factory hands in the small light-industry sector which had just come into existence, making straw goods or cigarettes.

By the turn of the century, when Livingstone was writing, a well established female lifestyle had emerged among the second generation of free black women. In her analysis of the life histories of a sample of such women, Erna Brodber summarises their distinctive traits as "emotional accommodation" (the ability to adjust without trauma to changing domestic units and/or relationships), independence and authority. She sees their preferred self-image as that of the successful small business woman, living independently within a closely knit community, or at the head of an extended family which could include her own children as well as those of other relations or even strangers, and in which the presence of a joint permanent male head of household was often not desirable and by no means essential.[3] Between 1881 and 1921 this pattern was reinforced by the migration of thousands of Jamaican men overseas as contract labourers to Panama or Central America because of high rates of unemployment at home. Since the majority of lower-class women were self-employed or worked as domestics, the shortage of wage labour locally did not affect them in the same ways that it did men. It was not uncommon for women to be the sole visible financial mainstay of the family as their men often worked far away, returning home only between contracts to idle away the time until another job opportunity arose. This arrangement preserved for the women a degree of sexual and economic independence, and men who did not maintain contact with their families while they were employed abroad were likely to find on their return that they had been displaced by someone else in their women's affections.

Given this background, it is not difficult to surmise how the Jamaican lower-class woman came to be perceived by the rest of the society as both unusually industrious and sexually promiscuous. The bourgeois role of the woman as wife and mother, removed from the productive sector of the economy and bound, by economic necessity rather than choice, to sexual fidelity to a single man and a subsidiary role within the family unit, was not only unattractive but also totally impractical for the Jamaican lower-class woman, who had to find a mate within a constantly shifting and often unemployed male population. Such a lifestyle was considered unchaste and sinful by the dominant culture, in which the Victorian ideal of family life was revered. On the other hand, it was these very women who appeared to work hardest, and hard work was perhaps only second to chastity in the Victorian hierarchy of values. For the dominant culture these traits presented a contradiction in terms, and it is not overstating the case to say that nearly all Jamaican creative writing before 1920 is taken up with trying to resolve this contradiction in a way that would rationalise the position of women in Jamaican society in terms acceptable to the dominant culture.

The preoccupation with the position of women can be gauged by the titles of some of the early novels which made use of social realism: *Becka's Buckra Baby* (1904), *Marguerite, the Story of the Earthquake* (1907), *One Brown Girl* (1909), *Jane's Career* (1913) and *Susan Proudleigh* (1915). Each of these novels describes the life-style of at least one lower-class female character, and the woman's independent spirit is generally played off against her sexual and economic needs. Dialect poems and poems about the lower class tend also to use female *personae* more often than male ones and in both types of poem the woman is usually presented in her working environment rather than a domestic setting. One of the earliest poems on record of this nature is "Tropica's" "Nana," a tribute to the faithful, old-fashioned Nanny to whom, during slavery, the upbringing of the master's children was almost wholly entrusted. "Tropica" evades the necessity of dealing with the servant's personal economic situation or sexual proclivities by concentrating exclusively on Nana's usefulness to her employers. The poem opens with an *"ubi sunt"* motif in which the poet recalls Nana as a relic of an age in which all things were better and more enjoyable:

> With the old homes are going
> The nanas of past days,

With their gay stiff-starched kerchiefs
And dear old-fashioned ways;
They disappeared with other
Quaint things too good to last;
And seldom now we see them
Those pictures of the past!

Throughout the poem there is a tendency to equate the faithful servant with quaint *things* rather than with people, and to see her as an object within a particular setting. This is summed up in the poem's closing stanza in which Nana's absorption in the lives of her charges, as story teller, nurse, protector and admiring observer from the kitchen of "young missis' " social triumphs, culminates in her beatification as a "faithful guidepost."[4]

Not all attempts to describe and account for the woman in her role as worker in early Jamaican literature, however, show such disregard for the individuality of the women they portray. H.G. de Lisser, for example, in *Jane's Career*, gives an insight into the situation as it actually existed for those women who attempted to assert their individuality from their subservient position as domestic servants.[5] The first part of the novel deals with Jane's life as a "schoolgirl" or apprentice servant with a Kingston woman called Mrs. Mason whose dictatorial attitudes toward her employees and her unreasonable demands are satirised by the author as typical characteristics of the Jamaican, coloured middle class. Rather than portraying Jane and the other domestic servants, whose lives he describes in the novel, merely as victims of exploitation, de Lisser emphasizes the extent to which they fought back against their employers and the system in general. Jane is exploited by Mrs. Mason and seduced by Mrs. Mason's nephew, Cecil, but when she leaves the Mason household she does so in a calculated manner which leaves Mrs. Mason discomfited and Cecil out of pocket. At several points in the novel, de Lisser describes verbal battles between working women and their employers in which, at the level of language, the workers often come out the victors. Jane's personal sufferings at Mrs. Mason's hands are ultimately the experiences which change her from a naive country girl to a determined and independent city woman, and at no point does the novel descend to sentimental protest writing in which women are portrayed as cowed or defenceless.

The stress on the verbal ability of working women to defend themselves as well as the tools of their trade can also be seen in early dialect poems presenting women in their working environment; whether it be the prostitute's defence of her right to choose her customers in McKay's "Midnight Woman to Bobby"; or the peasant woman's defence of her right to sit with her goods in the street car in MacDermot's "Market Basket in the Car." "Why? doan't I pay me car-fare?/ Tuppence—same fe we two?/ What you da mek up you face for?/ You tink I is frighten' fe you?" Or the fruit vendor's defence of her right to a spot on the pavement in McKay's "Apple Woman's Complaint." In each of these dramatic monologues, the woman's ability to "give as good as she can take" is stressed.[6]

In poems describing women at work, rather than reproducing their speech, there is a tendency to associate the female figure with "masculine" images of strength or aggressiveness: In McKay's "Pay-day" for example, we are given vignettes of the various women owed money by the police for their services, waiting to be paid off. There is the mess cook, who waits, "Wid a lee pice of old clot'/ 'Pon her curly glossy hair,/ Print frock an' old bulldog boots/ Tatters all t'rough wear an' tear." As well as the prostitute: "See de waitin' midnight girl/ Wid her saucy cock-up lips,/ An' her strongly-built black hands/ pressed against her rounded hips." The references to the strength of the girl's hands and the mess cook's "bulldog boots" leave an impression of physical strength rather than coyness in the former or motherly succor in the latter.[7]

When the early Jamaican writers come to treat the sexuality of the working woman and its relationship to their economic position, there is less unanimity in their use of imagery and their implied moral position. Claude McKay, in his Jamaican short stories in *Ginger Town*, written after he left Jamaica in 1912, sees the strength and industry as well as the free sexual appetites of the Jamaican women he portrays as natural and wholesome aspects of the rural Jamaican setting. He associates their lifestyle with a sort of primal innocence, shattered only by the intrusion of the values and morals of the dominant culture. In "The Strange Burial of Sue" the story centres on the death from overwork and (it is implied) a possible miscarriage of a "strong brown peasant woman." Sue's free-loving ways are overlooked by her husband and tolerated by the rest of the community until a young loon whom she has helped through his first sexual experience turns sour and slanders her reputation openly. This forces Sue, her husband and the local church to take a public stand on her private life. Though her husband stands by her and takes out a lawsuit against her defamer, Sue is read out of church. Her spirit fails, and she becomes obsessed with a sense of guilt for having brought her husband into disrepute on account of her actions:

> During the interval before the time fixed for the hearing of the case Sue was strangely restless. She developed a mania for toting heavy loads on her head, although there were Turner's mules and horses to do that, and a girl who stayed and worked with them for her keep. She would bring in heavy logs of firewood from the forest and insist on chopping and splitting them herself. She heaved upon her head baskets of yams and bunches of bananas as if they were the weight of a feather pillow. She rode the vicious kicking mule down and over the hills from the local market until he sweated white. She worked in the

fields as never before, digging and planting like a farm-loving man. She used to place bets sometimes to demonstrate that she could equal or even surpass a man's work, but the way she carried on now seemed a little mad. As if she wanted to burn up all her splendid strength.[8]

The comparison between Sue's behaviour now and earlier descriptions of her working and helping others to work, draws the parallel between Sue's earlier joyful sexuality compared to her new feelings of guilt and the fanatical attitudes of the local parson towards what he considers her sexual aberration. When Sue finally dies from guilt and overwork, the parson refuses to bury her from the church and tries to use her graveside funeral as the excuse for a sermon on hell fire and damnation. Instead Sue's husband takes over the service and turns it into a community testimonial in which Sue's virtues of generosity and strength are recounted by her friends. Thus in death Sue's good name is redeemed and she is returned in the communal memory to the state of pre-lapsarian innocence in which she had lived and loved.

In his novels, H.G. de Lisser also satirizes the moral values which the dominant culture tried to impose on working-class women but here the satire is double-edged, as he sees both middle-class values and lower-class morals as signs of the imitativeness and inferiority of colonial society. He makes this point fictionally in *Jane's Career* in describing an argument between Jane and Sathyra as they pass the brightly lit houses of the well-to-do in the tram car:

> "It must be nice to be a white lady," [Jane] observed to Sathyra, "an' to have white gentlemen to take care of you an' give you whatever y'u want. Then you doan't have to work, an' you can put on a new dress every day, an' eat what you like. An' when you go to church you doan't have to walk, but can drive in a car or a buggy. Doan't you wish you was white?"
>
> "Of course," replied Sathyra, "though some of de white ladies is as ugly as sin, an' them doan't all so happy as you wants to believe. I know them quarrel with them husban's, an' cry an' fret; and as them is married an' have to keep up them positions, them can't do as them like, as we can. If a lady husband beat her, she have to stand it, for if she leave him everybody will talk about it, an' she won't like dat. But if our "friend" beat us, we can send him 'bout his business, though I know some gurl that put up wid anything. It wouldn't be me, though! I am independent, an' I wouldn't meck any man do what him choose wid me. But if I was a white lady I suppose I would have to put up wid it, so it is better I am what I am.[9]

The debate continues with Jane maintaining that there are after all compensations in a woman being beaten by her own husband rather than by a casual friend who recognises no responsibilities toward her, and Sathyra pointing out that most of the advantages Jane sees in marriage could be gained through a judicious alliance with a white man as a lover. Though it is evident that de Lisser enjoys the opportunity of shocking and satirizing his middle-class readership under the guise of demonstrating his characters' point of view, something of his underlying contempt for the lower class comes through in his reduction of the argument between Sathyra and Jane over marriage to the level of whether it is better for a woman to be beaten by her husband or her lover. Yet Sathyra is clearly making a statement for the independent black woman as compared to the privileged but dependent white woman.

MacDermot attempts to defend the morality of the lower-class woman by presenting her as more sinned against than sinning. He is militant in his championing of the servant girl Fidelia Stanton in *One Brown Girl*, who loses her job rather than acquiesce to her employer's sexual advances. However his ambivalence with respect to the morals of the lower classes surfaces in his inability to see any positive aspects in the lifestyle of those of his characters who do not share Fidelia Stanton's preference for chastity. In *One Brown Girl* and *Becka's Buckra Baby*, sexual permissiveness tends to be associated with laziness, vain ambition (for example Becka's aunt's pride in the "Buckra" baby she has had for a white man) or, curiously, racial impurity—suggested in his emphasis on the chaste Fidelia Stanton's "pure Coramantyn descent" and his portrayal of mulatto women in *One Brown Girl* as particularly susceptible to seductive advances.

Both MacDermot and de Lisser imply that lower-class women saw sexual relationships purely in terms of their financial benefits, and that they would rather live as kept mistresses than work for a living. MacDermot, for example, portrays Ada in *One Brown Girl*, a former lady's maid, as seeing no alternative, given her degree of education and relatively fair complexion, to becoming the mistress of one of two men who can afford to keep her in the style she considers her social right. This partial vision of the life-style and aspirations of working women may have been one of the ways in which creative writers rationalised the threat to socially approved standards of behaviour which the independent spirit of the lower-class women presented. If the woman's sexual alliances could be presented as a debased form of the marital contract rather than an aspect of her greater economic self-reliance, then assumptions about her moral and cultural limitations remained intact. De Lisser's *Jane's Career*, for all its sympathy for Jane and satire of the Jamaican middle class, ends with the author distancing himself from his heroine as he describes with heavy irony the imitation white wedding that she finally succeeds in achieving after living with Vincent Broglie for several years. This gives Jane an *entré* into the same middle class which the novel has satirized already as petty and exploitative in its presentation of Jane's first employer Mrs. Mason. But the social dead-end is, on closer examination, one of the author's making, as it is he who has created the fictional society in which his character's only form of salvation lies in the financial security and social ostentation of a middle-class marriage.

De Lisser's contemporary, Claude McKay, from his different social and ideological perspective, is able to suggest a different quality of experience in his presentation of lower-class aspirations towards social security. In "The Strange Burial of Sue" Sue's marriage to Turner after her life of economic independence and sexual freedom is explained in the following terms:

> He was such a sure prop to her. Surely she would never dream of comparing much less measuring him with any of the bucks with whom she dallied. Who else on that mountain top would have given her the solid security and freedom that Turner did? She knew the history of her mother and of her own girlhood. Turner had taken her child by Sam Bryan as his own. He was going to educate her a little, and how proud she would be to see her daughter become a postmistress or a school mistress. [10]

Here the desire for social and economic security goes further than a mere wish for pretty clothes or respectability; the author stresses the freedom which Sue maintains within the relationship as equaling any social benefits that will accrue to her illegitimate daughter as the result of Sue's marriage. Elsewhere he emphasizes the distinction the villagers make between Sue's sexual generosity and the promiscuity of the undiscriminating village whore "Stinky-sweety," as if to underline the existence of values within the community which recognise limits on personal freedom even if these do not coincide with those preached by the parson. The fact that Sue is not "kept" by Turner, but works as an equal partner with him in the fields suggests the existence of a relationship which is mutually rewarding from an economic as well as an emotional point of view.

By contrast, the sexual freedom of de Lisser's female lower-class characters and their independence of spirit are used as qualities which work against the interest of the their men-folk. One of the most consumate achievements in his first two novels, *Jane's Career* and *Susan Proudleigh*, is the way in which the women play off their various suitors against each other to win the greatest financial security. While harping on the industry, resourcefulness and physical attraction of the black woman, de Lisser portrays her male partners as lazy, confused or unnecessarily aggressive by contrast. He also uses the woman's desire for social security at a personal, individual level to thwart the attempts of the men to organise politically or industrially as a group or class. In *Jane's Career*, Jane's lover Vincent Broglie is faced with the choice of either losing Jane to the factory manager at her place of work, or breaking the strike at the newspaper printery where he works in order to offer Jane protection and financial security. Broglie's decision to break the strike gains him a rise in pay and the confidence of his employers, and as a result he wins Jane and eventually marries her. The reader is encouraged to associate Jane's advice to Broglie to break the strike with her superior good sense.

In *Susan Proudleigh*, the pattern is repeated and elaborated as we follow the heroine through two marriages and three affairs. In each case the prize of Susan's attention goes to the man who shows the least inclination to challenge the system. Our identification with the attractive and courageous heroine deflects our attention from de Lisser's anti-working class perspective. By making common-sense and the ability to work hard feminine traits as opposed to the masculine act of going on strike, de Lisser is able to denigrate the attempts of black men to organise themselves politically and at the work place without seeming to write negatively about the black race as a whole. In reality lower-class West Indian women were often at the forefront of political action and the labour movement but, as most of them were self-employed or engaged as servants, there were few opportunities for them to use industrial strike action on their own behalf, and it was therefore easy to interpret industrial unrest as a uniquely male aberration.

With the emergence, after the First World War, of a black middle class, whose social values were derived from the dominant culture, the "good life" for the Jamaican woman came to be seen as one of so-called leisure. The black Jamaican woman who aspired to middle-class status was encouraged to see herself as being fulfilled in the role of wife and mother, or, if she could not marry, in chastity and good deeds. Instead of writing about women as workers and free sexual agents, the writers in post-war Jamaica portrayed women in domestic settings, as ideal figures whose conflicts were likely to be between marriage and the service of God rather than a choice of lovers. Such idealised images were not uncommon in earlier literature.[11] However, they had invariably been associated with white female characters. The appropriation of these images to describe black and brown women must therefore be seen as the expression of a legitimate—if misguided—wish on the part of the new black bourgeoisie to claim for itself the prerogatives of virtue and refinement from which their race had until now been excluded.

One of the familiar concepts of ideal womanhood celebrated by writers of this period was the idea of the Virgin Madonna. The paradox is central to Astley Clerk's poem "The Queen Mother," which he dedicates to his wife. In it, Clerk pays homage to the childless wife, who fulfills nevertheless the ideal role of motherhood on account of her love for all children, and is apotheosized to the status of "Queen Mother" in heaven: "Glitt'ring the crown that they place on her head,/ Rich, gleaming with jewels rare;/ For each gem is the love of a child's pure heart,/ A setting fair of the love-god's art,/ Fit symbol for her to wear." Other poems of this period extend the ideal women as mother to include the celebration of woman as the protector of all vulnerable life. Another of Clerk's poems, "The Lady of the Birds," is

dedicated to fellow-poet Arabella Moulton Barrett. The poet is led
intuitively, like the Magi to the birthplace of Christ, to the lady of the birds in
her garden, where she is surrounded by living things. Her tenderness to animals is "pictured in the Beauty, rich and full,/ Hung round about her doors
by Nature's hands."[12]

Few of the poems of this period portray women working or even engaging
in domestic tasks. In one of Constance Hollar's poems, for example, she
celebrates the saintliness of her grandmother, portraying her in a static, rapt
posture which gives no hint of her occupation or household virtues:

> Hair brushed on either side her face
> And such a look of quiet grace
>   In liquid eyes of brown
> A bible open on her knee
> It is thus I often see
>   My grandmother
> My lovely little grandmother

Mother love and love of God replace passion or sexual desire as themes,
and love poems concentrate on abstract concepts and the unattainability of
the loved object. J.E. Clare McFarlane writes, for example, of Beauty:

> To me thou seemst a thing divine,
> Moulded for reverence, not desire;
> Kindling within my Being's shrine
> The flame of an aspiring fire,
> Seeking to reach a purer air;
> That leapeth upward, leapeth higher,
> From sordid longing's dull-red flare
> And smould'ring confines of despair.

And love for M.M. Ormsby is

> Life-music; not the noise of market-place,
> Or sullen silence, but the sweet bird-songs,
> And whispering leaves, the wave-wash on the shore,
> The sigh and scent of flowers, the floating clouds,
> And all that makes for perfect harmony.

While her sister, Stephanie Ormsby, warns of desire:

> Children cry for the moon.
> Yet . . . if the moon itself were given?
> Shines forever the unattained;

> But oh! the dark of Desire gained
> At cost of the light that showed us Heaven
> . . . Too soon![13]

One of the consequences of the emergence of this new chaste idealized female figure in Jamaican literature is the transference of overtly sexual references from poems dealing with human love to poems dealing with sensations not directly related to women. McFarlane, for instance, in "Dawn" personifies the sunrise as a woman and lover, creeping softly to his "couch." Sexually charged imagery is also to be found in poems dealing with spiritual ecstasy, for example Joan Richmond's "What Hast Thou Done?" One senses in such poems, however, an element of sublimated desire:

> What hast thou done to me dear heart that I no more have power
> To shield my naked quiv'ring soul from mortal eyes but fore
> Thy searching gaze I must lay bare
> All in me that's divine:
> Why does my spirit roam afar from its accustomed place?
> When through the silence thou dost come to woo it face to face
> And then it seems a glorious thing
> To merge my life with thine.[14]

Such explicit, albeit unconscious, sexual imagery invites speculation as to the consequences of the new standards of morality within Jamaican society for those women whom it affected most directly—the black and coloured women who did not marry and whose moral conditioning prevented them from seeking sexual fulfilment outside of marriage as their mothers and grandmothers had done. Social studies of Jamaican middle-class society between the wars and after often draw attention to the disproportionate number of unmarried black women within the Jamaican middle class. They attribute this to the tendency of Jamaican men to marry upward on the colour scale, rejecting well-educated women of their own shade or darker in preference to fairer-complexioned women or foreign white women through whom they could increase their social prestige in Jamaican circles.

Although few literary works deal directly with the problems of those "left on the shelf," there is one fascinating social document from this period, written by the poet J.E. Clare McFarlane, which addresses this phenomenon. In a full-length study entitled *Sex and Christianity* (1932) which was republished in England two years later as *The Case for Polygamy*, McFarlane puts forward the rather startling proposal that in Christian societies like Jamaica and England where women outnumber men, a man should be allowed the legal option of having more than one wife, so that no woman on account of the shortage of available spouses

should be deprived of the God-given blessing of bearing children or be left
to fend for herself economically in the world, thus risking the temptation of
falling into sin. "Under the old Mosaic law it would have been impossible
for such to go unmated and uncared for; must it them be supposed that the
Law founded on justice is more righteous and merciful than that founded on
love?"[15] The author is however unable to find any biblical sanction for
polyandry. Indeed he makes a point of emphasizing the extent to which
multiple sexual relations in the case of a women pervert the laws of nature
and of man.

McFarlane's preoccupation with female faithfulness within marriage and
abstinence outside of it finds expression in each of his three major narrative
poems, *Beatrice* (1918), *Daphne* (1931) and *The Magdalen* (1957).
Beatrice opens on an impassioned diatribe by Beatrice's father who
suspects his wife of having been unfaithful:

> What has thou done!—O Dora, love of my boyhood,
> Dream of my wasted youth, and joy of my manhood,
> What has thou done! with deepest bond of affection,
> Bound to my heart and cherished with fond adoration.
> Hast thou to jealousy bartered my love?—Oh my darling
> What hast thou done!—How can I ever forgive thee!
> Over my pride the mask of shame is now falling.
> Over my name the hideous shroud of Dishonor
> Falling from hands I loved forever is resting;
> Over my life the burning east-wind is blowing,
> Blasting my love, my pride, my name and my honour.[16]

And the poem ends with Beatrice's death by drowning after she has
confessed her unfaithfulness to her childhood sweetheart during his long
absence overseas. Her death brings about the tearful reunification of her
estranged parents. In *Daphne* the emphasis is placed on "spiritual" rather
than physical faithfulness between man and wife. Daphne's devotion to and
moral support of her husband during his service to his country as a soldier is
held up as an example of ideal virtue. Even after her death, her example
remains to protect her husband from spiritual despair.

In *The Magdalen* McFarlane reconstructs a chaste love affair between
Christ and Mary Magdalen, citing scriptural evidence for his interpretation
of the gospel story.[17] *The Magdalen* is an ambitious but unsuccessful
poem from a technical point of view, as McFarlane's concern with maintaining the decorum of his theme and at the same time expounding polemically his
ideas about female virtue overburden the poem with verbal and aesthetic
clichés which are not redeemed by any sense of profundity as they are at
moments in his other poems. However, McFarlane's preoccupation with
female characters and sexual purity, though usually worked out in poems

which make use of Biblical or classical settings, seems as much a symptom of his age as de Lisser's preoccupation at an earlier date with the sexual habits of lower-class women had been.

The poet who approaches the question of the status of women in Jamaican society most directly and most originally during this period is Una Marson. Her work is probably best considered in the context of the changing social situation at the end of the 1930s rather than in the context of the work of McFarlane and his associates who had grown to maturity before the First World War. One of the side effects of the large numbers of unmarried Jamaican middle-class women at this period was an increase in the number of educated black women in careers. Standards of education for women in Jamaica had taken rapid strides between the wars with the founding of a number of boarding schools for girls in various parts of the island. [18] The poet herself is a typical case in point. Educated at Hampton Girls School, Una Marson was one of several sisters well known for their intellectual ability. During the 1930s she founded a magazine for women called *Cosmopolitan* aimed at encouraging local stenographers and female clerical employees to take a wider interest in cultural matters. Some of Marson's earliest poems, published in her first collection, *Tropic Reveries* (1930), give an idea of how distasteful the role mapped out for the average Jamaican middle-class woman must have seemed to an ambitious and spirited girl: [19]

> To wed, or not to wed: that is the question:
> Whether 'tis nobler in the mind to suffer
> The fret and loneliness of spinsterhood
> Or to take arms against the single state
> And by marrying, end it? To wed; to match,
> No more; yet by this match to say we end
> The heartache and the thousand natural shocks
> That flesh is heir to; 'tis a consummation
> Devoutly to be wish'd. To wed, to match;
> To match, perchance mismatch: aye there's the rub;
> for in that match what dread mishaps may come,
> When we have shuffled off this single state
> For wedded bliss. . . .

In another light-hearted parody, this time of Kipling's "If," Marson elaborates on some of the "rubs" attendant on marriage:

> If you can love and not make love your master,
> If you can serve yet do not be his slave,
> If you can hear bright tales and quit them faster,
> And, for your peace of mind, think him no knave;

> If you can bear to hear the truth you tell him
> Twisted around to make you seem a fool,
> Or see the capstan on your bureau burning
> And move the noxious weed and still keep cool.

Such poems are of slight literary merit but their use of other literary sources is indicative of the wider scope of women's education during this period. Indeed the poems, like most parodies of this nature, were probably written while Marson was still at school for the entertainment of school friends who would have been familiar with her literary sources as well as appreciative of her poetry's theme.

Several of the poems in *Tropic Reveries* attempt to deal with the problems of loneliness and frustration experienced by single women, well enough educated to converse as equals with men but unlikely to be considered suitable candidates for the roles of wife or mistress. "Illusion" describes a familiar crisis within a platonic friendship. The poem's bland almost banal rhyme scheme reflects the triviality of the every-day conversation which goes on while underneath quite different emotions are concealed:

> You said 'twas lovely weather
> I said 'twas lovely too,
> But I thought of your beauty
> Tell me, of what thought you?

In "The Waves" the poet uses the relentless beating of the sea against the shore as a metaphor for frustrated physical desire:

> I sit and idly wonder as the waves
>   beat on the shore,
> If the surging waves of passion will
>   beat for evermore;
> Will call in vain for answer from the
>   dawn of day to night
> And call again till day breaks with her
>   glorious purple light.

The constant repetition of this kind of theme in many of the poems in this early collection, often in works of negligible poetic achievement, suggests that Marson herself was still very close to the experiences of loneliness and frustration she describes.

In the poems in Marson's later collection, *The Moth and the Star* (1937), the poet seems more firmly in control of her art technically and achieves a greater degree of detachment from and emotional control over her themes.[20] Many of these poems were written during or after her first extended stay in

England where she worked for the exiled Haile Selassie and the League of Coloured People, and the poems show a new awareness of the relationship between feminist issues and questions of black identity in West Indian society. In "Kinky Hair Blues" one of a number of poems in the collection which make use of dialect (a rare phenomenon at this date), Marson uses the rhythms of Afro-American blues to describe the dilemma of a black girl, who finds herself unable to make an impression on the men of her circle without distorting her self-image by straightening her "kinky" hair:

> Gwine find a beauty shop
> Cause I ain't a lovely belle.
> The boys pass me by,
> They say I's not so swell.
>
> See oder young gals
> So slick and smart.
> See those oder young gals
> So slick and smart.
> I jes' gwine die on de shelf
> If I don't mek a start.
>
> I hate dat ironed hair
> And dat bleaching skin.
> Hate dat ironed hair
> And dat bleaching skin.
> But I'll be all alone
> If I don't fall in.

The poem catches the metre, the patterns of repetition, and even the minor key of the blues—a form traditionally associated with a sublimation of social impotence through artistic virtuosity. The combination of Jamaican dialect with African-American rhythms suggests a connection between the problems of the black Jamaican and Marson's new awareness of the wider racial struggle. Similar sentiments are expressed in poems like "Black Burden" which begins "I am black/ And so I must be/ More clever than white folks" and "Cinema Eyes" in which a mother tries to warn her daughter against repeating her mistakes and identifying with white ideals of beauty seen on the screen.

Though several poems in this collection carry on the themes of loneliness and frustration of the earlier collections, new poems such as "Repose," "The Heart's Strength" and "Fulfillment" assert the positive values of self-reliance and platonic love which, in the earlier collection, had not been able to compensate for the pain of being "left on the shelf." Una Marson's best known poem is probably "Confession," a defiant statement of her independence of spirit which drew the censure of McFarlane when it appeared as manifesting "the spirit of post-war Jamaica with its feverish search for sensation."[21] Like much of Marson's poetry, "Confession" with lines like: "I regret nothing—/ I have lived/ I have loved/ I have known laughter/ And dance and song,/ I have wept,/ I have sighed/ I have prayed,/ I have soared/ On fleecy clouds . . . " suffers from stylistic defects which suggest that though the mood and reality had changed, Marson was still searching for an idiom which could completement the new spirit of the age.

By 1939 the black Jamaican middle class had established itself securely enough to begin to challenge the cultural norms and political power of the ruling white colonial elite. Fired by the increasing militance of the working classes which led to violent upheavals throughout the Caribbean in 1938, educated Jamaicans began to take a new literary interest in the figure of the working-class woman as a symbol of revised racial and socio-economic values.[22] The trend can be observed in the poems celebrating black beauty written at this time which carry on the rejection of "white" cultural values expressed in Marson's poetry. George Campbell's "Mother" which describes a peasant woman bathing in a river, uses the naked figure of a black women with a baby in her arms as a symbol of Mother Africa, "stronger than old boulders, older than what moulders." In other poems Campbell attempts to coin images to describe what he considers the unique quality of the black woman's beauty, inadvertently creating in the process a new but equally confining stereotype of the black woman:

> Your blackness seeps through me
> It wets like dew
> It comes upon me like a lovely night.
> You are not here
> Your blackness stays round me like rich perfume.
> All space black dew.
> Your absence beautiful against my loins
> Oh! lovely woman like a velvet night!

Campbell's most memorable poem to make symbolic use of the black woman is "History Makers," in which the common sight, along Jamaican roads, of women in various stages of pregnancy carrying out the most arduous of physical tasks connected with road mending, the breaking of stones with pick-axes, is used as an image of the woman's strength and powers of endurance as well as of her historic role as mother of a strong race:

> Women stone breakers
> Hammers and rocks
> Tired child makers
> Haphazard frocks

Strong thigh
Rigid head
Bent nigh
Hard white piles
Of stone
Under hot sky
In the gully bed.

II
No smiles
No sigh
No moan.

III
Women child bearers
Pregnant frocks
Wilful toil sharers
Destiny shapers
History makers
Hammers and rocks.[23]

The vivid impressionistic images seem to freeze the figure of the woman in the action of bearing down on the rock, and are able to accommodate the poet's sense of the women as both victims and shapers of history. The line arrangement and the division into stanzas creates a pattern of stress and pause that imitates the regular motion of the women's axes in stanza one; the slowing of their movements as a result of fatigue in stanza two with its protracted pauses; and the renewed vigour and determination of the women's movements in the closing stanza. The strenuousness of their work is seen in the context of their economic independence as "wilful toil sharers," while the moral outrage of their physical exploitation even during pregnancy is balanced against their pivotal role as the mothers of future generations. The idea of the women as shapers of their country's roads and destinies is linked to the final image of them as both the hammers which provide the power and the rocks which receive the blows.

By contrast, creative writing by women about women during this period does not idealise its subjects. Instead the writers concentrate on the black women's sensual and economic oppression and use the female figure as a symbol of social injustice in the wider community. Una Marson's "The Stonebreakers" provides an interesting contrast to Campbell's visionary treatment of the same subject in "History Makers." By choosing the form of dramatic monologue, Marson approaches the women workers from within their consciousness rather than as heroic symbols, from the outside, as Campbell does:

"Liza me chile, I's really tired
Fe broke dem stone,
Me han' hat me,
Me back hat me,
Me foot hat me,
An' Lard, de sun a blin' me."

"No so, Cousin Mary, an' den
De big Backra car dem
A lik up de dus' in a we face.
Me Massa Jesus knows it,
I's weary of dis wol'—

"But whey fe do, Cousin Mary,
Me haf fe buy frack fe de pickney dem,
Ebry day dem hab fe feed.
Dem wutless pupa tan roun' de bar
A trow dice all de day—
De groun' is dat dry,
Not a ting will grow—
Massy Lard, dis life is hard.
An' so—dough de work is hard
I will has to work fe pittance
Till de good Lard call me."

"Liza me chile, I's really tired
But wha fe do—we mus' brok de stone
Dough me han' dem hat me
Me back it hat me,
Me foot dem hat me
An' de sun it blin' me—
Will—de good Lard knows
All about we sorrows."[24]

Marson's poem indicts men as well as an unjust socio-economic system for
the oppression of working-class women by its juxtaposition of the image of
the "buckra" car sweeping past the workers and raising the dust and that of
the "wutless pupa" throwing dice all day instead of looking for work to help
support his family. The women's sense of resignation to their fate is
expressed in the slow, tired rhythms of their dialect speech ("Me han' hat
me, Me back hat me") and their fatalistic reliance on divine compassion.
    Marson's insistence on the victimization of the working-class woman
may have been a response to the increased hardship within the working
class and especially among working-class women during the depression
years as the domestic market was flooded with men pushed out of jobs in

North and Central America. In addition, the prosperous small-farming sector, traditionally a female-dominated activity, had been undermined by the take-over of the banana industry by foreign monopolies like the United Fruit Company. This reduced many small farmers to the level of wage labourers and drained resources away from the modestly prosperous pre-war agricultural towns described by McKay in his Jamaican short stories, undermining in turn the other staple rural occupations of women as seamstresses, bakers and craftswomen. The results were an acceleration of the rate of rural-urban migration; a relative dearth of cheap foodstuffs in the city; an increase in the number of women wholly dependent on men for their upkeep or the upkeep of their children; and an upsurge of religious fatalism and escapism among working-class women. Marson's evocation of the communal release of the possession rituals of the predominantly female spiritual sects in "Gettin' de Spirit" emphasizes the cathartic effect of the religious ecstasy through which many women attempted to sublimate their social and economic impotence:

> Lord gie you chile de spirit
> Let her shout
> Lord gie you chile de power
> An' let her pray . . .
> Shout sister—shout—
> Halleluja—Amen
> Can't you feel de spirit
> Shout sister—shout

Religious sublimation of the socio-economic reality is also a characteristic of the poetry by middle-class women about their working-class sisters. In this context it is used as a way of shifting social responsiblity for economic conditions away from the concerned middle-class woman who could see no other solution for relieving her sister's economic burden. Marson opts for such a resolution in "Going to Market," for example, which ends by supporting her subject's faith in "a heaven/ Where there are no hot fields/ And hotter highways," and where "the great God Himself/ Will wipe all tears/ From your eyes."[25]

Perhaps the most ambitious poem by a female author of this nature is Vera Bell's "Ancestor on the Auction Block." Like Marson's "Going to Market," the poem begins by expressing guilt and shame as the poet confronts not only her social responsibilities in the present but also her connections with the working class through their joint origins within slave society:

> Ancestor on the auction block
> Across the years your eyes seek mine

Compelling me to look.
I see your shackled feet
Your primitive black face
I see your humiliation
And turn away
Ashamed.

Across the years your eyes seek mine
Compelling me to look
Is this mean creature that I see
Myself?
Ashamed to look
Because of myself ashamed
Shackled by my own ignorance
I stand
A Slave.

After this compelling statement of the conflict however, Bell attempts a resolution through the invocation of a shared sense of human dignity and purpose transmitted through the participation of the speaker and her ancestor in the divine will:

I look you in the eyes and see
The spirit of God eternal
Of this only need I be ashamed
Of blindness to the God within me
The same God who dwelt within you
The same eternal God
Who shall dwell
In generations yet unborn.

The vagueness of the conventional terms in which the "spirit of God eternal" is defined leaves one with the impression that, after all, the problem posed by the poet in her opening stanzas has ultimately been evaded. The poem's closing stanza attempts another form of resolution similar in some respects to Campbell's synthesis in "History Makers," by which the woman's humiliation and labour is rationalised as the beginning of the Jamaican society's struggle for dignity and independence:

Ancestor on the auction block
Across the years
I look
I see you sweating, toiling, suffering
Within your loins I see the seed

> Of multitudes
> From your labour
> Grow roads, aqueducts, cultivation
> A new country is born
> Yours was the task to clear the ground
> Mine be the task to build.[26]

In spite of the comforting downward cadence of the last two lines however, this stanza also loses touch with the central issues of the poem. There seems to be a *non-sequitur* in the logic through which the poet rationalizes her sense of her ancestor's humiliation by reference to her own nationalist ideals. Unlike Campbell's "History Makers" the poem seems unable to accommodate the idea of the women as victims *and* shapers of history in a single image so that the assertion of progress is made by suppressing the awareness of shame rather than through a creative fusion of the two ideas.

It would seem therefore that though a number of women writers of this period approach in their work a sense of identification with their female counterparts in the lower class, none of them is able to achieve the artistic balance between empathy and optimism suggested in the perhaps accidental virtuosity of Campbell's "History Makers": What is more, the women writers as a group ultimately reject confrontation with the society or with men as a way of dealing with the problems of working-class women and concentrate instead on voicing the women's complaints or extending religious comfort to the women whose hardship they describe. Their tendency to withdraw the women they present from active participation in the fight for social reform anticipates the subordination of female and working-class figures to a concern with the identity crisis of the middle-class male in the nationalist literature written by men in the 1940s and for most of the next three decades in West Indian writing. One can deduce the reasons for this shift from George Campbell's poem "Smells Like Hell," in which the familiar image of the women breaking stones—"One million children from women breaking stones"—is contrasted with the image of "[T]he little beauty with the peanut brain . . . all the childless, well slimmed down." Here the educated or privileged middle-class woman is evaluated negatively in comparison to her hard-working, child-bearing lower-class sister. Campbell's comparison suggests two things. In the first place, the lower-class woman has become a depersonalised symbol evoked to express the West Indian male's sense of social injustice or a romantic notion of the dignity of labour. At the same time the middle-class woman is reduced to a negative stereotype and made the scapegoat for the failings of the entire black bourgeoisie.

These two views of Jamaican women imply that middle-class Jamaican men no longer saw women as contributing either physically or intellectually to the process of resistance to colonialism or social injustice. Indeed the typical middle-class woman is now presented as a thorn in the flesh of the committed middle-class man who wishes to protect the "helpless" women of the working classes and to assert his own ego against the emasculating strategies of the dominant culture. In this way de Lisser's earlier stereotype of the apolitical female is perpetuated but given a reversed significance as the Jamaican male attempts to establish his right to participation in the political decision-making process of his community. Though the lower-class woman is honoured in several poems of this period, not a single male author puts forward a positive image of a woman of his own social status in his poetry.[27] Indeed, a new recurring theme in the fiction of the late 1940s and early 1950s is the lack of a shared sense of vision between male and female partners in a relationship, and the predominantly male protagonists of such works are presented as having to turn in on themselves for strength and support. This theme is central to the problematic middle section of V.S. Reid's *New Day* (1949), the first Jamaican novel to focus exclusively on a male protagonist. The first part of the novel deals with Davie Campbell's involvement in the Morant Bay Rebellion of 1865, while the last part deals with his grandson's emergence as a political leader in the 1940s. The middle section is taken up with the narrator's presentation of the marriage between Davie and the beautiful Haitian mulatto, Lucille, and their attempts to found a utopian society on one of the small cays off the coast of Jamaica. The first encounter between Davie and Lucille occurs as she enters the Morant Bay parish church at the side of the hated Custos Aldenburg:

> 'Member I remember how I stood looking on her eyes, on her hair, and saying to myself, "Johnny O, is summer moon it, shining on Maroon Hole, and silver lights are a-twinkle at the bottom o' dark waters."
>
> And then I saw that her eyes were resting on Davie. Davie it was I knew, for I saw her looking long over my head, and when I turned and looked too, there was my bro' David. My bro' stands there looking on Lucille Dubois as if other people were not here at all, at all.
>
> *Watch them, Johnny O!* Stallion eagerness is a-ripple Davie's flank against me shoulder. The sun has brought silver to the black of Lucille's hair, her lips suck at the blood-plum that is not there.[28]

Reid's lyrical evocation of Lucille's intoxicating beauty contains more than a hint of sexual danger and recalls the stereotype of the mulatress as sexually wanton and temperamental so often used in de Lisser's historical novels and "pot-boiler" romances. The initial electricity between Davie and Lucille involves the latter willy-nilly in Davie's escape from the redcoats to the offshore island where he later founds his utopian colony. Predictably, the fun-loving Lucille wilts in this environment. Her "woman's" inability to do without laces, parties and admirers in this austere community, whose economic basis is the farming of manure droppings left by the island's colonies of *guango* birds, is opposed to the rigidity of Davie's ideals for political reform. Lucille's refusal to share her husband's vision is ultimately the cause of her shipwreck on the coast of Cuba during a storm which blows up while she is being entertained on board a visiting cargo ship by the debonair Captain Grantley. During the storm the Captain is killed and, in Cuba, Lucille is mistaken for a common ship's whore. Our final picture of her is as a prostitute in a Kingston brothel where she meets the narrator once more before her drunken death during the great earthquake and fire that destroyed much of Kingston in 1907. The fictional story of Davie and Lucille is inserted into Reid's historical novel as a cautionary tale about the dangers of political extremism, and Lucille's tragedy is blamed on her husband's unbending fanaticism. However, the symbolic opposition of male strength to female weakness, so alien to earlier literary presentations of the Jamaican woman, is taken for granted in the narrative in a way that suggests that a new view of female character had become the norm in Jamaican society.

A similar development can be noted in the poetry of Louise Bennett.[29] Though Bennett maintains the old view of the working-class woman as more than a match for her oppressors at the level of language, her poems tend to show women using men as surrogates for their aggression and, at a first glance, she seems to follow the bias of Jamaican men in her presentation of women as apolitical. In "Uriah Preach" for example, Bennett recounts the vicarious pleasure taken by a Jamaican women in the accomplishments of her children and especially in her son's ability to use his occasional ascent to the pulpit to lambast the family's enemies:

> Fe me fambly is not peaw-peaw,
> Me daughta Sue dah-teach,
> An wen rain fall, or Parson sick,
> Me son Uriah preach!
>
> . . .
>
> Him climb up pon de pulpit, him
> Lean over, him look dung,
> Him look pon all we enemy
> An lash dem wid him tongue!

The woman's pride in the poetic justice of her son's scriptural attacks on her enemies is a comic version of the religious escapism expressed earlier in the poetry of Marson and Bell. In "Me Bredda," an irate woman who has failed to get a job as a domestic servant forces her would-be employer to placate her with two weeks' wages by threatening to call in her imaginary brother to settle the matter physically:

Oonoo call me bredda fe me,
Beg you tell him come yah quick!
Tell him bring him pelt-you-kin cow-cod
an bus-you-open stick!

Here again the woman shifts the responsibility for physical confrontation to
a male figure, implying that the woman herself no longer considers the
threat of her own action sufficient to terrify the housewife she abuses.

Though Bennett often works through apolitical female figures who are
more likely to react to the cut of a politician's clothes than what he says, she
often expresses a womanist perspective on topical issues and her poems
take note of social reforms intended to improve the position of women. In
"Bans of Oman," for example, she celebrates the founding of the Jamaican
Federation of Women in the 1940s aimed at bringing together women of all
classes, describing the clothes and social status of the women who flock to
support it as "high and low, miggle suspended." Poems like "Solja Work"
show the consequences of a local military presence for Jamaican women.

Bennett is one of the first creative writers to register the increase of female
oppression which was one of the consequences of the male assertion of
racial and political power during the nationalist movement of the 1940s and
1950s. Her poem "Pinnacle" satirises the new chauvinism of men towards
women as it manifested itself within the Rastafarian movement, which in
other respects has had such a profound and in many ways beneficial effect
on Jamaican attitudes to language, race and spiritual values. Written after
the brutal destruction of one of the first Rastafarian communities by the
Jamaican government, the poem delights in the humiliation of one of the
male members of the sect who had formerly used his Rastafarian
convictions to terrorise his woman:

Mass John come back fram Pinnicle
Yuh want see him head Mumma
Yuh kean tell ef it meck o' hair
Or out o' constab-macka.

Him tell we dat him get wey
Wen de police meck de raid;
Him crawl pon him belly like worm
Fe four mile, him soh fraid.

Him really have heart fe come back,
Atta him treat May soh bad!
Sell de po' woman li' Jackass
An start gwan like him mad.

Black up har two y'eye, bus har nose
An starve har fe so lang
She nearly dead, because she hooden
Goh jine him Rasta gang.

She say she hooden fegive him
'Cep him go dung pon him knee,
She get har wish, far him dah-lidung now
Flat-flat pon him belly.

Bennett's satirical resources however are limited to what she can authentically express through the resonances of a specific social reality and way of speech, so that in her dramatic monologues she can only be as positive about women as she thinks the character through whom she speaks is in real life. In a more recent poem she has described what she considers the philosophy of the Jamaican woman:

Jamaica Oman know she strong,
She know she tallawah,
But she no want her pickney dem
Fi start call her "pupa."

So de cunny Jamma Oman
Gwan like pants-suit is a style,
An Jamaica man no know she wear
De trousiz all de while!

So Jamaica Oman coaxin
Fambly Budget from explode
A so Jamaica man a sing
"Oman a heaby load!"

This presentation of the female point of view elucidates Bennett's own method in the early poems, by which she is able to assert a sense of female strength under the guise of using male surrogates and seeming to acquiesce in ideas about female weakness. The fact that she feels constrained to work through such masks, however, gives an indication of the extent to which the attitude to women in Jamaican society had become that expressed in the song she quotes in her poem on Jamaican women: "Oman a heaby load!"

Jamaican literature between 1900 and 1950 is unique within the English-speaking Caribbean in its close documentation of every step in the changing perception of the West Indian woman by its writers. In Trinidad by contrast, although a powerful sense of the strength and independence of the lower-class woman is expressed in the short fiction written by the *Beacon* group in the 1930s, there is no middle phase comparable to the idealistic writing of MacDermot, Clerk and the Ormsby sisters to help explain the transition from the protrayal of the woman as economically and sexually aggressive to the later treatment of women in the work of Naipaul and Selvon as marginal/antagonistic facets of the male personality. In Guyanese literature, Mittelholzer's portrayal of dominant matriarchal figures in his historical novels as well as his use of female protagonists as late as 1953 in *The Life and Death of Sylvia* suggests that any patterns developed for Jamaican society and its literary perception of women cannot be automatically transferred to other literatures of the region, although a basic pattern of male protagonists taking over from female figures in the literature published after 1950 remains true for the region as a whole. What the wealth of evidence for the almost obsessive concern with the female figure, before the emergence of an internationally recognised school of West Indian writing in the 1950s, demonstrates most conclusively is the extent to which the "typical" West Indian novel, with its middle-class male protagonist and its theme of cultural alienation is in fact a comparatively recent phenomenon. Both male and, to a lesser extent, female writers since 1940 have minimised the social and intellectual contribution of the West Indian women in much the same way that the 1930s Jamaican poets attempted to play down the sexual and economic independence of their female subjects. An understanding of the stages of development in the early literary presentation of women in Jamaican writing goes a long way towards explaining the reassertion of female subjects and themes in new and contemporary (1980s) West Indian writing by both male and female writers.

NOTES

1. W.P. Livingstone, *Black Jamaica: A Study in Evolution* (London: Sampson, Low Marston & Co., 1899), pp. 46-47. Livingstone himself seems to qualify his criticism partially later in his study when he notes: "A robust, active and independent class (the women) appear unconscious of any hardship in the arrangement which transfers to them so large a part of the burden of life. It gives them a certain power apart from sex (sic), over the men, which in the circumstances is perhaps essential. It would seem that nature has counterbalanced the weakness of sex by supplying them with constitutions stronger even than the male. The one drawback is a tendency to neglect giving proper attention to the duties of maternity and the responsibilities of the household" (pp. 220-221).
2. See Rhoda Reddock, "Women and Slavery," paper presented at the Institute for Social Studies, The Hague, Holland, 1980.

3. See Erna Brodber, "Profile of the Jamaican Free Woman," paper presented at the Institute of Social and Economic Research, U.W.I., Mona, Jamaica, May 1980.

4. "Nana" by Mary Wolcott, in *The Island of Sunshine: Verses by "Tropica"* (New York: Knickerbocker Press, 1904) p. 39. In his article on "Creative Literature of the British West Indies During the Period of Slavery," *Savacou*, I: 1 (June, 1970), Edward Brathwaite notes a similar tendency to depersonalize black figures in pre-Emancipation literature. He cites "Monk" Lewis's description of a black girl, Mary Wiggins, which ends, "Mary Wiggins and an old cotton tree are the most picturesque objects that I have seen for these twenty years" (p. 52).

5. This aspect of *Jane's Career* is discussed at length in Kenneth Ramchand's introduction to the Heinemann Caribbean Writers Series reprint of the novel (1972).

6. Thomas MacDermot, "Market Basket in the Car," in *Orange Valley and Other Poems* by "Tom Redcam" (Kingston: The Pioneer Press, 1951), p. 28; Claude McKay, "The Apple Woman's Complaint," in *Constab Ballads* (New York: Black Heritage Library Edition, 1972), p. 57.

7. "Pay-day," by McKay, in *Constab Ballads*, p. 52.

8. Claude McKay, "The Strange Burial of Sue," collected in *My Green Hills of Jamaica and Five Jamaican Stories*, ed. Mervyn Morris (Kingston: Heinemann Educational Books Ltd., 1979), p. 157. The story first appeared in *Ginger Town* (New York, 1932).

9. De Lisser, *Jane's Career*, pp. 108-109.

10. McKay, "The Strange Burial of Sue," in *Green Hills,* pp. 156-157.

11. See for example Becka's sunday school teacher in MacDermot's *Becka's Buckra Baby* or the Salvation army major in *One Brown Girl*.

12. Astley Clerk, "The Queen Mother," in *Voices from Summerland*, ed. J.F.C. McFarlane (London: Fowler Wright, 1929), p. 53; and "The Lady of the Birds," p. 49.

13. Constance Hollar, "My Grandmother," in *Flaming June* (Kingston: The New Dawn Press, 1941). J.E. Clare McFarlane, "Beauty," in *Summerland*, p. 147; M.M. Ormsby, "What is Love?" in *Summerland*, p. 233; Stephanie Ormsby, "Desire," in *Summerland*, p. 247.

14. McFarlane, "Dawn," in *Summerland*, p. 133; Joan Richmond, "What Hast Thou Done," in *The Yearbook of the Poetry League of Jamaica* (Kingston: New Dawn Press, 1939), p. 8.

15. McFarlane, *Sex and Christianity* (Kingston: The Gleaner Company, 1932), p. 26.

16. McFarlane, *Beatrice: A Narrative Poem in Classical Metre* (Kingston: The Times Printery, 1918), p. 3.

17. McFarlane, *The Magdalen: The Story of Supreme Love* (Kingston: The New Dawn Press, 1957), pp. 17-18 and p. 43.

18. De Lisser makes a point, for instance, in several of his inter-war novels, including *Haunted* and *The Sins of the Children* of giving his heroines the benefit of an education at well known local girls schools. For a fuller discussion of de Lisser's novels about educated women of this period, especially of *Myrtle and Money* (1942), his sequel to *Jane's Career*, see my article on H.G. de

Lisser in Daryl Dance (ed.) *Fifty Caribbean Writers: A Bio-Bibliographical and Critical Source Book* (Westport, CT: Greenwood Press, 1986).

19. The following poems from Una Marson's *Tropic Reveries* (Kingston: The Gleaner Company, 1930) are quoted: "To Wed or Not to Wed," p. 81; "If," p. 83; "Illusion," p. 54; and "The Waves," p. 6. For a fuller account of Marson's exceptional life and work, see Erika Smilowitz, "Una Marson: Woman Before Her Time," *Jamaica Journal*, 16, 2 (May 1983), pp. 62-68.

20. The following poems from Una Marson's *The Moth and the Star* (Kingston: The Gleaner Company, 1937) are quoted: "Kinky Hair Blues," p. 91; "Black Burden," p. 93; and "Confession," p. 63.

21. See McFarlane, *A Literature in the Making* (Kingston: The Pioneer Press, 1956), p. 94.

22. For a fuller statement of the cultural consequences of this socio-political re-orientation, see V.S. Reid, "The Cultural Revolution in Jamaica after 1938," address delivered at the Institute of Jamaica, ca. 1978.

23. Poems from George Campbell's *First Poems* (Kingston: City Printery, 1945) are quoted in the following order: "Black Mother," p. 37; "Your Blackness Steeps Through Me," p. 36; "History Makers," p. 61.

24. Marson, "The Stonebreakers," in *The Moth*, p. 70.

25. Marson, "Gettin' de Spirit" and "Going to Market," in *The Moth*, pp. 76 and 89.

26. Vera Bell, "Ancestor on the Auction Block," in *Focus* (1948), p. 187.

27. Conversely, male protagonists are invariably presented in favourable terms— at their weakest, they are portrayed as sensitive individuals, torn between their class/family loyalties and their desire for social justice, cf. Roger Mais' *Brother Man* (1954). In *Black Lightning* (1955) Mais goes a step further and thematizes the problem of human interdependence as perceived through the typical male/strong female/weak dichotomy. His condemnation of his protagonist's egotistical strength anticipates the re-examination and questioning of this pattern in more recent Caribbean writing—for example Earl Lovelace's *The Dragon Can't Dance* (1979), George Lamming's *Natives of My Person* (1972) or, less centrally, the Anna passages of Derek Walcott's *Another Life* (1972).

28. V.S. Reid, *New Day* (Kingston: Sangster/Heinemann, 1970), p. 38. (First published 1949).

29. The following poems from Louise Bennett's *Jamaica Labrish* (Kingston: Sangsters Ltd., 1966) are quoted: "Uriah Preach," p. 203; "Me Bredda," p. 190; "Pinnacle," p. 121. "Jamaica Oman" is quoted from an unpublished manuscript.

Wives and Other Victims: Women in the Novels of Roy A.K. Heath

Mark A. McWatt

It is necessary to point out from the beginning that all the characters in the novels of Roy A.K. Heath are victims. They are depicted as victims from birth, certainly from the beginning of the novels, and their condition is not alleviated at the end. These characters are victimized principally by large, anonymous forces beyond their control such as history, fate or passion—but these forces are not named or described in any detail by the author; rather they are left deliberately vague or understated. For instance, while the novels are roughly dated (*A Man Come Home* and *The Murderer* are set in the post-independence period in Georgetown, Guyana, and the Armstrong Trilogy begins in the 1920s and ends around the 1960s), there is no attempt to describe a historical context for the predicament of the charaters in the way, for instance, that the specific date of Jean Rhy's *Wide Sargasso Sea* is crucial to an understanding of that novel. One might get from Heath's novels something of V.S. Naipaul's sense of a historically determined futility in the lives of the characters, but Heath never explains this the way Naipaul constantly does, by reflecting on the society and the past and by dwelling at length on such historical causes as the failed myth of Eldorado.[1] Edward Brathwaite also, in all his major poetry, portrays the way in which ordinary West Indians were victimized by events in the past, but he concentrates on the cyclic movements of history and his volumes of poetry all end with affirmations of new beginnings which suggest a break in the cycle of victimization.[2] No such affirmations are to be found in Heath; rather there is a sense in which his characters are victimized by the author himself, by his deliberate choice of a particular mode of writing—which I have identified elsewhere[3] as "tragic irony, a fiction of victims and

223

scapegoats, rather than heroes." It is as though Heath were focussing relentlessly on only half of what Wilson Harris calls "the victor victim stasis"[4]—we have the victims and the stasis, the victor (or the agency responsible for the victimization) is perhaps implied but never stated in the novels.

The world of a Roy Heath novel is therefore very bleak, though this is not quite the bleakness of the literary conventions of the absurd, where characters are either only too painfully aware of their predicament, or else their mechanical and unmotivated speech and actions create explicit diagrams of their own despair.[5] Heath's characters, in spite of their inescapable victim status, attempt to live "normal" lives and pursue very ordinary goals—such as wealth or simple domestic comfort. This contrast between the ordinariness of the characters and their lives and the extra-ordinariness of the context of gloom in which they live, can often create a sense of deformity in the writing, a sense that the situations and events described do not ring quite true or seem somehow unreal—as do all effects that have been cut off from their causes.

It is necessary to be clear about this particular context in which Heath's characters exist and to realize that none escapes victimization of some sort. The thoughts and actions of the male protagonists in the novels—whose lives all end either in insanity or in violent or squalid death—demonstrate their astonishing lack of freedom as well as the mystery as to its cause. Armstrong, in *From the Heat of the Day*,[6] would clearly like to live an ordinary married life with Gladys, his wife, but he is subject to unexplained irritability and uncontrollable rages:

> Suddenly Armstrong found himself struggling with a wave of irritability that seemed to have no causes. . . . Why could he not accept things as they were . . . (p. 32)

There is also the accumulated guilt caused by these failings, which in turn fuels further unintended violence:

> Armstrong's wife had uncovered in her husband a host of guilty feelings whose existence he had never before suspected. The intemperate punishment of Boyie for a minor misdeed was evidence of a brutality that had nothing to do with his own nature. Yet at the time *he felt he could not act otherwise.* (p. 107)

The key phrases here are "that seemed to have no cause", "why could he not accept?" and "he felt he could not act otherwise"—which indicate a lack of motivation for, and control over, one's actions. There is perhaps the sense, here, on the reader's part, that where there is insufficient reason for a character's action, he is being acted upon—*manipulated*—by the author. I am sure this is not what Heath intends, but cutting the reader off from the source of the malaise in the novel only causes him or her to speculate the more about it. We know that Armstrong feels very much subject to notions of social status. He moves house at night, so that the shabbiness of his furniture might not be noticed; he is very conscious of the fashionable and unfashionable neighborhoods of the city; when he's in financial straits, he insists on eating and dressing well while his family goes hungry, because he is the one who goes out into the world and must keep up appearances. He is puzzled by his friend Doc's anger at being treated as an inferior by a white man:

> Armstrong could not understand his friends's excitement. A show of obsequiousness in the presence of his superiors was as natural (to Armstrong) as expanding and contracting his chest. (p. 88)

From such evidence one can perhaps speculate that the force oppressing Armstrong and rendering him unhappy has to do with society, but it is a force that has been internalised, it is not locatable anywhere out there in the Georgetown he inhabits; it commands him from within—it is in his head and in the heads of all members of Heath's claustrophobic Georgetown society, they have been conditioned to believe in petty distinctions of class and status and are ruled by these invisible laws. In the end one can perceive this kind of understated truth building, in novel after novel, to a very powerfully hostile statement about the evils of colonial society and its residual absurdities in the minds of the people long after the "colony" has become "independent." In terms of the internal conflict and the lack of control over one's actions, each of Heath's characters is a microcosm of the larger community, a "micro-colony" in fact, flailing helplessly in the grip of forces it does not understand nor control.

It is easy to see how, in this context, the woman becomes a double-victim. She is victimized by all of the forces we have been examining so far, and then she is further victimized by men. If Armstrong is driven and derided by the colonial system inside his head, then Gladys, his wife, and all the women in the novels are subject not only to the colony-in-the-mind, but also to the sexist principles that govern domestic relationships—to the "man-in-the-head." Armstrong's sister tells Gladys that:

> It was a man's world. Women were not in a position to change it (p. 94).

In *The Murderer*[7] Gemma addresses Galton Flood in her letters, before they are married, as "my tormentor," and she says:

... You men lock women up in small places and expect them to be
normal. These fires burning inside me are not normal. My dreams
aren't normal; the way I walk isn't normal. If I were normal I would
open the window and scream until something burst. There is an East
Indian girl living here who did that a little while ago. Her parents sent
for the pharmacist, who gave her some medicine and a sedative. Like
all men he believes there must be a medicine for every condition. I and
many women like me could tell that she couldn't take it any more, her
parents, the music in the streets at night, the sounds from the dance
hall down the road, the short skirts she was forbidden to wear and a
hundred and one little things. (p. 50)

This is one of the most specific statements, in the entire *oeuvre*, about the
way women are victimized, not only by individual men, but also by a world
designed or devised by men. It is worth noting, however, that in spite of her
perspicacity, Gemma still marries her "tormentor," who before the novel
ends becomes her murderer. The suggestion is that the woman is trapped no
matter what she does—the pervasive and pernicious influence of society
and of the male ego are inescapable. "Men are so strong!" Genetha[8] remembers her mother, Gladys Armstrong, saying. This is a statement that is
both true (when one considers the doubly colonized minds of Heath's
women) and at the same time spectacularly untrue (when one considers
objectively the pathetic weakness of "heroes" like Armstrong). Standard
sexist notions pervade the society in which these people live. When Genetha
becomes the mistress of the ne'er-do-well Fingers, people immediately
notice and comment on the change in her disposition:

The people she worked with noticed the transformation, as did the
neighbours and shop-keepers. "She getting it, dat's why", one of them
said to a customer who remarked how well she was looking. (p. 15)

In the minds of these people, it is natural that a woman's well-being should
be dependent upon a physical relationship with a man. The women are
expected, not only to do all the domestic chores, but also to be responsible
for the integrity and security of the family: "The security of the family has
always been bought at the expense of women, (Genetha's) mother once
remarked to her paternal aunt" (p. 43). But Genetha rejects the status of
wife and mother precisely because she can see the futility of that kind of
sacrifice:

Yet her mother having acted as a doormat all her married life, had not
attained any worthwhile stability, either for herself or for the rest of
the family. (p. 43)

Without ever mentioning the cruelties of the past, it seems clear nevertheless, that Heath's domestic situations are reenactments of the historical conditions of slavery and indenture in their emphasis on labour and sacrifice without reward. Even the "reward" of a husband's tenderness and affection puts the woman into the condition of servitude and denies her any individual worth. In Heath the family becomes a kind of hell for the women. This condition is stated very well by Deen, one of the lesser female characters in *One Generation*.[9] Deen is so overwhelmed with the task of trying to care for a family of eight children (to say nothing of Ramjohn's grandiose requirements) on her husband's small salary, that she wearily says:

> "Is what all you trying to do to me?" she asked weakly, while her husband took the belt from her. "You know nothing," she said, and sank wearily to the floor, "nothing. You never even see one o' your children born; and whenever I in labour you go under the house with a bottle of rum and cry like a child. If I go an' dead you'd buy a bottle o' rum an' do the same thing. An' the nex' day you'd make Asha do all the work an' say how good she is."
>
> She bent double, her head almost touching the floor and her teeth chattering.
>
> "I don't know what you all want with me. You all trample me from morning to night and then you say I don't sing no more. . . . I feel so cold . . . " (pp. 140-141)

It is clear that the domestic situation is the focus of Heath's fictional concern; the home and the family—terms transformed into the most vicious and cruel arena of human activities. The home and the family become traps for the humans involved, but especially so for the women. I've chosen to entitle this paper "Wives and Other Victims," because it suggests the centrality of the domestic situation in Heath's novels at least much as it indicates the inescapable victimization of women.

I am suggesting that women in the novels fit into a kind of continuum of categories, which might be stated as follows, in descending order of respectability:

> maiden aunts
> wives/mothers
> single girls
> mistresses
> servants
> prostitutes

All the women in Heath's novels fit into one or other of these categories, and although they live in and assign nuances of respectability or disgrace within

various gradations of the continuum, the irony is that they are all in fact
equal in terms of their status as victims. Society allows a maiden aunt to
appear more virtuous or respectable than a mistress or a prostitute, but
Heath makes clear that she is victimized in precisely the same way.

Maiden aunts figure prominently in the Armstrong trilogy. Gladys
Armstrong's two sisters have escaped what they regarded as the sordid
traffic in flesh that characterizes all the other categories of women, but they
have not been set free from desire, they are derided by their unsatisfied
physical longings and take out their frustrations by being cruel to those they
profess to love; Genetha, loveless and desperate, visits her maternal aunts,
but the deathlike atmosphere of the house and the uncomprehending
coldness of the women preclude any attempt on her part to ask for help.
Genetha also has a maiden aunt on her father's side and she does go to live
with her while Fingers is supposedly having their house repaired, but the
aunt torments her with complaints about the way she (the aunt) was used
and cheated by Genetha's father. This indicates that she has not lived a life
free of victimization by men, and that its effect lingers in a horrible and
sadistic streak. This aunt admits that she wants Genetha to suffer for her
father's sins:

> But the sins of the father will be visited on the children. You and you
> no-good brother will come to a bad end. I'll pray for you and you will
> go under wishing you were never born! Look round you and see what
> I'm left with. I use enamel plates, like a range-yard woman, have to
> empty my own po! And I was once respected in Anandale. Who
> respects me now? Who can respect a woman who does empty her own
> po? God is my witness that I've never had a moment's peace since he
> stripped me of everything I had. (p. 58)

This shows that the aunt is victimized not only by her brother, but also by
her own sense of social status; It seems that what she cannot forgive is her
apparent slippage down the steps of the continuum. She feels tainted by her
proximity and resemblance to the "lower orders" of women since she must
"empty her own po" and eat off enamelled ware like a servant.

Central to an understanding of Heath's portrayal of women in his novels
is an understanding of the role of wife and mother. It is a painfully ambiguous
role, for it is that towards which the woman generally aspire, and yet it is the
role that most relentlessly traps and diminishes them. In Heath's first novel,
A Man Come Home,[10] we are presented with the picture of the Foster
ménage, consisting of Foster himself, both his wife and his mistress serving
simultaneously under the same roof and their several children. The wife, the
prior of Foster's two attachments, puts up with the situation because she
can do no better in a man's world. There are no really independent women
in Heath. We are, rather, in the same kind of social circumstances which

trapped and victimized a whole string of Jean Rhys heroines in the early novels. There is simply no provision for a woman outside of some species of relationship with a man.

We have already seen how Gemma, although aware of the trap of marriage to Galton, enters it nevertheless and is increasingly subjected to his cruelties. It is true that Galton is seriously disturbed mentally, but that disturbance only emphasizes or symbolizes the disorder that is the male ego itself. Galton is severely sexually repressed—this is evident before they are married when he is first sexually aroused by her. Instead of going to her in the room next door, he is seized with an uncontrollable urge to lick the flowers on the wallpaper and smash down the walls—an incident which Wilson Harris refers to as "the symbolic rape of premises."[11] After they get married Galton's repression continues to be an obstacle to their relationship: "He insisted she wear underclothes in bed—even during their acts of intimacy" (p. 78). And we are also told: "Not once had he fondled Gemma's breast, in the belief that he would be engaging in an abnormal practice" (p. 95).

Galton's marriage to Gemma is therefore foredoomed. When he discovers that his wife had had an earlier sexual experience with an older man he cruelly drags her away from the fairly comfortable suburban house they were living in and installs her in a bleak and filthy room in a tenement building in the slum area of Albouystown. Later, when he discovers that she is unfaithful to him, the reader recognizes that he is incapable of any other solution but to kill her. Perhaps the saddest point about Gemma's tragedy is the realization that in Heath's fictional world, she would have fared no better and perhaps considerably worse if she had not married Galton. The notion of happiness or security within the role of wife is illusory, but the same is true of all roles.

Gladys, Sonny Armstrong's wife in *From the Heat of the Day* is not allowed the reprieve of an early death like Gemma; she gives her life in the service of Armstrong, slowly and painfully, wondering from time to time what was the meaning of it all:

> Separation from Armstrong was unthinkable, and when he fell into the abyss the chain that bound their lives would drag her with him. She searched for a reason for this terrible liaison, but could not find one. Things were just so. There was a sky and an earth; there was the wind and the Sun, and there was marriage. (p. 140)

In thinking about the lives of her servants, Gladys broods on the fate of woman:

> Why was Marion not as ambitious as Esther? . . . Her only goal appeared to be to get married and bring children into the world. Was that really all there was to life for a woman? (p. 45)

Gladys's dissatisfaction with the physical aspect of her role as Armstrong's wife is obvious in the fantasies of sexual self-abasement that she has and also in the fact that she foolishly confides these to the servants:

> You know, sometimes I feel like giving myself to the ugliest man that passed by," she once said to Marion. "I mean I could choose the ugliest from the first twenty and invite him into the house and cook for him and then allow him to do with me whatever he wanted." (p. 98)

These details seem carefully chosen by Heath to define the psychological effect of Gladys's victimization—the spiritual brutalization she has undergone at the hands of social circumstance and pretentiousness and at the hands of the man who is her husband. Her aims and desires, though conspicuously modest, are nevertheless depicted as unattainable:

> more powerful than the desire to escape death, deeper than the longing for happiness, was the longing to be herself, but in being herself to lose nothing; to wear the clothes of her choice, make friends with anyone who happened to be passing, and thereby discover her own true desires, her own morality. (p. 161)

When the role of wife is overlapped by that of mother the problems appear to be compounded. Ramjohn's wife in *One Generation* is, as has already been pointed out, a good example of a woman victimized in her role as mother. She ends up a pathetic suicide at the bottom of a well. Galton Flood's mother, in *The Murderer* provides and interesting variation on the theme of victimization. Heath shows us—with the psychological acuity that is one of the novel's major strengths—that the mother is the one largely responsible for Galton's disturbed state; with little acts of mental cruelty that are shown to have major consequences in the hero's adult life, she inflicts upon the child Galton the punishment really intended for the sins (real and imagined) of her husband. Galton has vivid memories of his mother's tirades:

> his earliest memory was of his mother belabouring his father in a frenzy of anger. He recalled how he looked on, paralysed with fear, and how, afterwards he wanted the world to come to an end. He was only three then. (p. 87)

She seems to resent the very fact that Galton's father married her and then enclosed her within the walls of the family home. Her inferior status as a woman and mother produces in her an enormous irritation and she retreats into a narrow religiosity, from which perspective she regales Galton with his father's sins:

> Your father is a gambler, Galton. He's steeped in sin and shame and
> God's mercy is turned away from this house. Kneel down and pray for
> your father and beg God to spare us . . . (p. 139)

Later on she punishes Galton for reporting that he has seen a group of
Indian women suckling their infants in full view of passers-by. She makes
him say a prayer "in which he asked to be forgiven for his evil thoughts" (p.
173). These details indicate that the mother compensates for the sense of
hurt, humiliation and victimization that she feels by visiting upon her son a
comparable mental cruelty and sense of distress. A particularly revealing
passage occurs towards the end of the novel, when Galton is haunted by the
recurring scenario of the murder he committed (p. 186)—only, in his
haunted vision, it is his mother that he sees in the role of murderer (instead
of himself) and his father as the victim (instead of Gemma).

The category of single girls, as exemplified by the characters of Melda (*A
Man Come Home*) and Genetha (*Genetha*) seems to slip quickly and easily
down one rung into the 'lower' category of mistress, which brings the
woman more obviously into contact with—and therefore under the control
of—men. The case of Melda's slippage down the continuum illustrates
clearly the way in which a woman can be the victim of both sexes.

When the young Melda announces to her mother Christine that she is
pregnant, and refuses to discuss the matter, Heath portrays, in his powerful,
understated technique, how the mother's own anger and anxiety overflow
into a terrible violence:

> Christine could hear her daughter brushing her hair. Somehow the
> thought of Melda sitting in front of the mirror in her slip, pulling the
> brush down on her hair as if nothing has happened, infuriated her . . .
> Snatching the brush from Melda's hand she brought it down on her
> head and back several times. Melda's arms were raised above her
> head one moment and covering her face the next, until she fell to the
> floor at her mother's feet. Only then did Christine stop. (p. 36)

This single destructive act, itself born out of the insecurity and fear inherent
in the victim status of the woman, becomes eloquently demonstrative of the
tragic helplessness of Heath's women, as both Christine and Melda are
forever trapped by its consequences. Melda miscarries, becomes mentally
deranged and ineligible for marriage; she becomes a burden on her mother
who, out of guilt and a grimly controlled pity, is forced to stand helplessly by
while Melda is shamelessly seduced and repeatedly subjected to the sexual
predations of her brother's friend Gee. Heath conveys perfectly the sense of
desperate longing and expectation with which Melda awaits Gee's visits,
and the graphic description of their lovemaking, together with the fact that it
is silently observed by Christine, constitute the most powerfully expressive

evidence of the way the woman is victimized in her own intimate, domestic sphere.

In *Genetha*, the final novel of the Armstrong trilogy, the eponymous heroine undergoes a fate similar to that of Melda's. Driven by physical desire into the arms of the shiftless Fingers, she finds the terrible, narcotized despair of her previous, unattached existence replaced by great anxiety over her new relationship interspersed with only brief moments of physical pleasure (hardly more than the moments of euphoria she used to experience during her solitary, self-inflicted doses of "a mildly poisonous substance", p. 2)

Fingers' act of robbing Genetha of her family home and possessions becomes the precipitating factor for a bout of temporary insanity;[12] she spends time in an asylum and upon release is unemployable. It is interesting to note that the escape—however illusory for the woman—into the role of "career woman" with its suggestions of independence and a certain status, is never really explored in Heath's fiction. Genetha, before she is robbed and abandoned by Fingers, comes closest to this kind of role, but her life as a working girl is nevertheless characterized by emptiness and desire, and the attempts to alleviate the one and fulfill the other lead, as we see, to ruin. The desperate Genetha eventually falls into the clutches of Esther, a former servant of her parents, now the madam of a brothel; from there her decline into the final category of the continuum is swift and inevitable.

Heath emphasizes the victimization of women by the fact that the tug always seems to be in a downward direction—towards further humiliation and degradation. The irony here is that even if there were the possibility of "upward" mobility in the continuum we have been examining, that would have meaning only in terms of the kind of society and social concerns *within* the novel; from the reader's perspective the prostitute is no more a victim than the mistress, the wife or the maiden aunt. The upscale categories have social status of a kind, but that is seen to be a cruel and inadequate substitute for a sense of genuine independence and personal worth, which seem to be denied to women at all levels.

The fact is that the social hierarchy may be considered to be in large part responsible for enforcing the victimization of women—with its built-in suggestion that movement can only occur in one direction; what is it worth for a servant, for instance, to try to move up the ladder and become a kept-woman or a wife when Heath has been careful to show that she has had at least vicarious experiences of these categories. Gladys Armstrong's servants have witnessed the bitterness and emotional chaos at the heart of that domestic situation and Marion has even served as confidante for the depraved fantasies of Gladys. Servants such as these are intimately aware of the sterility and victimization that characterize the married life of their mistress, and someone like Esther might well discern a greater chance for "freedom" in the *demi-monde* of the brothel. Esther may be feared and disreputable in the second half of *Genetha*, but at least she is financially independent and wields a kind of power—even over the daughter of her former employer.

The social hierarchy also serves to keep women apart. There is a conspicuous absence of warmth and compassion among the women in Heath's novels, a refusal to help each other or to work together. Instead they are all in futile competition for status in a man's world, just as the men themselves are in futile competition for status in accordance with their colonized mentality. In the end both men and women are victims, but the difference between the two is perhaps best illustrated by the two stories that Genetha tells to Michael towards the end of the novel. Michael is an early suitor, rejected because of his joylessness and religious snobbery; he is now a married man fascinated by the aura of the "fallen woman" now worn by his former girlfriend:

> I'll tell you two stories, Michael. My younger aunt is always telling me family stories. A few days ago she told me about their brother. I didn't even know I had an uncle; but they're not supposed to talk about him. When he was still at school he was always saying, "All I want is a gun and a dog." My grandfather doted on him and wouldn't shut him up when he talked like that, although Grandmother and my aunts were frightened at his threats to run away as soon as he could afford to buy a gun and a dog. He passed all his exams with distinction, and at eighteen left school to go abroad to study medicine. But during the holidays he went off into the bush—just as he said he would do—with an old hunting gun he bought from the vet who lived next door, Mr. Bruce. The last my grandparents and aunts heard of him was that he had married an aboriginal Indian. It's not an exciting story, but it keeps haunting me: a gun and a dog. . . . You'll like the second story, Michael. My aunt said that a man went abroad and returned with a European wife. Every day she came out with him to his work-place by cab. She then took him home again the same way. And you know what she did while he was at work?
>
> "What?"
>
> "She waited in the cab all those hours while he was at work, with only the cabbie for company. (pp. 146-147)

The stories indicate that perhaps a man might manage to flee society and its oppressive rules and structures, but the women remain trapped, theirs is a life of waiting and dependence on men. There is the suggestion, in this story of the lady who waits in the cab, that a woman has no separate existence, she must define herself and her status and ultimate worth in terms of a man. Perhaps this is why Genetha continues to be haunted by the first story—of escape to a world outside the stifling confines of the coastal city—escape into the bush, the freedom of the hinterland.

In this regard it is worth noting that there is one brief idyllic section of the novel which deals with just such an escape; it is entitled "A Season in Morawhanna." In this small riverside settlement Fingers and Genetha enjoy the happiest moments of the novel. More importantly, however, it is at Morawhanna that they meet the only really free woman in the Armstrong trilogy. References to Sybil occupy perhaps eight pages, but she remains a haunting portrayal of what is, in the context, an exciting possibility: her freedom is emphasized in the fact that she swims naked in the river, she is close to the Amerindian folk, she not only supports herself with her job as a school teacher to the Amerindian children, but she is the only one capable of keeping them at school (as the authorities discover when they try to fire her). Heath emphasizes her difference from the other women in the novel by referring to her as a "spirit-child" and by making her presence and her personality acutely disturbing to Genetha, who is attracted to her (almost wild) freedom, but at the same time the social conditioning of her Georgetown upbringing causes her to be repelled by that same freedom.

Sybil here is much more of a device for emphasizing Genetha's entrapment in her world than a full character in her own right, but she indicates what is perhaps the only avenue of possible escape from the claustrophobia and victimization that is the monotonously predictable condition of all the women in Heath's novels. Such an Avenue of escape is again suggested in Heath's latest novel, *Orealla*, where the title and internal references suggest an idyllic amerindian settlement in the interior; but the novel and its victim-characters, remain firmly trapped in the unforgiving Georgetown society we have seen in all the other novels.

NOTES

1. See especially V.S. Naipaul's *The Loss of Eldorado* (London: Andre Deutsch, 1969) and also "The Two Faces of Eldorado: Contrasting Attitudes towards History and Identity in West Indian Literature" by Mark McWatt, in *West Indian Literature and its Social Context* (Barbados: Dept. of English, U.W.I., 1985).
2. Edward K. Brathwaite, *The Arrivants* (Oxford: OUP, 1967).
3. Mark McWatt, "Tragic Irony—The Hero as Victim: Three Novels of Roy A.K. Heath" in *Critical Issues in West Indian Literature*, ed. Smilowiz and Knowles (Parkersberg, OH: Caribbean Books, 1984), pp. 33-47.
4. The term occurs in several places in Harris's essays, but see especially "Interview with Wilson Harris" in *Kas-Kas*: Interviews with Caribbean Writers in Texas (Austin, TX: African and Afro-American Research Institute, 1972), pp. 43-55.

5. I'm thinking about such works as the novels of Sartre and Camus and the theatre of Samuel Beckett.

6. Roy A.K. Heath, *From The Heat of the Day* (London: Allison & Busby, 1979). All references are to this edition.

7. Roy A.K. Heath, *The Murderer* (London: Allison & Busby, 1978). All references are to this edition.

8. Roy A.K. Heath, *Genetha* (London: Allison & Busby, 1981), p. 15. All references are to this edition.

9. Roy A.K. Heath, *One Generation* (London: Allison & Busby, 1981). All references are to this edition.

10. Roy A.K. Heath, *A Man Come Home* (London: Longman, 1974). All references are to this edition.

11. Review of *The Murderer*; Wilson Harris in *World Literature Written in English*, Vol. XVII, No. 2, p. 656.

12. Although there were obviously several predisposing factors, including childhood experiences and her more recent treatment by her father and brother. In this sense she conforms to a pattern of insanity among heroines of West Indian fiction as examined by Evelyn O'Callaghan in "Interior Schisms Dramatised: The Treatment of the 'Mad' Woman in the Work of Some Female Caribbean Novelists," appearing elsewhere in this volume.

Woman as Life or "Spirit of Place". Wilson Harris's Companions of the Day and Night

Joyce Stewart

Woman changes like water in our hands, she is shrewdly protean.[1]

In each of Harris's novels we find the woman treated according to her historial, geographical and cultural location, and according to the psychological climate of the period, but used as an abstraction or collective symbol. For instance, Mariella in *Palace of the Peacock* represents the spirit of the surviving Amerindian people, enslaved, abused, pursued and robbed by the Europeans, yet still maintaining an unbeaten and unfathomable spirit. In *Heartland* the Amerindian ability to endure and adapt is epitomised by the lonely figure of the Amerindian Woman who, with little assistance, gives birth to a child, the symbolic future. In *Da Silva da Silva's Cultivated Wilderness*, the women are typical of contemporary career women facing a set of problems new and peculiar to our age: while Kate faced the choice of motherhood or abortion and all the attendant trauma, Jenine combined a career with being a lover, prospective mother, and financial and moral supporter of her husband through his less lucrative but essential creative career.

The problems here concern a world where the real hope comes from a joint functioning of male and female; from the realisation that neither is inferior to, or independent of, the other; and from the recognition that the "mutual joy of flesh and blood . . . the immortal presence they ceaselessly conceived into existence through each other." (*Da Silva* p. 48) Magda of *The Whole Armour* is a product of the need to adapt in post-colonial times

237

in order to survive and grow. She is the result of colonialism and its unimaginative immigration policies which made racial mixture inevitable without removing the racial tensions and hatred which typified Guyanese/ Caribbean society as it emerged from slavery and indenture. Each "woman" embodies a representation of the cultural norms and expectations of her society at a particular time in history, yet beyond that, each allows the possibility of change and development.

In 1975 when *Companions of the Day and Night* was published (this was also the year in which the World Conference of International Woman's Year was convened in Mexico City) the position of the Mexican woman was no different from that of women in most of the rest of the world:

> ... the Mexican considers woman to be an instrument, sometimes of masculine desires, sometimes of the ends assigned to her by morality, society and the law. ... In a world made in man's image, woman is only a reflection of masculine will and desire. When passive, she becomes a goddess, a beloved one, a being who embodies the ancient stable elements of the universe: the earth, motherhood, virginity. When active she is always function and means, a receptacle and a channel.[2]

Although it was only in 1958 that women in Mexico voted in the presidential elections for the first time, by 1975 women crowded universities, wrote, painted, practised medicine and studied nuclear engineering. In short "women range from bureaucrats high in the administration to servile Indians who are beasts of burden at the man's command."[3] Yet, as observers like Octavio Paz and Irene Nicholson point out, the underlying fundamental attitudes to women remain. The legacy from a Roman Catholic Europe is that "woman is a domesticated wild animal, lecherous and sinful from birth, who must be subdued ... and guided by the reins of religion."[4] The woman who is subdued is good, the one who remains active is bad. On the other hand the Mexican's mythology has taught him to recognise as inherent in the woman the elements of mystery and seduction, to see her natural value and to appreciate the good feminine influence; yet he still considers her to be a dark, secret, passive being to whom he attributes no individuality. Paz describes the current conception, which he admits is false and therefore creates problems of communication and relationships, yet keeps the woman above being a mere object, thus:

> She is an idol ... mistress of magnetic forces whose efficacy increases as their source of transmission becomes more passive and secretive. ... Woman does not seek, she attracts, and the centre of her attraction is her hidden, passive sexuality ... she is a symbol ... of the stability

and continuity of the race. In addition . . . she also has the important social role . . . to see that law and order, piety and tenderness are predominant in everyday life.[5]

Unfortunately, because it is created out of man's subconscious projected image, the 'idol' is vulnerable, subject to his moods. "Woman" therefore, remains an idea, and should she try to become fully human, risks being made a victim of male outrage:

> Woman is an idol, a goddess, a mother, a witch, or a muse . . . but she can never be herself . . . she can only conceive of herself as an object . . . never her own mistress. Her being is divided between what she really is and what she imagines she is . . . dictated by family, class, friends, religion and love . . . if they attempt a free choice it must be a kind of jail break.[6]

In *Companions of the Day and Night*, Harris takes up these conflicting ideas. His ultimate aim is to force a reconsideration of Mexico's history in order to make clear the importance of all its aspects, whether popularised or stifled, so that we may learn something new from it. But first he forces a re-evaluation of the nature and role of the woman as prescribed by the institutions of the church, law, and society; and this re-evaluation becomes the vehicle for reconsidering history. What emerges is not a new "hard-and-fast" definition of the woman, modern or otherwise, but the awareness that her psyche cannot be separated into entities of good or evil, physical or spiritual. It must be seen as a compound of all. For while situations may demand that she play the madonna, she is also capable of being the whore should the need arise, and vice versa. The reality is that the woman has a human identity as great as that attributed to the man; that what constitutes "woman" or the feminine "other" as described by Paz is as vital as the masculine part, that neither male nor female, weak nor strong, can continue to exist on its own.

In the Mexican context, religion was the major shaping force of the idea of "woman." Harris sets out with this fact in mind, to re-examine the Roman Catholic and Aztec religions, and to draw lessons from them which should be applied thoughtfully to a new understanding of woman. Two cautions are reiterated: "vision is unsuspected, glimpsed proportions through objects of nature and history," (p. 13) and "What matters is a capacity to revise. . . . " (p. 47)

The Christian Church which disseminates religion, is regarded by its followers as feminine and good. The Roman Catholic Church, which is part of the Christian Church, branded woman as evil, yet found the woman indispensable to the spreading of the teachings of the church (here Harris alludes to the Virgin of Guadeloupe, used to popularise Christianity among the Mexicans, and to the nuns who were able to outwit political systems by going underground). The question arises as to where these features, the good and the evil, begin and end. The novel also shows the inseparability of the two elements through the fact that both Roman Catholicism and the Aztec religion were prostituted during the conquest of Mexico. Yet the syncretic religion that has emerged has become a force for good, a cohesive element supporting and leading the people into revolution and a new life, and shaping the modern state. Harris's suggestion seems to be that, as the features of religion have evolved, so too the features of "woman" have evolved and must be recognised and accepted for the good of "man". Harris puts this caution in Sister Joanna's mouth: "What matters is a capacity to revise . . . however painful that may be . . . to respond to self-contradictory tongues all rolled into one." (p. 47) This is the only method that allows growth and avoids frustration, for whereas in Europe there is established "a well-defined finished doctrine," (p. 49) in Mexico "a cleavage exists within the ethics of sacrifice," (p. 49) which can only be filled by a rebirth of ideas, a rebirth made possible when we strip "away from it a body of encrusted habit that trades on the exploitation of culture by culture." (p. 50)

The artist's model who is presented to us at the start of the novel as a total person, "the best in these parts," (p. 24) becomes as the work progresses, our gateway into re-evaluation of given concepts. We look anew at the idea of the virgin, and through the artist's vision we are encouraged to see that the original virgin appealed not because of a remote purity, but because of the similarity she bore to a living, feeling, warm-blooded woman. In the artist's conception, the model or ideal of the virgin sold to us was unnatural, "painted, sculpted with precision . . . a marvel. Flesh-within-flesh, ghost-within-ghost . . . worth her weight in gold." (p. 22) The idea and object to which these qualities belonged was in the present context "unfinished," still devoid of human-ness and feeling, to all intents—dead. There is the need to replace it with a human figure, human in its ability to care, to feel, and to evoke those feelings in man, as well as capable of giving life and warmth. Hence the artist drew his model from life. To bring about this change in outlook, our Fool is hypnotically freed from the present by the fire eater's ritual chanting, and is taken into a world made possible by the imagination. He felt the unfinished nature of the virgin as an "ageless material hollow, the marks of which he carried;" (p. 22) and the psychological result was that he felt "smeared" and "unclean." This contact with the unconscious,[7] though brief, had the effect of starting the mending in the Fool's psyche, promoting a closer rapport with his "other" female side. As he returned to the "stable element" (p. 23) he could not forget the brief perception of the value of the "passion of the senses," (p. 23) and this helped him to find that the true woman is not only virgin, but also possesses that sensuous element that makes man feel as an emperor:

... the intense spring of man when the arm of a goddess, her leg, her face, enmeshes him. And the chain of fire within him/within her confirms all that is intimate, all that is unbearable, within his reach, beyond his reach. (p. 24)

The excursion into the subconscious also had the effect of forcing the Fool to look further into the past, to

... descend still further beneath imperial shadow into rejected abysses, rejected goddesses, sacrificed priestesses under the floor of the church. Long, long ago when her flesh was the bread of spring. (p. 25)

This further looking helped him to perceive and to accept how vital that feminine element is to man and to his continuity. In fact this realisation and acceptance freed him from fear of extinction, from fear of the past and the present, and from fear of the future. Unfortunately (or realistically) his vision is still blocked by preoccupation with the physical and the urge to possess, to which the fire eater had first appealed.

There is great contrast between the ideal woman according to the artistic vision of the fire eater and the vision of Hose the guide. While the fire eater may be seen as a warm-blooded revolutionary, Hose is described as being of cold disposition, having one foot in the grave and the other in the past, bound by tradition and respectability. His view of women therefore comes as no surprise: Octavio Paz's description of the Mexican male fits him well. The great lady or 'model' is characterised by virgin passivity, hence his respect for Sister Beatrice in her role as nun, and his disapproval of her participation in the Easter parade. She, he believes, should never have assumed what he sees as a masculine role. Incongruously, his respect for her seemed heightened by the rape which she suffered, and which in no way damaged her virgin aspect, since she was not mentally co-operative. There is also the suggestion that he respects her because she is devoid of, or at best above sexuality, but events prove that this is the way Hose wants his ideal woman to be, while the reality is different.

If one sees the convent as a symbol of asexuality or as a denial of sexuality, then the nun by staying there, played the expected role while being willing to play another. She "possessed the capcity to revise." (p. 47) Therefore, when the hidden convent was exposed during the time that she was still a young woman and the other nuns fled, she remained to assume another important role: "to involve herself in the rituals of the day." (p. 40) It was during this period of active involvement that the interaction with the male element took place, the sexual side became temporarily important and she became pregnant. But that the "virgin" passive nun changes roles and conceives is not strange when one is reminded of the evidence put forward by Jung to prove that men and women possess components of their sexual opposites, and that these components are used simultaneously but in unequal proportions for a part of life; that later the previously lesser used aspect comes into prominence. More importantly, Jung points out that the changes become more noticeable in the psychic realm.[8] The young nun was simply asserting her stronger but suppressed side when she seemed to assume the role of the male, while at the same time she lived up to what is expected of the female, conceived and gave birth. In this way Harris supports his thesis on the necessity for positive interaction of the "male" and "female" elements if life is to be productive.

The Fool's situation as he looked for what he considered to be his feminine other is echoed in the "mythological" natural history of Mexico, and the story of the Sleeping Lady and Popocatapetl.[9] Like Popocatapetl, the Fool remained in danger through a narrow vision and fixation on an idea, of perpetrating his own extinction—he became involved in a search for the 'woman' only to pursue her physical self, so reducing her to the status of barren whore. As he met a woman (who could have been his companion of the night before) emerging from the church, he connected her with the dust and aridity of the convent[10]—the place which denies femininity—and the accumulated indoctrination from the past makes him turn away from her. In his experience, the sensual woman of the type with which he had spent the night and with whom he had penetrated paradise, had a place distinct from the church. The "woman" for whom he was looking must be reduced to an object without spirituality before he could be comfortable with her. The woman with an unexplored or virgin side "was not the woman he was looking for." (p. 33)

Eventually, for the Fool, Harris makes the difference between the fire eater's artist's-model-whore and Hose's artist-model-virgin disappear. The fire eater's model is everyman's woman/mother, Hose's model is everyman's ideal/idol, but for Harris both women come from the same place, and furthermore, the whore is the grand-daughter of the idol. While the Fool studied Hose and his attitude, he was able to see himself, his ideas, obsessions and susceptibilities—the product of the collective unconscious —mirrored in the guide:

> . . . The Idiot saw his lips move to a painted lesson, as if he were . . . immersed in the living fate of all guides into the past—to which one succumbs—to settle for the past as if it were the moral paint and skin of the present, as if the past reflected in the present had no bearing on the present except to adorn the present with facts, figures, appearances, commodities of love like a solid unbroken mirror through which one glimpses nothing but reflects everything. (p. 39)

The Fool presents us with a woman whose action in giving herself freely to him, fulfilling the natural role of woman, freed him from his fear of the future and gave him hope. Yet this positive action earned her the brand of deviant. Hose presents us with a woman whose life, in the main, seems to deny the natural role of the woman, who had to be raped for her femininity to be known, and who assumed a masculine role in defiance of the moral and social codes which said that "she should never have done it." (p. 41) Her action as a religious revolutionary was invaluable in promoting positive change in the static system which was in danger of extinction. Sister Joanna commends her:

> ... She tried to face a future everyone feared and shrank from ... Beatrice may appear to have achieved little ... and in the beginning there were elements in it which were deplorable and savage, ... the seed she has sown in terribly, terribly important. (p. 48)

In effect, this religious revolutionary action was complementary to that of the nameless whore, in that they both defied rigid moral and social codes and so succeeded in reawakening sensibilities in others. The Fool's renewed consciousness, the encouragement given by Sister Joanna and the artist, teach us to "respond without bitterness" to the voices "of saints, devils, and angels" as parts of one voice, since this tolerance of all roles allows us to understand "the drama of ... humanity." (p. 47)

The chapter called "Door into the Creation of the Gods" calls to mind Harris's essay "Reflection and Vision" in which he writes:

> What is controversial and difficult to establish is the reality of vision, as the imaginative writer or artist occupies a reflected object, not as an absolute formula, costume or investiture around each living moment of time, but as a doorway into apparently eclipsed proportions one needs to unravel in some degree, if the living body of the present is to be capable of some measure of detachment from the past as well as a relatedness to the past.
> ... without such a confrontation there can be no deepseated recreative transformation of the problematic present into a future that is more consistent with a genuine response to the miracle of life. . . .[11]

The discussion on the all inclusive nature of woman as seen by the writer is reflected in this "creation of the God's" through a discussion on the catholic nature of religion; and as the fixed attitudes toward the woman are represented through the nun and the whore, so attitudes towards life—history, change and growth—are represented through the artistic view of religion, in particular, this reconstructed Aztec faith and worship.

The religious icons of the past he sees reflected in the present are those of the Aztec worship of the gods of nature (sun, moon, rain, wind, etc.) As the Fool ascends the Pyramid of the Sun and contemplates the Aztec fixation on the sun as the life giver, and the preservation of life through the taking or denial of life, he senses that more than the power of the sun is needed to ensure life:[12] there is the vital value in the contributions of all the other elements which made the world possible, exemplified in the complex nature of the same Aztec religion. At Teotihuacan where all go to worship the gods, the most imposing pyramid was that of the Sun,[13] but the others were not neglected. In fact, according to Brasch, during the hey-day of the Aztecs, the pyramids of the various gods were all connected at the top by wide avenues along which the priests and worshippers moved. The Fool, as he fell from the precipice of the sun, experienced the feeling of being "connected" with all the gods as "high priest of all the elements." (p. 58)

Harris singles out the god of rain, the most benign and "feminine" of all the gods, to show that element as being equally important as the sun—the most "masculine"—to the survival of life; to infer the need for both the masculine and the feminine parts. Tlaloc's function was to give water in the right quantity for the seed to break through and grow. As the Fool redirected his mind away from the sun god, he "fell . . . into imperial mist" (p. 85)[14] and became the medium of the god of rain, a lesser spirit, symbol of the past within a new world, indiscriminately shedding life-giving substance on the world. The "rain" drenched both him and the indifferent city, which in turn ignored both him and the god. They were left "beached" and "abandoned." In this role as the neglected god/life giving spirit, the Fool forgot his particular location, and taking on the aspect of universality, he could have been in any metropolis where the falling rain and the collected pools of water are temporarily lit up by the lights of moving vehicles. He perceived through this "light" that in our world of advanced technology, there was little spiritual contact between past and present, between male and female. Also that in this age the natural is dominated by the man-made, and that one aspect of life—the stronger or the masculine—is respected, and herein lies our problem. The reflection of the god in the pools of water shows how the feminine contains the masculine, and reflects it for the world to admire. As the past is at once drowned and saved by the present, so the masculine is given life by the feminine. So is indicated the inseparability of the two. He does not fail to recognise that though the rain god has this feminine power to spread fruitful showers on both the spiritual and the physical worlds, there is a chasm that prevents the giving and receiving of the full benefits. What is needed is a spiritual link—represented in the watery, star-studded reflection —between the two worlds, so allowing harmonious contact. The spiritual link exists, but must be given a chance to surface.

Harris completes the involved reflection by drawing an analogy to a barren, fleeting, whoring relationship in which male and female senses are either dead or asleep, or indifferent. It amounts to "a glimpsed repudiation of passive man-condition to passive woman-condition in hollows of culture within the passing night." (p. 61) The Fool perceives that to the extent that genuine intercourse and vision take place, each world benefits; each sees itself in the other: "water wears . . . fire and fire wears the . . . heart of rain . . . to make day out of night." (p. 59) Conversely, the elements remain separate where no productive dialogue occurs. There is a picture of a woman exposed to the elements, seeking but not finding much shelter in the shadow of the male monument. She, only half illuminated by the patches of man-made light, moves across the empty square, and for a while the shadow cast on her is one of sexual domination as the shadow of the monument was imitative of the "out thrust arm, out thrust foot . . . reflection of the coercive embrace that made her look unutterably forlorn. . . . " (p. 61) Her journey suggests attempts to gain comfort and recognition by other means which hold out doubtful promise: first she pauses at a dress shop, seeking comfort in appearance; next, she seems drawn to education as a solution when she stops at a bookstore to contemplate the illustrations that "held her a moth to a candle." (p. 62) One realises that nothing in the world of men captures or explains the nature of woman. Her vulnerability is evident in the expression "animal staring into a bullet," (p. 63) because only by being captured can her spirit be free, since it is then understood. She eventually vanishes into the stale, empty, unimaginative masculine world:

> Reflected crackle, tin drum of pavement . . . orange streetlamp. Clockwork herald of dawn. Herald of garish beauty shed by street-lamp like a light that dresses cell and prison and bed into sacrificed elements.
>   . . . sense of mutual chasms . . . growing indifferent to each other in the . . . blind square of sex. (p. 63)

The Fool, in trying to find her, met with and interviewed a collection of men—workers and idlers, would-be politicians and revolutionaries without a sense of direction. For a while she hovered in sight on the outskirts of this gathering, so that the Fool was in a position to observe her. She did not thrust herself on them, but they could have taken notice of her if they had desired. He never reached her, because he became submerged in the world of his kind, side-tracked from his goal and embroiled in a barren discussion of politics and revolution and empty institutions; by what he describes as "everything that models the shape of the world we live in." (p. 65) The Fool attempted to voice his creative artistic vision to a company that was not ready to understand. He preached to an insensitive collection of "workmen' that:

> We need to see FROM WITHIN the roles that are played by others in our name, and in the name of the nameless forgotten dead, the nameless forgotten living. ME. YOU. We need to regress into our most formidable and implacable rituals for they dress us up like mummified children at a fair . . . " (p. 65)

But he was conquered by his own weakness—his own shame at the passion he felt "as though passion were born of elements . . . that one was ashamed to recall." (p. 65) He had in fact reverted to the side of his psyche represented by Hose, but he is not devoid of hope in that he realised his own insensitivity to the "female" and that he was responsible for allowing himself to be trapped by the deadness and insensitivity which he had inherited; that

> He had followed her across the city from Emperor Square through emperor death into this entanglement in sovereign hero, brute death in the overcoat of a dead workman whose name had long been forgotten at the heart of insurrection . . . the idiot was imbued afresh by the terror of banal lip, banal dialogue with earth as he sank into unwritten, unspoken reserves, codes, bodies, window dressing, overalls, bullets, factories . . . " (p. 65)

He, as man, had merely crossed from one continent to another, but had failed to free his mind from the old conditioning, and until he accomplished this, he would never "fathom in its entirety" what it meant to be "Born of woman." (p. 68)

NOTES

1. Geoffrey Wagner. *Five For Freedom: A Study of Feminism in Fiction* (London: Allen and Unwin Ltd., 1972), p. 15.
2. Octavio Paz. *The Labyrinths of Solitude: Life and Thought in Mexico.* Trans. by Lysander Kemp (London: The Penguin Press, 1976), p. 27.
3. Irene Nicholson. *The X in Mexico* (London: Faber and Faber, 1965), p. 115.
4. Paz., p. 28.
5. Paz., p. 29.
6. Paz., pp. 185-186.
7. According to C.G. Jung in his discussion on the anima, a concept of woman is inborn in man. This constitutes his weaker side—unknown, unconscious and therefore projected onto his opposite. An inherited collective image of woman exists in man's consciousness, with the help of which he apprehends the nature of woman. *Two Essays in Analytical Psychology.* Collected Works of C.G. Jung, Vol. 7, p. 188.
8. Jung describes this feature in *The Structure and Dynamics of the Psyche.* Collected Works of C.G. Jung, Vol. 8, p. 397ff.

9. There are probably a number of versions of the story. One version is available in *Mexico: a City of Contrasts*, by Ralph Brasch, Longmans, 1967, pp. 194-195; and another in Irene Nicholson's *The X in Mexico*, p. 117. Both versions acknowledge a love affair and death by suicide for at least the male when he failed to have the woman.

10. Wilson Harris. *Companions of the Day and Night* (London: Faber and Faber, 1975), p. 40; and R. Brasch, pp. 176-177.

11. Wilson Harris. *Explorations: a selection of talks and articles 1966-1981*, edited with an introduction by Hena Maes-Jelinek (Denmark: Dangaroo Press, 1981), p. 84.

12. The legends of ancient Mexico demonstrate that the worlds of matter and spirit are co-existent and each has something which the other needs. According to the legend of the Five Suns, the earth has already seen four suns—earth, air, fire, water. Each died because it stood alone. Only when the separate elements came together did we have the living sun of today. This sun is immortal only if man attains the redeeming quality, a union of the spiritual and the material. Irene Nicholson, *Mexican and Central American Mythology*, Revised Edition (Newnes Books, 1981), p. 53ff.

13. Brasch gives details of the pyramid, p. 133ff.

14. When the Fool falls to the land of mists he enters the lowest of the three heavens to which the Nahua dead were supposed to go. This was "a kind of paradise where happiness was of a very earthly variety but purer and less enhanceable." It was a sensual world where the good things of life abounded, and also a place where rebirth took place. The idea was that after four years here the soul returned to normal life. Beyond this were the places for those who had learnt to live outside the physical bodies, and the House of the Sun, the ultimate heaven, for those who had achieved full illumination in the search for happiness.

Victim and Accuser: Contradictory Roles of Women in Gabriel Garcia Marquez's Cronica de una muerte anunciada

Amparo Marmolejo McWatt

Je suis la plaie et le couteau
Je suis le soufflet et la joue
Je suis les membres et la roue
Et la victime et le bourreau.

—Baudelaire

Only those not familiar with Gabriel García Márquez's works will question his right to be considered a Caribbean writer. If the fact of having been born in the village of Aracataca on the Caribbean coast of Colombia does not give him that claim in his own right, there are other aspects that certainly do. In his own words

> . . . strictly speaking, [the Caribbean] goes as far as the southern part of the United States (on the north), to Brasil in the south. This shouldn't be thought of as the delirium of an expansionist. No: the Caribbean is not only a geographical area as is, of course, believed by geographers, but a very homogeneous cultural area.
>
> In the Caribbean the original elements of the early beliefs and the magic conceptions that existed prior to the time of discovery were augmented in the following years by the profuse variety of cultures

249

that came together as a magic syncretism whose artistic interest and
fecundity are inexhaustible. Although the African contribution came
about through force and humiliation, it was fortunate.[1]

García Márquez has pronounced himself on many occasions and
obviously in his entire literary works as a writer born and brought up in the
Caribbean, a fact to which he attributes his "frustration"[2] when he says:
" . . . I have never been able to create anything more astonishing than
reality itself."[3]

It is this Caribbean reality with its "cronistas de Indias,"[4] with the
"indian crossed with chinese,"[5] and the "green Hindus"[6] which makes
more difficult the writer's task, which according to García Márquez is to
"make that reality a believable one."[7]

That reality has many common contact points within the whole region as
considered by García Márquez. One of these points is the theme of the
legend of "EL DORADO" which has been treated by English Caribbean
writers such as Wilson Harris from Guyana, and V.S. Naipaul and Michael
Anthony from Trinidad. It is a historic fact that three Spanish conquistadores
met in the savannah of Bogotá—in the heart of Colombia—in 1538 on their
search for "EL DORADO." In any case the Spanish involvement with the
quest for "EL DORADO" is detailed at some length in V.S. Naipaul's *The
Loss of Eldorado*.[8] As can clearly be seen, Gabriel García Márquez is a
Caribbean man not only by birth and feelings but by the fact that the themes
and concern of his works are shared among other Caribbean writers.
Certainly as far as themes related to women are concerned, he reflects
nothing but the Caribbean woman's situation, with the roles assigned to her
by history and society as well as her preoccupations and achievements. He
says of women:

> Women hold the order of the species with an iron-fist, while men go
> out in the world determined to carry out the infinite craziness that
> makes history.[9]

After reading *Crónica de una Muerte Anunciada*[10] the reader might be
left with a feeling of uneasiness and perplexity as far as the behaviour of
Angela Vicario—the girl involved in this case of honour—is concerned. At
the beginning of the novel, Angela appears to the reader as an innocent girl,
completely subject to the values of society and in need of male protection.
By the end of the novel we find that the same Angela is a strong and
spiritually resourceful woman who is "master of her own destiny."

Angela's name is derived from the Greek "Angelus" which means
"messenger," a name of which Bayardo San Roman approved; the first time
he saw her while having his "siesta" he said "Tiene el nombre bien puesto"
(p. 40) ("The name suits her.") She is the girl of humble origin, whom

Bayardo has decided will become his wife, the girl who will be central to the tragic events of the novel.

Angela Vicario had been brought up and educated in order to fulfil the specific role of a woman in a society where distinct roles and codes of behaviour were assigned to its members depending on whether they were men or women. This division in roles can clearly be appreciated in the functions that the father and mother of Angela performed in their society according to pattern established by tradition and the past.[11]

The image that García Márquez projects of Angela's father—Poncio Vicario—highlights this tradition: " . . . era orfebre de pobres, y la vista se le acabó de tanto hacer primores de oro para mantener el honor de la casa." (p. 43) (He was a goldsmith for poor people and he lost his sight making all those beautiful golden objects in order to maintain the honour of his family.) But García Márquez presents us with a "blind father" who obviously is handicapped in the fulfillment of his functions as "the man of the house." One wonders to what extent the author intended to identify, in Poncio Vicario, the blindness and the unfairness that the concept of "machismo" generates.

Angela's mother on the other hand follows the pattern that society and tradition have assigned to women with respect to the family. García Márquez describes Angela's mother in the following terms:

> . . . su madre había sido maestra de escuela hasta que se casó para siempre. Su aspecto manso y un tanto afligido disimulaba muy bien el rigor de su carácter. Se consagró con tal espíritu de sacrificio a la atención del esposo y a la crianza de los hijos, que a uno se le olividaba a veces que seguía existiendo. (p. 43) (Her mother had been a school teacher until her marriage put an end to her career for good. Her gentle and somewhat afflicted appearance disguised very well the severity of her character. She consecrated herself with such spirit of sacrifice to look after her husband and the bringing up of the children that one forgot that she continued living.)

From this statement about Purísima del Carmen, the reader can clearly see that devotion, dedication and the spirit of sacrifice constituted the foundation of her relationship with her husband and her children. 'Los hermanos habían sido criados para ser hombres. Ellas habían sido criadas para casarse." (p. 43) (The brothers have been brought up to be men. The girls have been brought up to get married.) It was said of Pura's daughters that they could make any man happy because they have been brought up to bear suffering. Significantly, suffering is another of the elements that women in this society are trained to embody and endure. The girls receive an education which seeks to prepare them for marriage. They are trained in domestic chores that will allow them to play the role of wife and mother.

Angela is no exception and she, as would be expected, was brought up within rigid discipline and in the catholic religion. Having been brought up in the catholic religion means that she must arrive at her wedding day with her virginity intact.

> The blessed virgin is still the highest symbol of the latin american unmarried female and virginity the highest symbol of femininity; to give it away is the highest expression of dedication.[12]

Virginity is a concept highly praised by the Catholic religion and is promoted in the society through various religious groups such as the Legion of Mary.

Although prepared almost from birth to marry, it is important to note that Angela was never in agreement with the wedding that had been forced on her by her family which was more charmed than she was by Bayardo: "Era Angela quien no quería casarse con él." (pp. 47-48) (Angela did not want to marry him.) From the narration of the way events developed towards the wedding it is clear that she dreaded the occasion: "me parecía demasiado hombre para mí" (p. 48). (He looked too much of a man for me.) Besides, knowing that she was not a virgin, Angela feared this wedding because she knew that Bayardo would feel obliged to behave in accordance with the code of honour "Nadie hubiera pensado, ni lo dijo nadie, que Angela Vicario no fuera virgen . . . había crecido junto con sus hermanas bajo el rigor de una madre de hierro." (p. 52) (Nobody would have thought it, neither was it said that Angela was not a virgin . . . She had grown up with her sisters under the severity of an iron-mother.) This concept of virginity was so important, that Angela considered killing herself rather than settling for the shameful situation of "being brought back home" (ser devuelta a casa) by Bayardo for not being a virgin. "Lo único que le rogaba a Dios es que me diera valor para matarme . . . pero no me lo dió." (p. 52) (The only thing I asked God for, was to give me enough courage to kill myself . . . but he didn't.) Angela had entrusted to her girl friends the secret that she was not a virgin—although she never named the man responsible—and these friends persuaded her not to tell her mother about it and instead instructed her how to pretend to be a virgin on her wedding night. Angela, years later, referring to her wedding night, told the narrator: "No hice nada de lo que me dijeron—me dijo—, porque mientras más lo pensaba más lo me daba cuenta de que todo aquello era una porquería que no se la podía hacer a nadie, y menos al pobre hombre que había tenido la mala suerte de casarse conmigo." (p. 119) (I didn't do anything they told me because the more I thought about it, the more I realized that that was the kind of dirty trick I would not play on anyone, least of all the man who had the misfortune to marry me.) It is clear that Angela was a scrupulous person and had a "decencia pura escondida dentro de la estolidez de sus prejuicios" (p. 119) (real decency hidden in the stupidity of her prejudices) which did not allow her to go ahead with the farce in which she had been instructed by her friends, solely in order to appear to possess a carefully preserved virginity. So Angela let the events take their course, ready to suffer the consequences of her error. Only the narrator's mother seemed to appreciate Angela's behaviour: "mi madre fué la única que apreció como un acto de valor que hubiera jugado sus cartas marcadas hasta las últimas consecuencias." (p. 57) (My mother was the only one who appreciated as an act of courage that Angela played her marked cards to the last consequence.)

Angela behaved in this way in spite of the humiliation she knew she would be subjected to when Bayardo took her back home for not complying with the norms of traditions, with the demands of society. She rebelled against norms and patterns established by tradition and acted instead in accordance with her own higher convictions of truth and honesty.

A different and unexpected dimension of Angela's personality emerged, however, following the series of events; that is Angela as a prosecutor/judge. Finally, aware of the code of action that governed this situation, Angela sentenced Santiago Nasar to death, when she pronounced his name as the man responsible for her defloration:

> Ella se demoró apenas el tiempo necesario para decir su nombre. Lo buscó en las tinieblas, lo encontró a primera vista entre los tantos y tantos nombres confundibles de este mundo y del otro, y lo dejó clavado en la pared con su dardo certero, como a una mariposa sin albedrío cuya sentencia estaba escrita desde siempre (p. 65) (She needed only the necessary time to say his name. She looked for it in the darkness and she found it at the first glance among the very many easily mistaken names of this world and the next, and she left it pinned down on the wall with her well aimed dart, like a trapped butterfly whose sentence was written forever.

Angela's attitude as a judge in this instance seems irreconcilable with the Angela we discussed above, in whom the dedication to truth and honesty weighed more than the pressure and prejudices of the society. Why did Angela give Santiago Nasar's name, when everything else within the novel points to his innocence? This is a question we must ask before proceeding further, and it constitutes perhaps the central mystery of the novel. Could it be explained as a mischievous reflex, an instinct for the victimization of another as a compensation for her own status as victim? Baudelaire in his translation of *Notes Nouvelles sur Edgar Poe* says:

> "il y a dans l'homme ... une force mysterieuse dont la philosophie moderne ne veut pas tenir compte; et cependant, sans cette force innommée, sans ce penchant primordial, une foule d'actions humaines

resteront inexpliquées, inexplicables. Cette force primitive, irrésistible, est la Perversité Naturelle, qui fait que l'homme est sans cesse et a la fois homicide et suicide, assassin et bourreau.[13]

(There is in a man a mysterious force which modern philosophy does not want to take into account; however, without this unnamed force, without this essential inclination, loads of human actions will remain unexplained, inexplicable. This primitive, irresistible force is the Natural Perversity, which makes man continuously and simultaneously homicidal and suicidal—murderer, and executioner.)

Porché, in his book *Baudelaire. Histoire d'une âme*, mentions this point, as a contact point in the works of both Baudelaire and Poe:

"On trouve également chez les deux frères ces impulsions indéfinissables, que Poe a représentées comme des inspirations diaboliques dûe à la présence, dans l'âme humaine, d'un démon particulier qu'il appelle 'le démon de la perversité' "[14]

(We also find in the two brothers these indefinable impulses which Poe indentified as diabolic inspirations due to the presence in the human soul of a particular demon which he refers to as Demon of Perversity.)

It is possible to consider that Angela's behaviour was motivated by this "démon de la perversité." Even if we accept that Angela succumbed to such an inexplicable and perverse instinct when she named Santiago as her "autor," the question still remains, why Santiago? He personified the "macho" *par excellence* and therefore Angela saw in him, perhaps, a symbol of male pride and power. As a "macho" he enjoyed certain sexual privileges denied to women in a society where double standards regulate the life of its members.

Female resentment of Santiago is clearly shown. Victoria Guzman—lover of Ibrahim Nasar, Santiago's father and then maid in the Nasar house—said of Santiago: "No ha vuelto a nacer otro hombre como ése. Era idéntico a su padre. Un mierda." (p. 17) ("No man like that has ever been born again. He was just like his father. A turd.") She describes how the "macho" Santiago does not miss any occasion to show his power—in this case, sexual power: "Andaba solo, igual que su padre, cortándole el cogollo a cuanta doncella sin rumbo empezaba a despuntar por esos montes." (pp. 117-118) (He used to walk along, just like his father, plucking the flower of any wandering maiden who came into bloom in those bushes.) This feature of "machismo" was previously stressed by the author in his novel *La Mala Hora*[15] when Don Sabas referring to his sons said "Dicen que mis hijos se llevan por delante a cuanta muchachita empieza a despuntar por esos montes, y yo digo: Son hijos de su padre." ("It is said that my sons get every little girl who comes into bloom around this place and I said: like father, like son.") Santiago, good looking, rich and with all the attributes of the "macho" made the concept of machismo incarnate in himself. Angela then, moved perhaps by the "démon de la perversité" acted positively to avenge her own humiliation and at the same time to destroy the machismo concept as symbolised in Santiago. In this way Angela takes her revenge on society's values and becomes a redeemer of the female population.

So far we have seen several distinct stages in the metamorphosis of Angela's character: First, the humble girl "que tiene el nombre bien puesto" (whose name suits her) who had been born like the great queens of history, with the umbilical cord wound around her neck (p. 44), but this Angela "tenía un aire desamparado y una pobreza de espíritu que le auguraba un porvenir incierto" (p. 45) (had a helpless air and a poorness of spirit that predicted for her an uncertain future). It is this Angela who is in need of protection, the girl that Bayardo has chosen as his wife. Angela, knowing that she is not a virgin, and that she must get married to Bayardo according to what has been decided by her family, faced the consequences that her lack of virginity inflicted upon herself and her family. One saw an honest Angela, victim of her society. Then, Angela was forced into the role of accuser, as she had to name her seducer.

Finally, we meet an Angela quite different from the others. After the exodus of the Vicario family to La Guajira—in the Caribbean Coast of Colombia—and 23 years after the tragedy, Angela "era tan madura e ingeniosa que costaba trabajo creer que fuera la misma." (p. 116) (She was so mature and resourceful that it was hard to believe that she was the same Angela.) García Márquez continues: "Lo que más me sorprendió fué la forma en que había terminado por entender su vida." ("What surprised me the most, was the way she had ended up understanding her life.") Angela's mother, a product of that society of double standards, "había hecho más lo posible para que Angela se muriera en vida, pero la misma Angela le malagró sus propósitos porque nunca hizo ningún misterio de su desventúra" (p. 117) (had done everything possible so that Angela would experience death while still alive, but the same Angela had spoiled her plan because she never made a mystery of her misfortune). The mother-daughter relationship between Pura and Angela after the tragedy was marked by a note of rebellion and resistance on Angela's part. Pura, on one hand, was consumed with the notion that Angela must suffer and be punished for her error and the family's disgrace, as well as for her own personal disappointment in the child she raised. Angela's mother experienced a sensation of failure because she did not fulfill the task of keeping Angela's virginity intact until her wedding day. Angela had been educated "bajo el rigor de una madre de hierro" (under the strictness of an iron-mother) within the norms and patterns of the society, in order to fulfill the role that society had assigned to

her. In spite of Pura's efforts, Angela disturbed the social order and the tradition of her society, bringing a feeling of failure and shame to her mother. The
daughter was openly rebellious and refused to act the part of the contrite
sinner in order to please her mother. According to C.G. Jung:

> . . . resistance to the mother can sometimes result in a spontaneous
> development of intellect in which the mother has no place. Its real
> purpose is to break the mother's power by intellectual criticism and
> superior knowledge, so as to enumerate to her, all her stupidities,
> mistakes in logic and educational shortcomings.[16]

Angela's attitude now goes to prove the validity of Jung's statement,
especially considering the evaluation that García Márquez gives of her, 23
years after the drama: "no tenía nada en común con la que habían obligado a
casarse sin amor a los 20 años" (p. 117) (. . . she didn't have anything in
common with the 20-year old girl they had pressed into a loveless
marriage). Angela put an end to the power and influence that Pura had
exerted over her for so many years when she defined her as: "Una mujer
consagrada al culto de sus defectos" (p. 121) ("A poor woman consecrated
to the cult of her faults"). The fact that Angela finally defined her mother in
this way, indicates the extent to which her personality has changed. The
events that led to her disgrace may seem tragic from one perspective, but
they also seem to have occasioned her growth and development as a
woman.

A nice touch of irony on García Márquez's part is the way he makes clear
the fact that Angela, who—had she been the pure virgin that Bayardo
wanted—might easily have been condemned to a life of servitude to her
"macho" husband, was saved by breaking society's law. Her disgrace was
precisely what afforded her the opportunity for growth and development. It
is this change in Angela's personality that C.G. Jung calls "rebirth"
(Renovatio).

> Rebirth may be a renewal without any change of being, inasmuch as
> the personality which is renewed is not changed in its essential nature,
> but only its functions or parts of the personality, are subjected to
> healing, strengthening or improvement.[17]

García Márquez confirms this rebirth in Angela: "Nació de nuevo" (p.
121) (She was born again) and moreover heightens the irony by revealing to
us the secret that Angela had fallen in love with Bayardo from the moment
he took her home. "Se volvió lúcida imperiosa, maestra de su albedrío, y
volvió a ser virgen sólo para él, y no reconoció otra autoridad que la suya ni
más servidumbre que la de su obsesión." (p. 121) (She became brilliant,
imperious, master of her destiny, and was virgin again just for him, and

didn't recognize any other authority but her own, nor any other servitude than that of her own obsession).

It is perhaps the supreme irony of the novel that she gets in the end not only exactly what she wants—and on her own terms—but precisely that which was denied her by all the forces in society when she was considered impure and in disgrace. Her triumph therefore, is over not only 'machismo', masculine pride, but also over traditions and the values of society itself. The only element over which she does not triumph is time, which has by the end of the novel transformed her physical beauty into that of a "mujer con antiparras de alambre y canas amarillas" (p. 116) (woman wearing a wire-frame glasses and yellowish-gray hair).

Obviously, Angela accepted her fate and learned to endure it. " . . . nunca hizo ningún misterio de su desventura" (p. 117) (She never made a mystery of her disgrace). She spoke quite freely about her "tragedy" with the exception that she never revealed the secret—who had been really responsible for her loss of virginity because "nadie creyó que en realidad hubiera sido Santiago Nasar" (p. 117) (Nobody really believed that it was Santiago Nasar).

On one occasion Angela saw Bayardo in the hotel of the port " . . . Lo vió pasar a su lado sin verla y lo vió, salir del hotel" (p. 121) (She saw him pass next to her without seeing her and she saw him leave the hotel). This was the event that upset Angela and stirred up anew her feelings for Bayardo. "me volví loca por él—loca de remate" (p. 121) (I went mad with love for him—raving mad). In order to express her feelings for Bayardo, Angela started a correspondence with him that lasted seventeen years. She never got an answer from him; then he turned up on her doorstep bringing with him "la maleta de ropa para quedarse, y otra maleta igual con casi dos mil cartas que ella le había escrito. Estaban ordenadas por sus fechas, en paquetres cosidos con cintas de colores y todas sin abrir" (p. 125) (a suitcase with his clothes to stay and another similar suitcase with almost two thousand letters that she had written to him. They were in bundles according to their dates and tied up with coloured ribbons, all unopened).

This unlikely ending might make one wonder about the reasons for so much confusion, and for the killing of Santiago and the presence of the elements that disturbed the order and the tradition in that society—if in the end we are presented with a happy ending. As Gerald Guinness puts it: "Such events do not happen in South Kensington or off the Bois de Bologne to be sure, but then South America is not like other places as it has been García Márquez's remarkable achievement over the years to make us see."[18] Beyond such comfortable and superficial distinctions of geography and culture, however, the ironies discussed above go some distance towards explaining García Márquez's purpose. The novel undertakes nothing less than the story of a woman's growth towards selfhood and genuine independence. The Angela we see at the end is the final product of a revolutionary process, both in the context of society and of the creative imagination of the author. According to Marquez's own judgement he considers this work to be his best: " . . . logré con ella hacer exactamente lo que quería. Nunca me había ocurrido antes." (I have achieved with *Crónica*, exactly what I had set out to do. It had never happened to me before.) " . . . necesitaba escribir un libro sobre el cual pudiera ejercer un control riguroso y creo haberlo logrado con *Crónica de una Muerte Anunciada*."[19] (. . . I needed to write a book over which I could exercise rigorous control and I believe I have achieved it with *Crónica de una Muerte Anunciada*.) The novel satirizes society's values but it also celebrates the spirit of a woman.

Considering the case of Angela that we have been examining in this paper, and after looking at each and every one of the facets of her personality, one would consider it impossible to assign Angela a place within any one archetype or any fixed pattern. There is a richness of personality and an unpredictability of behaviour, and in Angela these facets of her character interact and modify each other. There is a dynamic in her actions, seemingly fluctuating from positive to negative: she is herself an innocent victim at one moment and she condemns an innocent man the next; she is vulnerable and in need of protection at the beginning and at the end she is master of her own destiny. All this fluctuation in human behaviour can perhaps be seen in terms of what Wilson Harris, the Guyanese writer describes as "the necessity to digest and liberate contrasting spaces."[20] García Márquez making use of the "contrasting spaces" showed us how Angela has rebelled against her society and its traditions which have considered women as inferiors, and where the values of the past, along with tradition, have made them victims and exploited beings for centuries.

> That the roles of exploiter and exploited breed polarization rather than the hard-won annunciation of new forms of community through self-knowledge is perhaps a failure of imagination to sense within a dynamic concert of energies a capacity which relates to the values of the past but runs counter to those values as static cultural imperatives.[21]

Her image is that of a woman, a human being within the spectrum of possibilities, both positive and negative: she has her "démon de la perversité". But it is through the "dynamic concert of energies" to which Harris refers, that she achieves a rebirth, a renewal, a knowledge of herself, and it is this, therefore, that is the message of the story. Her name means messenger, and she conveys her message to a society which to a large extent, continues to regulate the lives of its members according to traditional values, making the process of renewal very difficult.

One of the tragic ironies of modern man is his implacable conviction that traditional values are static. Thus when traditions erode they seem to have no other function but to engender oppression even though that erosion—unpalatable as it sounds—serves to release a new economic architecture of achievement in a concert of peoples.[22]

NOTES

1. Gabriel García Márquez, "Fantasía y Creación artística en América Latina y el Caribe" in *Texto Crítico*, 14 (July-Sept. 1979) p. 7. All translations are my own.
2. Ibid.
3. Ibid.
4. Idem., p. 4.
5. Gabriel García Márquez and Plinio Apuleyo Mendoza, *El olor de la Guayaba* (Bogotá: Editorial la oveja Negra, 1982), p. 55.
6. Ibid.
7. Gabriel García Márquez, "Fantasía y Creación artística en América Latina y el Caribe" in *Texto Crítico*, 14 (July-Sept. 1979).
8. V.S. Naipaul, *The Loss of Eldorado* (London: Andre Deutch, 1969).
9. Gabriel García Márquez and Plinio Apuleyo Mendoza, *El olor de la Guayaba* (Bogotá: Editorial La Oveja Negra, 1982), pp. 112-113.
10. Gabriel García Márquez, *Crónica de una Muerte Anunciada* (Bogotá: Editorial La Oveja Negra, 1981). All page numbers in the text refer to this edition.
11. For a discussion of this aspect of the novel, see Amparo Marmolejo-McWatt, "Men, Women and the Concept of Honour in Gabriel García Márquez's *Crónica de una Muerte Anunciada*" in Bulletin of Eastern Caribbean Affairs, II:1 (September 1985) I.S.E.R., University of the West Indies, Cave Hill, Barbados, pp. 1-12.
12. Julius Rivera, *Latin America: A Sociocultural Interpretation* (New York: Irvington Publishers, Inc., 1978), p. 51.
13. Charles Baudelaire, "Notes Nouvells sur Edgar Poe" in *Selected Critical Studies of Baudelaire*, ed. D. Parmée (Cambridge at the University Press, 1949), p. 54.
14. Francois Porché, *Baudelaire. Histoire d'une âme* (Paris: Flammarion Editeur, 1944), p. 217.
15. Gabriel García Márquez, *La Mala Hora* (Buenos Aires: Editorial Sudamericana S.A., 1974), p. 102.

16. C.G. Jung, *The Archetypes and the Collective Unconscious*, Translated by R.F.C. Hull, Vol. 9, Part 1 (New York: Pantheon Books Inc., 1959), p. 91.

17. Ibid., p. 114.

18. Gerald Guinness, Review of *Crónica de una Muerte Anunciada* in *San Juan Star* (Sunday Magazine), Puerto, Rico, May 21, 1981, p. 11.

19. Gabriel García Márquez and Plinio Apuleyo Mendoza, *El Olor de la Guayaba* (Bogotá: Editorial La Oveja Negra, 1982), pp. 64-65.

20. Wilson Harris, "A talk on the subjective imagination" in his *Explorations* (Denmark: Dangaroo Press, 1981), p. 57.

21. Ibid., p. 64.

22. Ibid., p. 65.

PART THREE
Caribbean Women Writers.
Redefining Caribbean
Literature

In this section, there are eight studies of Caribbean women writers as individual artists set in a context, like the others in this volume, of critical approaches that are womanist/feminist and so geared to the reading of the woman's story. We have included writers from English-, Spanish-, and French-speaking Caribbean nations, writers based both in the islands and abroad. There are definite and unplanned omissions, largely because of space and obviously, because as the collection grew, it became clear that the entire volume could be devoted to Caribbean women writers and this was not the original intent. For this section, then, we claim to do no more than offer the reader a variety of approaches to the reading of specific Caribbean women's texts along with presenting some idea of the scope of the developing body of Caribbean women's literature. While Part One discusses women writers in broad historical sweeps or with specific themes in mind, Part Three attempts a closer reading of individual author's works.

Our focus here is how the growing body of literature by Caribbean women is redefining the canon of Caribbean literature. We begin, then, with an interview with Cuban poet Nancy Morejon, titled "A Womanist Vision of the Caribbean" in which Morejon makes it clear that she prefers Alice Walker's term "womanist" to feminist as her perspective on women in society and history. Along with discussing her own impetus to writing, she identifies a number of women, mainly poets, who are writing in Cuba.

Another exploration comes from Marlene Nourbese Philip: "The Absence of Writing or How I Almost Became a Spy." A Canada-based

Caribbean writer, she discusses the limitations and challenges of using the imagery and words of English which she calls a "father tongue (vis-a-vis a mother tongue), the language of the white male colonizer." The positioning as black and female, away from the locus of power, fostered an "absence of writing" among women in her community which the Caribbean woman as writer must address and overcome. Michelle Cliff makes a similar argument in The Land of Look Behind *(Trumansburg, New York, The Crossing Press, 1986). In a way then, this absence that Marlene Philip talks about becomes emblematic of the whole space that the body of Caribbean women writers is filling. Taking possession of language assures the woman some control of her story.*

Carolyn Cooper's essay on Erna Brodber is significantly placed next. In its bringing together of the oral and written narrative and the implications of the use of folk tradition for the Caribbean writer, the essay offers us one of the primary modes by which Caribbean women's creativity is expressed. Cooper looks specifically at the "Afro-Jamaican Folklore Elements in Erna Brodber's Jane an Louisa Will Soon Come Home." *It is from Brodber, and this work, that the* kumbla *metaphor which serves as our title is derived. That Brodber, as Carolyn Cooper reveals, utilizes Jamaican folklore textually is aesthetically significant, given again the oral culture which is the mode of existence and discourse of the majority of Caribbean women. Carolyn Cooper too discusses the* kumbla *and its meaning for the character Nellie.*

The whole question of oral culture and storytelling *is carried over into Abena Busia's "This Gift of Metaphor: Symbolic Strategies and the Triumph of Survival in Simone Schwarz-Bart's* The Bridge of Beyond" *which argues that "[it] is the essential feature of Telumee's story that she tells it" for in the telling she triumphs. Throughout the narrative, Busia argues, story-telling connects generations, orders, heals, and saves.*

Maryse Condé's first novel is the subject of Vèvè Clark's "Developing Diaspora Literacy: Allusion in Maryse Condé's Hérémakhonon." Vèvè Clark argues that through Veronica, the reader is drawn into a "network of personal and cultural signs and images" which "unites through discourse the four corners of the African Diaspora." The essay ends with a brief reference to Condé's second novel Un Saison à Rihata *and forms an interesting complement to Clarisse Zimra's essay, in Part One, which refers to Condé's recent* Segou *and the whole re-writing of Francophone Caribbean history.*

Twin issues come out of Janice Lee Liddell's discussion, "The Narrow Enclosure of Motherdom/Martyrdom: A Study of Gatha Randall Burton in Sylvia Wynter's The Hills of Hebron." *One, a discussion of the limitations in circumscribed definitions of motherhood; the second, the re-examination of a writer who continued to make major contributions to Caribbean political discourse while her novel remained outside the critical pale—not part of the canon of Caribbean literature. This novel by Sylvia Wynter again validates the thesis that the work of some women writers (for instance, that of Zora Neale Hurston,Kate Chopin) frequently seems to lie awaiting the heightened consciousness of a new generation of reader/critics to be appreciated.*

A discussion of the development of women's theatre in the Caribbean is taken up in Elaine Savory Fido's "Finding A Way to Tell It: Methodology and Commitment in Theatre About Women in Barbados and Jamaica." The importance of the Jamaican theatre group "Sistren" to the insertion of specific woman-focused, themes, methods, and structures into Caribbean theatre is discussed along with the production of the play "Lights"in Barbados. The development of a theatre which posits a female view and courts a challenging female response, the need to expand some of the boundaries across race, gender and class is expressed in this essay. Theatre in the Caribbean with the creative attempts of people like Barbara Gloudon in Jamaica is clearly being re-energized by the centralizing of the woman's story and the woman's voice and perspective.

Finally, Giovanna Covi challenges with Kincaid the whole notion of "the canon." She shows in "Jamaica Kincaid and the Resistance to Canons" that there is a revolutionary thread running through Kincaid's work which heralds a new generation of Caribbean writers evoking and redefining locus and logos: challenging accepted notions of the self, gender, race and history.

A Womanist Vision
of the Caribbean.
An Interview.

Nancy Morejon (with Elaine Savory Fido)[1]

Rebirth	**Renacimentio**
Daughter of ocean waters	Hija de las aguas marinas,
asleep in that womb,	dormida en sus entranas,
I am reborn	renazco de la polvora
out of the gun-powder	que un rifle guerillero
sown over the mountain	esparcio en la montana
by a guerilla rifle	para que el mundo renaciera a su vez,
so the world in its turn	que renaciera todo el mar,
might be reborn,	todo el polvo,
and the vast sea	todo el polvo de Cuba.
and all the dust,	
all the dust of Cuba.	

ESF: Woven into this poem, which is from your book *Where The Island Sleeps Like a Wing*[2] are some elements which figure in your work generally: the idea of woman's culture, of the watermaid, is woven into the conception of rebirth, with the result that both the woman and African experience are emphasized. Do you see these things as important in your work?

NM: Yes, I think this short poem expresses many things or the most important things in my poetry . . . you talked of the watermaid which is very important for Caribbean literature and poetry. I do believe so, and when I'm talking about the sea, and about waters it is a very old thing that comes from the Bible up to now. I believe I do it in a very Caribbean style. I cannot deny that for us the ocean and the sea are somehow related with the transplantation of the African slaves to our region-this is one of the most important connotations of the word. The birth or rebirth conception is related to women but I would like to say that I wouldn't talk about a woman's culture in this respect. In this region particularly we are concerned with a mixture of culture given by ourselves to ourselves. I think it is very important in these times for us to read a Caribbean literature written by women because in our tradition we have had the male view of the Caribbean and we have to recognise now that these male views have been sometimes only sexual: a view that has limited women to sex. I believe women writers or Black women writers in the Caribbean and everywhere give a very special touch to their literature. I'm not talking as a feminist because I wouldn't say I am one, but you cannot deny objective facts, in your creativity, and I think that maybe a Caribbean male would be very far from the vision I have in "Rebirth."

ESF: Let me ask you here what exactly you mean by the term *feminist* since there are so many different meanings now . . .

NM: I guess there are sometimes words which are a trap . . . In our Western world there are certain feminist movements that I respect very much as a woman, but sometimes they don't go to the real point of our time and our societies. They develop ideas that belong maybe best to a consumer society. I think the task of a womanist (let's talk with Alice Walker's term which I love very much) in our region should be something related to our society and to our history. We cannot import certain patterns of these movements from Western Europe or developed countries because we are underdeveloped countries.

Anyway, in my literature, it is very important that I am a woman. It would be nonsense to say I'm not, or that I think women don't write in a very special mode and with a special experience and charge, because in our case for the first time in centuries women are facing their own problems by themselves. That is a historical fact in our world. But I think there are some confusing ideas about being women and men, and sometimes there are some tensions, artificial tensions, created by these naive movements and these may create a confusion among ourselves in this region which I think is not good for us. We have to see our mistakes in female and male relations and we have to learn every day, whilst having a deep feeling towards our society and our history. In the case of this poem "Rebirth," I feel this is a very Caribbean poem, and at the same time it is a very Cuban and a very American one. I talk about the guerrilla rifle which is an urgent image of our present, so I think it has these mixtures of values that appear in life and poetry—and I love that, because I think our Caribbean culture is very mixed.

ESF: I thought you would say something like that, that you would not see male and female as separate. In fact I see in your Grenada poems[3] very much an archetypal woman who has a relationship not only to the situation but with some of the male figures in the poems. This female presence is very important and gives another perspective on your vision of Grenada. But I wanted to ask you how you started as a poet . . .

NM: I began to write poetry as a child. I was nine years old. I did not know I was writing poetry. It was at a certain workshop at the Senior High School in Havana that I had a meeting with a Spanish professor—we were working on Homer's *Odyssey*, and I had to write a kind of paper on Book I2, dedicated to Polypheme, the one-eyed giant. After that I had a very interesting conversation with my teacher. Maybe she assumed I was someone very gifted for literature. She asked me if I loved poetry, if I loved literature and I said yes, I'd read everything I had to read in my classes. She said do you have a diary? I said yes I do; she told me to bring it the next day. So two or three days later, I brought my diary. So at the next meeting she said, do you know that you write poems? Because in this diary there are notes but there are poems too. You're going to be a poet. You have to be very aware of that. You have to read very much, the right poets, in your own language, which is Spanish and then we will meet. It was true-but until the age of 13 or 14 I did not know that what I was writing was poetry. This awareness of being a black writer did not come just like that; it came through a process in which my self-consciousness was in relation with my environment. We have had a very wide and lush process of revolutionary ideals in our island, we discovered that we used to belong to a Third World. In fact we were not white people in the sense of conquerors, but mixed people, coloured people, so these conceptions made me change and made me know that my writing could give many of these new ideas to myself and to my people. That is the way I started to have an awareness-it was something very spontaneous through the years since I was 17 years old up to date . . . and it is a process which I think is still unfinished.

ESF: Where do you think your poetry might go next? Do you see any new developments?

NM: I would like my poetry to be a tool for everybody. That's a high aspiration but I would say sometimes my poetry cannot reach that level—there are some poems in which I get it but others in which I don't . . . My aspiration is that poetry should be a very communicative way of loving everybody and sharing experience, even bitter experience, but I think bitterness is something related to love—even when you are bitter about some things it means you want to have them—you love them in a way. So I think of poetry as a means of acknowledgment, a means of changing people and giving people new ideas that really can help them find their own identity. I think poets should create beauty also to teach people to see beauty, because in the old times, in the past, we were not allowed to enjoy beauty . . . beauty was something given to us through the Western world and through perished patterns. I think one of our duties is to make an awareness that beauty is a very concrete thing, something that could be found in everyday life—it is not something that is so far you cannot touch it. That is a difficult task for any poet, painter or artist in our time—beauty.

ESF: This concept of love, too, which you talk about, which seems for you to be about relations between male and female, between races, between Cuba and the rest of the Caribbean and the rest of the world, isn't this a healing direction which you want and talk about? You seem always to see relationships between one thing and another . . . I sense you search to bring things together . . .

NM: Yes, I think of love in both senses—both humankind love and heroical love. I think love is conceived in each culture in a very concrete way. In the Caribbean we have a mixture (and we can take from any other cultures) so we have to be aware of that. When I talk of love as a Caribbean person I'm talking in a very wide and large aspiration . . . I'm talking about brothers, sisters, you know—I see the Caribbean as a whole family . . . so I want this family to enjoy life and their own identity but I do think also that having this idea of love reduced to arrows is important which is why in my love poems there are many images of water and sand—these are tropical words which my country gave to me. But I want to talk about the kind of love which is not concerned with flesh but in the larger sense—I like that kind of love very much.

ESF: I feel that very much coming through the poetry. But what of other writers in Cuba, women writers especially . . . ?

NM: There is a boom. When I started to write I was something weird, but now there are many young ladies who write very well. This boom is in poetry. I would like to talk about a certain tradition in which women have written very good poetry, from the 19th century. Then in the 20th century we have had Dulce María Loynaz, Mirta Aguirre, Fina Garcia Marruz, Rafaela Chacón Nardi, Carilda Oliver Labra, and in the last 25 years, we have had poets like Georgina Herrera, who is a poet I love very much, Excilia Saldaña, Reina María Rodríguez, Marylin Bobes, Cira Andres . . . these are poets who have been giving a very fresh breath to our poetry. In the case of the novel and the short story, I think with both women and men there is a problem of the genre recently. I don't know why, these manifestations have been suffering a kind of sclerosis, though I think we are recovering from that . . .

ESF: That is both women and men are having difficulties with forms of fiction?

NM: Both . . . no one can do it very well but in the case of poetry I do believe we have been increasing our maturity as a national expression—these young women are very devoted to their womanist condition and they love their country—and for them poetry is very important as a revolutionary process . . . I think that poetry has been a way of expressing their feelings.

ESF: And most of these younger women poets are Black poets too?

NM: Yes, ... there are many others ... for instance we have a very interesting workshop movement and there are many architects, engineers, black and white, women who have professions now and they are very interested in writing poetry and so we have this boom ...

NOTES

1. This interview was conducted in front of video cameras at U.W.I., Cave Hill, in October, 1985 and the resulting discussion was in need of some editing to make sense as a written document, though I have tried to stay faithful not only to Nancy Morejon's words wherever possible, but to the spirit and form of her lively conversation. I was assisted in the transcription of the Spanish names by my colleague, Amparo Marmolejo-McWatt.
2. The Black Scholar Press, 1985.
3. *Grenada Notebook (Cuaderno de Granada)* Tr. Lisa Davis. (New York City: Círculo de Cultura Cubana, 1984.)

The Absence of Writing
or
How I Almost Became A Spy

Marlene Nourbese Philip

I came to writing as a way of life rather late, although like most women, before coming out as a writer I had been in the closet for many years, secretly filling book after book with thoughts, ideas, poems, curses, diatribes and whatever else would come to mind.

Having left a somewhat secure and very conservative profession for writing, I often look back and wonder why I had never had the slightest indication as a child or adolescent that this way of being in the world, that is writing, was what I wanted. Many of the reasons for that lie in a colonial childhood in the Caribbean.

If as a child I had been given a word association test related to careers, the word writer would have drawn a blank. Being a spy in fact was a much more realistic occupation for me, especially after having read of the exploits of Mata Hari. Within the realm of possibilities, writing did not exist. For the black and brown middle classes of which my family was part, and in the wake of independence and its heady promises, aspirations ran to the professions like medicine, law, nursing, teaching accounting. Girls as well as boys were groomed and coached for these, in a highly competitive school system. Sexism made itself manifest in other ways.

As a high school student I was vaguely aware of V.S. Naipaul who at that time, must have been gaining a reputation. *He* was a writer, but it meant nothing to me; furthermore, he was Indian and, in the context of Trinidad at that time, in the eyes of Blacks, this would have been a strike against him.

It wasn't that books were a novelty, for I grew up surrounded by books and, living in the city, access to the library was easy. Books there were, but others wrote them. I read them.

271

I don't think that I was unique in my attitude to writing and I'm quite sure that of the twenty or so girls in my sixth form class not one considered writing as a career, or thought of being a writer. And this was at a school which, if I'm to be partisan, was the best in the island. The profession, vocation, career—call it what you will—of the writer did not exist for us. This, it could be argued, was to be expected since the material rewards of a writer are often insignificant and precarious when compared with that of professionals. For the large and predominantly Black nation, upward mobility was seen to be solely via education. To become a doctor, lawyer, teacher or professional civil servant was tangible proof that servitude and all its unpleasant memories had been left behind if not eradicated. The sooner they could put these memories behind them and become more like the upper classes the better. Writing therefore was not perceived as particularly efficacious in the process.

In my painfully slow development as a writer I have come to a greater awareness of the political significance of language and believe that only in understanding the role of language in a colonial society can we understand the role of writing, the writer, and perhaps why writing was not—and still, to a large degree, is not—recognised as a career, profession or way of being in the Caribbean or among Caribbean people resident in Canada.

What follows is my attempt to analyse and understand the role of language and the word from the perspective of a writer resident in a society which is still very much colonial, whose recent history is colonial and one which continues to cast very long shadows.*

Fundamental to any art form is the image, whether it be the physical image as created by the dancer and choreographer, the musical image of the composer and musician, the visual image of the plastic artist or the verbal image, often metaphorical, of the writer and poet. I confine myself for the most part to the concept of image as it relates to the writer. However, while it may be quite easy to see the role of image as it relates to the visual artist, it may be less so with respect to the writer. The word "image" is being used here to convey what can only be described as the irreducible essence of creative writing and it can be likened to the DNA molecules at the heart of all life. It is being used here to refer to all verbal techniques and methods used by the writer to convey meaning and non-meaning at the source of which is the process of imag-ination. These techniques have been formulated into different groups—comparison,simile, metaphor, metonymy, symbol, allegory, fable, myth—but whatever the name given, the function of the image remains the same: that of fuelling the artist's imagination.

---

*No discussion of writing or literature of New World people of African heritage is complete without mention of the oral tradition. That, however, is deserving of its own analyses and for reasons such as continuity of argument and length of paper must be omitted from this essay.

The power and threat of the artist, the poet, the writer, lie in just this ability to create new images, images that speak to the essential being of the people among whom and for whom the artist creates and which, if allowed free expression, succeed in altering the way a society perceives and, eventually, its collective consciousness.

When in the early 1900s, Picasso and his fellow artists entered their so-called 'primitive stage' they employed what had traditionally been an African aesthetic of art and sculpture and succeeded in permanently altering the sensibilities of the West toward this aesthetic. It did not necessarily increase the understanding or tolerance of the West toward Africans and Africa but people began to perceive differently.

The art form, the images that comprised this aesthetic, was previously thought to be primitive, naive, ugly and consequently has been dismissed not only by the Western alien but by the very Africans themselves living outside of Africa, so far were they removed from their power to create, control and even understand their own images. The societies in which they lived lacked a certain kind of matrix which has at its source the autonomy of the image maker—in most cases white and male—and for whom language and image become what they should be, a well balanced equation.

Caribbean society has been a colonial society for a much longer time than not and the role of image, image-making and image control are significant. These societies may be identified by:

(a) a significant lack of autonomy in the creation of images.

(b) opposition by the ruling classes both at home and abroad to the creation of images that challenge their image-making powers and the status quo

(c) restriction of indigenously created images to marginal groups, e.g. Reggae and Calypso.

At the heart of all creative writing therefore is the image, the basis for which is the word or word symbol as I prefer to describe it. The success of the execution of this image, be it poetical or in the extended metaphor of the novel, depends to a large degree on the essential tension between the image and word or words giving voice to the image. Tension is created by the interplay of image and word—image-creating word, word giving rise to further image and so on. This process is founded upon familiarity with word and image, "familiarity" being used here in the sense of being kin to, a part of, related to. What is assumed here, but probably should not be, is also growing familiarity with being and how it relates to the outer world.

If this process is as it should be, then the autonomous image-maker serves the function of continually enriching the language by enlarging the store of images and in particular metaphorical image. If we accept that living language continually encapsulates, reflects and refines the experiential life and world view of the tribe, the race of society, and if we accept that the poet, the balladeer, the storyteller, the singer, expresses this process in her work—apart from becoming within herself the metaphor for this development—then we must accept that this process becomes one way in which a society continually integrates and transcends its experiences positive and negative. For it is through those activities—poetry, story telling, singing and music—that the tribe's experiences are converted and transformed to image and to word almost simultaneously and from word back to image again. So metaphorical life takes place: so the language becomes richer, the store of metaphor, myth and fable enlarged, and the experience transcended not by exclusion and alienation, but by inclusion in the linguistic psyche, the racial and generic memory.

The progenitors of Caribbean society as it exists today created a situation such that the equation between image and word was destroyed. The African could still think and image. She could still conceive of what was happening to her, and in stripping her of her language, in denying the voice expression, and in denying the voice the power to make and simultaneously express the image, this ability and power was effectively stymied. That bridge that language created, the cross over from image to expression, was destroyed if only temporarily. Furthermore, alien and negative images were supplied to replace those recently removed and, irony of all ironies, when the word/image equation was balanced again, this was to take place through a language that was not only experientially foreign, but also etymologically hostile and expressive of the non-being of the African.

So, the resulting situation becomes one in which the African is decontextualised, except in so far as her actions generate profits for the owners, and the language within which the decontextualisation flourishes is in itself at best a decontextualised one for the African and at worst alientating. The language therefore served to push the African further away from the expression of her experience and consequently the meaning of it.

Once the image making power had been removed or damaged by denial of language and speech, the African was the forced back upon the raw experience without the linguistic resources to eventually transcend it.

The African in the Caribbean could move away from the experience in time, could even acquire some perspective upon it, but the experience, having never been reclaimed and integrated metaphorically through the language and so within the psyche, could never be transcended. To reclaim and integrate the experience required autonomous image makers and thereby a language possessing the emotional linguistic and historical resources capable of giving voice to the particular images arising out of the experience. The English language did not possess those resources and in fact, as mentioned earlier, articulated the non-being of the African over and above her function as a chattel and unit of production.

I would further argue, that it is impossible for any language that inherently denies the essence of any group or people, to be truly capable of giving voice to the images of experiences of that group, without tremendous and fundamental changes within the language itself. But, in the present case, the experience and image of that experience could only be expressed through the English language and, there was no possible expression of the experience within any African linguistic group.

Essentially therefore, what the African would do is to use a foreign language, expressive of an alien experiential life; a language comprised of word symbols that, even then, had affirmed negative images about her, one which was but a reflection of the experiences of an ethnocentric world view. This was to eventually become her only language, her only tool to create and express image about herself and her life experiences, past, present and future. The paradox of this acquisition is that the African learned both to speak and to be dumb at the same time, to give voice to the experience and image, yet to remain silent; and that silence has had profound effect upon the English speaking Caribbean artist working in the medium of words.

Speech, voice, language, word are all ways of being in the world, and the artist working with the image and giving voice to it is being in the world. The only way the African artist could be in this world, that is the New World, was to give voice to this split image of voiced silence. Ways to transcend that contradiction had to and still have to be developed, for that silence continues to shroud the experience, the image and so the word.

One of the ways around this was to become a wordsmith, forging new and different words in the vortex of New World slavery. It has been said that "language for us is not a distillation of our past," which is true if by that is meant standard, Queen's or King's English as we know it, because that language, for all the reasons given above, can never be a distillation of *our* past. But what the ordinary African, the African on the Papine bus or the Port of Spain route taxi or Toronto subway, produced from the only linguistic behaviour allowed her, i.e. functionality in the English language is truely and surely a distillation of our past. It may not be the clearest distillation, but a distillation it remains all the same.

The formal standard language was subverted, turned upside down, inside out and sometimes even erased. Nouns became strangers to verbs and vice versa; tonal accentuation took the place of several words at times; rhythms held sway. This used to be and sometimes still is referred to as bad English, broken English, patois, dialect or ideolect, but it is also the living legacy of an experience, the living legacy of a people trying and succeeding in giving voice to their experience in the best and sometimes the only way possible. We may even suggest that the havoc that was wreaked upon the English language metaphorically expresses the experience of the African being brought to the New World and all the havoc that that entailed for them.

Language then becomes more than a distillation; it is the truest representation, the mirror image of the experience.

Not possessing any other language by which the past may be repossessed, reclaimed and possibly transcended, English in its broadest spectrum must be made to do the job. To say that the experience can only be expressed in standard English—if there is any such thing—or only in Caribbean English—there is such a thing—is in fact to limit the experience, for it is in the continuum of expression, from standard to Caribbean English, dialect or ideolect, that the veracity of the experience lies.

Subversion of the language has already taken place. Much more must now be attempted. If we accept some of the earlier premises, that at the heart of the languages lies the image, metaphorical or otherwise, and that to the artist falls the task of articulating and presenting this image to the people, then the attack most be made where any true change is only ever possible, at the heart of language the image and the simultaneous naming of it. The African artist in the Caribbean and in the New World must create, give voice to and control her own images.

This is essential to any group, person or people but more so for the African in the New World, since in a sense our coming upon ourselves, our revelation to ourselves in the New World, simultaneous with a re-presentation of ourselves by a hostile imperalistic power, articulated in a language endemically and etymologically hostile to our very existence. In a very real sense, it can be argued that while at the same time as learning the English language, the African learned of her non-being, her lack of wholeness.

However, the experience of the African in the Caribbean and the New World is now part of the English collective experience just as England is part, for better or worse, of the African experience (in the same manner, for instance, that Germany will always be part of the Jewish collective experience and vice versa). That experience expressed in the language—a language common yet experientially different for both groups—has been and continues to be denied, hence terms like broken or bad English or good English, all of which serve to alienate the speaker further from her experience. If the language is to continue to do what language must do—to name and give voice to the experience and image and so house the being—the experience must be incorporated in the language and the language must begin to serve the re-creation of images.

When, for instance, we hear certain words and phrases, such as thick lips, kinky hair, and all the many images associated with blackness, we conceive certain images—mainly negative for which there are certain historical and sociological reasons. The role of the African artist in the Caribbean and the New World lies in re-creating the images behind these words so that the words are being used newly. It is not sufficient to write in dialect, for too often that remains a parallel and closed experience, although a part of the same language. The language has in fact to be destroyed, dislocated and acted upon so that it begins to serve our purposes. It is our only language, our mother tongue, or maybe it would be more accurate to say, ours is a father tongue.

The African in the Caribbean and New World is as much entitled to call the English language her own, as the Englishman in his castle. However, just as we have had to make *that* image our own, so too must he be made to acquire our images since we are both heirs to a common language albeit to different linguistic experiences. Our experiences have touched, in both negative and positive ways, and we remain forever sensitive to each other through the language.

For too long however we have been verbal or linguistic squatters, possessing adversely what is truly ours. If possession is in fact nine tenths of the law, then the one tenth that remains is the legitimisation process. It is probably the hardest part that yet remains, this reclaiming of our image-making power in what has been for a long time foreign language, but it must be done.

It is perhaps ironic that the descendants of a society where the word and the act of naming was the focal point, the fulcrum of societal forces, should find themselves in a situation where the word, *their* word was denied them. With the withering of the word, however, not only did the images die but the capacity to create in one's own image died also. Surely that is what the artist does—she creates in her own image. This is what the African artist from the Caribbean and the New World must now do—create in her own image— and in so doing eventually heal the word wounded by the imbalance of the word/image equation. This can only be done by consciously restructuring, reshaping and if necessary destroying the language. So that eventually there can be a healing of the word, wounded by the dislocation of the word/image equation. When that equation is balanced and unity of word and image is once again present, then will we have made the language our own—not before.

Postscript

I call this a postscript and not a conclusion because the issues raised here are still very much undefined. How does one begin to destroy a language? How does one replace the image behind the word? Those questions are still unanswered and will probably remain so for a long time. Being aware of them may heighten one's awareness of the job one sets out to do as a writer of African Caribbean heritage using the English language—a language which may be more fittingly described as a father tongue (vis-à-vis a mother tongue), the language of the white male colonizer.

The linguistic rape and subsequent forced marriage has resulted in a language capable of great rhythms and musicality; one that is and is not

English and one which is among the most vital in the English speaking world today.

It is perhaps ironic that a critique of the use and role of English in a particularly brutal historical context should be written in standard English, but that in itself throws into sharp relief the dilemma described above. It is to some degree answered by my argument that the English language in its complete range belongs to us and whatever mode best suits the communication should be used. I am not completely satisfied with this answer, and given that odd and brutal coincidence of events that has placed me here in the New World, my quest as a writer/poet is to discover my mother tongue, or whether or not peoples such as us may ever claim to possess such a thing.

Since I continue to write in my father tongue, what I need to engender by some alchemical process (alchemy: from *al-kimiyá*, the art of the black and Egypt) a metamorphosis within the language from father tongue to mother tongue. In that process some aspects of the language will be destroyed, new ones created.

At the risk of being reductionist, I see the issue as being one of power and so one of control. Writing entails in many areas: control of the word, control of the image (as argued above), control of information, and, perhaps as important, control in the production of the final product. For a female and a Black living in a colonial society, control was absent in each of these areas, and hence the lack of recognition of writing as a possible vocation or profession.

For the many like me, Black and female, it is imperative that our writing begin to recreate our histories and our myths, as well as integrate the most painful of experiences—loss of our history and our word. The reacquisition of power to create in one's own image and to create one's own image is vital to this process which can only serve to emphasize that which we have always known, even in the darkest hour of the soul, when everything conspired to prove otherwise, that we belong most certainly to the race of humans.

Afro-Jamaican Folk Elements in Brodber's Jane and Louisa Will Soon Come Home

Carolyn Cooper

The landscape of Erna Brodber's *Jane and Louisa Will Soon Come Home* is largely that of rural Jamaica, a setting in which family ties are complicated by the sinuous bonds of colour and class; a context within which an oral tradition of long-time story, family history and pure gossip flourishes alongside the world of books and distant town. Brodber's narrative method exemplifies an interpenetration of scribal and oral literary forms: a modernist, stream-of-consciousness narrative voice holds easy dialogue with the traditional teller of tales, the transmitter of anansi story, proverb, folk song and dance.

Brodber's experiment in form is underscored by the writer's deliberately ingenuous assertion that *Jane and Louisa Will Soon Come Home* was not conceived as a novel: she set out to write a case study in Abnormal Psychology.[1] But literary critics have appropriated the work, recognizing in its dense patterns of allusive imagery, its evocative language and its carefully etched characterizations, the sensibility of the creative writer. The "functionalist" intention of the social psychologist appears divergent from the "structuralist" analysis of the literary critic. But, Brodber's "faction" can be categorized within a Neo-African folk aesthetic of functional form: literature as wordhoard, the repository of the accumulated wisdom of the community, the creative medium through which the norms of appropriate social behaviour can be elaborated metaphorically.[2]

The Afro-Jamaican folk ethos of *Jane and Louisa Will Soon Come Home* is evident in the organizing metaphors of the work, derived from the

279

folk culture, and in its primary theme: the healing of the protagonist Nellie, who travels to "foreign" to study, and returns home to a profound sense of homelessness, from which she is redeemed only when she comes to understand the oral accounts of her fragmented family history, and the distorted perceptions of female identity and sexuality that she has internalized in childhood. The therapeutic power of the word is the subject and medium of Brodber's fictive art.

Thus Brodber employs the central framing device of the creolized English quadrille dance, and the children's ring game derived from it, "Jane and Louisa Will Soon Come Home," to suggest, imagistically, the adaptive capacity of Neo-African folk culture in Jamaica, its conscription of English folk traditions for its own enrichment: fiddling with their dance! It is this very egalitarian resilience that the contemporary Caribbean intellectual needs to relearn. Kenneth Bilby, in his liner notes to the Folkways record album, "Bongo, Backra & Coolie Jamaican Roots," defines the mutuality of cultural exchange in the formation of Jamaican folk music thus:

> The folk music of Britain has influenced much of Jamaican folk music. Yet it is precisely in this cultural domain that cultural exchange seems to have been somewhat more even. Even in instances in which melody or form is directly traceable to England, the rendition is always very Jamaican in flavor. In music such as quadrille music or John Canoe music, this 'flavor' would seem to owe much to African-derived rhythmic attitudes.[3]

Similarly, Louise Bennett analyzes the process whereby the English ring games taught in schools, become incorporated into the body of Afro-Jamaican children's games:

> The real Jamaican games, (like the folksongs), have no personal authorship but have been handed down from one generation to another. These are very old games and they retain much of the African (Ashanti) flavour.
>
> Some of the old English games, like "Jane and Louisa," which are taught in schools have been taken up to the hills by the children and are now part of the "Ring Ding." But these are easily recognized as the dialect is less pronounced and the movements more controlled.[4]

Edward Brathwaite, developing his theory of creolization with the evolution of Afro-Jamaican culture illustrates, argues in "Folk Culture of the Slaves of Jamaica" that

> ... it is in the nature of the folk culture of the ex-African slave, still persisting today in the life of the contemporary 'folk,' that one can

discern that the 'middle passage' is not, as it popularly assumed, a traumatic, destructive experience, separating the blacks from Africa, disconnecting their sense of history and tradition, but a pathway or channel between this tradition and what is being evolved on new soil, in the Caribbean.[5]

Brodber herself, as social historian, asserts in her polemical essay, "Oral Sources and the Creation of a Social History of the Caribbean," that the Eurocentrically disposed Caribbean intellectual, like Nellie, must revitalize the severed linkages with the nurturing folk culture, for sanity's sake. The deliberate attempt to remember the past—both personal and racial/cultural—restores the breach of history. In her analysis of this essential process of recreating the significant past, Brodber distinguishes between the perspective of the historian and that of the novelist: the range of permissable distance from "fact" varies, and thus influences both point-of-view and the kind of *persona* each assumes:

> What conclusively separates these works (fiction) from history is the relationship of their writer's 'I' to his data. While the historian, having collected his data, leaves them to move logically to a conclusion, the creative writer can impose his own sense of justice, his own feelings upon the data and guide them to a conclusion which accords with his prejudice.[6]

Brodber's prejudice in *Jane and Louisa Will Soon Come Home* is to present a sympathetic account of Nellie's maturation from the inquisitive innocence of childhood, through the secrecy of adolescence to the delayed wisdom of adulthood. Female sexuality—the "hidey-hidey thing"[7]—in both its creative and destructive manifestations is the subject of much of the novel. The proverb "Woman luck de a dungle heap," is used to articulate the ambivalence of female identity, the implied fortuitousness of destiny and the hidden promise of a fated luck. The fear of premature pregnancy, with its shameful confirmation of covert, adult knowledge is a constant threat.

Aunt Becca, with whom Nellie goes to live in town, is the epitome of middle-class propriety: "Hoity toity Aunt Becca with her stockings bumped under her knee"; (p. 92). It is she who cautions Nellie when she asks for permission to go on a date to the Globe cinema with Baba, a male childhood friend, to see appropriately enough "Jack the Ripper":

> I know you're vex but think of me. What would I tell your parents if your life get stopped part way.

> Learn that lest you be weighed in the balance and found wanting. Learn that the world is waiting to drag you down. "Woman luck de a

dungle heap," they say, "fowl come scratch it up." But you save
yourself lest you turn woman before your time, before the wrong fowl
scratch you luck—(p. 17)

Though Nellie herself does not immediately fall by the proverbial
wayside, she does become gradually aware of the stories of women in her
family who have been weighed in the balance and found wanting. For
example, Sara Richmond, Nellie's mother is made to feel ashamed of her
sexuality by Becca's dog-like capacity to ferret out the salacious secrets of
her family:

> Aunt Becca's shaming eye ruled our roost. Aunt Becca's crinkly hair
> scooped away from her face, stuck out in a point barely touching the
> top of her shoulder like a fish tail in a trapped hair net. . . . Aunt
> Becca's round brown self, her thin lips pursed together like a
> shrivelled star apple.

> Sarah Richmond was ashamed that she had married Mrs. Becca
> Pinnock's brother rather than finish her exams; that she gave given
> him so many children and the wash belly she was carrying 'at this
> stage of her life' aborted itself at Aunt Becca's coming. (pp. 92-93)

But even prim and proper Aunt Becca has a literal skeleton in her closeted
past. The shame of her sterility is the antithesis of Sarah's fertility: her
aborted child is proof of her failure to integrate the irrational designs of
erotic love and the compelling constraints of rural respectibility; her
inability to understand her own sexuality:

> She is barren. Threw away Tanny's child and made herself a mule.
> Lived through his hatred . . . but you know that. Suffered Pinnock
> who suffered her because of what you call her khaki. But is she home?
> Is she at peace? . . . Spinning in purgatory, her soul, her heart and her
> baby are in thatched huts, perspiration and drums, praying for peace.
> (p. 133)

Nellie describes her own adolescent view of nascent sexuality—
menstruation, and the capacity for pregnancy which it heralds—as the
coming of "it." "It" is both the shameful metaphorical anonymity of
sexuality, and also the literal English translation of the Freudian *id*, the
irrational forces of repressed desires. Nellie's mother formally introduces
her to the subject in the evasive language of whispered euphemism: " . . . You
are eleven now and soon something strange will happen to you. When it
does go and tell your Aunt. . . . I needed cleansing" (p. 119). Thus Nellie is

somewhat prepared for "it" when it does come, and she even intimates the clandestine need for cleansing that it will require:

> We had known that 'it' would come one day but never thought seriously of, nor discussed its happening to us, though we knew all about its happening to other people. . . . We could tell when any of our women folk were about to have 'it'. We knew that when they sat down and made themselves whisper one to the other, they were talking about 'it'. . . . 'It' was a hidey-hidey thing! It made you whisper. (pp. 119-120)

Nellie's first sexual experience is indeed an exercise in degradation. She feels a sense of obligation and shame at the essentially commercial nature of her contact with the groping male hands:

> A dark movie house and his hands going where nobody else's have been. And you ought to have kicked this man out of your room, coming back on all sorts of transparent pretexts. You ought to have torn up the script and backed out. But he paid the taximan what you knew must have been his week's food, so you let him touch you. Shame. You feel shame and you see your mother's face and you hear her scream and you feel the snail what she see making for your mouth. One long nasty snail, curling up, straightening out to show its white underside that the sun never touches. (p. 28)

The diminished reptilian image of the "mekke mekke"[8] snail is, in context, appropriately repulsive. An Oedipal image of her father, feeding slime to the six year old Nellie, reinforces the distastefulness of her first sexual experience, especially its orality:

> My father is a clown. It is fascinating to watch this adult playing just for me. He wants me to play too. That is embarrassing: to hold masks for a big man to fool around in. I am to be the baby to whom he feeds the white slimy stuff. He lifts the spoon dripping slime to my mouth and I, freezing the rest of my body, let it on to my tongue so that he might speak. (p. 36)

The physical revulsion is the objective correlative of the emotional pain that both Nellie, and her guilt-induced phantom mother experience at the moment of the fall from sexual innocence. But the pain is the price of womanhood, of acceptance into the ranks of the normal. Masochistic frigidity becomes the prime female attribute:

You want to be a woman; now you have a man, you'll be like everybody
else. You're normal now. Vomit and bear it. Wearing my label called
woman. Upon my lapel called normal. (p. 29)

The anticlimatic despair of Nellie's first sexual experience, representing
as it does her disillusionment with the male, both father and lover, is
counterpointed with the chivalric images of courtly love celebrated in the
English quadrille dance, and the Ring Game of the Beautiful Garden. The
use of the quadrille dance, "Jane and Louisa Will Soon Come Home," as a
symbol of the power of art to colour ordinary social relations, is compelling:
"Figure Four. Beat the box Charlie. Rock and stomp. You own the whole
world. Rock and stomp. We out here looking but is not we. Is stage
audience. . . . Show her courtesy." (p. 102)

The circle formation of the ring dance, which like the square of the
quadrille dance define the locus of transformation, can become the
imprisoning trap from which escape is difficult. The concept of ambiguity,
metaphorically expressed in the paradoxical image of the *kumbla*, is
central to the meaning of Brodber's novel: "Your kumbla will not open
unless you rip its seams open. It is a round seamless calabash that protects
you without caring" (p. 123). The *kumbla*/calabash image symbolizes the
seductive power of the protective devices employed by Nellie and several
other women in the novel, to shield themselves from the stark sunlight of
adult knowledge, and its concomitant responsibilities. For, after the fall,
one must leave the beautiful garden and establish a home in the real world.[9]

The very obscurity of the Jamaican Creole word *'kumbla'* illuminates its
paradoxical usage in the novel. Frederick Cassidy notes in *Jamaica Talk*
that

> The folk speech has a special affinity, it would seem, for words
> involving sound-play of one sort or another. . . . There seems definitely to
> be something analogous to nicknaming by which a word is not kept in
> its full form but reduced in some way. . . . *coobla* is probably a
> reduction of *calabash*, which is what it means. The effect is
> thoroughly to disguise the source of such words. . . . [10]

This literal element of playful disguise, characteristic of the Jamaican
Creole lexicon, becomes a subtle linguistic metaphor in Brodber's novel:
The shaping of the *kumbla*, an act of creativity, is also the art of subterfuge,
a flowering of the spirit of the morally ambivalent Anansi: ". . . Anancy is a
born liar, a spinner of fine white cocoons, a protector of his children. Not to
worry, they'll survive. Anancy is a maker of finely crafted kumblas" (p. 24).

Two Anansi stories narrated in the novel together illustrate the paradoxical
meaning of the *kumbla*. In "Brer Nancy and Brer Tumbletud," Anansi's
selfishness causes him to trick Brer Tumbletud, his sawing partner, out of

having gravy with his food. When Brer Tumbletud rebels, and insists that he
isn't eating any more dry food, Brer Nancy "fire him one box. Him drop.
Eye kin over. Him dead. Hmmm" (p. 37). Alarmed at Brer Tumbletud's
immediate demise, and aware that no one is likely to want a murderer as a
partner, Brer Nancy decides to shout the question "—You hear any news
say Nancy kill Tumbletud oh—?" The reverberating question boomerangs
as a statement and puts Nancy in a spin. The image of "Nancy spinning
around in the woods" (p. 38), is an expression of entrapment in the
subterfuge of the *kumbla*.

By contrast, the story of Brer Nancy and his son Tucuma, caught
poaching in Dryhead's waters, is a positive acknowledgement of the
necessity of subterfuge to ensure safe passage. By assuming a variety of
disguises, Tucuma pretends to be five sons of Anancy, and thus tricks
Dryhead into agreeing to allow just one of Anancy's sons to row him home
and return in surrender with the boat. The formula that signals Tucuma's
assuming of the disguise is:

> Your face favour . . . go enna kumbla—
> To Dryhead and his court, this was a bad word that only a man so torn
> with grief would utter to his child. To Tucuma, it meant: find yourself
> a camouflage and get back into the store house. (p. 128)

But Nellie wants to remain too long in her protective *kumbla*, which is, in
part, the world of book-learning and the brittle rhetoric of political slogans.
Her young man, Cock Robin, full of hot air, goes up in smoke:

> My young man's got the spirit. He's turned over a new leaf. He's even
> changed his profession. He is going to get more learning so that he can
> better minister to his people. He gives half of his salary to his people.
> My young man talks in an unknown tongue. . . . words like 'underdevel-
> opment,' 'Marx,' 'cultural pluralism.' I love my young man. He's got
> the black spirit and it's riding him hard. Lead on Robin. Lead on. (p.
> 46)

This is a parody of I Corinthians, chapter 13, Paul's sermon on love, and it
foreshadows Cock Robin's ironic apotheosis.

It is Baba, whose elements are water and earth, metaphysically associated
with the folk traditions of curative obeah, who with the assistance of Alice,
Nellie's nurturing maiden-aunt, rescues her from the *kumbla* of mourning
in which she has buried herself:

> But the trouble with the *kumbla* is the getting out of the *kumbla*. It is
> a protective device. If you dwell too long in it, it makes you delicate.
> Makes you an albino: skin white but not by genes. Vision extra-

> sensitive to the sun and blurred without spectacles. Baba and Alice
> urged me out of mine. Weak, thin, tired like a breach baby. (p. 130)

Nellie's *kumbla* is also that of the retreat from sexuality: the fear of the
responsibilities of independence, and the fear of dependence on the wrong
male, expressed in riddling proverb:

> Black tinged woman, if you manage to hold your head up at all, you
> should freeze yourself in that position and wait to be lifted as the earth
> turns. Do not turn around on your own momentum; if you do so, you
> will fall. "Woman luck at dungle heap, fowl come scratch it up" but in
> the life of a black-spermed woman, it is a miracle that finds the right
> cock. So freeze yourself and wait and how better to wait than in the
> shade of a *kumbla*? (pp. 142-143)

It *is* a miracle that Baba, "this obeahman of an anancy" (p. 69) returns in
his nurturing role as healer, and assists Nellie in grounding herself, by
teaching her self-love. Baba, smelling of lime, with its capacity to 'run
duppy,' and its folkloric associations with asceticism, exorcises Nellie of
the ghost of Aunt Becca:

> He had spent a good long time in . . . pointing out to me that I was
> more than a cracked up doll. I had seen for myself that levitation was
> not for me. I had fainted. I was water. I belonged to the earth. I was not
> like Aunt Becca had said, 'wanting.' I had been weighed in the balance
> and finally found heavy enough to sink. (p. 69)

Baba, who dabbles in a "higher science" (p. 67) than Aunt Becca's
Anglican hypocrisies, takes the metaphorical curse of obeah off Nellie, by
the laying on of hands.

The healed Nellie dreams of a fish—a sign of pregnancy in Afro-
Jamaican folklore. But the fish is not yet ready to be delivered:

> Last night I dreamt I was carrying a fish, a large sized parrot fish, so
> large that it stretched my belly to the point where it became a square
> gold fish bowl with one fish stuck crossways in it. I could touch the tail
> where the nurse had prepared me but no amount of bearing down
> could give birth to it. Strangely enough, I felt neither sadness nor
> frustration nor even pain that the fish couldn't come for after all I could
> still see it. (p. 147)

Indeed, Nellie has the assurance that "It will come" (p. 147): the release of
the repressed desires of the *id*. And *she* is ready.

Aunt Alice, the antithesis of Aunt Becca, helps accomplish Nellie's readiness. She is the spirit messenger who acquaints Nellie in childhood with the science of herbal healing:

> I travelled with her, my Aunt Alice, my father's mother's sister Alice Whiting who never could settle down to housewifing but spent her earthly days visiting with and washing for the fading ones. I travelled with her inside that round and she showed me our gardens. . . . She made me taste the guinea hen weed and the leaf of life, for better vision, she said. (pp. 75-76)

It is important that it is Alice, the visionary, who fits together the jigsaw puzzle of their family history. Maureen Warner-Lewis in her study of "The Nkuyu: Spirit Messengers of the Kumina," contrasts the veneration of ancestors institutionalized in that Afro-Jamaican religion with the scholarly scepticism about the value of documenting the small-scale histories of family life:

> In kumina, harmony with the divine world is achieved primarily through ancestral spirits. . . . The concept of the 'living dead' provides African society with the major basis of its people's sense of continuity—as a family, a clan, and a nation. . . . Although West Indian history has, in recent years, become a respectable academic pursuit, the study of the life and history of the people of the islands is still in its infancy. Family histories and village chronicles continue to be, in general, of minimal importance to both historian and layman.[11]

Erna Brodber's *Jane and Louisa Will Soon Come Home* does chronicle the history of one rural Jamaican family, and it is of absolute importance to both historian and literary critic. For it affirms, with literary sophistication and historical precision, the fertility of the gardens of women, restored from deserted *kumblas*.

NOTES

1. For an account of the genesis of the work see Evelyn O'Callaghan, "Rediscovering the Natives of My Person": Review of Erna Brodber's *Jane and Louisa Will Soon Come Home, Jamaica Journal*, 16:3(1983) 61.
2. See, for example, Micere Mugo, "The Relationship between African and African-American Literature as Utilitarian Art: A Theoretical Formulation",

in Joseph E. Harris, Ed., *Global Dimensions of the African Diaspora*, (Washington, D.C.: Howard University Press, 1982), 85-93.

3. Kenneth Bilby, "Bongo, Backra & Coolie Jamaican Roots," (New York: Folkways Records, Album No. FE 4232, 1975), 1.

4. Louise Bennett, "Children's Jamaican Songs and Games," (New York: Folkways Records, Album No. FC 7250, 1957), 1.

5. Edward Brathwaite, "Folk Culture of the Slaves in Jamaica," (London: New Beacon Books, 1970), 4-5. See also *The Development of Creole Society in Jamaica* (Oxford: Oxford University Press, 1971).

6. Erna Brodber, "Oral Sources and the Creation of a Social History of the Caribbean", *Jamaica Journal*, 16:4(1983) 4.

7. Erna Brodber, *Jane and Louisa Will Soon Come Home* (London: New Beacon Books, 1980), 120. Subsequent references cited parenthetically in text.

8. Jamaican Creole word meaning "mucous"; decidedly negative connotations; usually used to describe the consistency of unpalatable food.

9. In Yoruba cosmology the calabash symbolizes the divine harmony of the male and female deities. Obatala and Oduduwa. This interpretation is, of course, ironic in the context of the novel. See Ojo G.J. Afolabi, *Yoruba Culture* (London: University of London-University of Ife, 1966), 182; 196.

10. Frederick Cassidy, *Jamaica Talk* (London: Macmillan-Institute of Jamaica, 1961; 2nd ed. 1971), 400.

11. Maureen Warner-Lewis, "The Nkuyu: Spirit Messengers of the Kumina," *Savacou* (Kingston: Gemini, 1977), 76-77.

This Gift of Metaphor.
Symbolic Strategies and the
Triumph of Survival in
Simone Schwarz-Bart's
The Bridge of Beyond

Abena P.A. Busia

Simone Schwarz-Bart's novel *The Bridge of Beyond*[1] is a celebration of life, manifest through a story told. The heroine, Telumee, has puzzled out a meaning for her life, and she shares it with us. It is the essential feature of Telumee's story that she tells it. In doing so she integrates the entire fabric of her life, by naming herself and each person in her life, and situating them all in time and place, on her island home of Guadeloupe. Throughout the text, and the life that the text embodies, words are a charged and living force, for good or ill, and silence can be tantamount to destruction or annihilation. Thus Telumee's story is a triumph simply because it exists as an ordered narrative. As a story told, it is a gift of life.

We can read this work as a story told for black women. The growing body of works by black women writers of the African diaspora, collectively, have strategic impact, for within these works our writers re/collect the separated fictions of our lives, in order to reclaim our stories and to re-write our histories. In doing this, they legitimise lives and world views which have hitherto been alienated and removed from narrative account, and become for us the manifestation of that voice re-found. Thus the reclamation of our voices through these texts has become a socio-political reality, a reality which is also placed as a vital theme *within* some of these works themselves. Simone Schwarz-Bart's *The Bridge of Beyond* is significant

289

not simply because it is given to us, but because within that gift we are bequeathed the story of a woman who has learnt to give an account of her life, and who can acknowledge why that, in itself, is a gift worth possessing.

Telumee's ability to give an account of her life is her singular victory. And within the framework of the text, and the contemporary social context, the triumph of this singular narrative becomes a collective celebration. For Telumee serves in her text as a kind of griot for people whose lives would otherwise remain unrecorded. Narrated in the space of one day, *The Bridge of Beyond* is a history spanning five generations of Guadeloupean women, told to us by the central character, Telumee, the fourth of the generations. The novel is a chronicle history in two parts, and significantly Telumee begins her account with *her people*; she first tells the story of the generations immediately preceding hers, so that when she reaches her own, she is already firmly a part of a people and a place. Telumee is very conscious of narrating the history of which her story is only a part.

The history of Telumee's people is reflected principally through the generations of women in her family; her story goes from great-grandmother, to grandmother, to mother, to daughter, to adoptive daughter. She is firmly rooted in a matriarchal culture, and that she *tells* the women's story is fundamental to the narrative structure of the text and its thematic coherence. In her representation of her struggle for autonomy within a community, while reflecting for us the insecurities of her economic status as a black woman in a post-slavery society, what she mirrors for us is the healing strength of the community of women. This strength is dramatized principally through the abiding nature of her folk and oral culture, in particular the deeply symbolic significance of the mastery over words. In the context of her own narrative, that Telumee speaks to us is a manifestation of her mastery over life and language. She accounts for her life, private and public, in place on her island, and generationally through time. And as her foremothers triumphed over physical and spiritual sorrows, so does she, and as a result, through her story, she gives herself a sense of liberty, and thus, of happiness.

In Telumee's community, words themselves are treated as an elemental life force, for words can create or destroy, alienate or sustain. She says of her own taciturn mother, "She looked on human speech as a loaded gun, and to use her own expression, talking often felt to her like an issue of blood" (p. 16). And though not all take heed and likewise guard their speech, Telumee herself responds to words as if embodied, and sometimes even vulnerable themselves. On one occasion, Elie, her childhood friend and future husband, shares with her his dreams for them both. Yet her response to his driving dream is cautious:

> I wouldn't say a word or utter a sigh, in case I gave voice to some evil
> influence that might prevent the dream from ever coming true, Elie's

words made me proud, but I would have rather he'd kept them to him-self, *carefully sheltered from bad luck*. (p. 47) (emphasis mine)

For to her, in voicing these dreams, Elie had endangered them. But though saddened, she is silent, 'guarding hope,' and the memory of one of her grandmother's stories comes to her then:

> And as I was silent, guarding hope, one of Queen Without a Name's stories came into my mind, the one about the little huntsman who goes into a forest and meets—'What did he meet, girl?'—he met the bird that could talk, and as he made to shoot it, shut his eyes, aimed, he heard a strange whistling sound:
>
> > Little huntsman, don't kill me
> > If you kill me I'll kill you too.
>
> Grandmother said the little huntsman, frightened by the talking bird, lowered his gun and walked through the forest, taking pleasure in it for the first time. I trembled for the bird, which had nothing but its song, and lying there on my rock, feeling at my side Elie's damp and dreaming body, I too set off dreaming, flew away, took myself for the bird that couldn't be hit by any bullet because it invoked life with its song. (pp. 47-48)

In the end this text itself is Telumee's own song. This story is her own life-invoking song, for having learnt to sing it, she demonstrates the self-same magical control over her life. In the end, like the bird, Telumee demonstrates through her 'song,' both literally and figuratively, that mastery over self and circumstance which can overcome the forces which conspire to betray one's life. Words can be dangerous, they can poison and wound, but, above all else, if we can learn not to be alienated by them, they can be harnessed as a life-protecting force.

Telumee learns to harness her words through an essential and insoluble spiritual union which reveals itself in the story through song and story-telling. The principal bonding relationship in this story is that between grandmother and grandchild, a tie reflected by the fact that in the telling, Telumee's autobiography becomes at one and the same time her grand-mother's biography. The fact that Telumee is situated in the text principally as storyteller serves to emphasize the grandmother's crucial role in her life, for within Telumee's own narrative, it is her grandmother who is presented as the storyteller. Thus it is Toussine who, by giving Telumee the comfort of words and the wisdom they contain, makes of Telumee a storyteller, and bequeaths to her the wisdom she finally transmits to us through autobiogra-phy. In a text wondrously conscious of the giving and receiving of words, Telumee's narrative teaches us to accept that there are words that separate, and words that bind. She passes on, as her legacy to us, that gift of metaphor which she herself received from her grandmother, and which served to liberate her own life.

Toussine is a story-telling grandmother whose songs and stories function as a key to an understanding of self and community; a key to internal strength to learn the ability to survive the vagaries of private history and, most vitally, as a key to unite her to the history of suffering of 'her people.' The wisdom Toussine bequeathes is a wisdom granted *through narrative*. Toussine's stories, often based upon the vital importance of words themselves, bestowing as they do the gift of the proper use of metaphor, aid Telumee to define herself, and anchor her life. The wisdom she bestows on Telumee through her stories is the gift of love and understanding, both of human nature, and of human history, for "against sorrow and the vanity of things, there is and will always be human fantasy" (p. 12). This gift is made possible through a shared sense of the significance of words, for good or ill. It is a shared communal sense of the power of words which enables Toussine to teach Telumee how she can learn to rule, rather than be ruled by them.

Telumee, like her grandmother Toussine before her, has been given a name by her community as a testament to the dignity of her survival. The grandmother, Toussine, was given her communal name as a tribute to her surviving three years of deep grief over the loss of her twin daughters burned by fire, and proclaiming that 'resurrection' with the birth of another child:

> They thought of the old Toussine, in rags, and compared her with the Toussine of today—not a woman, for what is a woman? Nothing at all, they said, whereas Toussine was a bit of the world, a whole country, a plume of a Negress, the ship, sail, and wind, for she had not made a habit of sorrow. Then Toussine's belly swelled and burst and the child was called Victory. And then the Negroes did rejoice. On the day of the christening they came to Toussine and said:
>
> 'In the days of your silks and jewels we called you Queen Toussine. We were not far wrong, for you are truly a queen. But now, with your Victory, you may boast that you have put us in a quandary. We have tried and tried to think of a name for you, but in vain, for there isn't one that will do. And so from now on we shall call you "Queen Without a Name" ' (pp. 14-15)

The child Victory, emblem of Toussine's survival and redemption from madness, whose birth represents her own mother's re-birth, is Telumee's mother. Telumee herself is named by her community when, after she survives desertion by her first love and the treacherous death of her second husband, she has sympathy still for the last man she befriends, who attacks her in his madness:

But when the dawn rose on Angel Medard's coffin, the dancing over, the violins put away, the people came to me and said, their faces full of serenity: "Telumee, dear, Angel Medard lived like a dog and you made him die like a man. Ever since you came to La Folie we have tried in vain to find a suitable name for you. Now you are very old to be given a name, but until the sun has set, anything may happen. So as for us, henceforth we shall call you Telumee Miracle." (p. 166)

This communal naming, an honour bestowed in many African communities, is an accolade of acceptance. And the very names they chose to give, and the reasons and manner of bestowal, underscore the fact of this being a community keenly sensitive to the metaphoric or signifying power of words as elemental forces which can affect life itself.[2] In the names they bestow, they acknowledge that force in all life, which must precede any visible—or audible—creative act.

There are two spheres of enslavement that Queen empowers Telumee to conquer through this recognition of the power of words: The danger of internal, metaphysical enslavement, and the fear of physical enslavement—both as a fact of historical reality, and in the sense of the inevitable hardships of labour through life itself. We can isolate a number of central conversations or stories the grandmother shares with her spiritual heir, which carry the lessons the young Telumee needs to internalize, in order to take herself through life on the island and situate herself, personally and historically. The first incident is a seemingly casual account of the way in which Telumee and her grandmother used to spend their Sunday mornings doing the washing at the riverside, along with the other women.

When souls were heavy and everything proclaimed the futility of the black man's existence, . . . darkness would descend on me and I would wonder if I hadn't been put on earth by mistake. Then I would hear Queen Without a Name whispering into my ear: "Come away, Telumee, as fast as you can. They're only big whales left high and dry by the sea, and if the little fish listen to them, they'll lose their fins! . . . Telumee, my little crystal glass, . . . *there are three paths that are bad for a man to take: to see the beauty of the world and call it ugly, to get up early to do what is impossible, and to let oneself get carried away by dreams—for whoever dreams becomes the victim of his own dream.*" Then she would set off, already murmuring a song, some beguine from the old days to which she would give a special inflection, a sort of veiled irony, the object of which was to convey to me that certain words were null and void, all very well to listen to but better forgotten. Then I'd shut my eyes and grip my grandmother's hand, and tell myself it had to exist, some way of dealing with the life Negroes bear so as not to feel it pressing down on one's shoulders day after day, hour after hour, second after second. (p. 30) (emphasis mine)

It is precisely a way of keeping one's fins, despite the big whales, that her grandmother proceeds, through the use of words best remembered, to transmit to Telumee. The walk up the path, holding hands, symbolizes the relationship between them, and her words and songs, like the proffered hand, enable Telumee to walk up the path of life. In a sense Queen Without a Name gives Telumee lessons on how to engage and control 'her gift for metaphor.'[3]

This lesson is imparted casually, as cited above, through the singing of songs—from dance to slave songs—and, crucially, through the weekly Thursday evening ritual recounting of stories. It was on Thursdays that Queen would tell those stories which anchored their lives:

> She opened before us a world in which trees cry out, fishes fly, birds catch the fowler, and the Negro is the child of God. She was conscious of her words, her phrases, and possessed the art of arranging them in images and sounds, in pure music, in exaltation. She was good at talking, and loved to do so for her two children, Elie and me. 'With a word a man can be stopped from destroying himself' she would say. The stories were ranged inside her like the pages of a book. She used to tell us five every Thursday, but the fifth, and last, was always the same: the story of the Man Who Tried to Live on Air. (p. 48)

This is the story of a man who takes all three of the paths it is bad for a man to take (pp. 49-50). And, after the telling, the grandmother would end with the admonition:

> My little ember, if you ever get on a horse, keep good hold of the reins so that it's not the horse that rides you: Behind one pain there is another. Sorrow is a wave without end. But the horse musn't ride you, you must ride it. (p. 50)

The essential message of this story is the mastery of internal enslavement.[4] Queen transmits, and Telumee learns, the importance of the necessity for control; it is essential to learn to ride your horse, rather than be ridden by it. "My Two Eyes" is not the Man's eyes, but, to his detriment, calling him so, makes him so. He loses the ability to see correctly for himself, until it is too late to take control over his own life. He substitutes dream for reality and gets carried away, in the end, where his will is not to go. It is crucial that Queen bequeaths this "key to the defence against alienation by the Symbolic,"[5] for it is a counter-balance to her other stories, in particular her lesson on the mastery of *external* enslavement.

The Man Who Tried to Live on Air is a story about the mastery of *internal* enslavement. But there are two dangers to be fought, those which are internal, as well as those which are external. Queen's stories and conversations are all metaphorical, but, like all myth and ritual, their function is to serve as a tool for salvation which manifests itself in human affairs. One has to find a means to come to an understanding of both the self and the community. It is for this reason that, in a community which has suffered the degradation of slavery, that devastated the faith in the collective self, Queen Without a Name also makes certain to give Telumee a tool which will help her comprehend the history of Slavery and its effects.

In this endeavour there is one other female voice heard in the conversation, that of Queen's lifelong friend, the healer, Ma Cia. *Together* these two old women prefigure Telumee's private and public life, as she learns to comprehend the stories they tell her in those respective spheres. That is, as Telumee 'mirrors' Queen Without a Name in her private self and thus finds peace and comfort even after Queen's death, she also grows to 'become' or take over Ma Cia's role in her public life, as she too becomes a respected witch and healer. Telumee's public education begins with the first question she asks about slavery on a vist she and Queen Without a Name pay to Ma Cia. In answering her, the old women have the following conversation:

But who would think, to see them all smiles, that the ancestor the White of Whites would take a Negro in his arms and squeeze him till his spleen burst?

"But what did he do that for?" I said, terrified.

Ma Cia thought for a while.

"Long ago," she said, "a nest of ants that bit peopled the earth, and called themselves men. That's all."

Queen Without a Name leaned up against Ma Cia and tried to take away some of her bitterness.

"Who can blame a dog for being tied up?" she said. "And if he's tied up how can you prevent him being whipped?"

"If he's tied up he ought to resign himself," said Ma Cia, "for he's bound to be whipped. For a long time now God has lived in the sky to set us free, and lived in the white men's house at Belle-Feuille to flog us."

"That is a fine word," said Grandmother. "And after that sadness here is another: to see the fire go out and the puppies playing in the embers."

"With your permission, my friend, I'd say it is a piece of sadness, not a whole one. The whole sadness was the fire. But the fire is out, and it's a long time now since the white of whites was in the ground, rotten meat that will not grow again. And even the embers will not last forever."

> Queen Without a Name, her eyes shining strange and feverish,
> gazed at me for a long while and said:
> "No, even the embers will not last forever . . ." (p. 38)

> [Later], Grandmother heaved a deep sigh that signified our visit was
> almost over, and Ma Cia, turning to me, child that I was, said, "Be a
> fine little Negress, a real drum with two sides. Let life bang and thump,
> but keep the underside always intact." Grandmother nodded, and we
> went back down the overgrown path, clinging to each other. . . . (p. 39)

At the end of that day Telumee comments: "For the first time in my life I
realized that slavery was not some foreign country, some distant region
from which a few very old people came . . . It had all happened here, in our
hills and valleys, perhaps near this clump of bamboo, perhaps in the air I
was breathing." (p. 39)

This conversation serves two functions. First, as in the story of the Man
Who Lived on Air, it uses metaphor to render intelligible forces which could
seem either inexplicable or uncontrollable, and encapsulates the range of
contradictions over the issue of slavery in its telling. In giving her a wisdom
through which she can define and re-define herself, the two women are
trying to teach Telumee Miracle that no aspect of her life, private or public,
need be either inexplicable or uncontrollable. It is key that the admonition
to make of herself a drum—the sacred and primary instrument of *within*-
group social communication in African heritage communities—follows the
conversation about the ills of slavery. In the first place it teaches Telumee
clearly that her life *is* hers to make of it what she will no matter the odds, and
it does this through a metaphor which instructs her both to protect herself,
and face the world at the same time.

It is those words that Telumee carries with her away from home which
save her and give meaning to her life in times of solitude and trial. Working
as a maid servant in the household of former slave owners, under
circumstances which deny the value of her existence, she is comforted by
the remembrance of Queen's songs and stories, and sustained by the
efficacy of Ma Cia's admonition (p. 60). In the face of a flurry of demeaning
racial insults from her mistress, it gives Telumee a way of protecting herself
so as not to let the words wound or destroy:

> I glided in and out between the words as if I were swimming in the
> clearest water, feeling the cooling breeze on my neck, my arms, the
> back of my legs. And, thankful to be a little Negress that was
> irreducible, a real drum with two sides, as Ma Cia put it, I left one side
> to her, the mistress, for her to amuse herself, for her to thump on, and I,
> underneath, I remained intact, nothing ever more so. (pp. 61-62)

This lesson is not easily learned, however. Internal strength comes, as the women suggest, only through suffering, and it is the whole community, in particular the community of women, who help Telumee comprehend and accept this. One example only should suffice as illustration.

Telumee at the start of her life assumed that she would be bound to one man, the husband of her childhood choosing. She is deserted by him. When this happens, she incarcerates herself in their marital home in a desperate grief, a grief which is annihilating because in her love, she has seen herself as mirrored in him. His rejection of her then becomes a fundamental self-negation. This is an error; it is Queen Without a Name who never ceases to reflect Telumee's real self, a tie that binds, even after death.[6] *This truth is dramatized by the fact that when Telumee in her grief, behaves as one dead, Queen Without a Name also becomes as one dying.* And it is the *women* of the community (not all of whom have necessarily been Telumee's closest friends or associates), who appreciate the import of this and help her come to life again, thus saving both her life and that of her grandmother. This happens one Christmastime, when the woman all gather outside Telumee's bungalow, at first on the opposite side of the street, but speaking loud enough for her to hear, and slowly move closer to give her solace:

> A few days before the holiday people began to go up and down in front of my cabin without saying anything, *just to prove to me that there couldn't be a gap in the weft*, and that however much I wanted to fly and become a wind I had two hands and two feet exactly the same as them. And then, when they went by my yard, it was as if they deliberately laughed louder than before, *some of them even singing cheerful songs and hymns of deliverance with such zest I wondered if they were singing only for themselves.* So they went to and fro in front of my cabin, and from time to time a would break away from the group, lift imploring arms heavenwards, and cry in a high-pitched voice, "Be born, come down to change our fates." And hearing her I'd have the strange feeling that she was *throwing me a thread in the air, throwing a light, light thread toward my cabin, and then I'd be visited by a smile.* (p. 109) (emphasis mine)

The way this passage is presented has several elements worth noting, given the liberating aspect of metaphor which runs throughout the narrative itself. In the first place, the women gather around Telumee's cabin just to prove that "there couldn't be a gap in the weft." The social import of this metaphor is to convey a community which remains intact; Telumee under all circumstances remains one of them, a part of the fabric of the weave. She cannot make herself disappear, and life must go on as before. The mention of the hymns of deliverance reminds us also of the grandmother's songs, sung to teach hope and endurance. Furthermore, they are sung for the simple reason that the mission is one of deliverance, and therefore given the power of metaphor, it is such hymns which must be sung. The strange feeling of having a thread thrown through the air to her reminds us of the original communal metaphor; it is this which weaves her in and binds her, she has let go, but they will not let it fall.

The entire incident takes place on Christmas Eve, rather than, as one would expect in a story about spiritual rebirth, at Easter the Feast of the Resurrection, *because* it is the feast of the Nativity. Telumee recognizes that the women wish to remind her that however much she wants to 'fly and become a wind', she too has "two hands and two feet". The women are there because they want to bear witness to her own personal nativity, for they are concerned about whether they will ever see her again as she used to be—in the flesh. The spirit cannot die, but Telumee's community believes that this earthly life can in some instances either be prolonged, as in the case of Ma Cia who is believed to have turned herself into a dog when her human bones became too weary, or shortened, as Telumee is in danger of doing to herself by refusing to live fully on earth as a human being. The question then, is whether or not Telumee will be restored to the life which she is not yet due to leave, and rejoin in the flesh the community of the living. For her to do this requires the energy of the women, energy which is not just physical, but is carried and conveyed through very specific restorative use of words. They come and repeat, as an incantation, that "she will come to shore," a declaration of faith, as with certain miracles, requiring the repetition of the correct words to bring about the desired result (p. 111).

At this point in her life, Telumee has become like the Man of Queen's story. She has let her horse ride her, and in this instance the horse is sorrow and self-abnegation. "I'd gone hunting," she says, "I'd lost both the dog and the hare, half of my soul was broken, and the other half abased . . . The moon had come out, and its light dulled and killed the beauty of the stars" (p. 112). Also, more crucially she tells us, *"they said that of all things in the world speech had become the most alien to me."* When she loses her sense of self, she loses her power to speak. But this visitation proves a crucial turning point. After the women depart, and Telumee is tormented one more time by her husband and his lover, she leaves her marital home for them, and returns to her true home, her grandmother's cabin. After several weeks of silence Telumee bestirs herself and goes for a cleansing bath:

> Then, dripping wet, I went back to the cabin, put on dry clothes, and said to grandmother: "Queen Queen, who says there is nothing for me in the world, who says such foolishness? At this very moment I have left my grief at the bottom of the river. It is going downstream, and will enshroud another heart than mine. Talk to me about life, Grandmother. Talk to me about that. (p. 114)

She turns from her false self to her true self, and the intervention by the women was crucial to her recovery.

After this desertion and healing, Telumee has a number of relationships; but she herself struggles for, and attains, a liberating economic independence, separate from that of the man she is either married to or living with at the time.[7] This independence is not only necessary, it symbolizes her increasing spiritual independence as it is nurtured in her by the women of her family and community. Telumee's opening and closing words bind her closely to the island whose history she both records and reflects. By the end of her life she has walked its breadth, crossed its rivers, cleared its forests, harvested its brutal canefields and lived in the shadow of its mountains. By the end, she is finally speaking from a fixed point which is also her home—the cabin in which she was raised by her grandmother. She has moved this cabin from site to site to its final resting place in the town by the edge of the sea. There is a strong and integral unity between the place, the natural world, and the people and their spiritual worlds, and in Telumee's life it is the women who have taught her how to speak of the bridges between them. Her situation at the end of her story is a testimony to the triumph of their survival.

The Bridge of Beyond opens with the words 'A man's country may be cramped or vast according to the size of his heart. I've never found my country too small.' Two hundred pages later, the last sentences are 'Sun risen, sun set, the days slip past and the sand blown by the wind will engulf my boat. But I shall die here, where I am, standing in my little garden. What happiness.' Yet in between those two statements we have had a record of a great deal of suffering, a great deal of pain, a lot of betrayal. What matters to Telumee in the story of herself and her people, is that by the end she is sure of who she is, and where she is, and it is the grandmother who has helped her learn both, *and taught her how to tell us this*. The miraculous Telumee does manage to make sense of her world, and she tells us, and her narrative is a testimony to the bond between women[8] for the articulation of liberty (pp. 168-170). Throughout the narrative, the guiding principle remains the same: to find the balance between alienation and annihilation. Both internal and external enslavement must be combatted. We must not be controlled either by our own dreams, or by those of others. Life is beleaguered, but in the end, both its pains and its joys must be weathered, and it is this triumph which is manifest through narrative. Telumee has withstood the 'rain and wind'[9] upon her, and knows she is 'not a statue of salt to be dissolved.' She therefore leaves us, although unable to comfort the forlorn Elie,[10] with a sense of joy in herself, and in her world. In spite of all the sorrows, her story is self-creation and a triumph; she has managed to:

> Puzzle out a story, a story with a meaning, with a beginning and an end, as you have to here below if you want to know where you are amidst the chaos of men's destinies. (p. 165)

NOTES

1. Simone Schwarz-Bart, *The Bridge of Beyond*, translated by Barbara Bray, (London: Heinemann, 1982). All page references given in the body of this text are from this edition.

2. Speech has always been significant in societies and cultures primarily sensitive to oral traditions. In the context of the African continent, this still remains true in very many aspects of life. Within the Western literary tradition, we could cite the example of Anglo-Saxon England, or of Ancient Greece, where Aeschylus in his *Oresteia* and Sophocles in his 'Oedipus' cycle base the dramatic impact of their plays on their audience's recognition of the difference between "good speech" and "bad speech."

3. It is this gift which, for instance, Toni Morrison says Sula lacks which makes her dangerous and imperfectly socialised. Toni Morrison, *Sula*, (New York: Bantam Books, 1975), p. 105.

4. For an elucidation of this point see Ronnie Scharfman: "Mirroring and Mothering in Simone Schwarz-Bart's *Pluie et Vent sur Telumee Miracle* and Jean Rhys' *Wide Sargasso Sea*," *Yale French Studies*, Number 62, (1981). This is a superb and truly illuminating study on this novel, in particular Ms. Scharfman's explication of the nurturing of Telumee as a speaking subject, a process rooted in the bond between granddaughter and grandmother.

5. *Ibid.*, p. 96.

6. The relationship between the two of them survives death, for the dying Queen declares "Can you imagine our life, with me following you everywhere, invisible, and people never suspecting they have to deal with two women, not just one?" (p. 119).

7. The question of solvency and financial independence is a crucial factor in a discussion of women's liberty. We have here, for convenience, concentrated on the spiritual aspect of liberty, as if that were totally distinct from security, but women need strength and independence in a context, and creating that context is a part of their struggle. It is important to emphasize therefore that this concentration on spiritual metaphor, for the purpose of this paper, does a disservice to Ms. Schwarz-Bart's novel, in which the control of metaphor is closely linked to the control over life,—not only spiritual but economic as well. The movements around the island recorded in this narrative, for instance, were primarily for pragmatic economic purposes, in which the women, Telumee in particular, were struggling to wrest control over their lives and attain financial independence and security, regardless of the role played by the men in their lives.

8. In *The Bridge of Beyond* we are given wonderful, touching portraits of such men as Xango, who married Toussine's mother to give her child a name though he knew she was not his, Jeremiah, Toussine's "fisher husband [who] had loved and cherished her and kept her safe in her affliction, when her hair was unkempt and her dress in rags," after the tragic death of their daughter, and the loyal Amboise who waited for Telumee many long years, offered her sincere friendship at her greatest need, and shared his last years with her. Nonetheless, the principal bonding relationship in this story is that between women.

9. The literal translation of the original French title of this novel *Pluie et Vent sur Telumee Miracle*, (Paris, France: Editions Seuil, 1972).
10. Fifty years after deserting her, Elie turns up in her garden seeking those words of comfort she cannot give. The narrative that is this text, takes place the day of his funeral shortly afterwards, when she come to terms with both the pain and the joy of her experiences.

Developing Diaspora Literacy: Allusion in Maryse Condé's Hérémakhonon

Vèvè A. Clark

Veronica Mercier, the protagonist of Maryse Condé's first novel *Hérémakhonon*, is a neurotic misfit. By her own volition, she becomes a displaced person, exiled for a finite period in an independent Francophone, West African nation. No expatriate of the usual sort, Veronica refrains from "going native" or flaunting her foreignness. She has come to Africa to soothe the broken ego inherited from earlier encounters in her native Guadeloupe and Paris. Veronica's quest for racial contentment turns to love for salvation. Once she has located her personal "nigger with ancestors" (49/24)[1], Veronica expects she will be healed. The indigenous setting and local politics would go unnoticed were the protagonist not drawn into them by four men and one boy: her lover, a supervisor, a colleague, a casual acquaintance and a student. Despite the stature of her academic training and social class, Veronica Mercier is a shadowy individual whose persona is revealed in halftones through the eyes of the men she meets. For Africans who have never known an Antillean, she is a walking enigma. Tormented by feelings of inadequacy, her thought processes remain fragmented throughout the novel, her speech muted, reflecting a deep sense of displacement. In this acute state of alienation, one particular figure of speech dominates Veronica's search for ancestral identity in West Africa. That device is allusion. A symptom of her inability to be present and accountable, allusion reveals the complexity of the protagonist's character while it structures discourse in the novel. As a result of the author's extensive use of allusion, she develops in her readers what one might call "Diaspora literacy."

Diaspora literacy is the ability to read and comprehend the discourses of Africa, Afro-America and the Caribbean from an informed, indigenous perspective. In such an environment, names such as *Sundiata*, *Bigger Thomas*, and *Marie Chauvet* represent mneumonic devices releasing learned traditions. The protagonist of *Hérémakhonon* demonstrates that Diaspora literacy is more than an intellectual exercise. It is a skill that requires social and political development generated by lived experiences. The author herself has undergone both the intellectual and experiential components of this phenomenon. Raised in Guadeloupe, having lived for many years in Guinea and Ghana, for periods in France and the United States, Maryse Condé has written extensively on the literature and socio-political culture issuing from four hemispheres of the African Diaspora.[2] In *Hérémakhonon*, it is clear that Veronica Mercier is literate regarding three of these regions, the Antilles, France and Afro-America. She is, however, naive when faced with the fourth—ancient and modern Africa. Veronica's education in Africa will depend on her willingness to grasp both literary and social texts so that, for instance, ancient and modern figures in African history, like *Bilissi* and a *Mwalimwana* may be understood in context.

Veronica belongs to an Antillean literary tradition that originated with Suzanne Lacascade's 1924 novel, *Claire Solange, âme africaine*, set in Guadeloupe.[3] Aspects of Veronica's character are unequivocally of the tradition, particularly when Condé parodies discourse and attitudes the literate reader will recognize as conventional in the corpus of Antillean literature by women authors. The theme of the black Antillean who confirms identity by loving a non-black pervades the writing by Antillean women and some men. The first love may well be a mulatto from the islands with whom marriage is taboo or risky given the norms of the society's class and color barriers. In a second stage of development on this theme, the heroine flees to Paris transferring to a Frenchman her previous attractions.[4] The confused protagonist drawn into political intrigue is another motif that has some background in Caribbean literature. Marie Chauvet's *Amour* (1968) depicts a character that, like Veronica, is lured into a situation that she neither understands nor controls.[5]

The new developments and techniques in *Hérémakhonon* are many. Condé challenges outright the myth of Africa that has dominated African Diaspora literature since the Harlem Renaissance (1918-28). Unlike other Antilleans, Condé's heroine actually lives and works in a post-independence African country. Veronica is critical of revolution, has not read the major African political philosophers such as Nkrumah and Fanon, and maintains her privileged class biases by seeking analogous conditions among the African ruling elite.

Condé has been adamant about the need for contemporary writers to break out of the narrative structures of the previous generation:

Nous sommes prisonniers de structures érigées par la génération
précédente et qu'on prétend nous voir respecter. Or, il faut les briser.
La libération de l'écrivain négro-africain, homme ou femme, passe
par là. Il n'est pas d'identité culturelle immuable. Toute identité
culturelle dépend de facteurs socioéconomiques. Même, toute identité
est liée en partie à la classe sociale.[6]

We are prisoners within structures erected by the previous generation
to which they claim we must conform. These structures must be
demolished—now. Liberation for the black African writer, man or
woman, follows just such a course. Fixed cultural identity does not
exist. Cultural identity depends upon economic factors. Indeed, all
identity is tied in part to social class distinctions.

Hérémakhonon is an intricate, experimental novel. It uses cinematic
perspectives and contrapuntal structures to convey the message of an
ambiguous journey.[7] Sudden shifts in time, scores of allusions and, on
occasion, the equivocal use of pronouns[8] require the reader to be active,
engagé, as it were.

The novel opens and closes in an airport. Veronica Mercier, an
unmarried instructor of philosophy, has just arrived in Africa. During the
brief three months she remains in the country before resigning her post,
Veronica has an affair with the Minister of Interior, Ibrahima Sory, a young
man from a renowned family. Ibrahima becomes Veronica's "nigger with
ancestors." He extends an open invitation to his villa *Hérémakhonon*
(literally "Await Happiness" in Mande)[9] located in the quiet, residential
quarter of the city. As the novel unfolds, the reader experiences at close
range from Veronica's perspective a series of disquieting political maneuvers
provoked by the opposing perspectives that Ibrahima and the school
supervisor, Saliou, represent. The reader leaves *Hérémakhonon* with the
sensation of having witnessed from the third row of a theatre a technicolor,
feature-length film.

The novel is divided into three parts during which the protagonist's
concept of time conflicts with political action in the novel. In part one, when
Veronica should be assimilating a new present, she retreats repeatedly to
the past. In part two, she comes into the present, but is confused by virtue of
her previous remoteness from current dilemmas. Her aloofness makes it
increasingly difficult for her and the reader to understand the sources of
dispute in the general political climate. By part three, Veronica has realized
her error:

J'ai pris un mauvais départ dans ce pays. J'aurais dû m'intéresser.
M'intéresser à ce qui se passait autour de moi. Tenter de comprendre

... Le pouvais-je? J'y serai peut-être parvenue si j'avais pu m'oublier,
mais m'oublier, je ne le pouvais pas ... (243-44/137)

When, in part three, Veronica seems to have caught up with the present by
going in search of its meaning, she is floating off again as she did in part one,
but this time forward toward her future return to Paris. Political intrigue
runs parallel to Veronica's time frame. In part one, Birame III, one of her
students, is arrested, and virtually disappears for the remainder of the novel.
In part two, a casual acquaintance, Amar, and Veronica's former boss and
friend, Saliou, are arrested in separate incidents. At one point, Veronica is
detained, but only for a short time. Her ties to Ibrahima Sory ensure her safe
and speedy release. The same is not true of any of the other three. In part
three, when Saliou is said to have committed suicide in his cell, and the
townspeople accept his fate without protest, Veronica departs abruptly for
home, Paris. Not out of fear so much as to maintain her self-respect, she
leaves for France, we imagine, to rejoin her lover Jean-Michel.

This skeletal account omits some of the more captivating fibers of the
narrative. Nearly one half of *Hérémakhonon* develops out of Veronica's
memory and imagination: scenes from childhood in La Pointe, Guadeloupe,
moments of scorn in Paris, references to ancient African history, to Afro-
American popular culture as well as flashes of wish-fulfillment. The last are
some of the most confusing sequences in the novel occurring as they often
do in the middle of a paragraph that has as its subject another theme entirely.
In part three, for example, Veronica fantasizes Saliou's safe release from
prison (279/156 and 282/157). Imagine her distress, and that of the reader,
when Veronica learns of Saliou's death soon after (300-301/168)!

Hérémakhonon is a chronicle of emotions and events. The narrative is
animated by a form of Socratic dialogue. Characters query Veronica, the
newcomer: Why have you come? Where are you from? The author chooses
not to place the responses in quotations, rather she incorporates them into
Veronica's thought processes. As the novel progresses, Veronica asks
herself some of the same questions and slowly directs her inquiries outward
toward the well-being of Birame III, Amar and Saliou. The absence of
dialogue is perhaps the most innovative technique in *Hérémakhonon*.
Although one leaves the novel with the memory of conversations, in effect,
Veronica has never uttered a word. Her silent monologue reads like a
journal where incoming data is meticulously documented, and the thoughts
of the diary-keeper registered in detail. The novel gives the impression that
Veronica is recording on audio tape special events from her African journey
that she will "play" for her Parisian friends. They would certainly recognize
her voice thereby eliminating the need to quote herself. This technique
explains the instances when Veronica, in an aside to the reader, specifies
who is speaking (198/109, 223/125 and 310/174).

Allusion and Narrative Technique

Maryse Condé has reinterpreted the customary role allusion has assumed in literature by using terms unfamiliar to a general readership without the aid of footnotes or a glossary. Consequently, *Hérémakhonon* includes, what may be for some, obscure references to Euro-America and to the African Diaspora as well as to the cultivated and popular arts from both cultures. *Mayotte Capécia* and *Mahalia Jackson* are treated as recognized references sharing a wealth of connotations comparable to *Swann's Way* and the *Douanier Rousseau.*

Allusions may be classified by cultural origin or by type. Attributions are made to ancient and modern African history (Agadja, Shaku Umar, Segou, Jomo Kenyatta, Kwame Nkrumah), to Euro-American culture (*le roseau pensant*, Fabrice, *Les Liaisons dangeureuses*, Shirley Temple, Ku Klux Klan), to Afro-American intellectual history and popular culture (Louis Armstrong, Mahalia Jackson, *Up From Slavery*, Topsy, James Brown) and to Caribbean elite and folk society (Belain d'Esnambuc, Frantz Fanon, Fidel Castro, Papa Legba, Marilisse).[10] More than one hundred and twenty-five allusions, both explicit and indirect, appear in the novel. Direct allusions cross cultural lines between Marivaux and Césaire, from Buñuel to the Supremes. Indirect allusions assume a level of sophistication in the reader. References to the *Pavane pour un enfant défunt, le roseau pensant, Eïa pour le Kaïlcédrat royal*, Scarlett O'Hara's maid and *l'Etat c'est moi* are wordplays leading the imagination to three continents—to Ravel, Pascal, Aimé Césaire, Claudia McNeil and Louis XIV.[11]

The function these allusions serve in the novel is to a large extent conventional. They expand the narrative or undercut ironically a previous statement. Expansiveness comes by way of associations: Africa to the Antilles, the Antilles to Europe, or Africa to its past and present. By way of example: from the beginning of the novel, Veronica identifies her father with a racial and professional type she labels the *marabout mandingue*, "vu à sept ans dans un Atlas Illustré. Et non pas du Sud du Dahomey ou du Nigéria qui ont pourtant largement payé tribut à ce qu'on appelle le Nouveau Monde" [seen in my history book when I was seven. And not from the South either, but from Dahomey or Nigeria, men who paid their fair share to what they called the New World] (12/3). This allusion becomes an epithet used throughout to refer to her father. It links her family immediately and ironically with a mythical, non-slave African aristocracy to which Veronica believes Ibrahima Sory belongs—and by association, her family as well. The repetition of this sobriquet aggrandizes M. Mercier much in the way that Paule Marshall's references to "The Mother" in *Browngirl, Brownstones* elevates the character out of the ordinary. For both Veronica and Selina, the epithet reifies the parent thereby absolving the daughter from remarking the similarity between parent and offspring. In *Hérémakhonon*, the *marabout mandingue* becomes a litany that slowly reveals the degree to which Veronica is like her father in some ways. She writes:

> Abdoulaye (a servant) se permet un sourire d'acceuil à ma vue. Qu'est-ce qu'ils doivent penser de notre duo, lui et le chauffeur derrière le masque du respect? Les domestiques, c'était le grand souci du marabout mandingue. Pas Mabo Julie (Veronica's nanny) qui faisait partie de la famille. Les autres. *Dans le fond, je suis bien sa fille* (282/157). [Emphasis added]

The correspondences between Africa and the Antilles are numerous. They establish a real rather than mythical linkage between the two regions in their present states. Comparisons between landscape (152-53/83), food (217/121), furnishings (138/75) and laughter (142/77) exemplify the associational role of allusion.

Africa's past is linked with its present through Veronica's readings of Mandinka epics. Names like Bakari Dian, Bilissi, Shaku Umar, Ber Kufa, Segou, Silamaka and Agossou that may appear hermetic to some readers are nonetheless familiar in African oral tradition.[12] These personages and places receive attention on an equal footing with more widely recognized figures of the twentieth century, the likes of Kwame Nkrumah, Jomo Kenyatta and Frantz Fanon. Relations between Euro-America and the Antilles take the form of confrontations. A literally *lesser* Antilles that Césaire evoked in 1939 when he wrote,

> Ceux qui n'ont inventé ni la poudre ni la boussole
> ceux qui n'ont jamais su dompter la vapeur ni l'électricité
> ceux qui n'ont exploré ni les mers ni le ciel
> mais ils savent en ses moindres recoins le pays de souffrance
> ceux qui n'ont connu de voyages que de déracinements . . .[13]

> [Those who invented neither powder nor compass
> those who could harness neither steam nor electricity
> those who explored neither the seas nor the sky but who know
> in its most minute corners the land of suffering
> those who have known voyages only through uprootings . . .]

remains fundamentally unchanged in Veronica's mind.[14] Two sets of comparisons predominate. One repeats Césaire's sentiment, while the other emphasizes why individuals raised in Antillean society travel to the metropole in search of culture. Veronica's parents and others of their class perceived the journey as pilgrimage, comparable to the Hadj of Islamic life:

... les séjours en metropole où on emmène les enfants écouter le grand air de Lakmé, admirer la Victoire de Samothrace et la Vénus de Milo moins les bras. ... Que de belles choses, les Blancs ont faites! ... Et nous? ... Nous? ... Eh bien, ils nous permettent de les admirer. Est-ce que ce n'est pas déjà beaucoup . . . (22-23/9)

The disdain in this passage is typical of the narrative voice in *Hérémak-honon*. Contempt pervades Veronica's attitudes as when she refers to the complicity of African kings like Tegbessuou and Agajda in the perpetuation of chattel slavery. The first of many references to these kings comes early in the narrative directly after the allusion to the *marabout mandingue*: "Le nouveau monde? Tout cela pour des perles de Vénise, des bouts de coton rouge, un orgue portatif à Agadja et un carrosse à Tegbessou ... " (12/3). And later, when Saliou welcomes her innocently to Africa, Veronica opines:

Bon, il efface d'un coup trois siècles et demi. Tegbessou et Agadja au lieu de rouler carrosse et d'apprendre leurs gammes ont disposé leurs hommes aux ponts stratégiques. On a rejeté les Blancs à la mer. Elle s'est rougie de leur sang. A Nantes et Liverpool, on met le feu aux négriers. Plus besoin d'eux (13-14/4).

Veronica's scorn is nowhere more apparent than in an imagined retort to her students:

... Mademoiselle de quel pays êtes-vous?

En fin de compte, ici aussi, mon premier cours est un exposé sur les Antilles. Les négriers quittent à nouveau la baie du Biafra. Tant de sang sur l'oeil glauque de la mer! Et les requins joyeux, ancêtres joyeux du Ku Klux Klan.

... On va bouffer du nègre! (44/21)

Whether uncommon or familiar, allusion in *Hérémakhonon* connects cultures and criticizes or ridicules certain manifestations of them. These functions are combined in allusions that refer to stereotypes. Veronica's Aunt Paula resembles a "Mahalia Jackson streetwalking before she became a gospel singer" (24/10) and at times Ibrahima's sister, Ramatoulaye, dressed in one of her expensive wigs, looks like "one of the Supremes" (218/122). In addition, her Directoire furniture reminds Veronica of her own family's elite tastes in Guadeloupe (138/75).

Allusion can be premonitory. When Veronica imagines how the hotel-keeper from Rouen, Jean Lefevre, will recall his African sojourn for friends back home, she writes: "ils parleront de l'Afrique qu'ils imagineront verte et feuillue comme un Douanier Rousseau" ["they'll talk of an Africa as green and leafy as a Douanier Rousseau"] (93/48). A page later we learn that Lefevre's parents were paint sellers, a realization that makes the allusion to the Douanier Rousseau seem fitting. The sense of naturalness is intentional, for the author effectively renders even the most unusual allusions familiar. This she accomplishes through repetition and simile. In addition to culturally referenced comparisons, there are others that are purely personal.

Not only is allusion a gathering of memories and projections, it is also a pedagogical tool. The author is testing her readers in references to Césaire's epic poem, *Cahier d'un retour au pays natal*: "Eïa pour le Kaïlcédrat royal" (27/12) or to Mayotte Capécia's autobiographical novels, *Je suis martiniquaise* and *La négresse blanche* (61/30). Allusions to Afro-American singers, James Brown, the Supremes and Aretha Franklin (188/103), given the context in which they are mentioned, examine the recognition value of popular culture within the Diaspora.

In part one, the reader is bewildered by the numerous references to Diaspora culture and registers them as symptoms of Veronica's disturbed state of mind. However, as the novel gains momentum, Veronica seems less muddled as allusions become a vehicle for expressing comparative culture and private simile. A juxtaposition of similes Veronica creates demonstrates that she is a very literate and observant woman indeed:

European Culture	*Diaspora Culture*
1. Ma vie ressemble à la promenade d'un couple de vieillards sur la Place de la Victoire. Du kiosque à L'Allée Centrale à L'Allée au Bord de la Mer. Et retour . . . (193/107)	1. La vie, c'est une mégère boiteuse. Elle fume la pipe, assise au seuil de sa case et quand je passe à sa portée, elle marmonne méchamment. Elle me jette un sort, et le sort qu'elle m'a jeté, je n'ai jamais pu le défaire. Voilà pourquoi j'erre d'un continent à l'autre, à la recherche de mon identite, dixit Ibrahima Sory, et trouvant des cadavres sur mon chemin (118/64).

Personal Experience
1. La vie est comme un champignon qui prolifère sur tout terrain. Sur l'humus noir et gras, le long du tronc moussu des vieux arbres, sous la pourriture des feuilles mortes (289/162).

European Culture	*Diaspora Culture*
2. Reste Pierre-Gilles, ce coopérant célibataire qui souvent traverse la rue pour bavarder et vider un verre. Je le sais homosexuel et amoureux d'un jeune Peul qu'il a pris à son service et tente de retenir prisonnier comme Albertine (194/107).	2. Pierre-Gilles est dans son lit . . . Il me regarde approcher avec une authentique terreur. Comme un paysan tranquille dans son champs, qui voit fondre sur lui Betsy ou Flora (275/153).

Personal Experience
3. La mer est bleue comme un dessin d'enfant. Et chaude. Comme un ventre de lapine (235/132).

In the space of a simile, the text embraces the Other, reproducing in literary form a phenomenon of bi-cultural life in the Antilles. The compulsion to absorb or reject aspects of one's culture defines bourgeois life in the Caribbean. Some persons assimilate easily through education customs derived from European, African, Caribbean and Afro-American societies, while others, particularly the peasantry, are sequestered in a purely creole world. When the peasant does confront the bourgeois, it is as a servant, like Mabo Julie, who ministers to the needs of the acculturated who can afford the luxury of extra-regional imagery. That Veronica can compare life equally to the predictable actions of an elderly couple strolling along the Place de la Victoire or to the words of a lame, old woman shaping the future; that Pierre Gilles' behaviour reminds her at intervals of the manipulative Marcel or a peasant rendered vulnerable by a hurricane are examples of a creolized mentality and elite upbringing. Unlike other confused heroines of Caribbean literature who attempt to eradicate entirely their provincial persona, Veronica, the rebel, illustrates the potential for dialogue between cultures as an antidote to mere assimilation.

The form of the similes cited above demonstrates how the creolization process shapes narrative technique in *Hérémakhonon*. Opposition, the unifying principle in the novel and in Caribbean society, reproduces the 'New' World creole experience. A dialectic of cultural imagery, of memory versus actuality occurs in the text at the level of narration, characterization as well as structure. Assimilation is, however, a minor motif; the major motivation becomes clear in the two similes from personal experience. These examples and other allusions emanate from a multiplicity of landscapes. The context of conflict in *Hérémakhonon* reflects the psychological and social predicament of exile in modern literature. The Caribbean mode has its own history. From the forced exodus of Africans that led to chattel slavery in the Americas, through individual departures for personal and cultural reasons, to contemporary political exile, leave-taking has haunted the Caribbean writer's thematic reserves for half a century. No wonder, then, that Veronica is most disturbed by the image of an African streetcleaner in Paris. He belongs to the underclass, the latest form of cultural disassociation in the Diaspora. For Veronica, he is reminder and sign of her own expatriation. Moreover, he is a modern-day Mabo Julie isolated from the Diaspora literacy which elites like Veronica enjoy and perpetuate. The streetcleaner is doubly exiled—from his point of origin and from the culture he serves. Though narrative technique suggests a culturally balanced dialogue in Veronica's character, her persona lacks plenitude. The absense of similes based on African imagery confirms that the African content of Veronica's personality remains undigested.

Allusion and Characterization

Allusion delineates the personality of the principal character. References to the African Diaspora in Paris, America and the Antilles depict the range and depth of Veronica's training. She is bright, has been educated in private schools and promoted with fanfare to the head of her classes. There is a character called Sia in Condé's second novel, *Une Saison à Rihata* (1981) who shares some of Veronica's intellectual and emotional being. The adolescent Sia is full of scorn. She spends hours alone rereading *Anna Karenina*. Veronica, too, must have been that sort of youngster, except that she favored *Les Liaisons dangereuses* (49/24). As an adult, she prefers to imagine experiences rather than live through them.

Although Veronica possesses a cultivated knowledge of Diaspora culture, she is, nonetheless, ignorant of political ideologies shaping contemporary occurrences. It is interesting to note that the references to Guadeloupean politics are few and insignificant. Militancy for Veronica is a caricature, at best a spectator sport remembered from her life in Paris.

A person accustomed to confronting reality on the printed page or in a prepared text, has a great deal of difficulty remaining focused upon the immediate. Dislocated dialogue becomes Veronica's mode of communication and propels the narrative in *Hérémakhonon*. The primary question, "Why am I here?" serves as a call and a motif that find response eventually in the major encounters of the novel. Africans ask Veronica, "Why are you here?" Those more distanced from her, like her students, ask simply, "Where are you from?" She remains a foreigner because she retreats into the past, and because she does not speak any of the five languages indigenous to the area. The call, "Who am I?" prompts several definitions. Veronica is a rebel, not a conformist; a feminist, not a *Marilisse* (a whore). By part two, Veronica labels herself a misfit or drop-out, *une voyageuse paumée* ("a down and out traveler") (126/68). This reader would call her an *originale*, a non-conformist and exotic specimen of Antillean culture or the arum flower referred to in part two of the novel (189/104). Veronica's responses to these many questions define who she is. Allusions help her arrive at realizations about her identity in quiet moments of reflection. References to her past disengage memories concealed on the unsteady path of her journey toward self-definition.

The references to her childhood in Guadeloupe are a delusion, for she will likely never return. Home is Paris. Home will not be the Africa she seeks. Instead, Veronica Mercier joins the band of exiles from the Diaspora and other parts of the world who survive (as did African slaves in the New World) "chacun enfermé dans sa solitude et son souvenir."[15] ["Each one confined to his own solitude and memory.]

More than a simple figure of speech, allusion is a silent interlocutor that informs the reader of the past by insinuating itself into this first person narrative. Allusion is also a trickster creating confusion on the one hand and associations on the other. The reader cannot remain passive, and becomes the confessor for whom Veronica has been searching. One is drawn imperceptibly into the mind of the protagonist and into the center of a two-sided political drama.[16] Moreover, allusion creates a bond between four unique black cultures in Europe, Africa, the Antilles and America. It is as much a presence in *Hérémakhonon* as are Ibrahima Sory, Oumou Hawa, Saliou, Jean Lefevre and Pierre-Gilles.

Allusion and Structure

Maryse Condé has remarked that she deliberately provided her novel with "an eye-witness appearance."[17] For that reason, *Hérémakhonon* is told from the first person view in an acutely present tense Africa. Allusion plays a major role in structuring discourse in the novel, not only by its presence, but by its absence. In each of the three parts, allusion is a sign of Veronica's inability to cope with immediate events and the implications they will have in the future. In part one, the narrative is short on the present and long on the past tense, primarily because Veronica envelopes herself in memory listening occasionally to acquaintances around her. She writes: "Saliou nous y voilà. Mais de quoi me parles-tu, Saliou? J'ai toujours eu ce défaut d'écouter très mal les autres." (31/14)

Listening and perceiving in *Hérémakhonon* are a challenge for both Veronica and the reader. Although the French language will permit Veronica access to some debates, discrete levels of discourse are lost to her because of her inability and seeming unwillingness to learn native speech. However, the major barrier to communication remains the struggle in the narrative between the immediate and memory; memory, the storehouse of Veronica's allusions. The conflict is unresolved by the end of the novel and yet subtle changes in the prevalence and type of allusions affect radically the design of *Hérémakhonon*.

Structures resembling musical composition reveal the relationship of allusive passages to the storyline. Each of the three parts of the novel is

identified with the music of a particular culture: part one, African/percussive;
part two, European/harmonic; part three, Afro-American/improvisational.
The melody of Veronica's daily encounters is muted by a counterbass of
intrusive images from Guadeloupe and Paris. Particularly this is true in part
one where the momentum of her activities is barely audible above the
deafening percussive beat of African city life. In part two, the narrative is
more sequential. Allusions are associational here, and the reader by now
accustomed to the sound of Veronica's connections. There is more
harmony in this section of the novel. In part three, as Veronica accepts
responsibility for her thoughts and actions by directing them outward rather
than inward, the melodic line improvises more than it did in either parts two
or one. Similar to the dissonant modes in new wave jazz, the bass line has
become secondary to the solo performance. This section represents
Veronica's entry as a "detective" into unknown political events. She enters,
of course, on her own terms, in her own voice, a fact which leaves her alone
in her knowledge and finally draws her away from Africa, back home, to
Paris.

Receptivity appears in Veronica's character when allusion disappears.
The absence of allusion signifies the degree to which she has come to terms
with the present. When she is not making comparisons or drawing the
reader away, she is involved with Ibrahima Sory at *Hérémakhonon* or
Birame III and Saliou at Saliou's home and at the school. Considered
together, these encounters mark the political awakening of Veronica during
the more lucid moments of her monologue. Her interest in the well-being of
certain characters comes, however, after the fact as a near philosophic
reflection. A series of interrogations from parts one through three read like a
medieval *ubi sunt* requiem for the dead: where is Birame III? Where is
Amar? Where is Saliou? Maryse Condé has said in an interview with Ina
Césaire that she was motivated to write *Hérémakhonon* because of the
number of her African comrades who were imprisoned, in flight or in exile.[18]
That concern is clear in the novel. Unlike the author, Condé, however,
Veronica is anti-political. She fears that she will lose her objectivity were
she to believe Saliou's crusade rather than the pro-government rhetoric of
Mwalimwana, Ibrahima and Ramatoulaye. There is a serious gap in
Veronica's political formation and in her knowledge of modern, independent
Africa. If one considers, for intance, the absence of allusions to 20th
century African writing, that she has not read Fanon's *Les Damnés de la
terre* and that, unwillingly, she will teach Nkrumah's political philosophy,
one begins to comprehend the parameters of Veronica's ignorance. She
prefers the ancient African epic to any of the above.

Welcome house as a theme remains ambiguous, for *Hérémakhonon*
stands for *accueil* and indulgence at once. Each of the principal characters
receives Veronica warmly, providing a place for her if she wishes to join

their number. Involvements with her and with their duties bring Veronica into an abrasive present. As a concept, *welcome house* also allows her to investigate carefully the past. At Ibrahima's villa and at the beach, she escapes the clamor in which the peasant and working classes in most African towns live their lives. Silence is a mandarin concept in Africa, and Veronica is unconsciously seeking that very environment.[19] It is therapeutic for her. Reflection means indulgence allowing the time and space to study how past injuries have affected the psyche. *Hérémakhonon* borrows from the eighteenth-century *conte philosophique* the notion of the edifying journey. In this case, it is a voyage of the mind. The lessons are multiple gathered from Africa to Afro-America, Guadeloupe, Paris and back. This modern adaptation could be called a psycho-political tale. And what are its morals?

Why does Veronica leave Africa? She says to preserve her self-respect: she feels guilty over Amar's imprisonment, she is ashamed of having ridiculed Birame III and ignoring Saliou when he was free to speak to her. Her formal education and lack of civic consciousness do not prepare her to live among them. She finds herself untutored when confronted with specific African realities rather than Négritude myth. Veronica Mercier leaves the unidentified, non-aligned country after a liminal period when she is neither here nor there. Having evaded her initiation into contemporary African political culture, she returns to Paris knowing that she must reassess her point of departure.

What does Veronica learn in Africa? She encounters a new set of images and the complexity of one African society. Friendship is the gift she brings home. Veronica has had few friends in the past. Her sisters were her enemies, her family and Guadeloupean society a mass of competing individuals. Her sole friend before she arrives in Africa was her lover, Jean-Michel.

What does the reader learn? There is a discrete message in each of the three parts of the novel. In the first, an exemplary tale describes the confusion accompanying one woman's personal problems. The reader is taken away from the immediate, captured and whisked away into a past that only Veronica finds logical. In parts two and three, the reader discerns a logic in the associations Veronica conjures up. Her engagement draws the reader into a network of personal and cultural signs and images. Even in her disturbed state, Veronica unites through discourse the four corners of the African Diaspora.

If one reconsiders Alain Locke's call in 1925 for communication with Africa, one recalls how he predicted the seminal role the "new negro" would play in fusing the Diaspora. Through Veronica, Maryse Condé has accomplished that feat in literature some fifty years after Locke's pronouncement. None of the male writers of the Indigenist, Harlem Renaissance or

Négritude movements achieved such an integration, for Africa remained mythical and remote for most of them.[20] The "new Negro," it would seem, is an Antillean woman.

Were another "new Negro" to follow Veronica Mercier to Francophone, Islamic Africa would that person benefit from the lessons of *Hérémakhonon*? That question is partially answered in Condé's second novel, *Une Saison à Rihata*. Some of the same themes and structures emerge—political intrigue, exiled characters from the Diaspora and shifts in narrative perspective. The characters in *Une Saison* are more developed, primarily because the novel is written in the third person. Moreover, the reader of Condé's second novel who has benefitted from the previous adventures of Veronica Mercier, recognizes certain character-types: the government official, the militant, exiled Antilleans and common people. And why? Between the publications of *Hérémakhonon* in 1976 and *Une Saison* in 1981, the story of Veronica Mercier's intellectual exchanges combined with her political education has tested and perhaps developed Diaspora literacy in readers hailing from any of the four hemispheres of Maryse Condé's world.

NOTES

[A summary of this article was delivered at the 1984 meeting of the African Literature Association. I am grateful to Janis Mayes of Syracuse University for a critical reading of the manuscript.]

1. The dual references to *Hérémakhonon* are to the pages in the French original (Paris: Union Générale d'Editions, 10/18, 1976) and the English translation by Richard Philcox (Washington, D.C.: Three Continents Press, 1982). In most cases quotations will be from the French original and no additional translations will be provided. Reviews and pre-1983 criticism include: A. Baudot, "Maryse Condé ou la parole du refus," *Recherche, Pédagogie et Culture*, 57 (1982), 30-35; Carole Bovoso, Review of *Hérémakhonon*, by Maryse Condé, translated by Richard Philcox, *Voice Literary Supplement* (November 1982), 3; David K. Bruner, Review of *Hérémakhonon*, by Maryse Condé, *World Literature Today*, 51:3 (Summer 1977), 494; Oruno D. Lara, Review of *Hérémakhonon*, by Maryse Condé, *Presence Africaine*, 98:2 (1976), 252-256; Myrna J. McCallister, Review of *Hérémakhonon*, by Maryse Condé, *Library Journal*, 107:10 (May 15, 1982), 1009; Zeini Moulaye, Review of *Une Saison à Rihata*, by Maryse Condé, *Présence Africaine*, 121-122 (1982), 426-428; K. Muhindi, Review of *Hérémakhonon*, by Maryse Condé, *Présence Africaine*, 124:4 (1982), 239-241; Juris Silenieks, "Beyond Historicity: The Middle Passage in Writings of Contemporary Francophone Caribbean Authors." In *Travel, Quest, and Pilgrimage as a Literary Theme*, Frans Amelinckx and Joyce Megay, eds. Ann Arbor, Michigan: Society of Spanish

and Spanish-American Studies, 1978, 269-279; Clarisse Zimra, Review of *Une Saison à Rihata*, by Maryse Condé, *French Review*, 56:1 (October 1982), 165-166.

2. David Bruner's review article, "Maryse Condé: Creative Writer in a Political World," *L'Esprit Créateur*, 17:2 (Summer 1977), 168-173 refers to several of Condé's writings for *Présence Africaine*. These and other Condé works include: "Autour d'une littérature antillaise." Review of *Encyclopédie antillaise et Littérature antillaise*, by Jack Corzani. *Présence Africaine*, 81:1 (1972), 170-176; Review of *Batouala*, by René Maran. *Présence Africaine*, 87:3 (1973), 212-213; Review of *Bonjour et adieu à la négritude*, by René Depestre. *Présence Africaine*, 116:4 (1980), 226-228; *La Civilisation du bossale*. Paris: L'Harmattan, 1978; "La femme antillaise et l'avenir des Antilles françaises." *Croissance des jeunes nations*, 241 (juillet-août, 1982), 33-35; Review of *A Knot in the Thread: The Life and Work of Jacques Roumain*, by Carolyn Fowler, *Caraïbales* by Jacques André and *Harlem, Haiti and Havana: A Comparative Critical Study of Langston Hughes, Jacques Roumain and Nicolas Guillen*, by Martha Cobb. *Présence Africaine*, 123:3 (1982), 218-224; "La littérature antillaise se porte bien." *Bingo*, 315 (avril 1979), 50-51; "La litterature féminine de la Guadeloupe: recherche d'identite." *Présence Africaine*, 99-100 (1976) 155-166; *La Parole des femmes*. Paris: L'Harmattan, 1979; Review of *No Easy Walk to Freedom*, by Nelson Mandela. *Présence Africaine*, 87:3 (1973), 215-217; *Le roman antillais*. Paris: Fernand Nathan, 1978; "La Question raciale et la pensée moderne." (Conférence du professeur Claude Lévi-Strauss). *Présence Africaine*, 78:2 (1971), 240-245; *Une Saison à Rihata*. Paris: Editions Robert Laffont, 1981; *Ségou*. Paris: Robert Laffont, 1984; "Survivance et mort des mythes africains dans la littérature des Antilles francophones." *Afrique littéraire et artistique*, 54-55, pp. 56-64; Review of *Text and Context: Methodological Explorations in the Field of African Literature*, from the Colloquium of 1973 by the Société Africaine de Culture. *Présence Africaine*, 105-106, (1978), 294-295; Review of *Les Travailleurs étrangers en France*, by Juliette Minces. *Présence Africaine*, 88:4 (1973), 230-232; "Trois femmes à Manhattan." *Présence Africaine*, 121-122 (1982), 307-315.

3. *Claire Solange, âme africaine* has received critical review in Jack Corzani's *La littérature des Antilles-Guyanes francaises*, Vol. V (Paris: Desormeaux/ L'Harmattan, 1978) and in Condé's anthology, *Le roman antillais*, Vol. II: 19-21 (Paris: Editions Fernand Nathan, 1977). A longer version of the section on Lacascade appeared in Condé's "La littérature féminine de la Guadeloupe: recherche d'identite," *Présence Africaine*, 99-100, 156-159. In *La Parole des femmes* (Paris: Editions L'Harmattan, 1979), Condé discusses Lacascade on pp. 28-30.

4. The theme is discussed by Condé in *La Parole des femmes, op. cit.*, 28-33, 36-39 and in "La littérature féminine de la Guadeloupe," *op. cit.* See also Merle Hodge, "Novels on the French Caribbean Intellectual in France," *Revista Interamericana*, 4:2 (Summer, 1976): 211-231; Joycelynn Loncke, "The Image of the Woman in Caribbean Literature," *Bim* 16:64 (December, 1978): 272-281; Ajoke Mimiko, "Nevrose et psychose de devenir l'autre chez la

femme antillaise a travers l'oeuvre de Michele Lacrosil," *Peuples noirs, peuples africains*, 32 (mars-avril, 1983): 136-146; Clarisse Zimra, "Patterns of Liberation in Contemporary Women Writers," *L'Esprit Createur*, 17:2 (Summer, 1977): 103-114.

5. Marie Chauvet, *Amour, colère et folie* (Paris: Gallimard, 1968).

6. Maryse Condé, "La littérature féminine de la Guadeloupe," *op. cit.*, p. 166.

7. The discussion of narrative structures that resemble cinematic techniques falls beyond the scope of the present study. One might begin such an analysis by observing how the protagonist presents reality in filmic terms at several crucial points in the text, for example pp. 196/108, 256-7/144, 291-2/163.

8. *Hérémakhonon*, pp. 21/8 and 131/71.

9. The English translation of the title may create some confusion because Welcome House is a figurative use of *here* (peace or happiness) and *makhonon* (await). According to native speaker, Lamine Savadogo of Mali, Heremakhonon indicates that one has overcome hardships and moved on toward happiness. That Ibrahima Sory so names his villa suggests that after the Revolution in his country, a new era of peace and friendship will prevail. Saliou and Yehogul believe differently, and act accordingly.

10. Allusions to African history are on pp. 12/3, 31/4, 47/22, 95/49 and 215/120; to Euro-American culture, pp. 30/13, 49/24, 182/100 and 286/160; to Afro-American culture, pp. 24/10, 27/12, 99/51, 142/77 and 188/103; to Caribbean society, pp. 15/5, 19/7, 38/17, 65/32 and 240/135.

11. I am referring to pp. 18/6, 30/13, 27/12, 69/34 and 166/91.

12. See the following pages for allusions to Mandinka epics: 12/3, 47/22, 95/49-50, 213/119 and 218/122. The more familiar ones have been collected by Lilyan Kesteloot with the assistance of Amadou Hampate Ba in Vols. 11, 13, 15 and 16 of the Littérature Africaine series published by Fernand Nathan, namely *L'épopée traditionnelle* (1971) and *Da Monzon de Segou* (1972).

13. *Aimé Césaire, The Collected Poetry*. Translated by Clayton Eshleman and Annette Smith (Berkeley: University of California Press, 1983) pp. 64-65.

14. In a thought-response to Birame III (26/11) Veronica writes:
    Birame III, de qui parles-tu? Qu'est-ce que tu racontes? Est-ce que tu ne sais pas que l'histoire ne s'est jamais souciée des nègres? Parce que preuves à l'appui, ils n'en valaient pas le coup. Pas trace de leurs doigts sur le Golden Gate, ou la charpente de la Tour Eiffel. Au lieu de prier à Notre Dame ou à Westminster Abbey, ils animaient un bout de bois. Ou s'inclinaient devant un serpent...

15. Maryse Condé, "Survivance et mort des mythes africains dans la littérature des Antilles francophones," *Afrique littéraire et artistique*, 54-55 (n.d.), p. 66.

16. Space does not permit a full analysis of the political motivations in the novel, however it is clear that the non-aligned government of Mwalimwana subscribes in theory to Nkrumah's *Consciencisme*. Even Veronica recognizes the divisions along class lines in the country:
    L'éloquence politique m'a toujours paru une chose abjecte. Depuis que le monde est monde, des hommes, on dit des leaders, n'est-ce pas? montent sur des plates-formes et promettent aux autres hommes des merveilles. Or, ils ne croient pas à leurs promesses. Oui, on me citera quelques idéalistes,

quelques illuminés qui y croyaient. Apparement qu'ils y aient cru ou non, ils n'ont pas pu les tenir, leurs promesses. Puisque *voilà où nous en sommes. Les uns opulents, les autres dans la merde.* Je sais, je dois me taire, moi, qui toujours ai refusé de prendre parti. Mais qu'est-ce qu'il aurait changé *mon engagement*, comme on dit? Pas grand-chose. Rien. J'écoute Mwalimwana. Dans l'espoir qu'entre les phrases creuses, redondantes à souhait, je décèlerai un message, une intention . . . (278/155). [Emphasis added.] This insight derives from a conversation with the new director at the school where Veronica teaches. He explains the history of Mwalimwana's rise to power and the role Saliou and others played in the Revolution (224-225/126).

17. *La Parole des femmes, op. cit.*, p. 124.

18. *Ibid.*, p. 125.

19. Luxury in the elite quarters where Ibrahima Sory and Ramatoulaye reside is not the environment Veronica is seeking, for too often it reminds her of the pretentiousness of Guadeloupe. She searches for stillness which comes at the seashore:

    . . . il y a des moments où l'on est content d'être loin de tout. Ce n'est pas une idée romantique. Solitude—silence—loin—du—bruit—de—la—ville. Non. Mais on a amassé des faits dans les coins de sa vie comme une ménagère malpropre des détruitus sous les meubles. Et on veut les regarder en face. (234/131).

20. Some women novelists have represented the personal quest cross-culturally. Zora Neale Hurston, Katherine Dunham, Marita Golden, Buchi Emecheta, Jean Rhys, Paule Marshall and Jacqueline Manicom among Afro-American, African and Caribbean novelists are the pioneers. However, not one of these writers has, like Condé, written simultaneously about the four corners of the African Diaspora. Male authors of African descent who have lived in or treated at least three areas of the Diaspora include René Maran, W.E.B. Dubois, Langston Hughes and Claude McKay.

The Narrow Enclosure of Motherdom/Martyrdom: A Study of Gatha Randall Barton in Sylvia Wynter's The Hills of Hebron

Janice Lee Liddell

The image of mother—giver and nurturer of life; teacher and instiller of values and mores—has indeed become of the most persistent of Caribbean archetypes. In the Caribbean, as in nearly every place in the world, any criticism of this most celebrated and procreative human role will more than likely be met with wild-eyed contempt by women and men, both of whom have so internalized the myths of motherhood as to ignore its harsh realities—for themselves, in the case of women; for women with whom they are personally familiar, in the case of men. It has been difficult for women—and practically impossible for men—to admit that this most honorable woman-destiny can be and usually is both restrictive and debilitating; that society's pressure to be "the good mumma" almost always obstructs more creative opportunities than it provides. Patriarchal societies have no inherent system of balance for the roles which women are capable of performing as they do for men. Men are nearly aways expected to be at least marginally accomplished in numerous social areas—fatherhood often the most marginal. But women must always be "good mummas" almost singularly. In fact, women very seldom can demonstrate their capacities to be a "good mumma" and a good "something else" unless the "mother spirit" is clearly evident in that "something else." The "mother spirit" is that which

... we see daily in our societies in grandmothers, in teachers, in police women, bus conductors, nurses and community workers, the mother as seen is the cosmic plan.[1]

Most of the memorable women of Caribbean literature are not only mothers; they are mothers whose sole purpose in life has been to provide for their child[ren]. George Lamming furnishes a classic prototype of Caribbean women in his enduring work, *In the Castle of My Skin* (1953). It is the mother of the main character, known only as G, who unceasingly and untiringly struggles to provide day to day necessities for her young child. In being the "good mumma," G's prototypical mother:

> Seized by the thought of being left alone, she would become filled with an *overwhelming ambition for her child*, an even greater defiance of the odds against her. Then she would be silent as she was now, or she would talk in a way that was mechanical while her meaning seemed to go beyond the words. She would talk about pulling through; whatever happened she would come through, and *'she' meant her child.*[2]
> [Emphasis mine.]

G's mother, like most Caribbean mothers, both real and fictional, inevitably is forced by her place within the society to sublimate the development of any other aspect of self. For her, the child is even more than extension of herself and her life; the child *is* her life, her reason for being. G's mother is demonstrative of the mother figure in patriarchal societies, in general, and in Caribbean societies, in particular, where little or no premium is placed on what a woman can produce unless it is from her womb or the stove. As sociologist, Victoria Durant-Gonzales, says, in these societies "mothering provides opportunities for rewards and achievement that cannot be provided elsewhere."[3] It can be said that the historical backdrop peculiar to New World black female parents, which can be traced back to slavery, coupled with the social reality inherent to all patriarchies, creates an almost immutable mother-as-victim syndrome, particularly in regions affected by struggling economies such as the Caribbean.

Where many Caribbean novels like Lamming's indeed romanticize the image of woman as mother, in at least one Caribbean novel this very real mother-as-victim syndrome is dealt with. Jamaican Sylvia Wynter, as the first Black woman novelist from the English-speaking Caribbean, creates, in her only novel, *The Hills of Hebron* (1962), an indomitable woman figure, in the form of Gatha Randall Barton. But it is Gatha who falls desperately into the throes of this self-sacrificing motherdom. Like the mothering situation itself, Miss Gatha is a paradox. She is an ideal as as Caribbean Black mother, the self-sacrificing, self-effacing woman-parent to a young self-centered, ungrateful, partially crippled man-child. At the same time, Gatha Randall Barton, within the Hebron settlement, becomes an anomaly, a woman who is a pillar of fortitude, resourcefulness and wisdom as the community's efficient leader. For most Caribbean women, the former role would certainly be the narrow enclosure from which there would be no easy means of escape, while the latter would not even be within the realm of consideration. Although for Miss Gatha both experiences are personal realities, she is caught fast in her narrow enclosure. Even with community acknowledgement, acceptance and approval of her "more masculine" leadership attributes, Gatha, having so completely internalized her function as mother, never attempts to escape or even to obvert this most sacred of women-roles. Instead, this function becomes the prime motivation for everything else in her life; her every accomplishment rests on the fragile relationship she has with her son, Isaac, and her desire to see him as Hebron's leader. Gatha can never be an independent and individuated personality herself because of her almost fanatical commitment to her son's destiny which serves to entrap her in society's small enclosure of motherdom. This, indeed, is the tragic flaw in an otherwise imposing, self-assured Caribbean woman.

The primary thematic concern of *The Hills of Hebron* is certainly not with women, although women, as in nearly every facet of Caribbean life, play significant roles in the communication of the novel's theme. The rites of passage of a Black community in the 1940s from post-slavery oppression and poverty towards physical, psychological and spiritual freedom is the basic concern of the novel. It is actually the story of Prophet Moses Barton, Gatha's husband, opportunist and visionary who, like the biblical Moses, leads his people out of a physical and psychological bondage. His Egypt is a small, decadent village called Cockpit Center. His exodus is to the hillside; to a landscape called Hebron where he will settle his Church of the New Believers of Hebron. Moses Barton, although depicted by Wynter with some farcical humor, is a forerunner of Jamaican "deliverers." Wynter tells us this; thus, we are never really expected to believe that Moses Barton's Black God, whom he promises "would be on their side forever," will actually deliver the Hebronites from inequity. Through the brief glimpses of a young labor leader, the author hints to us that the movement to liberation which Moses Barton inspires will be evolutionary:

> The words that the man spoke remained in their hearts, prepared them for the coming of others of whom he was only the foreruner, as Moses had been his.[4]

As the novel opens, a severe and enduring drought has all but devastated the tiny farming community. Without the small cash crops, not only is the economy of Hebron on the brink of ruin, but the community is also spiritually demoralized. In addition, there is rampant dissension within the

Church of the New Believers regarding the successor to the now deceased Moses Barton. By birthright, the position should belong to Moses' and Gatha's son. But Isaac, away at boarding school, is unable to assume the role of leader. It is within the context of these struggles in a poor, patriarchal, patrilineal society that we encounter the tenacious Gatha Randall Barton, Moses' widow; more importantly, Isaac's mother.

Gatha's initial struggle is apparent: to hold on to the leadership until Isaac returns. She does not trust any in the community to serve as interim leader; thus, she assumes the position herself. No woman is considered for the leadership position but Gatha manages to seize control of the tiny community. Actually, given the abject conditions of Hebron, it is not surprising that Gatha, the only member with money, is able to rise to power. The security she is able to provide is valued more, in this time of need, than the impotent tradition of patriarchy. What does become surprising, at least to those of Hebron, is *how* Gatha emerges as such a powerful force after the death of her husband.

> [She] emerged from her anonymity, stamped herself upon [the community's] consciousness. Whilst her husband was alive she had been something of a spectre at a feast, someone whose inability to laugh made them uneasy. But they had taken no more positive notice of her than a man takes of his shadow. Then all at once she was there; enforcing respect. (p. 13)

Gatha never attempts to hide her motivations. It is clear from the outset that her ultimate desire as leader is to see her son "fulfilled as she had never been, and now whilst he was young." She tells the congregation:

> I am going to help you, not because I want to, but because I have to. I am going to help you so that Hebron can continue and my son Isaac can have the lot of his inheritance, can have his father's vision to carry on. (p. 50)

That Gatha is able to ascend to power, though of little surprise given the circumstance, is no small accomplishment in a patriarchal/patrilineal environment such as Hebron. Though the *motivations* for her quest are not unknown to most women of her society, it is, nevertheless, the immediate goal of acquiring the position that best demonstrates her tenacity and determination. Female religious leaders are certainly not an anomaly in the Caribbean, but in Hebron no woman is even considered as part of the hierarchy of power. The prevailing attitude in Hebron, as in most patriarchies, is that women have their particular place and roles in society and should be kept in them. When the wife of the influential Hebronite, Hugh, Chief Recorder of the Church, announces to her husband that she is with child, his response is predictable: "So what? What else God make woman for?" When Obadiah, hand selected by Moses to succeed him, returns from his vigil where he had hoped to find the adulterer who impregnated his wife (we find later it is Isaac), he is denounced by this same influential Hebronite, Hugh, for his inability to control his wife:

> It's me, me who decided against you, took away the eldership from you. And you know why? . . . Because you let down Hebron . . . bring down God's wrath and the drought on us and all because of a woman whom you weren't man enough to keep in order. (p. 61)

But it is Gatha who demonstrates "what else God make woman for"; who is the one that no one within the community is "man enough to keep in order." Thus, Gatha in this regard is truly a source of inspiration for even the 1980s reader.

At first glance, Gatha appears no less opportunistic than her husband, but a closer examination reveals a woman capable in her own right of leading Hebron through these, its most difficult, times. She is a woman whose power and vision have been sublimated throughout her marital existence as she fulfilled the expected role of supportive wife, a pre-requisite to the role of middle-class motherdom. And even though her object reality does not translate into an actual Caribbean middle-class reality, Gatha's position in the community certainly does.

Gatha Randall Barton had always separated herself from the commoners of Cockpit Centre, home of the Hebronites before their exodus, and she is no closer to them when they settle in Hebron. She had always viewed herself as different from the other women of Cockpit Centre; had always viewed herself as socially above all the inhabitants of Hebron. Her ascendant position as leader only increases the chasm. It is Gatha's family background that provides her with fuel to fire the contempt she has for the villagers. Her great grandfather was a former slave, Cato Randall, an opportunist akin to Prophet Moses, who had, through insidious means, acquired both his freedom and a large plot of land which passed to his descendants. For Gatha it is this legacy that creates the social chasm between herself and everyone else in the village. Gatha views herself as the only member of Hebron's elite class, as evidenced by her attitude towards "the treasure" she brought surreptitiously to the community so many years ago. Against Moses' orders to sell all worldly possessions and leave behind all remainders of the past, Gatha manages to keep the apron given to her by her grandmother. That she is the only one in the community to possess a worldly treasure elevates her above the community members: "Miss Gatha had taken it up to Hebron with her as the one symbol to mark her difference from the others." (p. 85) Ironically however, her treasure—the uniform of menial women's work—is actually the symbolic equalizer between herself and the commoners; it connects her with the past of slavery and servitude, oppression and poverty which historically they all share.

The apron, perhaps even more significantly, serves as an instrument of open rebellion against the vacuous life that was hers with Moses.

> Whenever the urge for rebellion against Moses and his empty striving for glory with which she was, willy nilly, identified, came upon her, she would sit quietly on the bed, hold the apron in her hand and reaffirm her private betrayal . . . Gradually she changed from a shadow flitting to and fro in the house, tending her husband's wants, cushioning his occasional spells of self-doubt with her idolatry, to become an unknown presence, silently challenging his dominance, wearing it away like water chafing against stone. (p. 86)

With such an evolution, Gatha rises to the occasion and assumes the leadership with a prevailing authority and clarity of vision. Gatha takes over physically, but as well, she battles the spiritual fantasies established by Moses who

> . . . had led them up to Hebron, set himself up above them, made them believe that behind him there was God, black and made in their image and partial to them . . . [But] above them now was Miss Gatha and behind her the face of God was anonymous and not to be depended upon. (p. 65)

Gatha's goal, it must be remembered, is not to allure the community's total and blind commitment to some religious foolery. Hers is the "simple" and much more worldly goal of assuring that Isaac's return as heir and leader would not be to the morally and physically dessicated community that Hebron had become; her goal is to rebuild Hebron. thus, "[her] way would never be like that of Moses. She would never drug them with drums of glory. She would spur them to work." (p. 51)

Gatha is almost dictatorial in her command, giving "preemptory orders to the men," assigning each one of them to special tasks in the refortification of their community. She orders the women to their tasks of cleaning their homes, themselves and their children and to the praying "for rain as you never prayed before." The community women "accept[ed] their tasks, resigned and complaisant, [for] all would be well now that they had someone to tell them what to do."

Gatha's objective of making ready the community "so that when the rains came they would be able to begin their lives again, tidy and in good condition" is accomplished and eventually the rains do come, but not before Gatha is neutralized by disappointment and disillusionment. Isaac is not to return to Hebron. This discovery is made after Hebron's welcome processional had travelled all the way to the Cockpit Centre train station to meet the community heir. The letter sent in his stead was brief: "Isaac wrote saying that he had taken the money and gone away, that he was sorry, that he thanked his mother for all that she had done for him." The money was the treasure box left for Isaac by his father. Gatha had missed the money but had forced herself to believe that Isaac had hidden it safely away. This revelation of her son's treachery practically paralyzes her. On the return trip from Cockpit Centre,

> Miss Gatha no longer led them, but walked apart, separate not only from them but from their hopes and fears. Isaac was not coming back. Her mind could not reach beyond this. (p. 275)

Gatha is disoriented by the removal of her sense of purpose, for it must be remembered that although she has demonstrated exceptional leadership capabilities, the position as Elder of Hebron has not provided her with the personal fulfillment a Moses or an Obadiah would extract from the accomplishments. No, Gatha has been singleminded in her traditional motivation as a mother, which is why she is left so devastated. It is almost paradoxical that she herself could achieve such accomplishments as bringing order and unity to the dying Hebron and providing the members with food, water and renewed hope but despair so totally at her failure to fulfill the expected cultural norm of mother. Durant-Gonzales reminds us

> that by affirming and reinforcing the cultural expectation of child bearing and/or child rearing, many women enjoy social rewards and social recogition not attainable at the level from which [they] participate in economic production.[5]

Such is certainly the case for Gatha.

Even though her motives might be challenged, Gatha Randall Barton can perhaps be cited as the most "self"-determined, "self"-directed woman in the literature of the English-speaking Caribbean. But Gatha is clearly a victim. She is victimized by the incident of her birth in a particular time and place. She is born Black and she is born a woman which translates, with few exceptions, into minimal options in the Caribbean in the 1940s. Prior to marrying, Gatha ran her own small business (a fried fish stand) and was viewed within her community as an independent woman. However, after marriage, she emerged as victim to those contradictory ideal sex roles that plague the majority of women within the Caribbean.

In her study, "West Indian Female Status," Yolanda T. Moses suggests that even though "working class women [unlike their middle class counterparts] can and do take care of themselves economically," they are nevertheless slaves to the prevailing social restrictions and mandates. Yolanda Moses states:

> An argument that working class women are not bound by the same social restrictions as middle class women and therefore, there is little sex role conflict between women at this level is not borne out completely. There is, in fact, conflict for several reasons: 1) both males and females are aware of the cultural ideal for the role of the male as provider and protector . . . 2) due to migration of the male labor force, both historical and contemporary, males are not often physically present to assume their roles . . . 3) last and probably most important, women are actually perpetuating the ideology that males should provide economically for their mothers and sisters while they are not preparing them to do so. Instead of teaching them responsibility, independence and flexibility, the way they teach girls, they are smothering them with attention. While they (mothers) are socializing females to take care of themselves, the males with whom they are to interact and ideally depend on as husbands-fathers [and leaders] have not been taught those things . . .[6]

Gatha is certainly part and parcel of this Caribbean experience. Her husband is by no means a stable provider, yet while he is alive he is certainly head of the household. In addition, Moses is an unprincipled hustler. He makes his way on the backs of others. Even when Moses first sees Gatha, his approval of her respectability is simply a foreshadowing of his choice of her as his mate. She is clearly a potential asset to him.

> [Kate] felt his eyes on her and looked up. A curious power seemed to emanate from this stranger, and to draw her towards him. Her breasts rounded themselves under her frock. But he looked way from her as he noticed Gatha Randall, the strikingly ugly young woman who alone wore a uniform of respectability—boots and stockings and a long-sleeved dress with a high neckline. (p. 107)

The manner in which Moses obtained the land upon which to establish Hebron perhaps most reveals his unprincipled character. When Moses learns that Reverend Richard Brook, a colonial clergyman, has raped and impregnated his young maid, he creates an opportunity from a contemptible situation. He strikes an agreement with the white Reverend that he "would hush up the scandal, take the young girl, *her* sin, and her mother up to Hebron" [emphasis added] and in return the Reverend would secure for him an impressive but legally ineffectual document giving him the right to squat on the land of Hebron. The Reverend believes it is either Moses' innocence or ignorance that suggests such a ludicrous agreement. But, in fact, Moses realizes the Reverend has no real power to obtain the land free and clear but he also recognizes his own need to have even a pseudo-government sanction if he is to convince and convert the many disbelievers. Thus, when the Reverend secures for Moses the document of thick vellum paper with its enormous red seal:

> The Prophet vowed eternal secrecy and went his way, triumphant. He now held in his grasp the paper which was to root Hebron firmly in reality. The Lord had sent the white Parson as an instrument to ensure the success of his, Moses's mission. (p. 200)

This is the man to whom Gatha has committed herself. And he has touched her even more intimately. It is "Gatha, whom Moses had ignored and trampled on, before whom he had flaunted his paramours. . . . " One among many was the time when Prophet Moses took a young girl to the shed at the back of his shop where "he pulled at her skirt, urgently fumbling with the safety pin, and explained that the sacrifice of her virginity was necessary to their successful exodus into the promised land of Hebron." During which time:

> Miss Gatha knocked on the door and shook it violently. But Prophet Moses had locked the door when they entered, had snapped the padlock shut. . . . [He] did not cease the rise and fall of his body against hers, but called out that he was praying for the soul of a young Sister and could not be interrupted. Later on, when they came out, he compelled his wife to ask forgiveness of himself and Sue for unworthy suspicions and evil thoughts. (p. 11)

Gatha's marriage is, indeed, debilitating for her and contributes significantly to her victimization (characteristic of that of Black women in the Caribbean in the 1940s). Her rebellion against the oppression is empty and symbolic (remember the apron). She realizes early enough that she will never find fulfillment in the marriage, but it never crosses her mind to leave it. Divorce was not the road to freedom in her time and place. We find that it is only after Moses' death that Gatha's spirit comes alive:

> . . . Life with her husband Moses had introduced her to all the subtle variations of treachery in the human spirit; her own as well as others. . . . She had been too long shut away in the silence of the defeated not to spread her wings in the rare sunlight of triumph. (p. 48)

It is, thus, only after his death that she becomes free and able to seek the fulfillment which she will experience vicariously through Isaac's success as leader. But that which is designed to fulfill comes to enervate, and again she is victimized by her limited woman role. For it is her almost fanatical perception of her responsibility as mother, as well as the actual and tenacious pursuit of Isaac's birthright, that makes Isaac's flight so difficult for her to bear.

Ironically, though perhaps predictably, Gatha never realizes that her fulfillment is not inherently connected to the fulfillment of others. At the novel's end, Wynter shows Gatha's hope renewed when the spurious child of Obadiah's wife and her own son is presented to her.

> Only in her lap was there any warmth. She put her hands under the shawl, traced the outlines of the child's body. It was perfect . . . The sins of the fathers, then, had not been visited on the children? The fabric of her forebodings dissolved, and she wept. (p. 305)

The child, unlike Isaac, possessed no deformities and Gatha comes to believe that in his perfection, he must be the true redeemer of Hebron, after all. The much awaited rains, symbolic of renewal and rebirth, pour as "Miss Gatha cradled the child against her withered breasts . . . " And the reader leaves the novel knowing that, for better or worse, Gatha's grandson has provided her with new reason to meet new struggles and in so doing the potentially "[s]heroic" woman is once again enticed into self-sacrificing motherdom by her condition as a Black woman in her particular historical time and place.

NOTES

1. Margaret Hope, *Journey in the Shaping*, Report of the First Symposium on Women in Caribbean Culture, July 24, 1981, University of the West Indies, Cave Hill, Barbados, Women and Development Unit (WAND), 26.
2. George Lamming, *In the Castle of My Skin*. (New York: Macmillan Co., 1953), 10.
3. Victoria Durant Gonzales, "The Realm of Female Familial Responsibility." *Women and the Family*. (Cave Hill, Barbados: University of the West Indies, 1982), 14.
4. Sylvia Wynter, *The Hills of Hebron* (Essex, England: Longman Group Ltd., Longman House, 1966), 222. All other references will appear parenthetically in the text.
5. Durant-Gonzales, 14.
6. In *Women and National Development: The Complexity of Change*. (Chicago, University of Chicago Press, 1977), 9-13.

Finding a Way to Tell It: Methodology and Commitment in Theatre About Women in Barbados and Jamaica

Elaine Savory Fido

Methods and techniques are not very important. It is where they take you that matters. What becomes of the work is determined by the content and the consciousness one brings to the theme.[1]
—Honor Ford-Smith

One cannot approach art as one can politics, not because artistic creation is a religious rite or something mystical . . . but because it has its own laws of development, and above all because in artistic creation an enormous role is played by subconscious processes . . .[2]
—L.D. Trotsky

This paper is concerned with the fundamental opposition between aesthetic considerations and political direction which concerns all polemical artists, and which is central to the complex area in which feminism, radical theatrical experiment and involvement with race and class issues meet within the modern theatre of two islands in the Caribbean, Barbados and Jamaica. These countries are selected because there have been a number of attempts to deal with women's issues on the Barbadian stage in recent years, and of course, in Jamaica, the well-known and well-established group Sistren has justifiably drawn international attention to women's theatre in the region.

Perhaps some context is necessary so that the relation of this kind of theatre to the general development of West Indian drama and performance may be understood. I distinguish between theatre and drama as follows: theatre is anything performed and as such is the core of many traditional cultures and certainly of the African cultural continuum which contributes to West Indian societies. Theatre, then, is not only verbal performance, but singing, dancing, masking, mime, etc., indeed anything which assumes an audience. Drama is a particular form of theatre, and involves, as we recognise it today, a plotted and structured shape, a verbal record or script, and characterisation which normally engages in conflict, thus giving rise to tension which illuminates the play's theme and is brought to some conclusion by the end of the performance[3]. Drama is intended for performance but is usually recorded in script form from one enactment to another. In the colonial period, drama in the West Indies was usually an import from Europe, and followed the prevailing fashion of the play as understood in the metrople. In the 1960s, West Indian playwrights were producing dramas and farces of the domestic type[4], some set in houses and some in yards. These performances, intended obviously for a middle-class audience, existed alongside village and working-class ritual, festival, and story-telling which was theatrical. The history of development of present-day drama and theatre in the region is a history of the relationship between these two traditions. Trinidad Carnival (now joined by a number of other island festivals of a similar type) is a theatrical event which has increasingly influenced dramatists[5]. As the energy centre of West Indian theatre has moved from island to island[6] (depending on internal cultural developments or political circumstances), the styles of theatre and drama have gradually become more radically involved with the non-scribal, non-verbal languages of the region. This has happened to the extent that when the Barbadian director Earl Warner produced the experimental works about women *Lights I and II*[7], he called them "theatrical events" and not plays. Thus I see the development of feminist or gender-focussed theatre and drama as being linked importantly to other creative developments in the theatrical centres of the West Indies.

The need for a focus on women's issues in theatre has been very plain. From the beginning of West Indian dramatic writing, most plays have been written by men for predominantly male casts, and where women have been portrayed they have primarily reinforced the stereotypes of West Indian women prevailing in society. With the advent of a strong and resourceful women's movement in the region, which has been very evident in both Barbados and Jamaica in recent years[8], women involved in theatre and drama have begun to ask questions about the images of themselves portrayed on the stage and to desire to have a more complex and truer reflection of their reality created in theatrical performance. Although women, as directors, actors, and writers, have certainly importantly begun to effect this change, interestingly enough, some younger male directors and writers have also begun to respond to this challenge, in ways which show them to recognise women's issues as important not only politically but also as a new and experimental area of creative expression.

Within world theatrical development during the recent past, two kinds of theatre have been identified as reflecting on the one hand political direction as primary and on the other, aesthetic intention as primary. These are known, following Brecht, as popular theatre and art theatre respectively. Sistren, working out of Jamaica, is within the popular theatre movement, and has in fact participated in popular theatre developments within the Caribbean[9]. Popular theatre is people's theatre, or theatre which minimizes the division between audience and performance by various strategies (group composition of a work from improvisation, collective research on a chosen topic of central interest to a community, a declared intention that activism should result from the production)[10]. Sistren has a strong focussed commitment to social change, to which end the company has centred its work on the lives of working-class black Jamaican women. There is a powerful certainty within the company as to what they are about. The most influential of the group's directors[11] and the generally recognised creative force behind it, is Honor Ford-Smith, whose account of the methodology which Sistren has developed is important here. She lists eight stages in the growth of a Sistren work: (1) selection of a topic; (2) selection of a community in which the research can be carried out; (3) collection of material for the work; (4) improvisation, role-playing and games; (5) final selection of material; (6) making of a script by a writer (usually Ford-Smith herself); (7) rehearsal; (8) performance.[12] Despite Ford-Smith's apparent dismissal of form as secondary in the quotation which begins this essay, she and Sistren have worked hard to develop sophisticated techniques which assure their continued success because they deliver the message of the group in effective theatrical terms. Sistren has grown from an experimental theatre project involving Ford-Smith as tutor of the Jamaican School of Drama and a number of working-class Jamaican women to a complex organisation, run collectively, which includes

> a professional theatre group; a popular education project using drama as its main tool; a research project; a screen printing project and a quarterly magazine.[13]

Though Sistren is centrally activist in nature, the group was begun through the interaction of trained theatre tutors with untrained participants in the project, and the skills of the directors who work with Sistren, especially those of Ford-Smith, are essential to the survival of the group as an effective theatre company, even whilst now the expertise is not any longer confined to Ford-Smith and other directors but is spread amongst the professional actresses who have developed out of Sistren's original members. Indisputably, however, what gives the group its power and direction is political conviction:

> By confronting what has been considered indecent, irrelevant or unacceptable, we have begun to make a recorded refusal of ways in which our lives have been thwarted and restricted. [14]

The question remains, however, as to what happens to art forms when political considerations become more essentially present than aesthetic skill. Trotsky's point is a valid one, (although I would dispute his remark about art and mysticism or religious rite), and it succinctly emphasizes that the real value of artistic processes is to bring to the surface what is largely hidden from view and from understanding, rather than to concentrate on reiterating views which are clearly held by a body of people and which constitute a general position. Of course, in practice hardly any art lacks some sort of political content and hardly any political theatre lacks artistic skill, if it has any sort of success. But we can find ourselves deeply confused by the meeting point of art and ideology. Sometimes, within feminist art, there is anxiety about whether or not different strands of political engagement or experience are equally viable:

> A feminist tack is different from a feminine or women's perspective; a lesbian perspective is not the same as a heterosexual feminist one. This diversity is not a liability if, at the outset, different positions are acknowledged and discussed. [15]

Another temptation is to flatten out one set of political considerations when another is the centre of attention, thus ignoring the complexity of experience which actually makes all facets of the identity of an individual relevant to the comprehension of truth at all times:

> ... beyond class, race etc. there is a meeting place where the experience of womanhood makes private histories one experience-being a woman. [16]

It is significant that the director speaking here is Earl Warner, the male creator of the female-focussed work *Lights*. For him, the experience of working on this project was enlightening and broke new ground in his comprehension of women. Concerned lest he impose a male vision on the actors, he tried simply to record the experiences which were witnessed in the early sessions of the group making the work. Later his direction reflected his perception of the multi-faceted nature of women's lives in the Caribbean, although this resulted in a structure which was a little too episodic and scattered (including scenes which demonstrated adolescence, child abuse and incest, marriage, divorce, single professional life, lesbianism, motherhood, old age, prostitution, rape, violence, religious experience, relations between black and white women, menstruation, friendship between women, madness, the tensions of personal versus professional life, etc., etc..) But the one thing which the work never consciously took into account was the interaction between him, as a male director, and the actors, as women consciously attempting to deal with their female experience on the stage. I have no simplistic strictures to offer, certainly do not wish to confine directors to dealing with works which reflect their accidents of birth, but at the same time, interactions which are relevant to the politics of such a work as *Lights* are worth exploring consciously within the developmental process which makes the final performance. Similarly, Ford-Smith, although Jamaican, as her actors are, is white and middle-class, and this evident contrast of race and class has sparked comment in many contexts. Yet Sistren does not deal with this issue explicitly, and thus perhaps weakens the group's defence against the charge that a creative shape may be being laid upon the working-class women from the director, rather than letting the works develop out of a communal experience, which reaches past one kind of life. Precisely because *Lights*, like Sistren's work, was created out of research, improvisation, and script-making, there was control of the process which would have allowed for interaction between the various individuals constructing the play on a conscious level, as there is not when a director accepts to interpret a fixed script of a literary kind.

I do not want to seem here to be suggesting that any creative person functions on a stereotypical level, i.e. that a human involvement between actors and director is impossible, an involvement which transcends class, race, and gender from time to time. Nevertheless, I think it is instructive to try to clarify what constitutes the cultural vision of any director overseeing the creation of a work from scratch, and that this is important for the director as well, who ought to develop a conscious awareness of her/his creative identity. Peter Brook, in *The Empty Space* (1968), said that in popular theatre, supposedly freer of aesthetic confinement than other kinds of theatre,

A director is not totally free of responsibility—he is totally responsible —but he is not free of the process either, he is part of it.[17]

However, within Sistren's structure, and part of its ideology, is a feminist opposition to hierarchical modes of organisation, amongst which is the director-as-creator school of theatrical organisation, and in order to facilitate a more broad-based structure, the group operates as far as possible

communally, so that whilst Ford-Smith's expertise is a necessary part of a
Sistren work she directs, she is not as visible as Earl Warner, who is really
creating a director's theatre in his productions.

His vision in *Lights* did not go unquestioned. Margaret Gill, a perceptive
commentator on the arts, commented:

> Woman, like man, is after all only a person trying to understand and
> be understood by the world. Woman is not "the source", or the
> mystical centre or the "universal" anything . . . Perhaps this drama
> needed to be directed by a woman. Perhaps the women in the research
> group needed to be more different from one another in terms of class
> experience. Perhaps they needed to be more questioning. One thing is
> sure: Earl (Warner) needs to state his methodology of research very
> carefully. This is not a play.[18]

In the attempt to catch so many aspects of women's experience, *Lights*
seemed sketchy and impressionistic, sometimes unsure of its tone, especially in
the inclusion of popular songs (*Jesse, Come Home*, for example), with
unfortunate overtones for a feminist work.

But the importance of *Lights*, as of other productions dealing with
women's issues in Barbados, and of Sistren's work, is its raising of issues
which help to improve awareness of women's experiences in the Caribbean
and, hopefully, to undermine the stereotypical images of women with which
we daily live (the strong black mother/grandmother, the difficult wife, the
cold and ruthless executive woman, etc.). This is groundbreaking work and
makes space for other dramatists to create women more freely on the stage.
Recently, Trinidadian playwright Rawle Gibbon's play, *I Lawah*,[19] presented
a story of the Camboulay Riots in Trinidad of the late nineteenth century via
a plot which centered on the relation between a black woman and a white
creole woman. This presentation of women as restorers of a temporarily
defeated culture is a marked advance on the images of women in the works
of Derek Walcott, for example, which dominated the theatrical scene of the
previous generation.

One of the most exciting aspects of this innovative work is in fact the
working through of theatrical styles by groups engaged in women's theatre.
Sistren has experimented with techniques associated with African ritual
and has brought these into effective association with feminist feeling in
their *Bellywoman Bangarang* (one of their earliest works, 1977). In *Lights
1*, Warner designed the set as a huge womb, which gave a surreal effect. The
womb image, of course, was objected to by a number of women as being too
much of a cliché of woman's consciousness, and in the second version of the
production, Warner replaced it with a series of draped cloths. A good deal
of popular theatre uses song, dance, and mime to present reality effectively
and the productions of both Sistren's works and *Lights* utilise non-verbal

theatrical form extensively. This aesthetic innovation, which captures the vitality of folk culture and brings it into the modern, staged theatrical work, has, however, to be carefully used, so that it does not become a simplistic evasion of issues or contradictions, but rather an extension and emphasis for important political ideas, just as ritual, dance, and music had a deep significance in traditional contexts.

In this, contradiction plays a conscious part in modern traditional and artistic work, simply because our experience and our perceptions are no longer, for the most part, contained within traditional systems which have worked out, slowly in an integrated manner, the nature of the world and the moral significance of action and belief. Lizzie Borden, polemical and feminist filmmaker, commented on her work "Born in Flames" about the ghetto:

> The language is meant to be contradictory: any political position contains so many contradictions that it has to undercut itself within its own expositions.[20]

Not only is it likely that any political ideology contains contradictions, but the astute artist works with these consciously, to create a better engagement of the intelligence. When focussing on simple ideology, the artist is unlikely to reach that level of internal conflict which marks the state of modern life for most of us. There is nothing inherently conservative about the assumption that contradiction is important, for both Marx and Trotsky understood this well. Trotsky regarded a constant evolution of culture as a desirable ambition for post-revolution society, leading to a classless awareness of experience, "the first culture that is truly human." Brecht, of such importance to Third World dramatists, and one of the strong influences on Earl Warner, and the origin of an opposition between art and popular theatre, believed in a dialectical relation of audience to performance and in the central significance of contradiction, even where there is strong political commitment. Of course, the use of contradiction must be deliberate and controlled by the artistic vision, conscious and not accidental.

The truth of experience for many actual Caribbean women is full of poignant contradictions. In the search for material, of course, both Sistren's directors and Earl Warner in *Lights* turned to personal history, what Ford-Smith calls "testimony" and which is extensively recorded in Sistren's book *Lionheart Gal* (1986)[21], a collection of life stories of Jamaican women written for publication by Honor Ford-Smith. In the story "Rock Stone a River Bottom No Know Sun Hot", the narrator tells of her mother's battles with men, her disillusionment with them and her closeness to her daughter when they live alone together. "She cook meat and throw it inna one dish and di two a we eat out a one dish"[22]. The desire for relations with men is as strong as the bitter knowledge that these lead to pain,

abandonment, and disappointment, and the sense of hurt and betrayal
which the narrator's mother feels when she gets pregnant as a young girl
causes her to lock the girl out of the house. Love and pain are deeply
interwoven in these stories. During the research for *Lights*, personal
histories were brought to the group, stories of family tensions, eccentric
female relatives, difficult love affairs, of violations of trust, of survival in a
context of economic insecurity. What survived out of these stories onto the
stage was fragmentary and often in fact *Lights* used not original material,
but extracts from various literary works about women (including American
texts) which expressed particular themes[23]. One constraint which certainly
restricted the effectiveness of the work in terms of its revelatory nature as to
the reality of women in Barbados was that of time. Since the production was
hastily directed for the first production, there was little time to finish a
properly written script and this is why literature became a resource for
shaping a good many scenes. The trouble which Honor Ford-Smith took
with *Lionheart Gal*, and her expertise in shaping Sistren scripts for
production, give us a fine text to work with which takes the raw material of
personal testimony and turns it into a structured narrative.

I perhaps feel this very strongly because I directed Ntozake Shange's *for
colored girls who have considered suicide when the rainbow is enuf*
(1977)[24]. It makes a finished and poetic interpretation of personal
experience. Some of the stories in that work (again an experimental script
developed through improvisation and called a "choreopoem" and not a
play) are intensely moving, such as the story of the woman whose lover, a
Vietnam veteran, pushes her children out of a high window. The writing
holds the intensity well and contains it, letting the full horror of the man's
condition be revealed through careful verbal control:

> i stood by beau in the window/ with naomi reaching for me/ & kwame
> screamin mommy mommy from the fifth story/ but i cd only whisper/
> & he dropped em[25]

For colored girls . . . was written as a series of short scenes punctuated and
interpreted through dancing and through Shange's colour coding of the
rainbow in relation to black women, but the verbal texture of the work is the
major medium of its transmission. The skilled use of words can contain and
delineate contradiction, just as the trained and talented choreographer,
musician, or designer can portray experience through aesthetic achievement.
To deny the importance of aesthetic skill in theatrical work is to deny the
essential vehicle by which the work is conveyed to the audience. Ford-
Smith, despite her apparent dismissal of the importance of form in
comparison to ideology, has recognised in fact that there needs to be a
responsible collaboration between Sistren and theatre critics: she would
like to see them

work(ing) alongside us in workshops to debate performance structure and to help us develop a clearer relationship between popular art forms and a new Caribbean theatre.[26]

Given the small geographical scope of the individual Caribbean islands, and the interaction which goes on between theatre people within the region, such association should seem inevitable. Ford-Smith played, for example, the white creole girl in *I Lawah* with Warner's direction.

In 1985, Earl Warner directed a female-centred play, Norman dePalm's *Desirée*, a scripted one-woman drama about a single mother whose existence is bound by her baby, the church, and the need to enjoy her young life and whose violence to the child provides a shocking *dénouement* to the work. Interestingly, some Barbadian men were heard to remark that no woman could hold the stage for a whole evening in a play by herself, and the actor, Alison Sealy-Smith, certainly proved them wrong. But the play lacked balance, and it certainly seemed, as *Lights* did, to be trying to do too much in too short a space. The grim message of the work appeared to be that teenage pregnancy is destructive to mother and child, and at least in this way the work attacked the prevalent notion of maternity as a known good, and the selfless mother as a commonplace, which is strong in the region. The script lacked poise here and there, presenting a mimed sexual experience onstage, (always too difficult to achieve, as is rape, because the audience cannot deal with either an obvious faking of the physical act or a convincing, apparently real demonstration of it).

Uneven as the *Desiree* script was, at least it gave some shape to a statement which was a contribution to the theatrical presentation of women's issues. In directing a student production of an improvised piece of theatre, unscripted[27], which explored the experience of women students on the Cave Hill campus of the University of the West Indies, I discovered yet again that the lack of a script was a serious weakness (largely because the play was primarily verbal and the students involved in the acting were highly educated individuals with a strong sense of the written word, whose oral skills were not as strong as their ability to interpret a written script). Whereas any director would know whether his or her actors have the skills to be brilliantly improvisational, in the manner of the gifted calypsonian who works *extempore*, for the most part, in the Caribbean, theatrical production needs to record that improvisation out of rehearsal and shape it into a script for final production, which is the Sistren method of approaching play-making. Even in the oral mode, for example, in the poetry of Louise Bennett (Mis'Lou) of Jamaica[28], which is performed as an immensely effective piece of theatre, there is a written script which acts as the basis for the created interpretation which the author makes.

Of course, there is a strong tradition in the folk cultures of the Caribbean, as elsewhere in the Third World, of improvisation, and if this can be developed for the modern stage, then it works very well. However, the interference of education with the skills of oral retention, unselfconscious role-playing, and creative verbal play is very evident amongst the middle-class actors who are prevalent in the theatre across the Caribbean region. Sistren, despite acknowledging the importance of script, has a great advantage in the original impetus of the group being from the orally sophisticated part of society, i.e. the working class. It should therefore be clear from this that I am not advocating scripting as superior to improvisation in all circumstances, but that the absence of writers and of a script in conditions where actors might have a shaky grasp of oral theatrical skill, and a limited originality in extempore dialogue, is a failure of aesthetic shaping which can have a high cost to the production as a whole. Those highly talented performers, like Louise Bennett or Trinidadian Paul Keens-Douglas, who are able to hold an audience alone and with great success, are gifted in performance skills, but they, too, use scripting as a base for their theatrical delivery, even when, as in the case of Keens-Douglas, the script is actually less central to the experience the audience gets than the marvellous ability he has to manipulate accent, tone, and nuance in his voice.

I am concerned, then, to refute Ford-Smith's remark which prefaced this essay. In the development of women's theatre in the Caribbean, we need to explore every possible avenue of form, stretching aesthetic skill to the utmost, for only then can the deeper layers of our political perspectives be developed as dramatic/theatrical performance in the most sensitive ways. In this region, after all, with its immensely complex people and their cultural identities which are a result of mixing different races, nationalities, cultures, and languages as well as genders and classes, it seems to me that we can only struggle to capture that complexity as fully as possible, to do justice to the reality we live. The only way to do this is through full realisation of form as a medium for multi-faceted reality. My own feeling is that we now need to encourage the growth of writing by women dramatists or men who are sensitive to gender issues, but that this should by no means be directed along any particular polemical track. The free exploration of form and content is the most powerful way to create a new tradition, as we have seen for so many years in the work of the most celebrated (but sexist) of the West Indian theatrical practitioners, Derek Walcott.

NOTES

1. "Sistren—Women's Theatre—A Model for Consciousness Raising" *Journey in the Shaping* (Report on the first Symposium on Women in Caribbean

Culture, CARIFESTA Barbados 1981) ed. Margaret Hope, (WAND, Barbados n.d.) p. 58.

2. *Class and Art: Problems of Culture under the Dictatorship of the Proletariat* (Speech 1924) (New Park Publications, 1974) p. 18.

3. I do not intend here any comparative value to be placed on theatre and drama or any cultural possessiveness to be implied. Aware of the 1970s debates amongst African theatrical/dramatic scholars as to the limits and nature of African traditional ritual, festival and story-telling as drama, I am very opposed to trying to determine all traditional theatrical activity as drama, as if drama was the ultimate goal of development. I do not see drama as an evolutionary end of theatre. Theatrical sophistication is perfectly justifiable in its own right. However those who wish to understand the debates I refer to might consult the following: Yemi Ogunbiyi, ed. *Drama and Theatre in Nigeria* (Lagos, Nigeria Magazine, 1981); Michael Etherton, *The Development of African Drama* (New York, Africana Publishing Co., 1981); Michael Echeruo, "The Dramatic Limits of Igbo Ritual" in *Critical Perspectives on Nigerian Literatures*, ed. by Bernth Lindfors (Washington D.C., Three Continents Press, 1976).

4. For example, Douglas Archibald *The Rose Slip* (UWI, 1967); Cicely Howland (Waite-Smith) *Uncle Robert* (UWI, 1967); Errol Hill *Strictly Matrimony* (UWI, 1966).

5. This was famously discussed by Errol Hill in *The Trinidad Carnival* (University of Texas, 1972), where he expressed strongly a view that Carnival in Trinidad offered great scope for the modern dramatist there. Recently, Helen Camps set up a Tent Theatre in Trinidad and was developing musical dramas using old traditions of Carnival, and Rawle Gibbons, the Trinidadian dramatist now director of drama and theatre in UWI St. Augustine's creative arts programme, has in his plays always tried to use ritual and carnival as theatrical vocabularies central to the meaning of the work. Directors like Earl Warner and Kendal Hyppolyte turn to dancing, singing and music as well as verbal arts for their major effects.

6. Without wanting to simplify what is an overlapping tradition fuelled by inter-island migration of artistic people, it is easy to see high points of theatrical development as they have occurred in each country. Guyana came first, and many of the actors and technicians who were part of the flourishing of theatre there up to the early 1970's (Michael Gilkes, Clairmonte Taitt, Ken Corsbie etc) are now working on other islands. Then Trinidad, during the days of Walcott's permanent residence and involvement with the Basement Theatre Company and the Trinidad Theatre Workshop, made great strides. Jamaica was greatly helped in theatre by the establishment of the Jamaica Drama School, which has trained many theatrical artists up and down the region. Barbados and St. Lucia now have fluctuating but interesting theatre projects, which show the development of ideas and skills from previous works.

7. These works came from the same process which Ford-Smith developed from popular theatre methodologies for her own work with Sistren, i.e. research, improvisation, rehearsal, script, performance. The research began in 1984 and the first version was performed early in 1985. The following year a second version was created and toured. The full title was "If You Wait Until The

Lights Are Green, You'll Never Get Into Town", a quotation from one of the group's informants when speaking of women's needs to get on and do things for themselves.

8. From the point of view of the arts, the Carifesta symposium on women in Caribbean culture held in Barbados in 1981 was of vital importance, because it focussed attention of artistic women and their struggle to develop within the region. Also CAFRA (a feminist research association presently based in Trinidad with regional involvement) has a commitment to creative projects like the production of a poetry anthology.

9. They performed *Ida Revolt Inna Jonkannu Stylee* with the participants of the Caribbean Popular Theatre Exchange in 1985.

10. See Augusto Boal *Theatre of the Oppressed* (Pluto Press, 1979).

11. The majority of these are women (Hertencer Lindsay, Jean Small) but the group does occasionally involve male directors in their work.

12. "Sistren: Exploring Women's Problems Through Drama" *Jamaica Journal* 19:1 (Feb-April 1986)2 ff explores this process in detail.

13. Ibid., p. 2.

14. *Journey in the Shaping* (Report on the Carifesta Symposium on Women in Caribbean Culture Barbados 1981) Margaret Hope (WAND, Barbados n.d.) p. 58.

15. "Women's Theatre Program ATA: Creating a Feminist Forum," Jill Dolan *Women and Performance*, 1:2 (Winter 1984) p. 5.

16. Programme notes for *Lights* by the director, Earl Warner.

17. *The Empty Space* (Penguin, Harmondsworth, 1968) p. 122.

18. "Lights: A Review" *ISER Bulletin* (Special Issue on the Female Presence in Caribbean Literature) 11:1 (March-April 1985) pp. 82-3.

19. First performed for the Caribbean Writers Conference in London (Commonwealth Institute) November 1986, by the Pan-Caribbean Theatre Company, formed for that one production. The work was interpreted through Carnival modes and directed by Earl Warner.

20. "An Interview with Filmmaker Lizzie Borden" by Anne Friedberg. *Women and Performance*, 1:2 (Winter 1984) p. 43.

21. London: Women's Press, 1986.

22. Ibid., p. 46.

23. For example, the works of Toni Morrison, Jamaica Kincaid, Gloria Steinem, Christine Craig, Jean Rhys.

24. New York: Bantam Books, 1977. I interpreted the piece as a jazz movement, solo and group play interweaving. The work was originally separate poems put together as a performance after workshop improvisation.

25. Ibid., p. 64.

26. "Sistren: Exploring Women's Problems Through Drama," p. 12.

27. "Three's Company: Cave Hill Style" was built on the idea of a sitcom, playing consciously with subverting stereotypical behaviour and characters. In many ways this experience confirmed another, that of assembling a group of researchers, a writer (Rosemary McClaughlin) and a director and actors (Glenda Dickerman directed) to produce a work on women and religion for the NWSA Conference of 1984, held at Rutgers University, NJ, USA. The work which emerged, *The Most Secret Time* was a beautifully scripted poetic

exploration of the theme, interpreted by three strong actresses. The script was the core of the production.

28. See *Jamaica Labrish* (Kingston, Sangster's Bookstores, 1966). Labrish, or women's talk and testimony are both part of Jamaican culture and the Sistren group draws on both.

Jamaica Kincaid and the Resistance to Canons

Giovanna Covi

Derrida in *Positions*[1] speaks of the necessity of ridding oneself of a metaphysical concept of history, that is linear and systematic. His claim is for a new logic of repetition and *trace*, for a monumental, contradictory, multi-levelled history in which the *différance* that produces many differences is not effaced. Jamaica Kincaid's *At the Bottom of the River*[2] and *Annie John*[3] represent examples of writing that break through the objective, metaphysical linearity of the tradition. At the same time, her voice manages to speak up for her specificity without—in so doing—reproducing in the negative the modes of classical white patriarchal tradition. Kincaid's voice is that of a woman and an Afro-Caribbean/American and a post-modern at the same time. This combination is therefore not only disruptive of the institutional order, but also revolutionary in its continuous self-criticism and its rejection of all labels. Perhaps we could say that it is a voice coming *after* the struggles of the women's movement first for recognition and then for separation; the voice of the third "new generation of women" as Kristeva defines it:[4] an effort to keep a polyphonic movement in process in the attempt to be always already questioning and dismantling a fixed metaphysical order, together with a determination to enter history. Her narrative, in fact, is a continuous attempt to turn away from any definitive statement *and* to utter radical statements.

But together with Julia Kristeva in *Unes femmes,*[5] I would ask whose interest is it to have every woman speak like any other woman; what's the gain? Traditionally our language has been 'silence' because of the yet unshaken authority of the discourse of a sexist order. Under conditions of slavery, black women's creativity was often expressed through the art of quilting: does this history of repression imply that we should necessarily confine our voices within the boundaries traced for us by a patriarchal and

345

racist law? Is the imitation of the language of our oppressor and a total rejection of our historical heritage the only alternative? If the 'universal' of minority literature has been its marginality—as JanMohamed maintains[6]— if the Invisible Man had to celebrate his invisibility and define himself through it—now that Black literature is slowly being admitted into the canon, its criticism must resist the hegemonic pressures which seek to neutralize it by repressing its political nature, by levelling its discourse through a rational, apolitical, humanistic criticism. There, where the broken rhythm of jazz is a cry of protest against the symmetry of the racist division of society, or the autobiographical 'intrusions' and 'loss of control' of the narrator in a woman's novel serves as a voice of the private cracking into the authoritative objectivity of the public order, we now risk to find only a conformity to the catechism of one of the many new churches of literature.

The contemporary philosophical debate is increasingly developing around the theme of the crisis of reason.[7] Since Einstein's relativity theory, through Heidegger, Wittgenstein and Nietzsche, and psychoanalysis, but not without the Marxist and Feminist contribution, the metaphysical tradition of the centrality of the Subject is being questioned in stronger and stronger terms. A generic label used to describe this cultural atmosphere is the controversial and too fashionable 'postmodernism.' In literature, it refers to a negative thinking which has resulted in a questioning of the authority of the author (e.g., Barthes, Borges, Eco, Nabokov) and of the fiction/reality relationship (e.g., Pynchon, Coover, Calvino). Despite the disagreement on the denomination (suggested alternatives to 'postmodern literature' range from the apolitical 'metafiction', James Rothner's 'parafiction,' Raymond Federman's 'surfiction,' to the most recent and more politically oriented coinage suggested by Susan Strehle of 'actualism,' among others), in the U.S. critics are defining this avant-garde as almost exclusively white and male. If the postmodern claim to represent an attack against the Western tradition is acceptable as a fact, then how does one account for the absence of the voices of the minorities? Therefore we must question the tendency to take for granted the radicality of the postmodern ideology. Being cognizant that postmodernism itself has already been coopted into a canon that excludes and excommunicates, it wouldn't be surprising to discover that there are in fact postmodern minority writers. I will argue that the connotation of political radicalism associated with postmodernism is acceptable in so far as it opens up to include the specificity of those voices which have been historically discriminated against. I contend that Jamaica Kincaid, a black woman writer, is *radically* postmodern precisely because she is *also* postmodern, but not only so. Her voice, in fact, dismantles the symmetry of the metaphysical tradition in that it escapes all attempts to become domesticated under any label.

The main theme of her writings is the inquiry into the feminine role and racial difference.[8] Kincaid criticizes the very existence of sexual and racial difference, rather than the modes of their existence: there's no place left for reform; the change that is invoked is not one of guards, but of structure.

In *At the Bottom of the River*, at the end of "Girl" we are left with nothing else but a series of imperatives—from "wash the white clothes" to "always eat your food" (*BR*, p. 3)—interrupted by one accusatory question—"is it true that you sing benna in Sunday school?"—, followed by a list of prohibitions—from "don't sing benna" to "don't eat fruits" (*BR*, p. 3)—and by a list of directions—"this is how to sew on a button" to "this is how to behave in the presence of men" (*BR*, p. 4)—, then a few more prohibitions —"don't squat down", "don't throw stones"—and more directions culminating in, "this is how to make ends meet" (*BR*, p. 5). This is a prelude to the final condemnation of the girl as "a slut," not surprising in a story that is almost a 'chronicle of a slut foretold.' The list is spun out at the beat of drums, which provides the only comment to the message that, in a world in which "ends" are meant to "meet," girls are "bent on becoming sluts." The practice of making ends meet is the primary target of this ferocious critique which manages to expose the very origin of sexual role division—the rationality of an ideology of symmetry. The 'uncivilized' Lack-of-Reason— the sound of the African drums that beat within the lines—serves as a political commentary, as a cry of protest against the predetermined destiny of the girl.

Particularly fascinating is the story "Blackness" in which the disruption of binary oppositions is devastating: everything is ambiguous, multiple, fragmented. Blackness is the night that "falls in silence" as well as the racial color that "flows through [her] veins" (*BR*, p. 46), but above all it is what cannot be defined—a signifier that escapes its signified by a continuous shifting, "for I see that I cannot see" (*BR*, p. 46). It is identity together with annihilation of the self, "I am swallowed up in the blackness so that I am one with it . . . " (*BR*, p. 47). And the self is "powerful" at the moment when the "I" is "not at one with [it]self," and can say, "I felt myself separate." (*BR*, p. 47). This story ends in a crescendo that is a celebration of the narrative "I," but what kind of "I" is it who ends its song with the words, "I am no longer 'I' " (*BR*, p. 52)? "Blackness" disrupts the concept of identity as One—of phallic identity. Like the ambivalence of the mother's body that is One *and* Other at the same time (herself and the child she bears), this "I" can say: "the blackness cannot be separated from me but often I can stand outside it . . . blackness is visible and yet it is invisible" (*BR*, p. 46). It is neither the silence of the repressed Slave, nor the voice of the Master because, like "the silent voice," "conflict is not part of its nature" (*BR*, p. 52). And her child can stand in front of the mirror looking at her skin without color (*BR*, p. 49), while the "I" is "at last at peace," "at last erased" (*BR*, p. 52), living in the oxymoron of the silent voice.

Open, fragmentary, multiple and paradoxical is also the "frightening" "I" that, "like an ancient piece of history," "will leave room for theories"

(*BR*, p. 24) in the story "Wingless." It is at the same time "unaware," "defenseless and pitiful" (*BR*, p. 23), "primitive and wingless," and yet it has the strength to declare:

> I shall grow up to be a tall, graceful, and altogether beautiful woman, and I shall impose on large numbers of people my will and also, for my own amusement, great pain. But now. I shall try to see clearly. I shall try to tell differences. (*BR*, p. 22)

In the future—like the panoptic eye of the omniscient narrator of the logocentric tradition that can see from the God-like vantage point of above the world—she will "tell differences" and impose "great pain." The same "I" in the same story is, like her hands, "brown on this side, pink on this side" (*BR*, p. 27).

The questioning of the unity of the self reaches its climax towards the end of the collection:

> I stood as if I were a prism, many-sided and transparent, refracting and reflecting light as it reached me, light that never could be destroyed. And how beautiful I became. (*BR*, p. 80)

This is possible because it is set in the maternal context that blurs—as the lips of the female sex—the distinction between open and closed: "I saw a world in which the sun and the moon shone at the same time" (*BR*, p. 77). The maternal perspective overcomes the nihilism deriving from the dread that faces the contemporary man after—in Lacan's words—"the phallus has been unveiled and exposed to shame":

> For stretching out before him is a silence so dreadful, a vastness, its length and breath and depth immeasurable. Nothing. (*BR*, p. 68)

The tremendous strength of Kincaid's stories lies in their capacity to resist all canons: They move at the beat of drums and the rhythm of jazz, so that we may be tempted to coopt them under the label of Black Aesthetics as formulated by Amiri Baraka.[9] Yet, sometimes the feeling is more like that of a nursery rhyme—we listen to what Elisabetta Rasy[10] has theorized as 'feminine language': the nurse's language of sounds and silence which stands before and beyond the rational signifying words of the father. The language of the mother and child is expressed by Jamaica Kincaid in the story "My Mother" in these terms:

> My mother and I wordlessly made an arrangement—I sent out my beautiful sighs; she received them. (*BR*, p. 56)

All these stories are structured around the figure of the mother: the writer is constantly connecting artistic creativity to maternity in the effort to create a new representation of the feminine which includes the logic of maternal love. The commitment to this new ethics moves in the direction supported, among others, by Julia Kristeva and Luce Irigaray: bringing the maternal into the discourse of the father represents the new voice outside the dichotomy of sexual difference.

And again there is one more label tempting the critic: under the influence of Gates's formulation of 'signifying'[11] as the main feature of Black Aesthetics, one could conclude that *At the Bottom of the River* is a successful example of this Afro-American rhetorical strategy. Parody, repetition, inversion mark every single movement of Kincaid's narrative.

To add one more and last side to the "prism" of the new self, one could note the insistent refusal to stick to a definitive statement, by going back to the beginning again and again. "What I Have Been Doing Lately" ends where it begins and re-begins in the middle of its non-linear movement (*BR*, p. 43). Like in Coover's *Spanking the Maid* the ultimate order/meaning is never reached:

> On the sides of the deep hole I could see things written, but perhaps it was in a foreign language because I couldn't read them. (*BR*, p. 42)

And so the "I" reverses itself and turns to the maternal horizon: "I said, 'The earth has thin lips,' and I laughed" (*BR*, p. 42).

Kincaid's narrator "doesn't know anymore," she has "no words right now for how [she] feel[s]" (*BR*, p. 30), "no name for the thing [she] had become" (*BR*, p. 80). Yet, she manages to voice her NO in thunder to the existing order of things: "I said, I don't like this. I don't want to do this anymore" (*BR*, p. 45). Yet, she manages to find the strength and take the responsibility to relate to *this* from which she couldn't otherwise escape— she realizes—but through annihilation (*BR*, p. 81). Since nihilism, though cherished, is rejected, a strong and yet un-authoritative voice concludes the whole collection:

> how bound up I know I am to all that is human endeavor, to all that is past and to all that shall be, to all that shall be lost and leave no trace. I claim these things then—mine—and now feel myself grow solid and complete, my name filling up my mouth. (*BR*, p. 82)

It doesn't surprise, therefore, that the reviews show a great deal of uneasiness with *At the Bottom of the River*. Edith Milton finds "Miss Kincaid's penchant for apocalyptic imagery disturbing" and believes that "her imagery may be too personal and too peculiar to translate into any sort of sensible communication"[12]; for Anne Tyler the stories are "almost insultingly obscure";[13] Suzanne Freeman defines the writing as "quirky enough to challenge our very definition of what a short story should be" and notes that the risk is that very few readers may be willing to "decipher the secrets".[14] Unquestionably, the judgement belongs to the audience, but why should we pose this as so dumb? Anne Tyler accuses Kincaid of not "leaning forward and taking our hands and telling us a story"—should critics blame it on the authors if readers need to be taken by their hands? Some readers might prefer to engage in a discourse with the text, rather than joining a "Church-Book" where the "Priest-Author" reveals the Truth.

The reviews of *Annie John* are altogether more positive, but one wonders whether the different evaluation is not simply due to a different reading, rather than to a difference between the two books. While the critics of the first book seemed to be preoccupied with the question of whether the collection worked *as* short stories, the reviewers of *Annie John* entirely overlook the question of the determination of the literary genre to the point that John Bemrose calls it a "collection,"[15] Bruce Van Wyngarden[16] takes it for granted that it is a novel, and for Patricia O'Connor[17] it is an autobiographical narrative. All three praise the way it depicts life in Antigua and the coming-of-age of the protagonist.

O'Connor reports the author stating, "the way I became a writer was that my mother wrote my life for me and told it to me." She informs us that Jamaica Kincaid is from Antigua, which she left at seventeen, like Annie John, and her father, too, was a carpenter. In addition, both her mother and her daughter are called Annie. We have no reason to question the definition of *Annie John*'s material as 'autobiographical'—but what kind of 'autobiographical' writing is it? Indeed, it is hard to decide between 'collection' and 'novel', since the book, divided into eight "Chapters," is in fact divided into eight sections each with its own title and internal unity of plot, although their first-person narrative and protagonist is always the same and the setting remains the island of Antigua throughout.

Chapter Three provides us with a clue to interpret what Jamaica Kincaid means by autobiographical writing, an "essay" in this case written for class by the twelve year-old Annie: a metaphor of the entire "novel," it shows how "lies" must enter autobiography when this is meant for a public audience (*AJ*, p. 45). Exactly like *Annie John*, it focuses on Annie and her mother and opens with the description of the paradisiacal Imaginery pre-Oedipal period when the child believes herself to be part of the mother. This union is represented in the image of swimming in the sea: the mother was a "superior" swimmer while Annie "was sure [she] was drowning" when the water reached her knees, but she could swim around with her "arms clasped tightly around her [mother's] neck" (*AJ*, p. 42). The mother would "sing a song in a French patois" that Annie didn't understand or she wouldn't say "anything at all," but the daughter could enjoy "all the sounds" of the world by placing her ear against her mother's neck as if it were a sea shell. The second part of the narrative describes the symbolic separation, with the mother on a rock "tracing patterns" and the water between them. The words of the mother cannot pacify Annie's despair: she has a recurrent dream of the mother on the rock "tracing patterns" with the father. "And it must have been amusing, for they would always make each other laugh" (*AJ*, p. 44). The story is then a metaphor of the Oedipal crisis with the father splitting up the dyadic unity between child and mother and the coming into existence of the speaking subject as a consequence of the desire for the lost mother. It is, in other words, the entrance into the Symbolic which Annie cannot yet accept. Therefore, she imposes a fictional closure to her autobiographical essay: she has her mother shed tears and hold her, rather than simply speak, in order to soothe her anxiety. This "lie" is a return to the repressed union of the "old days," a hiding of the "bad" side of reality. Autobiography, in Jamaica Kincaid's writing, manages to give us a feminist voice that stresses personal experience over the authoritarian universal, without, in so doing, resulting in a demand for realism over modernism, or a poetic discourse, and posing the author as the transcendental signifier of the text, as its meaning and origin.

The pre-Oedipal unity in which the selves of mother and daughter are undifferentiated is the paradise of the first two Chapters of *Annie John*, before the "young-lady business" (*AJ*, p. 26):

> As she told me the stories, I sometimes sat at her side, or I would crouch on my knees behind her back and lean over her shoulder. As I did this, I would occasionally sniff at her neck, or behind her ears, or at her hair. She smelled sometimes of lemons, sometimes of sage, sometimes of roses, sometimes of bay leaf. At times I would no longer hear what it was she was saying; I just liked to look at her mouth as it opened and closed over words, or as she laughed. (*AJ*, p. 22)

The narrative keeps interrogating the relationship with the mother, also after "all this was finished" (*AJ*, p. 32) and after the realization that, despite the same name, the two of them are two separate selves—"She was my mother, Annie; I was her daughter, Annie" (*AJ*, p. 105), even after the mother has become "just a dot in the matchbox-size launch swallowed up in the big blue sea" (*AJ*, p. 148). "It doesn't matter what you do or where you go, I'll always be your mother and this will always be your home" (*AJ*, p. 147), says the mother in the end. The caring and nurturing mother is always there when we need her, even if we can't explain her presence, like the grandmother, Ma Chess who comes and goes "on a day when the steamer was not due in port" (*AJ*, p. 127), mysteriously.

The duality and non-linear temporality of the maternal cannot be comprehended by the causal discourse of history. Luce Irigaray, in *Ethique de la différence sexuelle*, notes that sexual difference rests on the inter-dependence between space and time: in the beginning was the creation of space, outside the subject-God who is time itself that materializes in the places of his own creation. Time is then interior to the subject; space is outside it. The feminine-maternal, being the place of creation, the container for the baby and the man, becomes deprived of her own place-identity-self. The consequent question is then, "How to figure the place of the place?" Traditionally, the woman has been *given* a place: the house within whose walls she has been confined. In *Annie John*, Ma Chess refuses this house of the patriarchal discourse and in so doing refuses to be placed within the symbolic order of sexual opposition:

> A house? Why live in a house? All you need is a nice hole in the ground, so you can come and go as you please. (*AJ*, p. 126)

As Kristeva theorizes in her essay, the time of feminine subjectivity is either cyclical or monumental—the repetition of biological cycles and the myth of the archaic Mother—rather than linear—historical. For a re-definition of sexual difference outside the traditional dichotomy, it is necessary to reconcile these separate conceptions of time and to redefine the time-space relationship. *Annie John* plays with realistic objective temporality: the adverbial phrase, "On the Sunday before the Monday" (*AJ*, p. 29) is the most visible example of the mocking of spatialized temporality operating within a narrative that never refers to a time outside that of its own story. There are no dates in this autobiographical 'novel', but only the age of the protagonist: rather than a universal interpretation of history, we have "a conversation piece":

> The rain went on in this way for over three months. By the end of it, the sea had risen and what used to be dry land was covered with water and crabs lived there. In spite of what everyone said, the sea never did go back to the way it had been, and what a great conversation piece it made to try and remember what used to be there where the sea now stretched up to. (*AJ*, p. 109)

Also the theme of colonialism is treated by deconstructing the Master-Slave dialectics upon which it rests: After mocking the English who didn't wash often enough—"Have you ever noticed how they smell as if they had been bottled up in a fish?" (*AJ*, p. 36); after having the English girl wear the dunce cap in class; after stressing that "our ancestors"—the "slaves"— "had done nothing wrong except sit somewhere, defenseless," she refuses to appropriate the Western conception of nation in order to express her anti-colonialism and notes:

Of course, sometimes, what with our teachers and our books, it was hard for us to tell on which side we really now belonged—with the masters or the slaves—for it was all history, it was all in the past, and everybody behaved differently now (*AJ*, p. 76),

not without adding with revolutionary strength that,

if the tables had been turned we would have acted differently; I was sure that if our ancestors had gone from Africa to Europe and come upon the people living there, they would have taken a proper interest in the Europeans on first seeing them, and said, 'How nice,' and then gone home to tell their friends about it. (*AJ*, p. 76)

This discussion is placed in the context of the wonderful fifth Chapter, where under the picture of "Columbus in Chains" Annie prints in Old English lettering, "The Great Old Man Can No Longer Just Get Up and Go." She will have to copy Books I and II of *Paradise Lost* for punishment. However, this does not prevent the book from ending with Annie leaving Antigua for England "forever."

Just like the imagery of death which pervades the "paradise" of the first chapters and dissolves as the problems rise in the central part of the book, everything is looked at in its multiple aspects. Grounded on personal experience, Jamaica Kincaid's writing nonetheless defies a realistic interpretation of her voice; it challenges any possibility of deciphering a single meaning by emphasizing multiplicity in what Roland Barthes would call,

an anti-theological activity, an activity that is truly revolutionary since to refuse to fix meaning is, in the end, to refuse God and his hypostases—reason, science, law.[18]

But for Jamaica Kincaid it certainly does not mean to refuse love as we can know it.[19]

When I write I don't have any politics. I am political in the sense that I exist. When I write, I am concerned with the human condition as I know it.[20]

NOTES

1. J. Derrida, *Positions* (Paris: Minuit, 1972).
2. Jamaica Kincaid, *At the Bottom of the River* (New York: Aventura, 1985). Hereafter cited in the text as *BR*.

3. J. Kincaid, *Annie John* (New York: Farrar Straus Giroux, 1985). Hereafter cited in the text as *AJ*.
4. Julia Kristeva, "Les Temps des femmes" (1979), trans. by Alice Jardine and Harry Blake as "Women's Time" in *Feminist Theory: A Critique of Ideology* ed. by N.O. Keohane, M.Z. Rosaldo and B.C. Gelpi (Chicago: University of Chicago Press, 1982), pp. 31-54.
5. Julia Kristeva, "Unes femmes," in *Les Cahiers du Grif*, 7 (1975).
6. A. JanMohamed, "Humanism and Minority Literature," *boundary 2*, XII:3 (Spring, 1984) pp. 281-300. See also Sylvia Wynter, "The Ceremony Must be Found: Beyond Humanism," pp. 19-70 in same issue.
7. Besides American deconstructionism influenced primarily by Jacques Derrida, I have in mind the philosophy of Hans Georg Gadamer, the Frankfurt School, Althusser, Wittgenstein, Vattimo and Lyotard among others, but above all the impact of feminist theory and its imposition of the private and the body on the theoretical discourse—the most significant theoretical achievement being the last book of Luce Irigaray, *Ethique de la différence sexuelle* (Paris: Minuit, 1985).
8. As a Caribbean black woman writer, she is likely to fall under the category 'Third World Woman': for a critique of this other monolith of the Western tradition I refer to the wonderful article by Chandra Talpade Mohanty, "Under Western Eyes: Feminist Scholarship and Colonial Discourse," in *boundary 2*, XII:3 (1984).
9. See, for example, his essays "The Changing Same" (1967) and "John Coltrane: Where Does Art Come From?" (1978). For a further theoretical discussion of this pattern of Afro-American poetics, cfr, also James A. Snead, "Repetition As A Figure of Black Culture," *Black Literature and Literary Theory* (London and New York: Pantheon Books, 1985).
10. See Elisabetta Rasy, *La lingua della nutrice* (Torino: La Tartaruga, 1980). This formulation rests heavily on Kristeva's articulation of the semiotic.
11. Henry Louis Gates, "The Blackness of Blackness: A Critique of the Sign and the Signifying Monkey," *Black Literature and Literary Theory*, pp. 285-321.
12. Edith Milton, "Making a Virtue of Diversity" *New York Times Book Review*, 89 (Jan 15, 1984), p. 22.
13. Anne Tyler, "Mothers and Mysteries" *New Republic*, 189 (Dec 31, 1983), pp. 32-3.
14. Suzanne Freeman, "Three Short Story Collections With a Difference," *Ms*, 12 (Jan. 1984), pp. 15-16.
15. John Bemrose, "Growing Pains of Girlhood," *Macleans*, 98 (May 20, 1985), p. 61.
16. Bruce Van Wyngarden, "First Novel," *Saturday Review*, 11 (May/June 1985), p. 68.
17. Patricia O'Connor, "My Mother Wrote My Life," *New York Times Book Review*, 90 (Apr. 7, 1985), p. 6.
18. Roland Barthes, "The Death of the Author," *Image, Music, Text*, ed. by Stephen Heath (London: Fontana, 1977), p. 147.
19. I wish to thank Ms. Jamaica Kincaid for her permission to publish this statement, which she made in a telephone conversation with me on April 3, 1986.

Afterword: "Beyond Miranda's Meanings: Un/silencing the 'Demonic Ground' of Caliban's 'Woman'" *

Sylvia Wynter

The point of departure of this *After/Word* is to explore a central distinction that emerges as the dynamic linking sub-text of this, the first collection of critical essays written by Caribbean women. This distinction is that between Luce Irigaray's purely Western assumption of a universal category, "woman", whose "silenced" ground is the condition of what she defines as an equally universally applicable, "patriarchal discourse," and the dually Western and post-Western editorial position of a projected 'womanist/feminist' critical approach as the unifying definition of the essays that constitute the anthology. The term *'womanist/feminist,'* with the qualifying attribute "womanist" borrowed from the Afro-American feminist Alice Walker, reveals the presence of a contradiction, which, whilst central to the situational frame of reference of both Afro-American and Caribbean women writers/critics, is necessarily absent from the situational frame of reference of both Western-European and Euroamerican women writers. Thus whilst at the level of the major text these essays are projected within the system of inference-making of the discourse of

---

*Editors' note: This is the first section of a much longer manuscript which could not be included here in its entirety, generated, in part, by our request for this afterword.

Feminism, at the level of the sub-text which both haunts and calls in question the presuppositions of the major text, the very attempt to redefine the term *feminist* with the qualifier "womanist," expresses the paradoxical relation of Sameness and Difference which the writers of these essays, as members of the Caribbean women intelligentsia, bear to their Western European and Euroamerican peers. This dual relation is expressed by both editors if not precisely in these terms. Thus if for Boyce Davies, the term *womanist* necessarily qualifies *feminism*, for Elaine Savory Fido, the unique positional situation of Caribbean women writers/critics, as expressed in their writings, is that of a *cross-roads*, that is, one in which they experience themselves as placed at a crossroad of three variables. These are, on the one hand, the variable of sex-gender, as well as of class, both of which they share with their European/Euroamerican counterparts—*class* in that many members of both intelligentsia groups are still one generation away from our non-middleclass origins, even where this is numerically truer of the intelligentsia of the still, until very recently, colonized Caribbean— and, on the other, the variable of "race" which of course strongly demarcates the situation of the Caribbean women intelligentsia, whether Black or White from that of their Western/Euroamerican counterparts.

I want to argue in this After/Word, from its projected "demonic ground" outside of our present governing system of meaning, or theory/ontology in de Nicolas' sense of the word[1] that it is precisely the variable "race" which imposes upon these essays the contradictory dualism by which the writers both work within the "regime of truth" of the discourse of feminism, at the same time as they make use of this still essentially Western discourse to point towards the epochal threshold of a new post-modern and post-Western mode of cognitive inquiry; one which goes beyond the limits of our present "human sciences," to constitute itself as a new science of human "forms of life."[2]

The German scholar Hans Blumenberg, in exploring the parallel epochal threshold which led from the European Middle Ages to the emergence of the modern world *pari passu* with the advent of Renaissance humanism and the Copernican Revolution, widens the concept of Thomas Kuhn's theory of "scientific revolutions." This theory, he argues, which describes "the breakdown of dominant systems as a result of their immanent rigorism," and the "downfall" of "the pedantic disposition of every school-like mode of thought" (with both breakdown and downfall leading "with fateful inevitability" to the "self-uncovering of the *marginal* inconsistencies from which doubt and opposition break into the consolidated field") can be capable "of generalization to a high level in relation to historical phenomena;"[3] and therefore to the shift/mutation of one age or epoch and its related, in Foucalt's terms, episteme,[4] to the other. And the central point I want to make in this After/Word is that the contradiction inserted into the consolidated field of meanings of the ostensibly "universal" theory of feminism by the variable "*race*," and explicitly expressed by the qualifiers of "womanist" and "cross-roads situation," of these essays points toward the emergent "downfall" of our present "school like mode of thought" and its system of "positive knowledge" inherited from the nineteenth century and from the Industrial epoch of which it was the enabling mode of rationality and participatory epistemology[5]; and that it does this in the same way as feminist theory itself had earlier, inserted the contradiction of the variable *gender* into the ostensibly "universal" theories of Liberal Humanism and Marxism-Leninism.[6]

Because these theories and their related "universalisms" had been erected on the apriori self-description of the human on the model of a "natural organism" [as the inversion of the Euro-Christian "image of God"], the variable "race" was/is constituted as an "object of knowledge" able to function in the system of symbolic representations (Levi-Strauss' "totemic schema," Marlene Philip's system of images as the human analogue of "the D.N.A. molecules at the heart of all life") as a central topos of our present system of meaning and its regulatory behavioral mechanism. For as such a *topos*, "race," functions to signify a system-specific mode of causality, that is, the causality of a "materialistic substrate" which not only acts so as to place genetically determined constraints on human behaviors, but also, above all, to *prescribe* a teleology—that is, to imply that "ends," now no-longer, after the full-fledged secularization of the European Enlightenment, set by the most remote watchmaker of Gods, are still extra-humanly set for the human by *nature*, in our case, by the constraints of nature and/or of history.[7] Thus, if, for Freud, as Irigaray dissects with respect to the variable of "sexual difference," biology was destiny, with the functioning of the "anatomical model" being described by Freud in a manner which prescribes behaviors,— "It seems" Irigaray writes, speaking ironically in Freud's voice," [. . .] you take the term *masculine* to connote *active*, the term *feminine* to connote "passive" and it is true that a relation of the kind exists for "the male sex cell is actively mobile and searches out the female one, and the latter, the ovum, is immobile and waits passively" . . . And I, Freud, have to tell you that the behavior of the *elementary* sexual organisms is indeed a model for the conduct of sexual individuals during intercourse. My way of envisaging . . . these . . . "things" would therefore imply that the psychic is *prescribed by* the *anatomical* according to a *mimetic order*, with anatomical science imposing *the truth of its model* upon psychological *behavior.*[8]—the variable of *race/racial* difference is, since the sixteenth century, even more primarily destiny. For with Western Europe's post-medieval, expansion into the New World, (and earlier into Africa), and with its epochal shift out of primarily *religious* systems of legitimation, and behaviour—regulation, her peoples' expropriation of the land/living space of the New World peoples was to be based on the secular concept of the "non-rational" inferior, "*nature*" of the peoples to be expropriated and governed;[9] that is, of an ostensible difference in "natural" substance which, for the first time in history was no longer *primarily* encoded in the male/female gender division as it had been hitherto in the symbolic template of all traditional and religiously based human orders, but now in the cultural-physiognomic variations between the dominant expanding European civilization and the non-Western peoples that, encountering, it would now stigmatize as "natives." In other words, with the shift to the secular, the primary code of difference now became that between "men" and "natives," with the traditional "male" and "female" distinctions now coming to play a secondary—if none the less powerful—reinforcing role within the system of symbolic representations, Levi-Strauss's totemic schemas[10], by means of which, as governing charters of meaning, all human orders are "altruistically" integrated.[11]

Nowhere in this mutational shift from the primacy of the *anatomical* model of sexual difference as the referential model of *mimetic* ordering, to that of the *physiognomic* model of racial/*cultural* difference, more powerfully enacted than in Shakespeare's play *The Tempest*, one of the foundational endowing[12] texts both of Western Europe's dazzling rise to global hegemony, and, at the level of human "life", in general, of the mutation from primarily religiously defined modes of human being to the first, partly secularizing ones. Whilst on the other hand, both mutations, each as the condition of the other, are nowhere more clearly put into play than in the relations between Miranda the daughter of Prospero, and Caliban, the once original owner of the island now enslaved by Prospero as a function of the latter's expropriation of the island. That is, in the relations of enforced dominance and subordination between Miranda, though "female", and Caliban, though "male"; relations in which *sex-gender attributes* are not longer the primary index of "deferent" difference[13], and in which the discourse that erects itself is no longer primarily "patriarchal", but rather "monarchical" in its Western-European, essentially post-Christian, post-religious definition. Therefore, in whose context of behaviour-regulatory inferential system of meanings, as the essential condition of the mutation to the secular, Caliban, as an incarnation of a new category of the human, that of the subordinated "irrational" and "savage"[14] *native* is now constituted as the lack of the "rational" Prospero, and the now capable-of-rationality-Miranda, by the Otherness of his/its *physiognomic* "monster" difference, a difference which now takes the *coding* role of sexual-anatomical difference, with the latter now made into a mimetic parallel effect of the former, and as such a member of the *set* of differences of which the former has now become the primary "totemic operator."[15]

Correspondingly, as the play reveals, with this ontological and epistemological mutation effected in the sixteenth century, the new physiognomic model of "race", (or, in the terms of Elsa Goveiá, the Caribbean historian, used in a critical 1970 essay on the integrative principles of Caribbean societies, the "ascription of race"),[16] was to begin that ongoing transformative meaning process by which it would come to function, within our contemporary, behaviour-regulatory theoretical models and systems of meaning, to provide, parallely to the earlier traditional sex-gender models of *anatomical* difference of truly "patriarchal" orders, the grounding "mimetic model" or totemic operator which now *primarily* describes/prescribes at the multiple levels of the global order, analogical behavioural relations of dominance/ subordination activity/passivity, theory-givers/theory-takers[17] between human populations/geographical races, cultures, and societal groups, i.e. ethnic, class, gender, sexual-preference, etc. The "mimetic model" or totemic operator therefore, which legitimates these relations in now *purely secular* terms, as relations ostensibly pre-ordained by the extra-human ends set by, firstly, in the narrative schema/story of the monarchical discourse of civic humanism (as enacted in *the Tempest*) by an allegedly universally applicable "natural law"[18], and later in the Malthusian-Darwinian-Haeckelian, narrative schema of a monist discourse of "social naturalism" or "biological idealism"[19], by, allegedly, evolutionary biology. Thus, if in the first schema of "civic humanism," the model of *physiognomic* difference was still attached to the model of religio-cultural difference - with the New World peoples and African slaves defined as "pagan sacrificers of other humans and as idolatious "cannibals"[20], in the second, the now purely *physiognomic* difference came to provide a *somatic* mode of difference which would function from the early nineteenth century onwards as the *primary* "totemic operator" of the principle of Sameness and Difference about which our present global, and now purely secular order, auto-regulates its socio-systemic hierarchies, including those of gender, class, sexual preference, culture—including, therefore, the processes central to literary scholarship itself and to its normative system of interpretative readings, which have been defined by Cary Nelson as that of "literary idealization" by means of which, in Euro-American "humanism" processes of literary transcendence (i.e. literature as "one of the finer things on earth" one which "exhibits at once a powerful realism about the human condition and a visionary synthesis of its highest ambitions") are attached "to the experience of only one race, one sex, a restricted set of class fractions within a few national cultures." With the experiences of most of the world's peoples "having to be, rule-governedly, within the parameters of the 'play'[21] of its interpretative readings," and regulatory system of meanings, "obliterated"[22]; as the experiences of the physiognomic Other, the "natives", and in their most "primal" form *niggers*. The systemic "obliteration" is central, therefore to the imperative which impels the counter-readings of these essays.

It is in this context that we can begin to approach the significance both of this collection of essays themselves as essays projected both from the hitherto "silenced" vantage point of the obliterated "experiences of most of the world's peoples" and from the vantage point of gender, that is of a Miranda now speaking in her own intelligentsia name—instead of in the

name of her monarchical father, and of *The Tempest's* Miranda's speech to
Caliban; that we can grasp the significance of her legitimated expropriation
of the right to endow his purposes—when he did not "savage" know "his
own meanings"—with "words that made them known," her expropriation
then of what Marlene Phillips defines as "image-making power." And here,
we begin to pose in this context a new question, the question not of the
absence of Caliban's legitimate fatehr as posed by Aimé Césaire and
commented on by Clarisse Zimra in her essay on Francophone Caribbean
women writers, nor even the question posed by Zimra herself, that of the
"silent presence of a mother not yet fully understood" which carries with it
the implicit project of "discarding the logos of the Father," and of replacing
it instead with "the Silent Song of the Mother," but a new question related
to a new project. This question is that of the most significant absence of all,
that of Caliban's Woman, of Caliban's physiognomically complementary
mate. For nowhere in Shakespeare's play, and in its system of image-
making, one which would be foundational to the emergence of the first form
of a secular world system, our present Western world system, does
Caliban's mate appear as an alternative sexual-erotic model of desire; as an
alternative source of an alternative system of meanings. Rather there, on the
New World island, as the only woman, Miranda and her mode of
physiognomic being, defined by the philogenically "idealized" features of
straight hair and thin lips is canonized as the "rational" object of desire; as
the potential genitrix of a superior mode of human "life," that of "good
natures" as contrasted with the ontologically absent potential genitrix—
Caliban's mate—of another population of human, i.e., of a "vile race"
"capable of all ill," which "any print of goodness will not take," a "race"
then extra-humanly condemned by a particular mode of Original Sin which
"deservedly" confines them to a "rock," thereby empowering the "race" of
Miranda to expropriate the island, and to reduce Caliban to a labor-
machine as the new "massa damnata"[23] of purely sensory nature—"He
does make our fire,/fetch in our wood, and serve in offices/that profit us"[24].
And since the empirical relation of rational humans to purely sensory
nature humans, and its related physiognomic-cultural model of difference/
deference will now serve retrospectively, as the *mimetic model* of an order
whose intra-group societal hierarchical structures have been pre-ordained
by an allegedly universally functioning code of natural law,[25] the "desire"
of the 'lower class' sailors Stephano and Trinculo can also only be *for*
Miranda, with their *optimal* "desire" also transferred form their own
"lower class" mates, to her. Hence the non-desire of Caliban for his own
mate, for Caliban's "woman", is, as Maryse Condé brilliantly suggests, in
another context, a founding function of the "social pyramid"[26] of the global
order that will be put in place following upon the 1492 arrival of Columbus
in the Caribbean; a function then of its integrating behaviour-regulatory
system of meanings and "semantic closure principle."

In this first phase of Western Europe's expansion into the Americas, Caliban, as both the Arawak and African "forced" labor needed by the mutation in the land/labor ratio which followed[27], and given the existence of rapidly available fresh supplies provided by the expanding slave trade in "negroes" out of the Europe-Africa-New World triangular traffic, had no need/desire for the procreation of his own "kind", since such a mode of "desire" would only be functional in the very much later stages for the master-population group's purpose, as the only secularly-theoretically "idealized" purpose which now mattered.

Hence the empirical logic of the absence from the play's character system of Caliban's woman, for its erecting of its plot upon the "ground" not only of her absence, but also of the absence of Caliban's endogenous desire for her, of any longing. All his desire instead is "soldered" on[28] to Miranda as the only symbolically canonized potential genitrix. Hence his first act of overt rebellion is his attempt to "people this isle with Caliban's"; his attempt to copulate with her. However, this rebellious possibility is not to be—for if the absence of Caliban's woman is a central function of the play's foundational ontology in which Caliban "images" the human as pure sensory nature and as appetite uncurbed by reason, whilst Prospero and the prince, Fernando, "image" the human possessed of a rational nature and therefore able to curb their lustful appetites, (with the ship's Boatswain and the sailors Stephano and Trinculo, lower down the scale between the two), then the metaphysically imperative elimination of the *potential* progeny of Caliban, must rule-governedly bar him from any access to Miranda as the potential genitrix of a "race" which, as the beneficiaries of both rational and sensory natures bequeathed them by Nature, must necessarily behave so as to effect the "ends" ostensibly implicit this differential legacy; that is, must ensure the stable dominance of the "race" of good natures over the "vile race" of Caliban's purely sensory nature, if the now secularizing behaviour—regulatory system of meaning, and its related "semantic closure principle" is to be stably replicated.

The absence of Caliban's woman is therefore an ontological absence, that is, one central to the new secularizing behaviour-regulatory narrative schema, or in Clarisse Zimra's term, mode of "story-telling"[29], by means of which the secular Laity of feudal-Christian Europe displaced the theological spirit/flesh motivational opposition[30] and replaced it with its own first secularly constituted "humanist" motivational opposition in history. That is, the rational/sensory opposition between a projected redeemed "race" of "gentes humaniores" as the bearers of a rational nature able to master their own sensory nature at the same time as they mastered—and mistressed—the "vile race" dys-elected by Nature to be bearers of a purely sensory nature, and the new secular *massa damnata* of the "vile race" themselves.[31]

To put it in more directly political terms, the absence of Caliban's woman, is an absence which is functional to the new secularizing schema by which the peoples of Western Europe legitimated their global expansion as well as their expropriation and/their marginalization of all the other population-groups of the globe, including, partially, some of their own national groupings such as, for example, the Irish.[32] Yet it was with this same secularizing narrative schema that they were also to effect that far-reaching mutation, in which they were to displace, not only their own *religious* version of the narrative schemas of good and evil and their modes of "story-telling",—that is, their own religious version of the behaviour-motivational schemas/stories, by means of whose opiate-inducing signifying meaning systems which function to trigger the neuro-chemical processes of what Danielli defines as the internal reward system of the brain[33] and to induce and regulate the collective set of "altruistic" behaviours by means of which each human model of being and related human orders are stably brought into, and maintained in, being—but *all* other religious versions to the marginally private, rather than centrally public, spheres of human existence.[34] And, if the latter schemas, religious and/or mythological, together with their projection of a transcendentally ordered behaviour-regulatory definition of good and evil, had hitherto functioned to stabilize and guarantee all human "forms of life", the new narrative schema, powerfully re-enacted in the plot-line of *The Tempest*, was to initiate the first form of a secularly projected definition of Good and Evil, and therefore of a secularly guaranteed and stabilized "form of life" or human order, now dynamically brought in to being by the collective behaviours motivated and induced by its (the schema's) oppositional categories of secular "good" (as rational nature incarnated in Prospero and Miranda) and of secular "evil" (as pure sensory nature outside of the control of rational nature incarnated in Caliban when his own "master, his own man.")[35] In other words, in this epochal threshold shift to the secular, the physiognomic (and cultural) difference between the populations groups of Prospero/Miranda and that of Caliban is now made to function, totemically, as a new, so to speak infra-scendental[36] oppositional principle of good and evil which is ostensibly as extra-humanly ordained (by Natural Law), as, before, the Spirit/Flesh opposition had been ostensibly pre-ordained by supernatural decree—rather than as, in both cases ordained by the imperative of the respective narrative schemas, and the "semantic closure of principle" of their respective behaviour regulatory systems of meanings.[37]

It is within this latter "real" imperative that the absence of Caliban's woman as Caliban's sexual reproductive mate functions to ontologically negate their progeny/population group, forcing this group to serve as the allegorical incarnation of "pure" sensory nature; that is, the group for whom the image of Caliban stands, i.e., the original owners/occupiers of the New World lands, the American-Indians, now displaced empirically and metaphysically reduced, by the new regulatory system of meanings, to a "native" savage Human Other status now central to the functioning of

the first secularizing behaviour - regulatory schema or motivational apparatus in human history. Whilst with the rapid decimation of the indigenous
Arawaks of the Caribbean Islands, Africans bought and sold as "trade
goods" were now made to fill the same slot in the behaviour regulatory
schema, as they were made to fill a parallel slot in the system of forced labor.
As such they too, as Caliban's women, are reduced to having no will or
desire that has not been prescribed by Prospero/Miranda in the name of the
existential interest of the population-group for whom the "images" of
Prospero/Miranda, stand. Given that the idealization/negation of both
groups is effected precisely by the dominant group's imposition of its own
mode of volition and desire (one *necessarily* generated from the *raison
d'etre* of its group—existential interests) upon the dominated; as well as by
its stable enculturating of the latter by means of its theoretical models
(epistemes) and aesthetic fields, generated from its increasingly hegemonic
and secularizing systems of meanings. In consequence if, before the
sixteenth century, what Irigaray terms as *"patriarchal discourse"* had
erected itself on the "silenced ground" of women, from then on, the new
primarily silenced ground (which at the same time now enables the partial
liberation of Miranda's hitherto stifled speech), would be that of the
majority population-groups of the globe—all signified now as the "natives"
(Caliban's) to the "men" of Prospero and Fernando, with Miranda
becoming both a co-participant, if to a lesser *derived* extent, in the power
and privileges generated by the empirical supremacy of her own population;
and as well, the beneficiary of a mode of privilege unique to her, that of being
the metaphysically invested and "idealized" object of desire for all classes
(Stephano and Trinculo) and all population-groups (Caliban)[38].

   This therefore is the dimension of the contradictory relation of Sameness
and Difference, of orthodoxy and heresy which these Caribbean critical
essays must necessarily, if still only partially, inscribe, and do inscribe with
respect to the theory/discourse of feminism, (as the latest and last variant of
the Prospero/Miranda ostensibly "universally" applicable meaning and
discourse-complex); the relation of *sameness and difference* which is
expressed in the diacritical term *"womanist"*. And if we are to understand
the necessity for such an *other* term (projected both from the perspective of
Black American women (U.S.) and from that of the "native" women
intelligentsia of the newly independent Caribbean ex-slave polities,) as a
term which, whilst developing a fully articulated theoretical/interpretative
reading model of its own, nevertheless, serves, diacritically to draw
attention to the insufficiency of all existing theoretical interpretative
models, both to "voice" the hitherto silenced ground of the experience of
"native" Caribbean women and Black American women as the ground of
Caliban's woman, and to de-code the system of meanings of that other
discourse, beyond Irigaray's patriarchal one, which has imposed this mode
of silence for some five centuries, as well as to make thinkable the

possibility of a new "model" projected from a new "native" standpoint, we shall need to translate the variable "race", which now functions as the intra-feminist marker of difference, impelling the dually "gender/beyond gender" readings of these essays, out of the epistemic 'vrai'[39] of our present order of "positive knowledge"[40], its consolidated field of meanings and order-replicating hermeneutics. Correspondingly, since this order/field is transformative, generated from our present purely secular definition of the human on the model of a natural organism, with, in consequence this organism's "ends" therefore being ostensibly set extra-humanly, by "nature", i.e.Haeckel's monism, neo-classical economics Natural Scarcity, Marx's "materialist" imperative of the "mode of production", Feminism's ... bio-anatomical "universal" identity[41], we shall need to move beyond this founding definition, not merely to *another* alternative one, nonconsciously put in place as our present definition, but rather to a frame of reference which parallels the "demonic models" posited by physicists who seek to conceive of a vantage point outside the space-time orientation of the humuncular observer. This would be, in our case, in the context of our specific socio-human realities, a "demonic model" outside the "consolidated field" of our present mode of being/feeling/knowing, as well as of the multiple discourses, their regulatory systems of meaning and interpretative "readings", through which alone these modes, as varying expressions of human "life," including ours, can effect their respective autopeosis *as such* specific modes of being. The possibility of such a vantage point, we argue, towards which the diacritical term "womanist" (i.e. these readings as both gender, and not-gender readings, as both Caribbean/Black nationalist and not-Caribbean/Black nationalist, Marxian and not-Marxian readings)[42] point, can only be projected from a "demonic model" generated, parallely to the vantage point/demonic model with which the laity-intelligentsia of Western Europe effected the first rupture of humans with their/our supernaturally guaranteed narrative schemas of origin,[43] from the situational "ground" or slot of Caliban's woman, and therefore of her systemic behaviour regulatory role or function as the ontological "native/nigger", within the motivational apparatus by means of which our present model of being/definition-of-the-human is given dynamic "material" existence, rather than from merely the vantage point of her/our gender, racial, class or cultural being.[44] In other words, if the laity intelligentsia of Western Europe effected a mutation by calling in question its own role as the ontological Other of "natural fallen flesh" to the theologically idealized, post-baptismal Spirit, (and as such incapable of attaining to any knowledge of, and mastery over, either the physical processes of nature or its own social reality, except such knowledge was mediated by the then hegemonic Scholastic *theological* interpretative model,) and by calling this role in question so as to clear the ground for its own self-assertion which would express itself both in the political reasons-of-state humanism (enacted in *The Tempest*), as well as in the putting in place of the *Studia Humanitatis* (i.e. as the self-study of "natural man"), and in the laying of the basis for the rise of the natural sciences,[45] it is by a parallel calling in question of our '*native*', and more ultimately, nigger women's role as the embodiment to varying degrees of an ostensible "primal" human nature. As well, challenging our role as a new 'lay' intelligentsia ostensibly unable to know and therefore to master our present sociosystemic reality, (including the reality of our "existential weightlessness" as an always "intellectually indentured"[46] intelligentsia), except as mediated by the theoretical models generated from the vantage point of the "normal" intelligentsia, clears the ground for a new self-assertion. This time, as one which brings together the human and natural sciences in a new projected science of the human able to constitute *demonic models* of congition *outside* what Lemuel Johnson calls, in one of the essays in this collection, the always non-arbitrary pre-prescribed, "designs of the measuring rod" in whose parameters both our present hegemonic interpretative and anti-interpretative models[46] are transformatively generated; one able in fact to take these designs of the measuring rod and their "privileged texts" as the object of our now conscious rather than reactive processes of cognition[47]. In effect, rather than only voicing the "native" woman's hitherto silenced voice[48] we shall ask: What is the systemic function of her own silencing, both as women and, more totally, as ''native'' women? Of what mode of speech is that absence of speech both as women (masculinist discourse) and as 'native' women (feminist discourse) as imperative function?

The larger issue then is of the ontological difference and of our *human* and *"native" human* subordination, hitherto non-conscious, to the governing behaviour-regulatory codes of symbolic "life" and "death." It is an issue which calls for a second self-assertion able to respond to the new metaphysical imperative, not now of altering nature, but of altering our systems of meanings, and their privileged texts, and, therefore, of abolishing Elsa Goveia's ascriptions of "race" and "wealth" (whose *particularisms* work to contradict the *universalism* of one-(wo)man,-one-vote), as well as those other ascriptions of the same totemic set which function to the same effect, i.e. culture, through the mechanism of literary scholarship's "idealized" (Cary Nelson) canonism,[49] religion, an allegedly "natural" erotic preference[50] as well as that of gender. The issue then of a second epistemological mutation—based on the new metaphysical imperative of the now conscious alterability of our governing codes, their modes of ontological difference and their rule-governedly generated behaviour-regulatory meanings, together with their always non-arbitrary "designs"[51] of interpretative readings —one able to complete the *partial* epistemological mutation of the first which ushered in our modern age as well as that first process of the non-conscious secularization of human modes/models of being, of whose order-maintaining discourses, the doubly silenced "ground" of Caliban's "native" woman, was a central meaning-coherence function; and of whose *incomplete epistemological mutation*, both the gender hierarchy of the ostensible equality of our symbolic contract, as well as of the "hard and uncomfortable life" of the, since the 1960's, now politically empowered Caribbean black and poor majority as noted by, and finely imaged in, Christine Craig's complex figure *Crow*, as both young woman metaphysically invested as the negative of normative object-desire, and old woman/Carrion bird with the garbage dump as food for both), as well as then, of the "hard and uncomfortable" life of all those who inhabit the global archipelagoes of hunger in the midst of a new technologically produced surfeit of global abundance,[52] are an imperative effect and consequence.[53] That is, the paradoxical effect of that first, incomplete, and now objectified, secularizing epistemological mutation:

> "There are phases of objectivation" Blumenberg wrote, "that loose themselves from their original motivation (*the science and technology of the later phases of the modern age provide* a stupendous example of this); and to bring them back to their human function, to subject them again to man's (the human's) purposes in relation to the world, *requires* an unavoidable counter-exertion. The medieval system ended in such a phase of objectification that has become autonomous, of hardening that is insulated from what is human. What is here called 'self-assertion' is the counter-move of retrieving the lost motives, of a new concentration on man's (human) self-interest."[54]

The appeal of the Abeng is therefore to the larger issue of retrieving the lost motives of our "native" human self-interest, and, increasingly degraded in our planetary environment, of our human self-interest. This issue, which clearly calls for a second counter-exertion, has been initiated, in its first transitional phase by these diacritically "womanist" essays as the counter exertion of a "native women" intelligentsia, who, by refusing the "water-with berries" strategy sets, of all our present hegemonic, theoretical models in their "pure" forms, based on their isolated "isms"[55], has enabled the move, however preliminary, on to the "demonic" and now unsilencing trans-"isms" ground of Caliban's woman. This terrain, when fully occupied, will be that of a new science of human discourse, of human "life" beyond the "master discourse" of our governing "privileged text", and its sub/versions. Beyond Miranda's meanings.

NOTES

1. See A.T. de Nicolas, "Notes on the Biology of Religion" in *Journal of Social and Biological Structures* 3, no. 2 (April 1980):225.
2. I have put forward this proposal in two earlier essays, but most fully in the second. See Wynter, "On Disenchanting Discourse: Minority Literature and Beyond" in *Cultural Critique*, The Nature and Context of Minority Discourse *Vol. 11.* Fall 1987, No. 7.
3. See Hans Blumenberg, *The Legitimacy of the Modern Age* (Cambridge, Mass.: M.I.T. Press, 1983).
4. See Michel Foucault, *The Order of Things: An Archaeology of the Human Sciences*, (New York: Vintage Books, 1973).
5. For the concept of "participatory epistemology" see Francisco Varela, *Principles of Biological Autonomy* (New York, North Holland Series in General Systems Research, 1979).
6. At the theoretical level "feminist" theory developed on the basis of its rupture with the purely economic and class-based theory of Marxism, thereby calling into question both the "universalisms" of Marxian Proletarian identity and of the Liberal humanist "figure of man."
7. See Blumenberg, op. cit. where he discusses the function of Darwinian thought in this articulation of the concept of ends set by nature and by evolution.
8. See her *Speculum of the Other Woman* (Ithaca: Cornell University Press), 1985, 15.
9. See Anthony Pagden, *The Fall of Natural Man: The American Indian and the Origins of Comparative Ethnology* (Cambridge, England: Cambridge U.P., 1982).
10. See Levi-Strauss, C. *Totemism.* (Harmondsworth: Penguin, 1969).
11. See J.F. Danielli, "Altruism: The Opium of the People," *Journal of Social and Biological Structures* 3, no. 2 (April 1980):87-94.
12. See D. Halliburton, "Endowment, Enablement, Entitlement: Toward A Theory of Constitution" in *Literature and the Question of Philosophy*, ed. A.J. Cascari (Baltimore: Johns Hopkins University Press, 1986) where he develops this concept of "endowment."
13. A play on the Deridean concept of "difference" where the temporal dimension is replaced by the stratifying/status dimension, making use of the concept of "deferent" behaviour which functions to inscribe difference, and to constitute "higher" and "lower" ranking.
14. See in this respect, the book by Jacob Pandian, *Anthropology and the Western Tradition: Towards an Authentic Anthropology* (Prospect Heights, Illinois: Waveland Press, Inc., 1985).
15. See for an excellent analysis of this concept, the book by Jenkins, Claude. *The Social Theory of Claude Levi-Strauss.* London: The MacMillan Press, Ltd., 1979.
16. See her essay, "The Social Framework" in *Savacou*, Kingston, Jamaica, 1970.

17. The analogy here is to the always *deferent* relation of the wife-taker category to that of the wife-giver category.
18. See Anthony Pagden, op. cit. for an analysis of this intellectual process which was to lay the basis of today's concept of "international" law.
19. See my discussion of this concept/discourse which is founding to our present order of knowledge in the Cultural Critique essay already cited.
20. See Pagden, op. cit.
21. The reference here is to the "freeplay" concept of the deconstructionists. As is clear, our counter concept is that the parameters of interpretation are always set, in the last analysis, by what we develop later as the mode of ontological difference and its related code of symbolic "life" and "death".
22. See Nelson, Cary. "Against English: Theory and The Limits of the Discipline in Profession," 1987, M.L.A. Publication.
23. The analogy here is to the Christian theological concept of the non-elect by predestination.
24. See William Shakespeare, *The Tempest*, ed. R. Langbaum, (New York: Signet Classic, 1964).
25. This code, developed from Aquinas' formulation of an ontological natural law able to be detached from its Christological base, will be central to the later mutation to the secular orders of things.
26. See her book, *La parole des femmes: Essais sur les romancieres des Antilles des langues françaises.* (Paris, Harmattan, 1979).
27. Europe's expropriation of the lands of the Americas initiated a land/labor ratio of a new unprecedented extent. Both the encomienda and hacienda and the plantation institution were the answer to this vast "enclosure system" by which the category of "native labor" and "native being" came into existence.
28. See the essay by Arnold Davidson where he quotes Freud's point about the plasticity of the "sexual instinct" and how it can be easily "soldered" on to specific objects of desire. See his essay, "How to do the History of Psychoanalysis: A Reading of Freud's *Three Essays On The Theory of Sexuality* in Critical Inquiry 13:2 Winter, 1987.
29. See the illuminating point made by Clarisse Zimra in her essay in this collection.
30. The proposal here is that the Spirit/Flesh opposition of medieval Europe functioned as the motivational mechanism of desire/aversion by means of which the secular laity were made desirous of attaining to being only through the baptismal model of medieval Christianity. See Walter Ullman's book, *Medieval Foundations of Renaissance Humanism*, (Ithaca, New York: Cornell Univ. Press, 1977).
31. The roots of contemporary racism are sited in this system of speculative thought that would be "materialized" in the *encomienda* and the *plantation* systems, since these institutions were to be based on this new secular post-Christian mode of legitimation.
32. Recent work by political scientists have begun to focus on the parallels between the discourses by means of which the New World Indians were expropriated and those by which the Cromwellian conquest and partial occupation of Ireland were also legitimated i.e. by the projection of a "by nature difference" between the dominant and the subordinated population groups.

33. In this respect see the original and illuminating essay by Danielli, James F. "Altruism and the Internal Reward System or The Opium of the People" in *Journal of Social and Biological Structures*, 1980, 3.

34. Even where in the case of the Ayatollah Khomeini, and Islamic fundamentalism this might seem not to be so, the religious tenets of Islam are now a *function* of a religious-nationalist ideology adapted from the West's process of secularization.

35. This then legitimates his subordination to "rational nature" incarnated in Prospero.

36. Coined on the model of transcendental, but this time, although also extra-humanly, but from below.

37. The concept of a "semantic closure principle" is borrowed from the biologist Howard Pattee's description of the integrative functioning of the cell. The proposal is that human orders *should* function according to analogous principles. See Howard H. Pattee, "Clues from Molecular Symbol Systems" in *"Signed and Spoken Language: Biological Constraints on Linguistic Forms,"* U. Bellugi and M. Studdert-Kennedy, eds. (Berlin: Verlag Chemie, 1980). 261-274, and "Laws and Constraints, Symbols and Languages" in *Towards a Theoretical Biology*, C.H. Waddington, ed. (Edinburgh, University of Edinburgh Press, 1972), 248-258.

38. The sailors' dream too, is to be king on the island and to marry Miranda.

39. The term is used by Foucault in his talk, *The Order of Discourse* given in December 1970 and published as an Appendix of the *Archaeology of Knowledge*, (New York: Harper and Row., tr. A.M. Sheridan-Smith, 1972). Here Foucault notes that Mendel's findings about genetic heredity were not hearable at first because they were not within the *"vrai"* of the discipline at the time.

40. In *The Order of Things*, Foucault points out that because "Man" is an object of 'positive knowledge' in Western culture, he cannot be an "object of science."

41. "Women" can only be co-identified as a universal *political* category on the paradoxical basis of their/our shared bio-anatomical identity.

42. The force of the term *womanist* lies in its revelation of a perspective which can only be *partially* defined by any of the definitions of our present hegemonic theoretical models.

43. With respect to the functioning of the narrative of origins in human orders, including the "evolutionary" narrative of origin of our own which also functions as "replacement material for genesis," see Glyn Isaacs, "Aspects of Human Evolution" in D.S. Bendall, ed., *Evolution From Molecules to Men*, (Cambridge, New York, C.U.P., 1983), 509-543.

44. The contradiction here is between "cultural nationalism" i.e. the imperative to revalue one's gender, class, culture and to constitute one's literary counter-canon, and the scientific question. What is the function of the "obliteration" of these multiple perspectives? What role does this play in the stable bringing into being of our present human order?

45. See Ullman, Walter op. cit. and Hans Blumenberg, op. cit. as well, as Kurt Hubner, *The Critique of Scientific Reason* (Chicago: The Univ. of Chicago Press, 1983), for the linkage of the rise of the natural sciences to the overall secularizing movement of humanism.

46. The term is Henry Louis Gates', and is central to the range of his work. See for

example, his use of a variant of this term ("interpretative indenture") in his essay, "Authority (White) Power and the (Black) critic" in *Cultural Critique*, Fall 1987, no. 7, 19-46.

47. That is, cognition outside of the parameters prescribed by our participatory epistemology (See Francisco Vorela, op. cit.) or the World View, integrative of all orders, including our own.

48. In a paper given as a panel presentation at the recent 1988 March West Coast Political Science Conference, Kathy Ferguson of the University of Hawaii pointed to the contradiction, for feminist deconstructionists, between the imperative of a fixed gender identity able to facilitate a unifying identity from which to "voice" their presence, and the deconstructionist program to deconstruct gender's oppositional categories.

49. The attack on the master canon, and the thrust to devise new canons by hitherto marginalized intelligentsia groups allow us to speak of canonism, as one of the ordering "*isms*".

50. The stigmatization of homoerotic preference, plays a key role in the projection of the idea of "natural" preference, which is founding to the inferential logic of the discourse of economics.

51. Again the point here is that interpretative readings occur within parameters set by the governing code, and are never arbitrary, even if the governing codes are.

52. The problem that faces the world is one of distribution. But if as we argue, economic distribution is a function, in the last instance of the *integration* of our present order, then the contradiction between the global surpluses of food enabled by the Green Revolution and the spread of massive world hunger reported by world agencies is an effect, not of an economic imperative, but of an order-maintaining one, i.e. of the imperative of its "altruistic" integration.

53. In *The Tempest*, Caliban accuses Prospero of having given him "water with berries" and stroked him when the latter arrived, thereby getting Caliban to show where the streams and food sources on the island were. The proposal is that all theoretical models function both as "knowledge" and as the water-with berries strategy sets of specific groups. I have developed this more fully in a paper - *Why We Cannot Save Ourselves In A Woman's Manner: Towards A Caribbean World View*, to be presented at the First Conference of Caribbean Women Writers and Scholars, and hosted by the *Black Studies Dept.* at Wellesley College.

54. The proposal here is since all the *isms* constitute a totemic system or set, the attempt to abolish any of these as an isolated ism is everywhere a "strategy set" of the specific group for whom, as in the case of Duvalierisme for the new Haitian black middle class, the abolition of a specific *ism* will be empowering. See with respect to feminism, Moraga and Anzaldua, op. cit.

REFERENCES

Blumenberg, Has. *The Legitimacy of the Modern Age*, (Cambridge MA: MIT Press, 1983.)

Burke, James, *The Day The Universe Changed*, (Boston: Little Brown and Company, 1985).

Cavalleri, Liebe, The Double-Edged Helix: Science in the Real World (New York, Columbia U.P., 1981).

Comfort, Alex, "Demonic and Historical models in Biology", in *The Journal of Social and Biological Structures* 3, no. 2, (April 1980: 207-216).

Condé, Maryse, *La parole des femmes: Essais sur les romancieres des Antilles des langues francaises*, (Paris, Harmattan, 1979).

Danielli, James F., "Altruism and the Opium of the People" in *Journal of Social and Biological Structures*, 1980.

Davidson, Arnold, "How to do the History of Psychoanalysis: A Reading of Freud's *Three Essays on The Theory of Sexuality* in *Critical Inquiry* 13:2, Winter, 1987.

Fanon, Frantz, *Black Skins, White Masks*, (1964, New York: Grove Press, 1967).

Ferguson, Kathy E. "Interpretation and Genealogy in Feminism." Paper presented at the Western Political Science Association Meeting, San Francisco, March 10-12, 1988.

Foucault, Michel, *Madness and Civilization: A History of Insanity in the Age of Reason*, (New York: Mentor Books, 1965).

Fanon, Frantz, *The Order of Discourse*, Appendix to *The Archaeology of Knowledge*, (New York: Harper and Row trans A.M. Sheridan-Smith, 1972).

Fanon, Frantz, *The Order of Things: An Archaeology of the Human Sciences*, (New York: Random House, 1973).

Gallop, Jane, *Reading Lacan*, (Ithaca: Cornell University Press, 1985).

Gates, H.L., "Authority (White) Power and the (Black) Critic" in *The Nature and Context of Minority Discourse II*, A.R. Janmohamed and David Lloyd eds. in *Cultural Critique*, Fall, 1987, No. 7.

Goveia, Elsa, "The Social Framework" in *Savacou*, U.W.I., Mona Jamaica, 1970.

Grassi, Ernesto, *Rhetoric and Philosophy: The Humanist Tradition*, (University Park and Sundon: Penn State Univ. Press, 1980).

Haeckel, Ernst, *Anthropogenie* (Leipzig, 1987), English trans. by Joseph McCabe as *The Evolution of Man*, (New York, 1910).

Halliburton, David, "Endowment, Enablement, Entitlement: Toward a Theory of Constitution" in *Literature And the Question of Philosophy*, ed. A.J. Cascardi (Baltimore: Johns Hopkins University Press, 1986).

Hubner, Kurt, *Critique of Scientific Reason*, (Chicago: The Univ. of Chicago Press, 1983).

Illich, Ivan, *Gender*, (New York: Pantheon Books, 1982).

Irigaray, Luce, *Speculum of the Other Woman*, (Ithaca: Cornell University Press, 1985).

Isaacs, Glyn, "Aspects of Human Evolution" in D.S. Bendall, ed., *Evolution from Molecules to Men*, (Cambridge, New York: C.U.P., 1983), 509-543.

Jenkins, Claude, *The Social Theory of Claude Levi-Strauss*, (London, The MacMillan Press, Ltd., 1979).

Kristeva, Julia, "Women's *time* in *Signs*, 7, no. I, (1981-1982).

Lamming, George, *Water with Berries*, (London: Longman, 1971).

Levi-Strauss, C. *Totemism*, (Hamondworth, Middlesex: Penguin, 1969).

Moraga, Cherie and Gloria Anzaldua, *This Bridge Called My Back*, (Watertown, Mass: Persephone Press, 1981).

Nelson, Cary, "Against English: Theory and the Limits of the Discipline" in *Profession*, 1987, M.L.A. Publication.

Pagden, Anthony, *The Fall of Natural Man: The American Indian and the Origins of Comparative Ethnology* (Cambridge: England, 1982).

Pandian, Jaboc, *Anthropology and the Western tradition towards an authentic Anthropology*, (Prospect Heights, Illlinois, Waveland Press, Inc., 1985).

Pattee, H.H., "Clues from Molecular Symbol Systems" in *Signed and Spoken Language: Biological Constraints on Linguistic Forms*, U. Belliegi and M. Studdert-Kennedy, eds. (Berlin Verlag Chemie, 1980 261-274.

Pattee, H.H., "Laws and Constraints, Symbols and Languages" in *Towards A Theoretical Biology*, C.H. Waddington 1987 ed., (Edinburgh, University of Edinburgh Press, 1972), 248-258.

Scott, Joanna Vechicrelli, "The Origins of Public Discourse on the Status of 'Natives' in English Political Thought: Playing the 'Irish Game'." Paper presented at the 1988 Annual Meeting of the Western Political Science Association, San Francisco, California, March 10-12, 1988.

Scubla, Lucien, "Contribution a la theorie du sacrifice" in *Rene Girard et le probleme du mal* in Deguy, M. and Jean-Pierre Dupuy, eds. *Rene Girard et le probleme du Mal* (Pans: Bernard Grasset, 1982), pp. 103-168.

Shakespeare, William, *The Tempest* ed., Robert Langbaum, (New York: Signet Classic, 1964).

Smith, Maynard, "Game Theory and the Evolution of Cooperation in *Evolution from Molecules to Men*, D.S. Bendall, ed. (Cambridge: C.U.P. 1983).

Ullman, Walter, *Medieval Foundations of Renaissance Humanism*, (Ithaca, New York: Cornell Univ. Press, 1977).

Varela, Francisco, *Principles of Biological Autonomy*, (New York North Holland Series in General Systems Research, 1979).

Wynter, Sylvia, "On Disenchanting Discourse: Minority Literature and Beyond in *Cultural Critique* (*the Nature and Context of Minority Discourse*) Vol. 11, Fall, 1987, No. 7.

Selected Bibliography of Criticism and Related Works*

Jeniphier R. Carnegie

Introduction

The original intention of this bibliography was to bring together critiques of the works of little known women writers in the English-speaking Caribbean. The literature surveyed for the preparation of the bibliography showed, however, such striking similarities in the treatment of literature written by women in the French, English and Spanish-speaking Caribbean, that it seemed desirable to include a sampling of criticisms from the other two language areas for purposes of comparison.

It appears that there is a common problem of under-representation of women's writings in the general body of literary criticism compared to the interest accorded male writers. For example, Maryse Condé says of Guadeloupe: "La Guadeloupe présente cette particularité de posséder plusieurs écrivains féminins. Si elle n'a pas encore produit d'écrivains aussi prestigieux que Césaire, de theoriciens politiques tels que Fanon, du moins la parole de ses femmes ne manque pas d'intérêt et de complexité."[1] ["A striking feature of Guadeloupean literature is that it includes the work of several women authors. Although the country has not yet produced any writers of the international standing of Césaire or political theorists of the like of Fanon, it may be said that the writing of its female authors is lacking neither in interest nor in complexity."]

In a similar vein, writing of the Hispanic Caribbean Virginia Ramos Foster states: "Hay abundancia de letras femeninas; lo que hace falta son más trabajos críticos."[2] ["While there is an abundance of creative writing by women, there is definitely a need for more critical works."] Elaine Fido, in referring to essays such as those presented in "The Female Presence in

---

*Editors' note: Compiled in 1987.

373

Caribbean Literature", writes: " . . . [these critics] seek to redress a balance, to look at Caribbean literature, male or female oriented, from a focus which is sympathetic to women and committed to the portrayal of their reality in literature."[3]

Thus Caribbean literary criticism in the period before the 1970's seemed to deal almost exclusively with the interpretation of writings by men. The stereotyped images of women created and conveyed by many of these writers tended to be the prevailing images which influenced attitudes to women even in real life.

During the internationally recognized decade of women, efforts were made to correct this unevenness. Feminist presses were established, conferences and seminars held so that issues which affected women could find public expression. In seeking to redress the imbalance, however, profeminist critics eschewed vindictiveness. Naomi Lindstrom in a bibliographic essay states: "Instead of an attack on male authors, there has been a renewed interest in and a vigorous promotion of female writers. Various activities have sought to bring women's writings the critical and popular attention they have often lacked."[4] Of the French-speaking West Indies Maryse Condé has this to say: "En résumé, on chercherait vainement a travers les romans des écrivains femmes des Antilles l'écho tapageur de revendications féministes et de la haine du mâle perçu comme dominant."[5] ["In short, the novels of Caribbean women writers do not appear to reflect a strident feminism or a hatred of the 'dominant' male."]

The content of this bibliography, then, in a measure reflects the recent kindling of interest in Caribbean women writers. The listing does not claim to be exhaustive. The main emphasis of material included is on the image and role of women in the literary works of male and female writers from the Francophone, Anglophone and Hispanic Caribbean. It is readily conceded that the cause of parity of treatment has not prevailed over a compiler's enthusiasm for the English-speaking Caribbean.

A special effort has been made to list seminar and conference papers, some produced by the non-traditional methods, the in-house cyclostyled papers, which are therefore likely to be little publicised. Papers presented by members of the University of the West Indies language and literature departments often fit into this category. The recent publication, *Journal of West Indian Literature*, should in time make studies such as these more readily and widely available.

Although the primary concern is with creative literature, some sociological and socio-political studies dealing with the status of women in the Caribbean are also listed, mainly in the Bibliographies and General Works section. Represented in this section are the ideas of writers such as Merle Hodge, Erna Brodber and Phyllis Allfrey, on subjects other than fiction. A few articles which discuss the image of women in calypsoes have also been included, the calypso being considered as a creative art form and a powerful vehicle for social commentary in Caribbean societies.

No attempt has been made in the arrangement of items to judge the literary merit of the authors whose works are discussed. All material, critical or biographical, which was found on the newer and little-known women writers of the Anglophone Caribbean, those whose works have not yet been subjected to critical scrutiny over time, has been included. In the Anglophone Caribbean, for example, except for Jean Rhys and Paule Marshall, most women writers have been given little critical attention.[6] Writers such as Erna Brodber, Lorna Goodison, Olive Senior, Zee Edgell, Merle Hodge, to name only a few of the contemporary women writers, must await publications such as the present one for an introduction to readers outside the Caribbean.

NOTES

1. Maryse Condé, "La littérature féminine de la Guadeloupe: recherche d'identité", *Présence Africaine*, No. 99/100 (1976), p.155.
2. Virginia Ramos Foster, "La crítica literaria de las profesoras norteamericanas ante las letras femeninas hispánicas", *Revista Interamericana de Bibliografía*, 30, (1980), p. 410.
3. Elaine Fido, "Introduction", *Bulletin of Eastern Caribbean Affairs* (Barbados), 11, No. 1 (March/April 1985), p. iii.
4. Naomi Lindstrom, "Feminist criticism of Latin American literature: bibliographic notes", *Latin American Research Review*, 15, No. 1 (1980), pp. 153-154.
5. Maryse Condé, *La parole des femmes: essais sur des romancières des Antilles de langue française* (Paris: Editions L'Harmattan, 1979), p. 39.
6. Elgin W. Mellown's bibliography on Jean Rhys is a very thorough work on that author (Elgin W. Mellown, *Jean Rhys: a Descriptive and Annotated Bibliography of Works and Criticism* (New York: Garland Publishing, 1984)). Whereas no bibliography of comparable scope exists for Marshall, Barbara Christian (Barbara Christian, *Black Women Novelists: the Development of a Tradition 1892-1976* (Westport, Conn.: Greenwood Press, 1980); "Paule Marshall (9 April 1929 -)", *Dictionary of Literary Biography*, c1984) and Eugenia Collier (Eugenia Collier, "The closing of the circle: movement from division to wholeness in Paule Marshall's fiction", in *Black Women Writers (1950-1980): a Critical Evaluation*, ed. Mari Evans (Garden City, N.Y.: Anchor Press/Doubleday, 1984)), among others, have helped to establish her reputation as a writer. By contrast, the works of women writers in the Hispanic Caribbean appear to have had greater exposure than those of the Anglophone writers. Virginia Ramos Foster, in her essay, is of the opinion that there is now a need for a more rigorous selection of those works which are deserving of deeper study. She cautions, " . . . debemos evitar el proceso mitizante de inflar y de sobrevalorizar toda y cualquier literatura femenina." (*loc. cit.*) [" . . . we should avoid the kind of unwarranted reverence which would involve according importance indiscriminately to *all* writings by women."]

BIBLIOGRAPHIES AND GENERAL WORKS

Alarcón, Norma and Sylvia Kossnar. *Bibliography of Hispanic Women Writers*. Chicano-Riqueño Studies bibliography series, no. 1. Bloomington, IN.: Chicano-Riqueño Studies, c1980. 86p.

Bell, Roseann P., Bettye J. Parker and Beverly Guy-Sheftall. "A selected bibliography of Caribbean women writers and general Caribbean literature including criticism, fiction, drama, and poetry." In their *Sturdy Black Bridges*. Garden City, New York: Anchor Press, 1979, pp. 410-417.

Brodber, Erna ed. *Perceptions of Caribbean Women: Towards a Documentation of Stereotypes*. Institute of Social and Economic Research (Eastern Caribbean). Women in the Caribbean Project, No. 5. Cave Hill, Barbados: ISER(EC), University of the West Indies, 1982. 62p.

Byrne, Pamela R. and Suzanne R. Ontiveros, eds. *Women in the Third World: a Historical Bibliography*. Santa Barbara, Calif.: ABC-Clio, 1986. 152p. [Chapter 6 - Women in Latin America and the West Indies]

Caribbean Documentation Centre. *A Selected Bibliography on Women and Development*. Port-of-Spain: ECLA Sub-regional Headquarters for the Caribbean, 1984. 34p.

Castro-Klarén, Sara. "La crítica literaria feminista y la escritora en América Latina." In *La Sartén por el Mango: Encuentro de Escritoras Latinoamericanas*. Ed. Patricia Elena González y Eliana Ortega. Rio Piedras, Puerto Rico: Ediciones Huracán, 1984, pp. 27-46.

Christian, Barbara. *Black Feminist Criticism: Perspectives on Black Women Writers*. New York: Pergamon Press, c1985, 260p.

_____. *Black Women Novelists: the Development of a Tradition 1892-1976*. Westport, Conn.: Greenwood Press, 1980. 275p.

Cohen-Stuart, Bertie A. *Women in the Caribbean: a Bibliography, Part Two*. Leiden, The Netherlands: Dept. of Caribbean Studies, Royal Institute of Linguistics and Anthropology, 1985. 246p.

Commissiong, Barbara and Marjorie Thorpe. "A selected bibliography of women writers in the Eastern Caribbean." *WLWE*, 17, No. 1 (1978), 279-304.

Cortina, Lyn Ellen Rice. *Spanish-American Women Writers: a Bibliographical Research Checklist*. New York: Garland Publishing, c1983. 292p.

Coulthard, G.R. *Race and Colour in Caribbean Literature*. London: Oxford, 1962. 152p. [See esp. Chapter VII, "The coloured woman in Caribbean poetry"]

Dance, Daryl, ed. *Fifty Caribbean Writers: a Bio-bibliographical and Critical Source Book*. Westport, Conn.: Greenwood Press, 1986. 530p. Includes bibliographies. [Includes articles on the works of Phyllis Shand Allfrey, Louise Bennett, Dionne Brand, Erna Brodber, Jean D'Costa, Merle Hodge, Marion Patrick Jones, Jamaica Kincaid, Jean Rhys and Sylvia Wynter]

Foster, David William. *Cuban Literature: a Research Guide*. New York: Garland Publishing, 1985. 522p.

Foster, Virginia Ramos. "La crítica literaria de las profesoras norteamericanas ante las letras femeninas hispánicas." *Revista Interamericana de Bibliografía*, 30, No. 4 (1980), 406-412. [Bibliographical survey]

Henry, F. and P. Wilson. "The status of women in Caribbean societies: an overview of their social, economic and sexual roles." *Social and Economic Studies*, 24, No. 2 (1975), 165-198.

Hodge, Merle. "Caribbean women face conflicting contradictory codes." *Caribbean Contact*, August 1985, 11, 13.

_____. "Whither the young Caribbean women." *Woman Speak* (Barbados), No. 17, April 1985, 4-6.

_____. "Young women and the development of stable family life in the Caribbean." *Savacou*, 13 (Gemini 1977), 39-44.

Hurston, Zora. "Women in the Caribbean." In *Voodoo Gods; an Enquiry into Native Myths and Magic in Jamaica and Haiti*. London: Dent and Sons, 1939, pp. 61-66.

King, Lloyd, ed. *La Mujer en la Literatura Caribeña*. St. Augustine, Trinidad: Dept. of French and Spanish Literature, University of the West Indies, [1984?].

Kemp, Yakini. "Woman and Woman Child: Bonding and Selfhood in Three West Indian Novels by Women." *Sage* 2:1(Spring, 1985), 24-27. [Discusses *Crick Crack Monkey, Beka Lamb* and *Jane and Louisa Will Soon Come Home*]

Knaster, Meri. *Women in Spanish America: an Annotated Bibliography from Pre-Conquest to Contemporary Times*. Boston: G.K. Hall, c1977. 696p.

Jackson, Richard L. *The Black Image in Latin American Literature*. Albuquerque: University of New Mexico Press, 1976. 174p.

Lindstrom, Naomi. "Feminist criticism of Latin American literature: bibliographic notes." *Latin American Research Review*, 15, No. 1 (1980), 151-159.

McCaffrey, Kathleen M. *Images of Women in the Literature of Selected Developing Countries*. Washington, D.C. Office of Women in Development, Agency for International Development, 1979. 220p. [Haiti and Jamaica among nations studied]

McKenzie, Hermione. "Introduction. Caribbean women: yesterday, today, tomorrow." *Savacou*, 13 (Gemini 1977), viii-xiv.

Mellown, Elgin W. *Jean Rhys: a Descriptive and Annotated Bibliography of Works and Criticism*. New York: Garland Publishing, 1984. 218 p.

Miller, Beth. *Mujeres en la Literatura*. Mexico: Fleischer Editora, 1978. 145p.

_____. "A random survey of the ratio of female poets to male in anthologies." In *Latin American Women Writers Yesterday and Today*. Ed. Yvette Miller, and Charles Tatum. Pittsburgh: Latin American Literary Review, 1977.

Miller, Yvette E. and Charles M. Tatum. *Latin American Women Writers: Yesterday and Today*. Proceedings of the First Conference on Women Writers from Latin America, 1975. Pittsburgh: Latin American Literary Review, 1977.

Ormerod, Beverley. *An Introduction to the French Caribbean Novel*. London, Heinemann, 1985. 152p.

Research Institute for the Study of Man. Library for Caribbean Research. *Women in the non-Hispanic Caribbean: a Selective Bibliography*. New York: Research Institute for the Study of Man, 1982. 12p.

Rowe, Maureen. "The woman in Rastafari." *Caribbean Quarterly*, 26, No. 4 (Dec. 1980), 13-21.

Rushing, Andrea B. "An annotated bibliography of images of black women in Black Literature." *CLA Journal*, 25, No. 2 (1981), 234-262.
_____. "An annotated bibliography of images of black women in Black Literature." *CLA Journal*, 21, (March 1978), 435-42.
Searing, S. *Introduction to Library Research in Women's Studies*. Boulder, Colorado: Westview Press, 1985. 257p.
Steady, Filomena C., ed. *The Black Woman Cross-culturally*. Cambridge, MA: Schenkman, 1981. 645p. Bibliography.
Woman Speak! A quarterly newsletter about Caribbean women. St. Michael, Barbados: Women and Development Unit (WAND), University of the West Indies.

FRANCOPHONE CARIBBEAN WRITERS

Bérnabé,Jean. "Le travail de l'ecriture chez Simone Schwarz-Bart." *Présence Africaine*, Nos. 121-22 (1982), 166-179.
Bruner, Charlotte and David Bruner. "Buchi Emecheta and Maryse Condé: contemporary writing from Africa and the Caribbean." *World Literature Today*, 59, No. 1 (Winter 1985), 9-13.
Bruner, David K. Rev. of *Hérémakhônon*, by Maryse Condé. *World Literature Today*, 51, No. 3 (Summer 1977), 494.
Cesaire, Ina. "La triade humaine dans le conte Antillais." *Présence Africaine*, Nos. 121-122 (1982), 142-153.
Charles, Christophe. "Evolution de la poesie féminine haitienne, 1876-1976." *Le Nouveau Monde*, supplément, 22 and 29 Octobre, 5, 12, 26 Novembre and 10 Décembre 1978.
_____. *La poesie féminine Haitienne (histoire et antologie). De Virgine Sampeur a nos Jours*. Port-au-Prince, Haiti: Editions Choucoune, 1980. 219p.
Condé, Maryse. "L'image de la petite fille dans la litterature féminine des Antilles." *Recherche Pédagogie & Culture*, 44 (1979), 89-93.
_____. "La littérature féminine de la Guadeloupe: recherche d'identité." *Présence Africaine*, No. 99/100 (1976), 155-156.
_____. "Man, woman and love in French Caribbean writing." *Caribbean Quarterly*, 27, No. 4 (Dec. 1981), ʼ31-36.
_____. *La parole des femmes: essais sur des romanciéres des Antilles de langue française*. Paris: Editions L'Harmattan, 1979. 136p.
_____. "La femme antillaise et l'avenir des Antilles francaises." *Croissance des jeune nations* 241(juillet-aout, 1982), 33-35.
Coulson, Sheila. "Politics and the female experience: an examination of *Beka Lamb* and *Hérémakhônon*." Paper presented at the Seventh Annual Conference on West Indian Literature at the University of Puerto Rico, March 25-28, 1987. 20 leaves.
Fanon, Frantz. *Peau noire, masques blancs*. Paris: Editions de Seuil, c1952. 237p.
Gardiner, Madeleine. *Visages de femmes portraits d'ecrivains: etude*. Port-au-Prince, Haiti: Prix Litteraire H. Deschamps, 1981. 199p.
Gautier, Arlette, ed. "Antillaises = West Indian Women." *Nouvelles Questions Feministes*, Paris. Special issue. No. 9/10 (Spring 1985).

Giletti-Abou, Marie-Josephe. "Imposture a la femme ou le raisonnement du n'importe quoi: apropos de *Femmes Antillaises* [Claudie Beauvue-Fougeyrolles], et de *La Parole des Femmes* [Maryse Condé]." *CARÉ* (Guadeloupe), 6 (May 1980), 173-176.

Hodge, Merle. "Novels on the French Caribbean intellectual in France." *Revista/ Review Interamericana*, 4, No. 2 (Summer 1976), 211-231.

Jeanne, Max. "French West-Indian Literature." *Présence Africaine*, Nos. 121-122 (1982), 135-139.

Laplaine, Jean. "Fantômes et fantasmagories de la négrité." Rev. of *Ti-Jean l'Horizon*, by Simone Schwarz-Bart. *CARÉ* (Guadeloupe), 5 (Jan. 1980), 151-156.

Latortue, Régine. "The black woman in Haitian society and literature." In *The Black Woman Cross-culturally*. Ed. Filomena C. Steady. Cambridge, Mass.: Schenkman Publishing, 1981, 535-560.

_____. "The woman in the Haitian novel." Diss. Yale University, 1982. 277p.

Legros, Gloria. "The image of women in Haitian popular music: the case of the mini jazzbands." Paper prepared [for] the 6th Annual Conference of the Society of Caribbean Studies, Hoddesdon, 1982.

Loncke, Joycelynne. "The image of the woman in Caribbean literature with special reference to *Pan Beat* and *Héré*makhônon." *Bim*, 16, No. 64 (December 1978), 272-281.

McCallister, Myrna J. Rev. of *Hérémakhônon*, by Maryse Condé. *Library Journal*, 107, No. 10 (May 15, 1982), 1009.

Manuel, Robert. *La lutte des femmes dans les romans de Jacques Stephen Alexis.* Port-au-Prince: Imprimerie Henri Deschamps, 1980. 119p.

Mimiko, Ajoke. "Néurose et psychose de devenir l'autre chez la femme antillaise a travers l'oeuvre de Michele Lacrosil." *Peuples noirs, peuples africains*, 32 (Mars-avril 1983), 136-146.

Ngate, Jonathan. "Maryse Condé and Africa: the making of a recalcitrant daughter?" *A Current Bibliography of African Affairs* 19:1 (1986-1987).

_____. "Reading Warner-Vieyra's *Juletane*." *Callaloo* No. 29, 9:4(Fall, 1986), 553-564.

Ormerod, Beverley. "The boat and the tree: Simone Schwarz-Bart's *The Bridge of Beyond*." In her *An Introduction to the French Caribbean Novel*. London: Heinemann, 1985, pp. 108-137.

Perinbaum, B. Marie. "The parrot and the phoenix: Frantz Fanon's view of the West Indian and Algerian woman." *Savacou*, 13 (Gemini 1977), 7-13.

Pluie et vent sur Télumée Miracle de Simone Schwarz-Bart. Textes/Etudes/ Documents. Paris: Editions Caribeennes, 1979. 129p.

Rice-Maximin, Micheline. "Some recent Guadeloupean poets and novelists." San Antonio, Texas. Trinity University, n.d. 31 leaves. Unpublished paper.

Risden, Winnie. "*The Bridge of Beyond* . . . a review." *Savacou*, 13 (Gemini 1977), 45-47.

Scarboro, Ann Armstrong. "Womanist perspectives in the novels of Maryse Condé." Boulder, Colorado, December 1985. 18 leaves. Unpublished.

Scharfman, Ronnie. "Mirroring and mothering in Simone Schwarz-Bart's *Pluie en vent sur Télumée Miracle* and Jean Rhys' *Wide Sargasso Sea*." *Yale French Studies*, No. 62 (1981), 96.

Tardiew-Feldman, Yvette. "Une romancière Haïtienne méconnue: Annie Desroy (1893-1948)." *Conjonction*, 124 (août 1974), 35-54.

Wilson, Betty. "Sexual, racial and national politics: Jacqueline Manicom's *Mon examen de blanc.*" Paper presented at the Seventh Annual Conference on West Indian Literature at the University of Puerto Rico, March 25-28, 1987. 10p. [Draft].

Zimra, Clarisse. " 'An actor without feet does not interest me': an interview with Guadeloupe's Sarah Maldoror, actor, film-maker, self-professed trickster and overall maverick, with notes and an introduction." Unpublished paper n.d.

――――. "Negritude in the feminine mode: the case of Martinique and Guadeloupe." *Journal of Ethnic Studies*, 12, No. 1 (Spring 1984), 53-77.

――――. "Patterns of liberation in contemporary women writers." *L'Esprit Créateur* (Lawrence, Kansas), 17, No. 2 (Summer 1977), 103. [Discusses the work of Michele Lacrosil and Jacqueline Manicom]

――――. "A woman's place: cross-sexual perceptions in race relations: the case of Mayotte Capécia and Abdoulaye Sadji." *Folio*, August 1978. Special issue on women writers.

ANGLOPHONE CARIBBEAN WRITERS

Abbott, Keith. "Some thoughts on Jean Rhys's fiction." *The Review of Contemporary Fiction*, B.S. Johnson/Jean Rhys number (Summer 1985), 112-114.

Abel, Elizabeth. "Women and schizophrenia: the fiction of Jean Rhys." *Contemporary Literature*, 20, No. 2(Spring 1979), 155-177.

Abraham-van der Mark, Eva. "Jean Rhys, de buiten-staander." *Bzzlletin*, No. 95 (April 1982), 22-28. [Biography of the late writer]

Aho, William R. "Sex conflict in Trinidad calypsoes 1969-1979." *Revista/Review Interamericana*, 11, No. 1 (1981), 76-81.

Allen, Zita. "Close but no cigar." Rev. of *Annie John*, by Jamaica Kincaid. *Freedomways*, 25 (1985), 116-119.

"Allfrey, Phyllis Shand." In *Caribbean Writers: a Bio-bibliographical-critical Encyclopedia*. Ed. David E. Herdeck. Washington, D.C.: Three Continents Press, 1979, 18-20.

Anderson, Paula G. "Jean Rhys' *Wide Sargasso Sea*: the other side/both sides now." *Caribbean Quarterly*, 28, Nos. 1-2 (1982), 57-65.

――――. "Jean Rhys' *Wide Sargasso Sea*: the other side/both sides now." In *Conference on Critical Approaches to West Indian Literature: a Compilation of Position Papers*. Ed. Roberta Knowles and Erika Smilowitz. St. Thomas, U.S. Virgin Islands: Humanities Division, College of the Virgin Islands, 1981, 237-239.

Andre, Irving W. "The social world of Phyllis Shand Allfrey's *The Orchid House.*" *Caribbean Quarterly*, 29, No. 2 (June 1983), 11-21.

Angier, Carole. *Jean Rhys*. Lives of modern women [series]. Harmondsworth, England: Penguin, 1985. [126]p. Bibliography. [A biographical study]

Apandaye, Eintou. "The Caribbean woman as writer." In *Sturdy Black Bridges: Visions of Black Women in Literature*. Eds. Roseanne P. Bell, Bettye J. Parker and Beverly Guy-Sheftall. Garden City, New York: Anchor Press, 1979, 62-68.

Ashcom, Jane N. *The Novels of Jean Rhys: Two Kinds of Modernism*. Diss. Temple University 1982. Ann Arbor, Michigan: University Microfilms, 1984. 245p. Bibliography.

Austin, R.L. "Understanding calypso content: a critique and alternative explanation." *Caribbean Quarterly*, 22, Nos. 2 & 3 (1976), 74-83.

Baer, E.R. "The sisterhood of Jane Eyre and Antoinette Cosway." In *The Voyage In: Fictions of Female Development*. Eds. Elizabeth Abel, Marianne Hirsch, and Elizabeth Langland. Hanover, New Haven: Published for Dartmouth College by University Press of New England, 1983, 131-148.

Barratt, Harold. "A shuttered cleavage: Marion Jones's tormented people." *WLWE*, 19, No. 1 (1980), 57-62.

Barrow, Christine. "Male image of women in Barbados." *Social and Economic Studies*, 35, No. 3 (1986), 51-64.

Barthold, Bonnie J. "Women: chaos and redemption." In *Black Time: Fiction of Africa, the Caribbean, and the United States*. New Haven: Yale University Press, 1981, 99-136.

Baugh, Edward. "Goodison on the road to Heartease." *Journal of West Indian Literature* (Barbados), 1, No. 1 (Oct. 1986), 13-22.

Berger, Gertrude. "Rhys, de Beauvoir, and the woman in love." *The Review of Contemporary Fiction*. B.S. Johnson/Jean Rhys number (Summer 1985), 139-145.

Berrian, Brenda F. "Snapshots of childhood life in Jamaica Kincaid's fiction." Unpublished paper. n.d.

Boxill, Anthony. "V.S. Naipual's *Guerrillas:* 'violate, humiliate, destroy her'." Cave Hill, Barbados, [1978?]. 10p. Unpublished paper.

Brandmark, Wendy. "The power of the victim. A study of *Quartet, After Leaving Mr. MacKenzie* and *Voyage in the Dark* by Jean Rhys." *Kunapipi*, 8, No. 2 (1986), 21-29.

Bromley, Roger. "Reaching a clearing: gender and politics in *Beka Lamb*." *Wasafiri*, 1, No. 2 (Spring 1985), 10-14.

Brown, Bev. E.L. "Mansong and matrix: a radical experiment." *Kunapipi*, 7, Nos. 2 & 3 (1985), 68-79. [Discusses the work of Zee Edgell and Jean Rhys]

Bulletin of Eastern Caribbean Affairs (Barbados), 11, No. 1 (March-April 1985). Special issue "The Female Presence in Caribbean Literature."

Calio, Louise. "A rebirth of the goddess in contemporary women poets of the spirit." *The New Voices* (Trinidad & Tobago), 12, No. 23 (1984), 41-51.

Campbell, Elaine. "An expatriate at home: Dominica's Elma Napier." *Kunapipi*, 4, No. 1 (1982), 82-93.

_____. "*In the Cabinet:* a novelistic rendition of Federation politics." *Ariel*, 17, No. 4 (Oct. 1986), 117-125.

_____. "Introduction." [to *Orchid House*, by P. Shand Allfrey]. London: Virago Press, 1982, pp. vii-xvi. [A new introduction to the novel which was first published in 1953]

_____. "Oroonoko's heir: the West Indies in the late eighteenth century novels by woman." *Caribbean Quarterly*, 25, Nos. 1-2 (March-June 1979), 80-84.

_____. "A report from Dominica, B.W.I." *WLWE*, 17, No. 1 (April 1978), 305-316.

_____. "Two West Indian heroines: Bita Plant and Fola Piggott." *Caribbean Quarterly*, 29, No. 2 (June 1983), 22-29.

Casey, Nancy J. Fulton. "Jean Rhys's *Wide Sargasso Sea:* exterminating the white cockroach." *Revista/Review Americana*, 4, No. 3 (1974), 340-349.

_____. "The liberated woman in Jean Rhys's later short fiction." *Revista/Review Interamericana*, 4, No. 2 (1974), 264-272.

_____. "Study in the alienation of a creole woman: Jean Rhys's *Voyage in the Dark*." *Caribbean Quarterly*, 19, No. 3 (1973), 95-102.

Christian, Barbara. "Paule Marshall (9 April 1929 -)." In *Dictionary of Literary Biography*. Ed. Thadious M. Davis and Trudier Harris. Detroit: Gale Research, c1984, 161-170.

_____. "Sculpture and space: the interdependency of character and culture in the novels of Paule Marshall." In her *Black Women Novelists: the Development of a Tradition 1892-1976*. Westport, Conn.: Greenwood Press, 1980, 80-136.

Cobham-Sander, C. Rhonda. "The creative writer and West Indian society: Jamaica 1900-1950." Diss. University of St. Andrews, 1981. [Chap. 4: Women in Jamaican literature 1900-1950, 175-252]

_____. "Getting out of the Kumbla: review of *Jane and Louisa Will Soon Come Home*." *Race Today*, 14 (Dec. 1981-Jan. 1982), 33-34.

_____. "Making it through the night." Review essay of *Because the Dawn Breaks*, by Merle Collins. *New Beacon Reviews*, No. 2/3 (Nov. 1986), 72-77. [Merle Collins is a poet from Grenada]

Collier, Eugenia. "The closing of the circle: movement from division to wholeness in Paule Marshall's fiction." In *Black Women Writers (1950-1980): a Critical Evaluation*. Ed. Mari Evans. Garden City: N.Y.: Anchor Press/Doubleday, 1984, 295-315.

Cooper, Carolyn. "That cunny Jamma oman: the female sensibility in the poetry of Louise Bennett." *Bulletin of Eastern Caribbean Affairs* (Barbados), 11, No. 1 (March-April 1985), 13-27.

_____. "The fertility of the gardens of women." Review essay of *Jane and Louisa Will Soon Come Home*, by Erna Brodber. *New Beacon Reviews*, Nos. 2/3 (Nov. 1986), 139-147.

Coulson, Sheila. "Politics and the female experience: an examination of *Beka Lamb* and *Hérémakhônon*." Paper presented at the Seventh Annual Conference on West Indian Literature at the University of Puerto Rico, March 25-28, 1987. 20 leaves.

Davies, Barrie. "Neglected West Indian writers." Rev. of *The Orchid House*, by Phyllis Allfrey. *WLWE*, 11, No. 2 (Nov. 1972), 81-83.

Davies, Carole Boyce. "Black woman's journey into self: a womanist reading of Paule Marshall's *Praisesong for the Widow*." *Matatu* (West Germany), Heft 1:1 1987):

_____. "Developing a Voice. Creative Modes in Caribbean Women's Fiction." MLA paper presented at the MLA Annual Meeting, December, 1986. 27pp.

_____. "The indictment of phallicism in Lovelace's *The Wine of Astonishment*." Unpublished paper, 1986.

_____. "The Mammy water figure in the African and Caribbean novel." In her "Oral tradition and the Anglophone African and Caribbean novel." Diss. University of Ibadan, 1977.

_____. Rev. of *Critical Issues in West Indian Literature: Selected Papers from West Indian Literature Conferences, 1981-1983*. Ed. by Smilowitz and Knowles in *Research in African Literatures* 18:2 (Summer, 1987), 229-232.

"Death of a native daughter." Editorial. *The Nation* (Barbados), Weekend ed., 14 Feb. 1986. [Tribute to Phyllis Shand Allfrey]

Dieke, Ikenna. "Caribbean literature: the female as personal and collective root. 2. Wilson Harris: the woman named Mariella." In his "Archetypal patterns in African, Afro-American and Caribbean literature." Diss. Southern Illinois University at Carbondale, 1983. Ann Arbor, Michigan: Microfilms International, 1986, 76-77, 88-93.

Down, Lorna. "Singing one's own song: woman and selfhood in recent West Indian fiction. Thesis (M.A.) University of the West Indies, 1985. 73 leaves. [Discusses *Beka Lamb*, by Zee Edgell, *Crick Crack Monkey*, by Merle Hodge, and *Jane and Louisa Will Soon Come Home*, by Erna Brodber]

Durix, Jean Pierre. "Review of *Jane and Louisa Will Soon Come Home*." *Afram*, 14 (1982).

Eko, Ebele. "Beyond the myth of confrontation: a comparative study of African and African-American female protagonists." *Ariel*, 17, No. 4 (Oct. 1986), 139-152. [Characters chosen for discussion include Selina Boyce of *Browngirl, Brownstones*, by Paule Marshall]

Elder, J.S. "The male-female conflict in calypso." *Caribbean Quarterly*, 14, No. 3 (1968), 23-41.

Emery, Mary Lou. "Modernism and the modern woman: a socio-critical approach to the novels of Jean Rhys." Diss. Stanford Univ., 1982. Ann Arbor, Michigan: Univ. Microfilms International 1984. 314p. Bibliography.

Espinet, Rambai. "A short account of the life and work of Phyllis Shand Allfrey." *Bulletin of Eastern Caribbean Affairs* (Barbados), 12, No. 1 (March/April 1986), 33-35.

Fido, Elaine Savory. "Christine Craig's most recent poems: a cause for celebration." Rev. of *Quadrille for Tigers*. *Caribbean Contact*, November 1984, p. 15.

_____. "Crossroads: Third World criticism and commitment with reference to African-Caribbean women poets." *ACLALS Bulletin*, 7th ser. 4 (1986), 10-25.

_____. "Feminist and womanist discourses: West Indian/American lesbian writers." [Paper presented at] Sixth Annual Conference on West Indian Literature. St. Augustine, Trinidad, May 1986. [19]p.

_____. Judgements on art and the macho aesthetic of Derek Walcott." *Journal of Commonwealth Literature*, 21, No. 1 (July 1986), 109-119.

_____., "The politics of colours and the politics of writing in the fiction of Jean Rhys." Paper presented at the Seventh Annual Conference on West Indian Literature at the University of Puerto Rico, March 25-28, 1987. 28p.

_____. "The psycho-pathology of motherhood in *Pan Beat*." Unpublished paper, 1986.

————. "Psycho-sexual aspects of the woman in V.S. Naipaul's fiction." In *West Indian Literature and its Social Context: Proceedings of the Fourth Annual Conference on West Indian Literature.* Ed. Mark A. McWatt. St. Michael, Barbados: Dept. of English, University of the West Indies, Cave Hill, 1985, 78-94.

————. "Radical woman: woman and theatre in the Anglophone Caribbean." In *Critical Issues in West Indian Literature.* Ed. Erika Sollish Smilowitz [and] Roberta Quarles Knowles. Parkersburg, Iowa: Caribbean Books, 1984, 33-45.

————. "Where do we go from here? An overview of present directions in gender-focussed criticism of Caribbean literature." Paper delivered at the Inaugural Seminar of the Women and Development Studies Programme, University of the West Indies, held at Mount St. Benedict, Trinidad, Sept. 7-20, 1986. 20p.

————. "Woman on women: how far to disclose?" *Bulletin on Eastern Caribbean Affairs,* 11, No. (March-April 1985), 35-44.

Finch, Jacqueline B. "Merle Hodge's *Crick Crack Monkey*: textual adroitness." St. Croix, U.S. Virgin Islands, College of the Virgin Islands, 1985. 17 leaves. Unpublished paper.

Ford-Smith, Honor. "Sistren: exploring women's problems through drama." *Jamaica Journal,* 19, No. 1 (February-April 1986), 2-12.

————. "SISTREN - woman's theatre - a model for consciousness raising." In *Journey in the Shaping. Report of the First Symposium on Women in Caribbean Culture - July 24, 1981.* Ed. Margaret Hope. St. Michael, Barbados: Women and Development Unit (WAND), University of the West Indies, 1981, 52-58.

————. "Women, the arts and Jamaican society: the work of SISTREN Collective in context." Paper presented at the Fifth Annual Conference of the Society of Caribbean Studies, 26-28 May 1981, at High Leigh, Herts., England.

Fullerton, Janet. "Women in Trinidadian life and literature." *The New Voices* (Trinidad & Tobago), 5, No. 9 (March 1977), 9-31.

Gilkes, Michael. "The Madonna Pool: (woman as muse of identity)." [Paper presented at] Sixth Annual Conference on West Indian Literature. St. Augustine, Trinidad, May 1986. 21p.

Gill, Margaret. *"Lights - a review." Bulletin of Eastern Caribbean Affairs,* 11, No. 1 (March-April 1985), 82-83. [Reviews the performance of a dramatic presentation about the lives of women, given in Barbados by the Stage One Players]

Gloudon, Barbara. "Fifty years of laughter. The Hon. Louise Bennett, O.J." *Jamaica Journal,* 19, No. 3 (1986), 2-10.

Gonzalez, Anson. "A new & important voice in Caribbean poetry: Olive Senior's *Talking of Trees." The New Voices* (Trinidad & Tobago), 14, No. 28 (Sept. 1986), 31-34.

Gonzalez, Sylvia. "Cramped creativity." Guest editorial. *The New Voices* (Trinidad & Tobago), 3, No. 5 (1975), 3-6, 31.

Goodison, Lorna. Interview. With Norval Nadi Edwards. *Pathways: a Journal of Creative Writing* (Jamaica), 2, No. 4 (Dec. 1984), 8-12 (Part 1); 3 No. 5 (Dec. 1985), 3-8 (Part 2).

Greene, Sue. "Six Caribbean novels by women." *New West Indian Guide*, 58, Nos. 1 & 2 (1984), 61-74.

Griffith, Cheryl. "The woman as whore in the novels of V.S. Naipaul." In *West Indian Literature and its Social Context: Proceedings of the Fourth Annual Conference on West Indian Literature*. Ed. Mark A.McWatt. St. Michael, Barbados: Dept. of English, University of the West Indies, Cave Hill, 1985, 95-106.

Guppy, Shuska. "Novel choice: *Wide Sargasso Sea*, by Jean Rhys." *Observer Magazine*, 4 November 1979, 130.

Gúzman, Daisy Santos. Rev. of *Abeng*, by Michelle Cliff. *Sargasso* (Puerto Rico), No. 2 (1984), 65-66.

Harris, Wilson. Interview. With Jane Wilkinson. *Kunapipi*, 8, No. 2 (1986), 30-45. [Harris comments on the women in his novels]

Harrison, Nancy R. "An introduction to the writing practice of Jean Rhys: the novel as women's text." Diss. Univ. of Texas at Austin, 1983. Ann Arbor, Michigan: Univ. Microfilms International, 1983. 516p. Bibliography.

Hemenway, Robert. "Sex and politics in V.S. Naipaul." *Studies in the Novel* (Denton, Tx.), 14, No. 2 (Summer 1982), 189-202.

Hodge, Merle. Interview. *Woman Speak* (Barbados), No. 18, July/December 1985, 6-7. [Discusses women in Trinidad]

_____. "Introduction." [to] *Perceptions of Caribbean Women: towards a Documentation of Stereotypes*. Institute of Social and Economic Research (Eastern Caribbean). Women in the Caribbean Project, No. 5. Ed. Erna Brodber. Cave Hill, Barbados: ISER(EC), University of the West Indies, 1982, viii-xiii.

_____. "The shadow of the whip." In *Is Massa Day Dead?: Black Moods in the Caribbean*. Ed. Orde Coombs. New York: Anchor Press/Doubleday, 1974, 111-[119].

Hope Margaret ed. *Journey in the Shaping. Report of the First Symposium on Women in Caribbean Culture - July 24, 1981*. Ed. Margaret Hope. St. Michael, Barbados: Women and Development Unit (WAND), University of the West Indies, 1981, pp. 52-58. [Report presents summaries of papers given, discussions and other oral presentations and performances under such broad topics as "Traditional art and images of the early Caribbean woman," "Caribbean woman in the twentieth century and the use of her art to express this reality" and "the Caribbean woman as artist today"]

Hunter, Charles. "Belize's first novel, *Beka Lamb*." *Belizean Studies*, 10, No. 6 (Dec. 1982), 14-21.

Insanally, Annette. "Contemporary female writing in the Caribbean." *The Caribbean Novel in Comparison*. Proceedings of the Ninth Conference of Hispanists, 7-9 April 1986, University of the West Indies, St. Augustine, Trinidad. Ed. Ena V. Thomas. St. Augustine, Trinidad: Dept. of French and Spanish Literature, University of the West Indies, 1986, 115-141. [Discusses the work of Hazel Campbell and Jamaica Kincaid]

_____. "Eroticism as an expression of the consciousness of self in Rosario Ferré's *Fabulas de la Garza Desangrada* and Lorna Goodison's *Tamarind Season*." Paper presented at the Fifth Conference on West Indian Literature.

St. Thomas, Virgin Islands, May 23-24, 1985. 13p.

_____. "Sexual politics in contemporary female writing in the Caribbean." Paper presented at the Seventh Annual Conference on West Indian Literature at the University of Puerto Rico, March 25-28, 1987. 17p.

James, Selma. *The Ladies and the Mammies: Jane Austen and Jean Rhys.* Bristol, England: Falling Wall Press, 1983. 96p.

Lawrence, Leota S. "The mother-child relationship in selected works of British Caribbean literature." *Western Journal of Black Studies*, 5, No. 1 (1981), 10-17.

_____. "Three West Indian heroines: an analysis." *CLA Journal*, 21, No. 2 (Dec. 1977), 238-250. [Discusses the work of Jean Rhys, Claude McKay and Merle Hodge]

_____. "Women in Caribbean literature: the African presence." *Phylon*, 44, No. 1 (Spring 1983), 1-11.

Leigh, Nancy J. "Mirror, mirror: the development of female identity in Jean Rhys's fiction." *WLWE*, 25, No. 2 (Autumn 1985), 270-285.

Lent, John A. "The Allfrey story." Appendix E of his "Commonwealth Caribbean mass media: historical, cultural, economic and political aspects." Diss. Univ. of Iowa, 1972. Ann Arbor, Michigan: University Microfilms International, 1985, 501-504. [Writer reports an interview with Phyllis Allfrey about the establishment and operation of the *Star* newspaper in Dominica]

Leseur, Geta J. "The Bildungs-roman in Afro-American and Afro-Caribbean fiction: an integrated consciousness." Diss. Indiana Univ., 1982. 230p.

Lindroth, Colette. "Whispers outside the room: the haunted fiction of Jean Rhys." *The Review of Contemporary Fiction*, B.S. Johnson/Jean Rhys number (Summer 1985), 135-139.

Loncke, Joycelynne. "The image of the woman in Caribbean literature with special reference to *Pan Beat* and *Hérémakhônon*." *Bim*, 16, No. 64 (December 1978), 272-281.

López de Villegas, Consuelo. "Matriarchs and man-eaters: Naipaul's fictional women." *Revista/Review Interamericana*, 7, No. 4 (Winter 1977/78), 605-614.

Lyn, Gloria. "Naipaul's *Guerrillas:* fiction and its social context." In *West Indian Literature and its Social Context: Proceedings of the Fourth Annual Conference on West Indian Literature.* Ed. Mark A. McWatt. St. Michael, Barbados: Dept. of English, University of the West Indies, Cave Hill, 1985, 130-140.

McWatt, Mark. "Wives and other victims: women in the novels of Roy A.K. Heath." Dept. of English, University of the West Indies, Cave Hill, seminar paper, 4 January 1986. 17p.

_____. "The whore-madonna figure in the early novels of Wilson Harris." *Bulletin of Eastern Caribbean Affairs* (Barbados), 11, No. 1 (March-April 1985), 59-69.

Mellown, Elgin W. "Character and themes in the novels of Jean Rhys." In *Contemporary Women Novelists: a Collection of Critical Essays.* Ed. Patricia M. Spacks. Englewood Cliffs, N.J.: Prentice-Hall, 1977, 118-136.

[Reprinted from *Contemporary Literature*, 13 August 1972, "with slight variations by the author", by permission of the publisher]

Milton, Edith. Rev. of *At the Bottom of the River*, by Jamaica Kincaid. *New York Times Book Review*, 15 June 1984, 22.

Mohr, Eugene V. Rev. of *Beka Lamb*, by Zee Edgell. *Revista/Review Interamericana*, 11, No. 4 (1981), 619-620.

Mordecai, Pamela. "A crystal of ambiguities: metaphors for creativity and the art of writing in Derek Walcott's *Another Life*." Paper presented to the Fifth Conference on West Indian Literature, College of the Virgin Islands, U.S. Virgin Islands, 1985.

_____. " 'Into this beautiful garden' - some comments on Erna Brodber's *Jane and Louisa*." *Caribbean Quarterly*, 29, No. 2 (June 1983), 44-53.

_____. "The West Indian male sensibility in search of itself: some comments on *Nor Any Country, The Mimic Men* and *The Secret Ladder*." *WLWE*, 21, No. 3 (Autumn 1982), 629-644.

_____. "Wooing with words: some comments on the poetry of Lorna Goodison." *Jamaica Journal*, 45 [1981?], 34-40.

Morgan, Paula Eleanor. "The love relationship: a study of male/female interaction in selected West Indian authors." Thesis M. Phil. Univ. of the West Indies, 1984. 393 leaves. Bibliography.

Morris, Mervyn. "The dialect poetry of Louise Bennett." In *Critics on Caribbean Literature*. Ed. Edward Baugh. London: George Allen & Unwin, 1978, pp. 137-148.

_____. "Louise Bennett in print." In *Conference on Critical Approaches to West Indian Literature: a Compilation of Position Papers*. Ed. Roberta Knowles and Erika Smilowitz. St. Thomas, U.S. Virgin Islands: Humanities Division, College of the Virgin Islands, 1981, 136-159.

_____. "On reading Louise Bennett seriously." *Jamaica Journal*, 1, No. 1 (Dec. 1967), 69-74.

_____. Rev. of *Quadrille for Tigers: Poems*, by Christine Craig. *Jamaica Journal*, 18, No. 4 (Nov. 1985-Jan. 1986), 62.

Nebeker, Helen. *Jean Rhys: Woman in Passage. A Critical Study of the Novels of Jean Rhys*. Montreal, Canada: Eden Press Women's Pubns., 1981. 223p. Bibliography.

Nunez-Harrell, Elizabeth. "Beauty from decay." Rev. of *The Orchid House*, by Phyllis Allfrey. *CRNLE Reviews J.*, No. 1 (July 1983), 97-99.

_____. "The paradoxes of belonging: the white West Indian woman in fiction." *Modern Fiction Studies*, 13, No. 1 (Summer 1985), 281-293.

O'Callaghan, Evelyn. " 'The bottomless abyss': 'mad' women in some Caribbean novels." *Bulletin of Eastern Caribbean Affairs*, Barbados, 11, No. 1 (March-April 1985), 45-58.

_____. "Driving women mad." Rev. of *Beka Lamb*, by Zee Edgell. *Jamaica Journal*, 16, No. 2 (May 1983), 71.

_____. "The outsider's voice: white creole women novelists in the Caribbean literary tradition." *Journal of West Indian Literature* (Barbados), 1, No. 1 (Oct. 1986), 74-88.

_____. "Rediscovering the natives of my person: a review of Erna Brodber, *Jane and Louisa Will Soon Come Home*", *Jamaica Journal*, 16, No. 3 (August 1983), 61-64.

_____. Rev. of *Summer Lightning and Other Stories*, by Olive Senior. *Journal of West Indian Literature* (Barbados), 1, No. 1 (Oct. 1986), 92-94.

_____. Rev. of *Woman's Tongue*, by Hazel Campbell. *Jamaica Journal*, 19, No. 2 (May-July 1986), 50-51.

_____. " 'Vive la difference': political directions in short stories by West Indian women writers." Paper presented at the Seventh Annual Conference on West Indian Literature at the University of Puerto Rico, March 25-28, 1987. 29p. [Discusses work of Olive Senior, Hazel Campbell, the Sistren collective, Opal Palmer Adisa]

Parker, Dorothy. "Review of *Jane and Louisa Will Soon Come Home*." *Black Books Bulletin*, 7 (1981-82), 57-58.

Pattulio, Polly. "Caribbean Chronicle." *Observer Magazine*, 22 July 1984. pp. 22-25. [On Phyllis Shand Allfrey]

Pearn, Julie. "Woman time to come - a portrait of four Jamaican women poets." Paper [prepared for] the Sixth Annual Conference of the Society for Caribbean Studies at Hoddesdon, 1982. [The poets - Louise Bennett, Lorna Goodison, Jarika Birhan and Claudette Richardson]

Plante, David. *Difficult Women: A Memoir of Three*. New York: Atheneum, 1983. 173p. [Includes Jean Rhys]

Pollard, Velma. "Cultural connections in Paule Marshall's *Praise Song for the Widow*." *WLWE*, 25, No. 2 (Autumn 1985), 285-298.

Porter, Dennis. "Of heroines and victims: Jean Rhys and Jane Eyre." *The Massachusetts Review*, 171, No. 3 (1976), 540-552.

Pyne-Timothy, Helen. "Perceptions of the black woman in the work of Claude McKay." *CLA J.*, 19, No. 2 (December 1975), 152-164.

_____. "Women and sexuality in the later novels of V.S. Naipaul." *WLWE*, 25, No. 2 (Autumn 1985), 298-306.

Reddock, Rhoda E. "Women and slavery in the Caribbean: a feminist perspective." *Latin American Perspectives*, (Winter 1985).

Reyes, Elma. "Women in calypso." *Woman Speak* (Barbados), No. 12, 1983. 12-13, 20.

Robinson, Jeff. "Mother and child in three novels by George Lamming." *Release*, Nos. 6 & 7 (1979), 75-83.

Rohlehr, Gordon. "The calypsoes of the thirties." From the Archives Gordon Rohlehr retrieves images of men and women. *Trinidad & Tobago Rev.*, 8, No. 1 (Dimanche Gras, March 1987), 9-10, 14-16 (Part One); *Trinidad & Tobago Rev.*, 9, No. 1 (Pink Poui, April 1987), 11-14 (Part Two).

Rutherford, Anna. Rev. of *Summer Lightning and Other Stories*, by Olive Senior, *Kunapipi*, 8, No. 2 (1986), 114-115.

Salick, Roydon. "Naipaul's treatment of the white woman." *Bulletin of Eastern Caribbean Affairs* (Barbados), 11, No. 1 (March-April 1985), 28-34.

Saney, Virginia A. "An examination of the image of the female in West Indian drama." Thesis M.A. Univ. of the West Indies, 1981. 122 leaves. Bibliography.

Savacou, No. 13 (Gemini 1977). ["Caribbean woman." Special issue. Ed. Lucille Mathurin Mair]

Schipper, Mineke, ed. *Unheard Words: Women and Literature in Africa, the Arab World, Asia, the Caribbean and Latin America*. London: Allison & Busby, 1985. 288p.

Senior, Olive. Interview. With Anna Rutherford. *Kunapipi*, 8, No. 2 (1986), 11-20.

Shipley, William M. "History's phoenix: black woman in literature." In *Afro-World: Adventures in Ideas*. Ed. O.R. Dathorne. Coral Gables, Florida: Association of Caribbean Studies and the University of Wisconsin, Wisconsin System, 1984, 15-23.

Shorey-Bryan, Norma. "The making of male/female relationships in the Caribbean." *Bulletin of Eastern Caribbean Affairs* (Barbados), 11, No. 2 (May/June 1985), 34-38.

Sistren Magazine. Kingston, Jamaica.

Smilowtiz, Erika S. "Una Marson: woman before her time." *Jamaica Journal* 16, No. 2 (1983), 62-68.

_____. " 'Weary of life and all my heart's dull pain': the poetry of Una Marson." In *Critical Issues in West Indian Literature . . .* Ed. Erika S. Smilowitz and Roberta Q. Knowles. Parkersburg, Iowa: Caribbean Books, 1984, pp. 19-32.

Spillers, Hortense J. "*Chosen Place, Timeless People:* some figurations on the New World." In *Conjuring: Black Women Fiction and Literary Tradition*. Ed. Marjorie Pryse and Hortense J. Spillers. Bloomington: Indiana Univ. Press, c1985, 151-175.

Springer, Keane. "Image of women in the work of Caribbean writers." Paper prepared for the Conference on Caribbean Women in Culture, Barbados, 1980. Unpublished.

Steen, L.J. van der. "De man-vrouw relatie in de Caraibische bellettrie." (Male-female relations in Caribbean novels). Thesis M.A. Utrecht, 1970.

Talbert, Linda Lee. "Witchcraft in contemporary feminist literature." Diss. Univ. of Southern California, 1979.

Thieme, John. " 'Apparitions of disaster': Brontean parallels in *Wide Sargasso Sea* and *Guerrillas.*" *Journal of Commonwealth Literature*, 14, No. 1 (August 1979), 116-132.

Thorpe, Marjorie. "Beyond the Sargasso: the significance of the presentation of the woman in the West Indian novel." Diss. Queens University, Kingston, Ontario, 1975. 91p.

_____. "Challenging the stereotype: a re-reading of Merle Hodge's *Crick Crack Monkey.*" Paper presented at Sixth Conference on West Indian Literature, St. Augustine, Trinidad, May 1986. 8p.

_____. "The problem of cultural identification in *Crick Crack Monkey.*" *Savacou*, 13 (Gemini 1977), 31-38.

_____. "Women in culture - a literary review." In *Journey in the Shaping. Report of the First Symposium on Women in Caribbean Culture - July 24, 1981*. Ed. Margaret Hope. St. Michael, Barbados: Women and Development Unit (WAND), University of the West Indies, 1981, pp. 47-51.

Tiffin, Helen. "Mirror and mask: colonial motifs in the novels of Jean Rhys." *WLWE*, 17, No. 1 (April 1978), 328-341.

Trescott, Jacqueline. "Jamaica Kincaid: words and silences." *International Herald Tribune*, 29 April 1984, 8.

Wickham, John. "On going through the red: a comment on *Lights*." *Bulletin of Eastern Caribbean Affairs* (Barbados), 11, No. 1 (March-April 1985), 80-81. [Reviews the performance of a dramatic presentation about the lives of women, given in Barbados by the Stage One Players]

———. "Some women in West Indian fiction." *The Barbadienne*, Barbados Souvenir Magazine for International Women's Year 1975, 21-22.

Williams, Cheryl. "The role of women in Caribbean culture." *Bulletin of Eastern Caribbean Affairs* (Barbados), 11, No. 2 (May/June 1985), 46-50.

Wilson, Lucy. " 'Women must have spunks': Jean Rhys's West Indian outcasts." *Modern Fiction Studies*, 32, No. 3 (Autumn 1986), 439-448. [Discusses the strong black female characters in Rhys]

HISPANIC WRITERS

Acosta-Belen, Edna. "Ideología e imagenes de la mujer en la literatura Puertorriqueña contemporánea." In *La mujer en la sociedad puertorriqueña*. Ed. Edna Acosta-Belen. Rio Piedras, Puerto Rico: Ediciones Huracán, c1980, 125-156.

———. "Ideology and images of women in contemporary Puerto Rican literature." In *The Puerto Rican Woman*. Ed. Edna Acosta-Belen. New York: Praeger, 1979, 85-109.

Albert-Robatto, Matilde. "Reflexiones en torno a la actual poesía femenina puertorriqueña." *Revista/Review Interamericana*, 12, No. 3 (Fall 1982), 462-473.

Arrillaga, María. "La narrativa de la mujer puertorriqueña en la década del setenta." *Homines*, 8, No. 1 (1984), 327-334.

Barradas,Efrain. Rev. of *Vírgenes y martíres*, by Ana Lydia Vega, and Carmen Lugo Filippi. *Revista/Review Interamericana*, 11, No. 3 (1981), 465-466.

Bryan, T. Avril. "Virginity: contrasting views in the works of Miguel de Unamuno and Gabriel García Márquez." In *La Mujer en la Literatura Caribeña*. Ed. Lloyd King. St. Augustine, Trinidad: Dept. of French and Spanish Literature, University of the West Indies, [1984?], 168-184.

Carter, Sheila. "Women in Carlos Guillermo Wilson's *Chombo*." In *La Mujer en la Literatura Caribeña*. Ed. Lloyd King. St. Augustine, Trinidad: Dept. of French and Spanish Literature, University of the West Indies, [1984?], 69-93.

Cypess, Sandra Messinger. "La dramaturgia femenina y su contexto sociocultural." *Latin American Theatre Review*, 13, No. 2 Supplement (Summer 1980), 63-68.

———. "Women dramatists of Puerto Rico." *Revista/Review Interamericana*, 9, No. 1 (Spring 1979), 24-41.

De Beer, Gabriella. "Femenismo en la obra poética de Rosario Castellanos." *Revista de Crítica Literaria Latinoamericana*, 7, No. 13 (1981), 105-112.

De Costa, Miriam ed. *Blacks in Hispanic Literature: Critical Essays.* Port Washington, N.Y.: Kennikat Press, 1977. 157p.

Engling, Ezra S. "The 'compact' woman in Any Lydia Vega's *Pollito Chicken.*" In *La Mujer en la Literatura Caribeña.* Ed. Lloyd King. St. Augustine, Trinidad: Dept. of French and Spanish Literature, University of the West Indies, [1984?], 94-107.

Feeny, Thomas. "Women's triumph over men in René Marqués's Theater." *Hispania,* 65, No. 2 (May 1982), 187-193.

Fernandez Cintron, Celia and Marcia Rivera Quintero. "Bases de la sociedad sexista en Puerto Rico." *Revista/Review Interamericana,* 4, No. 2 (1974), 239-245.

Fernández Olmos, Margarita, ed. *Contemporary Women Authors of Latin America: Introductory Essays.* Brooklyn: Brooklyn College Press, 1983. 101p.

_____. "Desde una perspectiva femenina: la cuentística de Rosario Ferré y de Ana Lydia Vega." *Homines,* 8, No. 2 (1984/85), 303-311.

_____. "El género testimonial: approximaciones feministas." *Revista/Review Interamericana,* 11, No. 1 (1981), 69-75.

Ferré, Rosario. "La cocina de la escritura." In *La Sartén por el Mango: Encuentro de Escritoras Latinoamericanas.* Ed. Patricia Elena González y Eliana Ortega. Rio Piedras, Puerto Rico: Ediciones Huracán, 1984, 137-162.

Gantt, Barbara N. "The woman of Macondo: feminine archetypes in García Márquez *Cien anos de soledad.*" Diss. Florida State Univ. 1977. 129p.

González, Iris G. "Some aspects of linguistic sexism in Spanish." *Revista/Review Interamericana,* 11, No. 2 (1981), 204-219.

González, Julio Ariza. "Approximaciones a la imagen trágica de dos personajes femeninos en *Cien años de soledad.*" In *La Mujer en la Literatura Caribena.* Ed. Lloyd King. St. Augustine, Trinidad: Dept. of French and Spanish Literature, University of the West Indies, [1984?], 130-141.

González, Patricia Elena, y Eliana Ortego, eds. *La Sartén por el Mango: Encuentro de Escritoras Latinoamericanas.* Rio Piedras, Puerto Rico: Ediciones Huracán, 1984. 173p.

Hancock, Joel. "Elena Poniatowska's *Hasta no verte Jesús Mío*: the remaking of the image of woman." *Hispania,* 66, No. 3 (Sept. 1983), 353-359.

Harkness, Shirley and Cornelia B. Flora. "Women in the news: an analysis of media images in Colombia." *Revista/Review Interamericana,* 4, No. 2 (Summer 1974), 220-238.

Harrison, Polly F. "Images and exile: the Cuban woman and her poetry." *Revista/Review Interamericana,* 4, No. 2 (Summer 1974), 184-219.

Hoberman, Louisa S. "Hispanic American women as portrayed in the historical literature: type or archetypes?" *Revista/Review Interamericana,* 4, No. 2 (Summer 1974), 136-147.

Homar, Susana. "Inferioridad y cambio: los personajes femeninos en la literatura puertorriqueña." *Revista de Ciencias Sociales* 20, Nos. 3-4 (Dec. 1978).

Hullebroeck, Joelle. "La mujer en los cuentos de Juan Bosch: sombra omnipresente." In *La Mujer en la Literatura Caribeña.* Ed. Lloyd Kind. St. Augustine, Trinidad: Dept. of French and Spanish Literature, University of the West Indies, [1984?], 151-167.

Insanally, Annette. "Eroticism as an expression of the consciousness of self in Rosario Ferré's *Fabulas de la Garza Desangrada* and Lorna Goodison's *Tamarind Season*." Paper presented at the Fifth Conference on West Indian Literature. St. Thomas, Virgin Islands, May 23-24, 1985. 13p.

Jimenez Wagenheim, Olga. "The Puerto Rican woman in the nineteenth century: an agenda for research." *Revista/Review Interamericana*, 11, No. 2 (1981), 196-203.

Kalina de Piszk, Rosita. "Escritoras costarricenses: Maria Fernández de Tinoco." *Káñina*, 5, No. 2 (July-December 1981), 28-36.

King, Lloyd, ed. *La mujer en la literatura Caribeña*. Sexta Conferencia de Hispanistas, 6-8 Abril 1983. St. Augustine, Trinidad: University of the West Indies, [1984?] 196p.

"The Latin American woman: image and reality." *Revista/Review Interamericana*, Special Edition, 4, No. 2 (Summer 1974).

Leal, Luis. "Female archetypes in Mexican literature." In *Women in Hispanic Literature: Icons and Fallen Idols*. Ed. Beth Miller. Berkeley: Univ. of California Press, 1983, 227-242.

López, Ivette. "Puerto Rico: las nuevas narradoras y la identidad cultural." *Perspectives on Contemporary Literature*, No. 8 (1982), 77-83.

MacLachlan, Colin M. "Modernization of female status in Mexico: the image of women's magazines." *Revista/Review Interamericana*, Special Edition, 4, No. 2 (Summer 1974), 246-257.

Magnarelli, Sharon. *The Lost Rib: Female Characters in the Spanish American Novel*. Lewisburg, Penn.: Bucknell Univ. Press, 1985. 227p.

Marmolejo-McWatt, Amparo. "Marianismo/machismo in the family of the Spanish-speaking Caribbean." Paper prepared for the UNESCO/ISER(EC) Seminar on Changing Family Patterns and Women's Role in the Caribbean, University of the West Indies, Cave Hill, November 24-27, 1986. Cave Hill, Barbados: Institute of Social and Economic Research (Eastern Caribbean), University of the West Indies, 1986. 16p. Bibliography.

_____. "Men, women and the concept of honour in Gabriel García Márquez's *Crónica de una muerte anunciada*." *Bulletin of Eastern Caribbean Affairs* (Barbados), 11, No. 1 (March-April 1985), 1-12.

Meyer, Doris and Margarita Fernández Olmos. *Contemporary Women Authors of Latin America. vol. 1*. New York: Brooklyn College Press, c1983.

Miller, Beth K. "Avellaneda, nineteenth-century feminist." *Revista/Review Interamericana*, Special Edition, 4, No. 2 (Summer 1974), 177-183.

_____. ed. *Women in Hispanic Literature: Icons and Fallen Idols*. Berkeley: University of California Press, c1983. 373p.

Miller, Shirley Isabelle. "Women in the novels of Gabriel García Márquez." Thesis M.A. University of the West Indies, 1984. 199 leaves. Bibliography.

Mora, Gabriela. "Narradoras hispanoamericanas: vieja y nueva problemática en renovadas elaboraciones." In *Theory and Practice of Feminist Literary Criticism*. Eds. Gabriela Mora and Karen Van Hooft. Ypsilanti, MI.: Bilingual, 156-174.

Neggers, Gladys. "Clara Lair y Julia de Burgos: reminiscencias de Evaristo Ribera Chevremont y Jorge Font Saldana." *Revista/Review Interamericana*, Special Edition, 4, No. 2 (Summer 1974), 258-263.

Nigro, Kirsten F. "Rosario Castellano's debunking of the *Eternal Feminine*." *Journal of Spanish Studies: Twentieth Century*, 8, Nos. 1 & 2 (Spring and Fall 1980), 89-102.

Nowakowska Stycos, Maria, ed. "New approaches to twentieth-century Hispanic women poets." *Revista/Review Interamericana*, 12, No. 1 (1982). [Selection of papers presented at a symposium sponsored by the Dept. of Foreign Languages, the School of Humanities and Sciences and the Afro-Latin Society at Ithaca College, New York, 3-4 April 1981]

Pereira, Joseph R. "Image and self-image of women in recent Cuban poetry." In *La Mujer en la Literatura Caribeña*. Ed. Lloyd King. St. Augustine, Trinidad: Dept. of French and Spanish Literature, University of the West Indies, [1984?], 51-68.

Pérez, Arturo P. "La mujer en dos novelas de Rosario Castellanos." *Cuadernos Americanos* (Mexico), 10 No. 38 (May-July 1979), 221-226.

Pescatello, Ann, ed. *Female and Male in Latin America: Essays*. Pittsburgh: University of Pittsburgh Press, 1974.

_____. "Preface. The special issue in perspective: the Hispanic Caribbean woman and the literary media." *Revista/Review Interamericana*, 4, No. 2 (1974), 131-135.

Rodríguez, Maria Cristina. "The role of women in Caribbean fiction." Diss. City University of New York, 1979. 371 leaves. Bibliography.

_____. "Tema y estilo en la poesía escrita por mujeres Puertorriqueñas en la década de setenta." In *Poetry of the Spanish-speaking Caribbean. Conference Papers*. 2nd ed. Third Conference of Latin Americanists, University of the West Indies, Mona Campus, Jamaica, 10-12 July, 1980. Mona, Jamaica: Dept. of Spanish, University of the West Indies, 1984, 1-18.

Rodríguez-Peralta, Phyllis. "Images of women in Rosario Castellanos's prose." *Latin American Literary Review*, 6, No. 11 (1977), 68-80.

Rose-Green, Claudette. "Feminist perspectives in Rosario Ferré's *Papeles de Pandora*." In *La Mujer en la Literatura Caribeña*. Ed. Lloyd King. St. Augustine, Trinidad: Dept. of French and Spanish Literature, University of the West Indies, [1984?], 108-129.

Santos Silva, Loreina. *"La pasión según Antígona Pérez:* la mujer como reafirmadora de la dignidad política. *Revista/Review Interamericana*, 11, No. 3 (1981), 438-443.

Smart, Ian I. "La mulatez y la imagen de la nueva mujer negra en la poesía de Nicolas Guillén." *Union*, Revista de la Union de Escritores y Artistas de Cuba, No. 4, 1983.

Thomas, Ena V. "Women and the national ethos in the drama of Francisco Arriví." In *La Mujer en la Literatura Caribeña*. Ed. Lloyd King. St. Augustine, Trinidad: Dept. of French and Spanish Literature, University of the West Indies, [1984?], 142-150.

Urbano, Victoria. *Five Women Writers of Costa Rica*. Beaumont, Texas: Asociación de Literatura Femenina Hispánica, Lamar University, 1978. 131p.

Vallbona, Rima de. "Trayectoria actual de la poesía femenina en Costa Rica." *Káñina*, 5, No. 2 (July-December 1981), 18-27.

Vega, Ana Lydia. "El no de las niñas: transgresión y subversión en los cuentos de tres narradoras Puertorriqueñas." In *La Mujer en la Literatura Caribeña*. Ed. Lloyd King. St. Augustine, Trinidad: Dept. of French and Spanish Literature, University of the West Indies, [1984?], 40-50.

Welles, Marcia L. "The changing face of woman in Latin American fiction." In *Women in Hispanic Literature: Icons and Fallen Idols*. Ed. Beth Miller. Berkeley: University of California Press, c1983, pp. 280-288.

Wong, Oscar. "La mujer en la poesía mexicana." *Plural*, 11, No. 11 (August 1982), 54-59.

Young, Ann Venture. "The black woman in Afro-Caribbean poetry." In *Blacks in Hispanic Literature: Critical Essays*. Ed. Miriam De Costa. Port Washington, N.Y.: Kennikat Press, 1977, 137-142.

_____. "Black women in Hispanic Amerian poetry: glorification, deification and humanization." *Afro-Hispanic Rev.*, 1, No. 1 (January 1982), 23-28.

Editors

Carole Boyce Davies has an ongoing commitment to feminist criticism of African, Caribbean and African-American literatures. She has published a number of essays in this area including "Mothering and Healing in Recent Black Women's Fiction" in *Sage: A Scholarly Journal of Black Women* 2:1 (Spring, 1985): 41-43, and initiated and co-edited *Ngambika: Studies of Women in African Literature* (Trenton, New Jersey: Africa World Press, 1986). More recent essays include "Finding Some Space: South African Women Writers" in *A Current Bibliography of African Affairs* 19:1 (1986-7): 31-45 and "Black Woman's Journey Into Self: A Womanist Reading of Paule Marshall's Praisesong for the Widow" *Matatu* (formerly *Nommo*, W. Germany) 1:1 (1987). Her other major research commitment is to oral tradition and literature. Her Ph.D. thesis from the University of Ibadan (1977) was titled "Oral Tradition and the Anglophone African and Caribbean Novel" and contains an extensive chapter on Caribbean Oral Literature. Recent publications in this area include "The Politics of African Identification in Trinidad Calypso *Studies in Popular Culture* 8:2 (1985): 77-94. Originally from Trinidad, she has degrees from the University of Maryland, Eastern Shore and Howard University. She is now Associate Professor with joint appointments in the Departments of English and Afro-American and African Studies at SUNY-Binghamton.

Elaine Savory Fido initiated this collection of essays. She is Senior Lecturer in African, English and Caribbean Literature at the University of the West Indies, Cave Hill, Barbados where she has taught literature since 1974. She taught at the University of Ghana from 1970-72 and was visiting lecturer at the University of Ibadan 1982-83 and in 1987-89 was Coordinator of Women's Studies (teaching and project) at U.W.I., Cave Hill. She has been involved in theatre in Barbados and women's issues and organizations in the Caribbean. She maintains an on-going research and writing commitment to women's writing in African and Caribbean literature. She is readying a collection of her poetry for publication, and has completed a play "Spirit" in which Jean Rhys appears as a character. Her published essays in these fields include "Judgments on Art and the Macho Aesthetic of Derek Walcott in *Journal of Caribbean Literature* 21:1 (July, 1986), "Radical Woman and Theatre in the Anglophone Caribbean" in *Critical Issues in West Indian Literature* Ed. Erica Sollish Smilowitz and Roberta Quarles Knowles (Parkersburg, Iowa: Caribbean Books, 1984): 33-45 and "Psycho-Sexual Aspects of the Woman in V.S. Naipaul's Fiction" in *West Indian Literature and Its Social Context*. Ed.

Mark A. McWatt (Barbados, UWI, Cave Hill, Dept. of English, 1985): 78-94. She introduced a special issue "The Female Presence in Caribbean Literature" of *Bulletin of Eastern Caribbean Affairs* 11:1 (March/April, 1985).

Contributors

Abena P.A. Busia is Associate Professor of English at Rutgers University. Born in Accra, Ghana, she has lived in Holland, Mexico and Oxford, England where she completed all her secondary and university education. She has worked as a visiting lecturer at Yale University. Her publications include: "Manipulating Africa: The Bucaneer as 'Liberator' in Contemporary Fiction" in *The Black Presence in British Fiction* edited by David Dabydeen (Manchester University Press, 1985); "Parasites and Prophets: The Use of Women in Ayi Kwei Armah's Novels" in *Ngambika: Studies of Women in African Literature*. Edited by Carole Boyce Davies and Anne Adams Graves (Trenton, N.J., Africa World Press, 1986); and "Miscegenation as Metonymy: Sexuality and Power in the Colonial Novel" (for "Essays in Honour of Prof. Kenneth Kirkwood") *Journal of Ethnic and Racial Studies*, Summer, 1986. Her poetry has appeared in *Summer Fires: New Poetry from Africa* (Heinemann, 1983), *Conditions: A Literary Journal of Black Women* and *Kunapipi*.

Jeniphier Carnegie is Reference Librarian at the main library, University of the West Indies, Cave Hill, Barbados. She is married with two sons and one daughter. She is Jamaican, has a B.A. Honors Degree in English from the University of the West Indies and a Bachelor of Library Science degree from the University of British Columbia. She has published *Critics on West Indian Literature: A Selected Bibliography*, Mona, Jamaica, 1979 and "Select Bibliography on the Works of Professor Elsa Goveia, Dr. Walter Rodney and Dr. Eric Williams" in *Bulletin of Eastern Caribbean Affairs* 8:2 (May/June, 1982) 47-62.

Vèvè Clark is Associate Professor of African and Caribbean Literature in the Romance Languages Department at Tufts University, Boston. She is co-editor of *The Legend of Maya Deren* and author of articles on the Antillean novel, Haitian performance and Afro-American dance. She is currently completing a book on Katherine Dunham.

Rhonda Cobham is a graduate of the University of the West Indies (Mona) and the University of St. Andrews in Scotland where she completed her doctoral dissertation on early Jamaican Literature. She worked for several years, and until recently, within the African Research Programme at the University of Bayreuth, West Germany. She has written essays on Erna Brodber and other aspects of Caribbean literature. A part time editor for the Woman's Press (London), she has co-edited a special issue of *Research in African Literature* on African Women Writers. Her most recent publication is *Watchers and Seekers: Creative Writing*

By Black Women in Britain. (London: Woman's Press, 1987). She recently joined the faculty of Amherst College in Massachusetts.

Carolyn Cooper is Lecturer, Department of English, University of the West Indies, Mona, Jamaica. She is a graduate of the University of the West Indies, Mona, Jamaica and the University of Toronto (Ph.D., 1976). Her primary research area is comparative black literature, secondary focus: oral discourse. Essays include "That Cunny Jama Oman: The Female Sensibility in the Poetry of Louise Bennett" in *Bulletin of Eastern Caribbean Affairs* 11:1 (March/April, 1985): 13-27.

Giovanna Covi has a degree in Anglo-American literature from the University of Venice, Italy. She is currently a graduate student at SUNY-Binghamton working on her PhD in English. She has published an article on Sylvia Plath in an Italian collection of essays on feminist literary criticism to which she has been committed since the beginning of her literary activity.

Sandra Messinger Cypess is Associate Professor of Spanish and of Comparative Literature at SUNY-Binghamton. Her work on Hispanic women writers and on Latin American drama has appeared in several journals, including *Modern Drama, Latin American Theatre Review, Texto critico of Mexico, Revista/Review Interamericana* of Puerto Rico. She has contributed chapters to other books dealing with Puerto Rican Literature (*The Puerto Ricans: Their History, Culture, and Society; Subversion de canones: La escritora puertorriquena ante la critica*) and women writers (on Griselda Gambaro of Argentina in *Dramatists in Revolt* and on Elena Garro of Mexico in *Woman as Myth and Metaphor in Latin American Literature*).

Lemuel A. Johnson, from Sierra Leone, is currently Professor of English and Director of the Center for Afro-American and African Studies at the University of Michigan, Ann Arbor He has also taught at Fourah Bay College, University of Sierra Leone. His publications include *Highlife for Caliban; The Devil, the Gargoyle and the Buffoon; The Negro Metaphor in Western Literatures.* His forthcoming book, *Unreturnable-Heaven: The Utopian Bent* is a study of politics in African, Caribbean and Latin American literatures.

Janice Lee Liddell received her doctorate in American Studies from the University of Michigan (Ann Arbor) in 1978. She has since taught at Clark College in Atlanta. In 1978, she received a United Negro College Fund Distinguished Scholars Award which afforded her the opportunity to conduct extensive research on women writers of the English-speaking Caribbean. For her research she travelled to Jamaica, Barbados and Trinidad. She is currently writing a work which focuses on contemporary West Indian women writers. She is also the very proud mother of two sons.

Amparo Marmolejo McWatt is Colombian, has a degree in Literature and Foreign Language from the University of Santiago de Cali (Columbia) and is a lecturer in Spanish at the Cave Hill (Barbados) campus of the University of the West Indies. She has published articles on Garcia Marquez and comparative literatures of the Caribbean. She currently completing research in the field of language and linguistics.

Mark A. McWatt studied at the Universities of Toronto and Leeds; his doctoral thesis is in the field of Commonwealth literature. He is Senior Lecturer in English and West Indian literatures at Cave Hill (Barbados) campus of UWI. He has published articles and reviews in the field of West Indian literature and is editor of the new *Journal of West Indian Literature.*

Pamela Claire Mordecai is a poet, children's writer, publisher and educator. She lives and works in her home country of Jamaica. She has published a good deal of poetry and as well has edited the poetry anthology *Jamaica Woman* with Mervyn Morris (Kingston, Heinemann, 1980). She is presently preparing a volume of Caribbean women's prose with her sister Elizabeth Wilson (Heinemann, forthcoming).

Nancy Morejon was born in Havana, Cuba in 1944, and graduated from the University of Havana, Cum Laude with an M.A. in French Language and Literature. She is a poet, a journalist, a translator, and works at present as Editor in the Union of Cuban Writers and Artists. She has written on Guillen and her book *Nationality and Race Mixture in Nicholas Guillen* received the National Enrique Jose Varona Prize in 1980. She has completed Cuban editions of Shakespeare and Moliere and has translated a number of major French writers into Spanish. She has published a number of volumes of poetry and her work has appeared in various anthologies. She is perhaps best known for her collection *The Island Sleeps Like a Wing* (Black Scholar Press, 1984) and *Grenada Notebook (Cuaderno de Granada)* Trans. Lisa Davis, (New York City, Circulo de Cultura Cubana, 1984).

Marlene Nourbese Philip is a New World writer/lawyer who has lived in Canada since 1968. She is the author of two books of poetry *Thorns* and *Salmon Courage* (Toronto: Williams Wallace, 1980 and 1983), *Harriet's Daughter* (Heinemann, 1988) as well as several essays, articles and reviews. In 1983 she was awarded a Canada Council Explorations Grant to write and produce a taped documentary, *Blood is for Bleeding (The Positive Values of the Menstrual Experience).* Ms. Philip's work attempts a fusion of the disparate threads that make up the New World experience.

Evelyn O'Callaghan is a Jamaican who studied in Ireland and England and now teaches West Indian and British literature at the University of the West Indies, Cave Hill, Barbados. She is interested in creole socio-linguistic patterns, late nineteenth and early twentieth century women writers in the West Indies. She recently completed a study guide for Zee Edgell's *Beka Lamb* and has published articles on Erna Brodber, creole socio-linguistic patterns in the West Indian novel and popular West Indian fiction.

Joyce Stewart is a first-class graduate from the English Department, UWI, Cave Hill, Barbados, and is currently writing a Ph.D. dissertation on Wilson Harris.

Elizabeth Wilson is a lecturer in French language and twentieth century Francophone literature in the Department of French, University of the West Indies, Mona, Jamaica. A Jamaican, she studied in Britain, France and the United States of America where she completed a doctoral dissertation at Michigan State University on "The Portrayal of Woman in the Works of Francophone Women Writers from West Africa and the Caribbean." She is currently working on a prose anthology of Caribbean women writing with Pamela Mordecai. In addition to women's writing, her research interest is comparative literature, particularly Caribbean and African literature. She has also co-authored language arts texts for Caribbean primary schools.

Sylvia Wynter is Professor of Spanish and Portuguese, and Afro-American Studies at Stanford University. She is a well respected Caribbean playwright, novelist, translator and critical thinker. Professor Wynter has authored major essays on humanism and postmodern theory such as "The Ceremony Must Be Found: After Humanism", *Boundary II*, Spring & Fall 1984. She is the author of one of the first novels by a Caribbean woman writer, *The Hills of Hebron*, 1962.

Clarisse Zimra is a regular contributor in the field of Caribbean literature. She is finishing a book on the inscription of history in the Caribbean narrative. She started as a traditional student of the abolitionist novel at the University of Aix en Provence but soon moved into the comparative study of disapora literature. She has taught in France, Great Britain, the United States, Vietnam; and more recently in Thailand where she directed the Comparative Literatures Program and lectured on Afro-American women writers at Chulalongkorn University in Bangkok. She is currently a professor in English at Southern Illinois University—Carbondale. Her peregrinations (and childhood in North Africa) convinced her of two things: One, that we are all (willing) prisoners of our socio-cultural parameters, gender being one variant. And, therefore, two, that all literary studies are comparative.